# ServiceNow Application Development

Transform the way you build apps for enterprises

**Sagar Gupta**

BIRMINGHAM - MUMBAI

# ServiceNow Application Development



First published: September 2017

Production reference: 1210917

Published by Packt Publishing Ltd.
Livery Place
35 Livery Street
Birmingham
B3 2PB, UK.

ISBN 978-1-78712-871-2

www.packtpub.com

# Credits

**Author**
Sagar Gupta

**Reviewers**
Manoj Jain
Jonathan Jacob

**Commissioning Editor**
Kartikey Pandey

**Acquisition Editor**
Meeta Rajani

**Content Development Editor**
Trusha Shriyan

**Technical Editor**
Akash Patel

**Copy Editor**
Safis Editing

**Project Coordinator**
Kinjal Bari

**Proofreader**
Safis Editing

**Indexer**
Pratik Shirodkar

**Graphics**
Kirk D'Penha

**Production Coordinator**
Shantanu Zagade

# About the Author

**Sagar Gupta** is the chief software architect and founder of Eworks Services Pvt. Ltd., central India's first ISO 27001-certified firm.

He leads a team of 50+ ServiceNow, BMC Remedy, AEM, Cloud, and BigData experts. He started his career building custom enterprise and service management applications in 2003 and has been working on the ServiceNow platform since the past 7 years. He has in-depth knowledge of the platform ranging from ITSM and ITOM to GRC, Security Operations, HR, Field Service, and IT Business Management.

Over the past several years, he has consulted numerous companies and conducted over 200 training sessions for Fortune 500 organizations such as GE, Dell, NetApp, IBM, Cognizant, Sapient, HCL, and EMC2.

He is also the lead engineer in the SnowEditor project and currently devotes most of his time helping companies improve their IT service delivery, modernize ITSM, automate processes, and build cloud-native applications on ServiceNow.

# About the Reviewer

**Manoj Jain** is a technical architect and has over 10 years of IT experience. He has immense knowledge of ITSM processes and platforms, such as ServiceNow and BMC Remedy.

He is certified in ITIL V3 Foundation and ServiceNow System Administrator. He has conducted over 50 training in past 7 years in ITIL, BMC Remedy and ServiceNow for clients such as GE, Cognizant, CSS Corp, and Persistent.

During his career, he has consulted more than 100 clients to implement better ITSM solutions using ServiceNow and BMC Remedy. He is currently focused on helping companies create better custom applications on cloud platforms such as ServiceNow.

# www.PacktPub.com

For support files and downloads related to your book, please visit www.PacktPub.com. Did you know that Packt offers eBook versions of every book published, with PDF and ePub files available? You can upgrade to the eBook version at www.PacktPub.com and as a print book customer, you are entitled to a discount on the eBook copy. Get in touch with us at service@packtpub.com for more details. At www.PacktPub.com, you can also read a collection of free technical articles, sign up for a range of free newsletters and receive exclusive discounts and offers on Packt books and eBooks.

https://www.packtpub.com/mapt

Get the most in-demand software skills with Mapt. Mapt gives you full access to all Packt books and video courses, as well as industry-leading tools to help you plan your personal development and advance your career.

## Why subscribe?

- Fully searchable across every book published by Packt
- Copy and paste, print, and bookmark content
- On demand and accessible via a web browser

# Customer Feedback

Thanks for purchasing this Packt book. At Packt, quality is at the heart of our editorial process. To help us improve, please leave us an honest review on this book's Amazon page at `https://www.amazon.com/dp/1787128717`.

If you'd like to join our team of regular reviewers, you can email us at `customerreviews@packtpub.com`. We award our regular reviewers with free eBooks and videos in exchange for their valuable feedback. Help us be relentless in improving our products!

# Table of Contents

# Preface

*ServiceNow Application Development* will focus on in-depth application development from designing forms to write business rules and client scripts to designing workflows on the world's fastest growing enterprise cloud platform. Global organizations such as GE, NASA, Intel, and Dell EMC are using the ServiceNow platform to quickly build enterprise-ready custom applications that run on the cloud. GE Capital, the financing arm of GE, delivers financial, intellectual, and human capital to its customers, around the world and to meet growing challenges they used ServiceNow to build a new cloud-ready Risk Vulnerability Assessment Tool (RVAT) in only six weeks. This developer-focused book will serve as a road map for you and your team on how to build cloud-ready applications, manage data in single system of record, build standard-based applications, and win customers' and IT users' satisfaction.

## What this book covers

`Chapter 1`, *Introduction to ServiceNow*, will help the reader get started with ServiceNow and gain access to a free developer instance from ServiceNow Developer Portal. The chapter is focused on getting the reader used to the platform and the basics of ServiceNow, such as UI, Login process, and some out-of-the box applications and features. The chapter will also help the reader brush up their knowledge about how ServiceNow is used within organizations.

`Chapter 2`, *User Administration*, explains how to create new users and associate them to a group. You will also learn how to assign roles to groups and users. Further, you will learn how to impersonate a user to test if our newly created users have access to correct applications and modules.

`Chapter 3`, *Data Management*, explains that managing tables and columns is one of the most common job administrators and developers have to perform when working on the ServiceNow platform. ServiceNow platform features various modules that can be used to create and manage tables and columns. In this chapter, you will learn how to create a new table from scratch, extend existing table and add fields (or columns) to new or existing tables. You will also understand the structure of existing tables such as task and cmdb.

`Chapter 4`, *Application Scopes*, explains that, when developing applications on the ServiceNow platform, developers need to take special care about the application scope they are working on. Applications help administrators and developers to combine different modules and features to deliver a relevant set of functionality. ServiceNow allows developers and administrators simple means to create and manage applications. In this chapter, you will learn how to create new applications. You will learn about the relationship between applications and scopes. You will also learn how to use applications to associate relevant information and access data from other applications.

`Chapter 5`, *Modules, Forms, and Views*, explains that ServiceNow platform easy-to-use features that allow administrators to create modules, and customize form and views. In this chapter, you will learn how to create different type of modules, customize the form layout, and quickly add new form fields to the table. You will also learn about various form field element types available in the platform including the reference field, journal field, date field and choice list. Furthermore, you will learn how to use form views to present same record in different manner to end-users based on their role.

`Chapter 6`, *Introduction to ServiceNow Scripting*, ServiceNow platform offers various scripting options to developers. This chapter, you will learn about different type of scripting options available in ServiceNow platform. You will learn about difference between server-side and client-side scripts. Furthermore, you will also learn how scripting works in scoped applications and get introduced to client-side and server-sideGlide APIs.

`Chapter 7`, *Client-Side Scripting*, will help you to learn how to create client-side scripts and what are the different ways to execute the client-side code. The readers will learn how to make use of the client-side Glide API and some of the most widely used functions available. You will learn how to create client scripts, UI policy, and UI script.

`Chapter 8`, *Server-side Scripting*, explains that server-side scripts and APIs can be employed to enhance server-side data processing and integration with different systems. Server-side scripts can also be used to perform database operations and perform large scripted imports. This chapter will help you learn how to create server-side scripts, and when and where the server side scripts comes in the scene when working with ServiceNow applications. The chapter will help you understand how to make use of the server-side Glide API and server-side artifacts like Business Rules, script-include, and data policy.

`Chapter 9`, *Jelly Scripting*, explains that in ServiceNow platform, Apache's Jelly syntax is used to render forms and UI pages. Jelly is Java and XML-based scripting and a transformation engine used to turn XML into executable code. The output is usually HTML and JavaScript code that is used by the browser to render elements on a page. This chapter will help you learn how to create UI pages, UI macros and formatters. You will learn how to make use of Jelly scripts to enhance our UIs and create custom controls and application property page.

`Chapter 10`, *Events and Notifications*, explains that in ServiceNow, Events are used to monitor changes or *events* by event handlers just like in any other programming language. Events in the queue are consumed by script actions or notifications, which in turn execute scripts or trigger notifications. Notification on the other hand, is an approach to send out e-mail to the end-users or external end-points. Any form or script sending out an email relies on the Notification feature of the platform. This chapter will help you learn how to trigger events when data changes and send out e-mail based on events.

`Chapter 11`, *Workflow Development*, explains that the ServiceNow offers a web based visual workflow designer known as Workflow Editor. A workflow is made up of activities and always consists of begin and end activities that marks the start and end of the workflow. This chapter will help you learn how to use many of the different available standard workflow activities including the REST activity and how to design, run and test your own workflow.

`Chapter 12`, *Debugging in ServiceNow*, explains that within ServiceNow you write both server-side and client-side code. The ways to troubleshoot them more or less remain same but the approach differs. This chapter will cover many different troubleshooting and debugging techniques available within the platform. The chapter will help you how to use many features to debug and troubleshoot scripts in ServiceNow platform and cover various topics such as Syntax editor, launching and using the Script debugger, JavaScript log and Field watcher.

`Chapter 13`, *Advanced Database Features*, ServiceNow platform offers many features to improve the performance and overall functionalities of ServiceNow applications. This chapter will cover features like relationships, indexing, full-text search, and overriding field properties. You will also learn features such as enabling auditing, restoring deleted records and Table rotation and data archiving.

`Chapter 14`, *Job Scheduling and Data Export-Import*, explains that as a developer you will always to be tasked to ensure data from various external systems can be brought into the platform with ease and this may require you to create scripted controls that can perform pre- and post-processing of the imported data. This chapter includes some of advanced development and administrative tasks that a developer must be aware of like scheduled script execution (SSE), and data export and import. More specifically, you will help how to schedule a script to run in the background, export data, import data using import sets, configure transform maps and use scripts to process imported data.

# What you need for this book

As ServiceNow is a cloud-based SaaS application, it can be accessed using most standard browsers. These are browsers that are supported by the UI16 of the ServiceNow application:

- Chrome
  Version: Latest public release
- Firefox
  Version: Latest public release
- Internet Explorer
  Version: 9 and above
- Microsoft Edge
  Version: Latest public release
- Apple Safari
  Version: 9.1 and above

There are some limitations when using Internet Explorer to access ServiceNow, including the following:

- Compatibility mode is not supported
- Setting security to **High** using **Internet Options** | **Security** tab is not supported and will make some ServiceNow applications and features inaccessible
- Internet Explorer 11 may face memory leak issues especially in Windows 7

Notifications in Connect are only available in Safari, Chrome and Firefox. Internet Explorer doesn't support notification feature.

Cookies must be enabled for the login feature to work. If you disable cookies, you will not be able to log in to the instance.

# Who this book is for

This book is indented for anyone who wants to learn how to develop software on the world's fastest growing enterprise cloud platform. Developers and administrator, who are already working on ServiceNow, can also use this book to brush up their knowledge of key development features.

# Conventions

In this book, you will find a number of styles of text that distinguish between different kinds of information. Here are some examples of these styles, and an explanation of their meaning.

Code words in text, database table names, folder names, filenames, file extensions, pathnames, dummy URLs, user input, and Twitter handles are shown as follows: "The `g_user` global object can be used to retrieve user session information in client scripts."

A block of code is set as follows:

```
function DemoCallBack(response) {
//javascript code
var answer = response.responseXML.documentElement.getAttribute("answer");
console.log(answer);
}
```

**New terms** and **important words** are shown in bold. Words that you see on the screen, in menus or dialog boxes for example, appear in the text like this: "Navigate to the bottom of the page and click on the **New** button in the **Database Indexes** related list."

Warnings or important notes appear in a box like this.

Tips and tricks appear like this.

# Reader feedback

Feedback from our readers is always welcome. Let us know what you think about this book-what you liked or disliked. Reader feedback is important for us as it helps us develop titles that you will really get the most out of. To send us general feedback, simply e-mail `feedback@packtpub.com`, and mention the book's title in the subject of your message. If there is a topic that you have expertise in and you are interested in either writing or contributing to a book, see our author guide at `www.packtpub.com/authors`.

# Customer support

Now that you are the proud owner of a Packt book, we have a number of things to help you to get the most from your purchase.

## Errata

Although we have taken every care to ensure the accuracy of our content, mistakes do happen. If you find a mistake in one of our books-maybe a mistake in the text or the code-we would be grateful if you could report this to us. By doing so, you can save other readers from frustration and help us improve subsequent versions of this book. If you find any errata, please report them by visiting `http://www.packtpub.com/submit-errata`, selecting your book, clicking on the **Errata Submission Form** link, and entering the details of your errata. Once your errata are verified, your submission will be accepted and the errata will be uploaded to our website or added to any list of existing errata under the Errata section of that title.

To view the previously submitted errata, go to `https://www.packtpub.com/books/content/support` and enter the name of the book in the search field. The required information will appear under the **Errata** section.

## Piracy

Piracy of copyrighted material on the Internet is an ongoing problem across all media. At Packt, we take the protection of our copyright and licenses very seriously. If you come across any illegal copies of our works in any form on the Internet, please provide us with the location address or website name immediately so that we can pursue a remedy.

Please contact us at `copyright@packtpub.com` with a link to the suspected pirated material.

We appreciate your help in protecting our authors and our ability to bring you valuable content.

## Questions

If you have a problem with any aspect of this book, you can contact us at `questions@packtpub.com`, and we will do our best to address the problem.

# 1
# Introduction to ServiceNow

If you are reading this book, it is probably because your company is planning to implement and customize the **ServiceNow** platform or you want to build a career around the fastest growing enterprise cloud platform. ServiceNow is a SaaS platform offered by ServiceNow, Inc. and used by global corporations such as **GE**, **Dell EMC**, **NetApp**, **Yahoo**, **Google**, **Aegis**, **Deutsche Bank**, **AstraZeneca**, **Red Hat**, **Siemens**, **University of San Francisco**, **Sony Pictures Entertainment**, **Intuit**, **Moody's**, **Diageo**, and so on. For the purpose of this book, we are going to assume that you work at ABCD, Inc. and your company's management has asked you to build a custom application on top of the ServiceNow platform.

ServiceNow allows companies to manage processes and create custom applications using a single system of record framework - meaning every application and all data stored in the platform follows the same framework and basic structure. ServiceNow platform comprises key product features such as **Service Management**, **IT Operations Management**, **Application Development**, **IT Business Management**, **Human Resources**, **Customer Service**, and **Security**.

- **Service Management**: Offers features used by your IT Service Desk to manage ITIL processes such as Incident Management, Change and Release Management, Problem Management, Service Level Management, Service Catalog, Knowledge Management, and Configuration and Asset Management along with features like reporting and administration, which extend across other features as well.
- **IT Operations Management**: Includes applications such as Discovery, Service Mapping, Event Management, Orchestration and Cloud Management.
- **Application Development**: Includes the core Platform and app development features such as Custom Applications, APIs, Portal Designer and Integration tools.

- **IT Business Management**: It includes applications such as Performance Analytics, Financial Management, Project Portfolio Management, Demand Management, Resource Management and Application Portfolio Management.
- **Security**: It includes features and applications related to Security Operations and **Governance, Risk and Compliance** (**GRC**)
- **Customer Service**: It includes applications such as Customer Service Management, Field Service Management and Knowledge Management.
- **Human Resources**: It includes the HR Service Management application.

Companies using the ServiceNow platform deploy one or more of the aforementioned product features. Service Management, Application Development Platform, and IT Operations Management are the most widely deployed features among ServiceNow customers.

In this book, we will be covering topics related to application development and customizing and extending features of Service Management applications such as Incident Management. As ServiceNow is a cloud-based platform, we do not usually need to install any special software on a client system. We can access any ServiceNow instance easily from anywhere using a computer or mobile with internet connectivity and the latest browser such as Microsoft Edge, Internet Explorer, Firefox, or Google Chrome. For administration and Development purposes, it is recommended that you use a desktop with the latest version of Chrome, which is what we will be using throughout this book to access our instance.

Fred Luddy founded ServiceNow, Inc. in 2003 (as GlideSoft, Inc.) and in Jan 2016 ServiceNow announced total revenues of US $1.0 billion for the fiscal year, 2015. It is one of the fastest growing companies and has a target to reach a market size of US $60.0 billion by 2020. You may find people referring to ServiceNow as GlideSoft, SNC, SNOW or `service-now.com`.

This chapter will help you get started with ServiceNow and gain access to a free developer instance from ServiceNow developer portal and understand the basics of ServiceNow such as UI, Users, and out-of-the-box applications and features.

This chapter will cover the following topics:

- Creating a ServiceNow developer account
- Launching a developer instance
- Understanding the ServiceNow platform login process

- Understanding the ServiceNow user interface
- An introduction to Service Management Applications
- ServiceNow platform architecture

# Creating a developer account

ServiceNow, Inc. offers developers a free instance of their cloud-based platform. To be able to develop a custom application, you first need to have your own instance of the ServiceNow platform. You can create a developer account and request a free instance by visiting the ServiceNow developer portal site at: `https://developer.servicenow.com`:

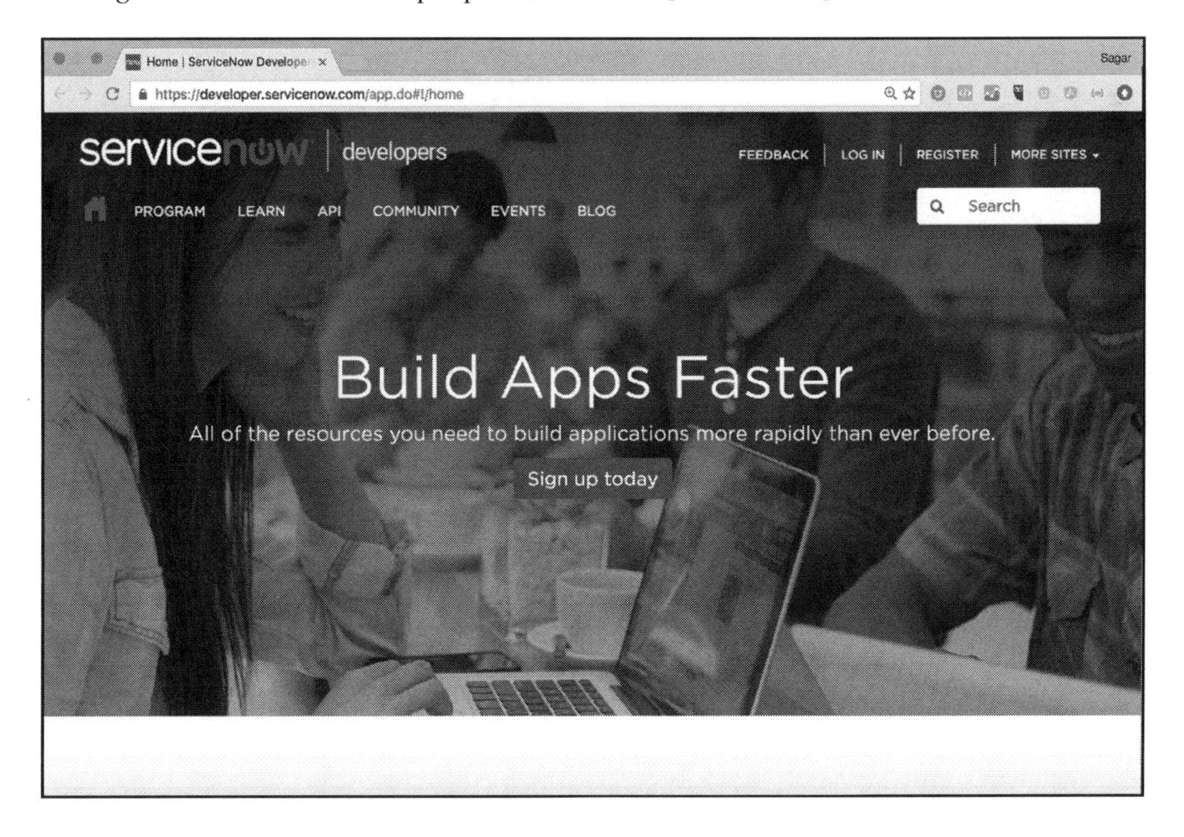

The registration process for the ServiceNow developer portal is fairly simple. You can click on the **REGISTER** link in the upper-right, if you are not already registered, and fill in your name, e-mail, and choose a password to complete your registration. Once you verify your email and are registered, you can log in to the ServiceNow developer portal and request an instance by clicking on the **Request Instance** button, as shown in the following screenshot:

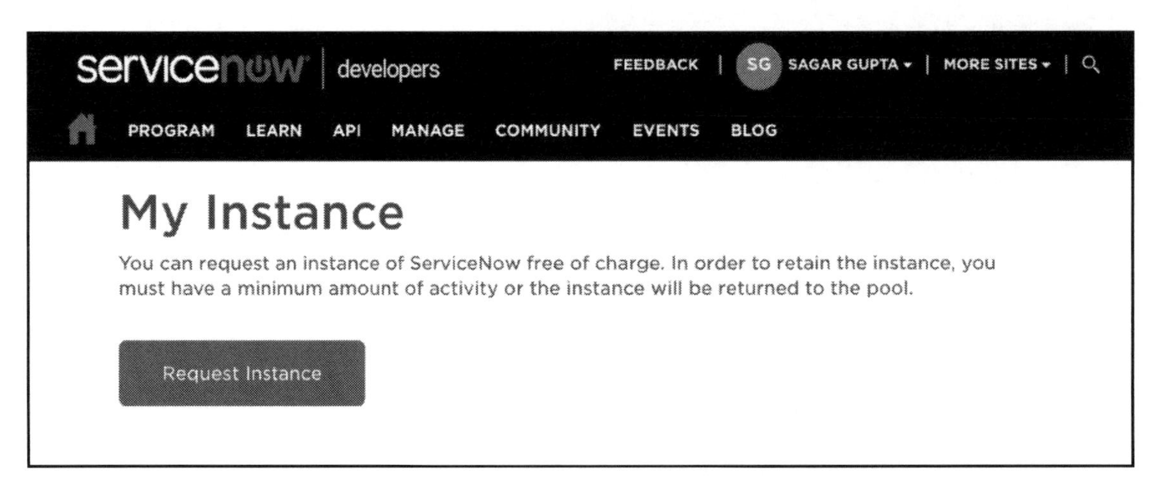

The link to request a new instance is visible on the left side of the dashboard page and is also accessible from the **MANAGE** | **Instance** menu link once you log in to the developer portal. You can only launch one instance per developer portal account.

## Requesting a new ServiceNow instance

You will be presented with a modal window, like the one shown in the following screenshot, to select a version of the ServiceNow instance you wish to launch. For the purpose of this book, we will be launching an instance running the **Istanbul** version of the ServiceNow platform. You can also select the latest version of the ServiceNow platform, which is **Jakarta**:

X

Which version of ServiceNow would you like?

Helsinki Release Notes | Istanbul Release Notes | Jakarta Release Notes

If you aren't sure which version to choose, start with Jakarta.
It's our latest available release and we have an instance ready for you to get started.

Release notes on the Istanbul version can be found at:
`https://docs.servicenow.com/bundle/istanbul-release-notes/`.
Release notes on the Jakarta version can be found at:
`https://docs.servicenow.com/bundle/jakarta-release-notes/page/release-notes/jakarta-release-notes.html`.

It may take a few minutes for the developer portal to assign you an instance. Once the instance is available, you will be presented with details of your instance - such as the URL of the instance, the System Administrator's username (by default `admin`), and an alphanumeric password. Make sure to save this information for future reference:

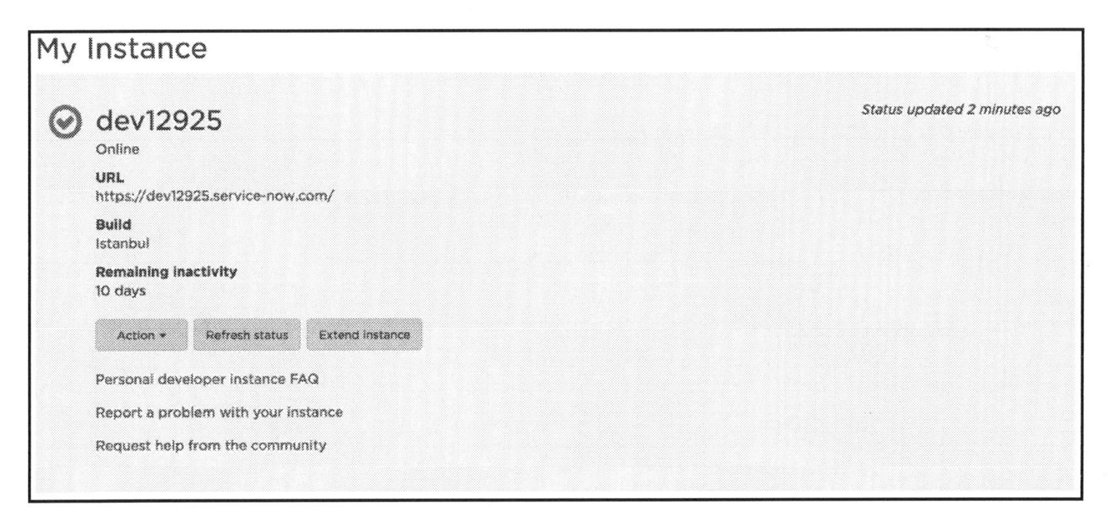

You will also be presented with the credentials to log in to your instance, as shown in the following screenshot:

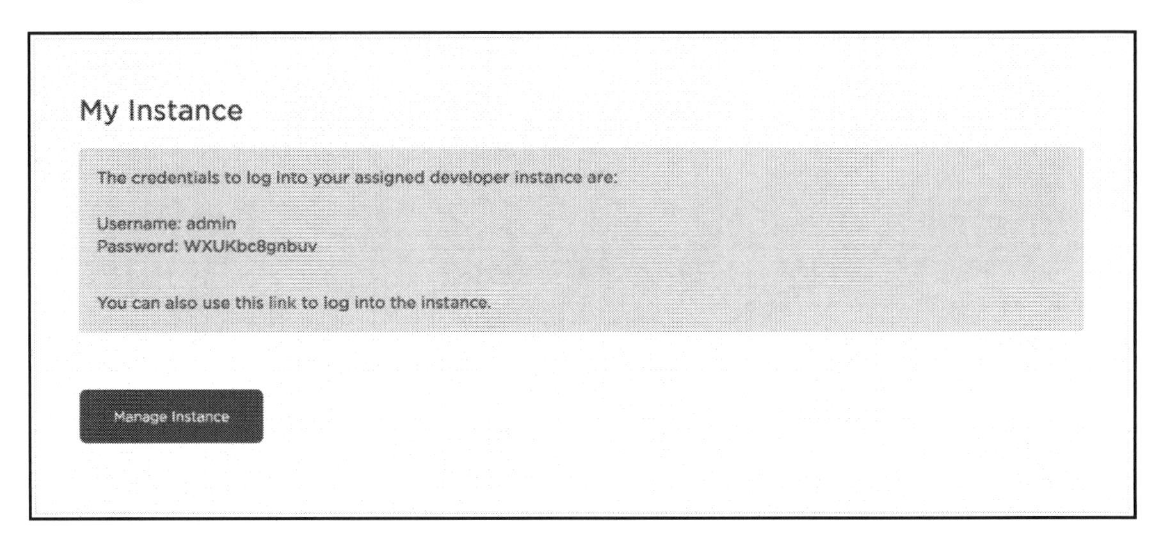

It may take up to 60 seconds to launch your instance, so be patient. Your instance may sleep or be reclaimed if there's no activity/usage for a few days. However, it is always easy to wake or request a new instance by visiting the **MANAGE** | **Instance** page in the ServiceNow developer portal. Each developer instance URL is different, but always has the `dev` prefix, and uses the `service-now.com` domain instead of `servicenow.com`. In case you forget your admin user's password, you can always reset it from the **MANAGE** | **Instance** page.

# Logging in to your instance

Now that you have your own personal developer instance, in the ServiceNow developer portal, you can click on the instance URL link to open and log in to your instance using the `admin` user credentials, as shown in the following screenshot:

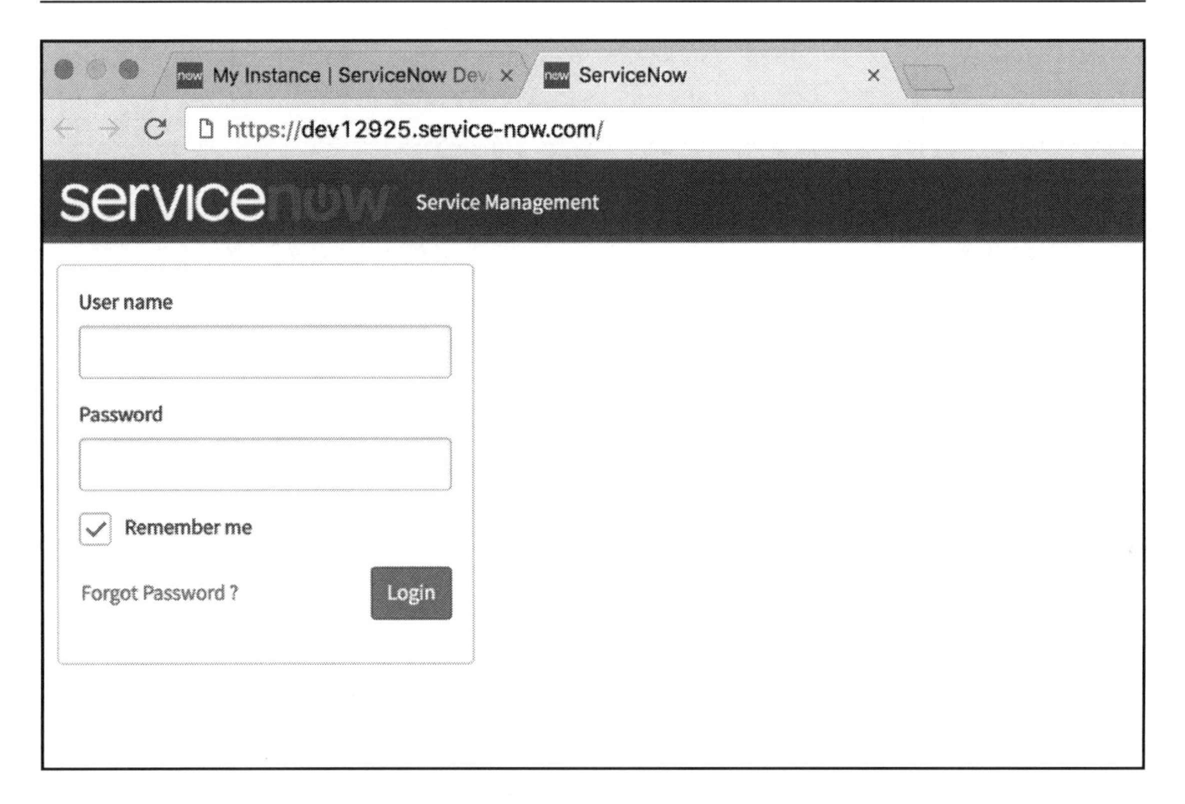


Enter your **User name** and **Password** to log in to your instance, and leave the **Remember me** checkbox checked only if you trust others who share your computer. If you are logging in to your instance for the very first time, it will prompt you to change your password. Every ServiceNow instance's URL is different. Instance settings, users, passwords, roles, applications, modules, tables, UIs, scripts, and so on available for one instance are unique to that instance. They can, however, be copied from one instance to another.

The first time you log in as `admin`, you are taken to the **System Administrator** homepage (**Dashboards**), like the one shown in the following screenshot:

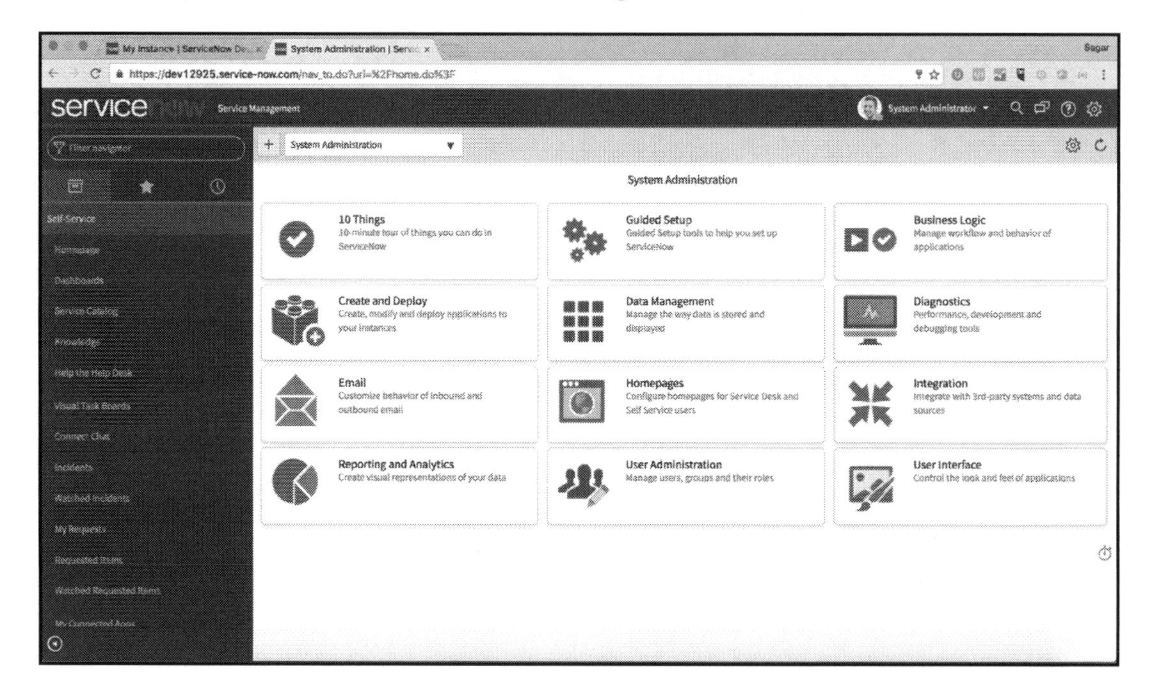


# Understanding the ServiceNow platform user interface

Just like any web-based application, we interact with the ServiceNow platform's application and modules through the user interface using a web browser. The version of UI that comes with the Istanbul release of ServiceNow is referred to as UI16. There are three main components of UI16: **Banner Frame**, **Application Navigator**, and **Content Frame**.

## Components of the user interface

The various components of the user interface are explained here:

- **Banner Frame (top header)**: The banner frame appears at the top of the interface. This is where you see the logo, global navigation, logged-in user's info, search and other tools, and a settings (gear/cog) icon at the extreme right. This settings gear icon is extremely useful for developers as it is used quite frequently during development:

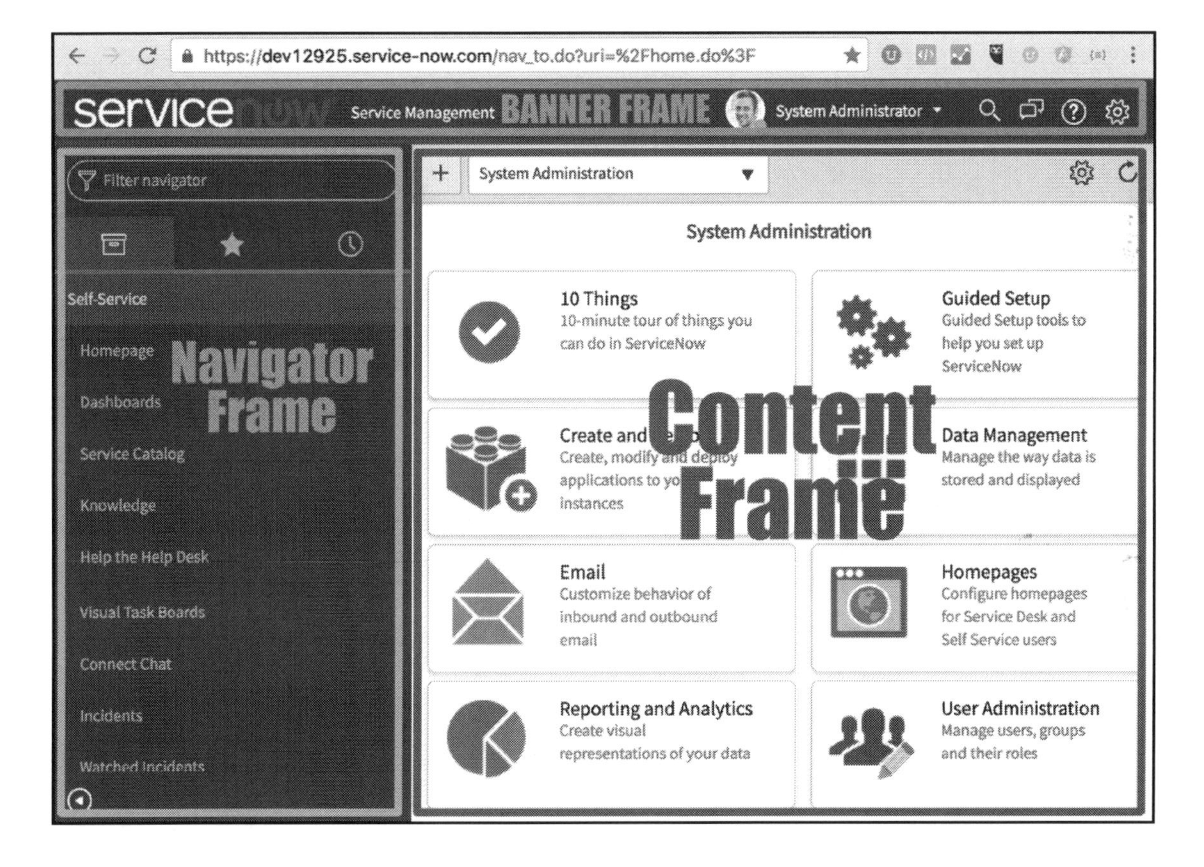

- **Application navigator (left navigation bar)**: This is where navigation links to different ServiceNow platform applications and modules are visible. It has a text filter box at the top, which allows us to filter through available navigation links. There are three tabs available in the left navigation bar:
    - The **Applications** tab contains a list of all of the applications and modules the logged in user has access to. Based on the user's role, each link has an edit icon and inactive star icon to its right. The edit link can be used to navigate to the edit module page, and the star icon can be clicked on to add or remove navigation entries to user favorites.
    - The **Favorites** tab lists all navigation links and items the logged in user has added to their favorites.
    - The **History** tab lists navigation links and items the logged in user has recently accessed.
- **Content Frame:** This is the main section of the user interface where pages, forms, list of records, dashboards, **Homepages** of all applications, and modules are loaded.
- It is possible to switch back to an earlier version of the user interface (UI15) by clicking on the settings gear icon in the far right of the **Banner Frame**, which will open up the **System Settings** modal window (more on this on next page), and then clicking on the **Switch to U15** button in the upper-right of the modal window. To switch back to U16, again click on the settings gear icon, and click on the **Switch to U16** button:

Version 15 of the UI features **The Edge**, which has been replaced by the Favorites (left-navigation) tab in version 16 of the UI, as shown in the following screenshot:

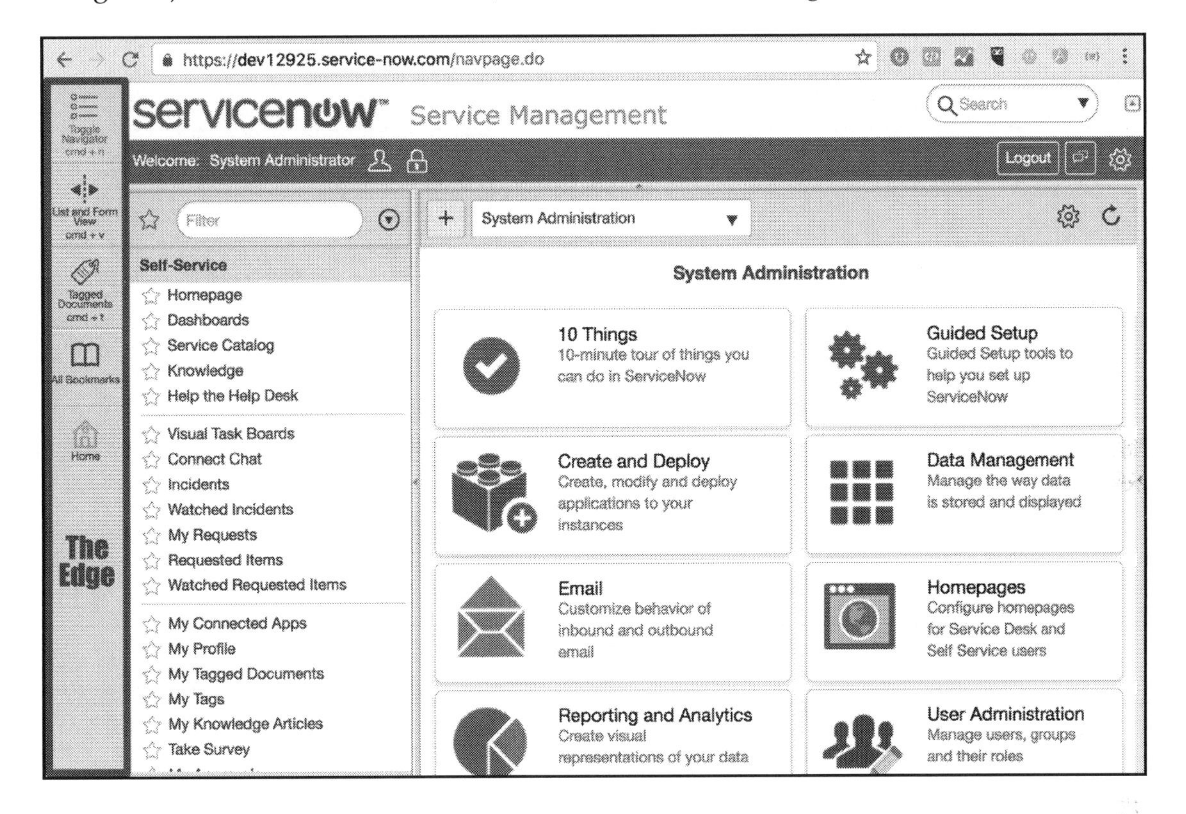

# System settings

The **System Settings** modal window is accessible (in UI16) by clicking on the settings gear icon in the **Banner Frame**. When you are logged in as **System Administrator** or a delegated developer, you will have the following settings available:

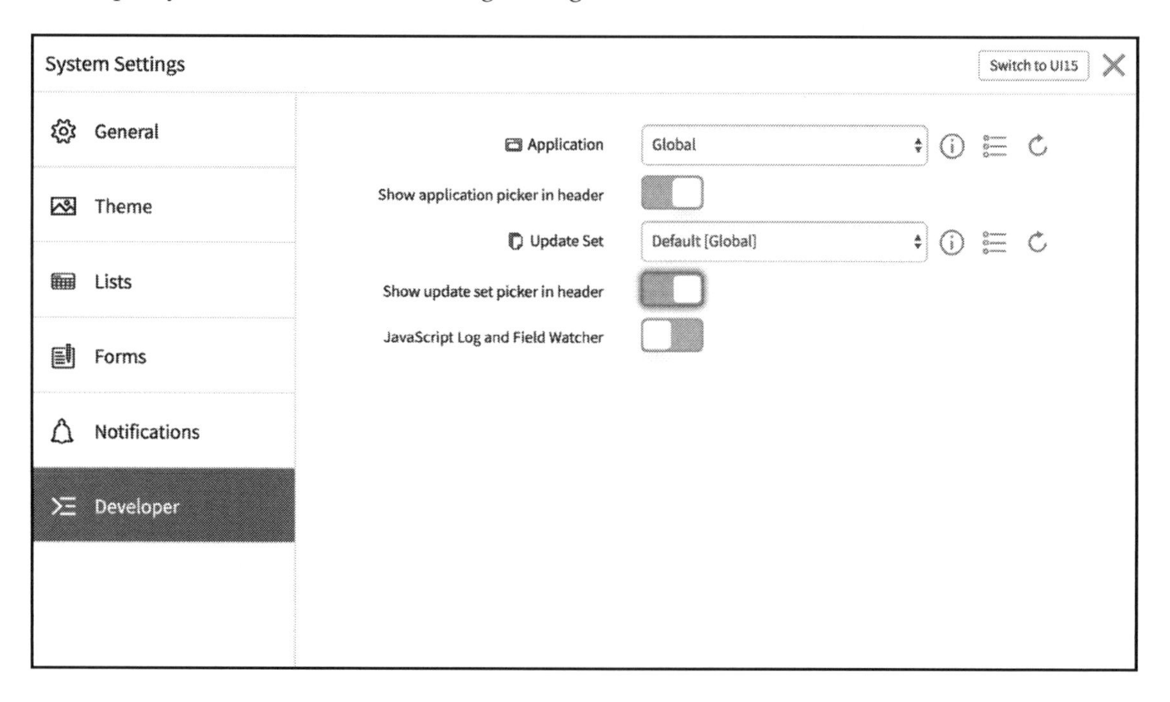


- **General**: Here you can change your time zone, view a printable version of the content frame, and change a few accessibility-related settings.
- **Theme**: Allows you to select and change your UI's theme color.
- **Lists**: Here you can change settings related to a list of records module pages:
    - **Wrap longer text in list columns**: If enabled, breaks long text into lines in order to minimize horizontal scrolling in the list of records module pages.
- **Forms**: This tab allows you to change how your Form UI loads and work:
    - **Tabbed forms**: If enabled, all related lists and sections on the form show up in tabs in all forms.
    - **Related list loading**: Allows changing how related lists load in the form. We can choose to load related lists **With the Form**, **After the Form,** or **On-Demand**.

- **Notifications**: This tab allows users to enable or disable mobile, desktop (web), e-mail, and audio notifications.
- **Developer**: This tab is only available to users with an admin role or a delegated developer. This tab allows developers to select their current **Application** and working **Update Set**. The following settings are available under the **Developer** tab:
- **Application picker drop-down**: Allows selecting an application scope and marking it as active. This prevents developers from making modifications to any other application other than the one that is currently selected. One ServiceNow instance can have more than one application scope defined but a user can work only on one of the scopes at any given time.
- **Show application picker in header**: If enabled, shows application picker drop-down in the banner frame. We will keep this setting enabled for the rest of our chapters.
- **Update Set picker drop-down**: Allows selecting an **Update Set** and marking it as active. **Update Sets** are like containers, which record changes to the selected **Application** scope and allows easy migration of changes to other instances and rollbacks. One application scope can have more than one **Update Sets** defined but only one marked as active.
- **Show update set picker in header**: If enabled, shows the **Update Set** picker drop-down in the banner frame. Keep it enabled for the rest of our chapters.
- **JavaScript Log and Field Watcher**: If enabled, shows the JavaScript Log and Field Watcher frame within the Content Frame.

After enabling **Show Application** and the **Update Set** picker in the header settings, both drop-down fields will appear in the banner frame, which will enable us to quickly change the active **Application** scope and **Update Set**:

The ServiceNow platform comes with a default **Application** scope named **Global** and a default **Update Set** under the global application scope named **Default [Global]**. We will be covering how the **Application** scope and the **Update Set** works in detail later in the book. One key thing to remember is that the **Application** scope is different to application menu links, which are visible in the left navigator and explained here:

The name of the **Update Set** is usually shown along with the name of **Application** scope it is part of in [square brackets.] So, the **Default** update set, which is part of global application scope, will appear as **Default [Global]** in the **Update Set** picker drop-down.

## Navigating through applications

The **Application Navigator** on the left of the user interface lists all applications menu and modules. An application menu is a set of related modules grouped together as a section, which can be expanded on click, and is denoted by an application label. Once expanded, it lists all modules (navigation links) available under it.

One of the most important aspects of the ServiceNow Application is that it can comprise of one or more modules of different types. Modules types are also referred to as navigation link types.

The administrator can easily customize the order and label of all **Applications** and **Modules**, as shown in the following screenshot:

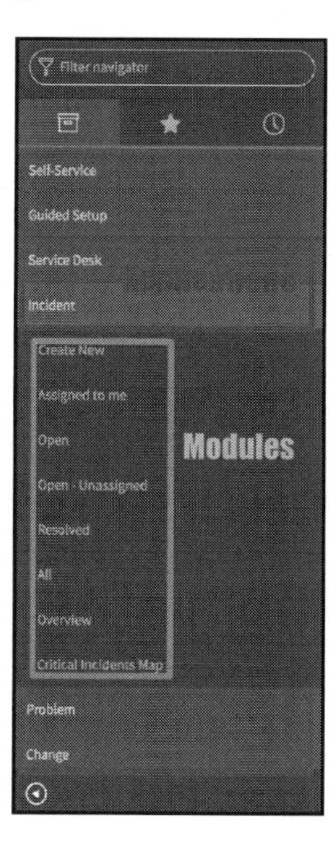

Even though we will be covering **Modules** in upcoming chapters, to completely understand different types of user interfaces available, we must go through some key types of modules available in ServiceNow.

In the preceding image, **Self-Service**, **Guided Setup**, **Service Desk**, **Incident**, **Problem**, and **Change** (marked in red) are all **Application** menus. The **Incident** application menu section is expanded and navigation links under it, including **Create New**, **Assigned to me**, **Open**, **Open - Unassigned**, **Resolved**, **All**, **Overview**, and **Critical Incidents Map** (marked in green), are visible and these navigation links are called **Modules**.

## Module UIs

- **New record**: A module that opens up a web form is referred to as a **New record** module. Clicking on many modules in ServiceNow, including the **Create New** navigation link under the **Incident** application, opens up a form like the one shown in the following screenshot, which allows you to insert a new record to a specified table. Every **New record** module is linked to a table in to which new and existing records are either inserted or updated. For example, the **New record** form of the **Incident** table, as shown in the following screenshot, can be used to insert new records into the **Incident** table:

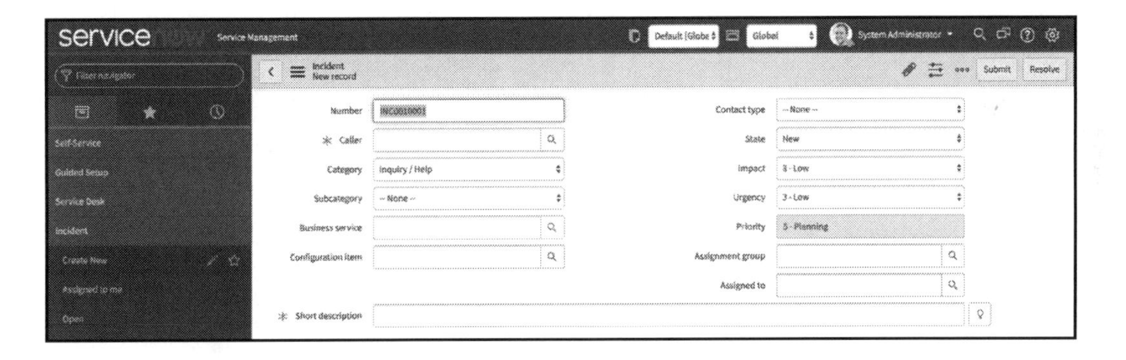

- **List of records**: Any navigation link that points to a page that lists records from a table or view is referred to as a list of record modules. A list of record modules can also be used to drill down into records using the search filters visible at the top of the page and can have pre-defined filters set during the creation of the module. Modules under the **Incident** application menu including **Assigned to Me**, **Open**, **Open - Unassigned**, **Resolved**, and **All** navigation links lists records from the **Incident** table and displays items in a grid format:

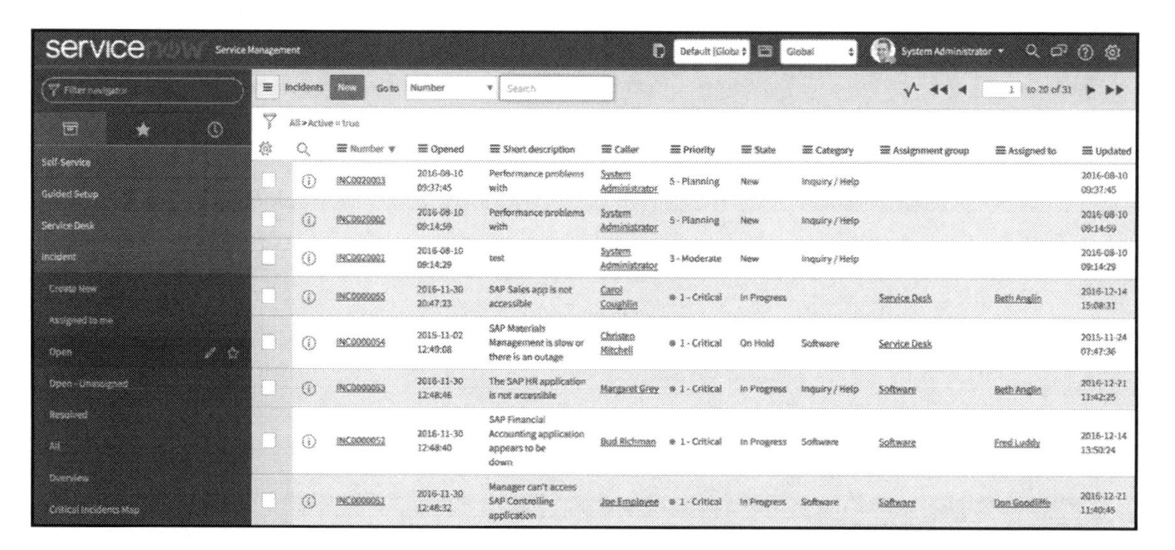


Lists of record modules usually have a **New** button in the upper-left, which allows you to insert a new record into the table list of records that the module is fetching its data from. Moreover, you will also find a filter icon, which can be clicked to open a query builder known as the Filter UI, as shown in the following screenshot:

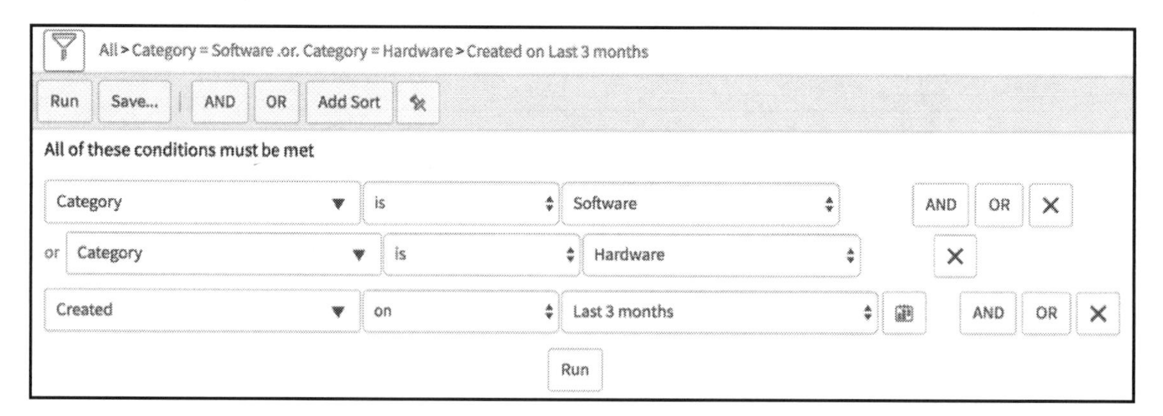

The list of records also features a quick search feature at the top section but unlike Filter UI, it can be perform a search only on one of the visible columns:

It also features a simple to use pagination UI in the upper- and lower-right, which allows you to quickly jump through records from one page to another:

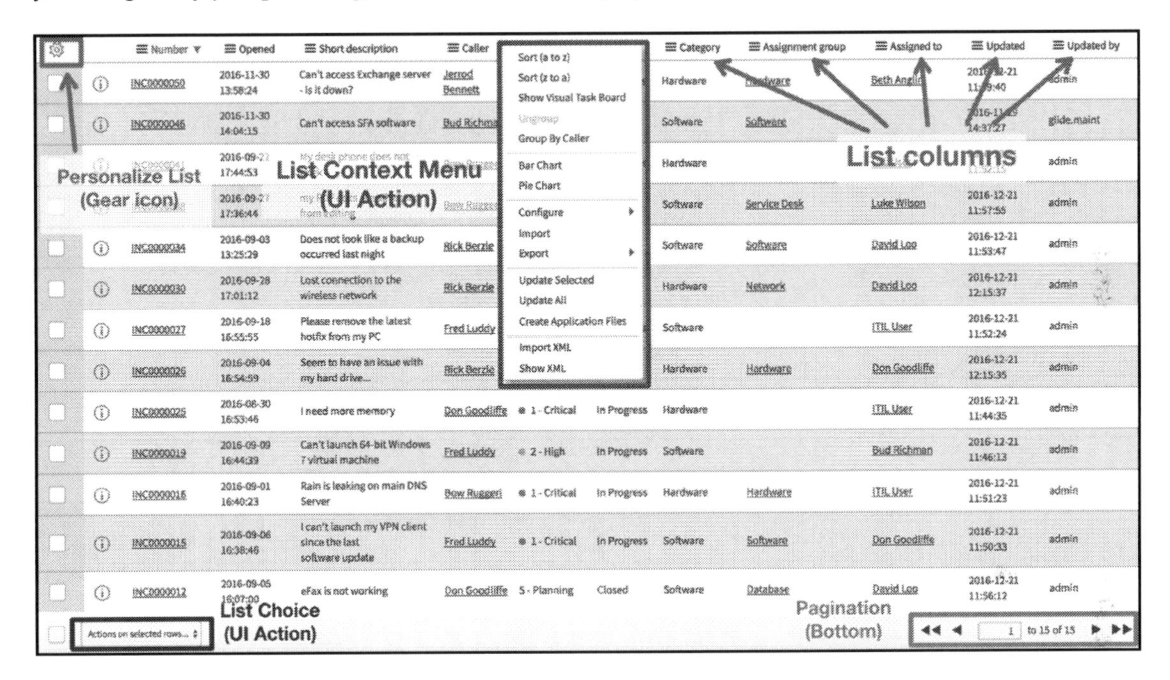


Apart from the Filter UI, quick search, and pagination UIs, the list of records module also features UI actions such as list choice and context menu, which are visible when we right-click on the list's column header. It also provides an efficient way to change the sorting order of the list, simply by clicking on the column name on the list's header.

Clicking on the gear icon at the upper-left of the list header brings up the **Personalize List Columns** modal window, allowing logged-in users to customize columns available to them in the list's grid. You can bring in the columns you want visible to the **Selected** list from the **Available** list of columns and click on the **OK** button to confirm your changes, as shown in the following screenshot:

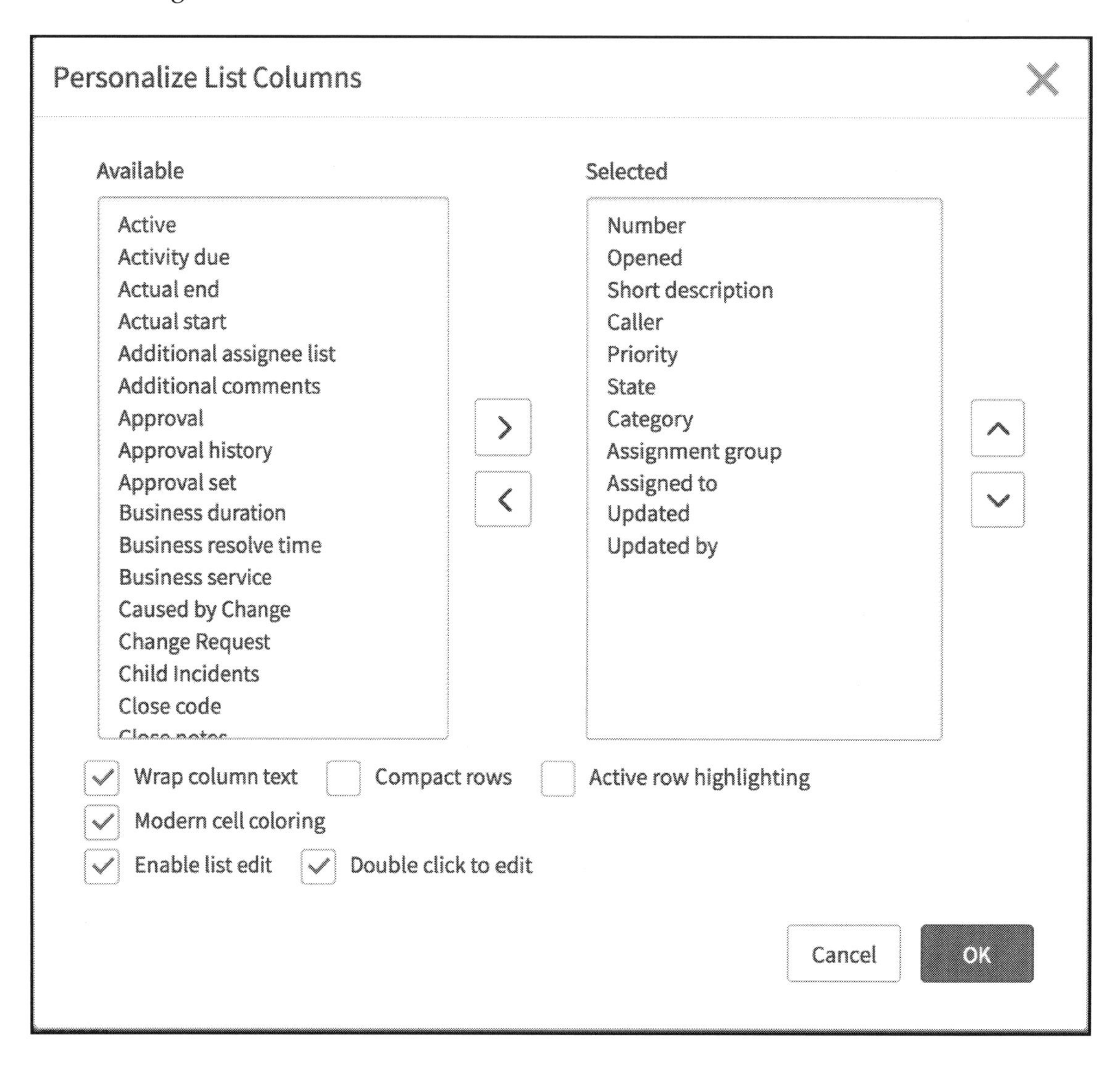

- **Homepage**: A navigation links (or module) that point to any dashboard-like page filled with graphs and widgets is referred to as a homepage. For example, the **Overview** navigation link under the **Incident** application menu loads a homepage like the one shown in the following screenshot:

- **Other available module/link types**:
    - Map page
    - Content page
    - Run a report
    - Separator
    - Single record
    - Survey
    - Timeline page
    - URL

# Form UIs

ServiceNow offers many different form UI elements , such as choice (drop-down), simple text, numeric, price, date, reference field, journal field, and so on, which can be used in forms and catalog pages. Different form UI types can be used to create one form. For example, the **New record** form of the **Incident** application, as shown in the following screenshot, can comprise text fields, reference fields, form buttons, header context menus, drop downs, form sections, list fields, and journal fields. Some of these fields can be marked as mandatory:

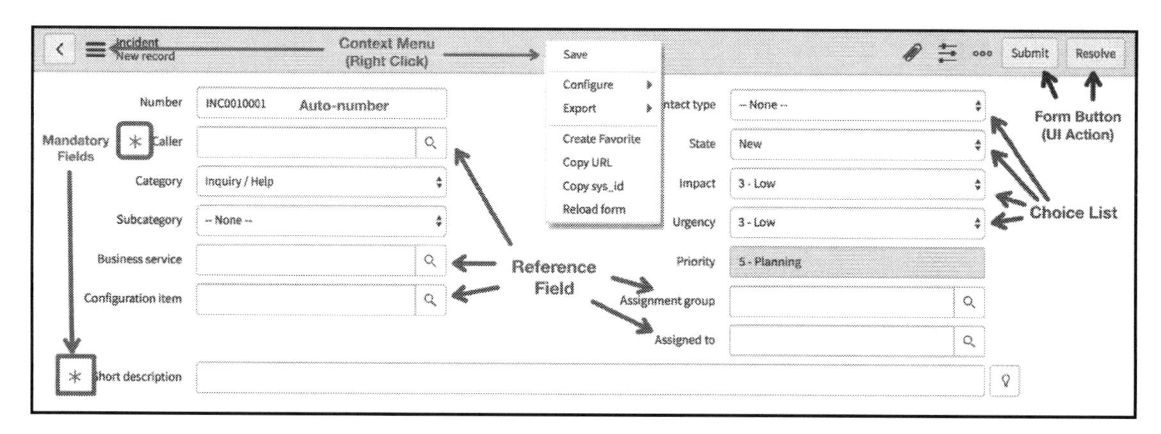


Some sections of the form are accessible via a tabbed interface as shown here:

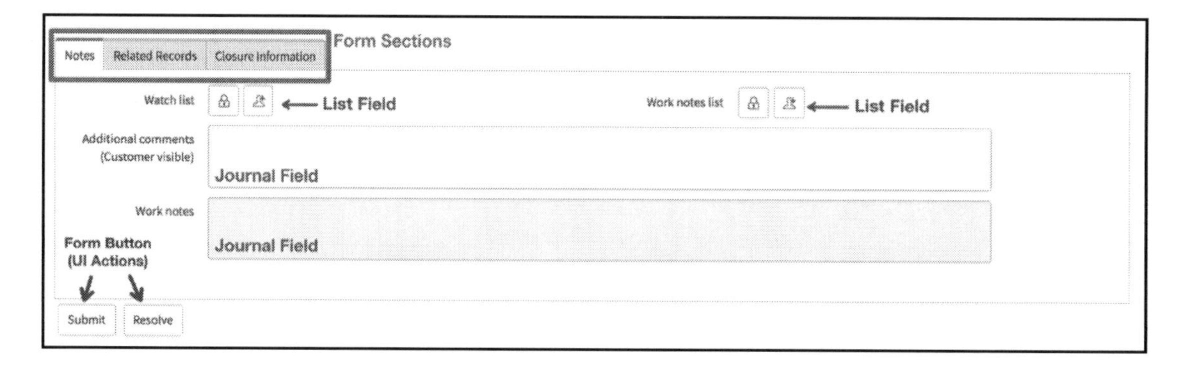

- Fields marked with * are mandatory fields.
- **Reference Fields** refer to a record in a separate table. It can also refer to a record in the same table. Example: In the previous screenshot, the **Assigned to** and **Caller** fields refer to records in the users table, whereas the **Assignment group** field refers to a record in the user groups table.
- **Form Sections** are used to remove the clutter from the page and arrange fields into meaningful tabs or sections.

We will be covering how to create different form fields and customize form layout in later chapters.

## Related List UI

Related lists are one of the most important UI elements available in form pages. A related list can be used to show lists of related records from either, the same or a different table. While we will be covering related lists in detail in later chapters, let us quickly understand how the related list UI works and how it can help augment the information available in any form:

1. Open one of the existing records in update (edit) mode in the **Incident Management** application by clicking on the **Incident Number**:

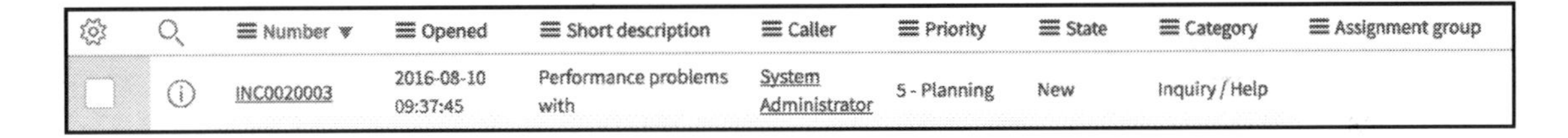

| Number | Opened | Short description | Caller | Priority | State | Category | Assignment group |
|---|---|---|---|---|---|---|---|
| INC0020003 | 2016-08-10 09:37:45 | Performance problems with | System Administrator | 5 - Planning | New | Inquiry / Help | |

2. Once you are in update mode, right-click on the form header to bring up the form context menu UI actions. From the list of options available, select **Configure** | **Related Lists**:

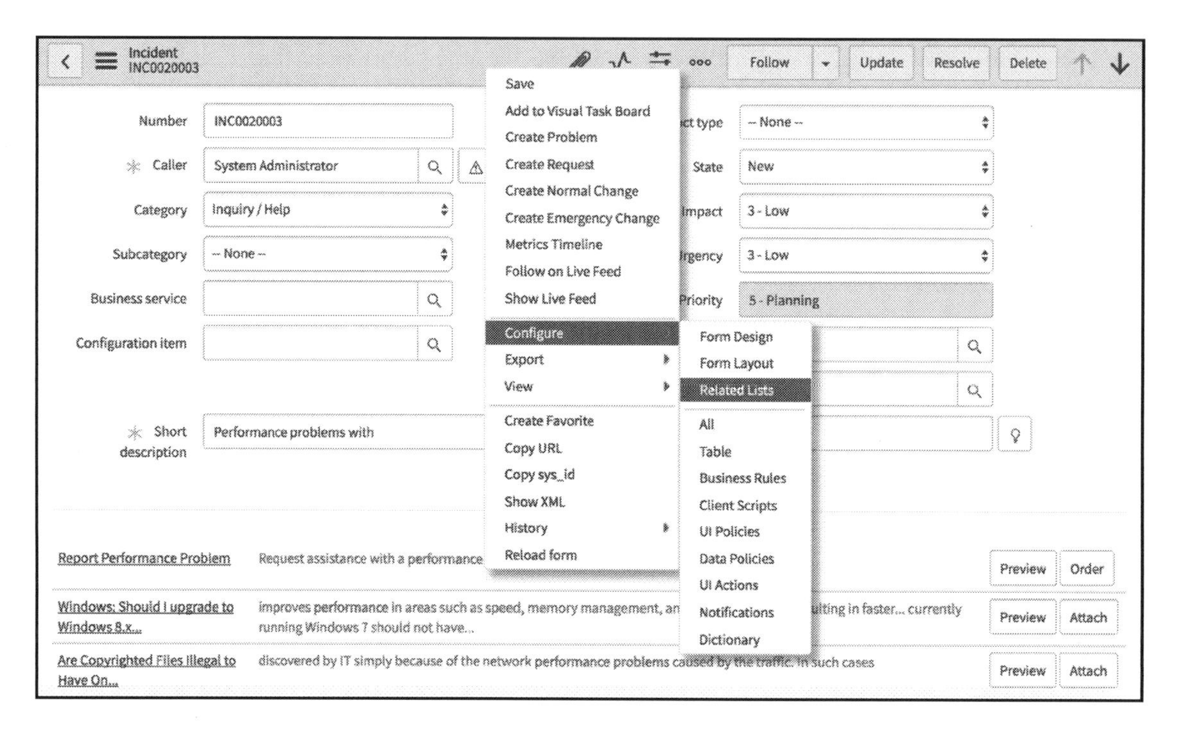


3. It will take you to a page with a special UI referred to as **slush-bucket**.

The slush-bucket UI is used on multiple pages in the ServiceNow platform. It allows you to select one or more records from a list of available records either by double-clicking or selecting a record and clicking on the > icon to add and < icon to remove.

4. From the list of **Available** related lists in the **Incident** table, bring **Incidents by Same Caller** to the **Selected** bucket:

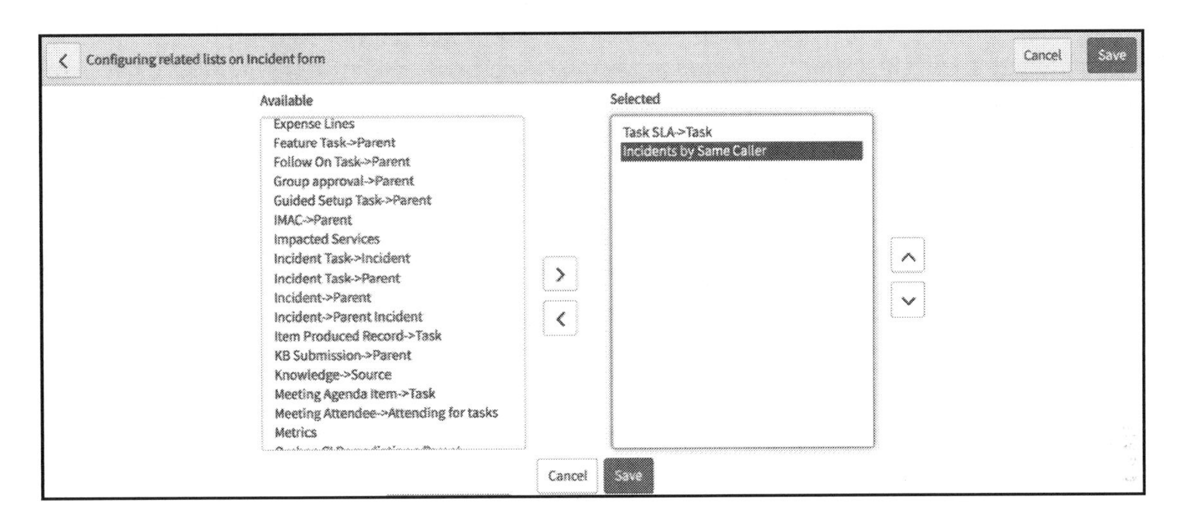


5. Then, click on the **Save** button and the system will take you to the **Incident** form again, where you can scroll to the bottom of the page to see the **Incidents by Same Caller** related list added to the form:

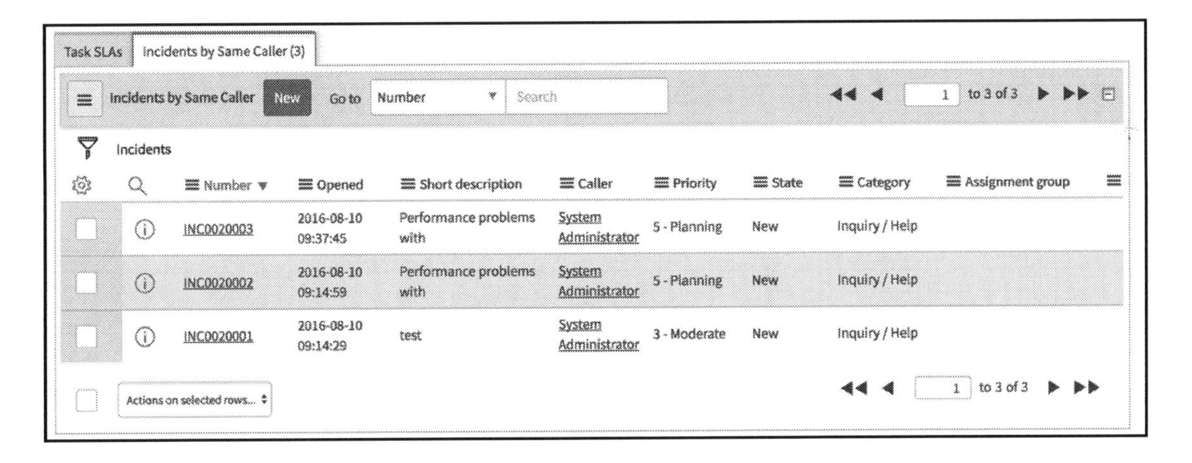

## Dot-walking

**Dot-walking** is a concept within ServiceNow that enables you to drill down to records, as in the Filter UI. When you are in the List of Records modules page, you usually end up using the Filter UI. The Filter UI lists all columns in the table. Like the **Incident** table, it lists Number, short description, created date, caller, and so on. Suppose we want to list all incidents by a **Caller** named **Joe Employee**. Using the Filter UI, it is quite easy to do this - simply select the **Caller** field as one of the filters and set the search value as **Joe Employee**:

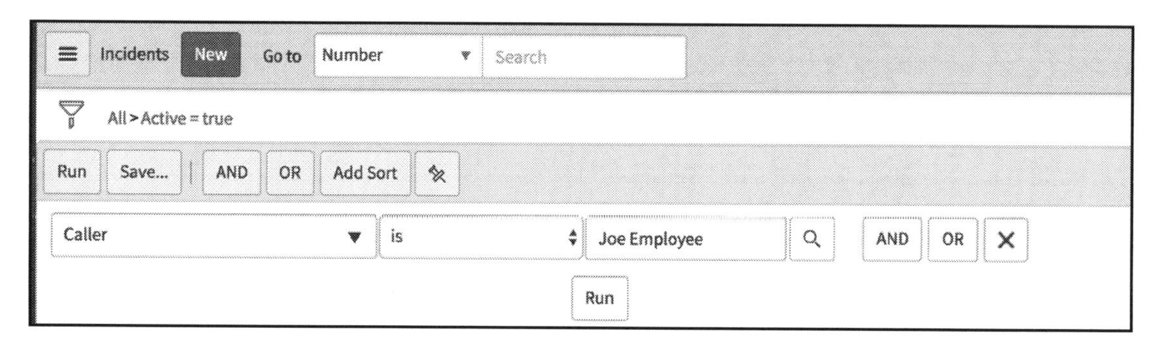


But what if we want to list records based on **Callers** who are from the sales department? We do not have a department field in the **Incident** table but we do have such a field in the user table. As we have learnt before in this chapter, the **Caller** field is of type reference and it is referring to a record in the users table. So, in order to list all Incidents of **Callers** who are from sales, we will employ a feature available in all Filter UIs called **dot-walking**:

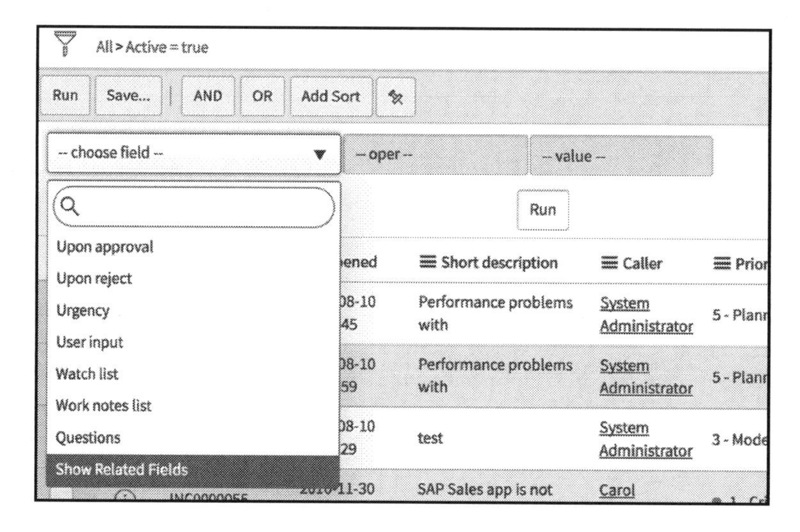

# Service Management applications

ServiceNow instance comes with many Service Management applications, which follow the ITIL v3 framework and allow you to manage processes such as incident management, change management, problem management, knowledge management along with configuration and assets management and service-level management.

These processes help in managing the life cycle of a ticket and are used in almost all IT service organizations. When you call your IT service desk and tell them that your Microsoft Outlook or some other software on your computer is not working properly, you are actually reporting an incident.

The Service Desk member (agent) will log an incident (ticket) on your behalf (IT customer) - provide you with an incident (ticket) number, and mention you as the caller, so that they can easily identify who reported the incident. People working with the **Incident Management** team are responsible for working on incidents. They will update the ticket as and when some work is done on the ticket so as to keep you informed about the progress. The service desk agents can quickly resolve the incident by looking for any existing relevant knowledge articles stored in the knowledge management database.

If the Incident Management team is able to resolve the incident, they will mark the ticket as resolved and you (the customer who reported the incident), can close the ticket. If you are unsatisfied with the work done, re-open the ticket or the ticket will auto close in about 3 days (default) if you do not take any action.

If the Incident Management team cannot resolve an incident, it is then assigned to the **Problem Management** team and a problem ticket is created, which is usually linked to the original Incident ticket. The task of the Problem Management team is to find the root cause of the issue and try to fix it permanently. They are usually senior level team members working with the IT Support Desk.

In cases where the Incident or Problem Management team cannot resolve the ticket or a change is required to close the ticket, a change request is initiated and the Change Management team is assigned to work on it. A change request goes through multiple levels of workflow and approvals. Approvals may be required in order to change or procure new software or hardware. Also, changing critical hardware like a router, email server, web server, or upgrading to a newer version may affect one or more client/customers. It is the duty of the Change Management team to ensure a smooth transition while lowering the effect on normal business functions.

Tickets (incident, problem, and change requests) are usually affected by Service Level Agreements. An SLA is an agreement between the customer and your IT support desk. ServiceNow allows administrators to define any number of SLAs based on any condition using the SLA definitions modules. If a ticket is resolved within a specified amount of time in the SLA, the ticket is said to have achieved the SLA, and if it fails to be resolved within the specified time, it is said to have breached the SLA. The Service Level Management application within the platform allows administrators to easily define multiple scenarios when **Service Level Agreements** (**SLA**), **Operation Level Agreements** (**OLA**), and under-pinning contracts get attached to a ticket.

ServiceNow also offers a means to automatically calculate priority of a ticket based on **Priority Lookup Rules**. If impact (for example, number of components depending on an item) is high and urgency is high, then we assume that priority is critical. Similarly, ServiceNow also offers a means to auto-assign tickets based on any condition using the **Assignment Rules**. Example: Suppose the category of an incident ticket is Network, in such cases, we can always automatically assign such tickets to a network group.

Another important application under Service Management is configuration and asset management. Configuration Management allows you to maintain a record for all configuration items in your organization like computers, laptops, routers, servers, racks, hard disk, network attached storage, printers, along with software component records like Apache, IIS, JBoss, SAP, MySQL, Oracle database instances, and so on.

Asset management, on the other hand, allows you to store software licenses and agreements and a list of hardware consumables like keyboard, mouse, and computers along with details like the user it has been assigned to.

# ServiceNow application architecture

In ServiceNow, applications represent packaged solutions designed to deliver and manage a business process like Incident Management, Change Management, Problem Management, and Knowledge Management:

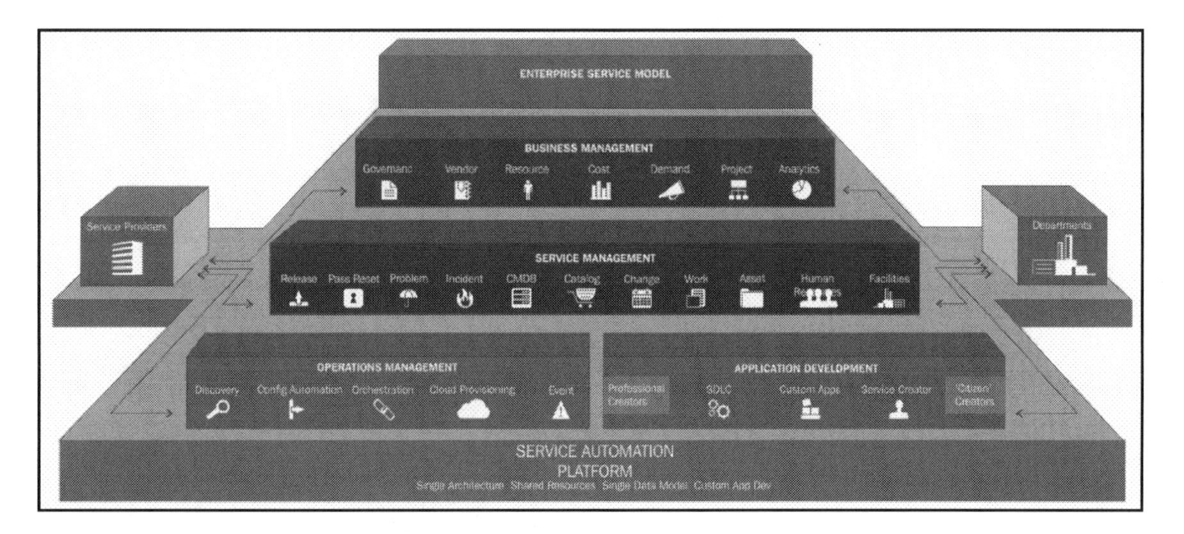


The ServiceNow platform has four major constituents - often referred to as a single source of *truth* by leaders at ServiceNow, Inc:

- Single architecture
- Shared resources
- Single data model
- Custom app development

# Single architecture

Every application in ServiceNow follows the same architecture consisting of one or more modules and pages accessing data from various sources and tables. ServiceNow offers several out-of-the-box standard applications such as incident, change, problem, and knowledge management - and all of these standard applications share the same common architecture. Each application in ServiceNow has one of more of these components: application record, tables, UI elements, application files, and integration services. We will be digging deep into these components in `Chapter 4`, *Application Scopes*.

## Shared resources

ServiceNow applications utilize system resources that are shared by all applications. These include user interface, security access control, workflow engines, reporting, and notification handlers along with system resources such as database, storage, and memory.

## Single data model

Each ServiceNow instance has its own database and is used to store data in tables comprised of various columns. While each application has their specific set of tables and columns, there are some tables like users, `cmdb_ci`, and tasks shared by many different applications. All records stored in tables are structured quite similarly with the column `sys_id` as the unique primary key thus enabling a single system of records that correlates all business services and processes throughout the enterprise.

While working on the ServiceNow platform, developers do not have to worry about how the database is set up or how tables are structured. On the other hand, administrators have access to many data management tools, giving them enough control over tables and data stored in them `Chapter 3`, *Data Management*.

## Advanced High Availability architecture

One of the most important contributing factors to the success of ServiceNow and reasons why enterprises trust it, is their **Advanced High Availability** (**AHA**) architecture. It is one of the key elements of ServiceNow; being able to offer a true enterprise cloud. Their multi-instance architecture along with Advanced High Availability is designed exclusively by ServiceNow to meet and exceed their enterprise customer's stringent requirements surrounding data security, availability, and performance.

ServiceNow's datacenters are designed to be available 24/7, 365 days a year and all data center components like servers and network devices are redundant and have multiple network paths to avoid a single point of failure. They back customer's production instances with multiple connections to the internet and load balance them within each data center. Furthermore, database servers in one data center are asynchronously replicated in real time to a peer data center within the same geographic region:

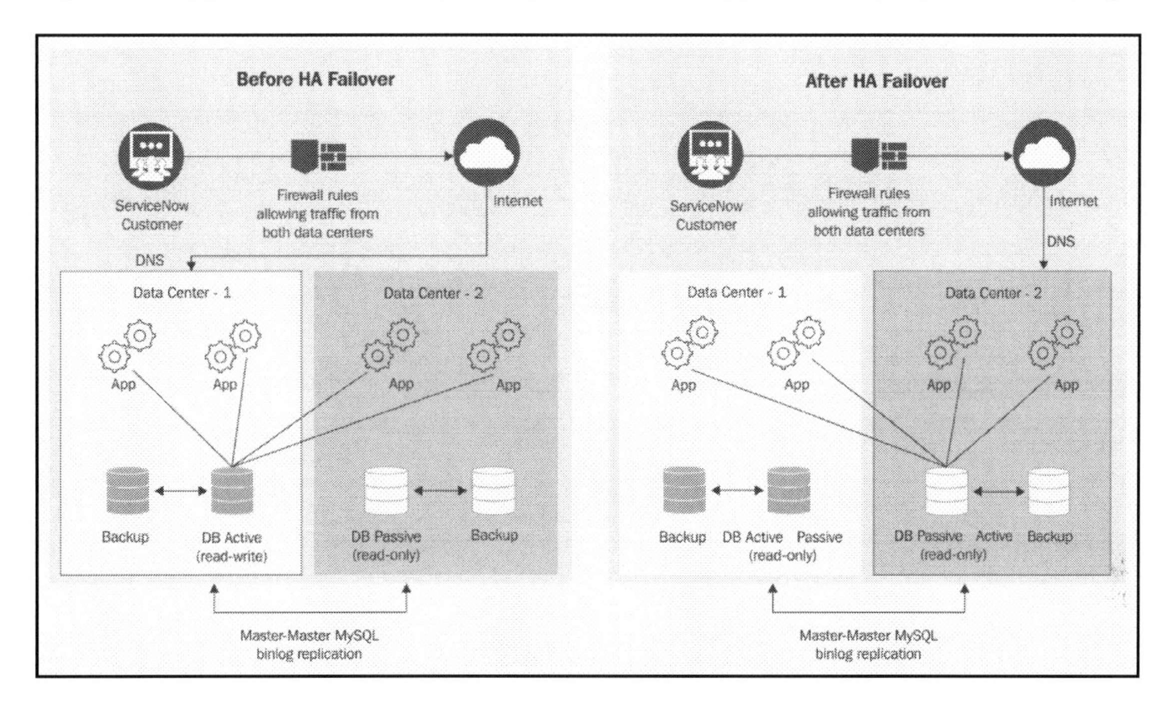


As of writing this book, ServiceNow operates a total of 16 data centers (eight pairs) in the following geographic locations:

- Asia Pacific Japan (APJ)
- Australia
- Europe
- Swiss (country-specific)
- Middle East and Africa (EMEA)
- North America:
    - America
    - Canada
- South America

Furthermore, to ensure data is never lost, ServiceNow conducts regular backups. The backup cycle consists of four weekly full backups and the past 6 days of daily, differential backups that provide 28 days of backups. ServiceNow doesn't rely on tapes and stores backup data to disk. Also, no backups are sent off site.

# Summary

In this chapter, we launched a ServiceNow instance and went through different user interface elements. This introduction of the user interface along with Service Management applications is a good starting point to get started working on the ServiceNow platform.

In the next chapter, you will go deep into users, groups, and roles, and all the possible user administration options available to us, making you aware of good user management practices.

# 2
# User Administration

Now that we have learned the basics of the ServiceNow platform, login process, and its user interface, let us dig deep into how to create and assign roles to new and existing users. As part of your project at ABCD, Inc, you are suppose to provide **Server Administrators** access to your newly procured ServiceNow instance and they should be able to access **Incident Management**, **Change Management**, **Problem Management**, and **Knowledge Management** applications.

In this chapter, we will learn how to create new users and associate them to a group. We will also learn how we can assign roles to groups and users. Furthermore, we will learn how we can impersonate a user to test if our newly created users have access to proper applications and modules.

**User Administration** is one of the easiest but most important functions an administrator and developer needs to perform. ServiceNow allows administrators various ways to manage users, groups, and roles using simple modules accessible through the User Administration application, as shown in the following screenshot on the right. Let us quickly go through the different modules available under the User Administration application:

- **Users**: Lists all users in the system and allows administrators to easily create or update user records and associate existing one to different groups or assign roles
- **Groups**: Lists all available groups and allows administrators to create or update group entries
- **Roles**: Lists all roles defined in the system and allows administrators to create or update role records
- **Logged in users**: Lists of users who are currently logged in to the ServiceNow instance
- **Active transactions**: Lists of transactions running in the foreground

- **All Active transactions**: Lists of transactions running in the system
- **Departments**: Lists departments defined in the system and allows administrators to easily create or update existing department entries
- **Locations**: Lists of all locations entries defined in the system and allows administrators to easily create or update existing location entries
- **Companies**: Lists of all companies defined in the system and allows administrators to easily create or update existing company entries
- **Location Map**: Plots all locations defined in the **Locations** module on to a Google Map
- **Countries**: Lists of countries defined in the system and allows administrators to easily create or update existing country entries

In this chapter, we will get started with ServiceNow User Administration and gain an in-depth understanding of how to create new users, and assign group and roles to existing ones.

This chapter will cover the following topics:

- Creating a new user
- Creating a new group
- Creating a new role
- Associating users to one or more groups
- Assigning roles to a group
- Impersonating as a different user
- Configuring location, department, and country

# Creating a new user

Every ServiceNow developer instance comes with some pre-populated demo data, which also includes some demo user accounts. In ServiceNow, all user records are stored in a table named `sys_user`:

1. Click on the **Users** module under the **User Administration** application to list all users in the system, as shown in the following screenshot:

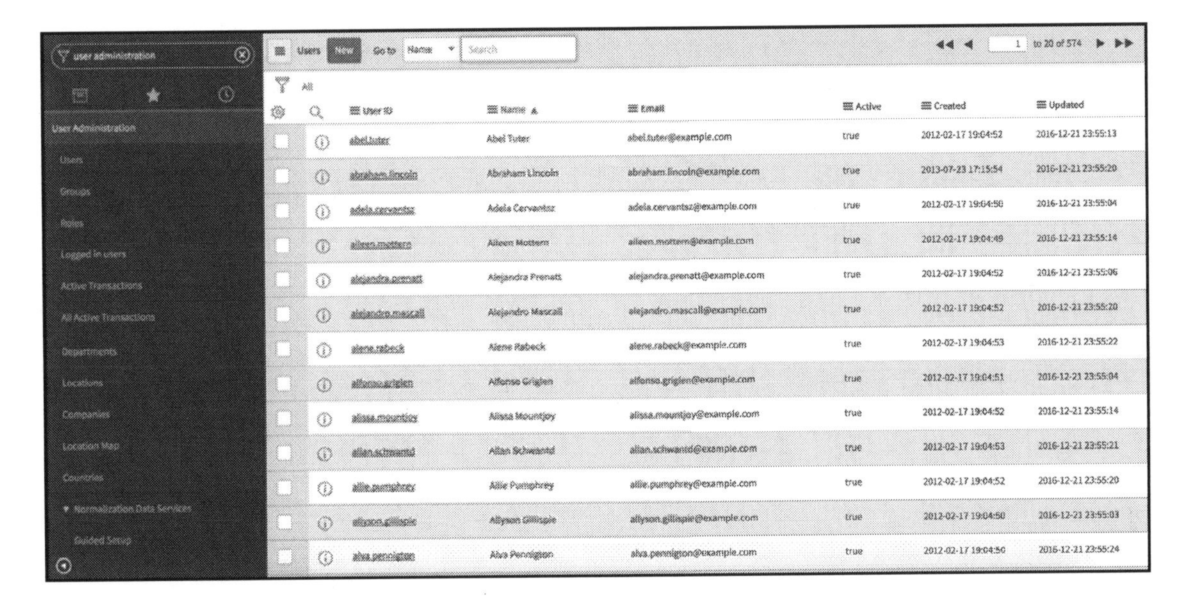


2. Click on the **New** button on the top left of the content frame to bring up the **User** table's **New record** form:

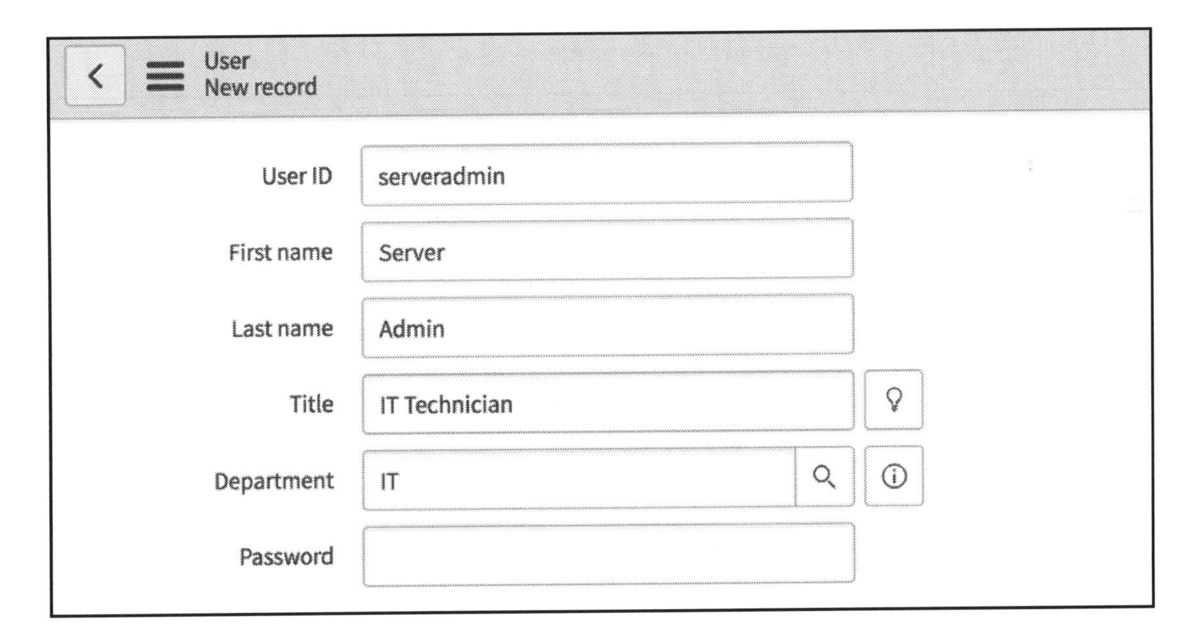

3. Fill in the **User ID**, **First name**, **Last name**, **Password**, and other fields as needed and click on the **Submit** button to create a new user. The **User ID** field is mandatory and must be unique and is also referred to as username.
4. Once you click on the **Submit** button, you will be brought back to the list of users page and will see a message confirming that the new user record has been created:

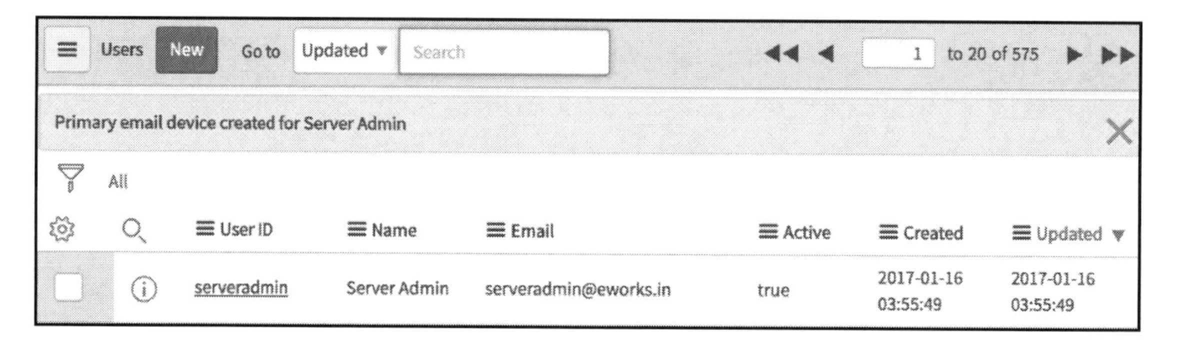


5. In the **List of Users** page, you will be able to see the new user we just created. Clicking on the **User ID serveradmin** will bring you back to the **User details** form in the **Update** mode, where it is possible to update a user's record, and assign roles and groups using related lists.

Users with the `user_admin` role can create and edit users, groups, and roles.

# Things to consider when creating a user

When we create a new user in ServiceNow, we need to consider the following key points:

- Make sure that each user is associated with a group
- Consider which fields are mandatory in order to ensure full and complete user profiles
- Use a unique user ID when creating new profiles or updating existing profiles
- Consider creating an ITIL-based role for each administrator or process owners for managing different types of tasks

Once we have created a new user account, we can create any new group or role that we would like to use or else we can also associate any of the existing groups and roles to the new user.

Most large companies usually integrate the ServiceNow platform with their identity provider services, such as active directory to import and periodically sync users into the Users table without having to manually create them.

# Creating a new group

A group in ServiceNow is a collection of users who share a common function within the organization. Creating and managing groups needs to be taken seriously as it can impact security and affect the end user's experience. Members of groups may perform tasks such as approving catalog requests, resolving incidents, or receiving email notifications.

Once we have created a new user, we need to create a new group and assign it to the new user. User groups are stored in a system table named `sys_user_group`, as shown in the following screenshot:

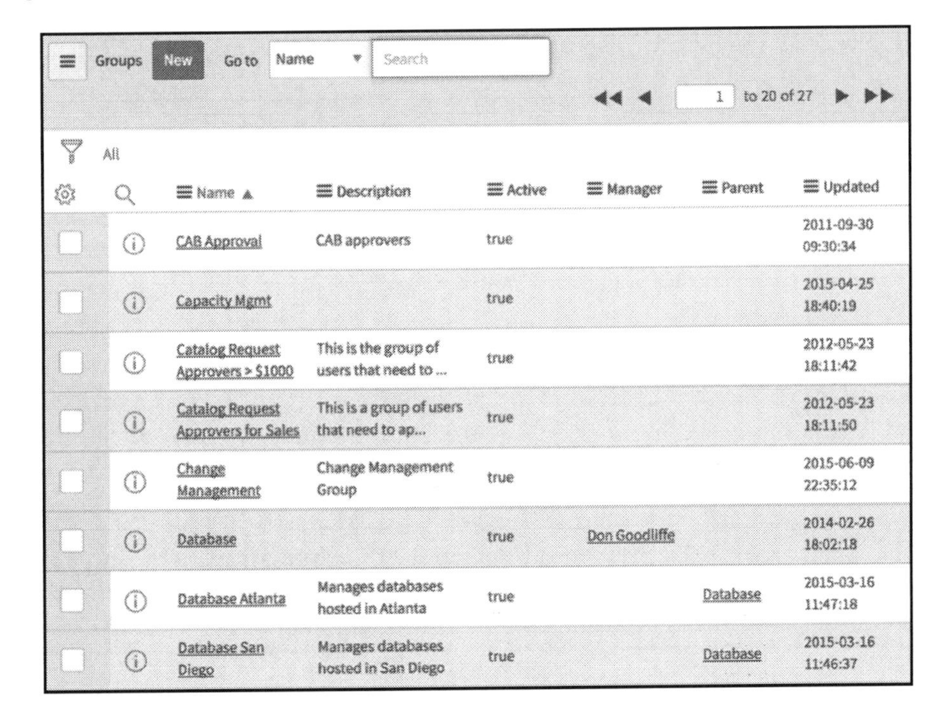


| Name ▲ | Description | Active | Manager | Parent | Updated |
|---|---|---|---|---|---|
| CAB Approval | CAB approvers | true | | | 2011-09-30 09:30:34 |
| Capacity Mgmt | | true | | | 2015-04-25 18:40:19 |
| Catalog Request Approvers > $1000 | This is the group of users that need to ... | true | | | 2012-05-23 18:11:42 |
| Catalog Request Approvers for Sales | This is a group of users that need to ap... | true | | | 2012-05-23 18:11:50 |
| Change Management | Change Management Group | true | | | 2015-06-09 22:35:12 |
| Database | | true | Don Goodliffe | | 2014-02-26 18:02:18 |
| Database Atlanta | Manages databases hosted in Atlanta | true | | Database | 2015-03-16 11:47:18 |
| Database San Diego | Manages databases hosted in San Diego | true | | Database | 2015-03-16 11:46:37 |

1. In the **User Administration** application, click on the **Groups** module to list all groups defined in the instance.
2. Click on the **New** button on the top left of the content frame to define a new group:

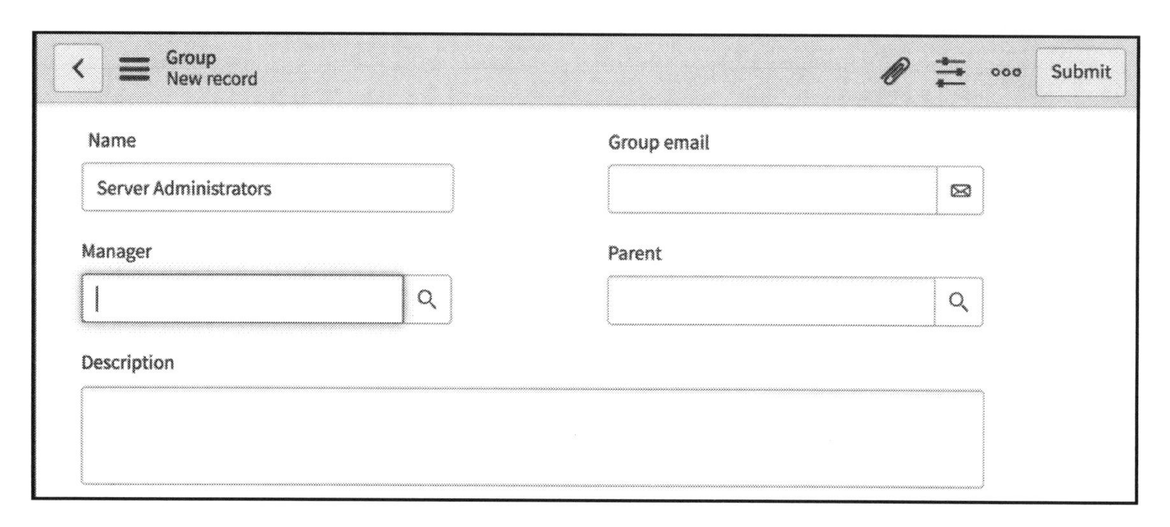


3. We will set new group's name as `Server Administrators`. Click the **Submit** button to create the new group.

In ServiceNow, groups can be hierarchal. If a group has a parent, the child group inherits the roles of the parent group. One of the key points to note here is that the members of the child group are not members of the parent group, which means that any ticket assigned to the parent group may not be visible to the child group; however, any ticket assigned to the child group will be visible to the members of the parent group.

## Creating a new role

In ServiceNow, roles are used to limit and control access to features in applications and modules. Once access to an application or module has been restricted by a role, any user group or user assigned to the role are granted access.

We can create a new role in the **Roles** modules under the **User Administration** application. The **Roles** modules will list all roles currently defined in the instance. Roles are stored in a system table named `sys_user_role`:

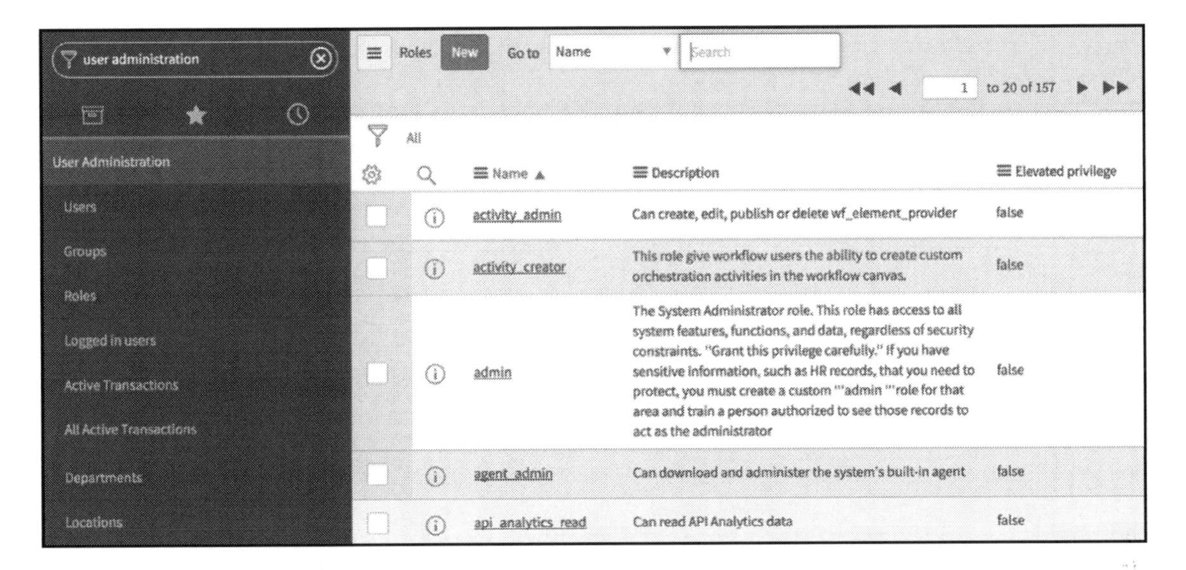


1. Click on the **New** button to bring up the **New Record** form and enter a name for your new role. In our case, we will set the new role as `servers` and click on the **Submit** button.
2. We will leave the **Elevated privilege** checkbox unchecked, which will be covered later in the book. The **New Record** form of the **Roles** tables is shown in the following screenshot:

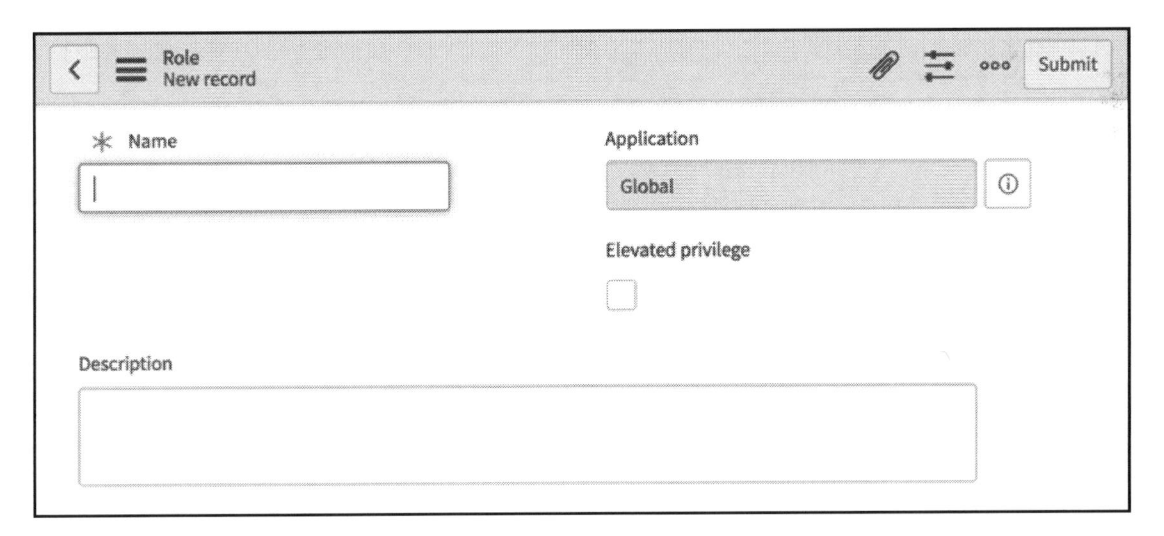

Roles can contain other roles and thus any access granted to a role is granted to any role that contains it. For example, the `knowledge_admin` role contains the role knowledge, as shown in the following screenshot. Thus, any application or modules that has a requirement of role *knowledge* will also be accessible by groups and users assigned to the `knowledge_admin` role:

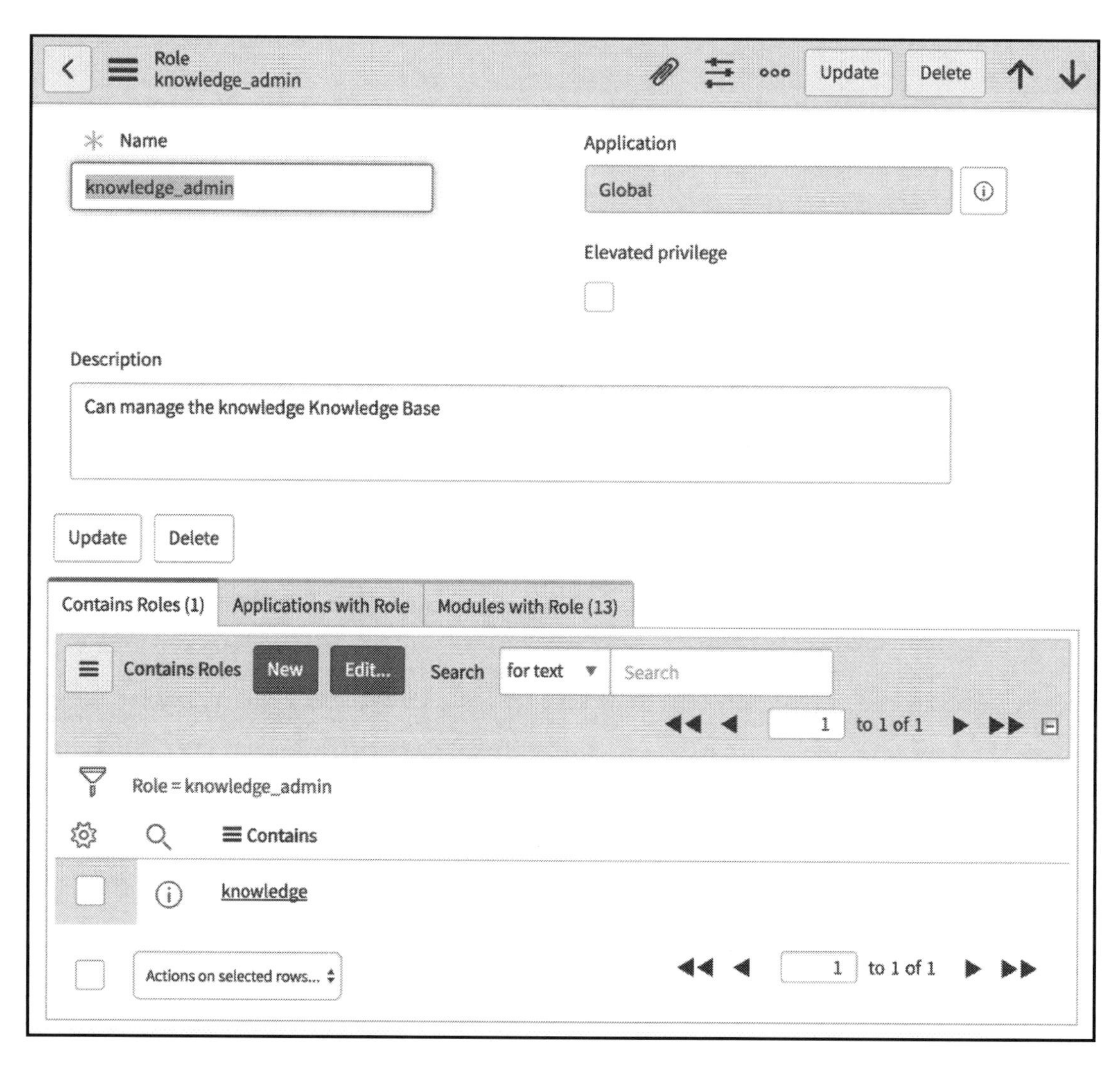

Once we have created a new role, we will assign it to a group. But first we will assign a user to a group.

## Associating a user to one or more groups

To make sense of the newly created user, group, and role, we need to associate them. While it is possible to assign a role to a user, it is not recommended. We will instead associate the user to a group and then we will assign some roles to that group:

1. Open the `serveradmin` user record from the **Users** module under the **User Administration** application menu and scroll to the bottom of the page where you see the **Groups** related list, as shown in the following screenshot, and click on the **Edit...** button to assign:

2. In order to associate a user to one or more groups, we need to pull the User's record from the **Users** module and **Edit...** the **Groups** related list:

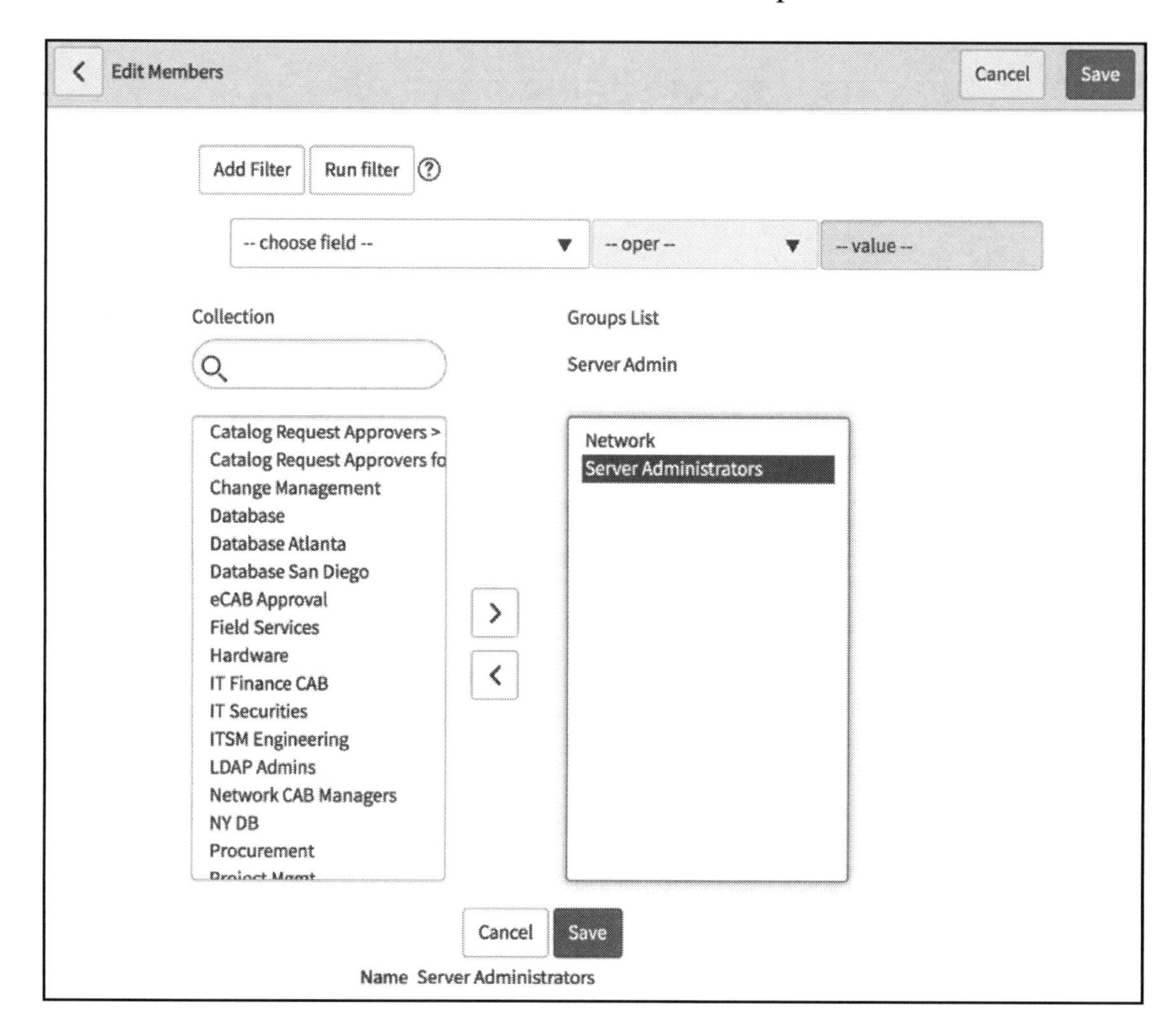


3. Click on the **Save** button once you have selected the required groups to be brought back to the users detail form.

It is possible to filter the collection of available groups by using the filter tools available on the top of the slush-bucket page. You can filter based on when the record was **Created**, **Created By**, or just about any other field available in the Groups (`sys_user_group`) table. We can also filter on any of the referenced fields, using the dot-walking we learnt in the previous chapter.

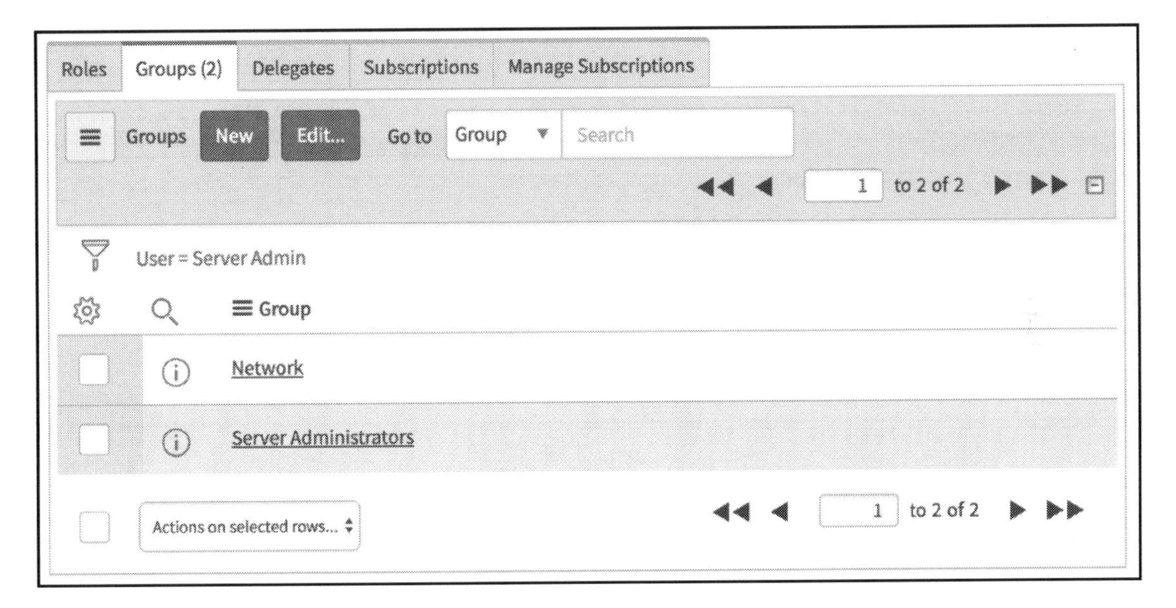


# Assigning a role to a group

We can add a role to a group to enable the group's members to be able to access the application or module restricted by a role. Assigning a role to a group is a fairly simple process; however, one must be careful while granting roles to groups, as it deals with Security and many other features. Once a role is assigned to a group, members of the group will be able to gain access to applications and modules:

1. Open the **Server Administrator** group we created previously through the **Groups** module and **Edit...** the **Roles** related list.

2. From the slush-bucket, find servers **Roles List** we created and bring it to the selected list on the right and click **Save**:

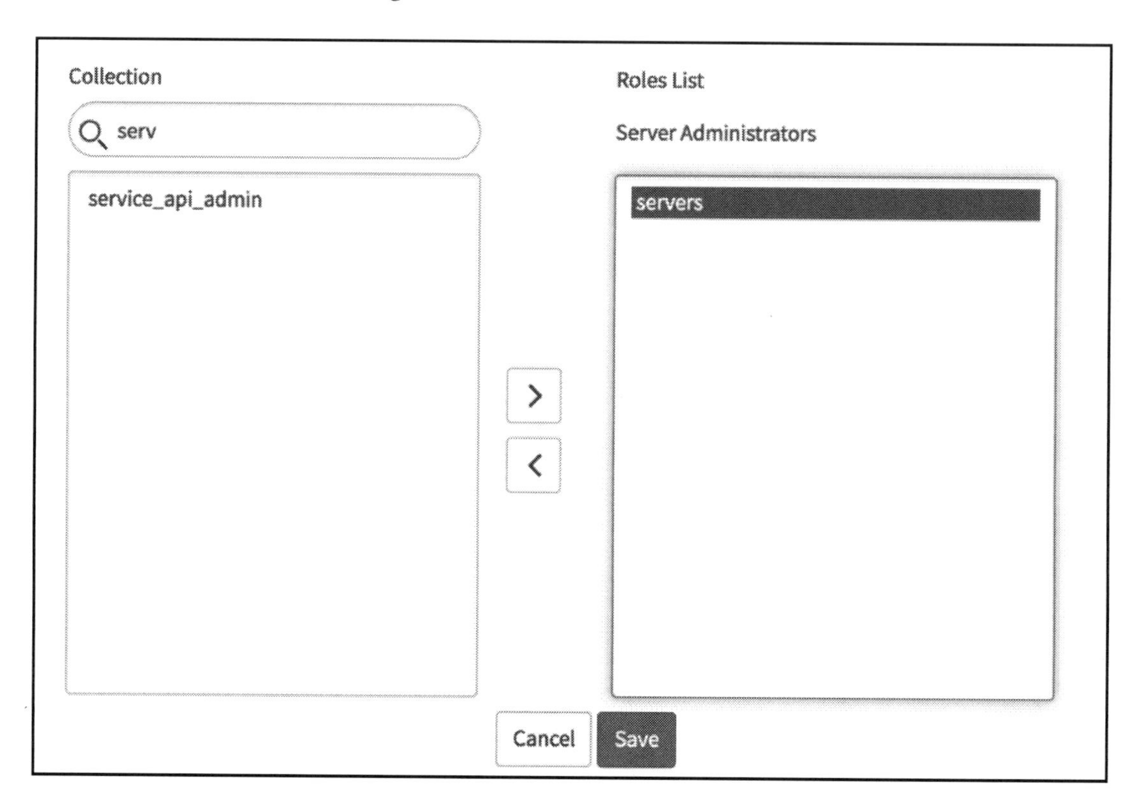


3. Once we add **servers** role to the group, we can see it appear in the **Roles** related list in the **Server Administrators** group detail page:

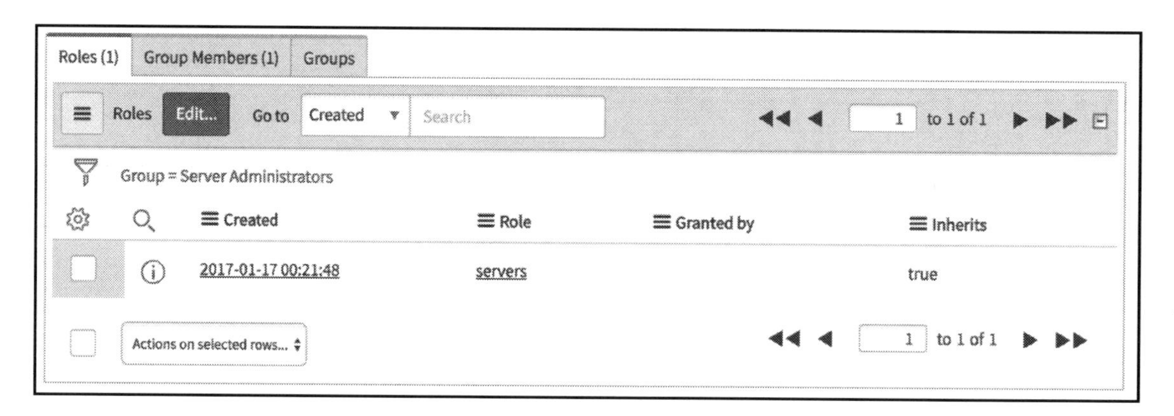

# Best practices for managing groups

There are four major aspects to consider when associating users to groups.

## Task assignments

In ServiceNow, assignment groups are the most common user group type consisting of one or more members. There exists an out-of-the-box relation between assignment groups and the *assigned to* field in different ServiceNow applications such as Incident Management, Problem Management, Change Management, or Service Catalog Management. In real-world scenarios, it's typically mandatory for the assignment group to be identified and populated on task records before a Service Desk user can perform any update to any task or ticket.

This assignment group field will allocate responsibility of working on the task to the selected team and any associated SLA will be attached to the ticket. If the assigned group is not responsible for working on the task, the group is now responsible for reassigning the task to a more suitable group.

There are many out-of-the-box assignment groups defined in the system including, but not limited to:

- Service Desk
- Software
- Network
- Database
- Procurement

These groups can also have a hierarchical structure employing the following parent/child group dependency:

- Software:
  - Microsoft
  - Adobe
- Database:
  - MySQL admins
  - Oracle database admins
  - DB backup admins
  - DB monitoring

# Approvals

When designing approvals in ServiceNow workflows, we have the option to select user approval or group approval. Over the past years working on ServiceNow, I've realized that it is always better to use group approvals as much as possible since it allows us to add or remove members from a group without any development and changes to the workflow. Even if this group only contains one person, it's still a preferred method. You can also create custom groups for approving any process. In any real-world scenario, it is always recommended to consider all different Approval groups and define them in the system and assign an appropriate role before going live with your application.

# Security

As a best practice, I recommend not to directly assign roles to any user. Instead, we should first create a relevant group, if one doesn't already exist, and assign roles to this group. A group can have multiple roles assigned and also roles can contain other roles as needed. These features give an immense level of flexibility to the administrators and ensure that things do not get complex.

Administrators can define the **Access Control List** (**ACL**) to limit read, write, create, and delete access for field data, records, and tables. With this granular security ability, you may need to create additional groups for elevated permissions (see `Chapter 5`, *Application Scopes*).

# E-mail notifications

Email notifications are another important aspect to consider when defining a group, which is sent during task assignments and updates. You can use these groups to automatically send an email letting users know that a task has been assigned to their group or about an update made to the task.

# Impersonating a user

Users with an *admin* or *impersonator* role can impersonate as any other user in the instance. This feature is useful for testing when making changes to applications and modules and to ensure proper security access.

There are three important user accounts that come by default with every developer instance:

- `admin`: The system administrator account with the *admin* role has access to all applications and modules
- `itil`: The Service Desk user with access to ITIL applications, such as incident management, problem management, change management, configuration management, service catalog, and so on
- `employee`: A normal user account with no role or group assigned and access to just the Self-service application

The user account `serveradmin` that we created is associated with the **Server Administrators** group and has a **servers** role granted. Let us try to impersonate as all of these users to see the differences:

To impersonate as a `serveradmin` user, when logged in as admin, click on the user info menu icon in the top Banner Frame and select the **Impersonate User** option. It will open up a small modal window titled **Impersonate User**:

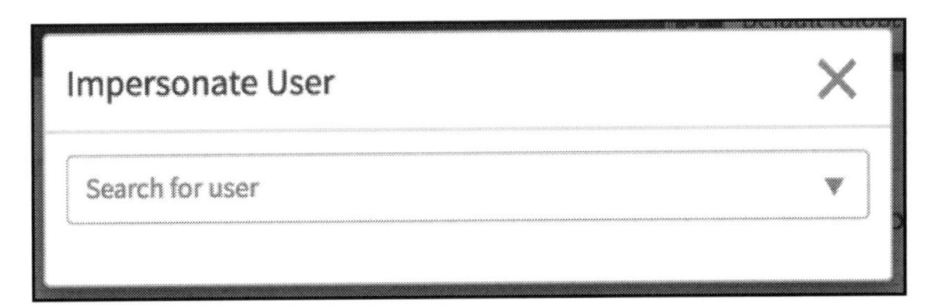

In the `Search for user` field start typing the name of the user and the auto complete text box will help you select the most relevant user. Select the `serveradmin` user from the auto complete list and the page will reload and log you in to the instance as a `Server Admin` user:

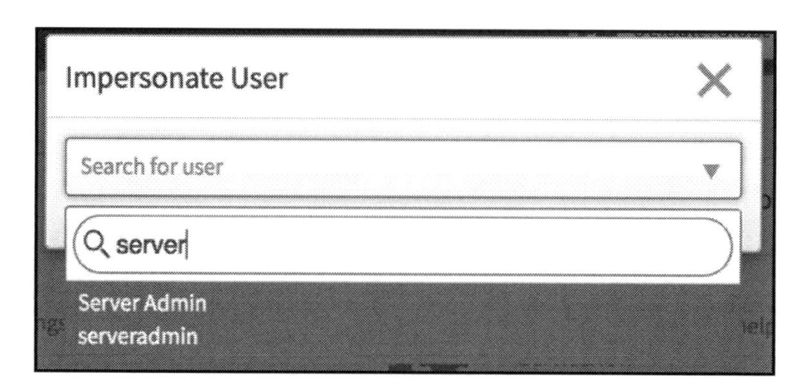


At this point, you will have access to only those applications and modules that are accessible by the user you are currently impersonating.

You can repeat the steps to impersonate to log in as the user `itil` and `ess` to see how impersonation works and how groups and roles available to a group can affect access to different applications, modules, features, and capabilities in ServiceNow.

Once you are done with your testing, you can login back as Administrator simply by selecting **Impersonate user** in the **User** menu and selecting the **System Administrator** account.

ServiceNow instance logs all impersonations in the system log and can be seen by all users with admin roles and should be used carefully only for testing purposes.

# Companies, locations, and departments

Companies, locations, and departments in ServiceNow can be defined very easily and is used to categorize users, groups, and roles. It helps in easily sorting and looking up users belonging to a particular department, location, or company.

The need to add multiple companies may arise depending upon how your company is structured and if you are allowing vendors, manufacturers, and suppliers to access the system. It is also useful to categories users, groups, and roles when a company operates out from many different geographic locations.

## Adding a department

Follow these steps to define a new department:

1. Navigate to **User Administration** | **Departments**.
2. Click **New**.
3. Fill in the following fields:
    - Name field must be populated
    - Description field can be used to mention detail about the record
4. Click **Submit**.

Similarly, **Companies** and **Locations** can also be added using the **Departments** and **Locations** modules available under the **User Administration** application.

## Associating a user with a department

Navigate to the **Users** modules under the **User Administration** application and open the `serveradmin` user record we created previously in the chapter.

In the **Department** reference field, either start typing the name of the **Department**, for example, IT or Human Resource, and select the appropriate **Department** name from the auto-complete suggestion list or click on the search icon on the right of the field to open a pop-up reference selector window:

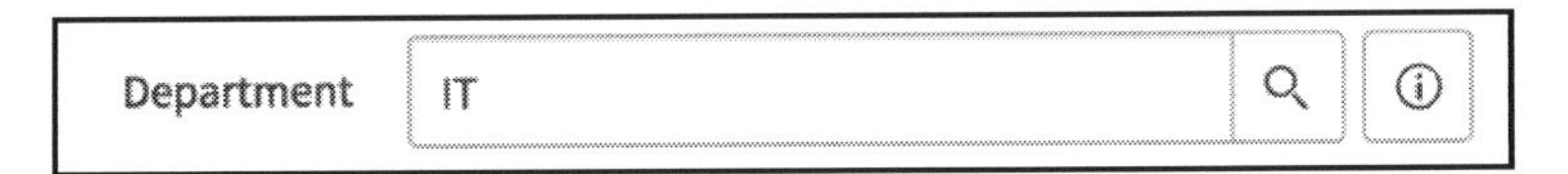


# Managing user sessions

ServiceNow offers multiple ways to manage user sessions. While administrators have the ability to impersonate any user, they can also completely lockout the user, make users inactive, or terminate any individual user session.

# Terminating sessions of a logged in user

The **Logged in Users** module under the **User Administration** application lists sessions of all the users currently logged in to the system:

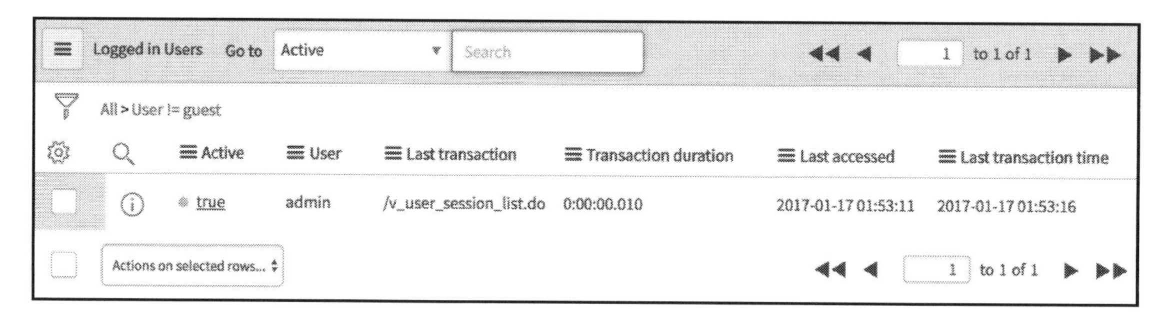


An administrator can view the details of any of the listed sessions by clicking on the info icon and read the entire session logs. It is possible to lock out a user's session by simply clicking on the **Lock Out Session** button on the **Session detail** page:

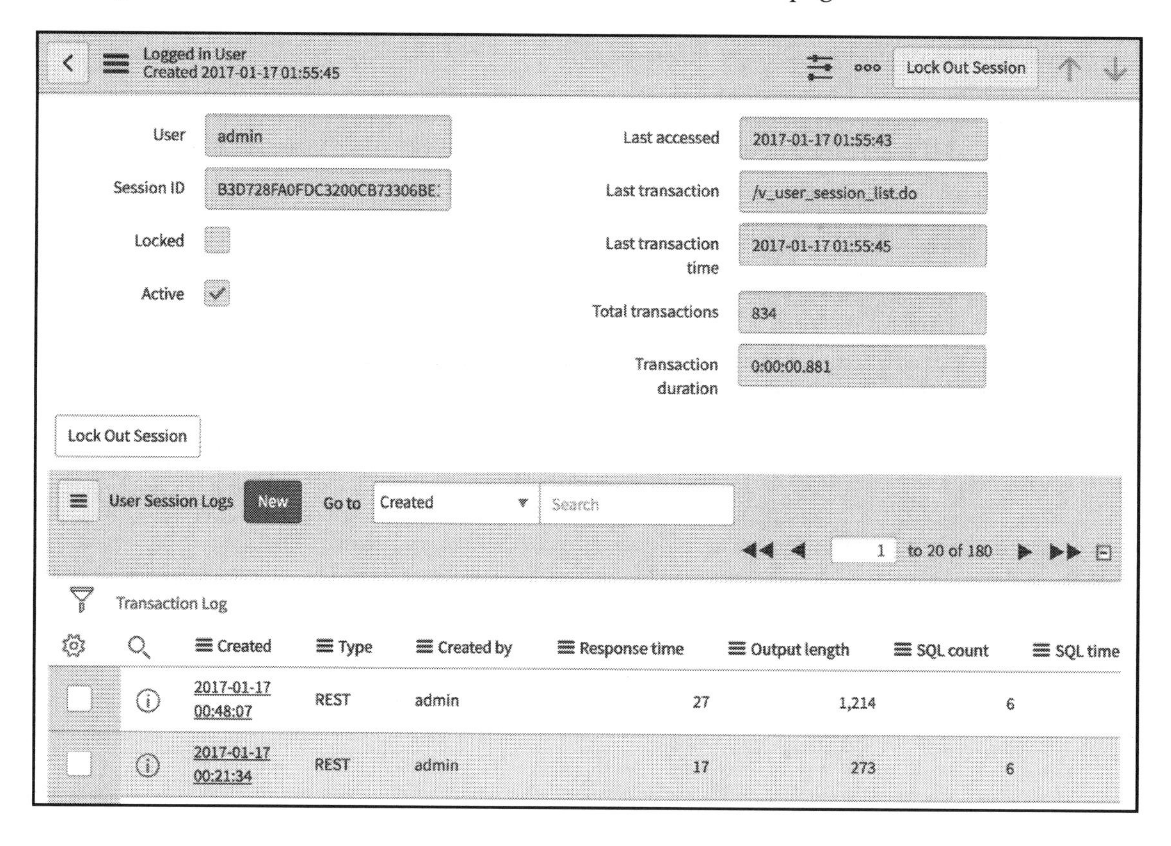

A user might have logged in from different browsers thus there may be a scenario where more than one session belongs to one user. When locking down sessions from the **Session detail** page, we are only terminating one of the sessions of the users. Also, the user can still log back in and start a new session, as they are currently not **Locked out** of the instance.

## Locking out a user

In the **Users** modules under the **User Administration** application, open the record of the user you wish to lockout and check the **Locked out** checkbox, as shown here:

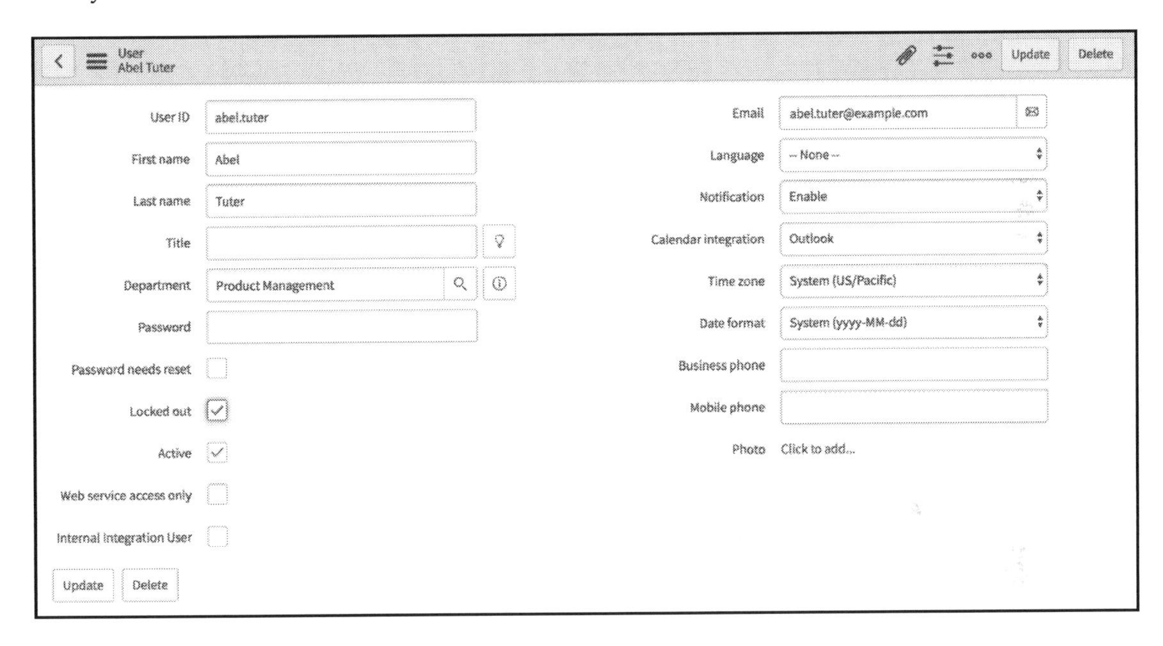


This will cause the user to remain active; however, they will be locked out of the system. Any attempt by the user to log in or generate actions through email will fail and all their existing user sessions will be terminated.

One important thing to understand here is that other users will still be able to open tickets on their behalf as the user is currently still active.

## Marking a user as inactive

To mark a user as inactive, open the Users module under the **User Administration** application, and open the record of the user you want to mark as inactive. Uncheck the **Active** checkbox and click on the **Update** button. Marking a user inactive hides them from all reference fields. Thus, no one can select the inactive user or request any task on their behalf, as shown in the following screenshot:

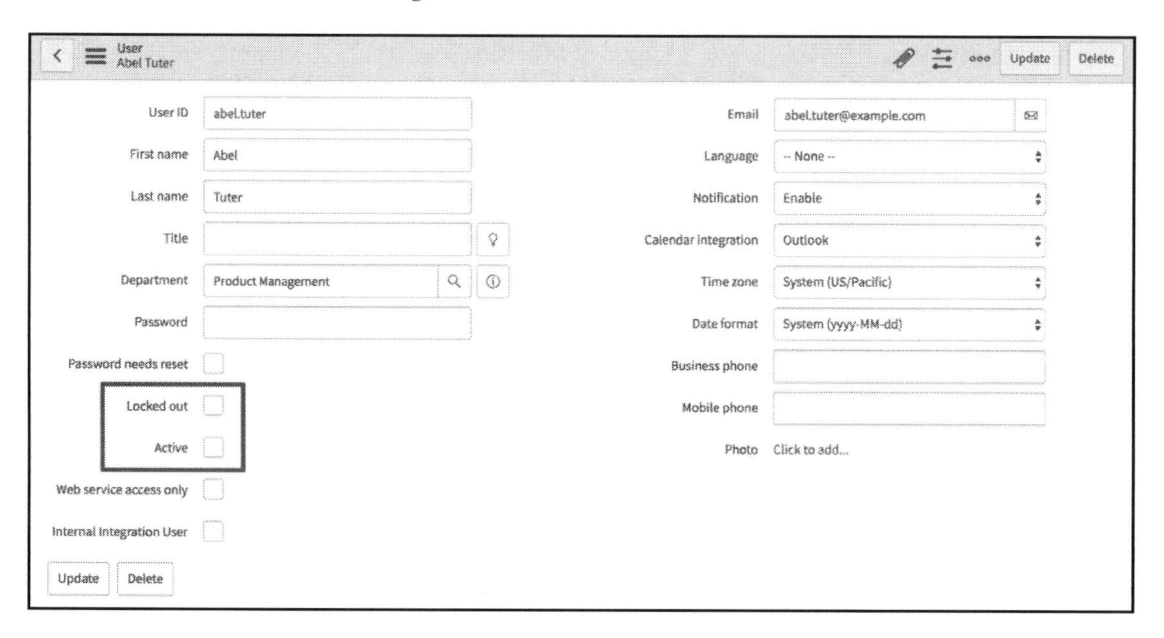


Furthermore, marking a user as inactive also executes a server-side script (**Lock Out Inactive Users** business rule), which in turn also set the locked out value to true thus causing the user's sessions to be terminated and being locked out.

# Summary

In this chapter, we learned how to create and manage users, groups, and roles and how this can affect access to different applications and modules. We also learned about best practices when creating users and groups and understood how to manager individual user sessions and lock out users when required.

In the next chapter, we will learn how standard tables are structured and the data dictionary can be used to perform simple database operations.

# 3
# Data Management

In the previous chapters, we learned the basics of the ServiceNow platform and how to perform user administration. Let us now dig deep into the concept of **data dictionaries** to understand how data is stored and segregated in ServiceNow. As part of your project at ABCD, Inc, you are supposed to create a custom table to manage all **point-of-sale** locations.

In this chapter, we will learn how to create a new table from scratch, extend existing tables, and add fields (or columns) to new or existing tables. We will also look at the structure of existing tables, such as `task` and `cmdb`.

Managing tables and columns is one of the most common jobs that administrators and developers have to perform when working on the ServiceNow platform. As ServiceNow is a cloud-based platform, direct access to the database isn't provided to customers. However, the ServiceNow platform features various modules that can be used to create and manage tables and columns.

In this chapter, we will cover the following topics:

- Database structure overview
- Using the **Tables & Columns** module
- Viewing the schema map
- Creating a new table
- Adding columns to a table
- Modifying column properties
- The `Task` table structure
- Creating a table that extends the `Task` table
- The configuration management (`cmdb_ci`) table
- Creating a new CMDB class

# Database structure

Like any other database-based application, information in ServiceNow instances is stored in structured and related tables, which consist of columns and rows of records. Tables can be related to each other in the following ways:

- **Extensions**: A table in ServiceNow may extend an existing table (parent class), thereby ensuring that all of the fields of the parent class are included as part of the child table. For example, the **Incident** table extends the `Task` table, and thus the Incident table has all of the fields that are available in the `Task` table.
- **One to many**: A table can consist of a field that refers to a record on another table. For example, the assigned to (`assigned_to`) field in the **Incident** record might contain a reference to a record in the users (`sys_users`) table. The **Reference**, **Glide List**, and **Document ID** field types can be added to create a one-to-many relation between two tables.
- **Many to many:** Two tables can have a bidirectional relationship when they both refer to a record stored in each another.
- **Database views:** This is a virtual relationship between two or more tables that can be used to generate complex reports.

In ServiceNow, a table that extends another table is referred to as a **child** class, and the table it extends is referred to as a **parent** class. Another table can further extend a child class if it is marked as extensible. In such a scenario, it is a table that is both a child and parent, as it extends and is also an extension of a table. A parent class that is not an extension of another table is called a **base** class.

# Key table-management modules

The following are the key features and modules available to manage tables and columns in the ServiceNow platform:

- **System Definition | Tables & Columns**: This module lists all the tables that exist in the ServiceNow instance in a single page. It offers a quick way to see a list of all the columns in a table, along with the attributes of each column, as shown in the following screenshot:

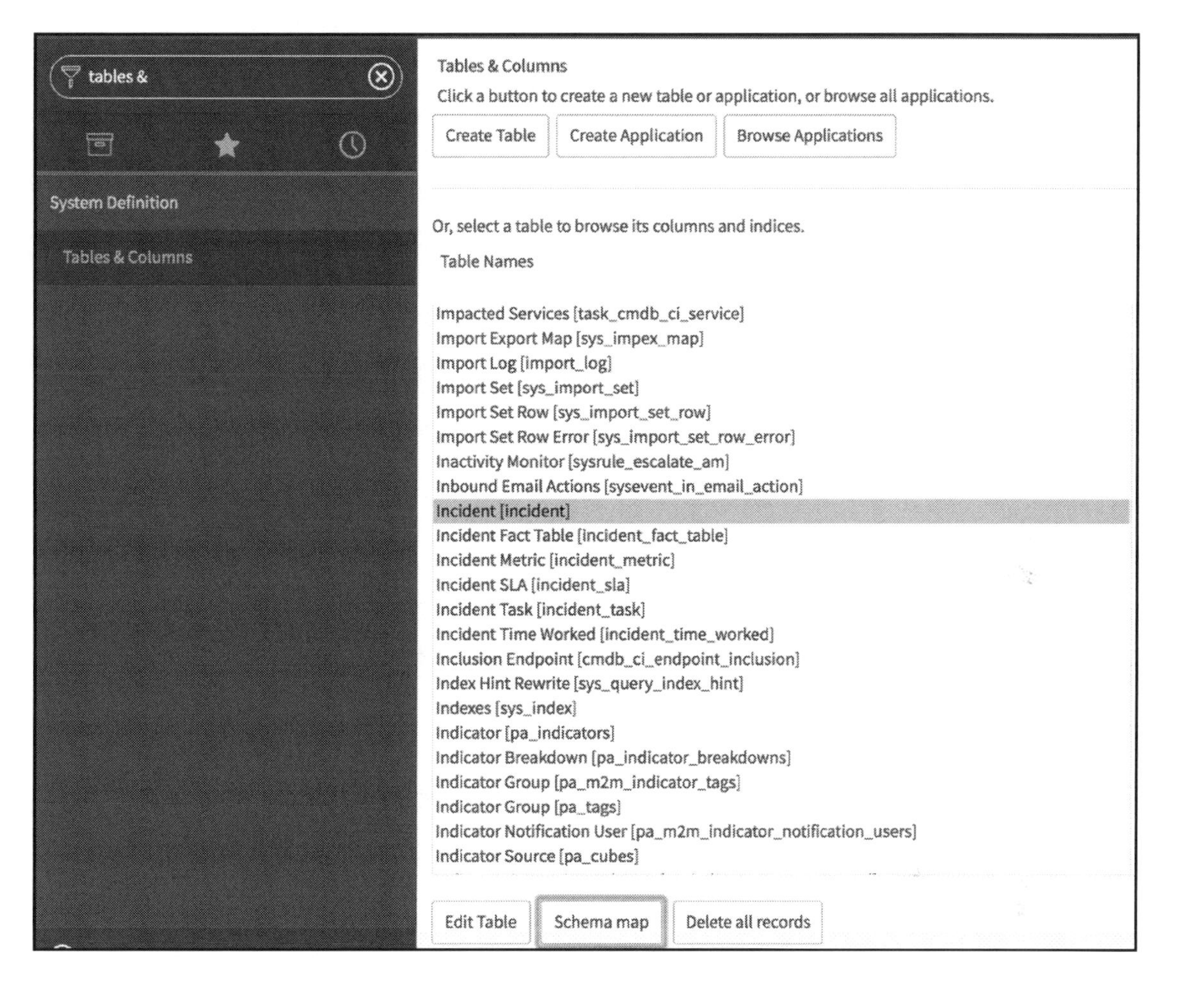


- **Schema map**: The schema map feature can be used to display relationships between tables visually, thereby helping you to understand the relation between tables and navigate through the database structure. As shown in the following screenshot, the schema map captures the following different intertable relationships:
    - Many-to-many relationships
    - Tables that extend other tables

- Tables that reference other tables through reference fields

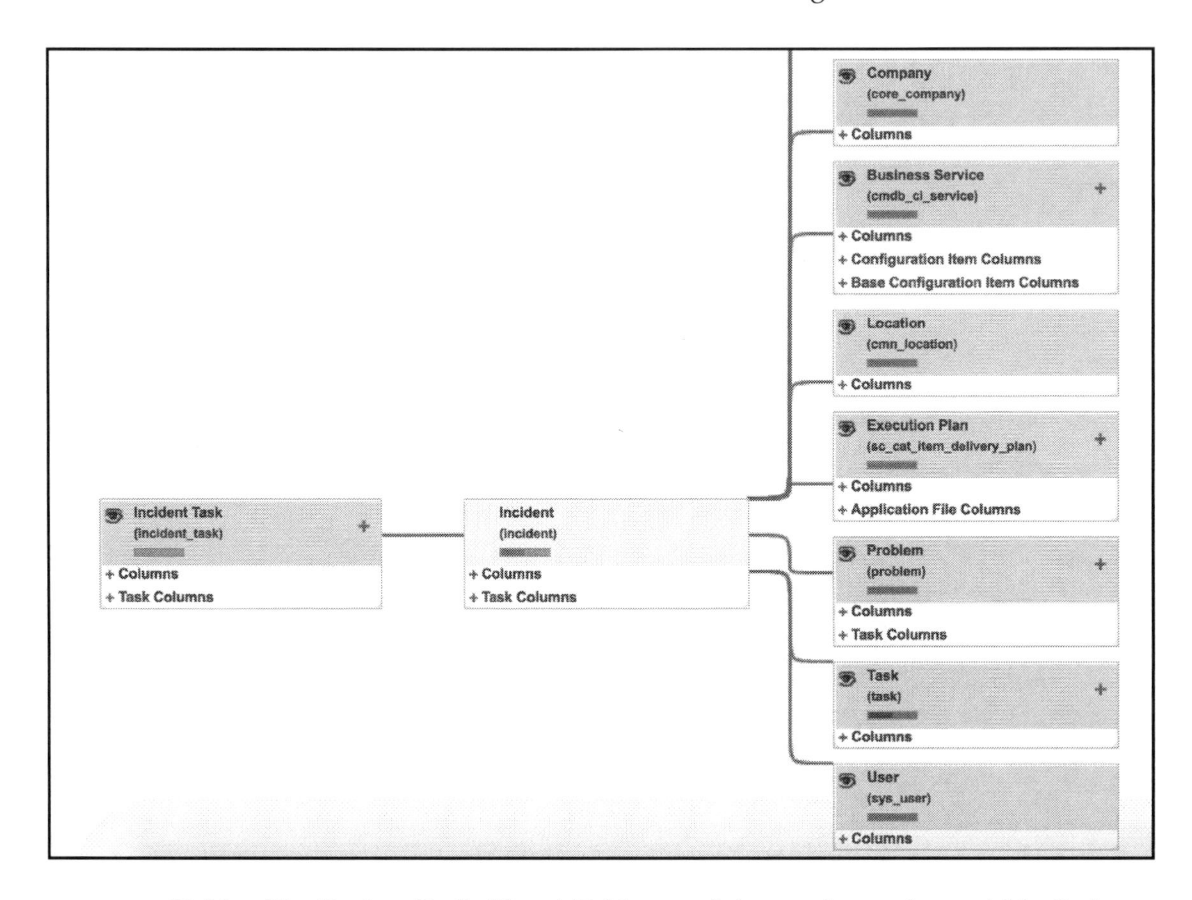


- **Tables**: The **System Definition** | **Tables** modules can be used to quickly find information about a table, such as its system name and the table that it is extending (**extended table**).
- **Dictionary**: The **System Definition** | **Dictionary** module lists information that defines the entire database schema. Dictionary is also referred to as the data dictionary.

# Tables & Columns

As mentioned previously, the **Tables & Columns** module lists all the tables in the instance in a single page, thus allowing developers to quickly view the list of tables and columns for any given table and access the attributes of any of its columns. As shown in the following screenshot, the **Tables & Columns** page is a special page that consists of the following three sections:

- **Table Names**: A list containing the labels of all the tables followed by the system name of the table within square brackets. For example, in the following screenshot, **Incident SLA** is the label, while `incident_sla` is the system name of the table.
- **Column Names**: This displays a list of columns available in the selected table. Each column has a distinctive icon that is based on column attributes, such as the element table. Clicking on the plus icon can expand the reference field columns:

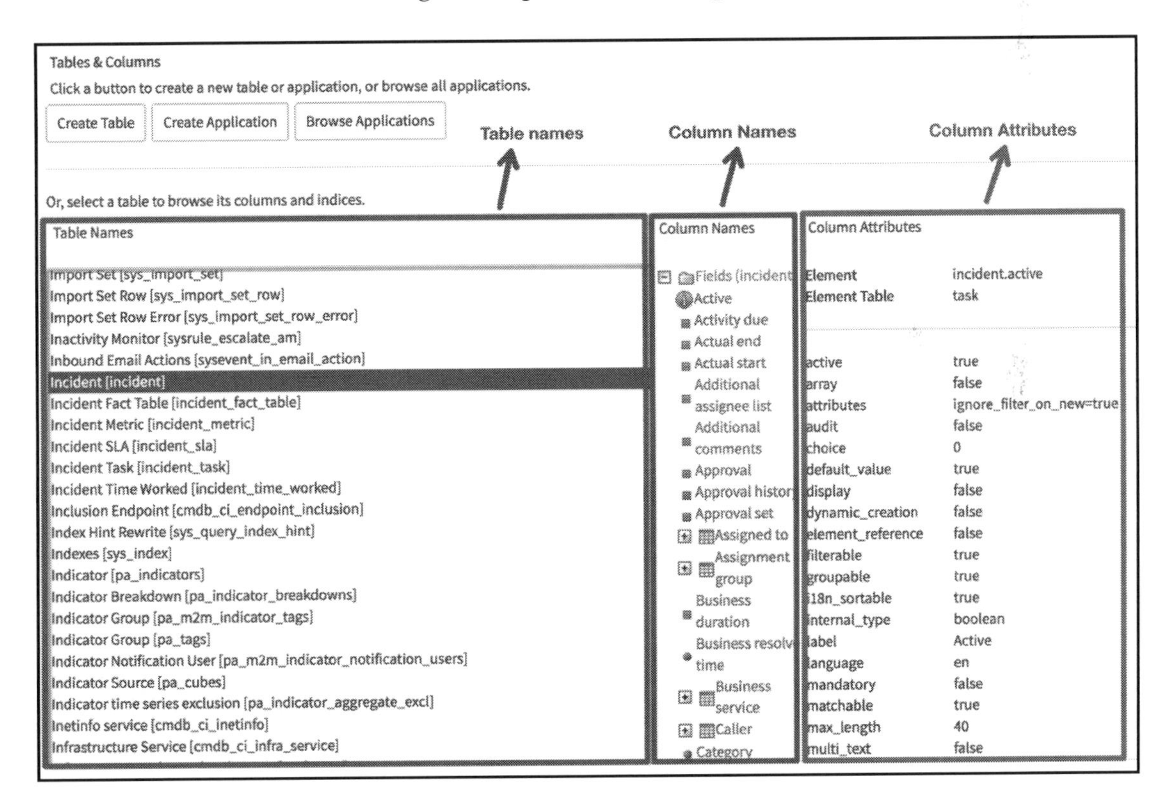

- **Column Attributes**: This is the rightmost section, where attributes of the selected column are shown. It usually consists of the type of the field, the system name of the element, and other field attributes based on the type of the selected field. If a field is extended from the parent class and is not part of the selected table, you may see a difference in the system name of the selected table and the **Element Table** attribute property.

# Schema map

The schema map feature allows you to view the relations between tables in a visual manner and explore the structure of the tables.

To view the **Schema map** for the incident table, in the **Tables & Columns** module, select the **Incident** table in the **Tables** names list and click on the **Schema map** button:

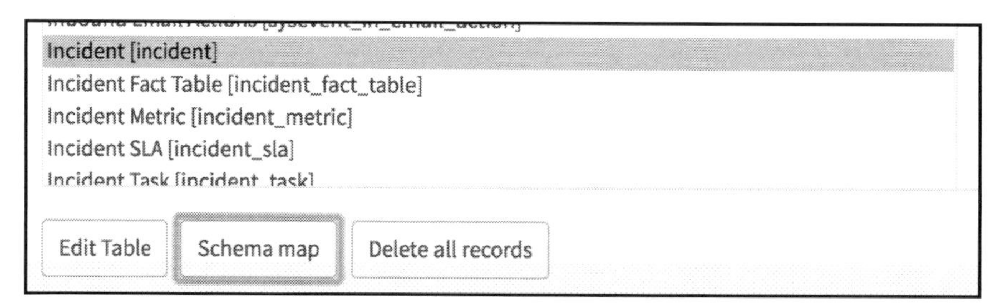

The schema map opens up in a new window or tab depending upon your browser settings. Ensure that you have your pop-up blocker disabled for your ServiceNow instance URL.

When in the **Schema map** page, we can quickly jump from one table to another using the document reference field available in the top-left corner, as shown in the following screenshot:

As shown previously, we can also use the check-box filters to show or hide interrelated tables based on their relationship type. The following filters based on relationship types are available to us:

- **Show referenced tables**: If checked, this displays all tables whose records are referenced from the current table
- **Show referencing tables**: If checked, this displays all tables that have a field that refers to the record of the current table
- **Show extended tables**: If checked, this displays the table (parent class) from which the current table (child class) is extended
- **Show extending tables**: If checked, this displays all tables (child classes) that are extending the current table (parent class)

In the schema map, we can click on the **+** icon next to the label **Columns** in order to see all the fields in the selected table:

**Incident**
**(incident)**

**– Columns**

| | |
|---|---|
| Business resolve time: | Integer |
| Caller: | reference to User |
| Category: | String |
| Caused by Change: | reference to Change Request |
| Change Request: | reference to Change Request |
| Child Incidents: | Integer |
| Close code: | String |
| Incident state: | Integer |
| Notify: | Integer |
| On hold reason: | Integer |
| Parent Incident: | reference to Incident |
| Problem: | reference to Problem |
| Reopen count: | Integer |
| Resolve time: | Integer |
| Resolved: | Date/Time |
| Resolved by: | reference to User |
| Severity: | Integer |
| Subcategory: | String |

**+ Task Columns**

To view the columns of the extended table (the parent class), click the **+** icon next to the extended table's name, shown in green in the following screenshot:

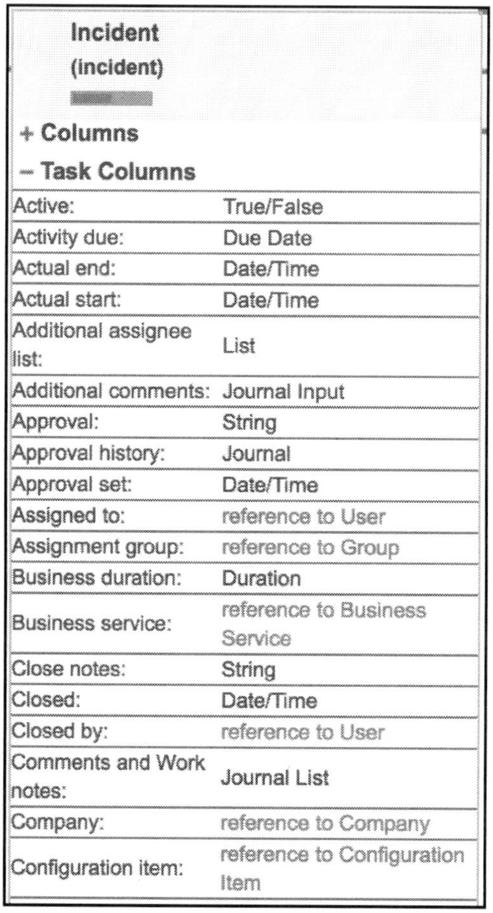

**Incident**
**(incident)**

**+ Columns**

**– Task Columns**

| | |
|---|---|
| Active: | True/False |
| Activity due: | Due Date |
| Actual end: | Date/Time |
| Actual start: | Date/Time |
| Additional assignee list: | List |
| Additional comments: | Journal Input |
| Approval: | String |
| Approval history: | Journal |
| Approval set: | Date/Time |
| Assigned to: | reference to User |
| Assignment group: | reference to Group |
| Business duration: | Duration |
| Business service: | reference to Business Service |
| Close notes: | String |
| Closed: | Date/Time |
| Closed by: | reference to User |
| Comments and Work notes: | Journal List |
| Company: | reference to Company |
| Configuration item: | reference to Configuration Item |

We can also click on any of the field's titles to open its dictionary definition (more on *Dictionary* later in the chapter). Clicking on the reference field links (in red) will take you to the schema map of the referenced table. For example, if you click on the reference to the **Configuration item** link, as shown in the preceding screenshot, you will be taken to the schema map of the **Configuration item** (`cmdb_ci`) table.

# Tables

We can use the **System Definition** | **Tables** module to access tables in the instance and quickly find the relevant tables using the list modules filters. The list of tables is the same as the list available in the **Tables & Columns** module; however, here they are accessible directly as a list module layout of the `sys_db_object` table. For example, in the following screenshot, we can filter on the **Name** column and list only the tables that start with the term **Incident**:

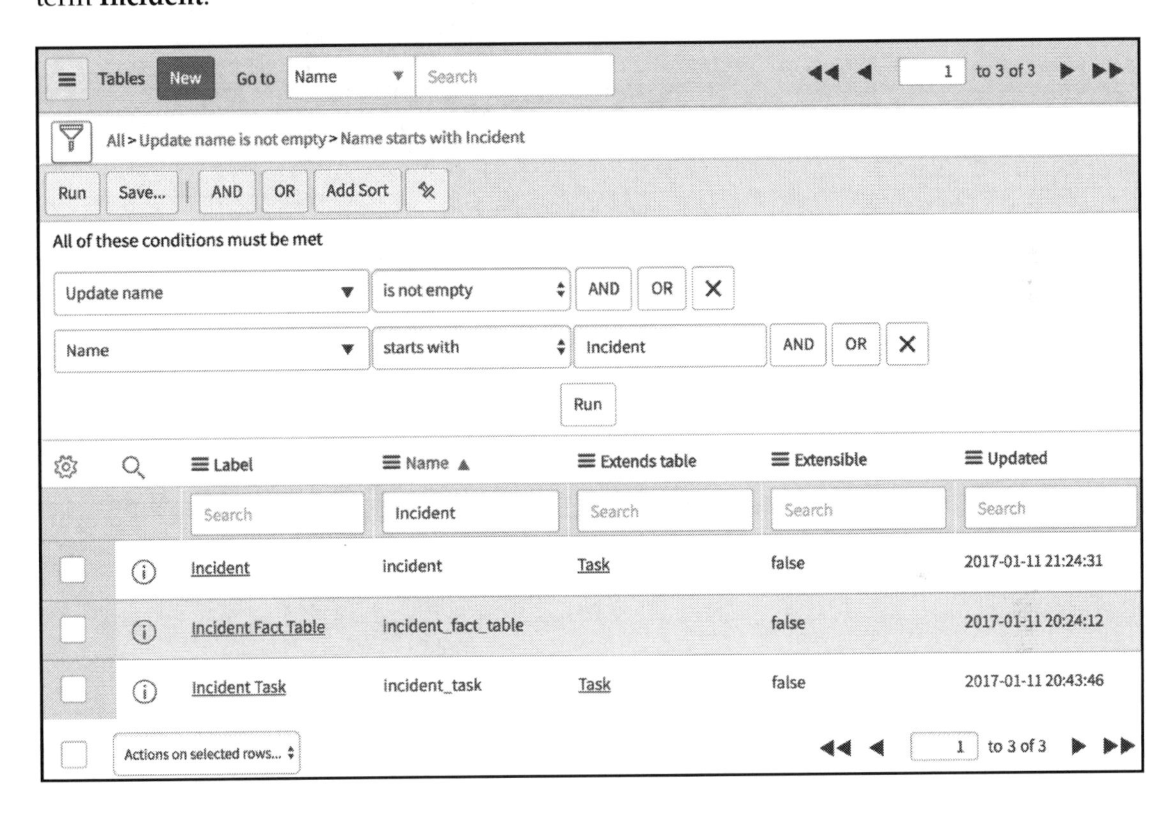

We can click on the label of the **Incident** table or on the info icon to open the selected record in a detailed view. Once the detailed form page loads, we can see a list of the columns in the tables, as shown in the following screenshot, under the **Columns**-related (embedded) list. The detailed view of the **Tables** modules also displays the name of the table the current table is extending from. Furthermore, we can click on the **Controls** tab to make basic changes to the table's basic properties:

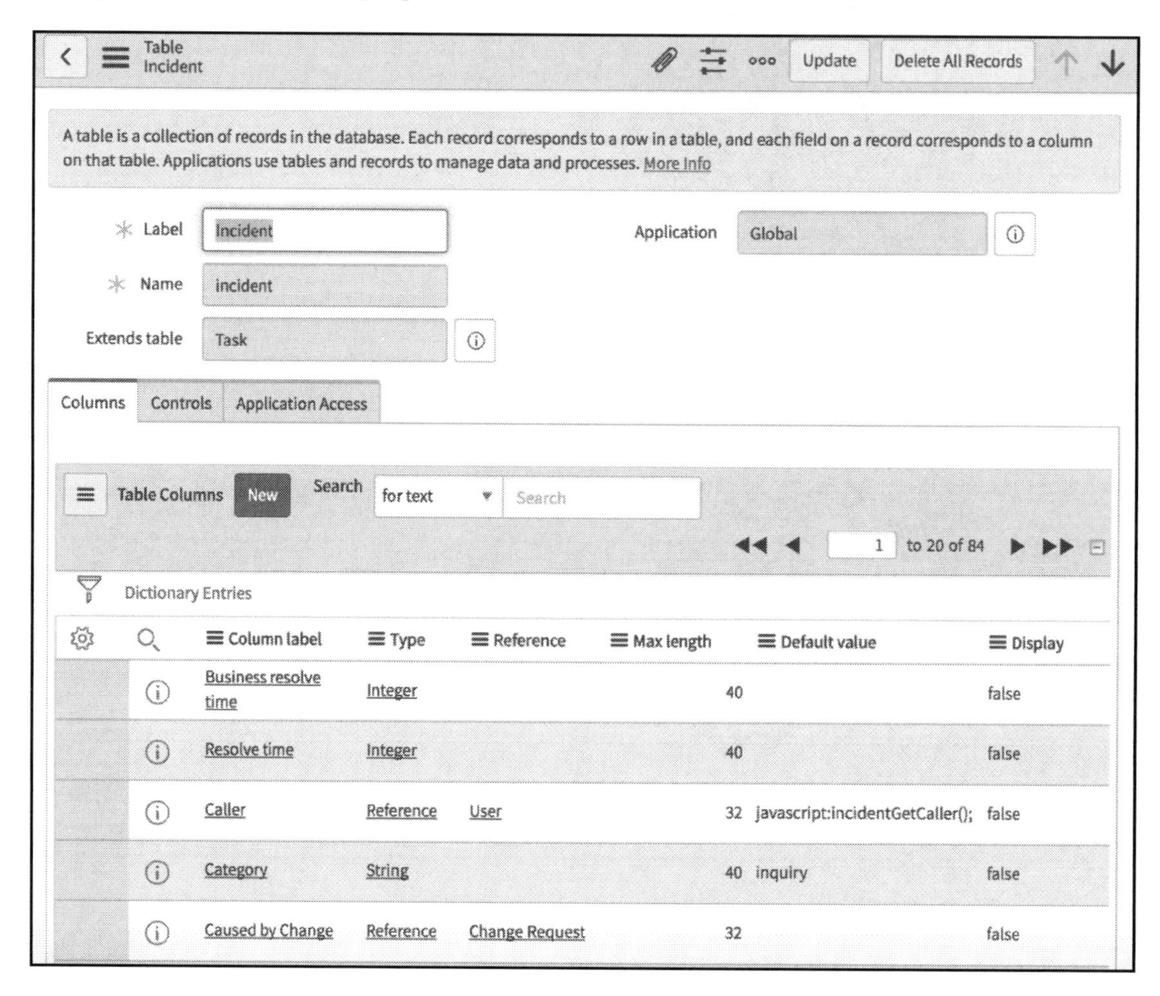

## Columns and rows

The columns of a table, also referred to as fields, are stored as **Dictionary Entries**, and are unique to each table. The `sys_id` column is the 32-character unique identifier field available in all ServiceNow tables. A parent class may have a set of columns; however, a child class can have its own set of columns, along with the columns it has inherited, by extending the parent class. Thus, the dictionary entry for a child class only contains the columns unique to the child class. We will cover creating columns in `Chapter 5`, *Modules, Forms, and Views*.

The dictionary entry of a child class contains the fields created explicitly in that child class and not the ones inherited from the parent class. So a record in the child class will have values in both the child class and all of its parent classes, which means that a record in the child class consists of a set of values spanning columns in all parent tables and that share the same `sys_id` value in the unique identifier field.

The system tracks record changes by the `sys_id` value and applies any change to all classes that have a record with the matching `sys_id` value. For example, if we insert a new record in the child incident table, a new corresponding record will also be inserted in the parent `Task` table, and both rows will share the same `sys_id`.

## Dictionary

The **System Definition | Dictionary** module has an entry for each table and column in the database. As direct access to the database is not provided to ServiceNow customers, the dictionary offers a way to access the information on the database schema. It is also referred to as the data dictionary.

The **Dictionary** module lists data stored in the `sys_dictionary` table, referred to as the dictionary entry. It is equivalent to the database dictionary property of the tables and column objects in any RDBMS.

It lists both the tables and columns defined in the instance, as shown in the following screenshot:

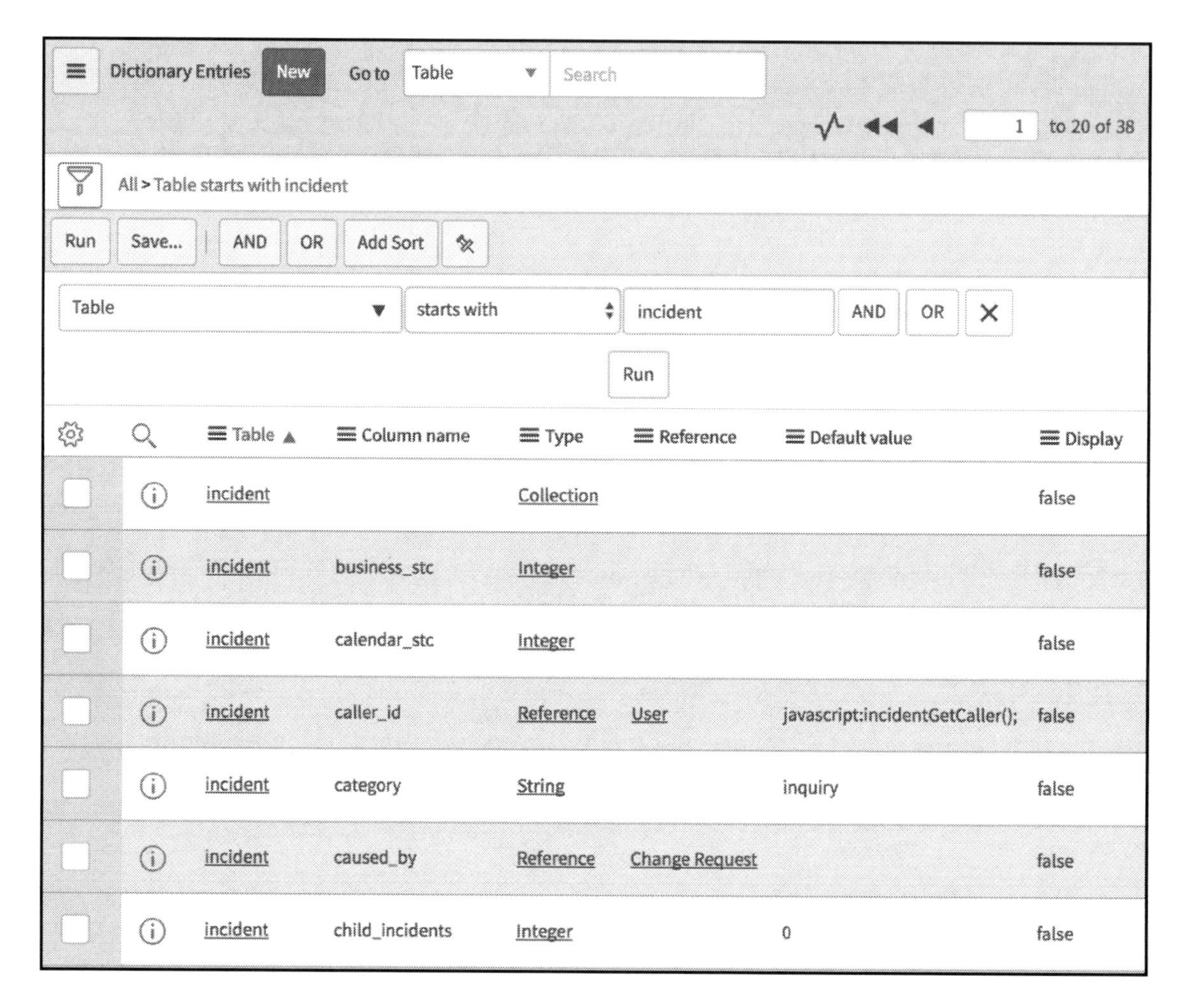


If the **Column name** field is empty and the **Type** field is set as **Collection**, then the record is a table's definition. As shown in the preceding screenshot, for the **Incident** table, the **Column name** field is empty and the **Type** is set as **Collection**-this means that the record is the dictionary definition of the **Incident** table, whereas other records belonging to the table incident have the column name and type set as something other than Collection - it means they are the dictionary definition of the columns (fields) in the **Incident** table.

We can click on the info icon next to the record of the **Incident** table definition (collection) to load in the form detail page. We can activate features such as the auditing and text index or set some advanced attributes in the detail form (see `Chapter 13`, *Advanced Database Features*).

Similarly, we can click on the info icon, as highlighted in the following screenshot, next to the definition of the `caller_id` field of the **Incident** table, to view and manage the dictionary properties of the field:

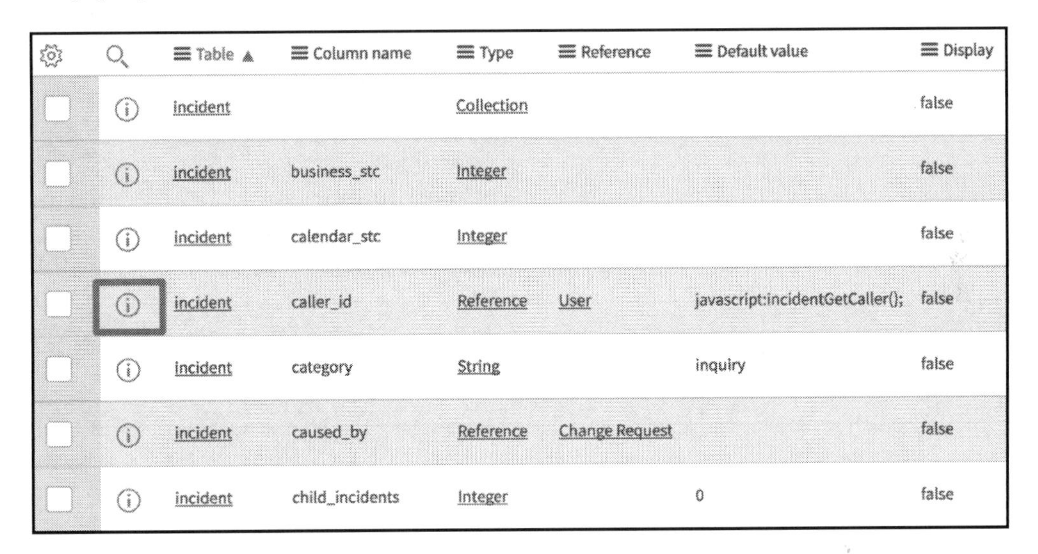

| Table ▲ | Column name | Type | Reference | Default value | Display |
|---|---|---|---|---|---|
| incident | | Collection | | | false |
| incident | business_stc | Integer | | | false |
| incident | calendar_stc | Integer | | | false |
| incident | caller_id | Reference | User | javascript:incidentGetCaller(); | false |
| incident | category | String | | inquiry | false |
| incident | caused_by | Reference | Change Request | | false |
| incident | child_incidents | Integer | | 0 | false |

Once the detail form page is loaded, we can modify field properties such as the field type, column label, or the table's display field by setting them as read-only or mandatory by simply editing the form fields:

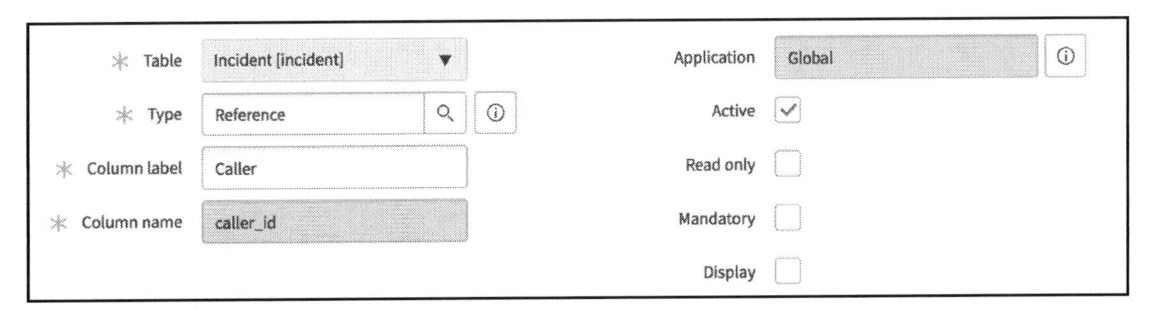


We will be covering the use of different related tabs in the **Dictionary detail** form in `Chapter 6`, *Introduction to ServiceNow Scripting*.

# Creating a table

Let us now create a custom table using the **Tables & Columns** module. There are multiple ways to create a new table. Either open the **Tables** module and click on the **New** button on the top, or open the **Tables & Columns** module and click on the **Create Table** button in the top section, as shown in the following screenshot:

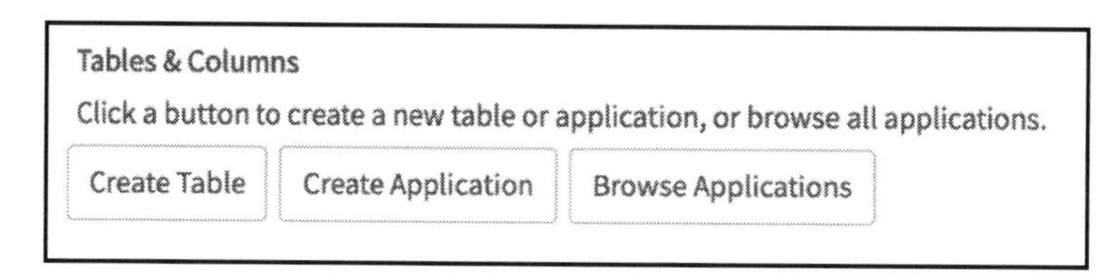


You will be presented with a **New record** form for the **Table**. To be clear, we are inserting a new record, using the following form, into a system-defined (out-of-the-box) table labeled **Table** (with the system name `sys_db_object`) to create a new table in our instance:

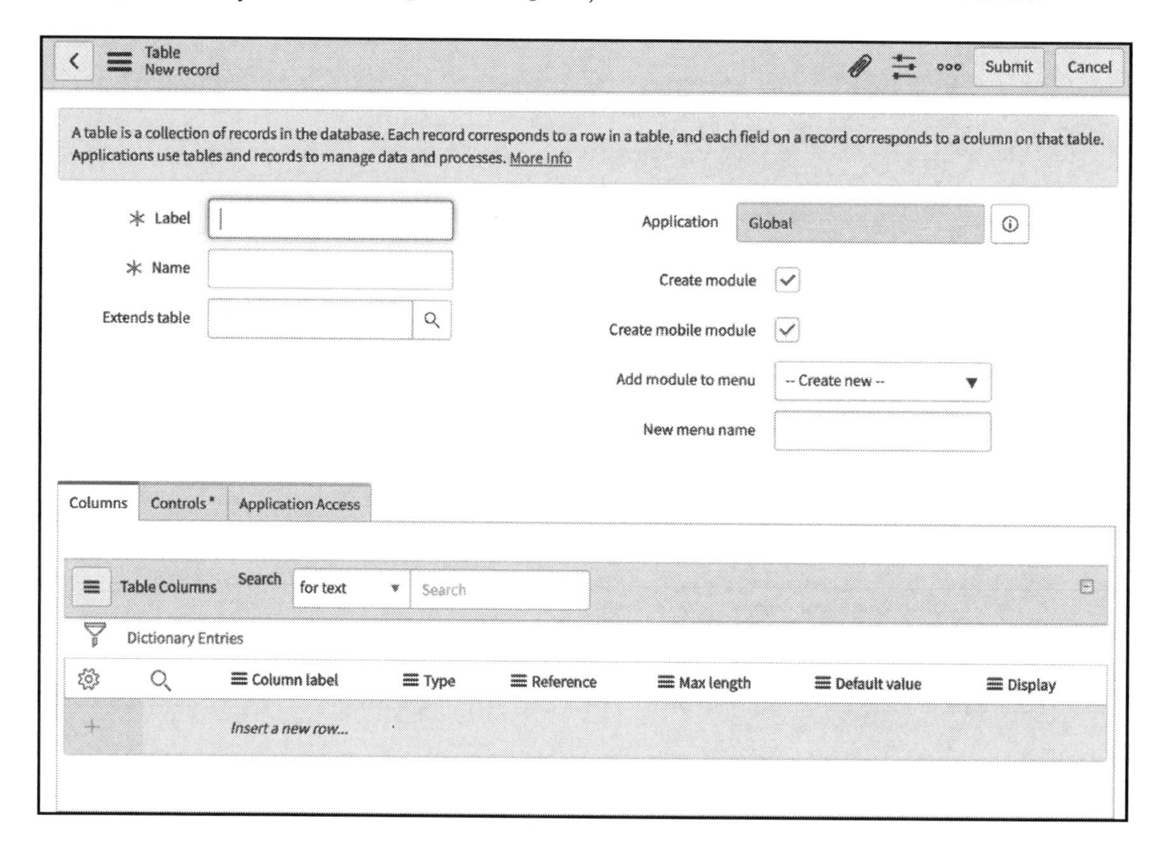

Let us populate the form fields with the following values to create our first custom table:

1. In the **Label** field, enter the label we want to give to our new table-that is, `POS Location`.
2. The **Name** field will be automatically populated for you when enter a value in the **Label** field and focus out of it. Note that the `u_` prefix will be added to the system name of your table. This is useful for distinguishing user-created tables from system tables. All user-created tables will have the `u_` prefix.
3. Leave the **Extends table** field blank.
4. Make sure that the **Create module** checkbox is checked.
5. Make sure that the **Create mobile module** checkbox is checked.
6. Ensure that **--Create new--** is selected in the **Add module to menu** field.
7. As shown in the following screenshot, set the **New menu name** field's value as `POS app menu` and click **Submit**:

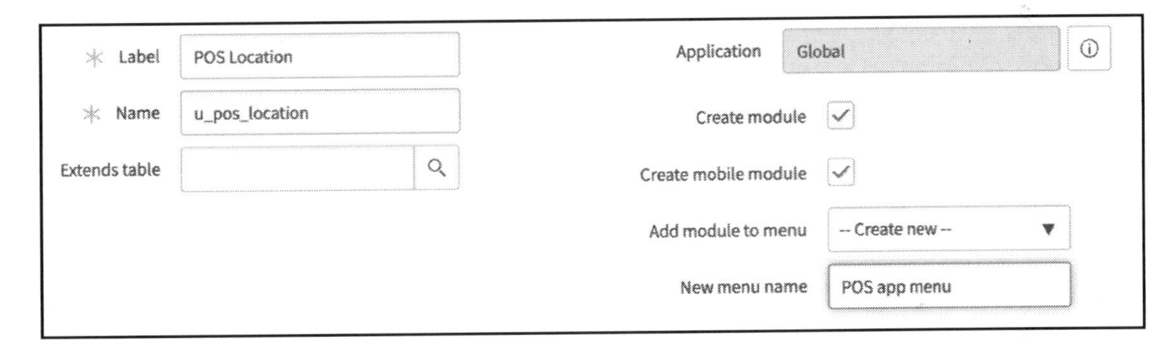


A new table with the label `POS Location` and system name `u_pos_location` will be created in our instance, along with a list of record modules and a new application menu in the left navigator section, as shown in the following screenshot:

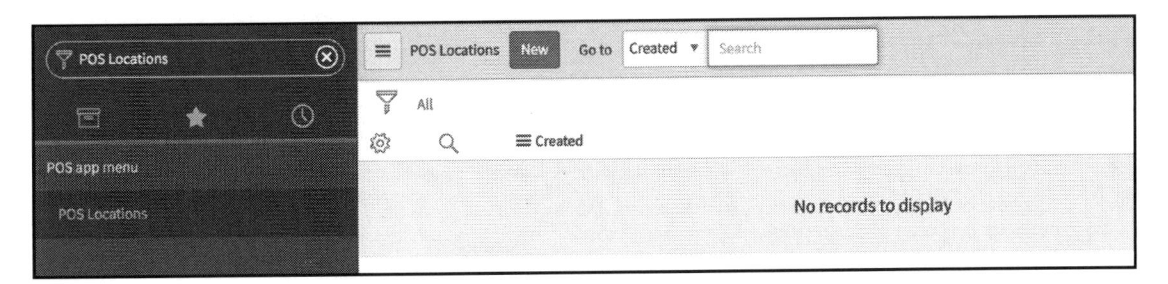

We can confirm that our new table has been created by opening the **Tables** module and searching for all the tables that start with the u_pos string, as shown in the following screenshot:

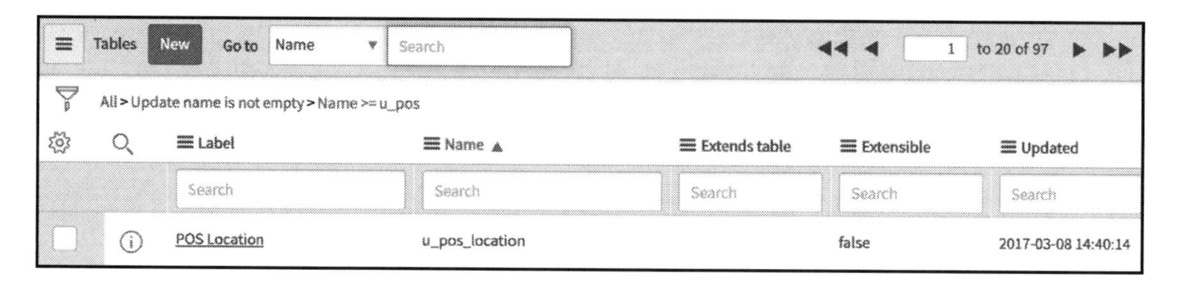


We can click on the info icon to open the POS Location table in the detail page, where we can make some basic modifications to elements, such as the table's label, and see a list of the existing columns:

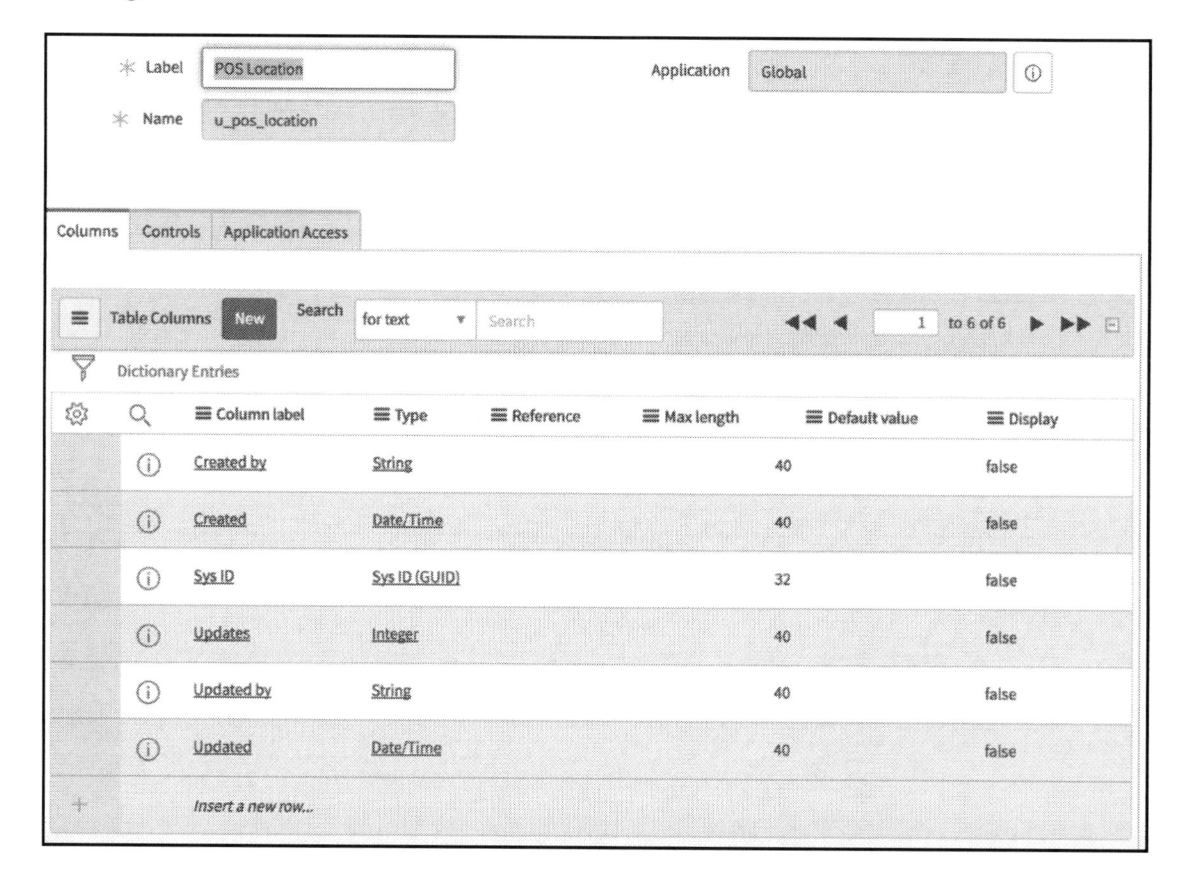

# Adding columns to table

In order to add new columns, open the table using the **Tables** module and under the **Columns** section tab, double-click on the **Insert a new record** text to insert a new entry in our new column. As this related list is pointing to the **Dictionary** table (`sys_dictionary`), any record that we enter in this embedded list will get stored into the **Dictionary** table as that is where information related to the columns is stored.

As shown in the following screenshot, set the value of the **Column** label field as `Location Name`, **Type** as `String`, and **Max length** as `40`, and click on the green check icon to confirm:

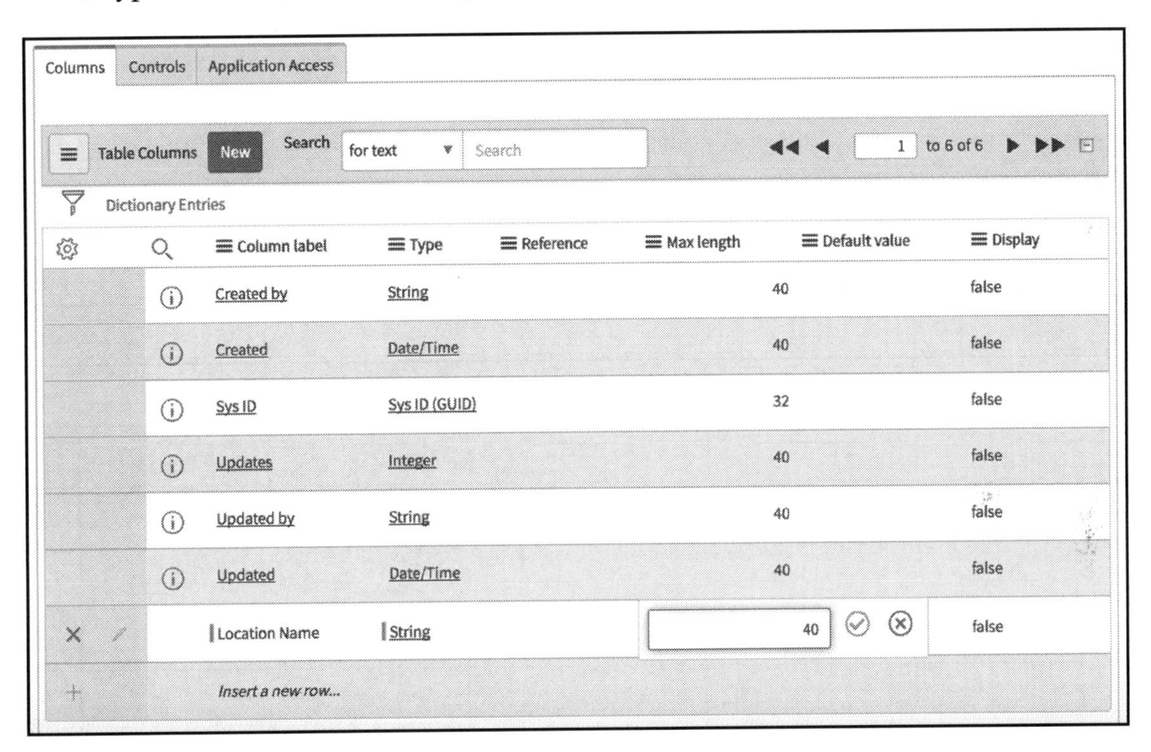


We can insert multiple new rows to create more than one column in one go before clicking on the **Submit** button.

As shown in the following screenshot, insert two more rows with the following values:

- **Column Label**: `Location Incharge`, **Type**: `Reference`, **Reference**: `User (sys_user)`
- **Column Label**: `Location`, **Type**: `Reference`, **Reference**: `Location (cmn_location)`

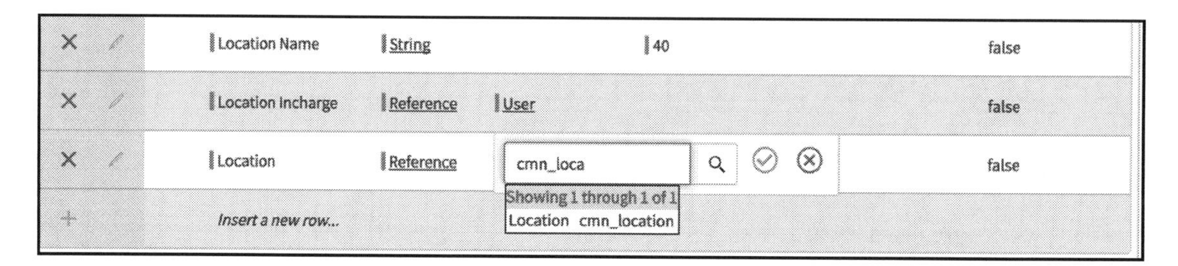


Once you are satisfied with the new column's label and type, click on the **Submit** button to confirm our changes and create three new columns in the `POS Location` table. You can reopen the table's record in the **Tables** module to confirm the creation of these new columns:

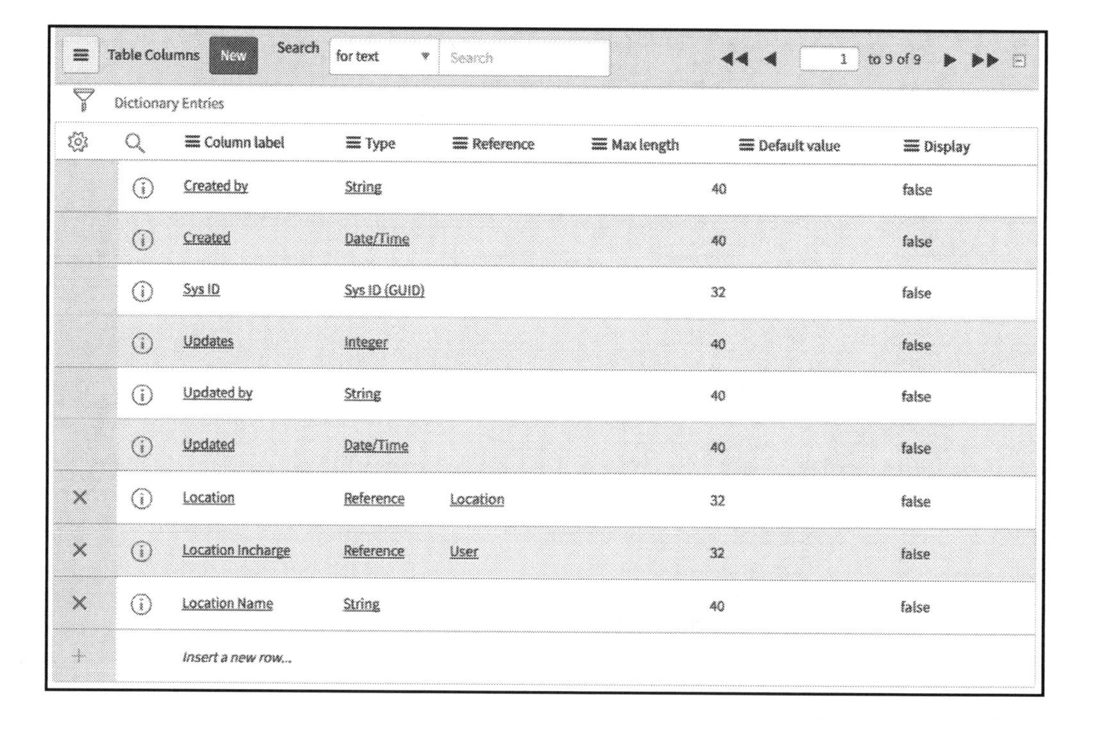

We can double-click on any user-created fields to change its label or other values, as shown in the following screenshot. Make sure to click the **Update** button again to save your changes:

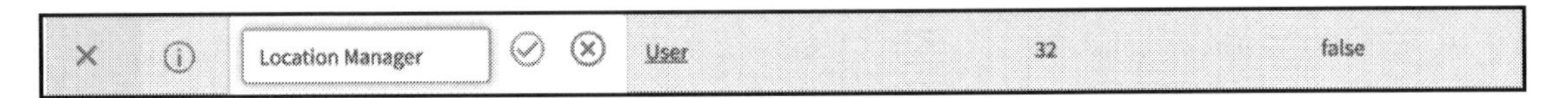


We can also click on the info icon next to each row to open up the record in the **Dictionary detail** form view.

## Modifying column properties

Clicking on the info icon next to the **Column** label in the previous screen will bring us to the **Dictionary Entry** form, similar to the one shown in the following screenshot. We can make the necessary changes to the properties or attributes of the column to our satisfaction:

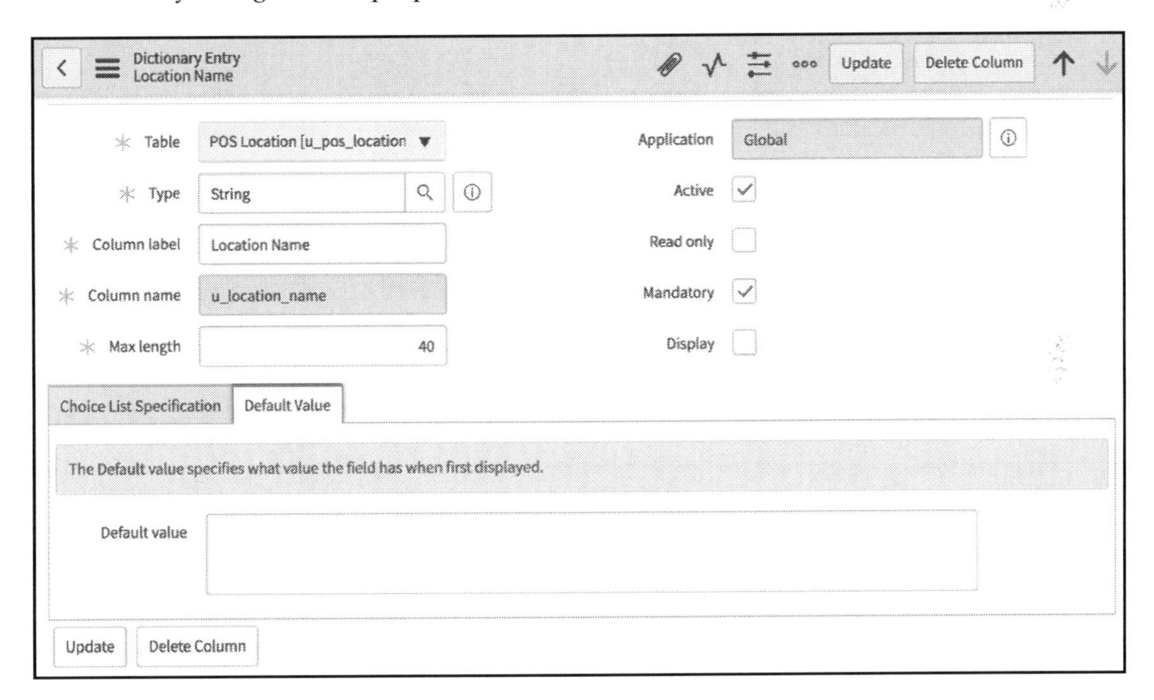


We can just edit the **Label** form field's value to change the label of the column, and similarly we can mark it as a mandatory field by simply checking the **Mandatory** checkbox. If required, we can also set a default value for our column. Once we are satisfied with our alterations to the column's dictionary entry, click on the **Update** button to save our changes.

# Task table

The `Task` table is one of the most important tables in the ServiceNow instance. Many tables extend the `Task` table. Thus, it is the parent class of many other tables, such as **Incident**, **Change Task**, **Problem**, and so on. Using the **Tables** modules, we can open the `Task` table entry to view a list of all available columns under the **Columns** tab, as shown in the following screenshot. We can optionally view the **Schema map** of the `Task` table to see all the tables that are extending and related to the `Task` table:

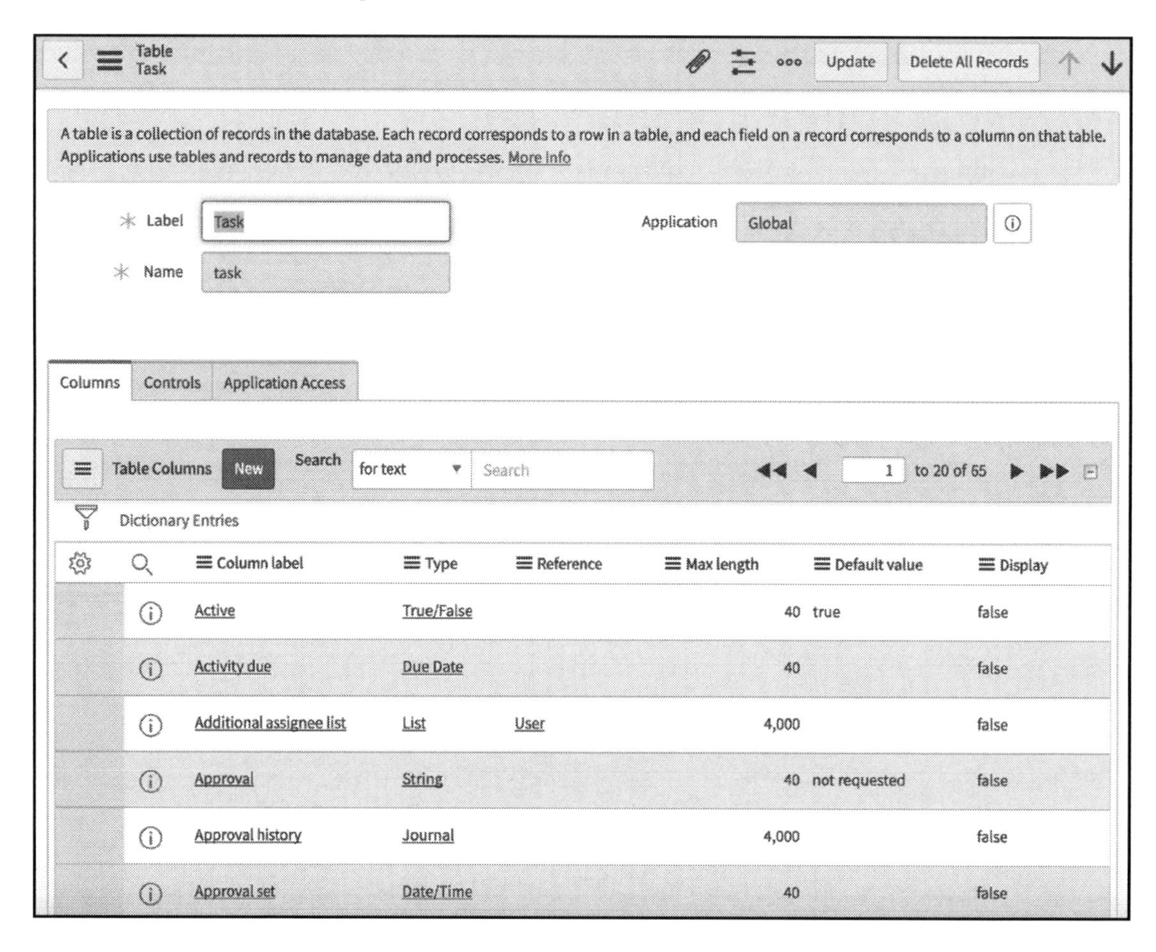


We can use the pagination on the top right corner of the list to browse through the entire record set. As always, clicking on the info icon will bring up the **Dictionary Entry** detail form page.

Furthermore, to view a list of tables that extends the `Task` table, as shown in the following screenshot, open the **Tables** modules again and use the quick filter on the top of the content frame to search for records where the **Extends table** starts with **Task** and press the *Enter* (return) key to perform the quick search:

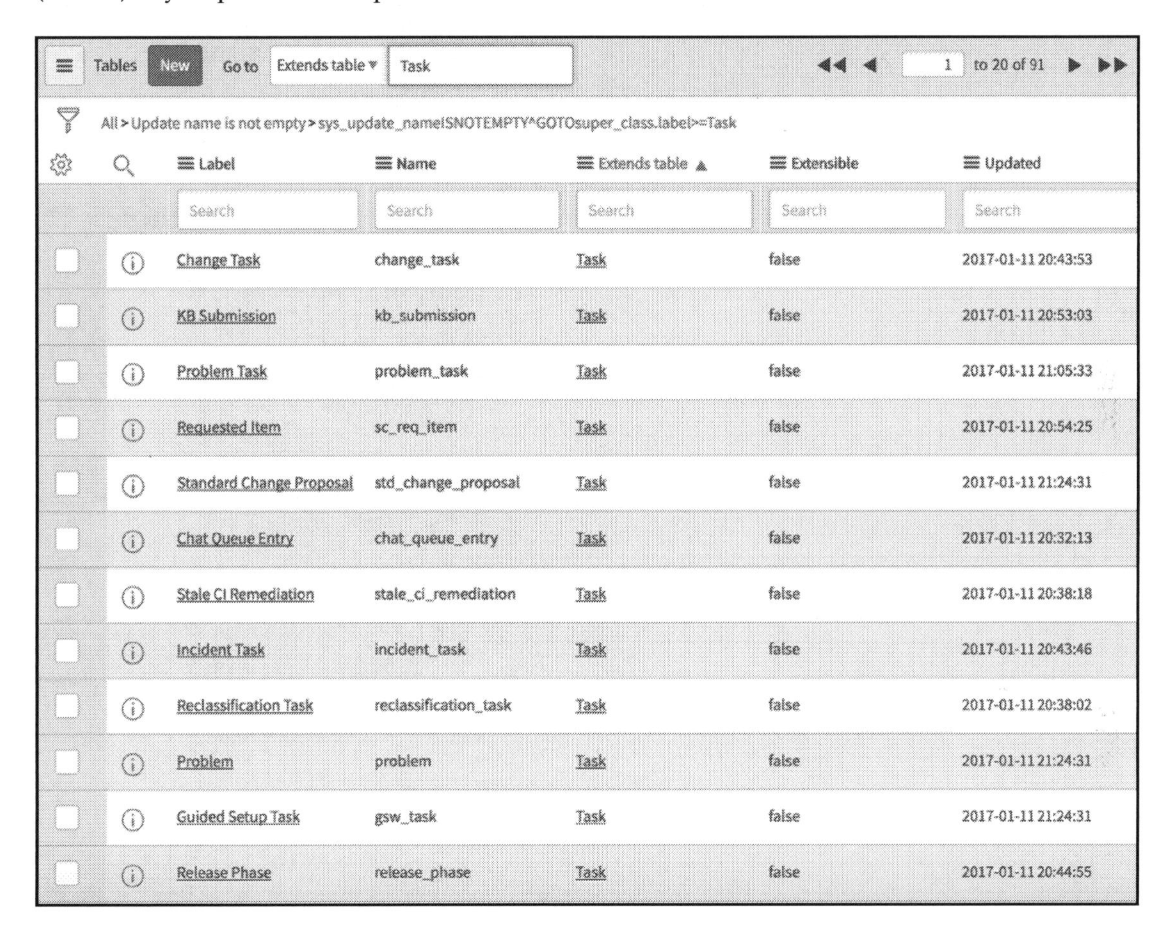


Let us now create a custom table that extends from the `Task` table.

# Extending the Task table

In order to create a table that extends from the `Task` table, we need to select the `Task` table as the `Extends` table that extends from it while creating a new table. Once a table has been created, it is not possible to change or specify a table to extend from. Extending the tables helps in reusing the fields and other features already defined in the parent class, and make them available in the child classes:

1. Open the **Tables** module and click on the **New** button at top of the content frame to open the **New** record form.
2. Enter the label of the new table as `POS Tasks` and select `Task` as the **Extends** table.
3. Ensure that the **Create module** and **Create mobile module** checkboxes are checked.
4. Finally, select the previously created **POS app menu** as the value of the **Add** module in the menu. This will ensure that the new modules that will be created will be added to the selected application menu:

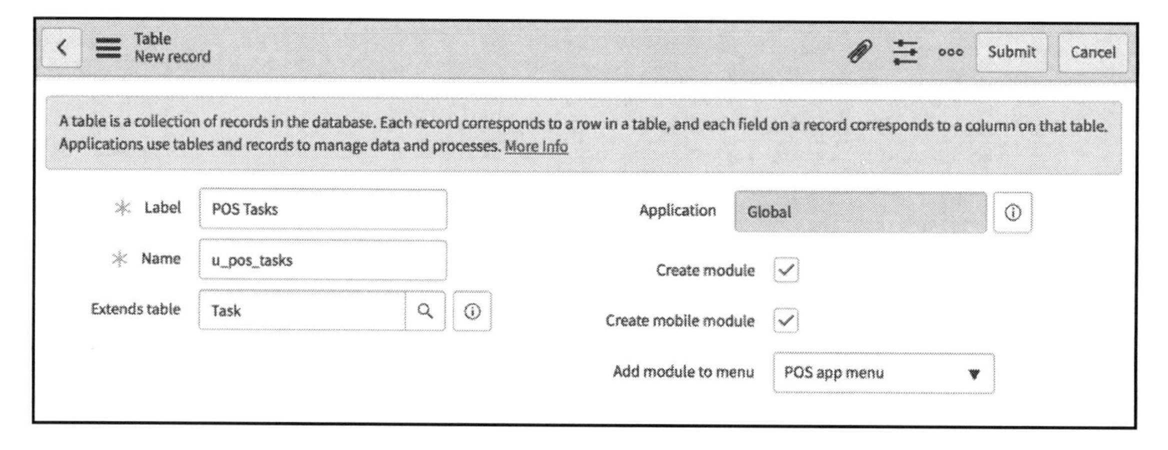


5. Open the newly created table record in the **Tables** module and ensure that the columns from the `Task` tables are all available in the `POS Tasks` table, as shown in the following screenshot:

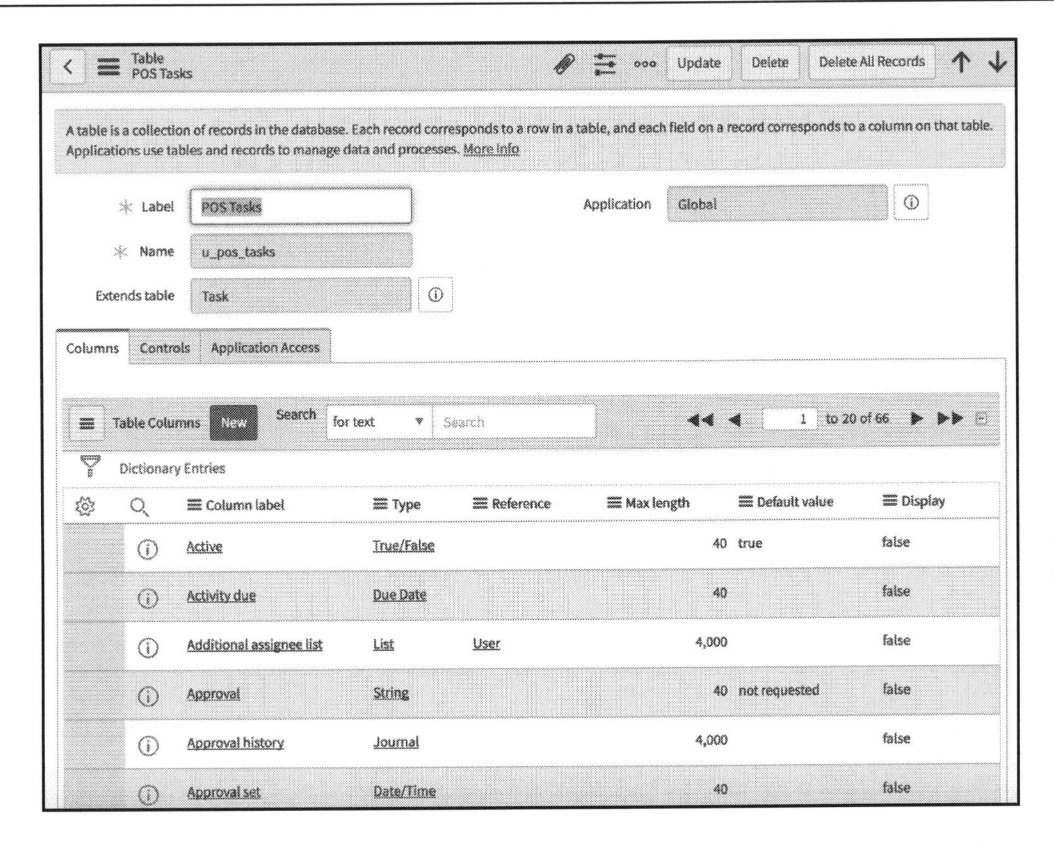


These columns are available in the `Task` table, and thus making changes to any of these columns will make the changes available to all the tables in the instance that is extending the `Task` table, unless the attributes of the extended columns are explicitly overridden.

It is also possible to add custom columns using the same steps explained previously under the topic *Adding columns*. The columns we add to the POS Tasks tables will not be available to the tables that are extending the `Task` table.

# Configuration management table

The configuration management application in ServiceNow is used to build and maintain the logical service configurations of the infrastructure and applications that support a service. In order to build applications surrounding the configuration management application, it is important to understand the architecture of the configuration management tables.

The logical service configurations are stored in the **Configuration Management Database (CMDB)**, and are mapped to the physical inventory in your organization. The CMDB consists of entities called **configuration items** (**CI**). A CI may be:

- **A physical entity**: Such as a computer or router
- **A logical entity**: Such as an instance of a database
- **Conceptual**: Such as a payroll service

The parent class of all CI classes in ServiceNow is the `cmdb` (**base configuration item**) table. It has some set of fields that are relevant to all configuration items. The `cmdb` table is extended by the a table named `cmdb_ci` (**Configuration Item**). There are over 90 tables/CI class definitions that extend the **Configuration Item** (`cmdb_ci`) table, and thus they also inherit the fields from the **base configuration table** (`cmdb.`) This is illustrated in the following image:

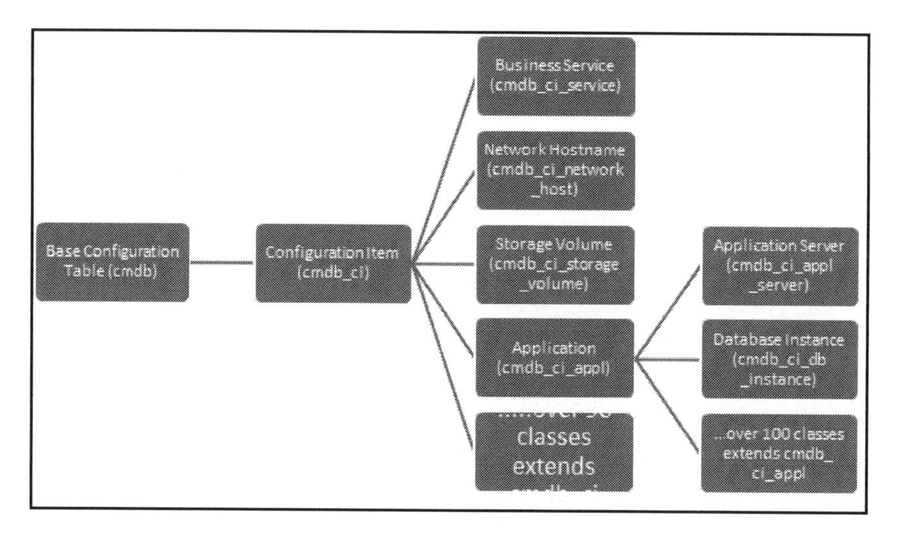


To see the relationships between tables (classes), we can always refer to the schema map. The **Database Instance** and **Application Server** tables extend the **Application** class, which in turn extends `cmdb_ci` and again extends the `cmdb` class.

# Extending the configuration table

While ServiceNow comes with numerous CI class definitions and a proper hierarchy, we may have a requirement where we have to define our own CI class definition.

Let us suppose that in our organization, we use the `Couchbase Database` server as a data storage solution for one of the projects. We may want to ensure that **Configuration Items** relevant to Couchbase are stored in a proper table. We need to ensure that a proper class is defined in our configuration management application. The process to do this is very similar to creating a new table.

Before we proceed with creating a new class, we must figure out where the class will fit in the existing hierarchy of our ServiceNow CMDB classes. We are already aware that the `Database Instance` class exists in our CMDB; however, we need to confirm if the `Couchbase Instance` class exists or not. To confirm this, let us first list all the existing classes that extend the `Database Instance` class. Now we can open the **Tables** module and apply the filter to find all tables that extend `Database Instance`, as shown in the following screenshot:

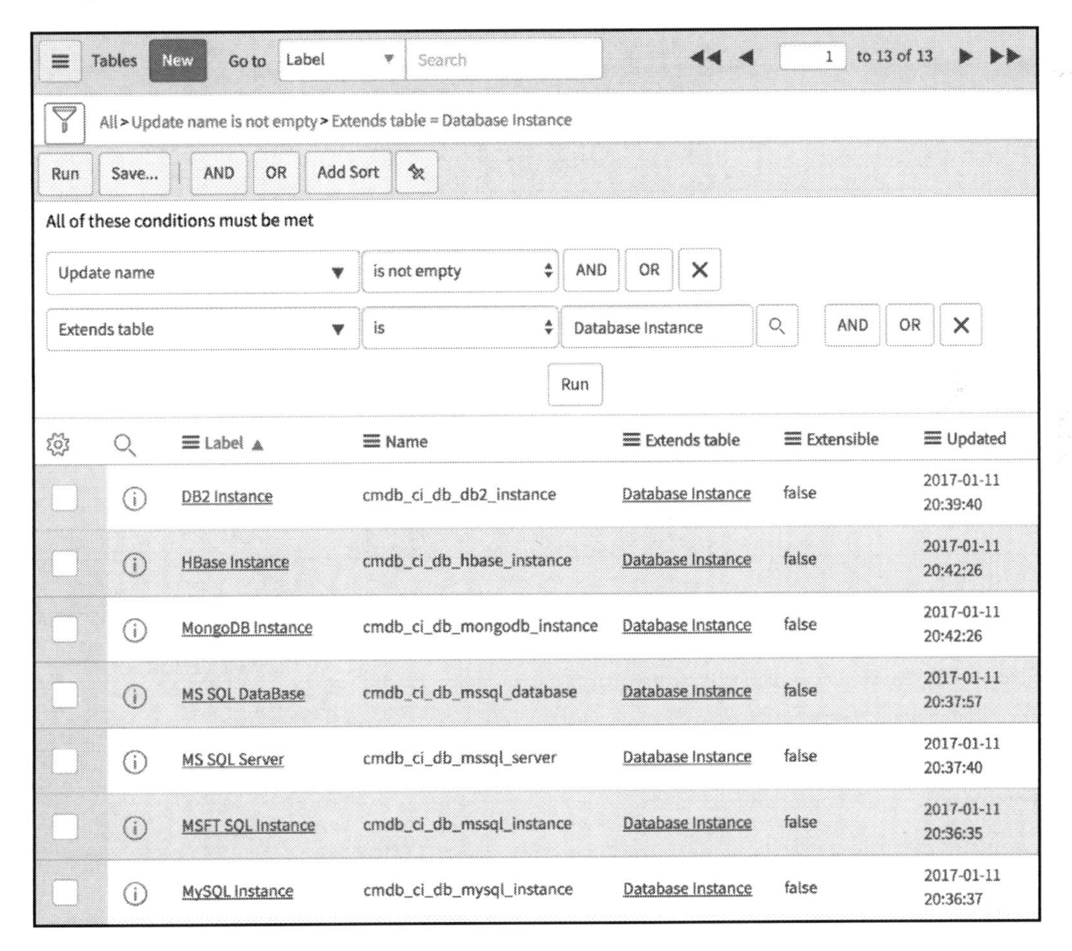

We can also use the **Class Hierarchy** section available in the **CI Class Manager** page in the configuration management application. To open the **CI Class Manager**, click on the link available in the left-hand side navigator, as shown here:

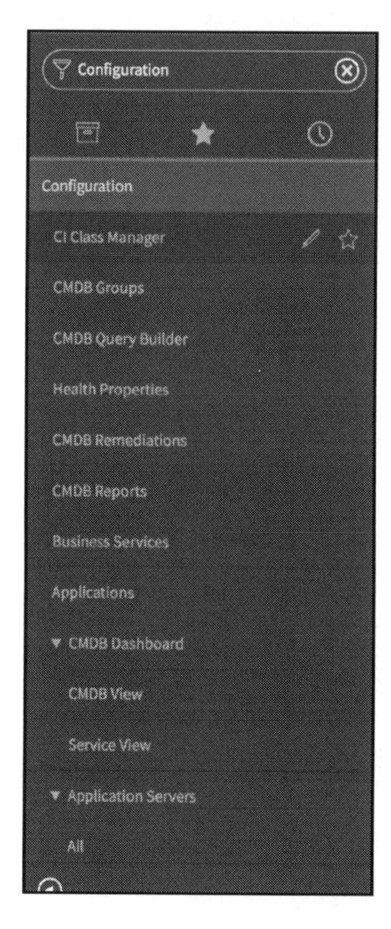


The **CI Class Manager** consists of the **Class Hierarcy** section on the left, the content section in the middle, and the **Advanced** section appears on the far left. The **Class Hierarchy** can be used to quickly scroll through the hierarchy of CMDB classes.

We can click on the arrow icon next to the `Application` class label to expand it and see all the child classes that extend the `Application` class. We can further drill down and click on the arrow icon next to the **Database Instance** to see a list of all child classes defined under it. We can click on the label directly to open the **Table** definition in the center section, as shown in the following screenshot:

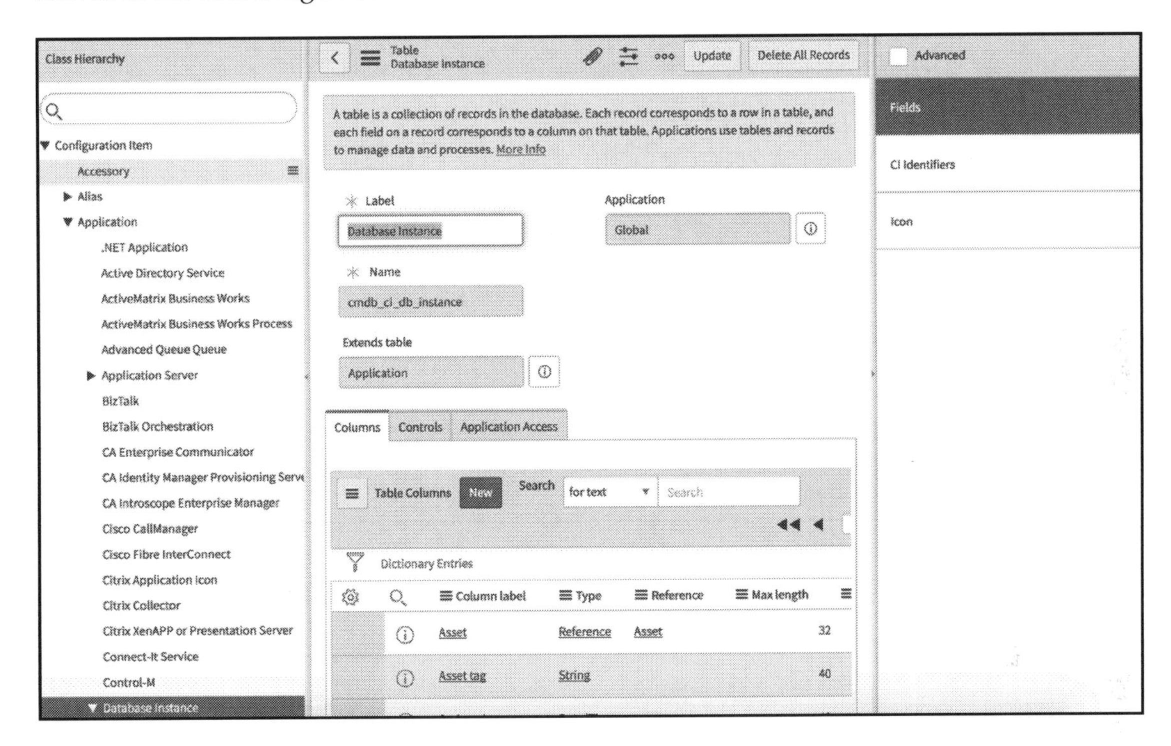


To extend the `Database Instance` class, move your mouse over to the top of the label and click on the menu icon that appears on the right of the label, as shown here:

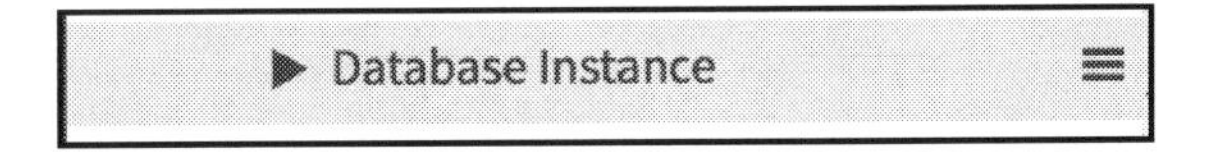

We will be presented with a menu, as shown in the following screenshot. Click on the **Extend** menu item:

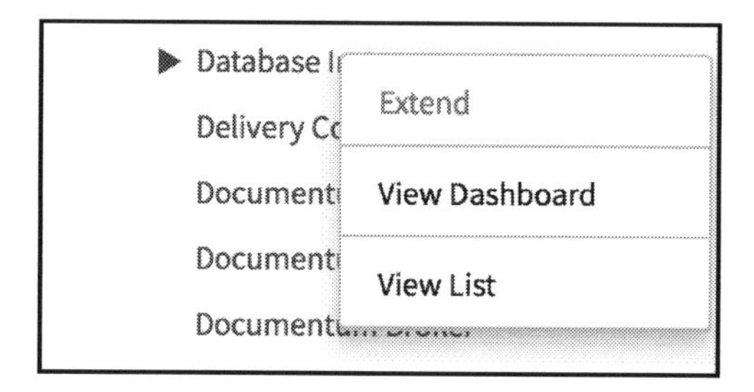


This is will open up the **Create a New Table** form in the **Contents** section. The process to create a new CI class is similar to creating a new table. We just have to ensure that we are extending a table that either extends one of the tables that has `cmdb_ci` in its parent class hierarchy, such as `Application`, `Business Service`, `Database Instance`, and so on, or we can directly extend the `cmdb_ci` table.

As shown in the following screenshot, in order to create a new CI class under the `Database Instance` in the class hierarchy, we must make sure our new table is extending from the `Database Instance` class. Click on the **Submit** button to finish creating a new CI class:

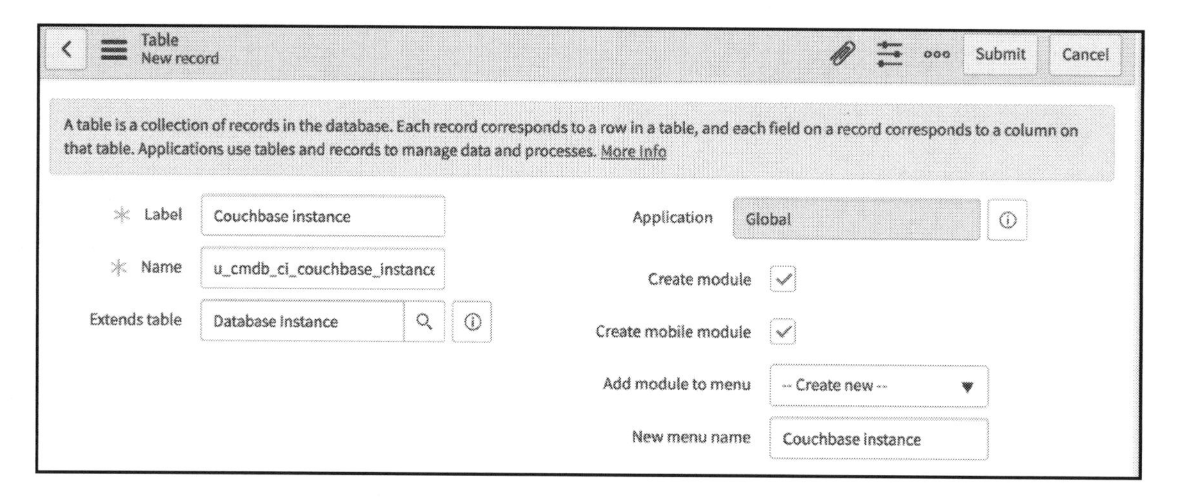

# Summary

In this chapter, we learned about the features available in ServiceNow to manage tables and columns in the instance. We learned how to use the data dictionary and **Tables** modules to create and manage tables and columns. We also learned about the structure of the `Task` and `Configuration CI` tables.

In the next chapter, we will learn how to create different applications and work in different application scopes.

# 4
# Application Scopes

So far we have learned the basics of the ServiceNow platform, user interface, user administration, and databases. Now we will understand the architecture of applications in the ServiceNow platform.

When developing applications on the ServiceNow platform, developers need to take special care of the application scope they are working on. Applications help administrators and developers to combine different modules and features to deliver a relevant set of functionality. For example, an application meant to manage sales may offer features related to managing leads, prospects, and customers. An application scope can restrict access to resources of an application. ServiceNow allows administrators the simple means to create and manage applications.

In this chapter, we will learn how to create new applications. We will also learn about the relationship between applications and scopes. Furthermore, we will learn how we can use applications to associate relevant information and access data from different applications.

This chapter will cover the following topics:

- Application architecture
- Creating a new application
- Creating an empty table in new application scopes
- Accessing information in different scopes

# Application architecture

Every ServiceNow instance has a suite of out-of-the-box applications such as **Incident Management**, **Problem Management**, **Configuration Management**, and **Knowledge Management**. These applications make use of different features of the ServiceNow platform such as the UI, access control, tables, workflows, client and server side scripting, and so on. This means, an application, as illustrated in the following screenshot, consists of many different records and files, which are referred to as application artifacts:

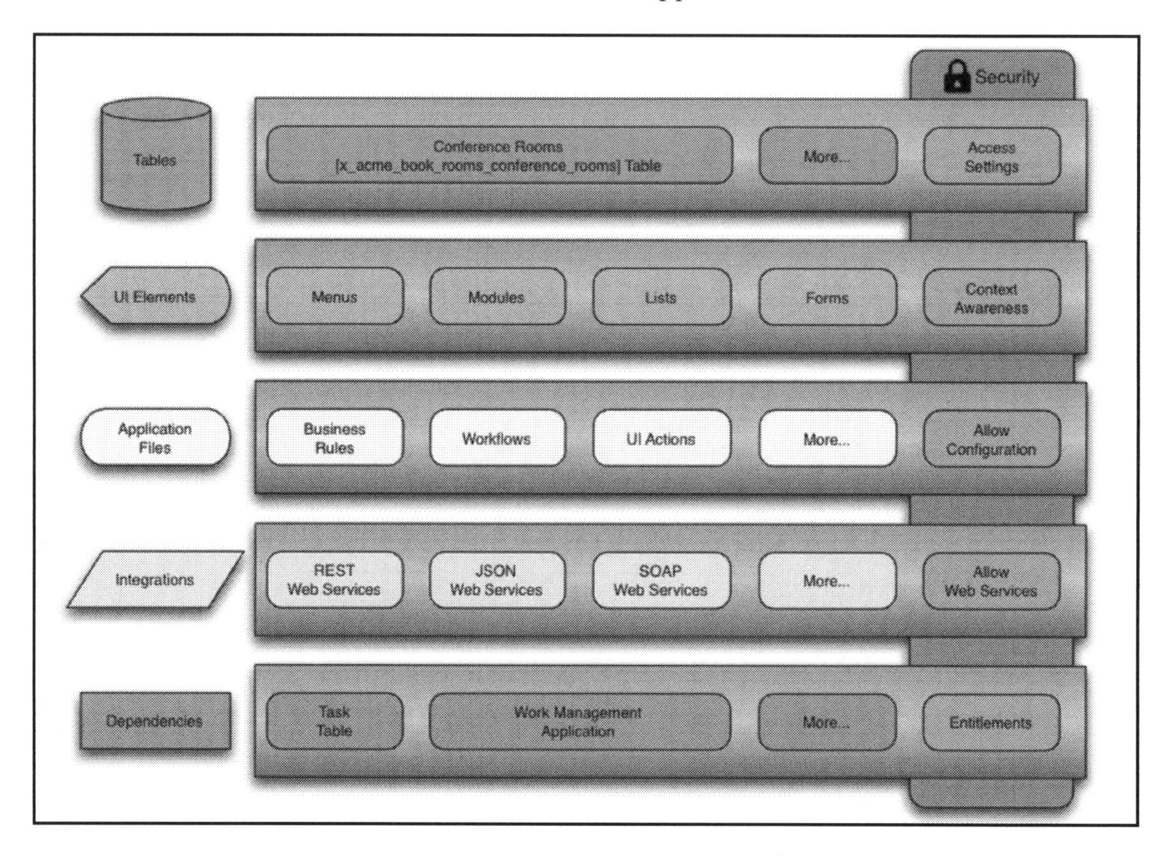

# Structure of an application

The primary record that defines an application is that of an application record. An application consists of the following parts:

- The primary application record
- Application scope
- Application versions
- Application tables
- Application dependencies (on other applications)
- Application files/scripts
- Fix scripts (`init` scripts)

# Application scope

Application scope ensures that applications do not interfere with one another. Each application in ServiceNow has its own corresponding application scope. All the artifacts of an application, such as business rules, tables, and forms, and so on, are created in the same application scope as the application.

Application scope ensures an application artifact in a different scope doesn't interfere with the functionality of applications running in other scopes unless granted explicit permissions.

There are two types of scope in ServiceNow:

- Private application scope
- Global scope

## Private application scope

This is the only kind of application scope available to administrators and developers when creating a new application. Applications created in private application scope implements application scoping. This means all the application artifacts created within the scope will create, read, write, and delete the application data.

The artifacts in private application scope have a unique namespace identifier with the following format: `x_[vendor-prefix]_[application-id]`.

A vendor prefix is a two to five characters long string that is unique to each ServiceNow customer. Your organization may own multiple ServiceNow instances, but the vendor prefix in all of those instances will remain the same, whereas the application ID is typically the application name with spaces replaced by underscores and could be up to *40* characters long.

### Global scope

Typically, out-of-the-box applications are part of global scope, along with any custom application developed prior to the application scoping feature prior to the Fuji version. Any developer can modify applications defined in global scope. However, global scope applications are not eligible to be uploaded to **ServiceNow Store**.

Application artifacts in global scope don't have any namespace identifier.

## Application versions

The version information is stored alongside the custom application record and is by the system to determine whether an update is available to the application. The version information of a custom application can be easily updated in the application record from the **System Application** | **Applications** module.

## Application tables

Each application in ServiceNow, whether in private or global scope, can consist of one more table. These tables may be used to store information related to application artifacts and data that a user may enter. For example, in the **Sales** application, we can create a table each to store leads, prospects, and customers information. Furthermore, when creating a new application a new role is also created in the system that restricts standard record operations such as create, read, write, and delete.

## Application dependencies

An application can be dependent on another application. In such cases, we can add applications to the dependent application related list in the application record to ensure that they have proper access to the applications it is dependent on.

## Application files

The application files consist of business rules, workflows, script includes, and other scripts that a developer may create to enhance the functionality of an application.

## Fix scripts

A fix script is similar to an init script that is executed on the server side when the application is either installed or upgraded.

# ServiceNow applications

The **System Applications** | **Applications** module lists all custom developed and downloaded applications in the **Develop** and **Downloads** tabs respectively. The following screenshot displays a list of applications downloaded from the ServiceNow Store:

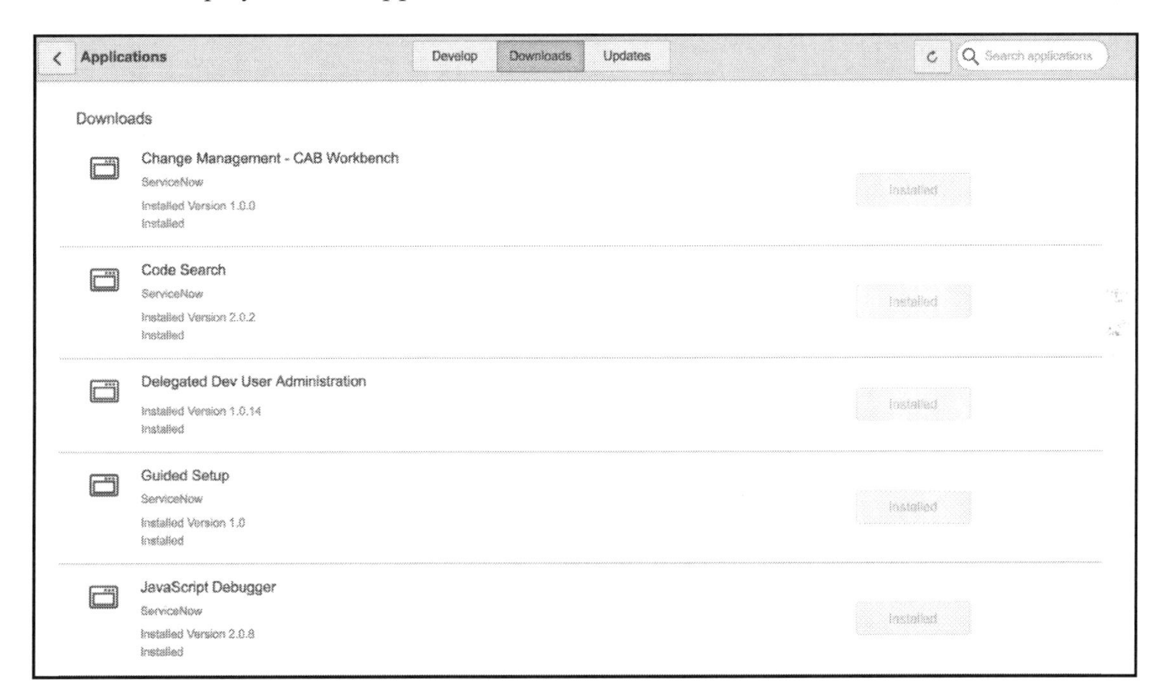

Clicking on an application name will take us to the application detail where we can see detail relevant to the application such as the application version, name, install date, and vendor name along with application files.

# Application picker

Before we dig deep in the applications, let us ensure that we have our application picker visible in the top banner frame. The application picker allows us to quickly identify and switch the application scope we are currently working on. If not, just as we discussed in `Chapter 1`, *Introduction to ServiceNow*, we can make it visible using the **System Settings** dialog box, as shown in the following screenshot:

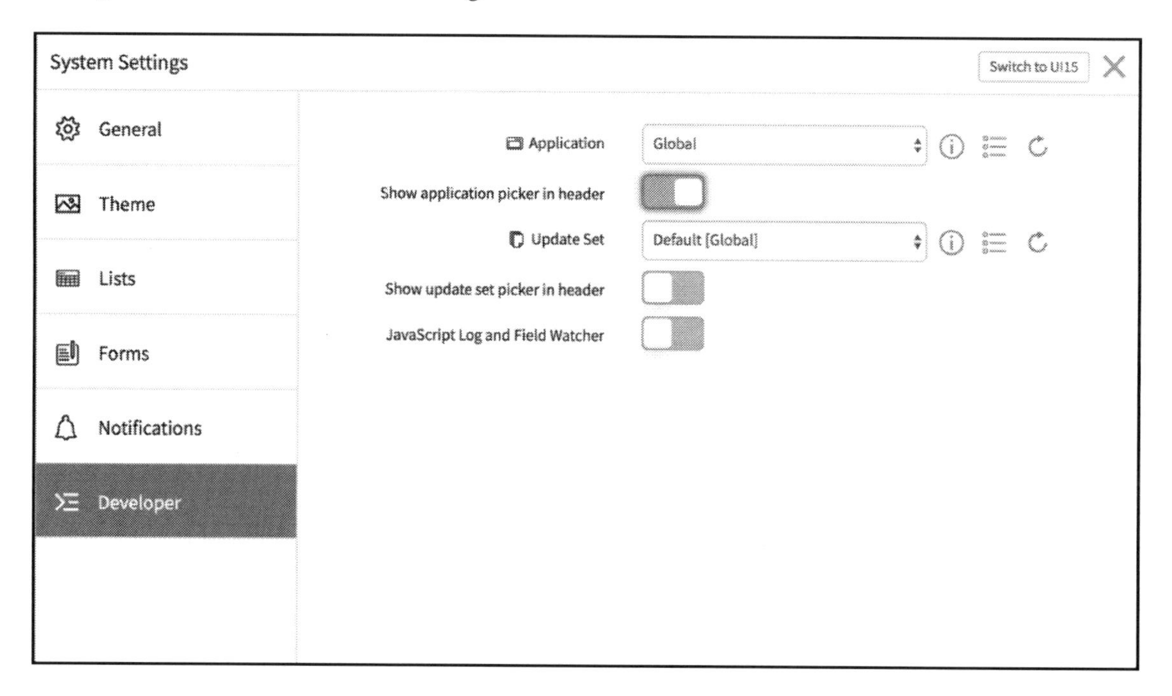


Marking the **Show application picker in header** checkbox as true will show the application picker drop-down field in the banner frame, as shown in the following screenshot:

# Creating a new application

To create a new application, open the **System Applications** | **Applications** module, as shown in the following screenshot, and click on the **New** button on the left:

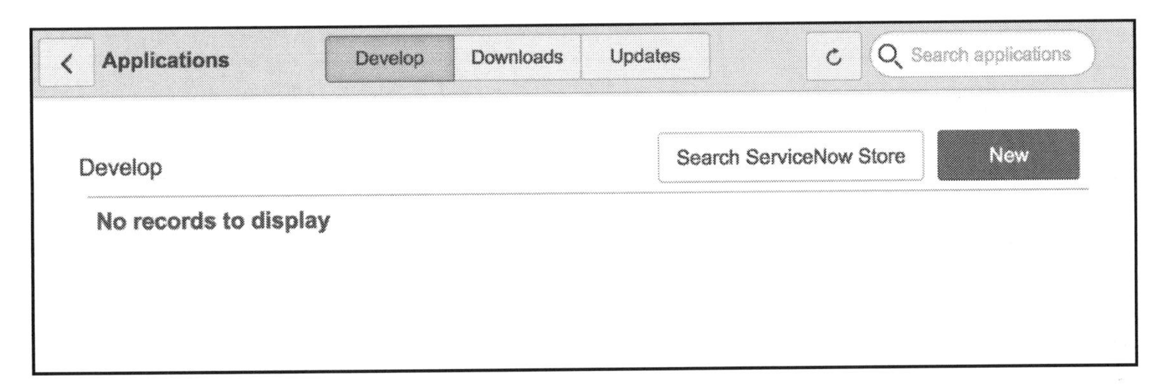


We will be presented with a new application wizard screen like the one shown in the following screenshot:

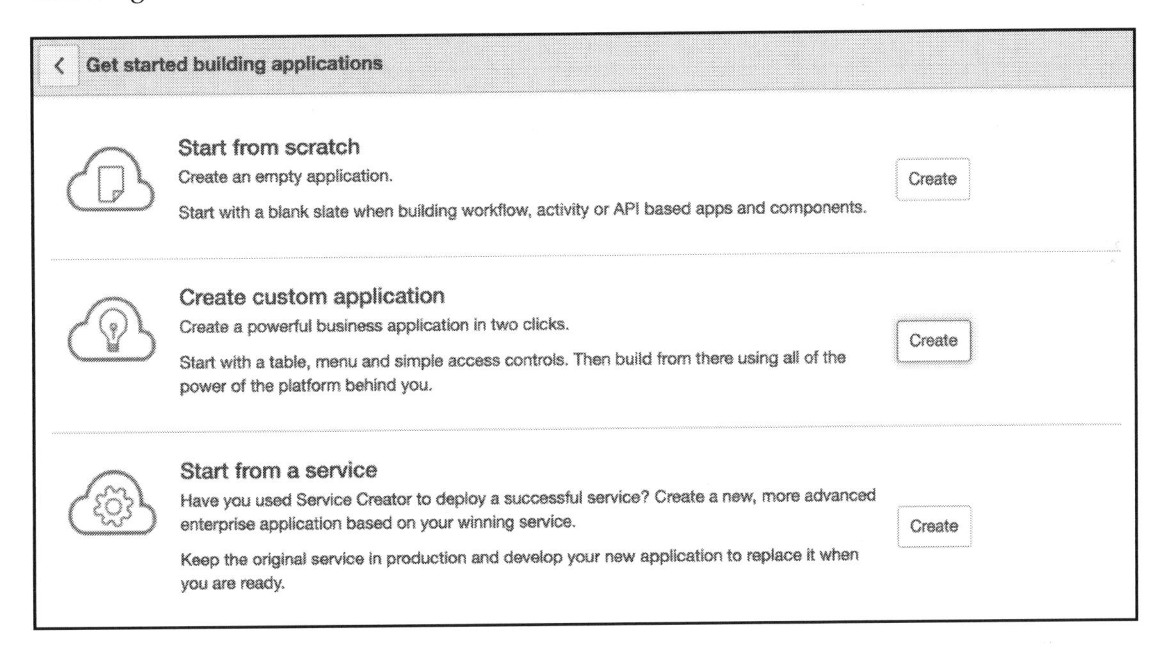

As we are interested in creating an application that requires a table to store data, we will select the second option to **Create custom application**. We will be taken to the **Create Application** page, similar to the one shown in the following screenshot:

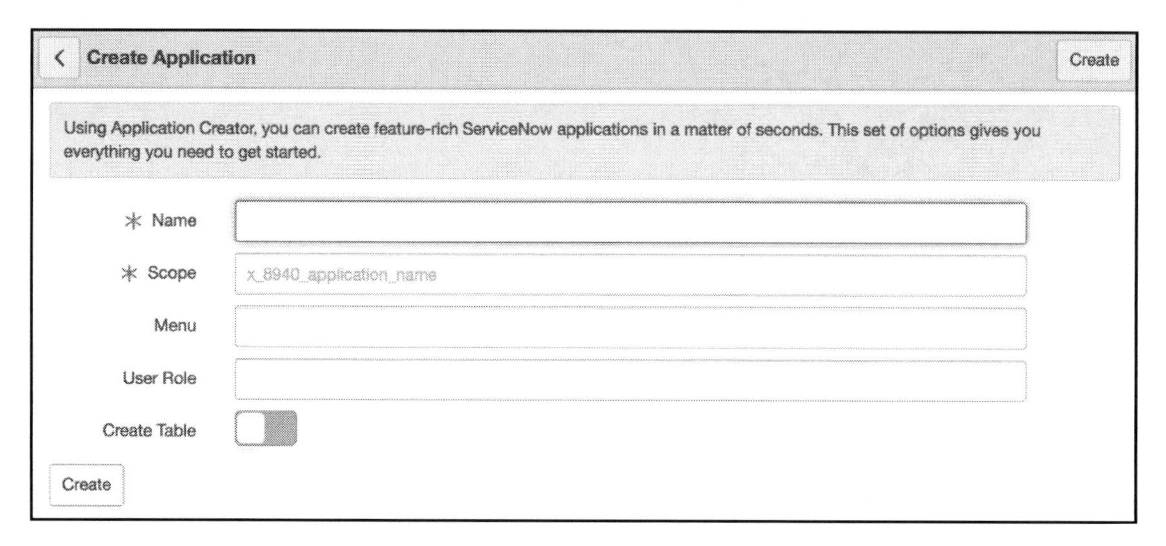


Let us populate the form fields in the **Create Application** page with the following values:

- **Name**: `Travel Booking Application Table`
- **Scope**: (auto filled)
- **Menu**: (auto filled)
- **User Role**: (auto filled)
- **CreateTable**: Set as `TRUE`

- Table section fields: (use auto filled values)

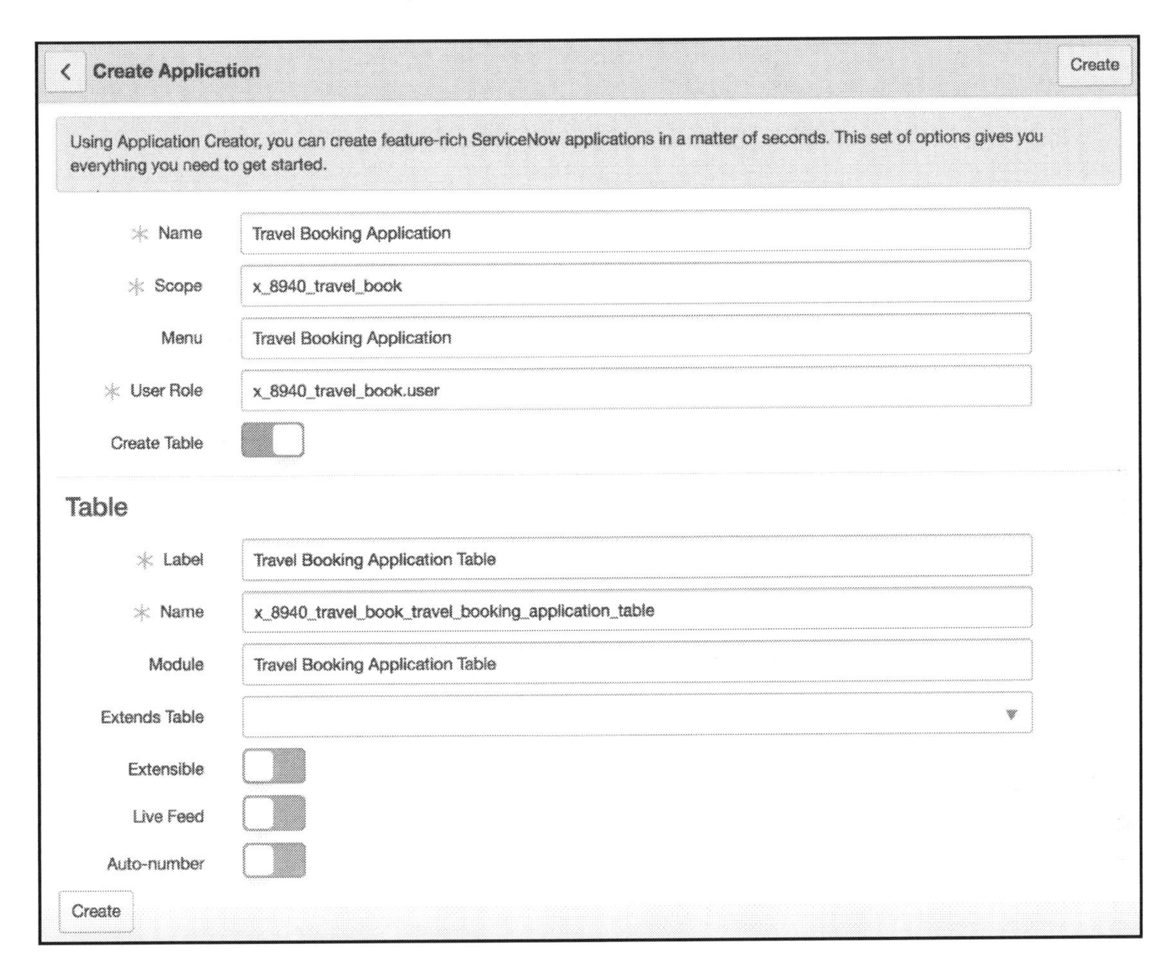


Click on the **Create** button to create a new application named `Travel Booking Application Table` along with the following artifacts:

- **An application scope**: The process will also create a new scope, as discussed earlier in this chapter. It will consist of `x_ prefix` along with the customer vendor code. This will also create a new table and user role.
- **A user role**: A user role in the format of `x_[vendor-prefix]_[app-name].user`.
- **A table**: A new table with an application scope namespace prefixed to its name.

- **Access control**: The table access control list defined for create, read, update, and delete operations.
- **An application menu**: With the access role requirement set to the user role created with the application.
- **A module**: A list of records type module linked to the newly created table and the access role requirement set to the newly created user role.

The artifacts such as user roles, table, and so on will use the scope name as the prefix. So while the custom table we created in `Chapter 3`, *Data Management* had a prefix `u_`, all tables in custom application have an `x_` prefix. This means that when we create a user role, business service, table, and so on in global scope, it doesn't have any namespace prefix in its name field.

Furthermore, the **Applications** column for all artifact records will have the value set to the application record when they are part of a private scope application. On the other hand, the value of the application is set to global application record when the artifact records are part of the global application.

We can go back to the **System Applications** | **Applications** module page to see our new application listed under the **Develop** tab, as shown in the following screenshot:

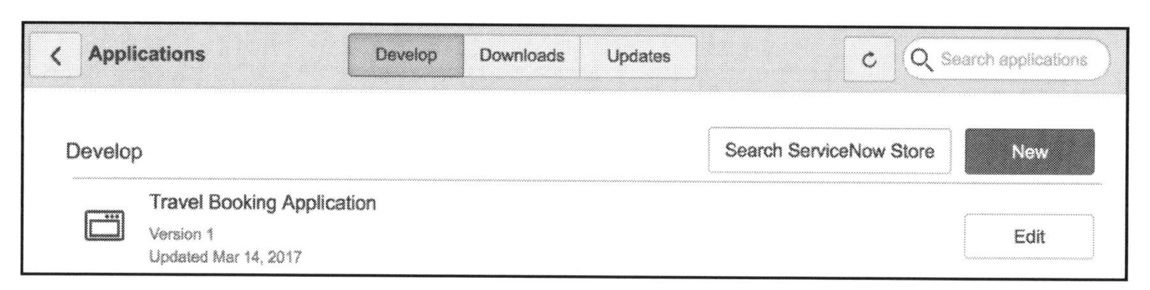


We can click on the **Edit** button next to the custom application to open it in **Studio**, which enables us to quickly create, edit, and manage application artifacts.

When we create a new application using the application creator, the application picker automatically switches to the application we just created.

# Creating application artifacts

Now that our application is created, let us also learn how to manually create a custom table in the new application scope using **Studio**, which is a web-based interface that enables administrators and developers to easily work on different artifacts such as tables, modules, roles, content pages, scripts, and so on of any custom ServiceNow application.

To create a custom table in a specific application, we must ensure that the correct application scope is selected in the application picker dropdown as shown in the following screenshot:

When in **Studio**, we can confirm the application scope we are working on by ensuring that the correct application name is shown at the bottom left corner. As shown in the following screenshot, we are currently working on `Travel Booking Application`. The version of the application is `1.0.0` and there are `10 Files (0 Unsaved)` as part of this application:

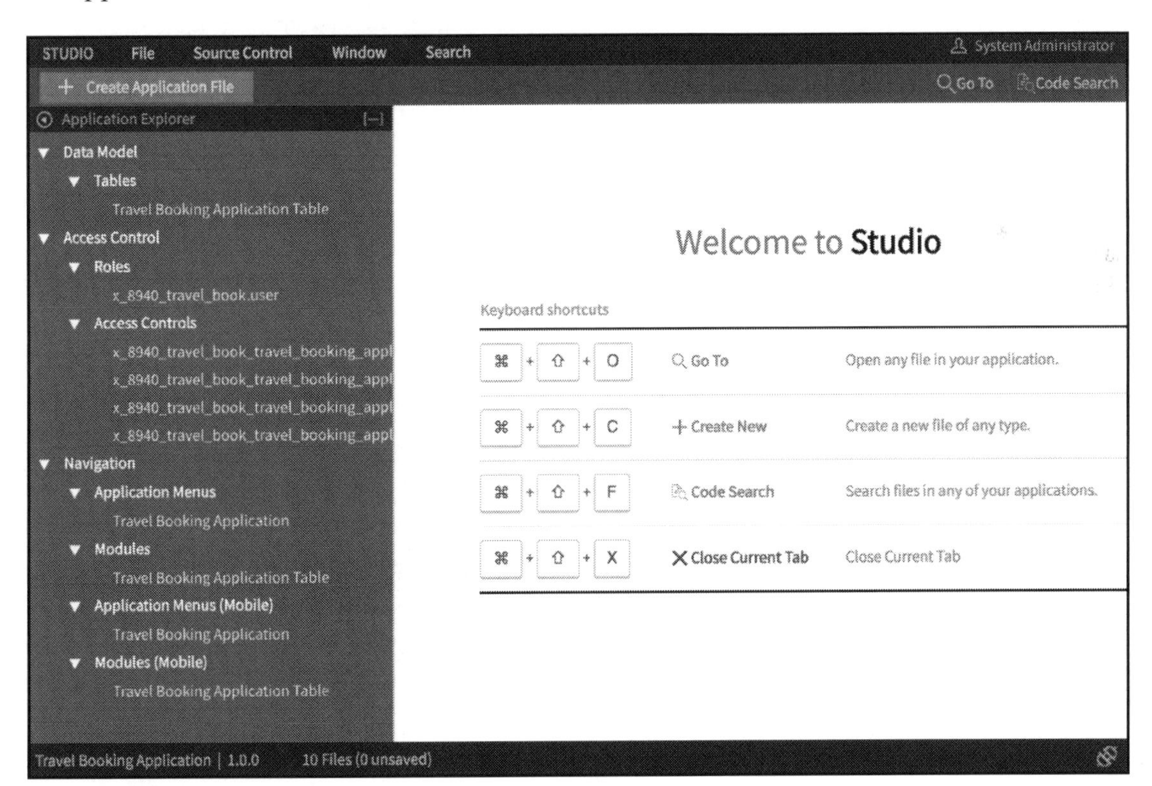

In **Studio**, expand on the **File** menu and click **Create File**, as shown in the following screenshot:

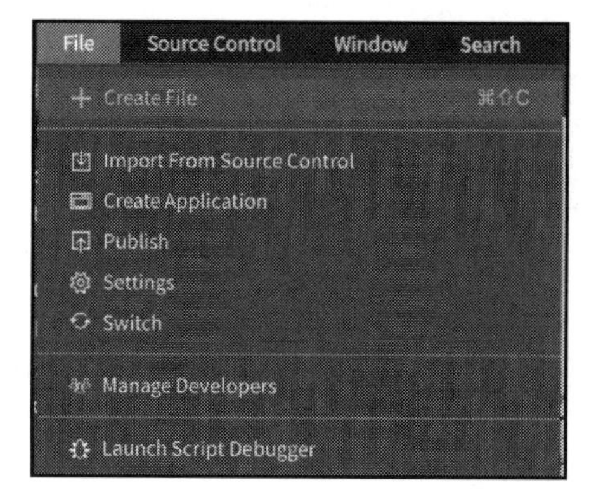


In the **Create Application File** dialog, select **Data Model** on the left as artifact category and **Table** as the artifact type, as shown in the following screenshot, and click on the **Create** button:

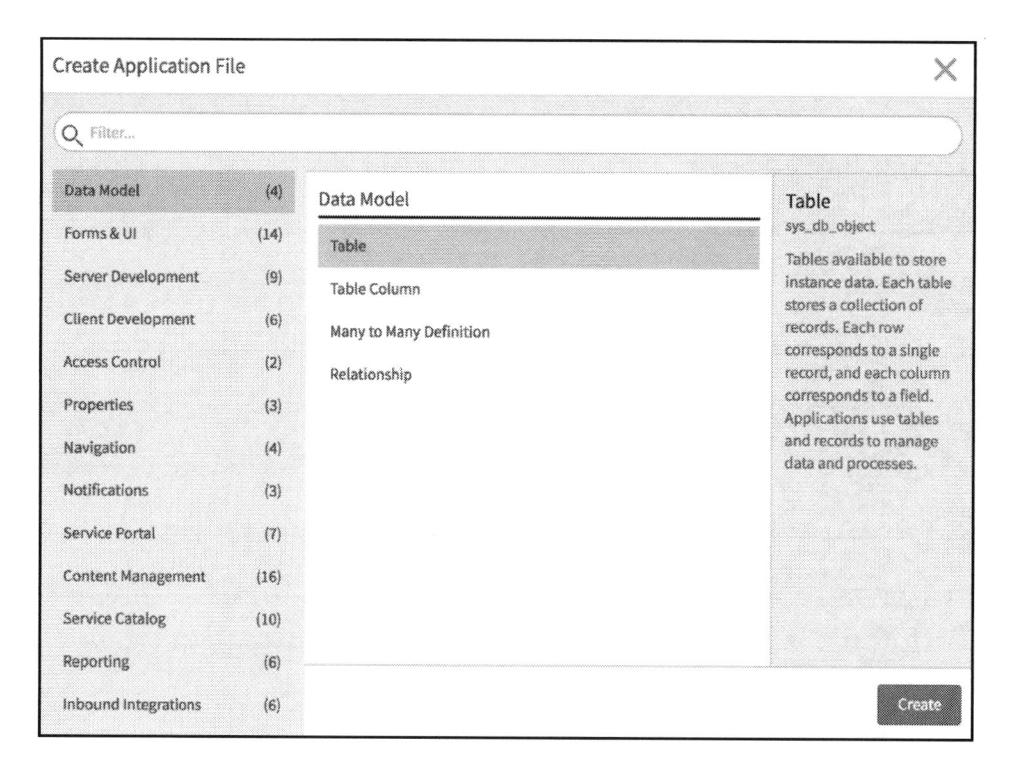

This will open the **Create Table** form in the main section of **Studio**, as shown in the following screenshot:

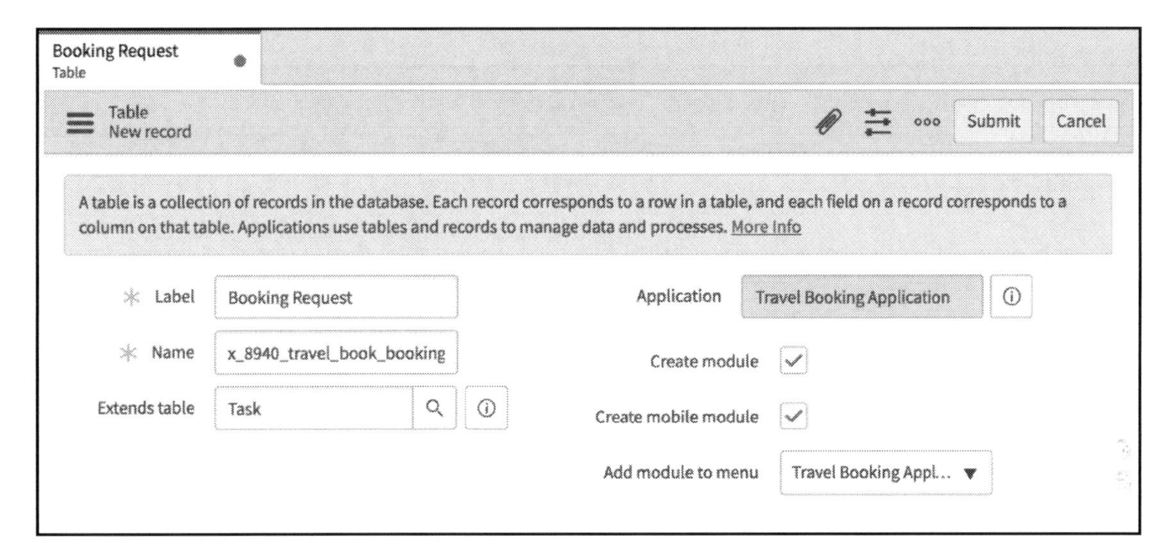


Let us populate the form with the following values:

- **Label**: `Booking Request`
- **Name**: (auto filled)
- **Extend stable**: `Task`
- Leave other fields to default

Click on the **Submit** button to create a new table named `Booking Request`. This will create a new table in the `Travel Booking Application` scope, which extends the fields from the `Task` table, as shown in the following screenshot:

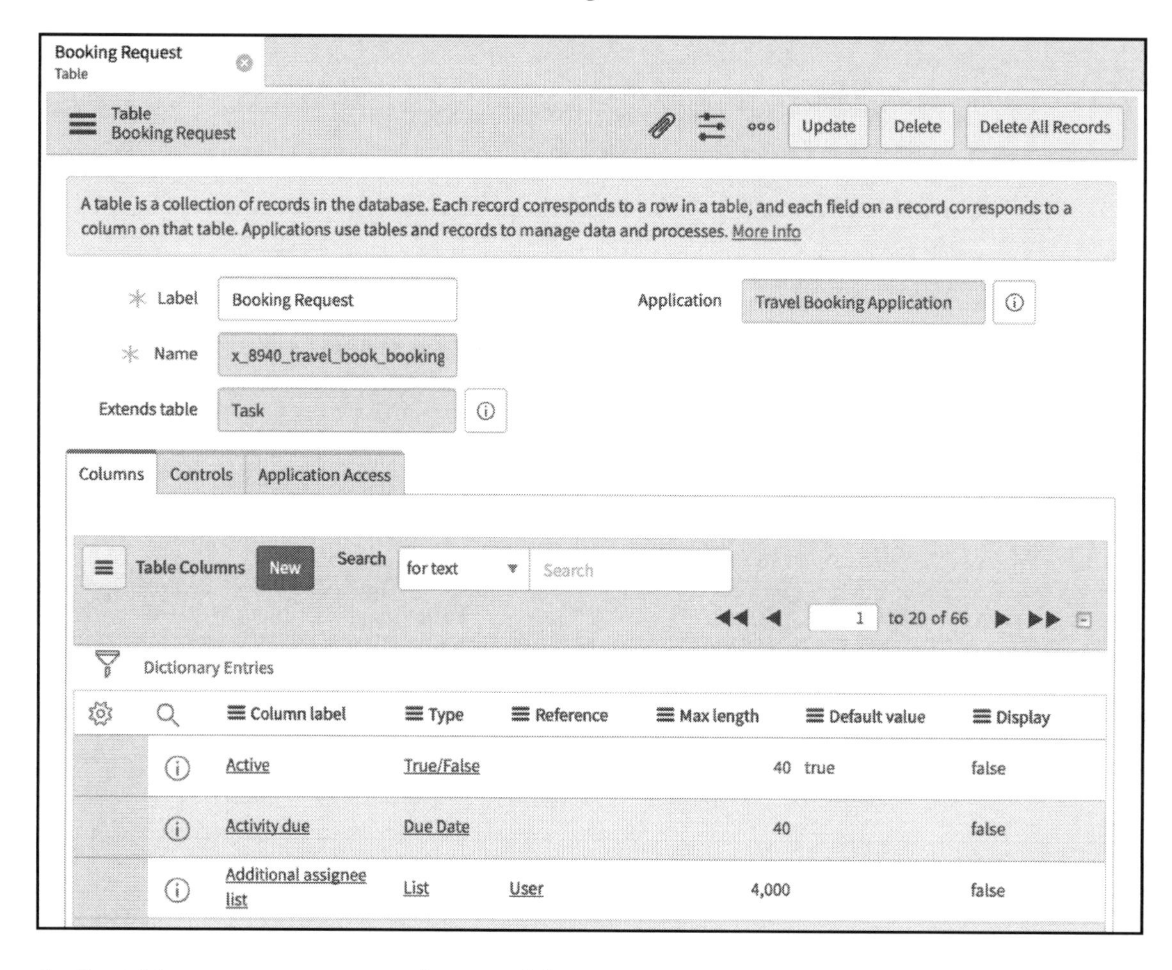


As the table `Booking Request` is part of the `Travel Booking Application` scope, we cannot edit the **Dictionary Entry** of the fields inherited from the `Task` table because task table belongs to the global scope.

Let us open one of the columns inherited from the `Task` table, say the **Activity due** field. Click on the info icon to open the record. We will now be able to see the **Activity due** record in the **Dictionary Entry** detail view; however, all fields will be read only, as shown in the following screenshot. This is because the **Activity due** field belongs to the global application scope and we are currently working on the `Travel Booking Application` scope:

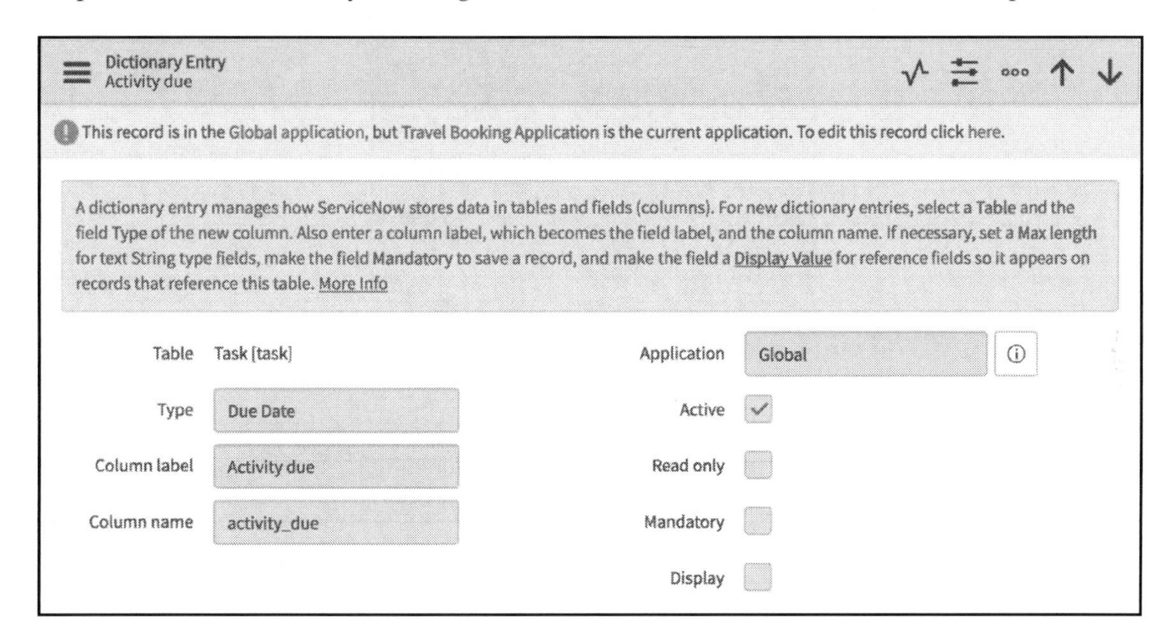

If required, to edit the artifacts that are part of the global scope we can switch to global scope using the application picker dropdown.

Let us now switch back to the main ServiceNow instance page and in the navigator search for the newly created `Travel Booking Application` and open the `Booking Requests` module:

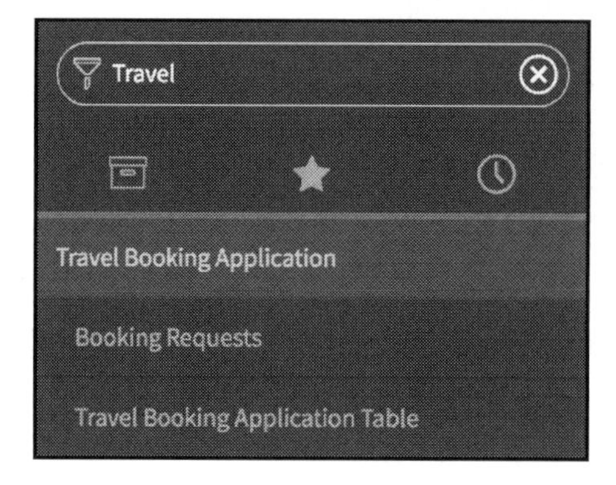


The `Booking Requests` module will present a list of records module similar to the one shown in the following screenshot:

As this is a newly created table, it obviously doesn't contain any records. Let us enter a new record in this table. To create a new booking request task, click on the **New** button. We will be presented with a **New record** form for the `Booking Request` table, as shown in the following screenshot:

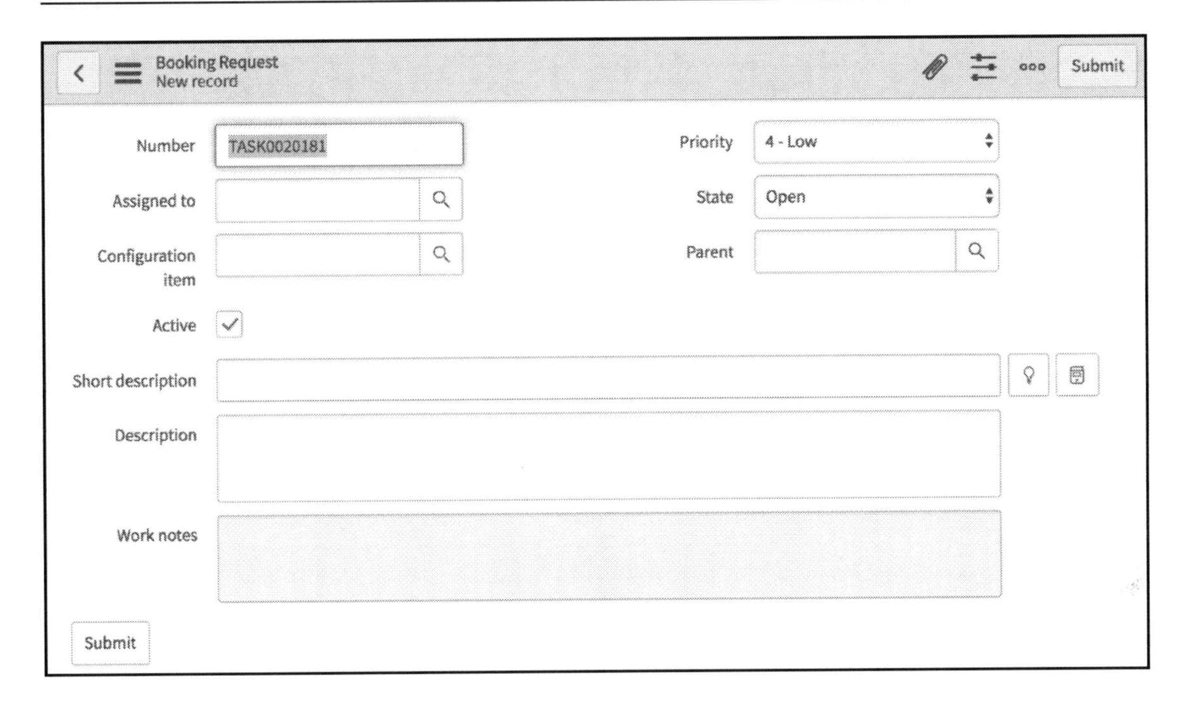


Let us populate the form fields with the following values:

- **Short description**: Demo booking request
- Leave other fields to default values

Click on the **Submit** button to insert a new record into the `Booking request` table. We can see the new record appear in our list of records module for the `Booking request` table, as shown in the following screenshot:

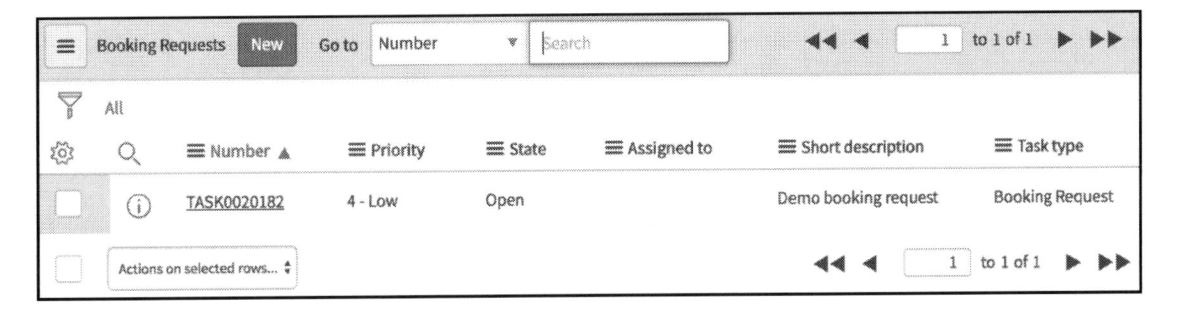

# Accessing information in different scopes

While access to records in the table is controlled by user roles and settings defined in ACL access to records from artifacts like business rules, workflow, script includes relies on **Application Access** settings, which are defined in the table module.

For example, a user can access the record we created in the `Booking Request` table as long as the user has the proper role granted. In our case, `x_8940_travel_book.user` user role must be granted to all users who wish to access records stored in the `Booking Request` table. This is true for users and groups; however, server-side scripts like business rules, script includes, and workflows have application scope set for each artifact entity.

The application scope field shows which application scope an artifact belongs to. In such scenarios, the **Application Access** settings of the table come into the picture. These can be used to allow access to records stored in the table from all application scopes.

We can set the table records to be accessible from:

- All application scopes
- This application scope only (the scope the table is part of)

## All application scopes

When we set the table records, accessibility to **All application scopes**, we can further restrict different table operations such as read, create, update and delete. Furthermore, we can check the **Allow access to this table via web services** to also allow table operations to be performed through web services.

The **Allow configuration** check box allows a table's configuration to be modified by artifacts in other application scopes.

We can allow read access to the data stored in the `Booking Request` table by simply ensuring the **Can read** check box is checked, as shown in the following screenshot:

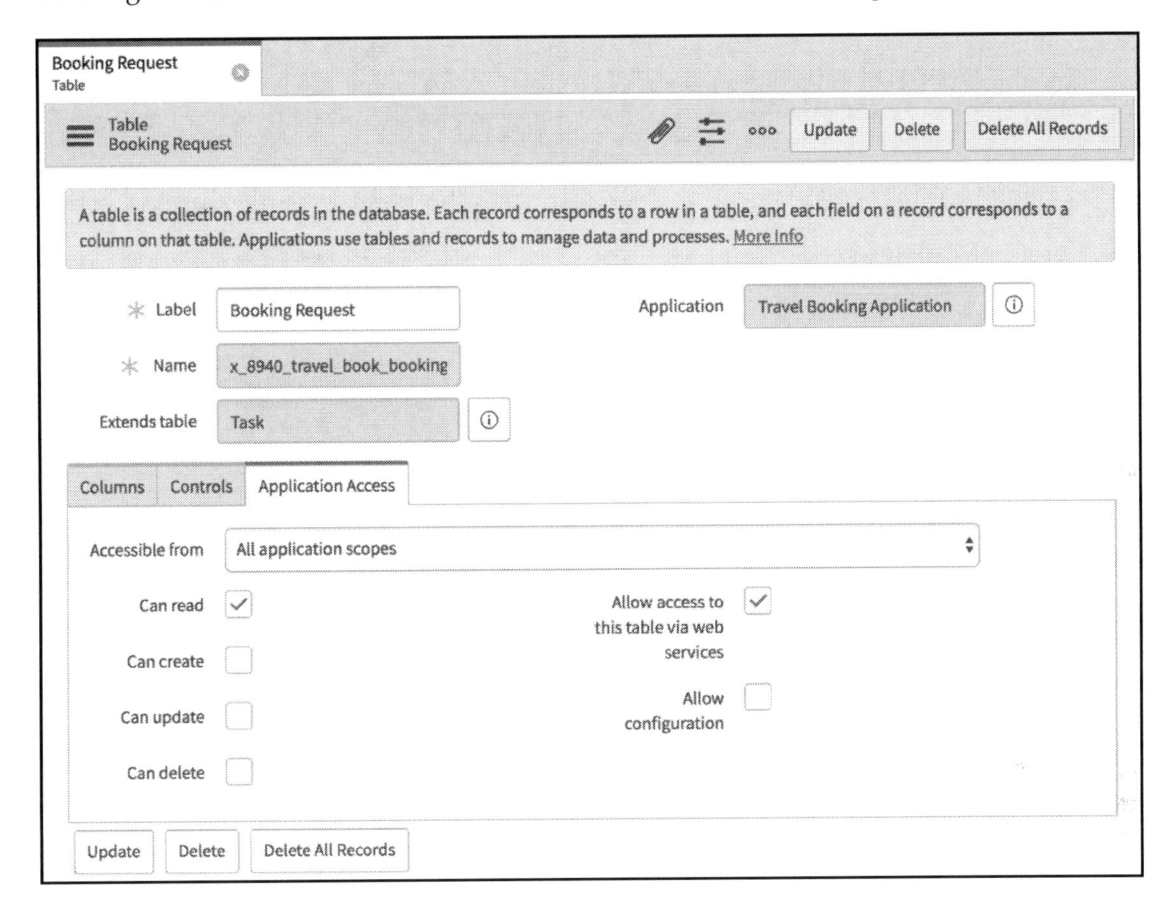

# This application scope only

Alternatively, we can set the table's record to be accessible only from the scope the application is part of. Setting the **Accessible from** field's value to **This application scope only** makes other fields in the tab read only, as shown in the following screenshot. Any artifacts that are part of the table's application scope can perform all table operations such as read, create, update, and delete:

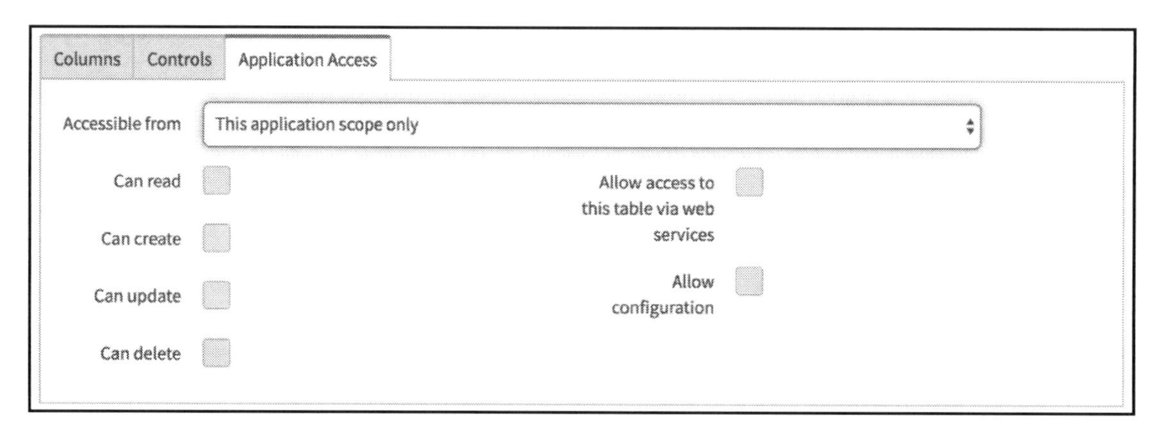


# Summary

In this chapter, we learned how to create custom applications. We learned how application scopes can ensure developers do not make changes to artifacts belonging to a different application and allow artifacts belonging to other scopes access to data. We also learned about the concept of the private and global application scope.

In the next chapter, we will learn how to create custom modules and how to customize the layout of a form and add custom fields to a table.

# 5

# Modules, Forms, and Views

So far we have learnt about user interface, user administration and databases, and how application scopes work. Now we will learn how to create modules, and customize forms and views.

ServiceNow applications are data oriented, which is why the ServiceNow platform offers us various ways to present data to end users by creating various kind of modules, which are accessible through navigational links available under each application menu in the left navigation pane. It also offers tools to modify the layout of forms and add various types of form field elements to the form. It enables us to present data to end-users in an efficient and easily understandable manner. Forms have the capability to present the same records to end-users in a different manner based on their role or other policies. For example, an end-user is only interested in limited amount of form fields when reporting a new incident; however, the service-desk person must have access to more data (form fields) in order to properly work on the incident. The ServiceNow platform offers easy to use features that allow administrators to create modules, and customize form and views.

In this chapter, we will learn how to create different types of modules, customize the form layout, and quickly add new form fields to the table. We will also learn about various form field element types available in the platform, including the reference field, journal field, date field, and choice list. Furthermore, we will learn how we can use form views to present the same record in different ways to end-users based on their role.

In this chapter, we will cover the following topics:

- Creating a new module
- Different module link types
- Managing module order

In this book, we will be using **Studio** to create these application artifacts; however, it is also possible to create these using the standard ServiceNow interface.

# Creating a new module

In the previous chapter, we created a new application named `Travel Booking Application` along with a custom table that inherited a task table named `Booking Request`. When we created the table, it automatically created new modules for us based on the options we had selected in the create table form. Now let us look at ways to create new modules manually using **Studio**.

# Using Studio

ServiceNow Studio offers a simple way to create new modules with just a few clicks:

1. We can open **Studio** by clicking on the **System Applications** | **Studio** navigation link.
2. When in, **Studio** interface, select the appropriate application you want to work on. In our case, we will select the `Travel Booking Application`, as shown in the following screenshot:

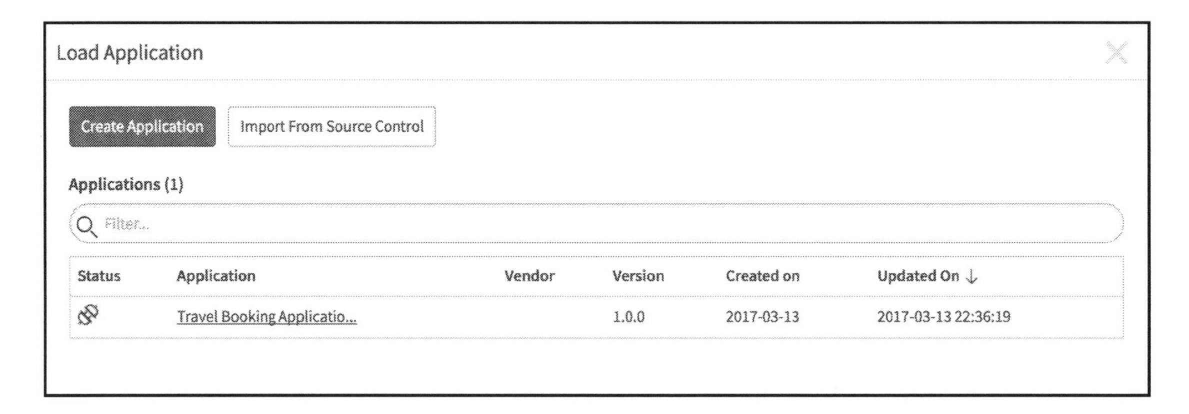

3. Once the application loads, click on the **Create Application File** button, shown in the following screenshot, to show the **Create Application File** dialog:

4. The **Create Application File** dialog, shown in the following screenshot, is one of the most important interfaces of the ServiceNow Studio as it is used quite frequently and allows developers to quickly select the kind of application artifact they wish to create:

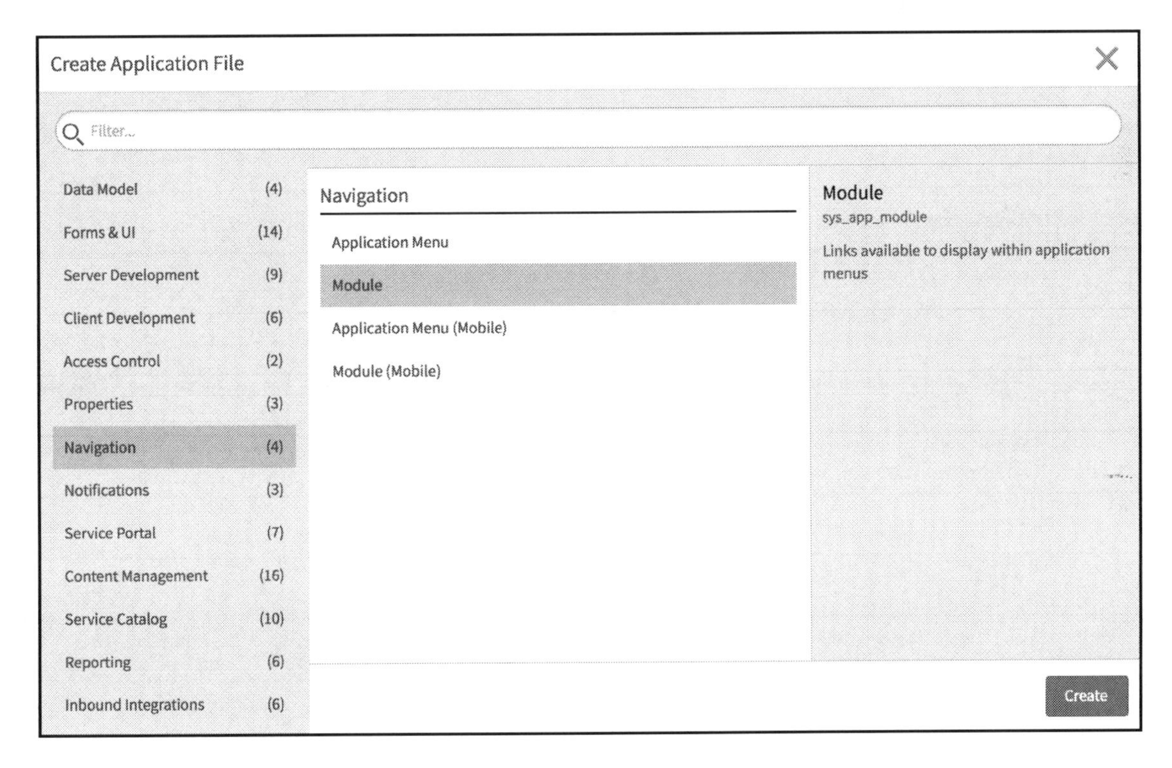


5. Select **Navigation** | **Module** in the dialog, as shown previously, and click **Create** to open the new module form.

The new module form, shown in the following screenshot, will automatically have the application field populated based on the current active application scope:

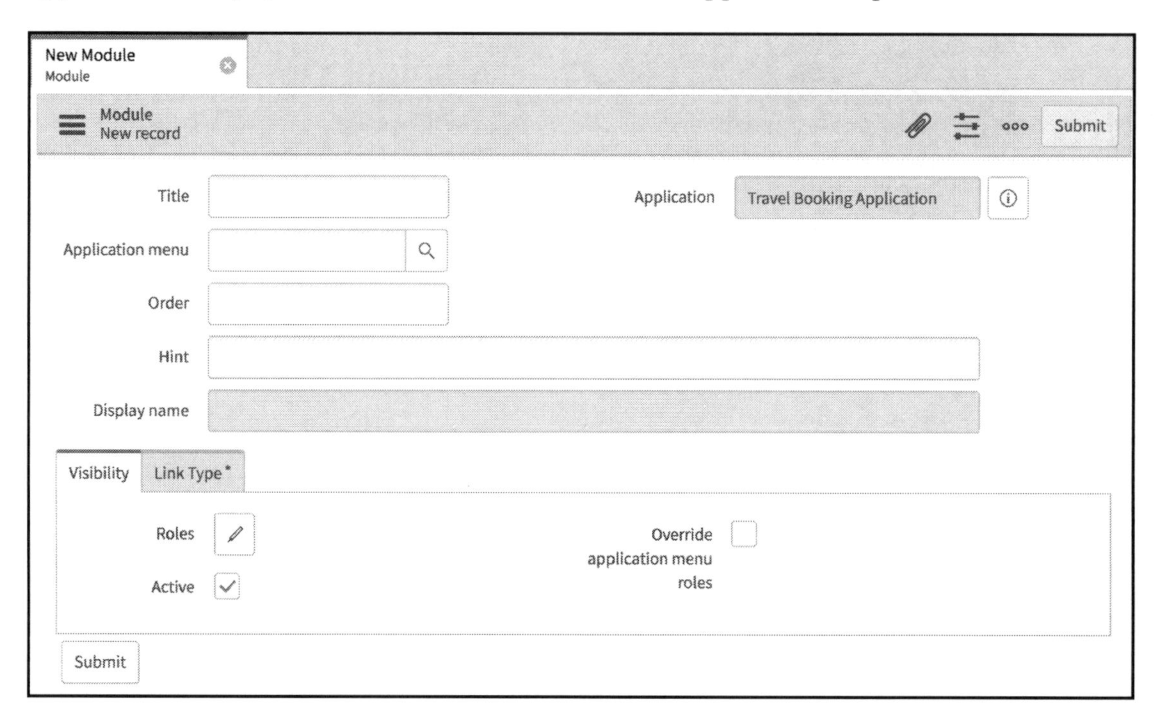


We need to populate other fields and specify the **Application Menu** name under which the module will appear in the left navigator frame. Fill the form with the following values:

- **Title**: `Unassigned Requests`
- **Application**: `Travel Booking Application`

Ensure that the **Active** checkbox is marked as checked and click on the **Link Type*** tab to make it active, as shown in the following screenshot:

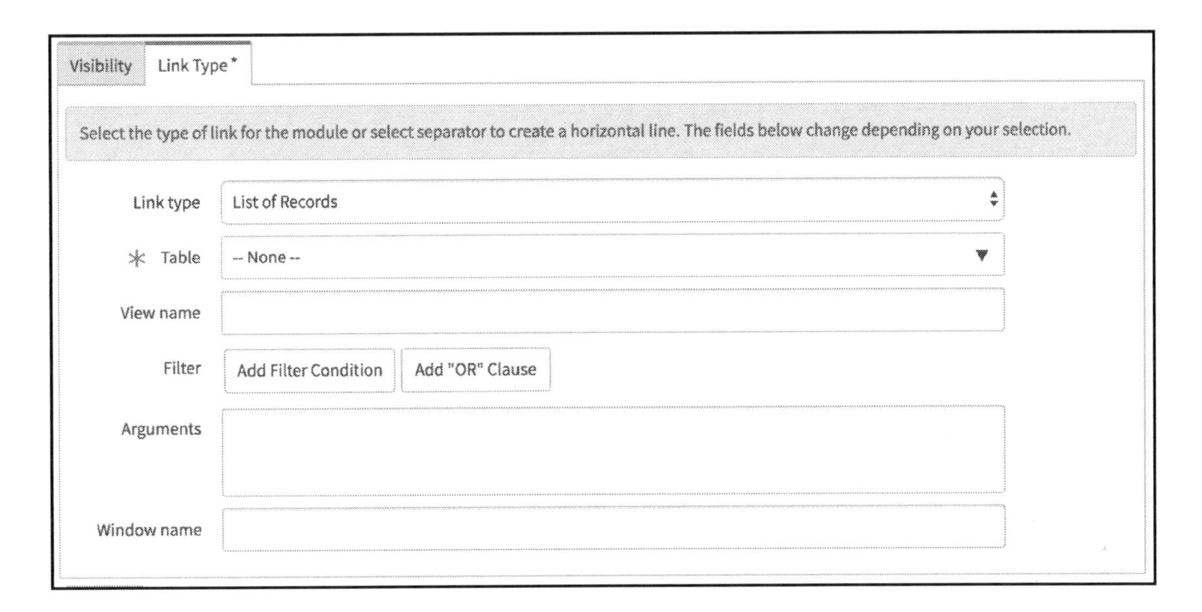


Continue filling in the form fields with the following values:

- **Link type**: `List of Records`
- **Table**: `Booking Request`
- **Filters** (as shown in the following screenshot):
    - **Assigned to** is empty
    - **Assignment group** is empty

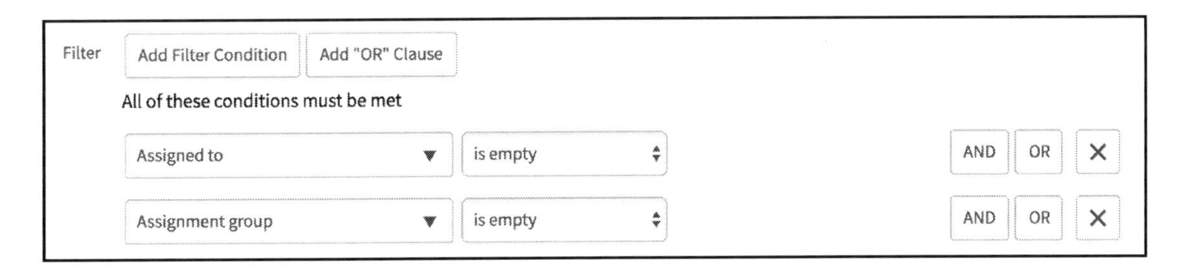


Link type is what sets the behavior of the module. A list of records link type is used to display records from a table. When we select a link type, the following fields will change based on our selection. We will cover different available link types in the next section in this chapter.

Click **Submit** to create a new list of records module named `Unassigned Requests` under the application menu `Travel Booking Application`, as shown in the following screenshot:

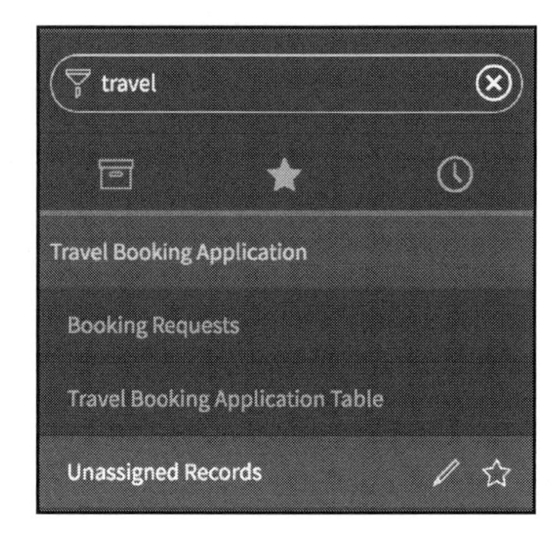

When we create any new module, we must specify an application menu under which the new module will appear. Modules are typically accessed using the left navigator. If you do not see the newly created module appear immediately in the navigator, try refreshing the page.

Let us now open our new module `Unassigned Request`. As it is a module with link type set as list of records, it will fetch data stored in the `Booking Request` table and show rows of records in tabular format, as shown in the following screenshot:

# Different module link types

Every link type has a different interface and functionality from the others. There are many different link types available in the platform. The following are the most commonly used module link types:

- List of records (see previous topic)
- New record
- Run a report
- Homepage
- Separator

# New records

A new record module can be used to direct end-users to a form that can be used to insert a new entry into a specified table. The left navigation link **Incident** | **Create New** is an example of a new record module. Creating a new record module is fairly simple and similar to creating a list of records module:

1. Open the **Create Application File** dialog in **Studio**, and select **Navigation** | **Module** and click **Create**.
2. Fill in the form as detailed here:
    - **Title**: `Create New`
    - **Application menu**: `Travel Booking Application`
    - **Link type**: `New Record`

- **Table**: `Booking Request [x_8940_travel_book_booking_request]`

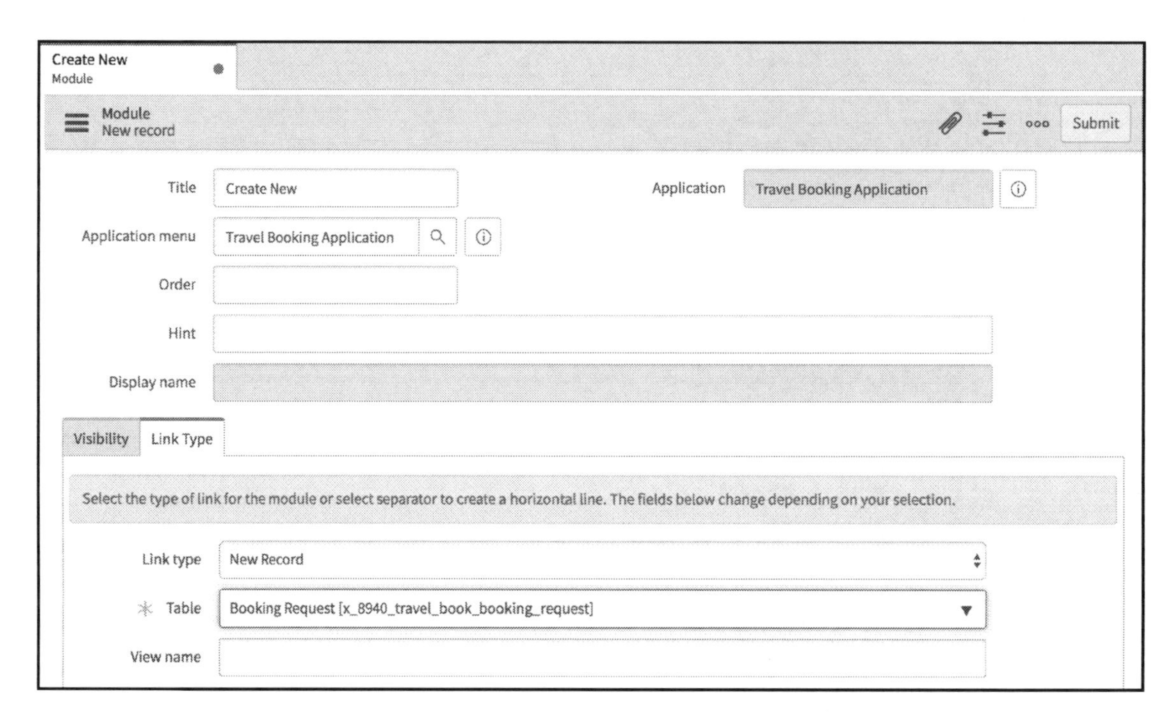


3. Click **Submit** to create a new module named **Create New** with link type new record. It will be visible in the left navigation menu under the `Travel Booking Application` menu, as shown in the following screenshot:

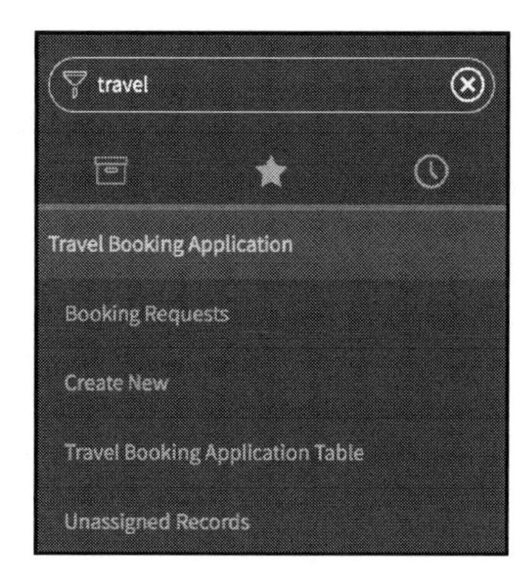

Remember, as mentioned previously, if the newly created module link is not visible in the left navigator pane immediately, either wait for a while or try refreshing the page. You may need to perform this action whenever you are adding an application menu or module.

4. Clicking on the **Create New** navigation link will directly take us to a form, which can be populated to create a new entry in the `Booking Request` table:

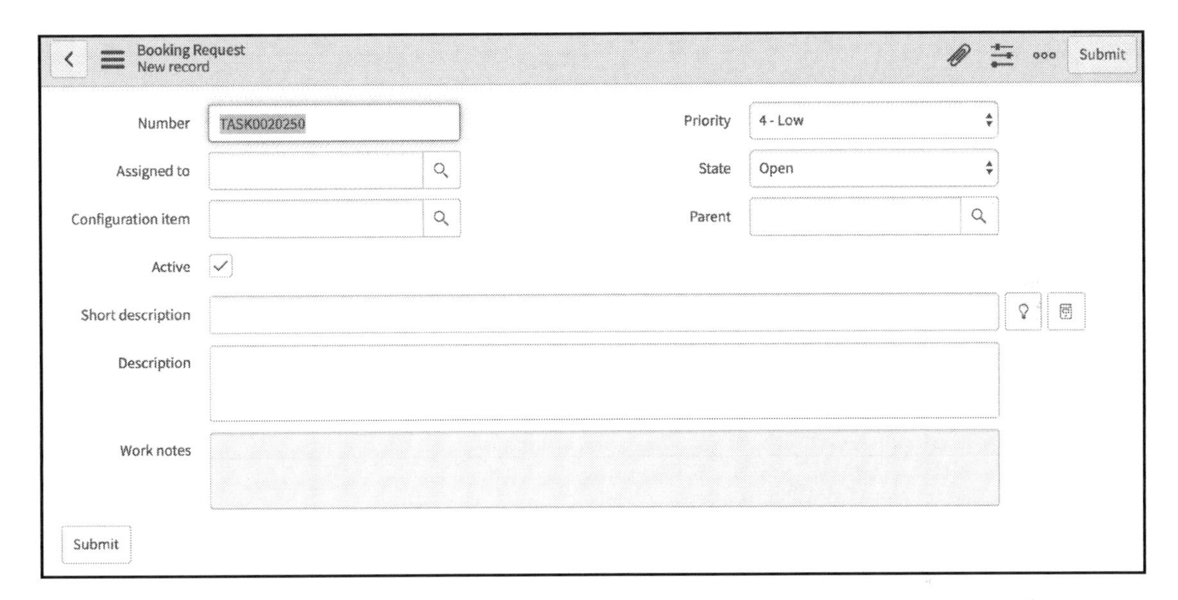


Let us test our new record form by populating it with the following values and clicking **Submit**:

- **Priority**: `3 - Moderate`
- **Short description**: `Testing new record form`

We will be taken to a list of records page for the specified table in the same view as shown in the following screenshot:

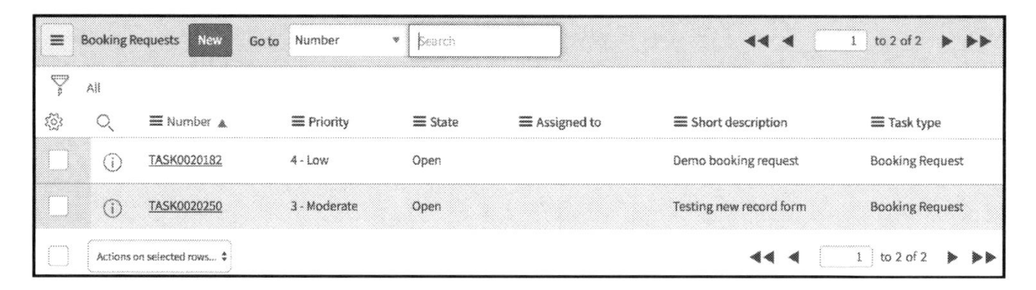


# Running a report

This type of module is used specifically to run an existing report. So let us first create a simple report for our table before we create the run a report module type. To create a new report:

1. Select the **Reporting** | **Report** in the **Create Application File** dialog window in **Studio**, as shown in the following screenshot, and click **Create**:

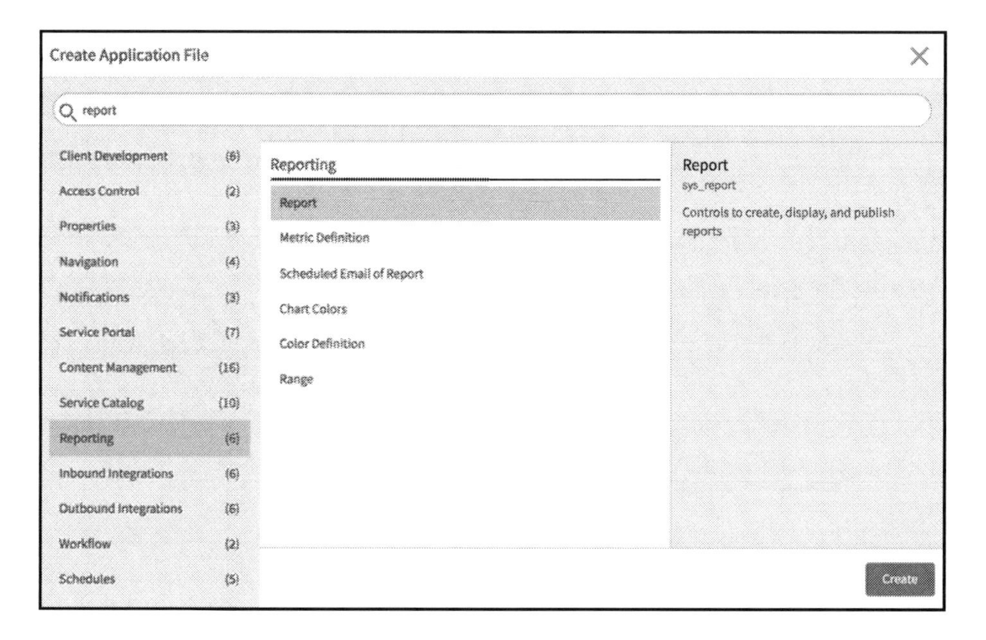

2. You will be presented with an interface suitable for creating reports. Fill in the form as detailed here:
    - **Title**: `Travel Booking Requests by Status`
    - **Table**: `Booking Request`
    - **Type**: `Bar`
    - **Group by**: `Priority`
    - Leave other fields as default
    - Set filters as: Active is true, see the following screenshot:

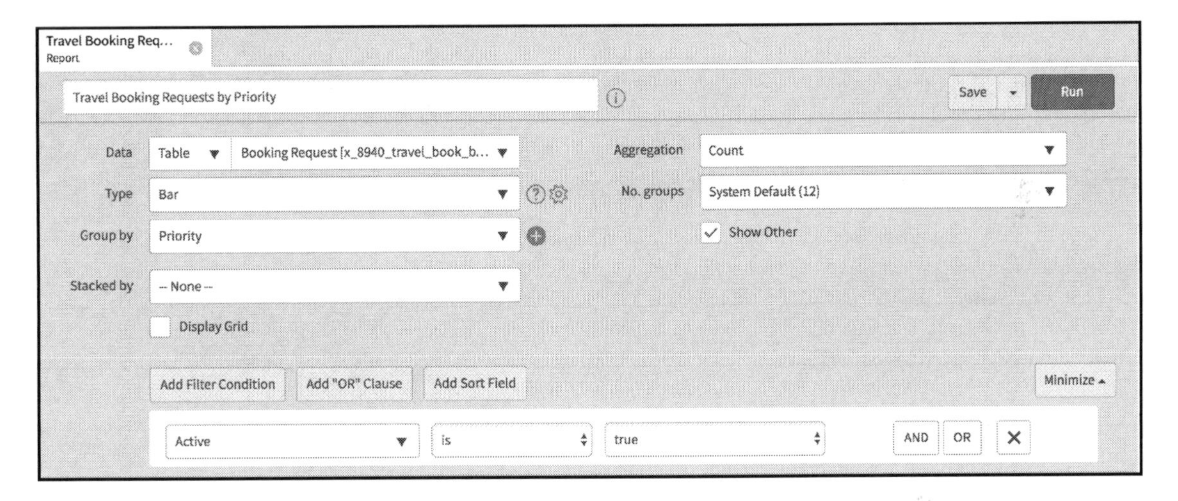


3. Click on the **Run** (on the top-right) button to generate our new report. It will generate a bar chart, similar to one shown in the following screenshot, as the **Type** of the report is selected as **Bar**.

4. Click on the **Save** button to be able to use this later:

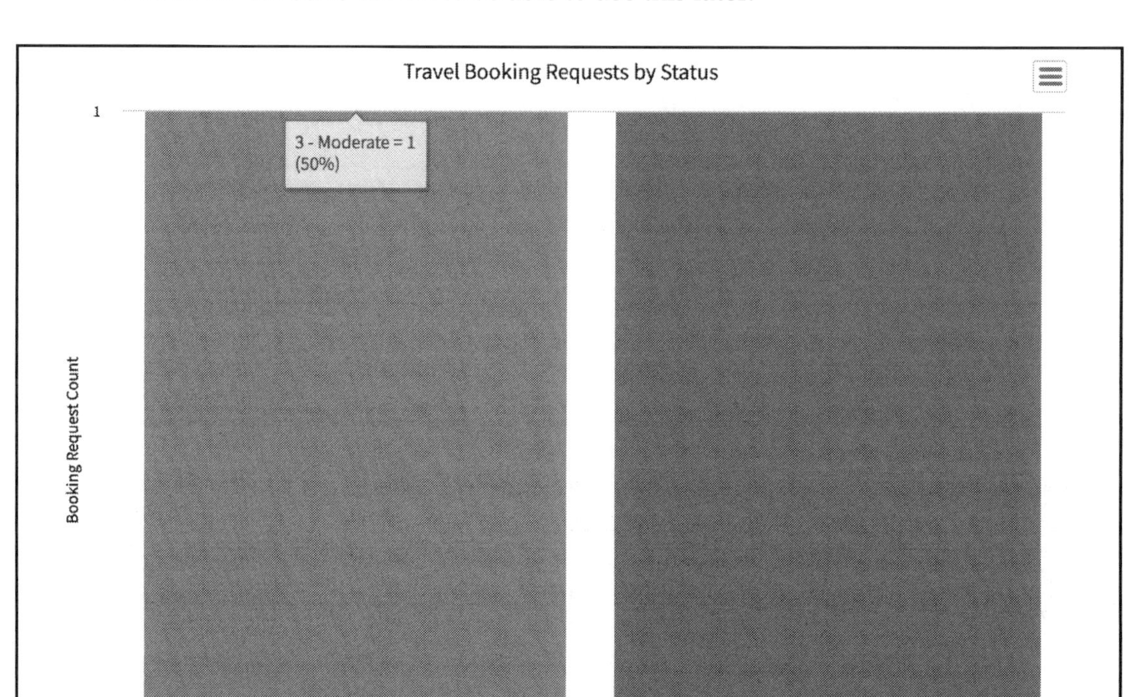


Similarly, create another report named `Booking Requests by State` by grouping the query by the **State** field instead of the **Priority** field.

Once the report is saved, we can now create a module of link type **Run a report**. Follow the steps mentioned here to create a new module of link type **Run a report**:

1. In the **Create New Application File** dialog window, select **Navigation** | **Module** and click **Create**.
2. Fill in the new module form as detailed here:
    - **Title**: `Booking Requests by Priority`
    - **Application menu**: `Travel Booking Application`
    - **Link Type**: **Run a Report**
    - **Report**: `Travel Booking Requests by Priority`

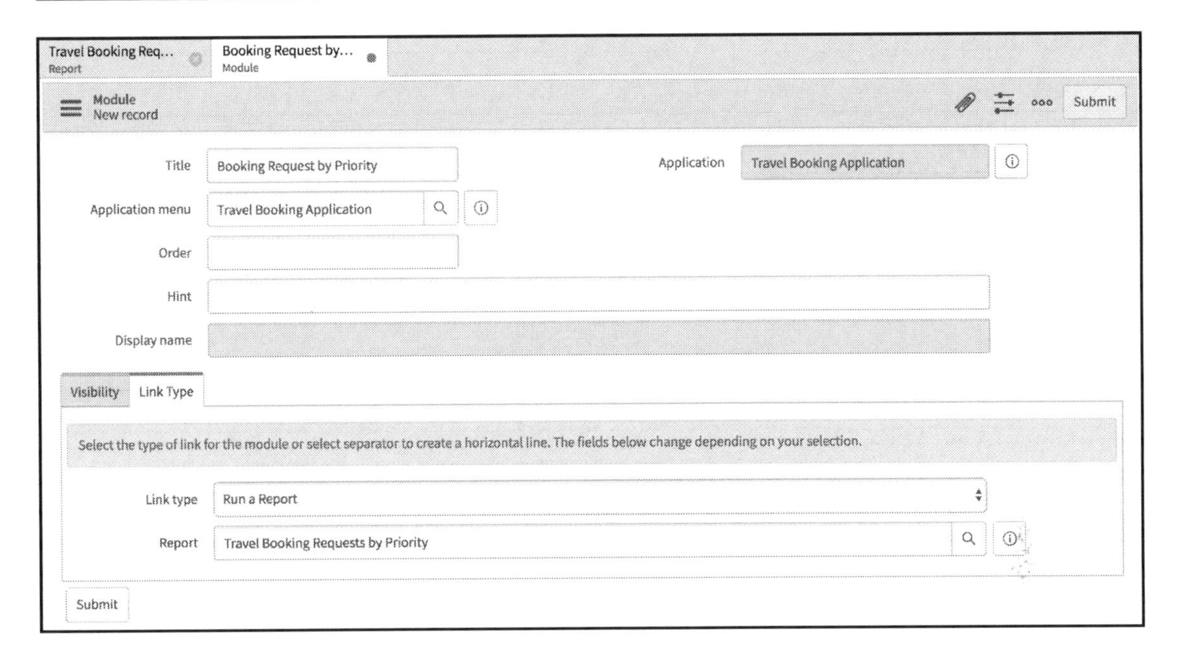


3. Click **Submit** to create a new module named `Booking Requests by Priority`. Once we create the module, it can be seen in the left navigation module, as shown here:

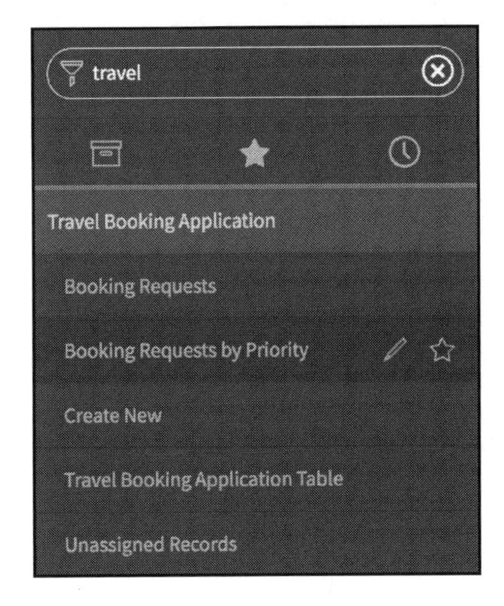

4. Clicking on the `Booking Requests by Priority` link will load and run the `Travel Booking Requests by Priority` report in the content frame, as shown here:

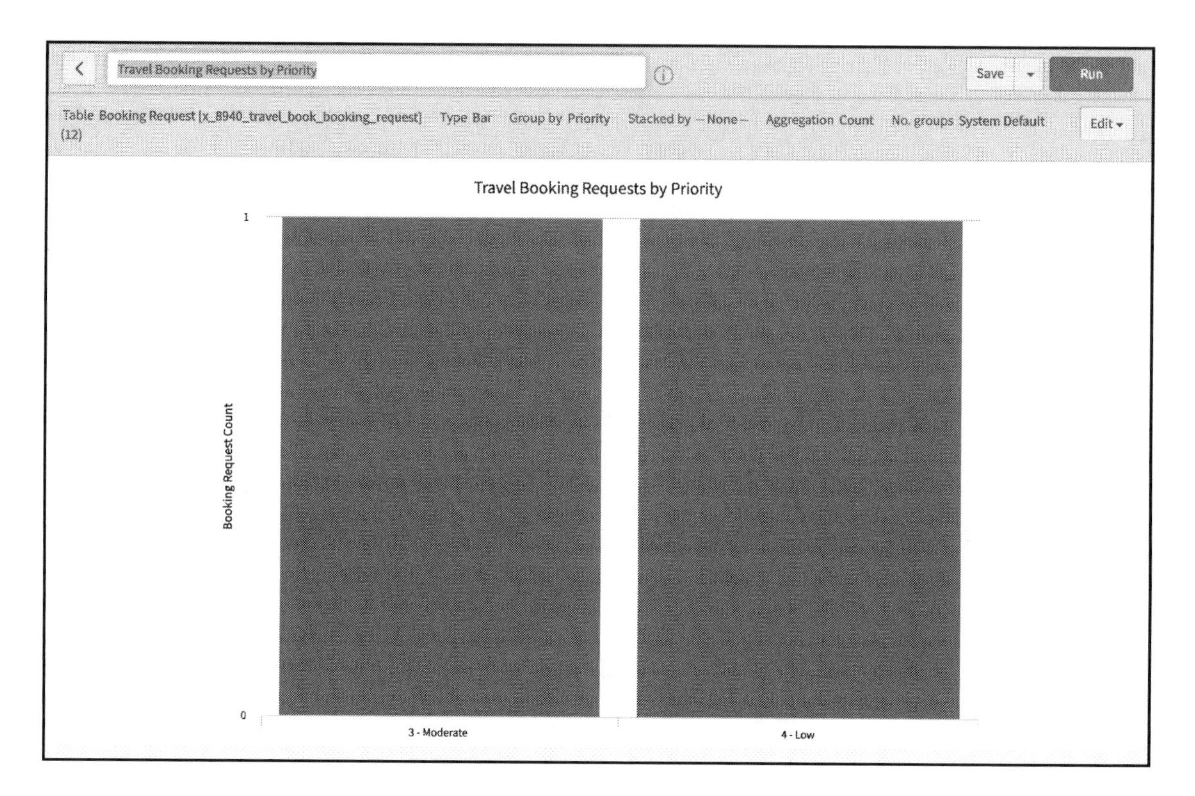


# Homepages

We can create navigation links that point to portal pages with content made up of graphs (created using the reports feature) and other elements such as a service catalog category, scrolling news widget, and so on.

The **Service Level Management | SLA Homepage** module, shown in the following screenshot is an example of a homepage link type:

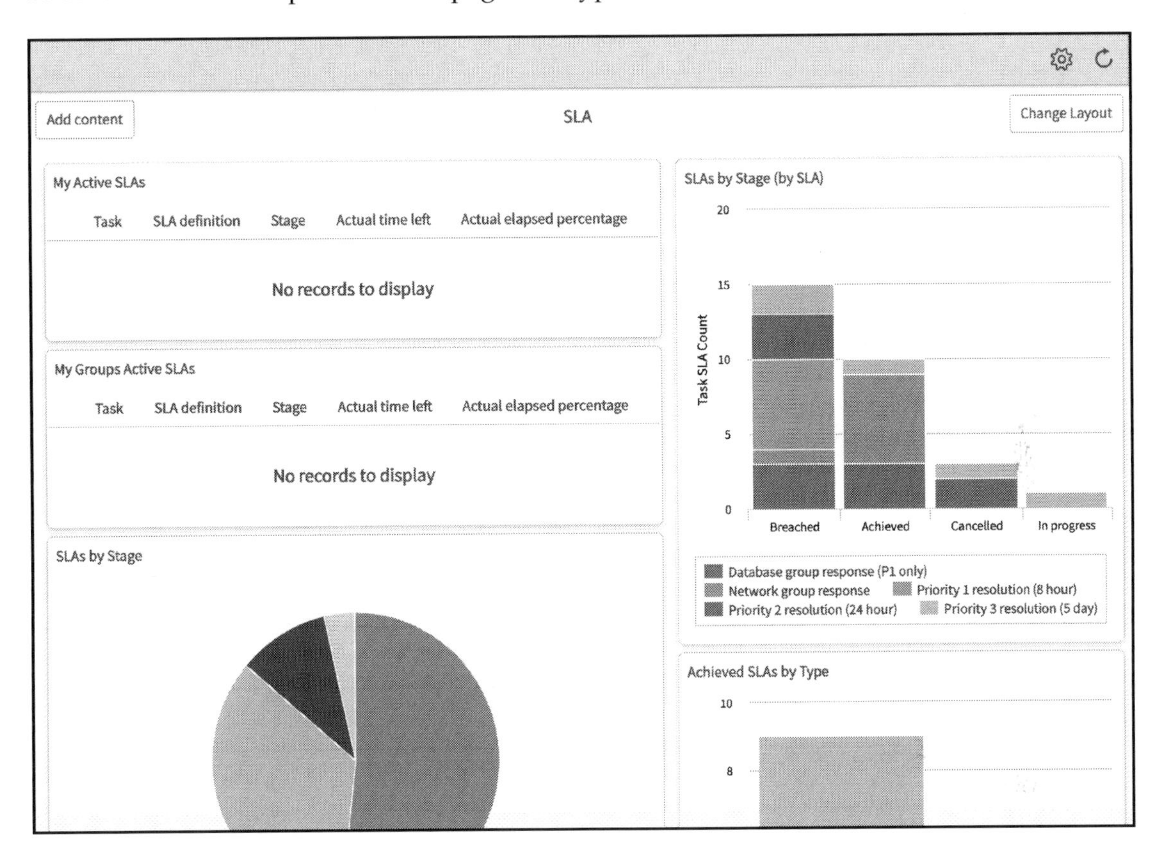


Creating a new **Homepage** module is as simple as creating the list of records module.

# Portal pages

To create a **Homepage** module, we need to first create an empty portal page. To make sense of a homepage, we must also add some content such as reports to the portal page:

1. Open **Studio** and in the **Create New Application File** dialog select **Content Management** | **Portal Page**, as shown in the following screenshot, and click on the **Create** button:

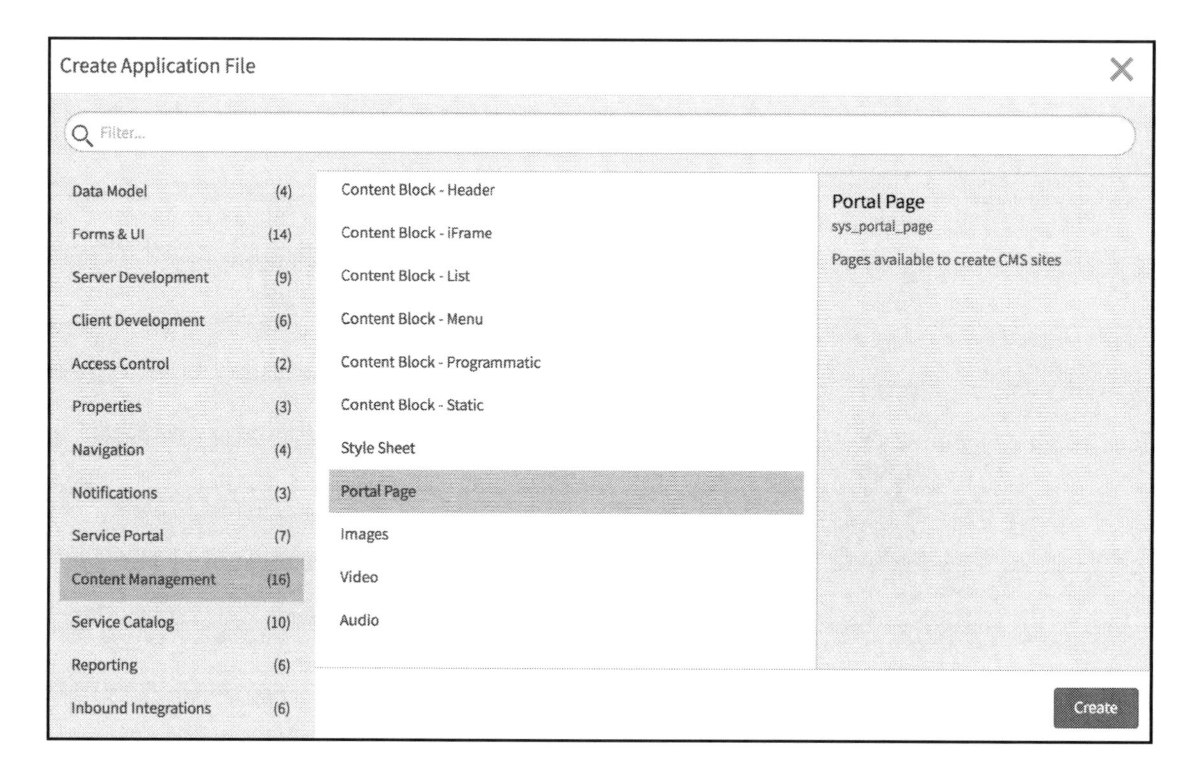


2. Then fill in the form with the following details:
    - **Title**: `Travel Booking Portal Page`
    - **Selectable**: Checked
    - **View**: `travel_booking_portal_page`
    - **Write Roles**: Leave blank (if required, grant role write permission)
    - **Read Roles**: Leave blank (if required, grant role read permission)

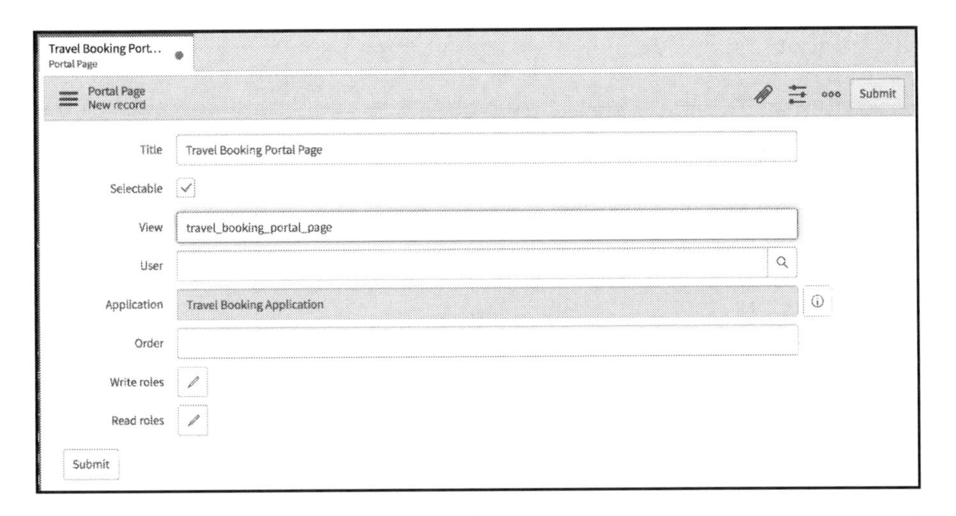


3. When a portal page is marked as **Selectable**,only then is it available to be selected as a homepage.
4. Each portal page must have the view name defined that is used to refer to it using scripts.
5. Click on **Submit** to create a new empty portal page.
6. Once the portal page is created, open the record, scroll down to the **Related Links** UI actions list, shown in the following screenshot, and click on the **Edit Homepage** related link. This will open the portal page to be edited for all users. This means, any changes that you make will be visible to all users:

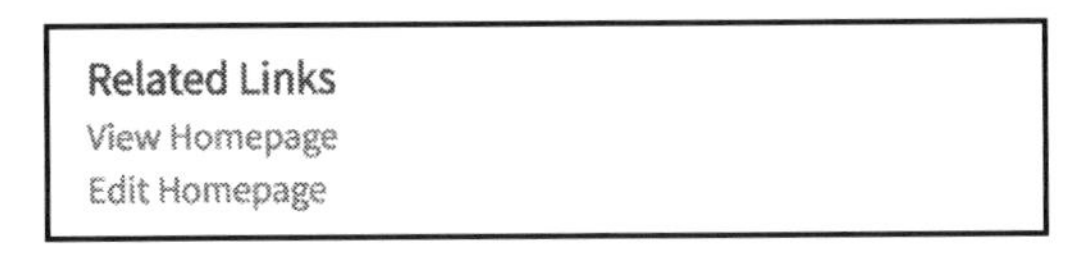


As shown in the following screenshot, an empty portal page will appear after clicking on the **Edit Homepage** link. The title of the page is displayed in the center:

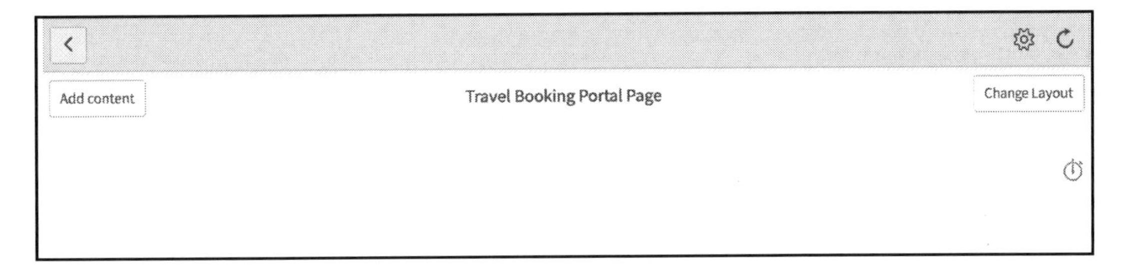

There are two buttons available on the top section of the page:

- **Change Layout**: This is used to change the layout (container style) of the portal page
- **Add content**: This is used to add content to the portal page

## Change layout

The **Change Layout** button allows us to change the layout of any portal page. The layout of a page defines the drop zone for any content. There are many different layout options available to us.

Click on the **Change Layout** button and to open the layouts selection dialog. Then, select the **2 rows: 3 equal columns and 2 equal columns**, as shown in the following screenshot option from the left section and click on the **Change** button:

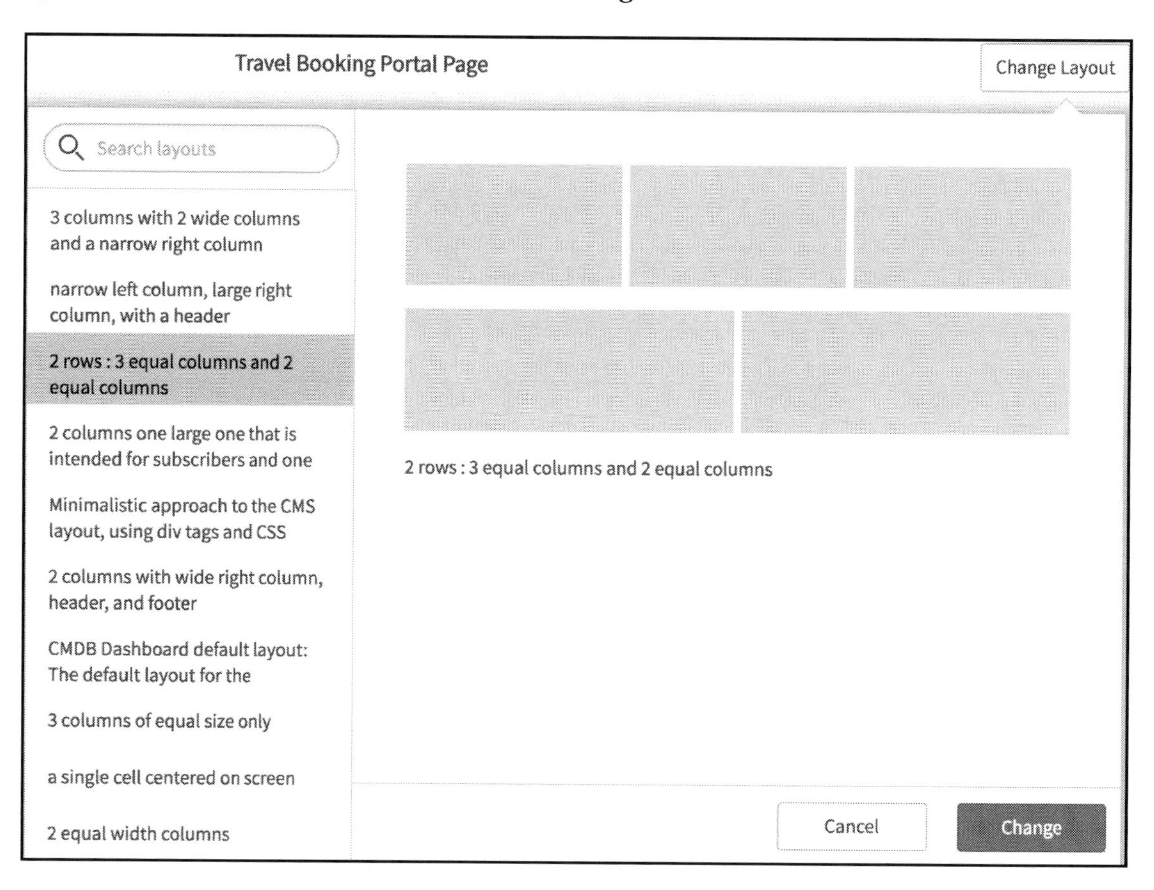

This will change the layout of the portal page and enable drop zones as specified in the layout definition. Now let us see how the drop zone works by adding some content to the portal page.

## Add content

Click on the **Add content** button to open the relevant dialog box, as shown here:

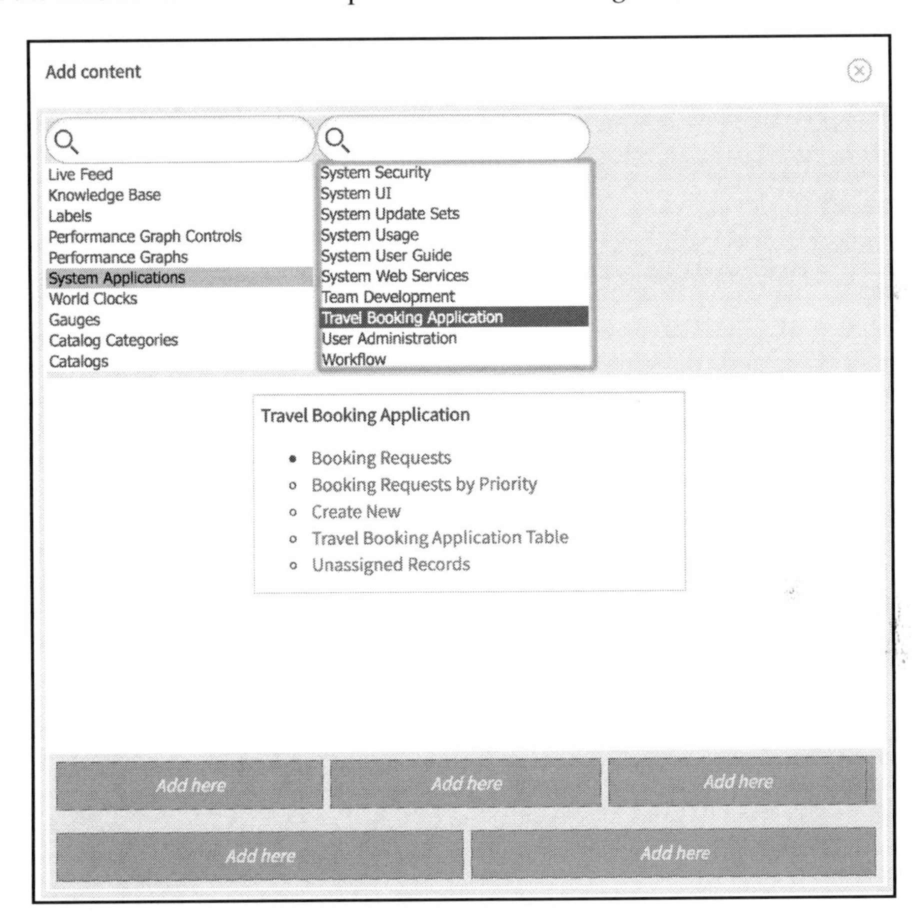


The **Add content** dialog box is divided into three vertical sections. The top section is where we select the type of content we want to add. The middle section allows us to preview the content we want to add. And the bottom section allows us to select a drop-zone, defined in the layout, where we want to add the content. Let us add content to each of these drop-zones.

In the **Add content** dialog box, select **System Application** | **Travel Booking Application** in the top section and click on the top-left **Add here** button as shown here:

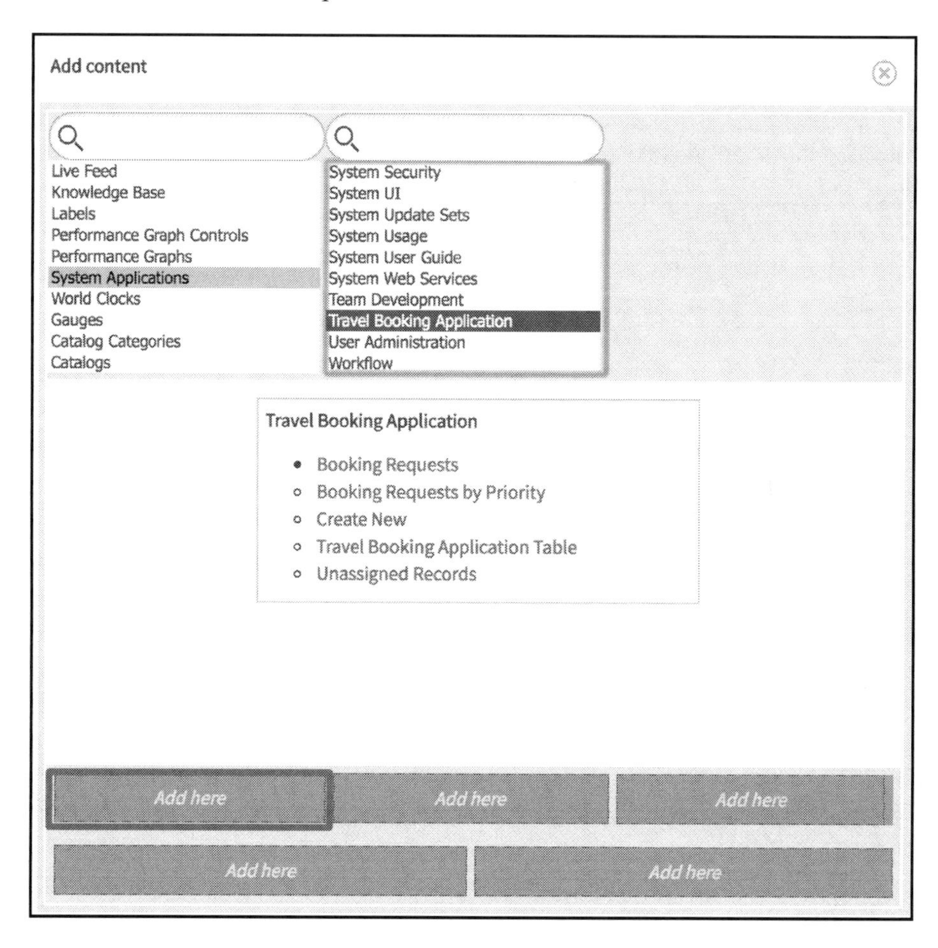


This will add the new content to the top-left drop-zone of the page. The new content will add the page immediately.

Add **World Clocks** | **World Clocks** to the top-middle drop zone and **Gadgets** | **System Information** | **Overview** to the top-right drop section by selecting the content and clicking on the relevant **Add here** buttons.

Let us add our report by selecting **Reports** | **Booking Request** | **Travel Booking Requests by Priority** and clicking on the bottom-left **Add here** button:

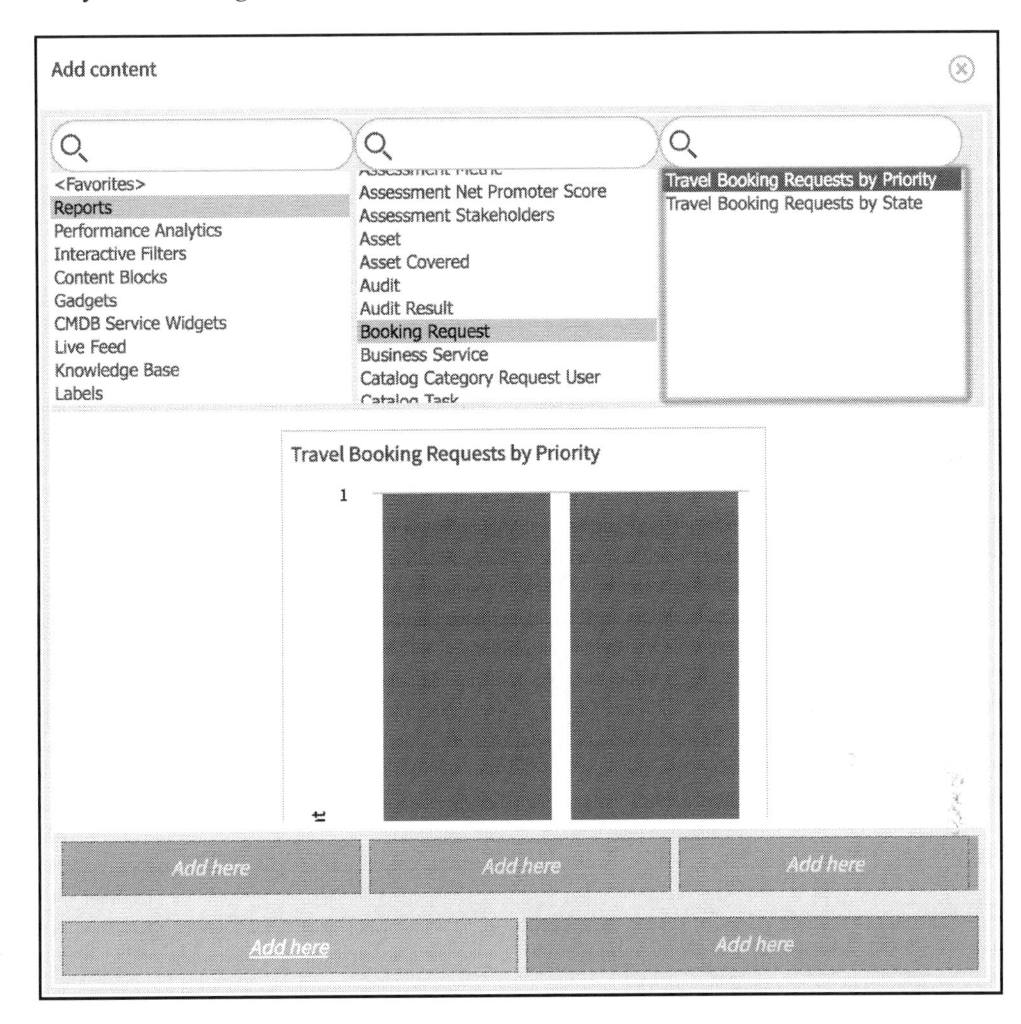


Similarly, add the **Reports** | **Booking Request** | **Travel Booking Requests by State** report to the bottom-left drop-zone by clicking on the corresponding **Add here** button.

Close the **Add content** dialog box to see the changes to our portal page. Based on your content, the portal page will look something similar to the one shown here:

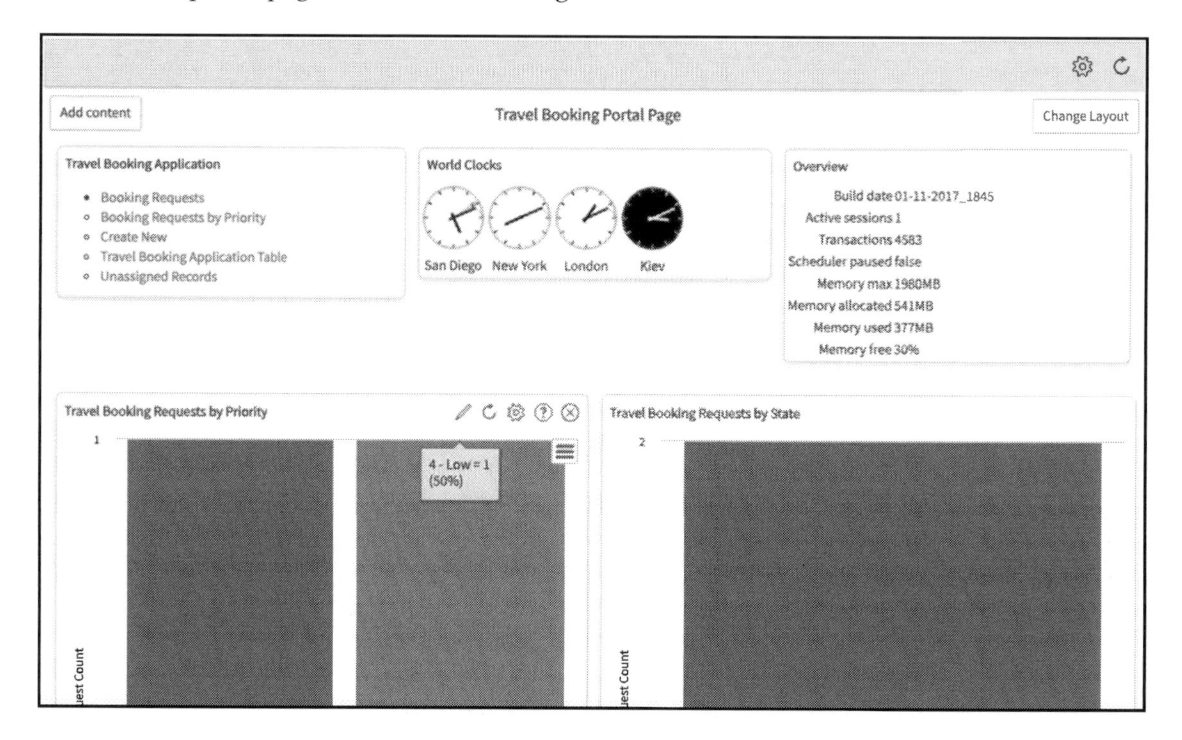


## Homepage modules

Let us now create a homepage module:

1. Open **Studio**, in the create application file dialog select **Navigation** | **Module**, and click **Create**.
2. Fill in the form as detailed here:
    - **Title**: `Overview`
    - **Application menu**: `Travel Booking Application`
    - **Link Type**: **Homepage**
    - **Homepage**: `Travel Booking Portal Page`

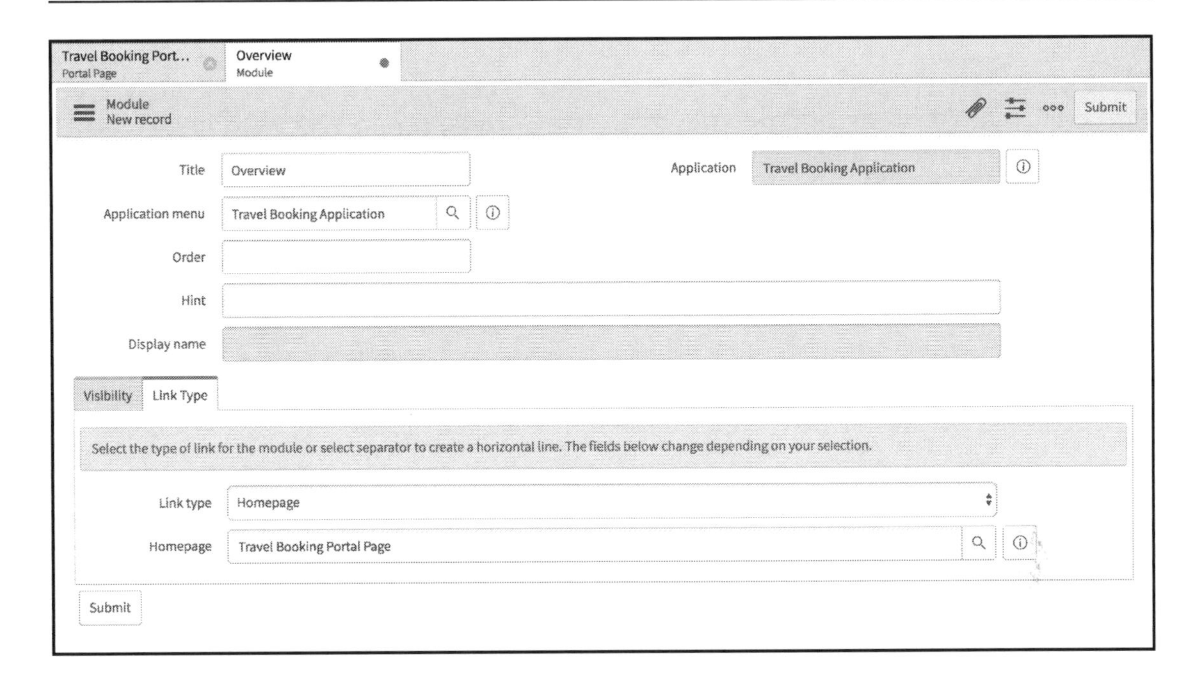


3. Click on the **Submit** button to create a new homepage module named `Overview`. The navigation link will appear under the `Travel Booking Application` menu, as shown here:

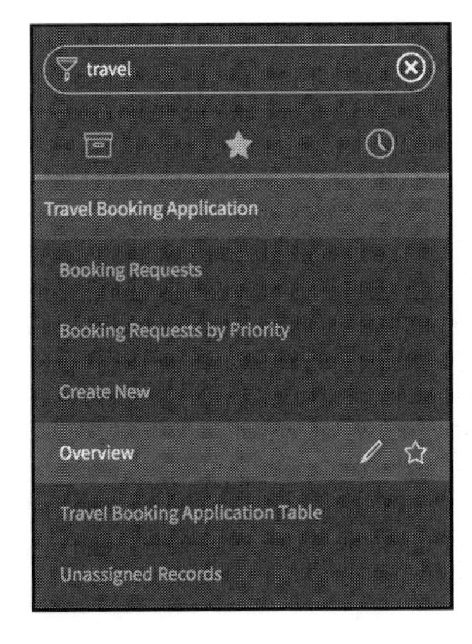

# Separators

Open **Studio** and in the create application file dialog window, select **Navigation** | **Module**. Fill in the form with the following details:

- **Title**: `Separator` (this can also be left blank when link type is separator)
- **Application menu**: `Travel Booking Application`
- **Link Type**: **Separator**

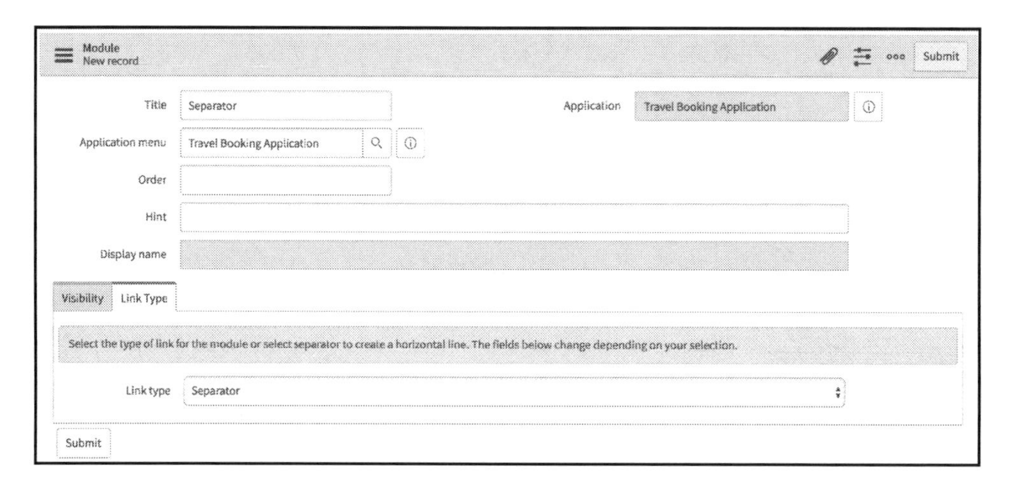


Click on the **Submit** button to create a new separator. This separator will appear under the `Travel Booking Application`. To ensure it is visible properly we must arrange the order of the modules available under the application menu.

# Managing module order

Let us arrange the order of the modules available under the `Travel Booking Application` menu:

1. In **Studio**, open the **Travel Booking Application** menu using the left file selector, as shown in the following screenshot:

This will open the record in the detail edit mode. Scroll to the modules related list, shown in the following screenshot to see all the modules available under the menu.

The cells of list are editable in ServiceNow by default. Clicking on cell highlights it and double-clicking will allow you to edit the cell's value without opening the row.

2. As we are interested in changing the order of the modules, let us double-click on the **Order** cells for each row and set the proper order as listed here:

   Module name Order

   - `Booking Requests`: 30
   - `Booking Requests by Priority`: 50
   - `Create New`: 20
   - `Overview`: 10
   - `Separator`: 40
   - `Travel Booking Application Table`: 90
   - `Unassigned Records`: 60

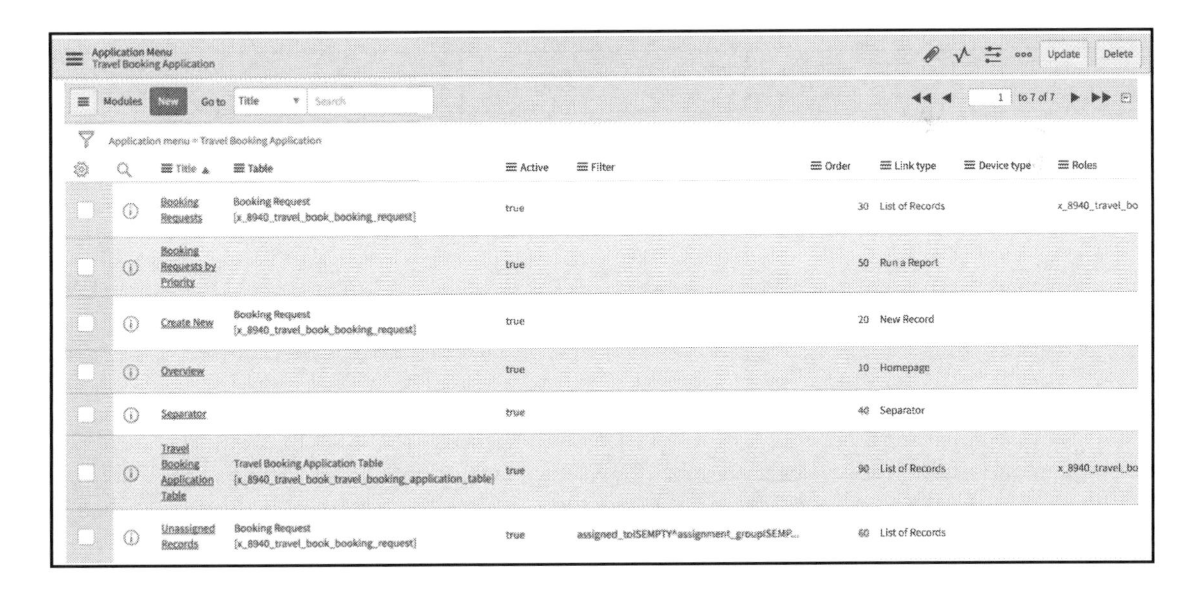

3. Once we have modified the order of the modules, we can confirm the changes by checking the navigator pane. If required, refresh the main ServiceNow interface and scroll to the `Travel Booking Application` menu. We will be able to see the list of modules appear in the proper order:

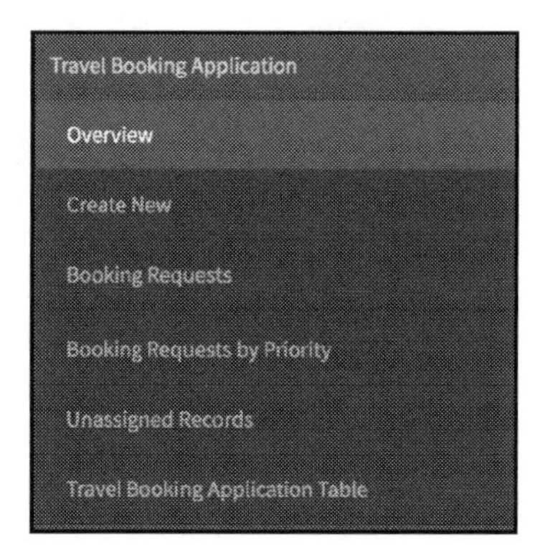


Unlike UI16, a separator is much easily more visible in UI15, as shown in the following screenshot:

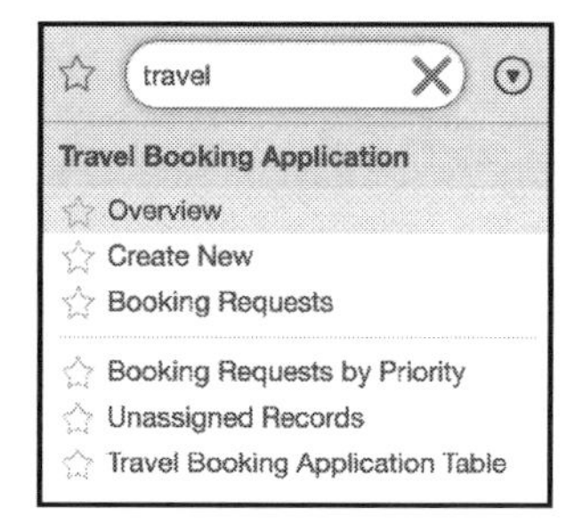


# Summary

In this chapter, we learned how to create different types of modules, including a list of records, new record forms, reports, and a homepage. We covered how to customize a homepage and add content. We also learnt how to user ServiceNow Studio to create application artifacts quickly and efficiently.

In the next chapter, we will learn about the basics of ServiceNow scripting and how to use scripting to enhance the functionality of the ServiceNow application.

# 6

# Introduction to ServiceNow Scripting

So far, we have learned about tables, application scopes, modules, and forms. In this chapter, we will learn how to employ scripts to enhance standard features in ServiceNow.

As we already know, ServiceNow applications are data oriented and we can create different kind of modules to present this data. We can employ scripts to enhance our instance beyond standard configuration and features. We can create scripts to automate some tasks and improve standard system functionality. ServiceNow allows developers to create different types of scripts, each enhancing a different aspect of the platform. For example, we can create a transform map script to parse data imported from a CSV file and create a unique automated importing feature that validates data in multiple tables. Scripts in the ServiceNow platform either execute on the server side or the client side (web browser).

In this chapter, we will learn about the difference between server-side and client-side scripts. We will also learn about different types of scripting options available in the ServiceNow platform. Furthermore, we will learn how scripting works in scoped applications.

In this chapter, we will cover the following topics:

- Different script types
- Execution order of scripts
- Client-side Glide API
- Server-side Glide API
- Scripting in scoped applications

In this chapter, we will learn about the basics of scripting in the ServiceNow platform. New applications, created in Helsinki or beyond, run in the JavaScript ECMA5 standard with compatibility mode enabled for older versions. Both server-side and client-side **Application Programming Interfaces** (**APIs**) are provided, which we can use in scripts to perform specific tasks. A basic understanding of JavaScript or any object-oriented programming language is required to understand ServiceNow scripting. We will be creating these different script types (artifacts) in the next few chapters.

# Different script types

ServiceNow offers various scripting options to the developer. While all scripts in ServiceNow are written using JavaScript and invoke relevant API calls, each script type offers a different functionality. The following are the key script types available in the ServiceNow platform, which we are going to cover in this book:

- **Business rules**: These are similar to database triggers and can be used to customize system behavior. They execute on the server side and run when a database action such as query, insert, update, or delete occurs. They can also be used to abort a database action. For example, business rules can be used as a server-side form validation wherein an insert or update database action can be aborted if the form validation fails.
- **Script actions**: These are a set of scripts that are executed whenever an event occurs. They have a condition field which, when set, must be true for the script to run. They can also be invoked by firing events from a workflow. Like business rules, script actions also execute on the server side.
- **Script includes**: These offer a way to create reusable classes and methods. These scripts execute only when called from other scripts such as business rules and script actions. We must create script includes whenever we create a script that we plan to reuse. Script includes can also be invoked from client scripts by marking them as client callable.
- **Transform maps**: Transform map scripts are executed on the server side when we perform an import operation on a table. Transform map scripts can help in importing a complex set of data into ServiceNow. They can also be used to automate and improve the process of importing CMDB data from external sources when auto-discovery tools are not employed.

- **Client scripts**: Client scripts are executed on the client side and their runtime environment is the user's browser. Client scripts are basically JavaScript code that run on the browser. They have access to the page and form elements and, like other client-side scripts, they also have access to the client-side Glide API available in the ServiceNow platform.
- **UI actions**: Using UI actions, we can create custom UI elements on forms and list module link types. These UI elements can be form and list buttons, related links, context menu items, or list choices. UI action scripts can run either on the client or server side, depending on the configuration of the UI action. If the **Client** checkbox is checked, the script executes on the client side and when it is unchecked, the page reloads and the UI action script executes on the server side, where it has access to server-side APIs.
- **UI policies**: UI policies can be used instead of client scripts to modify common behavior of form fields, such as toggling mandatory, visibility, and read only properties. They act on a specific table and are executed on the client side when the given condition turns out to be true.
- **UI pages**: Using UI pages, we can create custom pages that can be used standalone or as a component on another page. UI pages are made up of client scripts, server-side processing scripts, HTML, and Jelly. Jelly is XML-based preprocessing or templating code that turns XML into HTML.
- **UI scripts**: These are reusable client-side scripts comprised of classes and functions. They can be invoked from any client-side script. They are executed only when invoked from other scripts.
- **Workflow**: Any script or condition on a workflow executes on the server side. A workflow consists of multiple activities and can execute scripts at any point during its flow.

# Client-side scripts

A client-side script is JavaScript code that executes on the client, that is, the web browser. The client-side scripts have access to the form fields and the entire DOM. They can be used to show or hide form fields, related lists, or form sections and manipulate form values or perform client-side form validations. They are also used to perform AJAX calls and execute any valid JavaScript code.

# Server-side scripts

A server-side script executes on the server and has full access to other system resources and the database. Server-side scripts are used for server-side processing of data and extending the OOTB features of the ServiceNow platform.

# Execution order of scripts

Scripts in the ServiceNow platform are executed in the following order:

- **Before business rules**: Business rule scripts, with an order less than 1,000, configured to execute *before* the database operation
- **Before engines:** Workflow, approval, and other engines
- **Before business rules**: Scripts configured to execute before the database operation but with an order greater than or equal to 1,000
- **Database operation:** Insert, update, delete, or query operation
- **After business rules**: Scripts with an order less than 1,000 configured to execute *after* the database operation
- **After engines**: Text indexing and workflow engines (for deferred workflows)
- **E-mail notifications**: Notifications sent on an insert, update, or delete and event-based notification executed based on the order
- **After business rules**: Any scripts with an order greater than or equal to 1,000 and configured to execute after the database operation

# Client-side Glide API

The client-side Glide API exposes many different methods that can be used to customize the UI, access user sessions, and perform AJAX. Let us quickly go through the different client-side classes available in ServiceNow. We will be using these APIs in the upcoming chapters.

## GlideForm

The `GlideForm` JavaScript class consists of methods that can be used to customize forms and modify form data. There is no need to explicitly create an object of the `GlideForm` class. Instead, the `g_form` variable is a global object and is available and accessible from all client-side scripts.

The following are some examples of `GlideForm`:

- The `void setReadOnly` method of the `GlideForm` object can be used to make a form field read only. It accepts two parameters - `fieldname` and the `boolean` read only property:

```
g_form.setReadOnly("fieldName",true)
```

- The `void setValue` method of the `GlideForm` object can be used to change the value of a **Form** field:

```
g_form.setValue(fieldname, value)
```

# GlideUser

The `GlideUser` class contains methods and properties that can be used to retrieve session information related to the currently logged-in user and user roles. Similar to `GlideForm`, there is no need to create an explicit object of the `GlideUser` class. The `g_user` global object can be used to retrieve user session information in client scripts.

The following are some examples of `GlideUser`:

- The `g_user.userName` property can be used to retrieve the username of the currently logged-in user
- The `g_user.userID` property can be used to retrieve the `sys_id` of the currently logged-in user
- The `booleang_user.hasRole` method can be used to check whether the user has a specified role. It will return `true` if the user has the role and vice versa
- `g_user.hasRole('admin')//` will return `true` if the currently logged-in user has the admin role granted.

# GlideMenu

We can use the `GlideMenu` class to customize the options available in the form header context menu through the client scripts. The `g_item` object refers to the `GlideMenuItem` class.

The following are some examples of functions available in the `GlideMenu` class:

- `voidg_menu.clearImage`: This method can be used to specify which item will have its image removed from the display:

```
g_menu.clearImage(g_item);
```

- `void setDisabled`: This method can be used to mark a menu item as disabled:

```
g_menu.setDisabled(g_item)
```

# GlideList2

The `GlideList2` class can be used to customize and control the list behavior. It has many available functions that can be used in conjunction with UI actions. Some commonly used functions in `GlideList2` include the following:

- `String g_list.getChecked`: This method can be used to retrieve a comma-separated `sys_id` of the items that are checked in the list:

```
g_list.getChecked();
```

- `String getView`: This method can be used to retrieve the name of the current view:

```
g_list.getView();
```

# GlideDialogWindow

The `GlideDialogWindow` class can be used to create a modal dialog with specified content. The class can be referred from any other client-side script and is usually called from a UI action.

## Using the GlideDialogWindow class

We can show a new dialog window using the `GlideDialogWindow` class by creating an object of the class and passing the name of the UI page to render:

```
vargdw = new GlideDialogWindow('demo_ui_page');
```

This will create a new dialog window with the content of the window generated from the UI page named `demo_ui_page`.

To set the title of the glide dialog window, we can use the following code:

```
gdw.setTitle("A new title");
```

The preceding code will change the tile of the glide window. In order to resize the glide window, we can use the `setSize` method of the class, as shown here:

```
gdw.setSize(width, height);
```

The preceding code will change the `height` and `width` properties of the glide window. The `width` and `height` parameters must be valid integers.

In order to render the glide window onto the client, that is, the web browser, we must invoke the `render()` method of the class, as shown here:

```
gdw.render();
```

We can programmatically close the glide dialog window by calling the `destroy()` method:

```
gdw.destroy();
```

# GlideAjax

The `GlideAjax` class exposes methods that can be used to implement AJAX features without having to understand the low-level intricacies. We need to create a `GlideAjax` object in order to invoke server-side scripts.

Any working AJAX call requires both a client-side and server-side component. In this section, we will go through the overview of the client-side code and will be implementing and covering this in detail in the upcoming chapters.

In order to invoke AJAX calls within ServiceNow, we must first create an object of the `GlideAjax` class in the client-side script and initialize it with the name of the script include we want to use:

```
varga = new GlideAjax("DemoScriptInclude");
```

To pass parameters to the server-side script include code, we can set parameters using the `sysparm_` prefix in the `addParam` method, as shown here:

```
ga.addParam('sysparm_name','demoFunction');
ga.addParam('sysparm_username',"Bob");
```

In the preceding code, the first `addParam` method's key, `sysparm_name`, refers to the name of the public function, `demoFunction`, defined in the `DemoScriptInclude` class.

The second `addParam` method's key, `sysparm_username`, refers to the `username` variable on the server side. All variable names on the server side must have a `sysparm_` prefix on the client-side code when passing values using the `addParam` method of the `GlideAjax` class.

Once the skeleton to `GlideAjax` is set, to finally invoke the server-side code, we need to call the `getXML` method:

```
ga.getXML(DemoCallBack);
```

The callback handler is a normal JavaScript function with any code, as shown here:

```
function DemoCallBack(response) {
//javascript code
var answer = response.responseXML.documentElement.getAttribute("answer");
console.log(answer);
}
```

# Server-side Glide API

The server-side Glide API exposes many Java classes and methods on the server that can be used to extend the feature of the platform by exposing access to system resources and the database. Let us quickly go through different server-side APIs available in ServiceNow. Like the client-side API, we will be using these server-side APIs in the upcoming chapters.

# GlideRecord

`GlideRecord` is a special Java class exposed to enable developers to perform database operations by writing simple JavaScript code that executes on the server side. The `GlideRecord` class can be used to perform insert, update, delete, or query operations on the database. It can also be used to perform complex join queries, bulk delete, and update.

To create a GlideRecord object, we must specify the table we want to retrieve the data from. In the following example, passing the name of the table in the constructor of the object will create a GlideRecord object for the incident table:

```
var gr = new GlideRecord("incident");
```

A GlideRecord returned from the server is made up of rows of records and columns. Let us go through a list of the most commonly used methods available in the GlideRecord class.

## addQuery

Once we have defined the object of a table using the GlideRecord class, we can query to retrieve the records from the table:

```
gr.addQuery(fieldname, operator, value);
// fieldname is the name of the column the table or view
// operator as detailed in the table below
// value is the record's value we are looking for
```

## Available query operators

We can use the following 13 different JavaScript operators in the addQuery method:

| Operator | Type | Code example |
|---|---|---|
| = | Value of field must be equal to value supplied | addQuery('priority', '=' , 2); |
| > | Value of field must be greater than value supplied | addQuery('priority', '>', 1); |
| < | Value of field must be less than value supplied | addQuery('priortiy', '<', 3); |
| >= | Value of field must be equal or greater than value supplied | addQuery('priority', '>=', '2'); |
| <= | Value of field must be equal or less than value supplied | addQuery('priority', '>=', '2'); |

| `!=` | Value of field must not be equal to the value supplied | `addQuery('priority', '!=', '1');` |
|---|---|---|
| `STARTSWITH` | Value of field must start with the value supplied | `addQuery('short_description', 'STARTSWITH', 'CRIT');` |
| `CONTAINS` | Value of field must contain the value supplied | `addQuery('short_description', 'CONTAINS', 'Server');` |
| `IN` | Value of field must be equal to one of the values supplied as comma-separated list | `addQuery('category', 'IN', 'Software,Network');` |
| `ENDSWITH` | Value of field must end with the string supplied as value | `addQuery('short_description', 'ENDSWITH', 'Error');` |
| `DOES NOT CONTAIN` | Value of field must not contain the string supplied as value | `addQuery('short_description', 'DOES NOT CONTAIN', 'Server');` |
| `NOT IN` | Value of field must not be equal to the values present in the comma delimited list | `addQuery('category', 'NOT IN', 'Software,Network');` |
| `INSTANCEOF` | This is a special operator that can be used to query records of extended tables in the parent table.<br>We can query the task table to find all records that belong to the class incident or problem by passing the correct table/class name. | Example 1:<br>`var gr = new GlideRecord('task');`<br>`gr.addQuery('sys_class_name', 'INSTANCEOF', 'incident');`<br>Example 2:<br>`var gr=new GlideRecord('cmdb_ci);`<br>`gr.addQuery('sys_class_name', 'INSTANCEOF', 'cmdb_ci_computer');` |

## addNullQuery

Unlike addQuery, when using the addNullQuery method, we do not have to specify the operator and filter value. It is used to query records that contain NULL values. The following example will return all records stored in the incident table where the short_description field is NULL. While the addNullQuery method is used to build the search filter for the database operation, the query() method is used to trigger the database operation:

```
var gr = new GlideRecord("incident");
gr.addNullQuery('short_description');
gr.query(); //executes the query
```

## addNotNullQuery

This is similar to addNullQuery but returns records where the field value is NOT NULL. The following example will return all records stored in the incident table where short_description field is NOT NULL:

```
var gr = new GlideRecord("incident");
gr.addNotNullQuery('short_description');
gr.query();
```

## Applying multiple queries

We can apply multiple search queries, which act as AND clauses, by adding multiple addQuery, addNullQuery, or addNotNullQuery methods, as shown in the following example:

```
var gr = new GlideRecord("incident");
gr.addQuery('priority','<=','2');
gr.addQuery('active',true);
gr.addNotNullQuery('short_description');
gr.query();
```

## Applying an OR query

While it is easy to add multiple `addQuery` methods to our `GlideRecord` object, we need to add the `OR` condition in one of the existing `addQuery` method's object, as shown here:

```
var gr = new GlideRecord('incident');
var qc = gr.addQuery('category', 'network');
qc.addOrCondition('category', 'software');
gr.addQuery('priority', '1');
```

In the preceding code, we are creating a `qc` object as a reference to the `QueryCondition` object returned by `addQuerymethod`. Then we are using the `addOrCondition` method available in the `QueryCondition` class to form our `OR` clause. We can apply multiple `addOrCondition` to any `QueryCondition` object.

## Iterating over query records

Once we fire a query, the next important thing we need to be able to perform is iterating over the record set or query set retrieved from the database. Iterating over a query set can be done using the `next()` method, which acts as an iterator and returns `true` till there exists the next record; otherwise, returns `false` when there are no more records in the query set:

```
var gr = new GlideRecord('incident');
gr.addQuery('priority', '1');
gr.query();
while ( gr.next() ) {
gs.print( gr.getValue('number')+ " exists");  //number is a field in
incident table // the getValue method returns string
}
```

# GlideSystem

The `GlideSystem` class offers a number of methods to easily access system resources such as logging, user session, and data time function. `GlideSystem` is represented by the `gs global` object and is available for use on server-side scripts.

Let us go through some of the most widely used methods available in the `GlideSystem` class.

# getCurrentScopeName()

The `getCurrentScopeName` method can be used to retrieve the name of the currently active application scope. As `GlideSystem` is represented by the `gs global` object, we do not need to create an object of the `GlideSystem` class explicitly to use it; for example:

```
varscopeName = gs.getCurrentScopeName(); //will return the name of the
active scope
```

# log()

`gs.log()` logs a message to the system log and this method is useful for development and debugging important events in production. The `gs.log()` method accepts two parameters.

**Usage**:

```
gs.log(String message, [String source]); //source parameter is optional
```

**Example**:

```
gs.log("Business rule iteration started", "DemoBusinessRule");
```

# logError()

Similar to the `gs.log()` method, the `gs.logError()` method logs a message to the system log and saves it to the `syslog_table`; however, it categorizes the message as an error.

**Usage:**

```
gs.logError(String message, [String source]); //source parameter is
optional
```

**Example**:

```
gs.logError("Business rule execution failed", "DemoBusinessRule");
```

# logWarning()

Similar to `gs.log()`, `gs.logWarning()` logs an entry to the system log and saves it to the `syslog` table and categorizes it as a warning.

**Usage**:

```
gs.logWarning(String message, [String source]); //source parameter is
optional
```

**Example**:

```
gs.logWarning("Email field value not provided", "DemoBusinessRule");
```

# nil()

The `nil()` function of the `GlideSystem` class can be used to query the value of an object. It returns `true` if the value of the object is either null or empty; otherwise, returns `false`.

**Example:**

```
if ( current.short_description.nil() ) {  //checking if the value of the
filed is null
//some code
}
```

# now()

The `now()` method of the `GlideSystem` class returns the current date of the server; for example:

```
var gr = new GlideRecord("incident");
if (gr.get(event.parm1.toString())) {
// Set the value of the date field using setValue method of GlideRecord
object
gr.setValue('u_date1',gs.now() );
gr.update();
}
```

## print()

The `gs.print()` method, similar to `gs.log()`, writes a message to the system log; however, unlike the `log()` method, it doesn't write the message to the `syslog` table unless the debugging features are activated.

**Usage**:

```
gs.print(String message);
```

**Example**:

```
gs.print("Using print to write to system log");
```

## addInfoMessage()

`addInfoMessage` of the `gs` class can be used to add an information message to the current interactive user session. These session information messages are shown to end users at the top of the form and below any `addErrorMessage` entries.

**Usage:**

```
gs.addInfoMessage(Object message);
```

**Example:**

```
gs.addInfoMessage("Incident record successfully updated.");
```

## addErrorMessage()

`addErrorMessage` of the `GlideSystem` class can be used to add an error message to the current interactive user session. These session error messages are shown to end users at the top of the form and above any `addInfoMessage` entries.

**Usage**:

```
gs.addErrorMessage(Object message);
```

**Example**:

```
gs.addErrorMessage("Incident record successfully updated.");
```

# isInteractive()

A server script may get executed depending upon the database operation or some event. At times, it might be required to determine whether the script being executed is for an interactive user session. An interactive user session means that the user manually logged in using the sign-in screen. On the other hand, if it was a REST API or SOAP call that triggered the server-side script, the session is not considered to be interactive.

**Usage**:

```
gs.isInteractive(); //returns true if the session is interactive
```

**Example**:

```
if ( gs.isInteractive() ) {
// some code
}
```

# isLoggedIn()

This method is useful to determine whether the user is currently logged in. It will return `true` if the user is logged in or else return `false` if the user is not logged in or if the session has timed out.

**Usage:**

```
gs.isLoggedIn(); //return true if the user is logged in
```

**Example:**

```
if ( gs.isLoggedIn() ) {
//some code
}
```

# getUserID()

The `gs.getUserID` method is used to determine the `sys_id` of the currently logged-in user.

`sys_id` is the unique identifier column available in all ServiceNow tables, including any custom table created by an admin, and also the `sys_user` table, which stores user records.

**Usage:**

```
gs.getUserID(); //return the sys_id of the currently logged in user
```

**Example**:

```
gs.log( "The current logged in user ID is "+ gs.getUserID() );
```

# getUserName()

This method can be used to determine the username of the currently logged-in user.

**Usage**:

```
gs.getUserName(); //return the username of the currently logged in user
```

**Example**:

```
gs.log( "The record has been updated by "+ gs.getUserName() );
```

# getUserNameByUserID()

The `gs.getUserNameByUserID()` method of the `GlideSystem` class can be used to determine the username of a user by his `sys_id`.

**Usage**:

```
gs.getUserNameByUserID(String sys_id); //return the username if the user
with matching sys_id exist
```

**Example**:

```
varuser_sys_id = gs.getUserID();
gs.getUserNameByUserID(user_sys_id);
```

# eventQueue()

The `gs.eventQueue()` method can be used to queue an event for the event manager programmatically.

**Usage**:

```
eventQueue(String name, Object gr, String option1, String option2, String
event_queue)
```

**Example**:

```
if (current.operation() != 'insert' &&current.comments.changes()) {
gs.eventQueue('incident.updated', current, gs.getUserID(),
gs.getUserName());
}
```

The `current` object is the `GlideRecord` object of the row currently being inserted, updated, deleted, or queried. We will learn more about the `current` object in the *Business rules* section in `Chapter 8`, *Server-Side Scripting*.

# Scripting in scoped applications

The OOTB ServiceNow platform comes preinstalled with many different types of scripts which are required for proper functioning of the platform. When we create a script, depending upon our application scope selection, it will become part of either the global or some private custom application scope. We have already covered the benefits of creating an application scope instead of directly creating custom features in the global scope.

Writing scripts for scoped applications enables us to associate scripts to specific applications and features. It enables us to easily manage feature updates and migration. When we create an application, depending upon the selected application scope picker, the script becomes part of that selected application.

As discussed in previous chapters, each private application scope has its own application namespace, which is in the format of `x_[organization-code]_[app-id]`. All artifacts, including scripts, tables, and roles, belonging to the private application scope have the same application namespace prefix.

When creating scripts for scoped applications, the rule of the application scope namespace prefix does apply for all script types. However, the script include has a special configuration available that enables it to be used by other scripts in a different private or global scope. We will cover this in detail in the *Script includes* section in `Chapter 8`, *Server-Side Scripting*.

Similarly, as the tables are part of a specific application or global scope, the list of available tables, when creating a business rule, will be limited to those tables that allow their configuration to be changed from the outside. Again, we will see this in action in the *Business rules* section in `Chapter 8`, *Server-Side Scripting*.

# Summary

In this chapter, we learned about the basics of ServiceNow scripting. We also learned about the difference between server-side and client-side scripting. We also covered some important and regularly used methods available in client- and server-side client APIs.

In the next chapter, we will create client-side scripts and learn how to enhance the interaction of a user using the client-side scripting available in the ServiceNow platform.

# 7
# Client-Side Scripting

Now that we are aware of all the basic features of the ServiceNow platform, including the different scripting options available to us, let us start writing some client-side scripts to enhance our application.

As discussed in the previous chapter, client-side scripts are JavaScript code that execute on the browser and have access to the client-side Glide API. We can employ client-side APIs to enhance our instance beyond the standard configuration and features. Client-side scripts can be used to perform many different operations that execute within the client's browser and have access to the entire DOM along with the Glide API.

In this chapter, we will learn how to create client-side scripts and the different ways we can execute the client-side code. We will also learn how to make use of the client-side Glide API and some of the most widely used functions available.

In this chapter, we will learn how to create the following client-side scripts:

- Client scripts
- UI policies
- UI scripts

## Client scripts

Let us create a client script - our first client-side script. A client script is JavaScript code that is associated with a table and is executed when the form loads, a field value changes, or on form submit.

The type property of the client script controls how and when the client script code is executed. The following types of client script can be created:

- `onLoad`: The code is executed when the form is rendered on the client browser.
- `onChange`: The code is executed when the selected form field's value is changed. For the `onChange` type, we also need to specify a form field (column) along with the table.
- `onSubmit`: The code is executed when the form is submitted.
- `onCellEdit`: This type of client script is executed in the list module page. It is executed when the field is modified using the quick cell edit feature of the list grid by double-clicking on a cell.

To create a client script, open **Studio** and click on the **Create Application File** button. In the **Create Application File** wizard, select **Client Development** | **Client Script** and click on the **Create** button, as shown in the following screenshot:

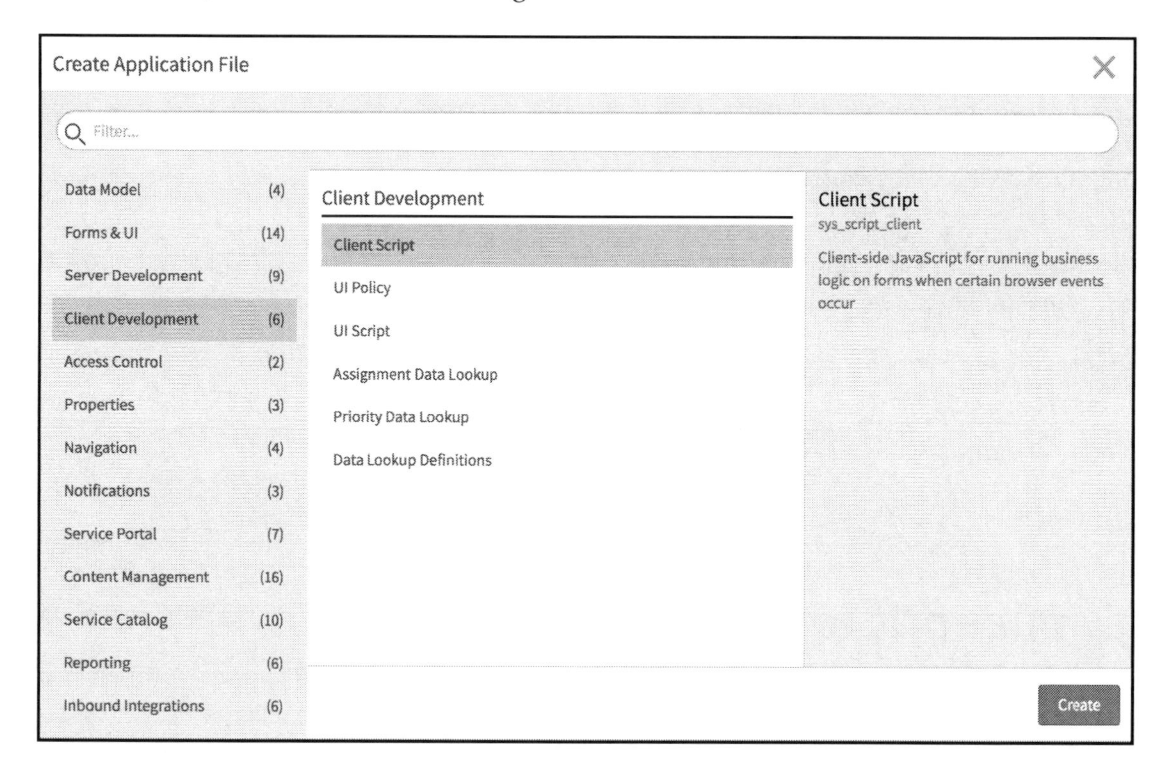

The client script form presents us with many fields; however, we write code only in the **Script** field. Other fields are used to define the properties of the client script, which in turn define how the client script will be executed.

# onLoad client scripts

Let us create a client script that will be executed when the form loads. For this, we need to specify a table in our instance; in our case, we will select the `Booking Request` table and specify the type as `onLoad`. The **UI type** field is to determine whether the script will be executed only on the **Desktop** UI, **Mobile** UI, or on both platforms. For our learning purposes, we will specify **UI type** as **Desktop**.

Marking a **Global** checkbox as checked makes the client script be associated with all form views of the selected table. If we uncheck the **Global** field, we can manually specify the name of a view to associate the script with. On the other hand, the **Inherited** field makes the script available to all the child tables that extend the selected table. For example, if we create a client script and apply it on the `Task` table, with the **Inherited** field checked, the script will be available to `Incident`, `Problem`, `Change`, and all other tables that inherit the `Task` table.

In the new client script form, as shown in the following screenshot, enter the following values:

- **Name**: `Hide return field on load`
- **Table**: **Booking Request**
- **UI Type**: **Desktop**
- **Type**: `onLoad`
- **Active**: Checked

- **Inherited**: Unchecked
- **Global**: Checked

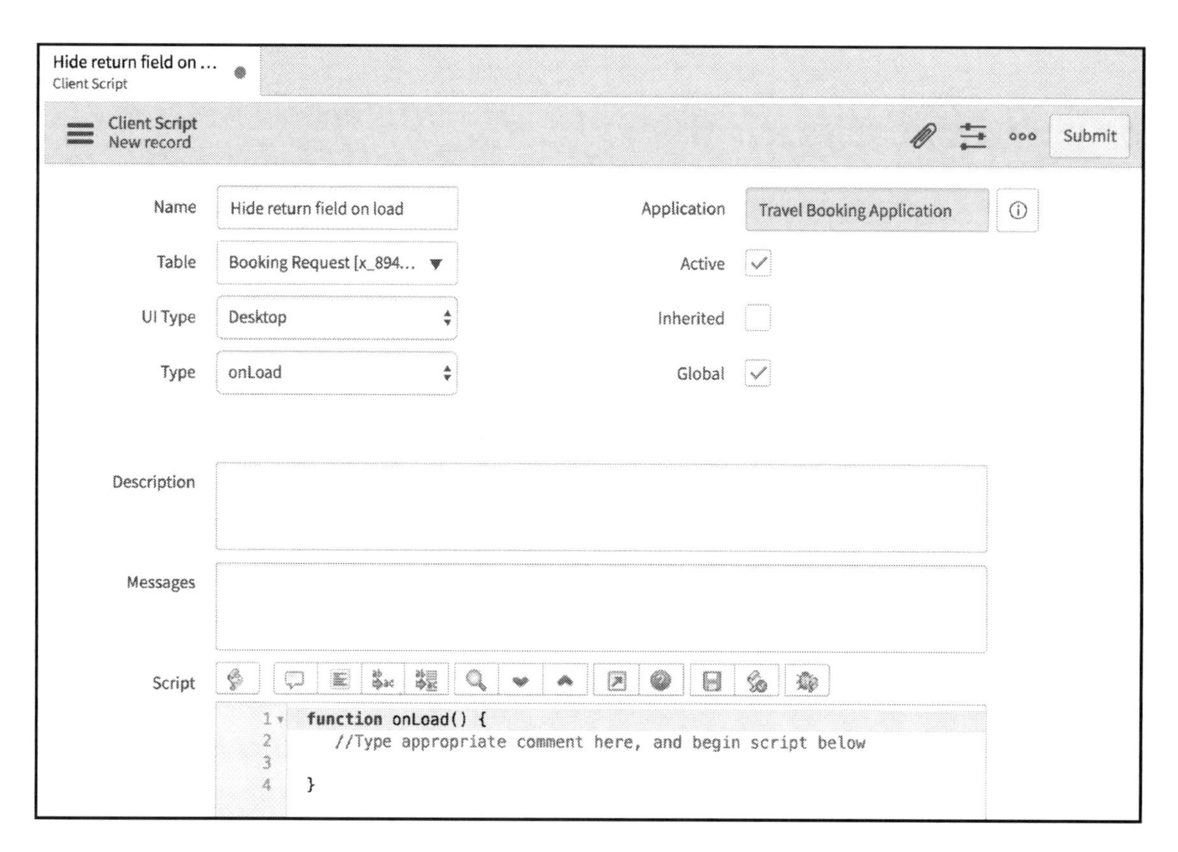


The **Description** field in the client script form can be used to write requirements or a code document about what the script is intended to do. This will not be visible to end users but can provide useful information to developers and system administrators. The **Messages** field can be used for developing localized applications, which we are going to cover in later chapters in this book. A client script must be marked as active in order to execute.

The **Script** field is where we write JavaScript code. The execution of the script depends upon the properties defined using the **Active**, **Type**, **UI type**, **Global**, **Inherited**, and the **Table** field. Let us describe our client script and write code that will execute when the form loads:

```
function onLoad() {
   //Type appropriate comment here, and begin script below
   //alert(g_form.getBooleanValue("u_is_return"));
if ( ! g_form.getBooleanValue("u_is_return")) {
  g_form.setDisplay("u_return_date",false);
   }
}
```

Make sure your table for which you are writing the script has custom fields for the **Return** checkbox and **Return Date** created using **Studio** and, if required, you can create these fields as explained in previous chapters. You can confirm the system name of the fields by going to the **Tables & Columns** module and selecting the appropriate table and column to see the system name. You must specify the system name of the table and columns when writing scripts. You cannot use the label of the database entities when writing scripts.

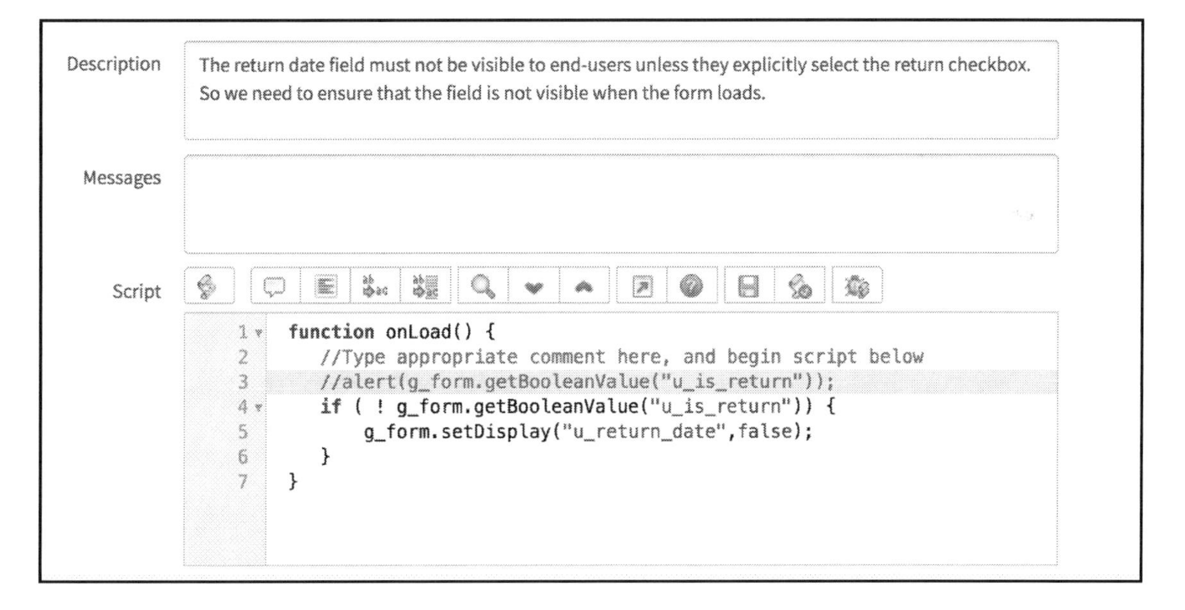

You can always use a JavaScript alert or the `console.log` method. However, ServiceNow offers different ways to log and debug output using different methods, including `gs.log("log something")`, which we are going to cover in later chapters.

Now let us test our client script by opening the **Booking Request** form in the main ServiceNow window. If everything goes well, the **Return Date** field should hide on page load. To test the new form, simply click on **Travel Booking Application** | **Create New** in the left navigation panel as shown in the following screenshot:

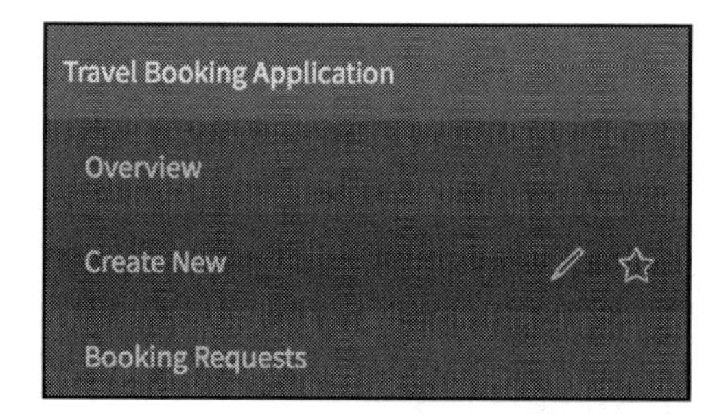


The new **Booking Request** form should open in the content pane and upon form load, we will notice the **Return Date** field will not be visible on the form, as shown in the following screenshot:

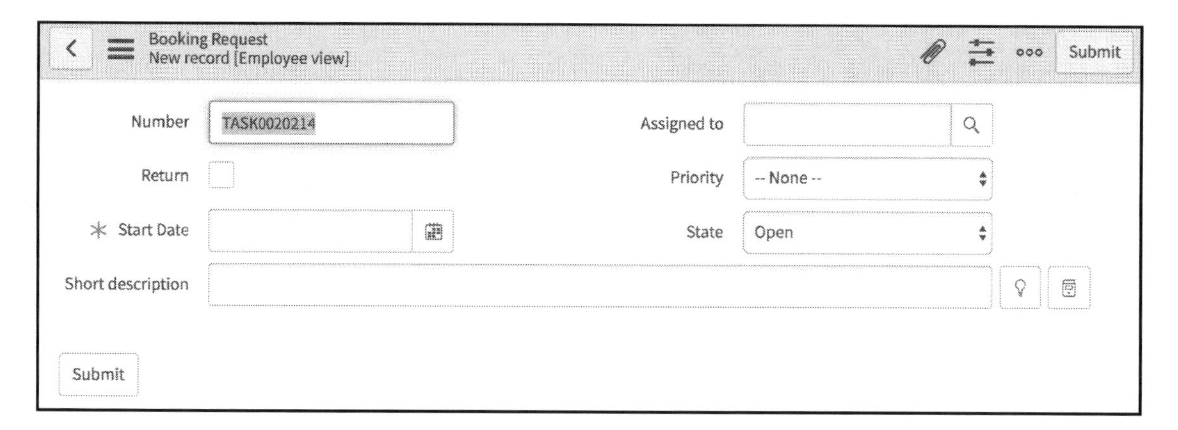

Let us now ensure that our client script is executed only for the **Employee view**, which we created in a previous chapter, and is not executed for the **Default view**. To do this, we need to open the client script in the **Studio**. Click on the **Hide return date field on load** record under **Client Development** | **Client Scripts** in the application explorer tree, as shown in the following screenshot:

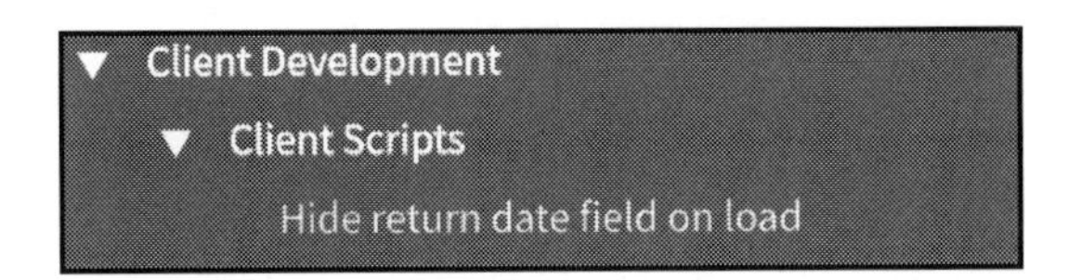


Now uncheck the **Global** checkbox in the form that opens up in the **Studio** and specify **Employee** as the view. Click the **Update** button to save and confirm our changes:

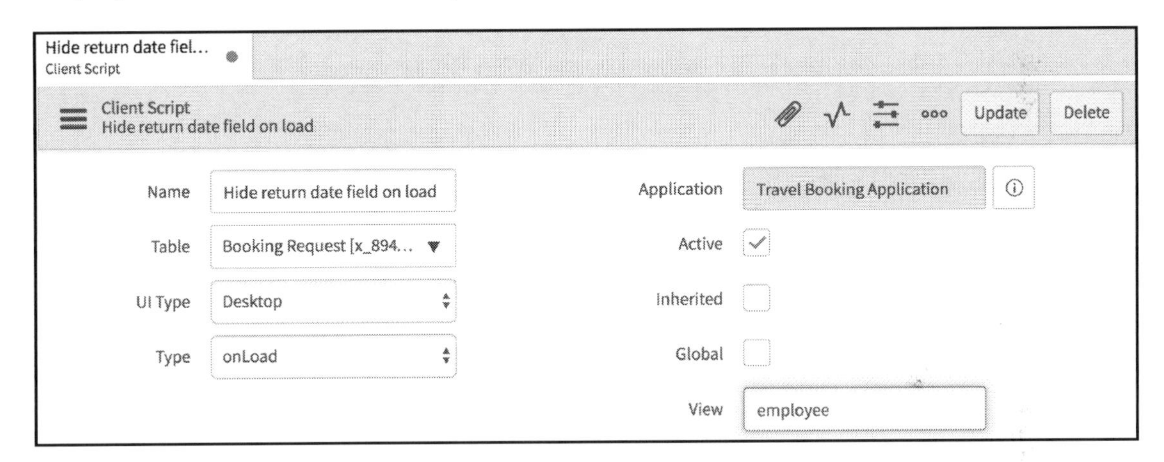


This will ensure that the client script is executed only when the form being loaded by the end user is attached to the table named `Booking Request` and the view specified in the module they are accessing is **Employee**.

To test changes and to ensure the code is executing only for the **Employee view**, we can try opening the **Create new module**, in **Employee view** as shown here, in the main ServiceNow interface, and subsequently try to open the new record entry form by navigating to the **Travel Booking Application** | **Booking Requests** module, and clicking on the **New** button on the list of records page:

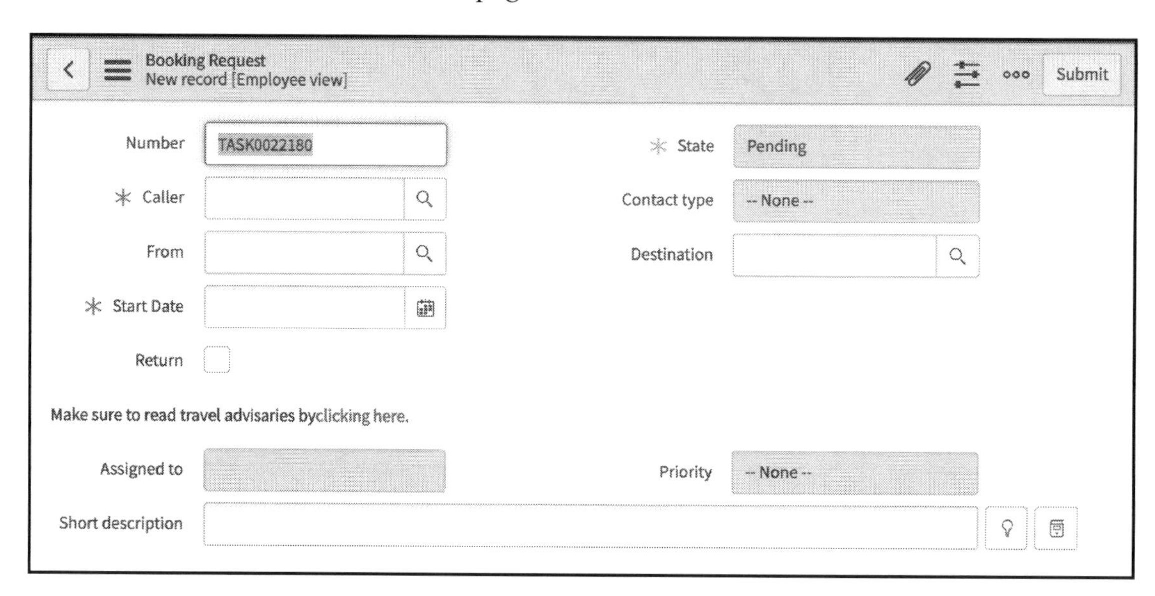


You must have created the **Create new module** and set it to open in **Employee view**, as explained in a previous chapter. If everything works well, then the new record form that opens up when we click on **Create new module** will execute our client script on form load. However, the new record form that opens up when we click on the **New** button in the list of records **Booking Requests** module will appear different and will not execute our client script code.

Now let us create another client script that will execute when we check the **Return** checkbox and cause the **Return Date** field to appear on the form. Also, when we uncheck the field, it should hide the **Return Date** form field again.

# onChange client scripts

Creating an `onChange` client script is similar to creating an `onLoad` client script. We need to specify the table and other properties just like in the `onLoad` script. However, the type field must be set to `onChange` and we need to specify the name of the field (column) on which the `onChange` client script will be applied.

Click on the **Create Application File** button in **Studio** and select **Client Development** | **Client script** and click **Create**. In the new client script form, as shown in the following screenshot, enter the following values:

- **Name**: `Toggle return date field`
- **Table**: **Booking Request**
- **UI Type**: **Desktop**
- **Type**: `onChange`
- **Field name**: **Return**
- **Active**: Checked
- **Inherited**: Unchecked
- **Global**: Unchecked
- **View**: `employee`

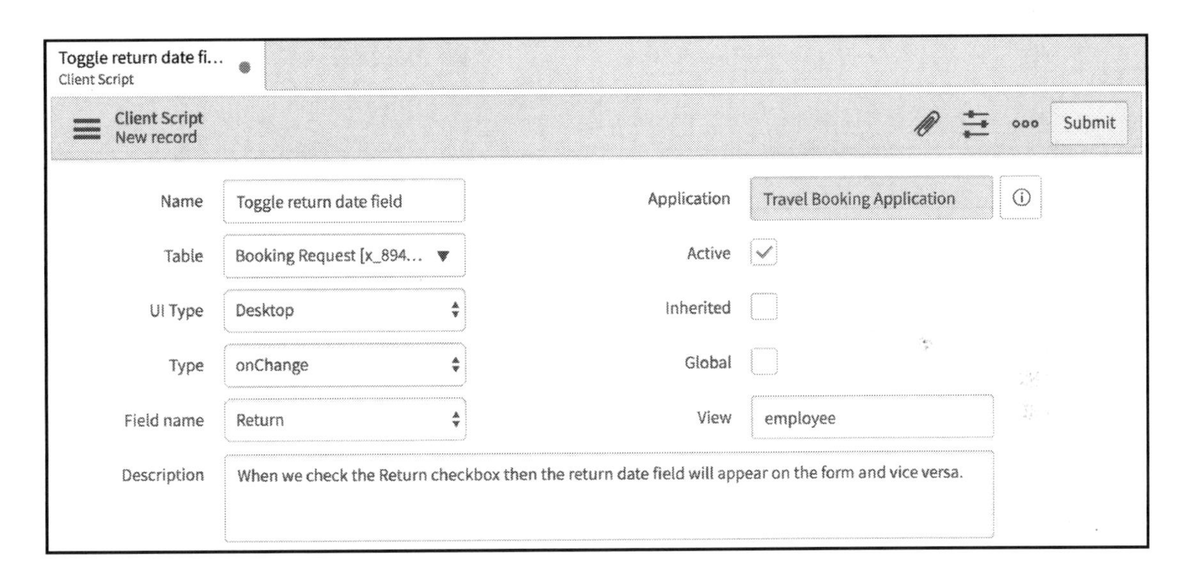


When we set the type of the client script to `onChange`, the **Script** field is automatically populated with the following code:

```
function onChange(control, oldValue, newValue, isLoading, isTemplate) {
if (isLoading || newValue === '') {
return;
   }

   //Type appropriate comment here, and begin script below

}
```

Let us first understand the variables available in the preceding script before we start writing our own custom client script code.

The name of the JavaScript function is `onChange` here, and there are the following parameters available:

- `control`: This is the reference to the form field object that triggered the `onChange` event.
- `oldValue`: The old value of the field before the `onChange` event was triggered.
- `newValue`: The new and current value of the field.
- `isLoading`: This is a special `boolean` parameter that tells the script if the `onChange` event is being triggered due to the page rendering. When the browsers renders the form fields and populates the field values, it automatically triggers the `onChange` event.
- `isTemplate`: This is another special `boolean` parameter that tells the script if the `onChange` event is being triggered due to the use of a template to populate the form fields.

The following part of the default code is used to exit the code execution if the change event is being triggered due to form rendering or use of templates:

```
if (isLoading || newValue === ''......) {
return;
   }
```

Now let us write our custom code to toggle the display of the **Return Date** field based on the value of the **Return** checkbox. Enter the following code in the **Script** field:

```
g_form.setDisplay("u_return_date",
    g_form.getBooleanValue("u_is_return") );
```

The entire form is shown here for your reference. Click on the **Submit** button to create the `onChange` client script:

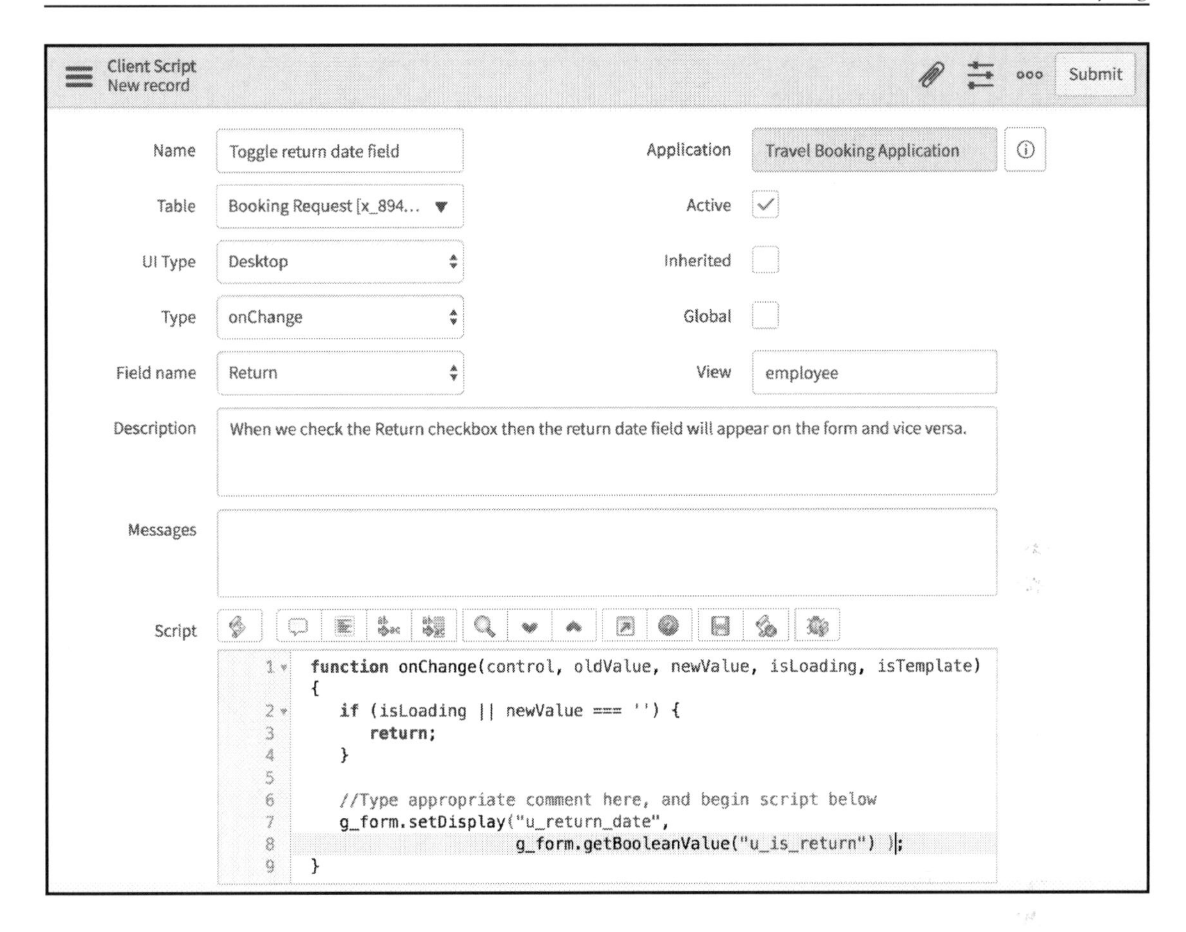


The entire code in the **Script** field is provided here:

```
function onChange(control, oldValue, newValue, isLoading, isTemplate) {
if (isLoading || newValue === '') {
return;
   }

   //Type appropriate comment here, and begin script below
g_form.setDisplay("u_return_date",
g_form.getBooleanValue("u_is_return") );
}
```

Now let us test our `onChange` client script by opening the **Create new** module, which is also using the **Employee view**.

If everything goes well, when we check the **Return** checkbox, as shown in the following screenshot, the **Return Date** field will appear and it will hide when we uncheck the **Return** checkbox:

Let us now also make the **Return Date** field mandatory when the **Return** field is checked and vice versa.

It must be noted that we must make the field non-mandatory using `setMandatory` false before we try to hide it using `setDisplay` or `setVisible`, otherwise these functions will not hide the field if it is marked as mandatory and has an empty value.

To set the field as mandatory, we will have to modify our code in our `onChange` client script to the one mentioned here:

```
function onChange(control, oldValue, newValue, isLoading, isTemplate) {
if (isLoading || newValue === '') {
return;
   }
   //Type appropriate comment here, and begin script below
   //Get the current boolean value of the return checkbox
varisChecked= g_form.getBooleanValue("u_is_return");
g_form.setMandatory("u_return_date", isChecked);
g_form.setDisplay("u_return_date", isChecked);
}
```

With the new code in place for the `onChange` client script, the **Return Date** field will also be marked as mandatory when we check the **Return** checkbox and hide when we uncheck the **Return** field. The red star icon next to the **Return Date** field, as shown in the following screenshot, indicates that it is a mandatory field:

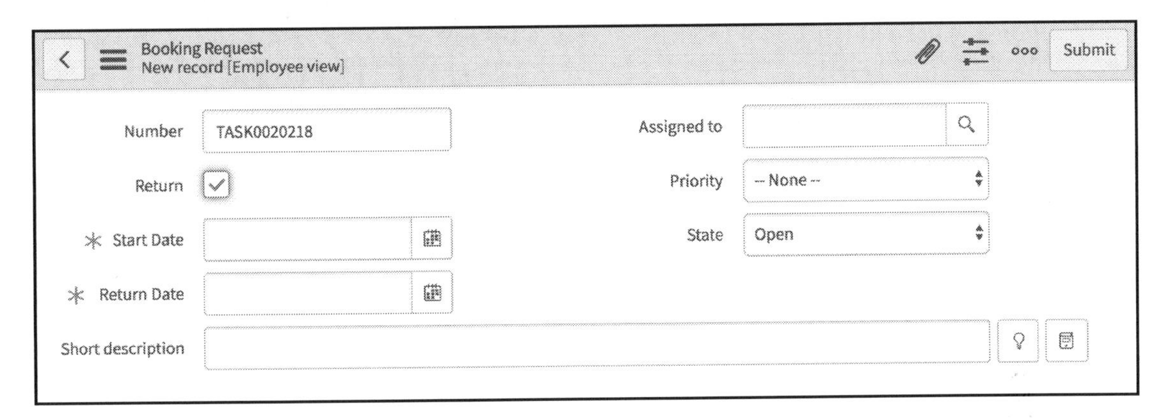


Let us now create another client script that will execute when we try to submit the form and check whether the date mentioned in the **Return Date** field is after the **Start Date**.

# onSubmit client scripts

The `onSubmit` client script is similar to the `onLoad` script. Unlike the `onChange` script, when creating the `onSubmit` client script, we do not need to specify the field as it is triggered when the form is submitted. Other properties, such as table, view, and type, must be set similar to the `onLoad` and `onChange` client scripts.

When creating the `onSubmit` client script, to compare **Start Date** and **Return Date**, we will leave the **Global** checkbox checked to ensure this script is executed for all views of the **Booking Request** table/form.

In **Studio**, open a new **Client Script** record form, as shown in the following screenshot, and populate the form fields with the following values:

- **Name**: `Compare start and return date`
- **Table**: **Booking Request**
- **UI Type**: **Desktop**
- **Type**: `onSubmit`

- **Active**: Checked
- **Inherited**: Unchecked
- **Global**: Checked

The code to be executed needs to be populated in the **Script** field, as shown in the following screenshot:

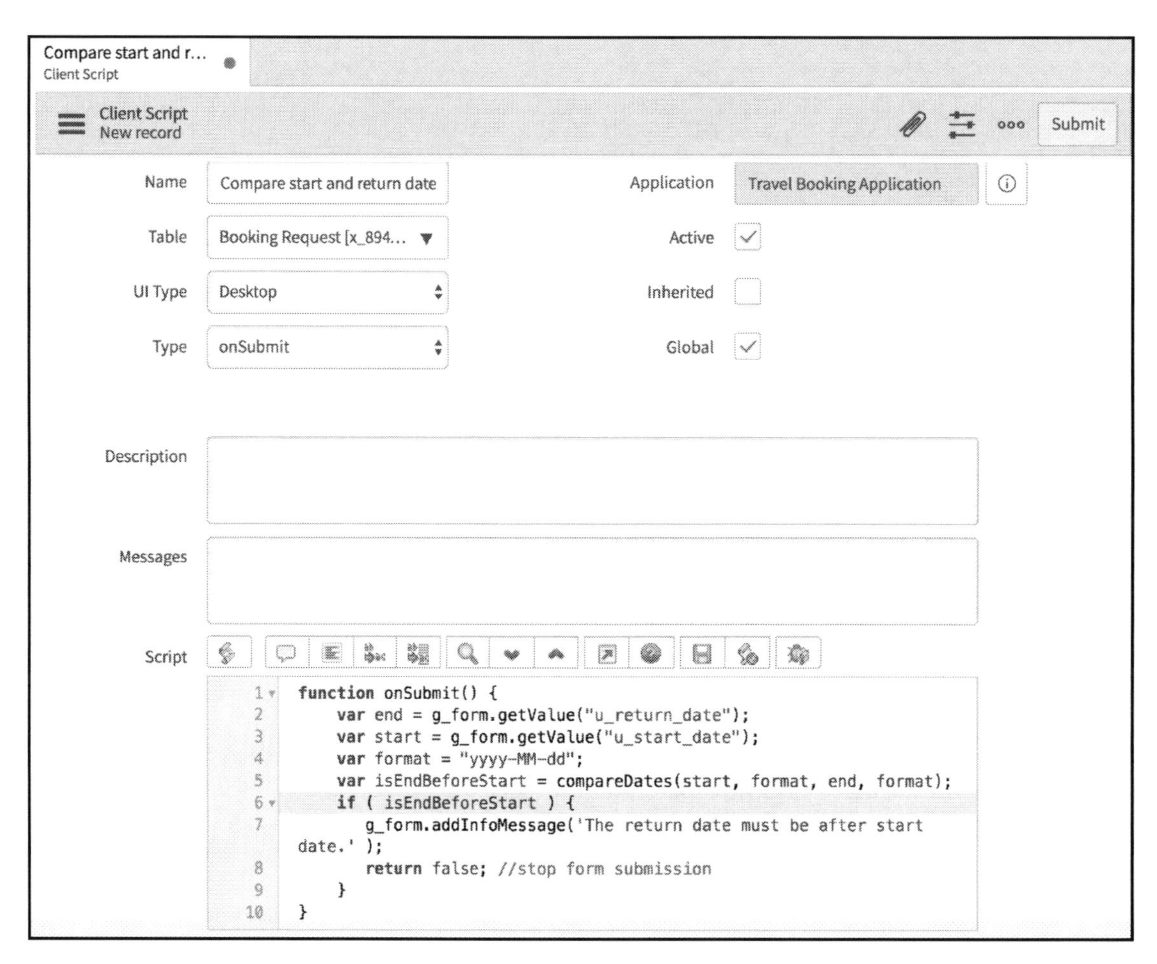

Here is the entire code that we are using to compare the **Start Date** and **Return Date** client scripts:

```
function onSubmit() {
var end = g_form.getValue("u_return_date");
var start = g_form.getValue("u_start_date");
  var format = "yyyy-MM-dd";
  varisEndBeforeStart = compareDates(start, format, end, format);
  if ( isEndBeforeStart ) {
  g_form.addInfoMessage('The return date must be after start date.' );
  return false; //stop form submission
    }
}
```

The `compareDates` function is available in the client code whenever the date or date time field is available in the form as part of the `calendar.js` JavaScript code included by the ServiceNow platform.

It accepts four parameters, namely **Start**, **Start Date** format, **End**, and **End Date** format. The format we are going to pass to the script is based on the date format we see when we select a date either in the **Start Date** or **Return** field. The `compareDates` function will return `1` if the **Return Date** is not after the **Start Date**. It returns `0` if the **Return Date** is after the **Start Date** and `-1` if either date format is incorrect.

The `g_form.addInfoMessage` function will add a descriptive information message to the form in order to inform the end user that the **Return Date** must be after the **Start Date**, as shown here:

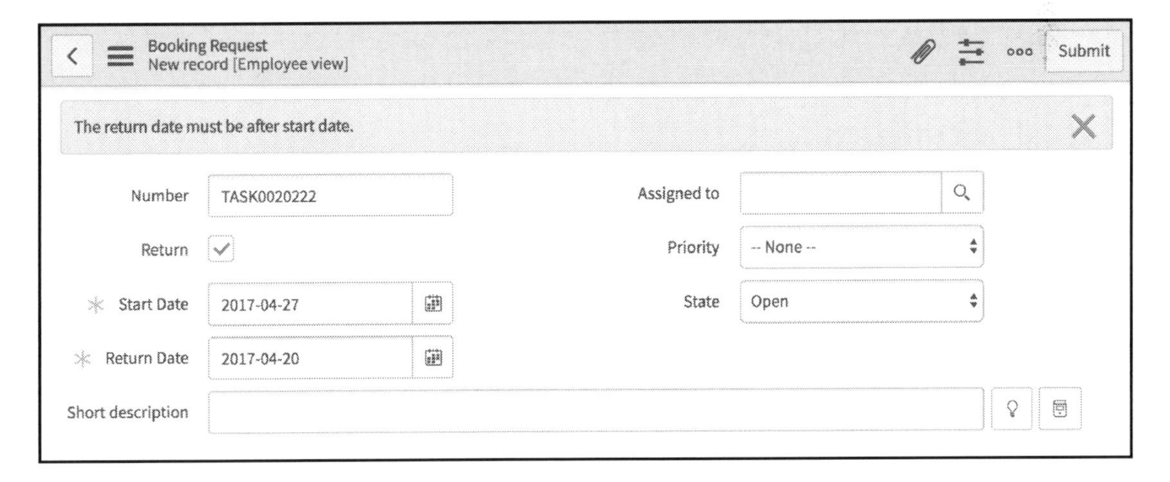

We can also use the `g_form.showErrorBox` function to show the following error message the specific field - in this case, **Return Date**:

```
g_form.showErrorBox("u_return_date", "Must be after start date.");
So the final code for the compare start and return date client script will
look like:
functiononSubmit() {
var end = g_form.getValue("u_return_date");
  var start = g_form.getValue("u_start_date");
  var format = "yyyy-MM-dd";
  varisEndBeforeStart= compareDates(start, format, end, format);
  if ( isEndBeforeStart ) {
  g_form.showErrorBox("u_return_date", "Must be after start date.");
  return false; //stop form submission
    }
}
```

The end user will be presented with a message right here, the **Return Date** field as shown here:

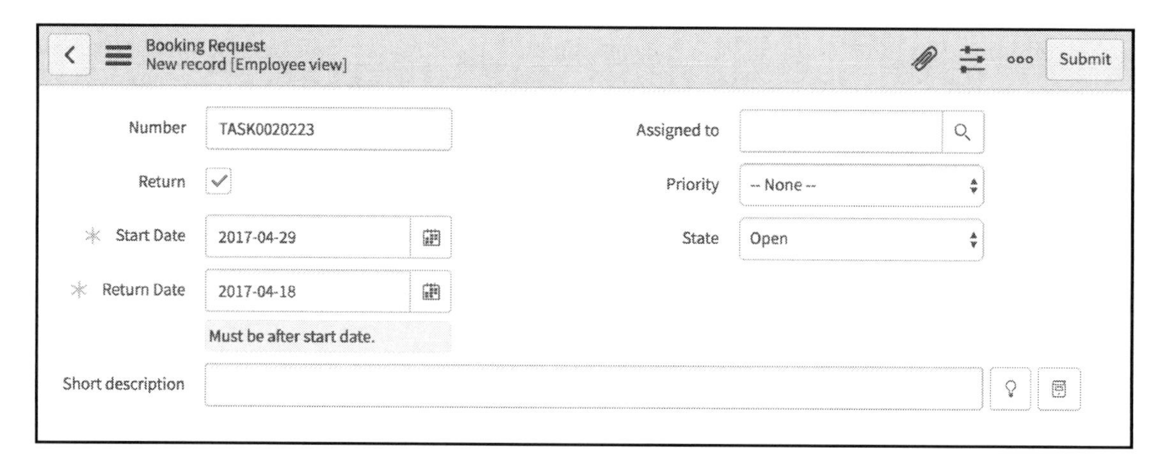


Similarly, now let us ensure the **Start Date** selected by the end user is after the current date. The entire code we will use in our client script is mentioned here:

```
function onSubmit() {
var end = g_form.getValue("u_return_date");
  var start = g_form.getValue("u_start_date");
  var format = "yyyy-MM-dd"; //format used in ServiceNow date fields
  var d = new Date();
varcurr= d.getFullYear() + "-" + (d.getMonth()+1) + "-" + d.getDate();
//format for current date will be yyyy-M-dd
  varreturnval= true; //default return variable
```

```
    //hide any existing error messages
    g_form.hideAllFieldMsgs("error");
    //check if start date is before current date
    varisStartBeforeCurr= compareDates(curr, "yyyy-M-dd", start, format);
    if ( isStartBeforeCurr ) {
    g_form.showErrorBox("u_start_date", "Must be after current date.");
    returnval=false; //flag form submission
      }
    varisEndBeforeStart= compareDates(start, format, end, format);
    if ( isEndBeforeStart ) {
    g_form.showErrorBox("u_return_date", "Must be after start date.");
    returnval=false; //flag form submission
      }
    return returnval;
}
```

As shown here, the end user will now be presented with an error message if the **Start Date** is before the current date, and similarly, if the **Return Date** is before the **Start Date**, an error message will be shown. The form will submit successfully if both dates are correct. That is, if the **Start Date** is after the current date and the **Return Date** is after the **Start Date**:

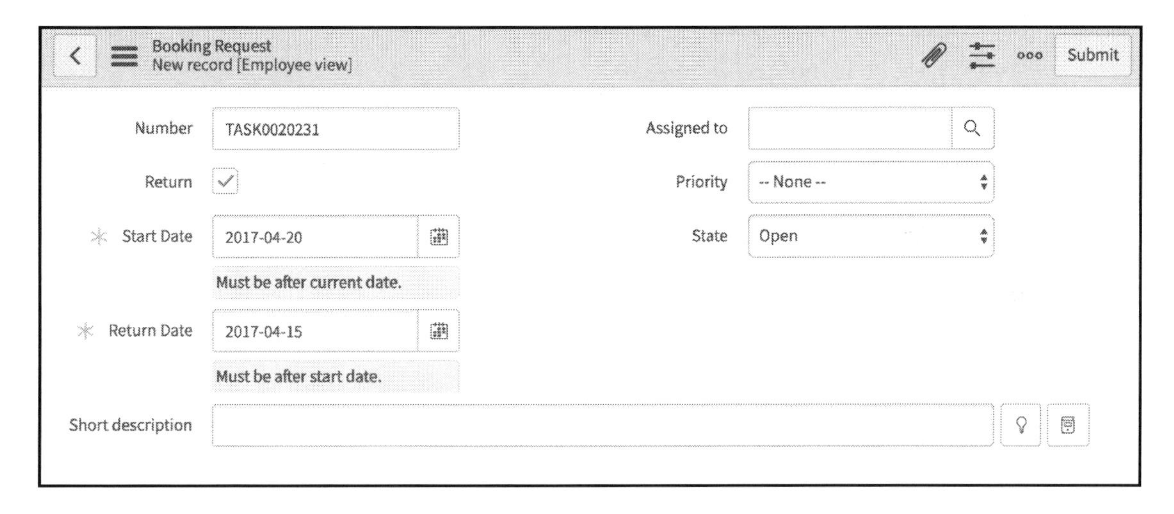

Now we have covered the client script, our first client-side script in the ServiceNow platform. Let us now learn about other types of client-side scripts available in the platform.

# UI policies

We can make use of the UI policy to toggle the display, read-only, and mandatory properties of a field when a certain criterion is matched. In essence, we can toggle the display of the **Return Date** field when the **Return** checkbox is checked without having to write any script using a UI policy.

Let us show or hide the **Return Date** field using a UI policy. If you recall, earlier in the chapter, we implemented the same feature using a client script; however, we applied it on the **Employee view**. Such a toggle feature is not yet available in the **Default view**. So now we will apply the UI policy to toggle the display of the **Return Date** field based on the value of the **Return** checkbox for the **Default view** instead.

The UI policy will change the display or edit properties of a field when the following three conditions are met:

- The UI policy is marked as active
- The field specified in the action is available in the form
- The conditions set evaluate to `true`

To create a new UI policy, open **Studio** and in the **Create Application File** wizard, select **Client Development** | **UI Policy**, as shown in the following screenshot, and click on the **Create** button:

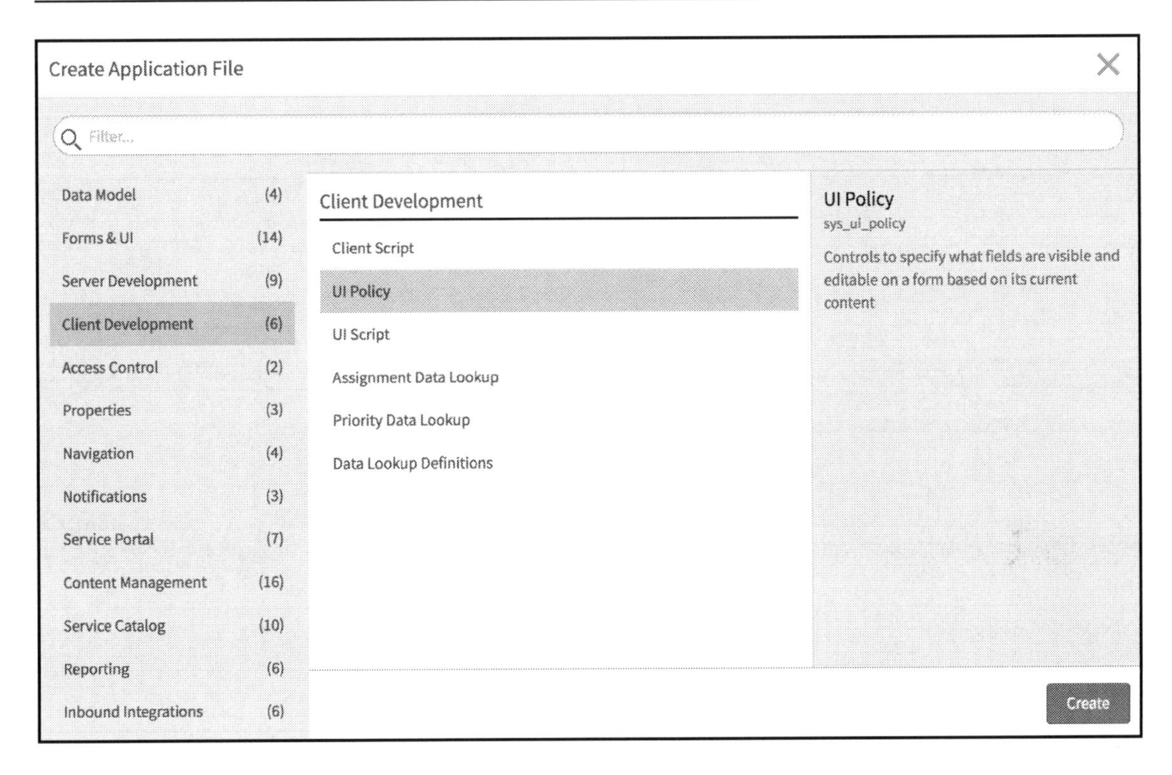


The UI policy new record form will open in the content section of the **Studio**. Now fill in the new record form with the following values:

- **Table**: **Booking Request**
- **Short description**: `Toggle return date display`
- **Conditions**: **Return is True**
- **Global**: Unchecked
- **View**: (leave blank)
- **Reverse if false**: Checked

- **On load**: Checked
- **Inherit**: Unchecked

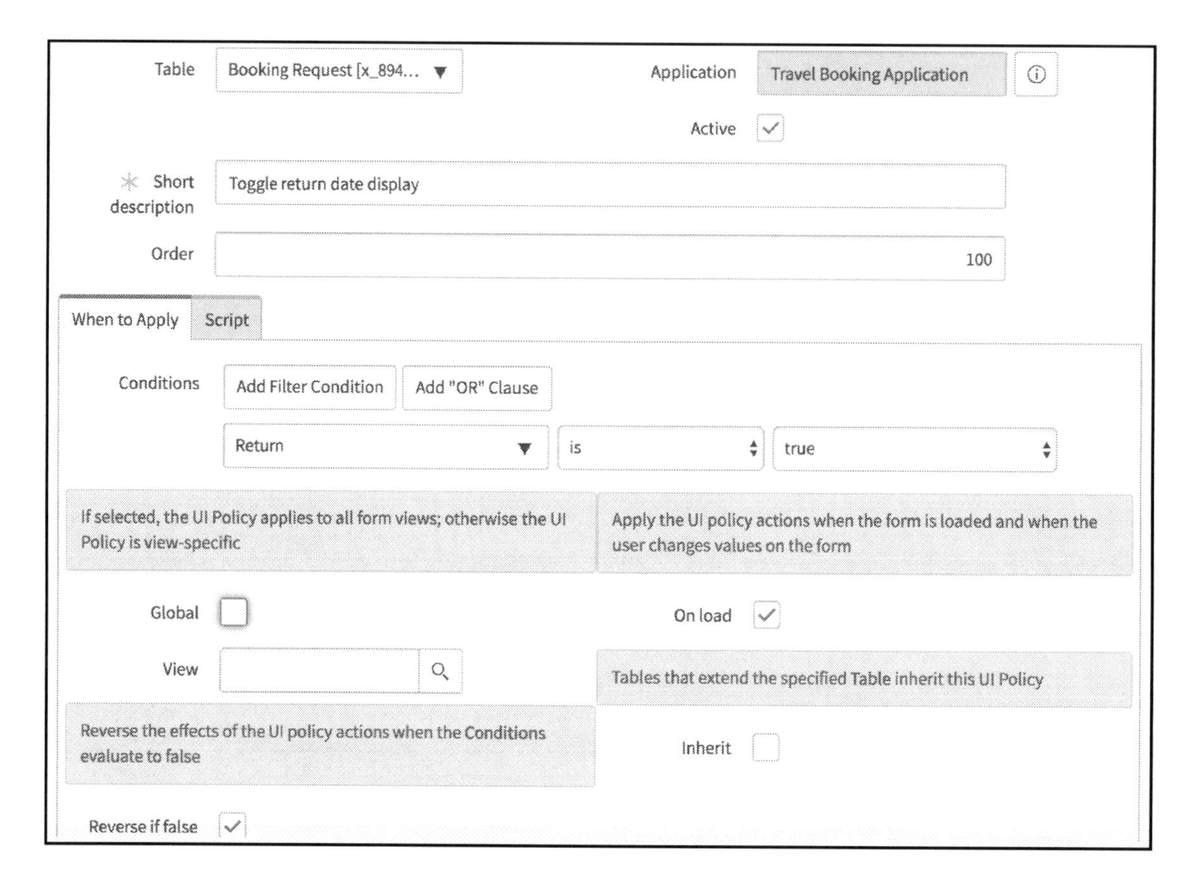


Marking the **Global** field as checked while leaving the **View** field empty will make the UI policy active only on the **Default view**. The **Reverse if false** field, when checked, will ensure the UI policy actions defined for the current policy will be reversed when the conditions set evaluate to `false`. We will see this in action next. Finally, the **Inherit** field, if checked, makes the current UI policy available to all tables that will inherit the current table, that is, the `Booking Request` table.

The conditions we have set are simple and will check whether the **Return** checkbox is checked or not. If the **Return** checkbox is checked, the condition will evaluate to `true`, otherwise it will evaluate to `false`.

Now click on the **Submit** button to create the UI policy and remain in the UI policy record in the **Studio**. Scroll down the UI policy actions related list and click on the the **New** button, as shown here:

The UI policy action new record form will open up in a new tab in the following screenshot. Fill in the new record form fields with the following values:

- * **Field name**: **Return Date**
- **Mandatory**: **True**
- **Visible**: **True**
- **Read only**: **Leave alone**

The other fields will be automatically selected for you, as shown in the following screenshot. Click on the **Submit** button to save the UI action policy. One UI action can have multiple UI action policies defined, each for a different field:

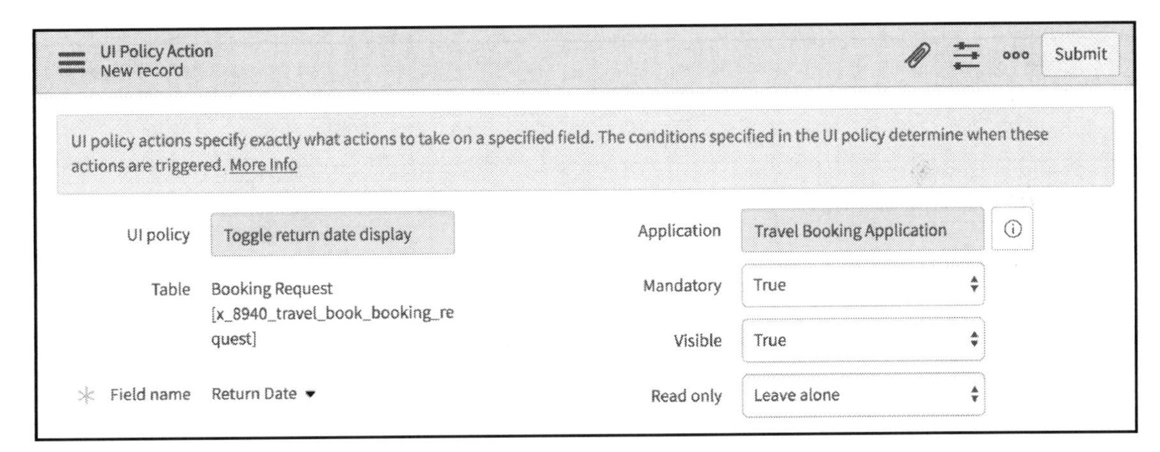

Now let us test the UI policy but open the new record form of the `Booking Request` table in the **Default view**. Switch to the main ServiceNow interface and open the **Travel Booking Application** | **Booking Request** module using the left navigation panel. Click on the **New** button on the top section of the list of modules page that opens up. This will bring up the new record form of the **Booking Request** table in the **Default view**. You can also ensure to switch to the **Default view** when you are in the list of record module by clicking on the menu icon available in the list header and selecting the correct view as shown here:

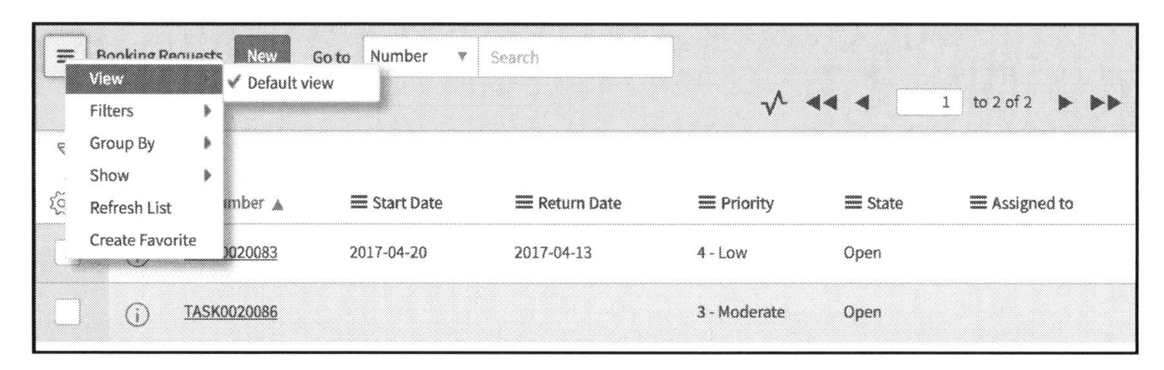


Now click on the **New** icon to open the new record form in the **Default view** as shown here. We can notice that the **Return Date** field is not visible. This is because in the UI policy definition, we have checked the **Reverse if false** checkbox. This is causing the effects of the UI policy action to be reversed when the conditions are not met:

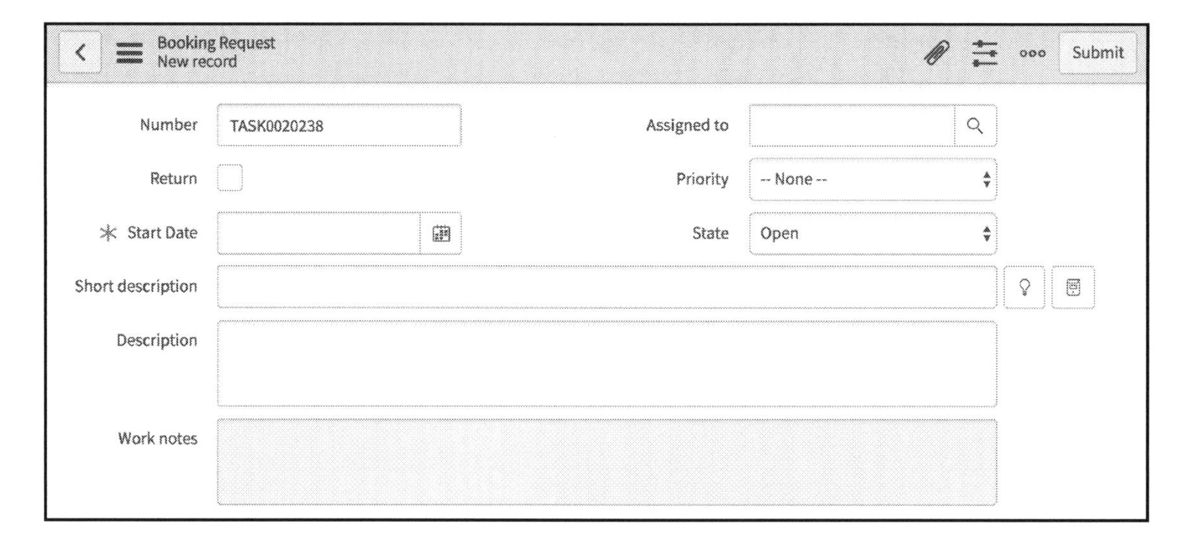

Also, as shown here, you will notice that checking the **Return** field is making the **Return Date** field visible and mandatory and vice versa without having to write a single line of code:

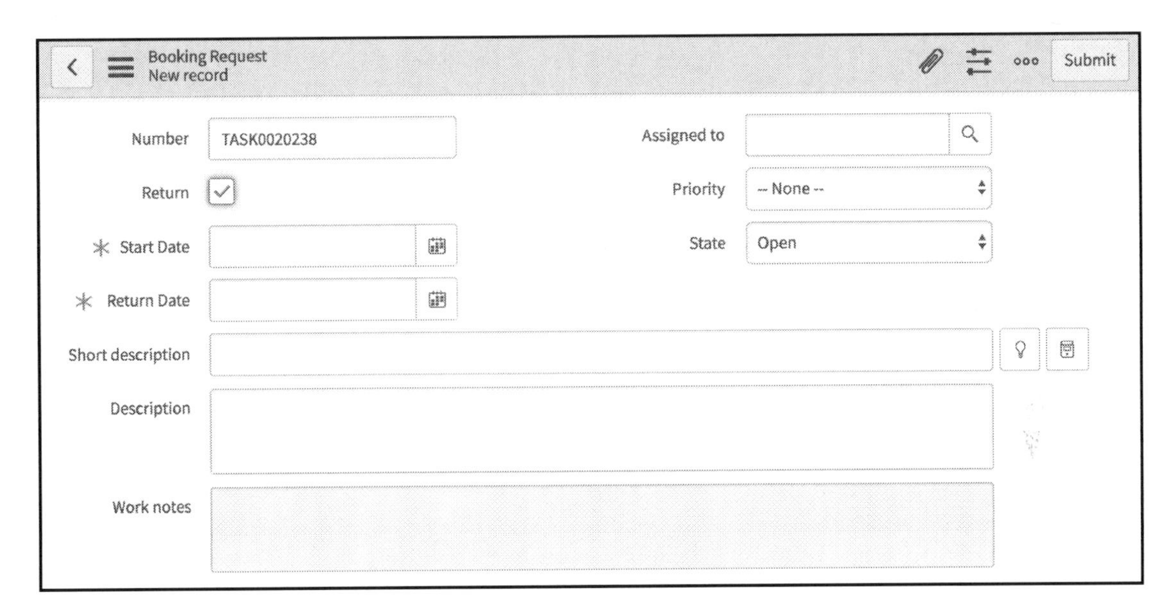

ServiceNow recommends using a UI policy instead of writing scripts wherever possible to show or hide fields and to mark them as mandatory or read-only.

# UI scripts

Let us now learn about another type of client-side script feature available in the ServiceNow platform, known as the UI script. The UI script is basically a bundle of JavaScript functions that may also include client-side Glide API calls.

The most important purpose of the UI script is to enable developers to create reusable code. The UI scripts are included and available in all the forms, list of record pages, and other modules. They can be referred to from any other client-side scripts, including the client script and UI policy. Because the UI script code is included in all the forms and page when marked **Global**, it is a recommended best practice to avoid creating a UI script unless it is really required.

As our intent is to create globally reusable client-side code, we will create the UI script in the **Global** application scope because only then will our UI script be accessible globally. The ServiceNow platform, starting with the Fuji release, doesn't support the creation of a global UI script in an application scope. A UI script defined in an application scope can be used along with UI macros and formatters. However, to make the script really reusable and accessible from all client-side scripts, we must create the UI script in the **Global** scope.

So first, we will switch to the **Global** scope using the application picker drop-down menu in the main ServiceNow interface as shown here:

If the application picker drop down is not visible, you can click on the cog icon on the far right and mark the **Show application picker in header** as `true` in the **System Setting** | **Developer** tab.

To create a new UI script, in the main ServiceNow interface, open the **System UI** | **UI Scripts** module, as shown here:

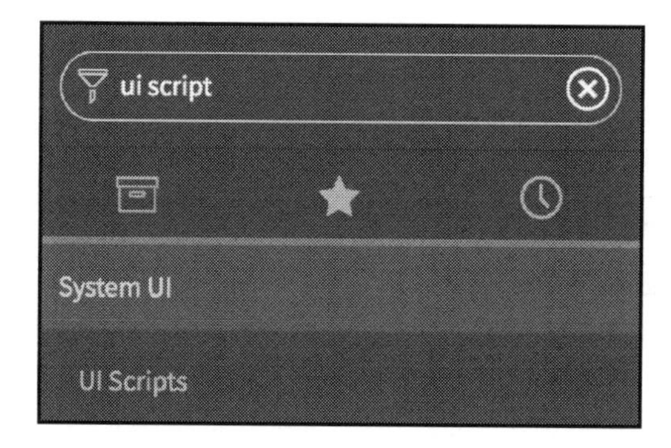


In the list of records page, click on the **New** button on the list header. The UI script new record form will open up, as shown here. Fill in the form with the following values:

- **Name**: `toTitleCase`
- **Global**: Checked
- **Description**: (Any meaningful description about the UI script)

Let us set the following JavaScript code that will be used in the **Script** field:

```
function toTitleCase(str) {
  return str.replace(/\w\S*/g, function (text) {
    return text.charAt(0).toUpperCase() +
      text.substr(1).toLowerCase();
  });
}
```

The new record form for the UI script in the **Global** application scope is shown here. The **Global** checkbox in the **UI script** form is to tell the platform that this UI script will be available in all the forms. The **Description** field can be used to add some meaningful information about the UI script, including some code documentation. We must ensure that the UI script is marked as **Active** and **Global** before we try to invoke it in any form. Click on the **Submit** button to create the global UI script in the **Global** application scope:

Now switch back to the **Travel Booking Application** scope using the application picker and open the ServiceNow **Studio** using the navigation panel:

In the **Studio**, we will now create a new client script that will execute when the **Short description** field on the **Booking Request** form is changed. To create a new client script in the **Studio**, in the **Create Application File** wizard, select **Client Development** | **Client Script** and click on the **Create** button. Populate the new record form, as shown here, using the following values:

- **Name**: `Change short desc to title case`
- **Table**: **Booking Request**
- **UI Type**: **Desktop**
- **Type**: `onChange`
- **Field name**: **Short description**
- **Active**: Checked
- **Inherited**: Unchecked
- **Global**: Checked

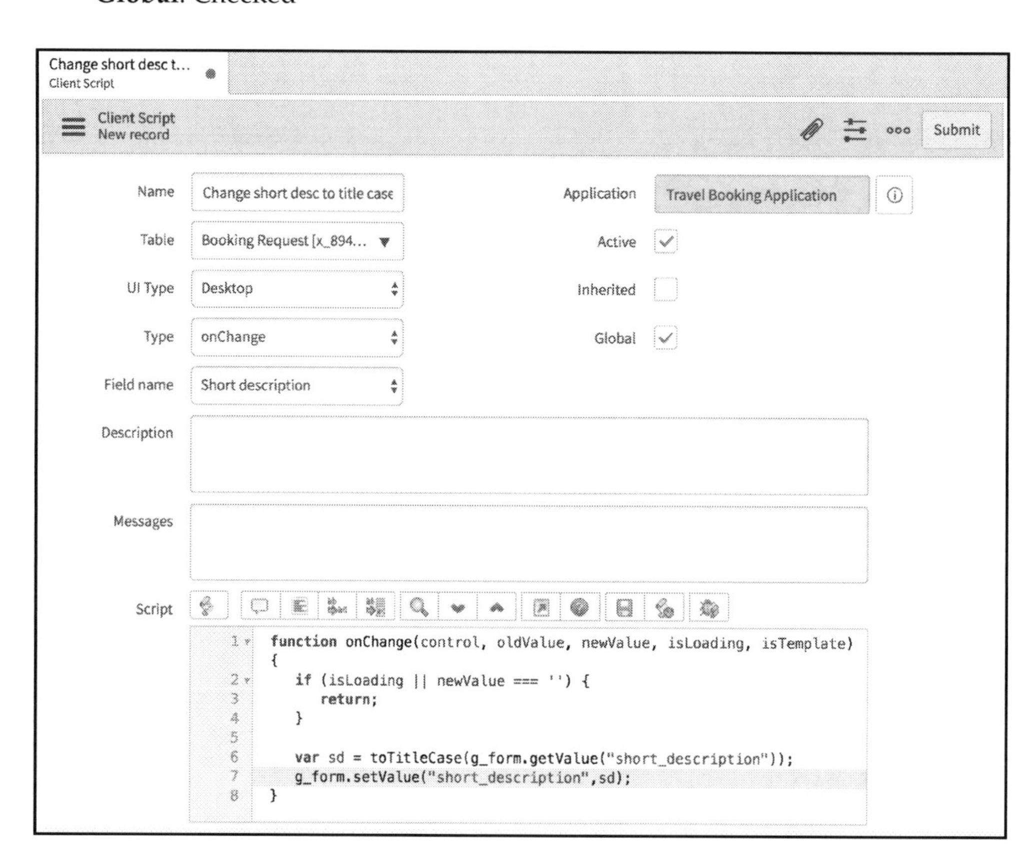

The following code will be specified in the **Script** field:

```
function onChange(control, oldValue, newValue, isLoading, isTemplate) {
if (isLoading || newValue === '') {
return;
   }

var sd= toTitleCase(g_form.getValue("short_description"));
g_form.setValue("short_description",sd);
}
```

Let us test our UI script and the client script in the **Booking Request** form by switching to the main ServiceNow interface and opening the **Booking Request New Record** form using the **Travel Booking Application | Booking Request** module and clicking on the **New** button.

In the **Short description** field, as shown here, type in some, value such as `i need to go to new york on 3rd of janurary`, and focus out of the field:

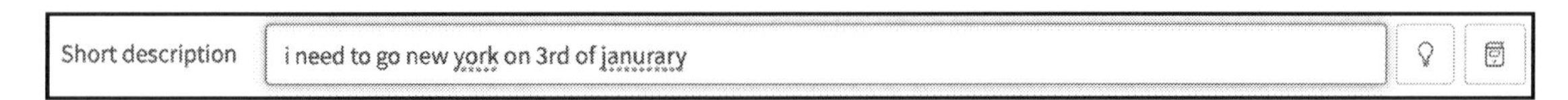


The `onChange` event handler defined in the client script must execute, which in turn will use the `toTitleCase` function defined in the global UI script to change the field's value to camel/title case, as shown here:

# Disabling client-side scripts

There may be times when we want to disable a particular client-side script. To do this, all we need to do is uncheck the **Active** field for the record. The script definition will remain in the system; however, it will not be attached to the form and execute.

For example, let us disable the `Change short desc to title case` client script. Open the appropriate record in the **Studio** using the application explorer on the left.

In the form that will open in the content area of the **Studio**, uncheck the active field and click on the **Update** button. Now when you change the **Short description** field, in the **Booking Request** form, the `onChange` client script will not execute, as it marked as inactive. We can mark it as active whenever we wish but for now let us leave it as inactive.

# Creating a scope UI script

To create a UI script for a scoped application, we need to use the **Studio** and, in the **Create Application File** wizard, as shown in the following screenshot, select **Client Development** | **UI script** and click on the **Create** button to open the relevant new record form:

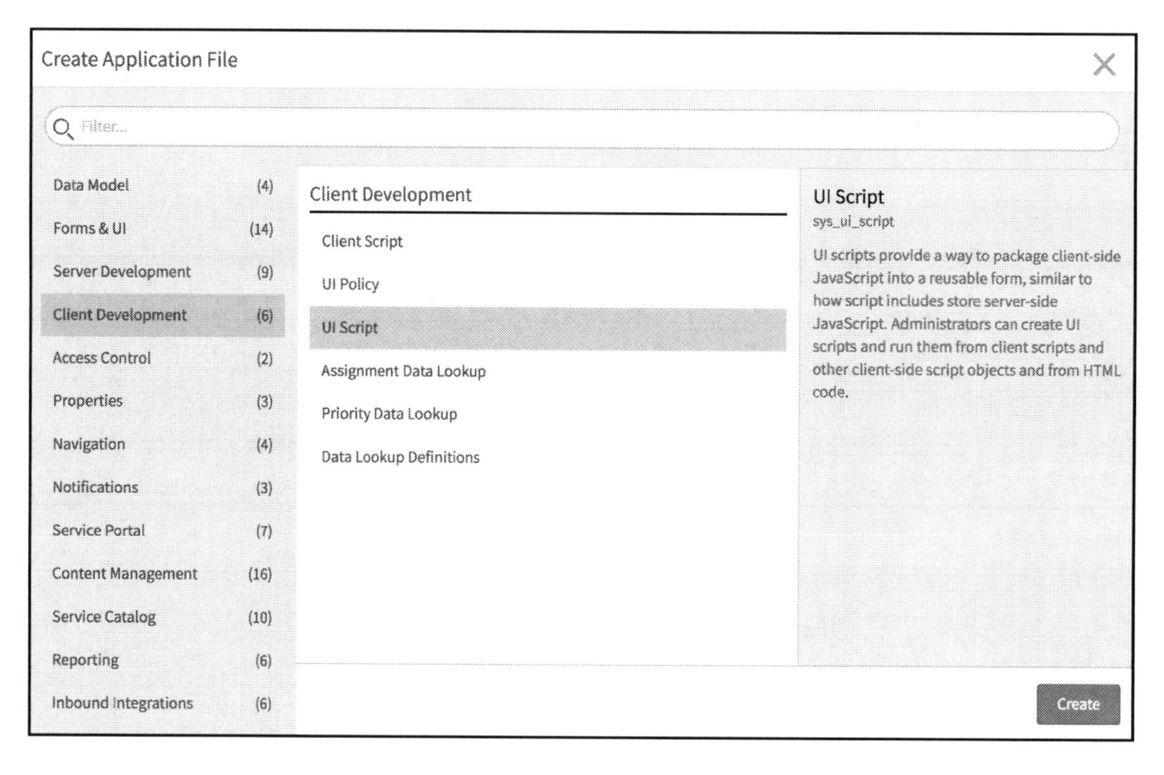


Now, in the new record form for the UI script, we can specify the script we would like to be available in client forms.

The UI scripts created under an application scope other than **Global** are not accessible in the forms automatically as they have to be explicitly included in the form using UI macros and formatters. We will be covering UI macros and formatters later in the book.

# Summary

In this chapter, we created client-side code, including client scripts, UI policies, and UI actions. We also learned about the different types of client scripts available and how to make use of the different properties of the client scripts. We also learned how to create global UI actions that can be invoked from any client-side code, including the client script.

Furthermore, we learned about UI policies and how they can be used to show or hide fields and modify the editable properties, such as mandatory and read-only, without writing any code. In the next chapter, we will learn how to make user of the server-side scripting features, such as business rules, and server-side Glide APIs, such as `GlideRecord`.

# 8
# Server-Side Scripting

Now that we have learned about scripting and created some client-side scripts in the ServiceNow platform, let us start writing some server-side scripts to further enhance our application.

As discussed in the previous chapter, server-side scripts are JavaScript code that executes on the server and has access to a server-side glide API. We can employ a server-side API to enhance server-side data processing and integration with different systems. Server-side scripts can also be used to perform database operations and perform large scripted imports.

In this chapter, we will learn how to create server-side scripts, and when and where the server-side scripts come on the scene when working with ServiceNow applications. We will also learn how to make use of the server-side glide API and some of the most widely used functions available in it.

In this chapter, we will learn how to create the following server-side scripts:

- Business rules
- Script include
- Data policy

## Business rules

Let us create our first server-side script-a business rule. A business rule is a JavaScript code that is associated with a table, runs on the server, and is executed before, after, or asynchronously when a record is inserted, updated, deleted, or retrieved in the specified table.

The following business rule new record form has many fields and tabs available when the advanced checkbox is checked:

- **When to run**
- **Actions**
- **Advanced** (this tab is available only when the Advanced checkbox is checked)

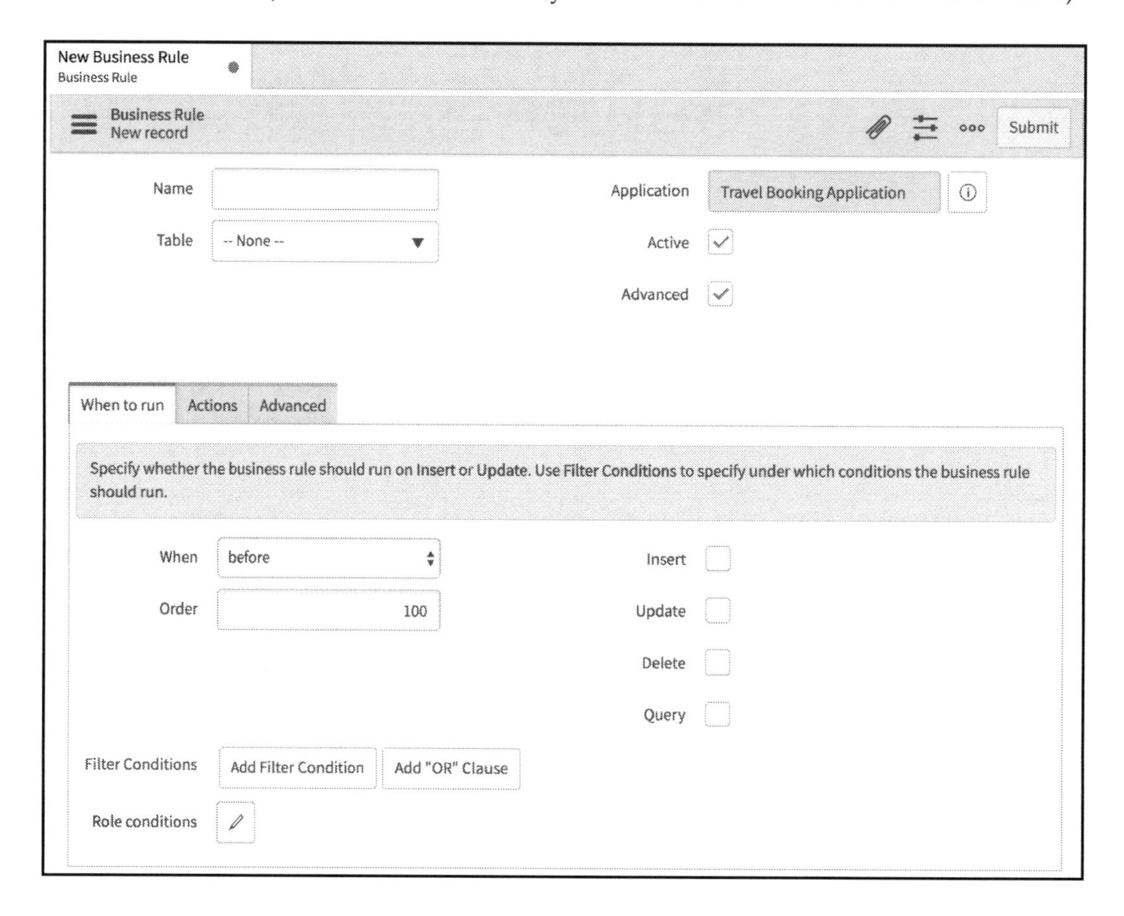


- The business rule can execute based on the kind of database operations selected. One or more of the following different operations can be selected:
    - **Insert**
    - **Update**
    - **Delete** (Only available when the **Advanced** field is checked)
    - **Query** (Only available when the **Advanced** field is checked and cannot be aborted)

- **When**: The **When** property is only available when the **Advanced** field is selected. When the **Advanced** field is unchecked, the **When** property defaults to **Before**. The **When** property of the business rule can be one of the following at any given time:
    - **Before**: This type of business rule can abort the insert, update, or delete operation
    - **After**: This type of business rule cannot abort any database operation
    - **Async**: Short for asynchronous
    - **Display**: Selecting this option makes the operation field default to query
- **Order**: The order in which the business rule executes
- **Condition**: The conditions set must match in order for the business rule to complete execution

Apart from when to run properties, we can also set actions that will be performed when the conditions are true and the business executes:

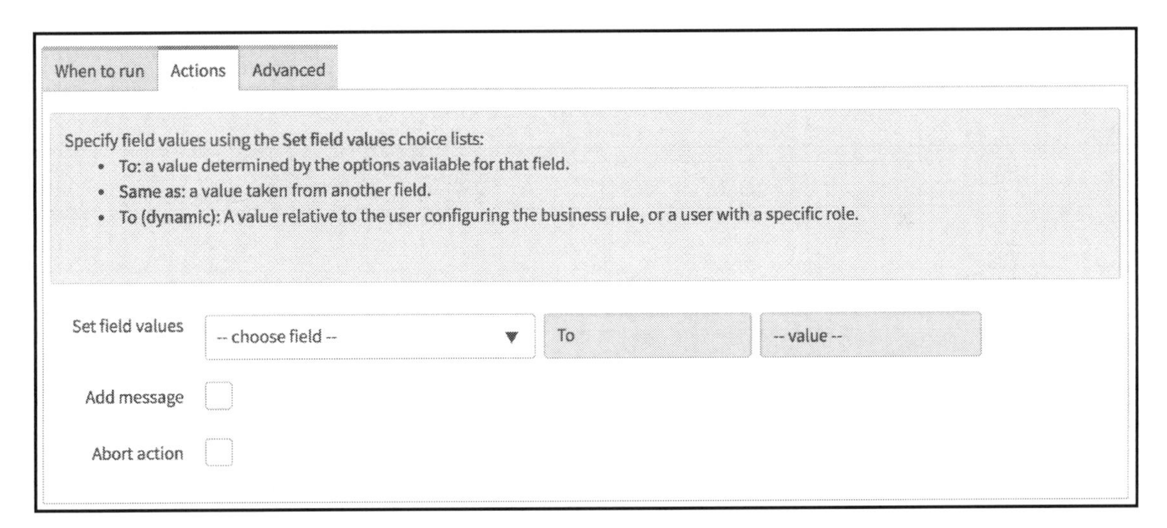


If the **Advanced** field is checked, we also get the ability to write server-side script, where we can also make use of the server-side glide APIs. For simple features such as changing the value of a field or aborting an insert, update, or delete operation, we can use the **Actions** tab instead of writing script.

Now let us create our first business rule that will alert the end user that there isn't enough lead time if the start date selected is at or before tomorrow. To create a new business rule, open **Studio** and in the **Create Application File** wizard, select **Server Development** | **Business Rule** and click on the **Create** button.

Once you are in the **Business Rule New Record** form, as shown here, fill in the form with the following values:

- **Name**: `Insufficient lead time for booking`
- **Table**: **Booking Request**
- **Active**: Checked

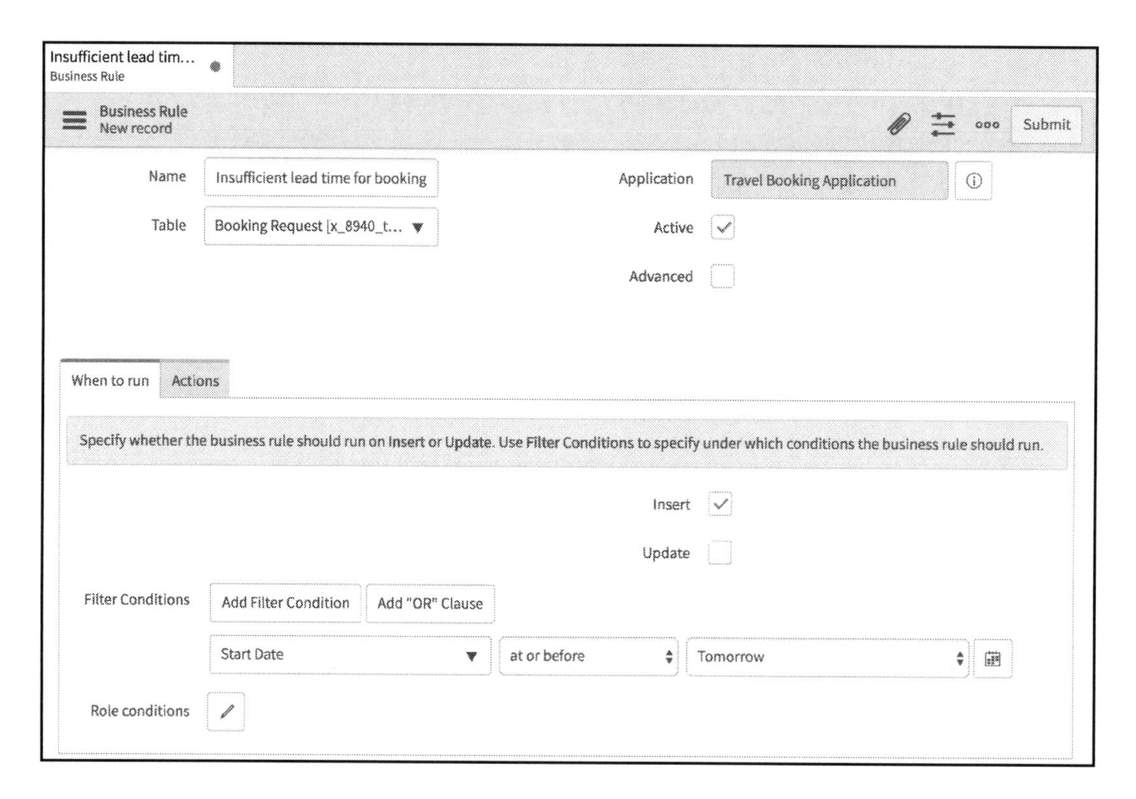


As shown in the preceding screenshot, in the **When to run** tab, fill in the following values:

- **Insert**: Checked
- **Filter**: **Start Date** | **at or before** | **Tomorrow**

In the **Actions** tab, set the following values:

- **Add message**: Checked
- **Message**: `It may not be possible to find you a suitable travel option. If possible, change the travel start date.`
- **Abort action**: Unchecked

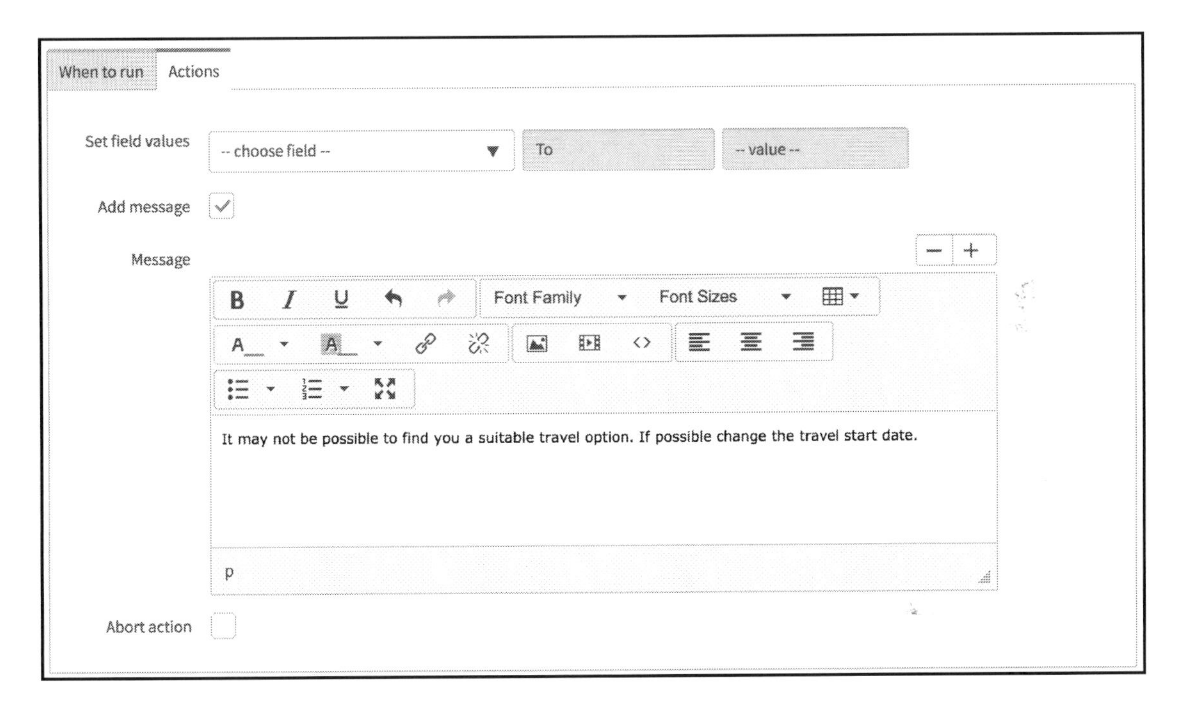


Click on the **Submit** button to create our first business rule, and to test it, switch to the main ServiceNow interface, open the **Travel Booking Application** | **Booking Request** module, and click **New**.

Fill in the **Booking Request New Record** form with the following details:

- **Start Date**: Select today's date
- **Return Date**: Select tomorrow's date
- **Short description**: `testing business rule`

- Click on the **Submit** button

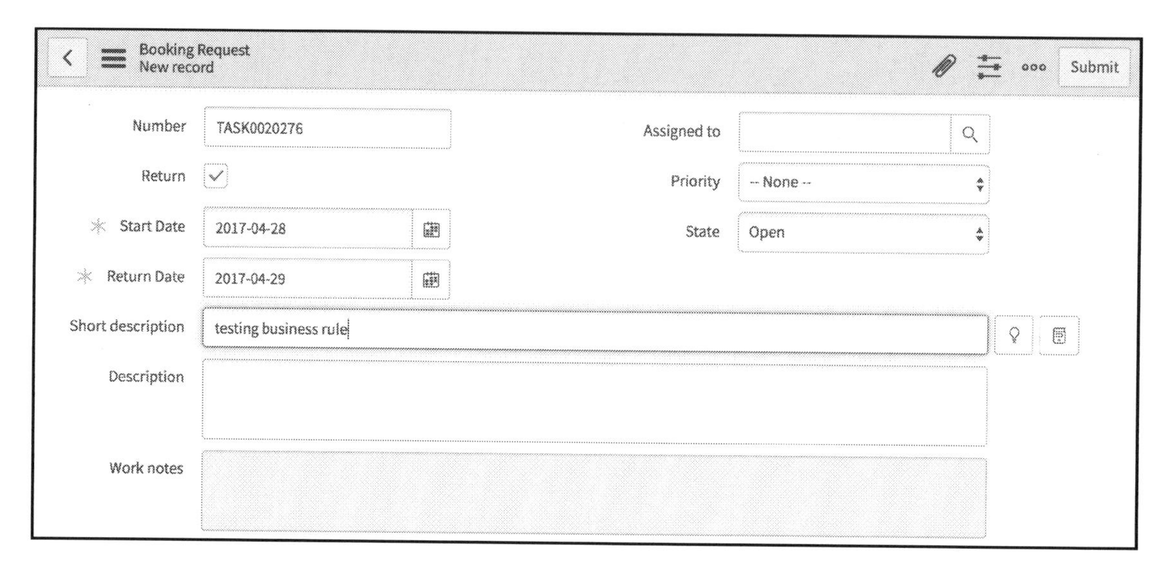


Once you submit the new record form, you will be taken to the business rules list of records module where you will see the message we have set in our business rule appear on top of the list, as shown here, because the conditions we set in the business rule matched:

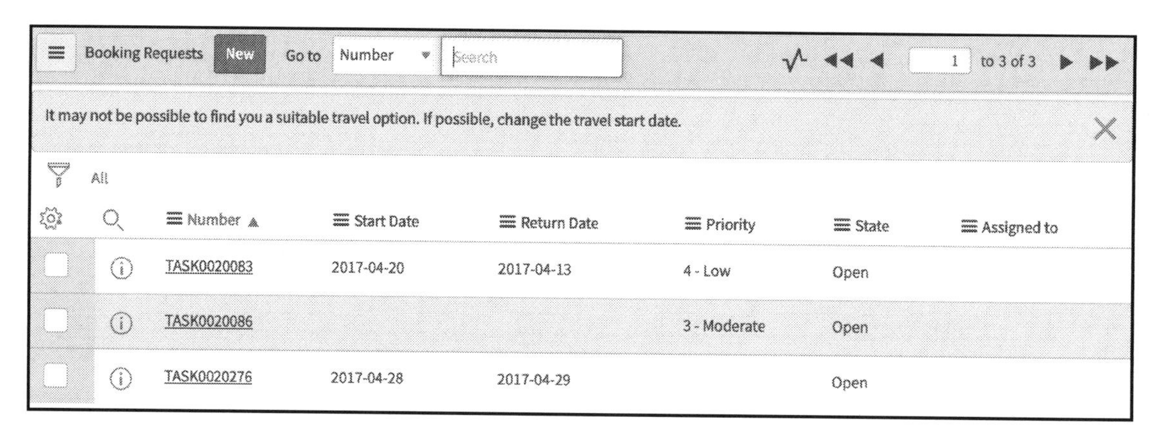


Business rules can also be used to overwrite the value passed in a form field, abort operations, and conduct database operations on any table. Let us create another business rule to do just that. However, before we proceed any further, we will add the following few fields to our business rule form: **Caller** (user), **Contact type**, **From** (location) and **To** (location).

To do this, open **Studio** and edit both views of the `Booking Request` table using the **Form Designer** by clicking on the form view name:

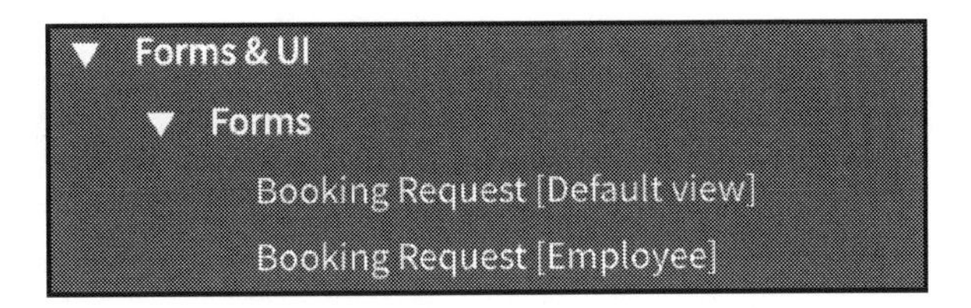


We will be creating the following three new fields to both form views:

- **From**: A new reference field linked to the `Location (cmn_location)` table:

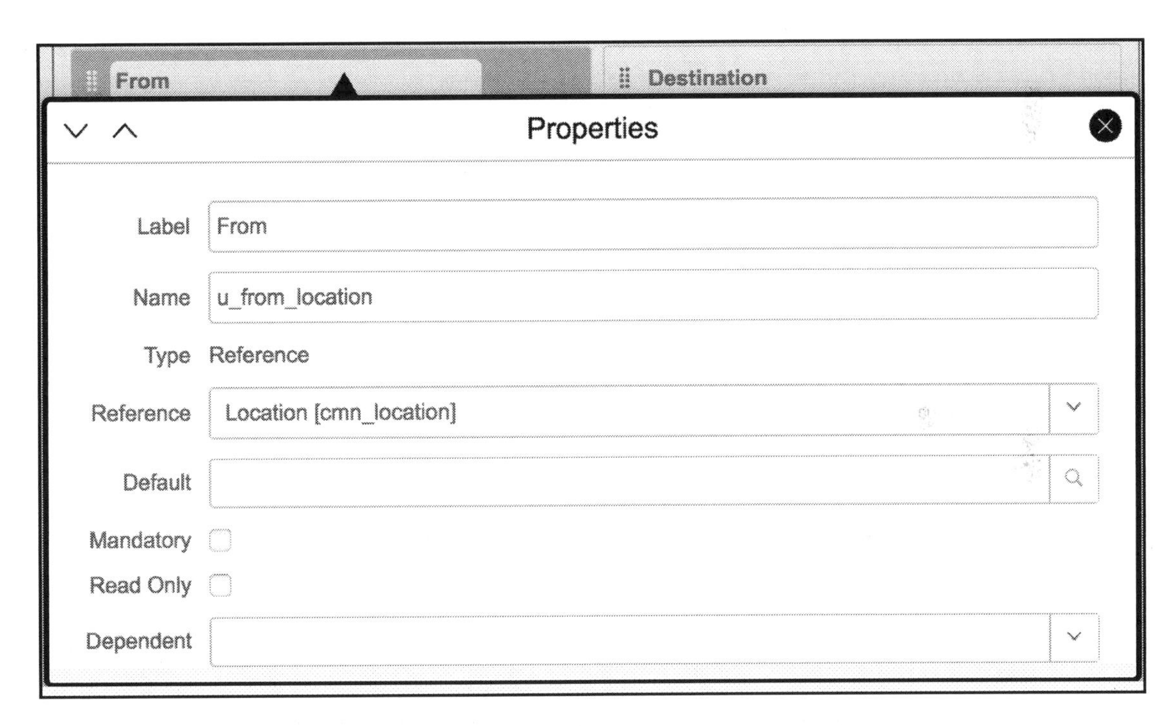


- **Destination**: Like the **From** field, this is another new reference field linked to the `Location (cmn_location)` table:

- **Caller**: A new reference field, which will be linked to the `Users (sys_user)` table:

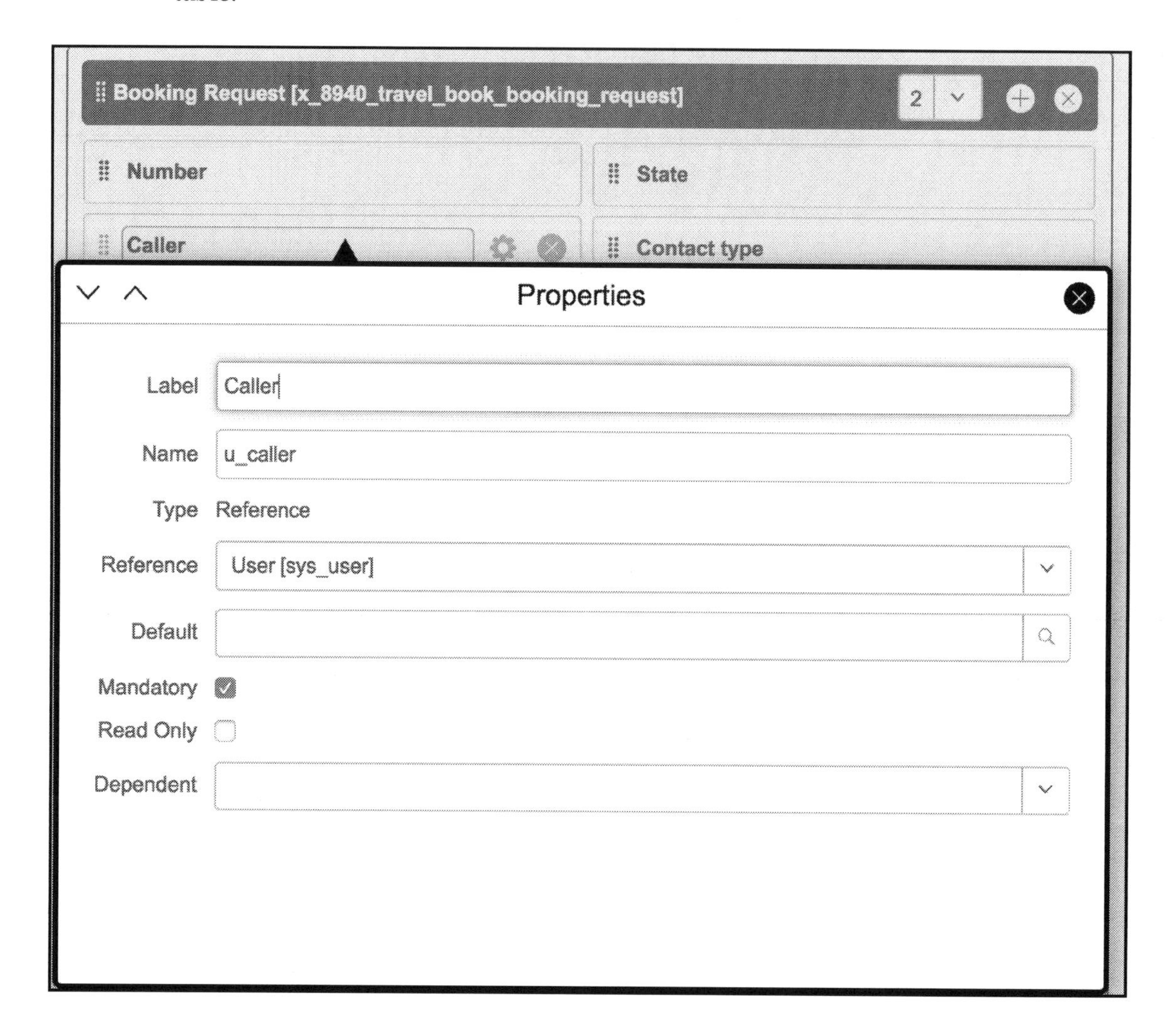

Additionally, we will bring in an existing column called **Contact type**, which is inherited from the `Task` table to the **Default** form:

- **Contact type**: As this field already exists in the table, we will bring it in to the **Default** form view using the **Fields** tab in the **Form Designer**:

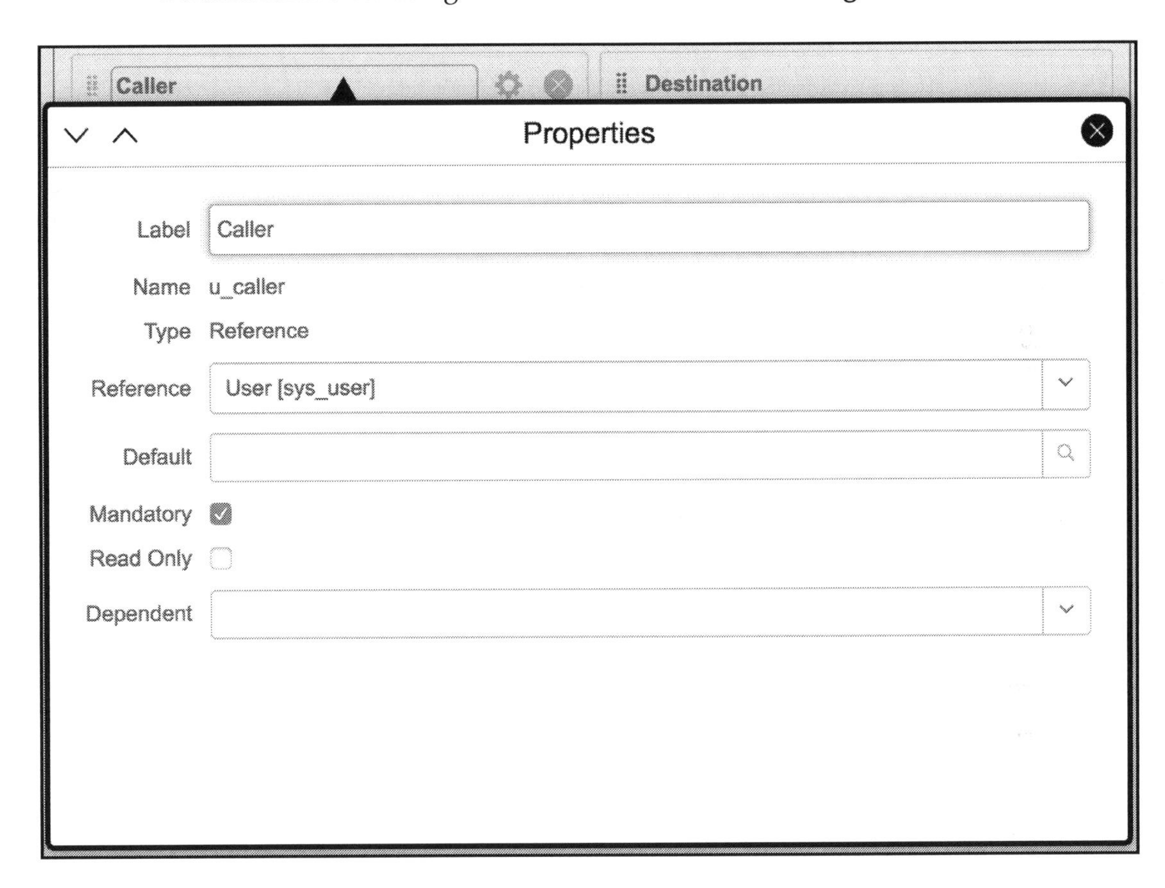

Now, the modified **Employee** form view should look like the one shown here:

Make sure that you perform similar changes in the **Default** view. Once we create a new form field in any view, it can then be reused in other views. So the **Caller**, **From**, and **Destination** fields that we created while changing the **Employee** view can now be reused using the **Fields** tab in the **Form Designer**. We can drag and drop fields from the **Fields** tab and from one section to another to present a better form with the required fields to the end-users.

Thus, the **Default** view will have one extra field available-**Work notes**. The **Contact Type**, **Assigned to**, **Priority**, and **State** fields will be marked as read-only in the **Employee** view by defining a new UI policy for the specific view; however, they will remain editable in the **Default** view.

The final **Default** form view of the `Booking Request` table should look like the one shown here in the **Form Designer**:

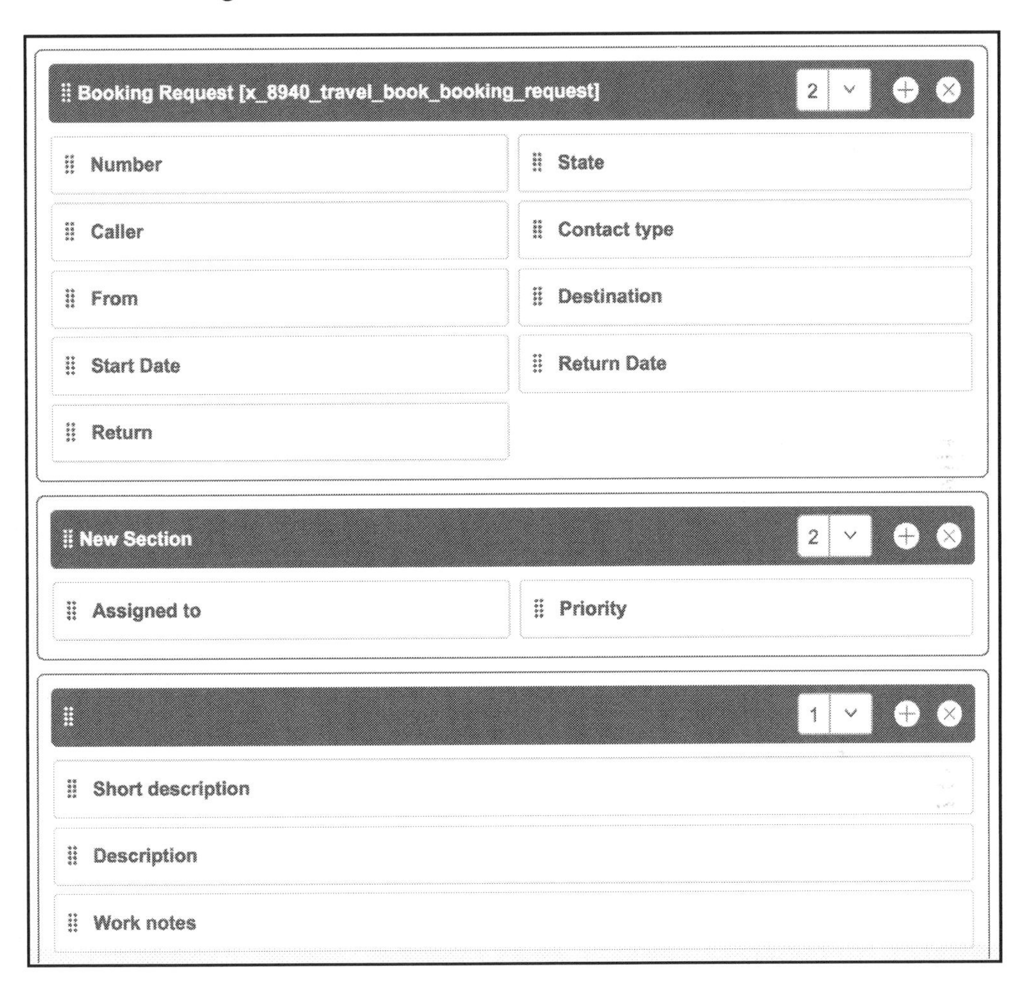


Once you have saved the changes to both the form views, switch to the main ServiceNow interface and confirm that our forms are working properly by creating some records.

Now let us begin creating our second business rule that will abort the current operation and execute script to perform a database operation based on certain conditions.

# Checking the booking requests by the same caller

We will now create a business rule that will execute *before* the insert operation and that will abort the operation when there is another request currently in a pending or open state that is made by the same caller. It will execute a script that will query the `Booking Request` table using the `GlideRecord` for the presence of another pending or open request by the same caller.

Let us now switch to **Studio** and open the business rule new record form by selecting **Server Development** | **Business Rules** in the **Create Application File** wizard.

Fill in the form with the following details:

- **Name**: `Booking request by same caller`
- **Table**: **Booking Request**
- **Active**: Checked
- **Advanced**: Checked
- **When**: **before**
- **Order**: `80`
- **Insert**: Checked
- **Update**: Unchecked
- **Delete**: Unchecked
- **Query**: Unchecked
- **Filter conditions**: (None)

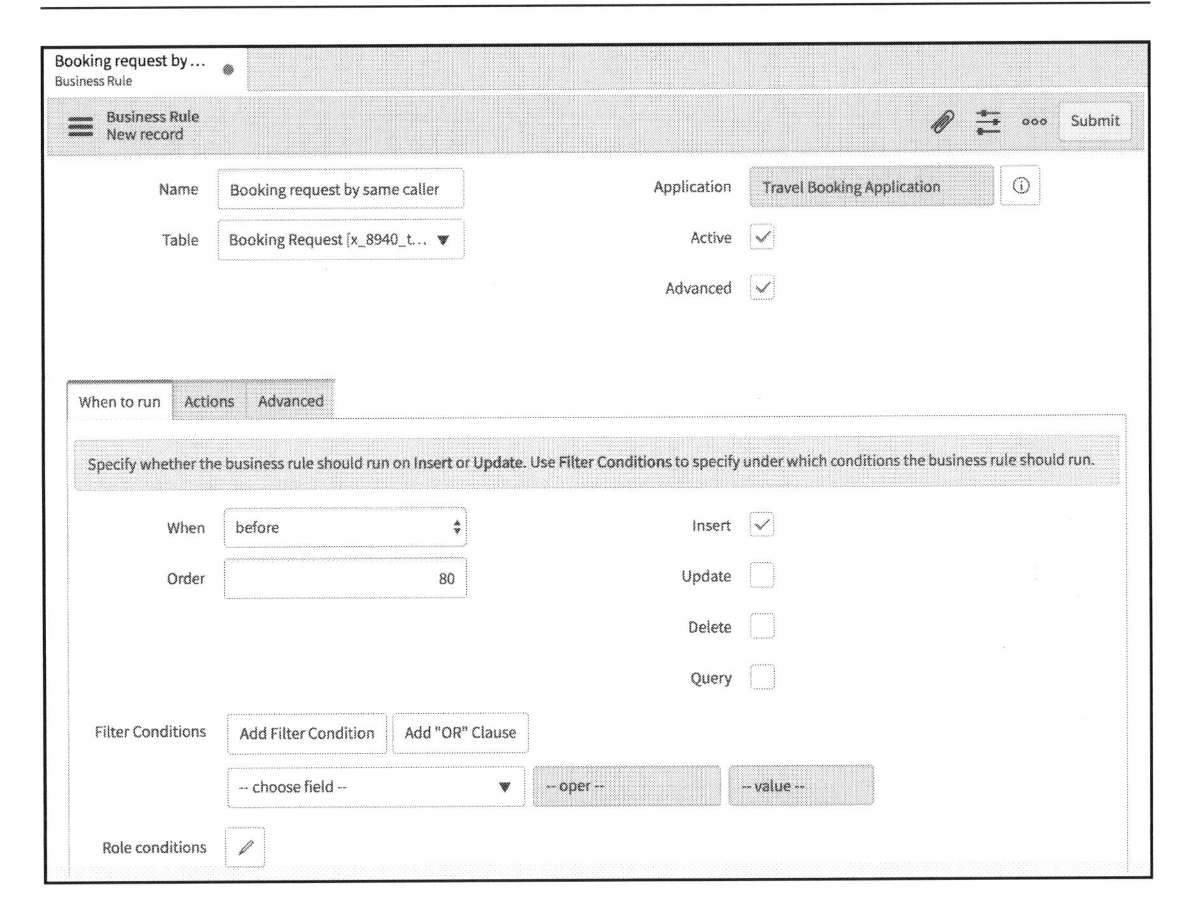


In this business rule, we set it to run **before** the selected database operation(s)-in this case, **Insert**. Marking a business rule to run before any operation gives it the ability to abort the operation. A business rule where the **When** field is set as **After**, **Async**, or **Display** cannot abort the database operation. That means we can abort only when the **before** option is selected in the **When** field. A before business rule can abort an operation by calling `current.setAbortAction(true)` from the script when the **Advanced** field is checked.

Under the **Advanced** tab, populate the script field with the following code:

```
(function executeRule(current, previous /*null when async*/) {
      // Add your code here
      var gr = new GlideRecord(current.getTableName());
      gr.addActiveQuery();
      gr.addQuery("u_caller",current.u_caller);
      varstate_qry = gr.addQuery("state","-5");
      state_qry.addOrCondition("state","IS","1");
      gr.query();
```

```
        if ( gr.hasNext() ) {
                gs.addErrorMessage("Unable to "+current.operation()+" the
record as there is already an existing travel booking request by the user
in pending or open state.");
                current.setAbortAction(true);
        }
})(current, previous);
```

The snapshot of the **Advanced** tab is shown here for your reference. Click on the **Submit** button to create a new business rule:

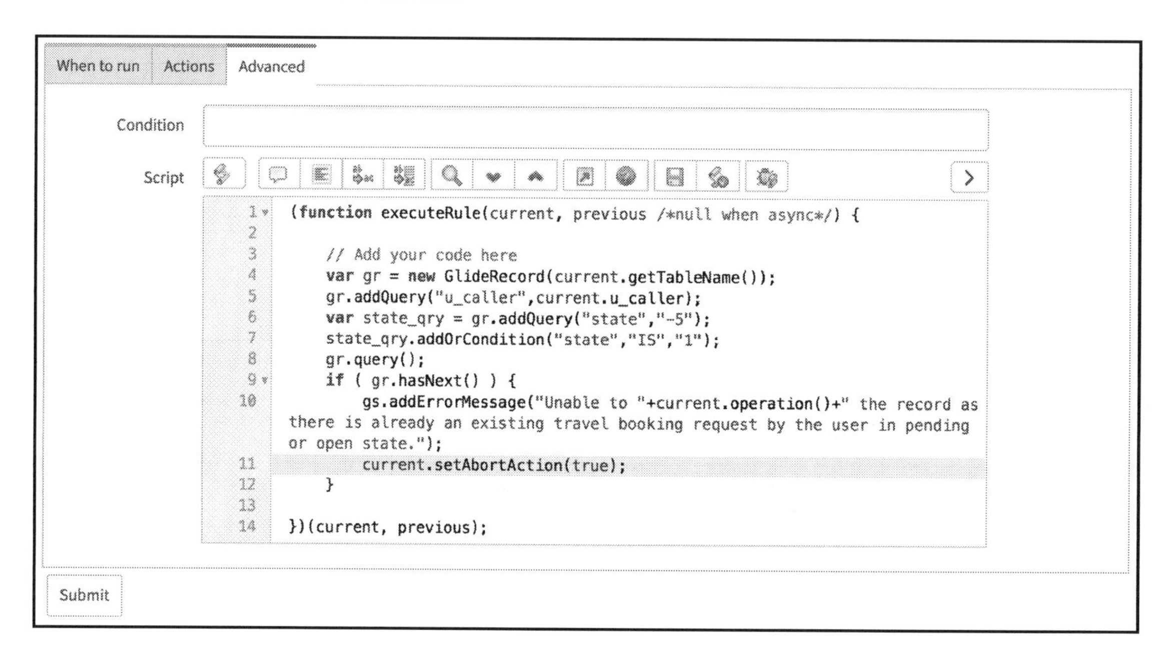


Let us now go and examine the code we specified in our business rule in detail:

- The `executeRule` is the function that gets executed when the condition defined in the **Filter Condition** field matches. If no condition is specified, then the business rule will execute every time for the selected operation and **When** criteria. It accepts two parameters: `current` and `previous`.
- The `current` object is a reference to the record currently being inserted, updated, deleted, or queried.

- The `previous` object is more useful in the update operation, and contains the values that are available in the record before the update operation was triggered (that is, before the form was submitted). The `previous` object is null if **When** is set as **Async**.
- The `current.getTableName()` function returns the name of the table on which the business rule is executing.
- The `GlideRecord(current.getTableName())` function creates a `GlideRecord` object that is going to perform a query operation on the specified table to find the records by the same caller.
- `addActiveQuery`, `addQuery`, and `addOrCondition` set the filter for our database query.
- The `gr.query()` method is what triggers the database operation and fetches records based on the filters we define using `addQuery` and related functions.
- `gr.hasNext()` returns a boolean if there is a record in the specified `GlideRecord` object after the `gr.query()` method. If there are no matching records, `gr.hasNext()` returns false; otherwise, it returns true when there are one or more matching records.
- `gr.addErrorMessage()` is a method available in the `GlideSystem` object, represented by `gs`, which sets an error message that is displayed to the end user when the form loads.
- `current.setAbortAction(true)` is the method that aborts the database operation.

To test the business rule, we will have to create multiple records by the same caller. The first record should get inserted without any issue. However, the second try should fail, as the business rule we just created will abort the insert operation because there is already a pending/open booking request by the same caller. On the contrary, if we change the caller to some other user, the insert operation should complete without getting aborted.

Let us switch to the main ServiceNow interface and create new records in the `Booking Request` table to test our newly created business rule.

Open **Travel Booking Application** | **Create new** module, as shown here, and fill in the form with the following values:

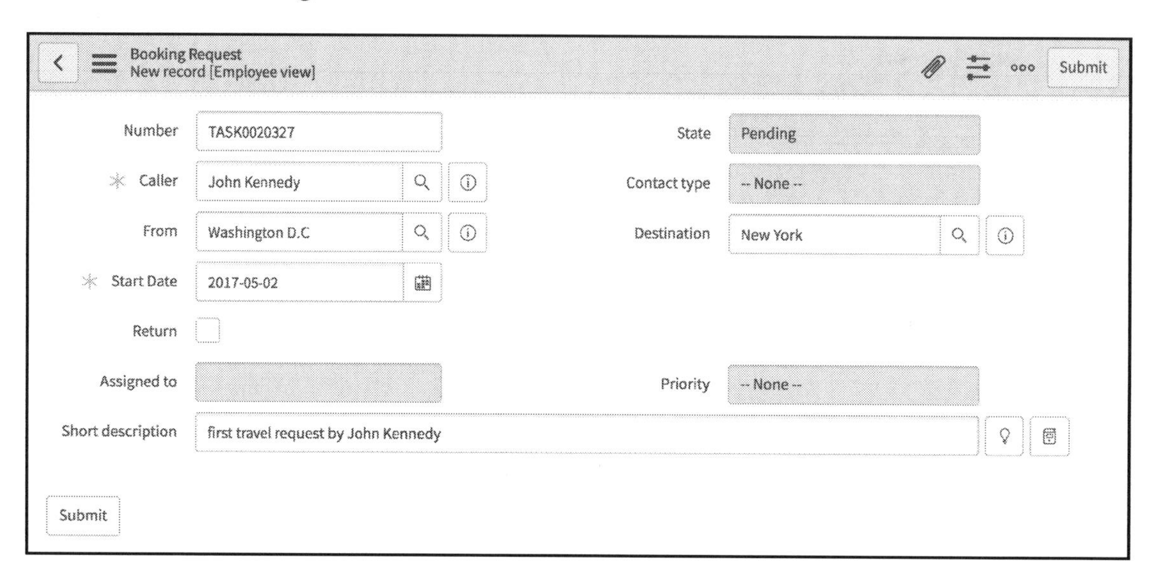


- **Caller**: `John Kennedy`
- **From**: `Washington D.C.`
- **Destination**: `New York`
- **Start Date**: (Any future date)
- **Short description**: `first travel request by John Kennedy`
- Click on **Submit** button

As this is the first booking request by the caller `John Kennedy`, the record will be inserted into our table without any problem. We can confirm this by finding the new record in the list of records module for the `Booking Request` table. Now let us try to create another booking request by the same caller, `John Kennedy`:

- **Caller**: `John Kennedy`
- **From**: `San Francisco`
- **Destination**: `Texas`
- **Start Date**: (Any future date)
- **Short description**: `this is second booking request by John Kennedy`
- Click on **Submit** button

This insert operation will fail this time, even though the **From** and **Destination** locations are different, because the business rule will be able to find another booking request by the same caller that is in a pending state and thus abort the operation and display the error message to the end user, as shown here:

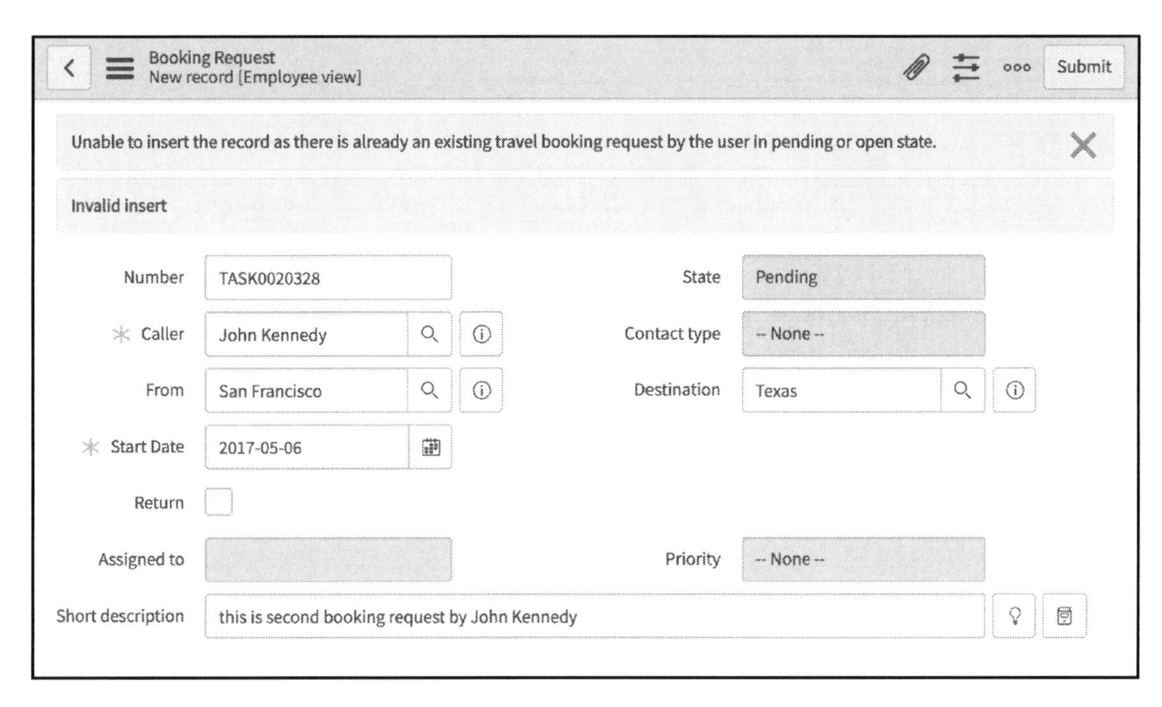


On the contrary, if we try creating a request for some other user for whom there are no pending or open booking requests, then the business rule will not abort it and the insert operation will work just fine.

Furthermore, if we open the first booking request by the caller `John Kennedy` in the default view and change the state to something other than pending or open, we will then be able to create another request by the same caller as the business rule will not be able to find any pending or open request by him.

So let us change the state of the first booking request to **Work in progress** by opening the corresponding record in the **Booking Request** form in the default view, as shown here:

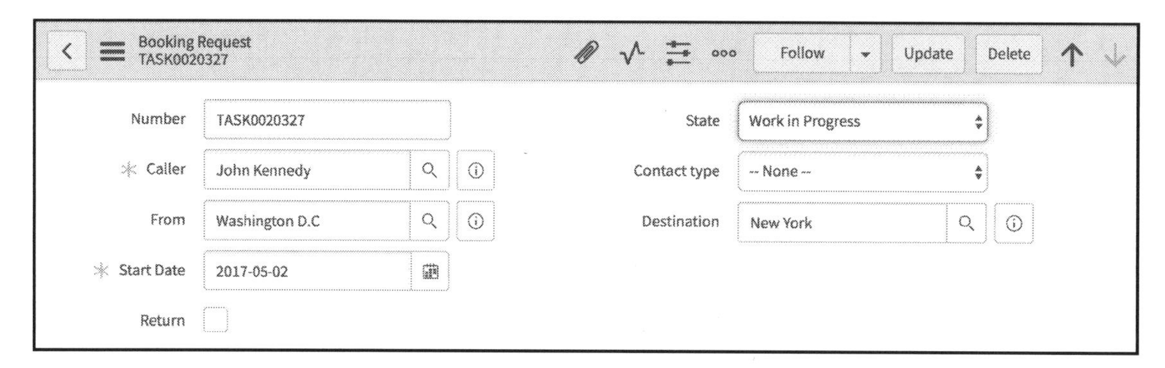


Now that there are no requests in a pending or open state by the caller `John Kennedy`, we should be able to create another request, as the business rule will not abort the operation because the `GlideRecord` will not be able to find any record that matches the query.

In this example, we used the advanced feature of the business rule to create a script that executes and accesses data from a ServiceNow table by creating a `GlideRecord` object.

# When to execute business rules

The **When** field on the **Business Rule** form is one of the most important fields when creating a business rule. It controls when the business rule will be run. The options available are described here, along with some use cases:

- **Before**: One of the most widely employed options when creating a business rule, along with **After**. It can be used for cases where we want to create server-side controls to override field values, perform checks or validations, and/or abort operation based on a certain condition. The execution of the business rule happens before the database operation is performed, thus it can be used for many different use cases, such as the ones we just mentioned. However, it is not recommended when the execution of the business rule takes a long time as it can delay the output to the end user, thereby impacting the overall experience of the platform.

- **After**: The execution of the business rule happens after the database operation is completed, and thus does not really work as expected when trying to abort the operation. **After** business rules are useful for executing post-database operation scripts that involve `GlideRecord` operations on related objects that need to be displayed immediately. Similar to **Before** business rules, **After** rules should not be used to execute very large scripts.
- **Async**: Business rules that execute **Async** can be used to execute large scripts, and are also useful for executing scripts that involve `GlideRecord` operations of related objects that do not need to be displayed immediately. **Async** is very useful for calculating SLAs, validating information from remote systems, triggering web service calls, and other scripts that may take more time than usual to execute. The execution of **Async** business rules happens in parallel to the database operation, and thus the previous object is not available during the execution and it cannot abort the operation.
- **Display**: The **Display** rules are executed when a record is queried and shown in a form. **Display** can be very useful in providing client-side scripts access to data that is not part of the form, such as values in columns that are not part of the form view, any server-side calculated values, or records stored in other tables. It utilizes a shared scratchpad object that is sent to the client along with the form. An example of the display business rule script that utilizes the scratcpad object, `g_scratchpad`, is shown here:

```
//display business rule example
g_scrathpad.someVariable = "some value";
g_scratchpad.secondVariable = "another value";
//we can also pass column values that are not part of the form
g_scratchpad.lastUpdatedOn = current.sys_updated_on;
```

# Preventing recursive business rule execution

As we are already aware, business rules can be triggered before, after, or asynchronously with database operations such as insert, update, delete, or query. One of the most important things we need to bear in mind when we create advanced business rules with scripts is that we should avoid creating an endless loop of business rule execution.

In the previous example, we made a business rule that was triggered when a record was inserted into a table, and we also performed a `GlideRecord` query operation from within the business rule. The table on which we applied the business rule and performed the `GlideRecord` operation is the same-**Booking Request**.

While our code worked successfully, we should usually avoid performing `GlideRecord` operations on the same table unless they are really needed. We should especially make sure that we do not call the `thecurrent.update()` method, as it may trigger the same business rule, thus creating an endless loop and causing the server performance to go down. Similarly, we should take care that we do not perform a `GlideRecord` insert or update operation on the same table. In some cases, the server may require a restart, which can only be performed by creating a request with the ServiceNow support service.

# The scope problem

When we write scripts in business rules, we should take extra steps to enclose all our code within a function to limit the scope of objects. If we do not encode the code within a function, any variable and other objects will be accessible from other server-side scripts, such as a script include. Consider the following code:

```
var gr = new GlideRecord("problem");
gr.addActiveQuery();
gr.query();
```

The preceding code defines an instance of the `GlideRecord` object named `gr`. If the code is not enclosed within a function, the `gr` object will be available in other server-side scripts, which can cause unexpected results and make things very difficult to debug. Hence, we must ensure that the code is properly enclosed within a function body, as shown here:

```
function abc() {
   var gr = new GlideRecord("problem");
gr.addActiveQuery();
gr.query();
}
abc();
```

Now the `gr` object is local and available only within the scope of the `abc` function. However, the `abc` function is not global, and if we use the same name elsewhere in script include or other scripts, it may cause conflict and unexpected results. To avoid such situations, we must follow a proper naming convention for functions and other global objects. A better name for the function could be `getActiveProblemRecs()` or `br_getActiveProblemRecs()`.

# Script includes

Let us now create our first script include. The script include usually comprises a set of JavaScript functions that can be called from any server-side scripts. Moreover, it is possible to mark a script include to be client callable, thereby making it possible for client-side scripts to make remote (AJAX) calls to script include code.

As part of this book, we will create a script include that will be client callable and create a client script that will make a call to the function defined in the script include when the value of the **Destination** form field changes. The client script will initiate an AJAX call to our script include and will tell the end user about the weather conditions in their destination location.

As of now, the weather conditions will be hard coded in the script include; however, in the later chapters, we will integrate it with an external weather service and provide end users with up-to-date weather information.

To create a script include, open **Studio** and click on the **Create Application File** button. In the **Create Application File** wizard, select **Sever Development** | **Script Include** and click on the **Create** button, as shown here:

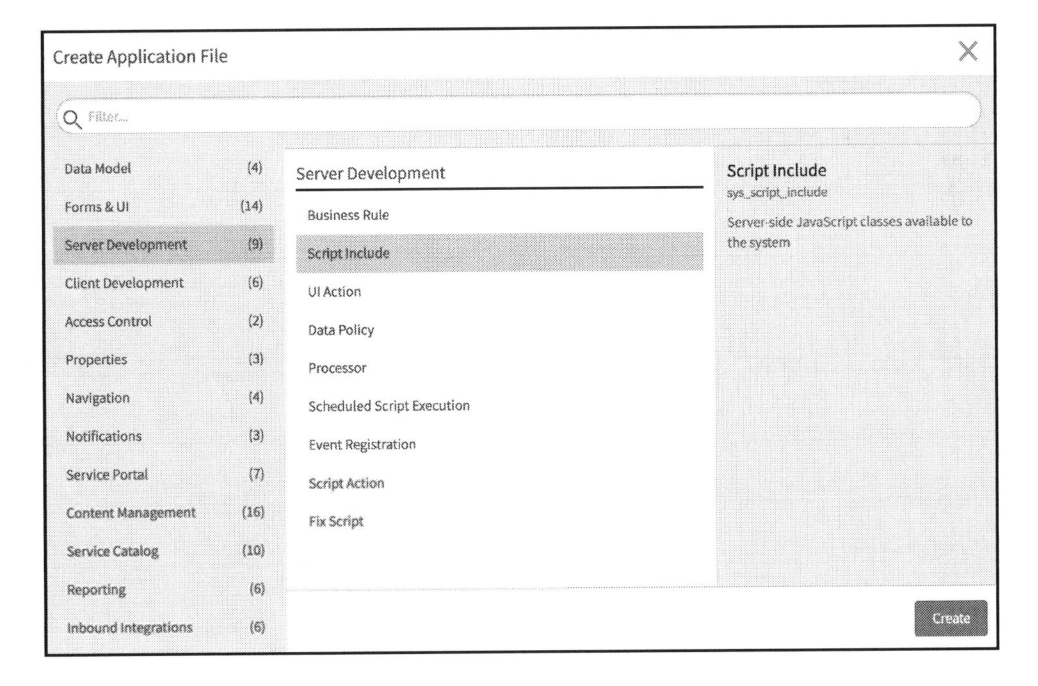

The **Script Include** form will open up in a new tab in **Studio**. We will write code in the **Script** field and set properties such as **Name**, **Client callable**, and so on in the other fields. Marking the **Client callable** checkbox as checked allows the client-side scripts to be able to invoke public methods defined in the script include. All functions of script include are usually public, except the ones that begin with an underscore symbol. The functions that begin with an underscore are private functions and cannot be invoked from client-side AJAX calls.

Fill in the **Script Include New Record** form with the following values:

- **Name**: `CheckWeather`
- **API Name**: (Autogenerated once we type a name)
- **Client callable**: Checked
- **Application**: **Travel Booking Application** (automatically selected)
- **Accessible from**: **This application scope only**
- **Script**: (As detailed here)

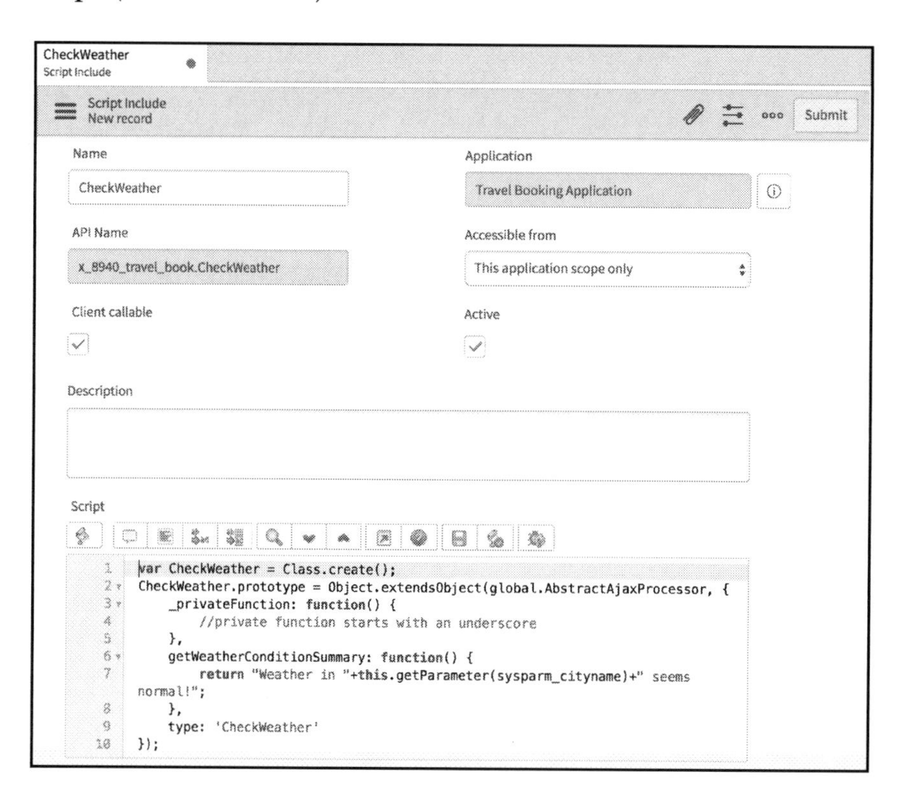

The code to be populated in the **Script** field is provided here for quick reference:

```
var CheckWeather = Class.create();
CheckWeather.prototype = Object.extendsObject(global.AbstractAjaxProcessor,
{
     _privateFunction: function() {
          //private function starts with an underscore
     },
     getWeatherConditionSummary: function() {
         return "Weather in "+this.getParameter(sysparm_cityname)+" seems
normal!";
     },
     type: 'CheckWeather'
});
```

In the preceding code, we created a new class named `CheckWeather` and set its prototype to extend the class `global.AbstractAjaxProcessor`. We extended the abstract AJAX class because we intend to create a client callable script include. Furthermore, we defined two functions. The `_privateFunction` is a private function as it begins with an underscore symbol and cannot be called from other scripts. The second function we created is `getWeatherConditionSummary`, which can be called from other scripts and accepts a parameter named `cityname`.

Let us now create a client-side script that makes the AJAX request to call the `getWeatherConditionSummary` function defined in the `CheckWeather` class.

Open a **New Client Script** form in **Studio** by selecting **Client Development** | **Client Script** in the **Create Application File** wizard and fill in the following values:

- **Name**: `Get destination weather summary`
- **Table**: **Booking Request**
- **UI Type**: **Desktop**
- **Type**: **onChange**
- **Field name**: **Destination**
- **Active**: Checked
- **Global**: Checked
- **Script**: (As detailed here)

We will use the following code in the **Script** field of our client script:

```
function onChange(control, oldValue, newValue, isLoading, isTemplate) {
if (isLoading || newValue === '') {
return;
   }
varloc = g_form.getReference("u_destination_location",getWeatherSummary);
}
function getWeatherSummary(destination) {
   varga = new GlideAjax("x_8940_travel_book.CheckWeather");
   ga.addParam('sysparm_name', 'getWeatherConditionSummary');
   ga.addParam('sysparm_cityname', destination.name );
   ga.getXML(CheckWeatherCallback);
}
function CheckWeatherCallback(response) {
var answer = response.responseXML.documentElement.getAttribute("answer");
g_form.showErrorBox("u_destination_location",answer);
}
```

The preceding code will invoke the AJAX call to the script include we created earlier in the chapter. The response will be shown as an error box message around the **Destination** field.

If the GlideAjax code seems difficult to understand, be a little patient. We will learn how to make similar client-server calls using RestAPIs and workflows in the later chapters, which will be much easier than understanding and writing GlideAjax code.

# UI actions

Let us now create a server-side UI action. A UI action can be invoked from different UI elements, such as form buttons, form list context menus, form-related links, list of records header context menus, list actions menus, or list-related links. UI actions are usually server-side code, and can make use of script includes and other server-side client APIs. However, it is also possible to mark a UI action to run on client- and write- and use-only client-side glide APIs.

For the purpose of this book, we will create server-side UI actions. Our goal is to provide a button on the top of the form, in the form header and context menu, to allow users to set the state of a pending or open booking request as a work in progress.

To create a new UI action, open **Studio**, select **Server Development** | **UI Action** from the **Create Application File** wizard, and click **Create**:

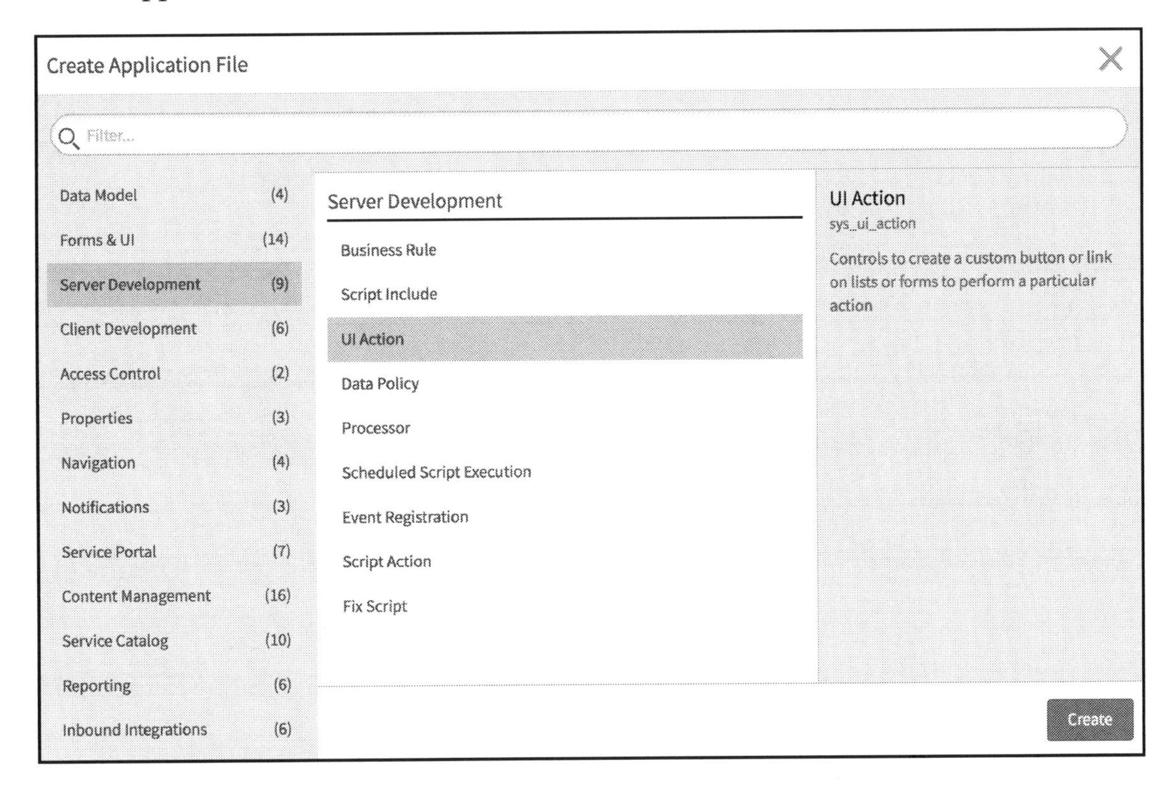


Fill in the **UI action New Record** form with the following values:

- **Name**: `In Progress`
- **Table**: **Booking Request**
- **Action name**: `mark_in_progress`
- **Show insert**: Unchecked
- **Show update**: Checked
- **Client**: Unchecked
- **Form button**: Checked
- **Form context menu**: Checked
- **Condition**: `javascript:(current.state==-5 || current.state==1)`
- **Script**: (As detailed here)
- **Protection policy**: **Read-only**

The script for the UI action is very simple and is comprised of just two lines of code:

```
current.state=2; //2 refers to work in progress
current.update(); //unlike before business rules explicit call to save the
form is required in UI actions
```

The **Form button** and **Form context menu** will appear when the condition we have defined in the UI action evaluates to true. The script will execute when we click on the **Form button** or the **Form context menu** we have defined using the UI action. All we are trying to do in the script is to mark the state field as a work in progress.

Let us test our UI action by switching to the main service now interface and opening an existing record in the `Booking Request` table. Open the **Travel Booking Application** | **Booking Request** list of records module and click on one of the existing records to open it in edit form. If the record is either in a pending or open state, then the condition defined in the UI action will match and we will be able to see a button and context menu entry in the form header.

The **In Progress** form button UI action will appear on the form header, as shown here:

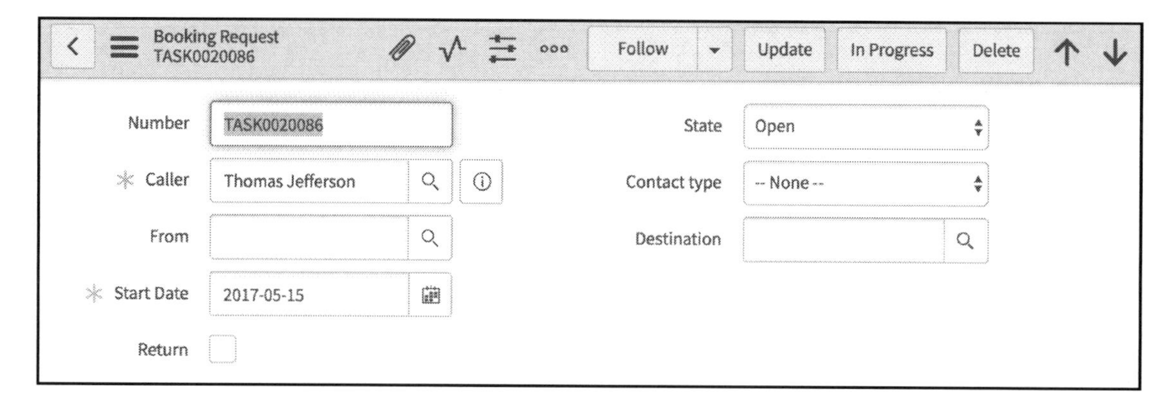

The **In Progress** form context menu UI action is shown here:

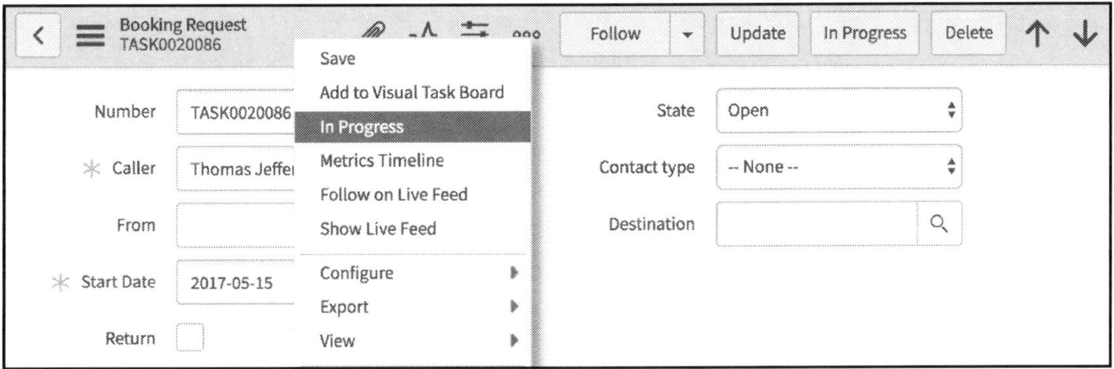

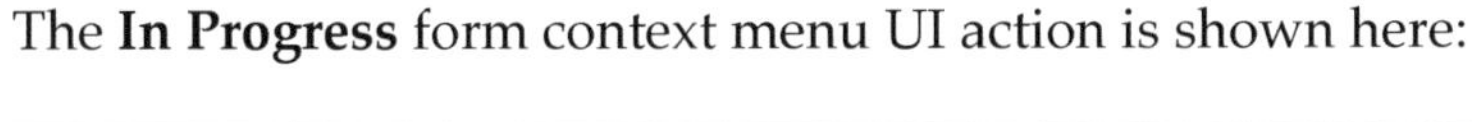

Similarly, we can create a form-related link and actions for the list of records modules by checking the different options available in the UI action form.

# Summary

In this chapter, we covered business rules, script includes, and UI actions. We learned about different types of server-side scripts and how to make use of the `GlideRecord` API to perform database operations. We also learned how to create a UI action that can be invoked from any client-side code, including the client script, using GlideAjax.

Furthermore, we learned about the options available when creating a business rule and understood when different conditions are available. In the next chapter, we will learn how to write Jelly scripts to enhance the user interface and how to use features such as UI macros and formatters.

# 9
# Jelly Scripting

Now that we have learned about and created some client- and server-side scripts in the ServiceNow platform, let us learn about UI pages and macros, along with Jelly scripts.

In the ServiceNow platform, Apache's Jelly syntax is used to render forms and UI pages. Jelly is comprised of Java- and XML-based scripting and a transformation engine used to turn XML into executable code. The output is usually HTML and JavaScript code that is used by the browser to render elements on a page.

In this chapter, we will learn how to create UI pages, UI macros, and formatters. We will learn how to make use of Jelly scripts to enhance our UIs and create custom controls.

In this chapter, we will cover the following topics:

- Jelly scripts
- UI macros
- Formatters
- UI pages

## Jelly scripts

Before we create any artifacts, let us first learn a bit about Apache Jelly and how it is used within the ServiceNow platform.

Basic knowledge of XML is important for this chapter. Apache Jelly follows XML syntax, and thus any developer with prior knowledge of XML, HTML, XHTML, or JavaScript should be able to learn it quickly. The project homepage is located at `http://commons.apache.org/proper/commons-jelly/`.

In the ServiceNow platform, Apache's Jelly syntax is used to render forms, lists, UI pages, and other elements in the browser. Jelly script is comprised of XML and HTML code. Jelly brings in its own set of XML tags, known as Jelly tags, using a specific XML namespace. ServiceNow has also implemented some extension to Jelly tags, referred to as Glide tags. The Jelly scripting is only used in UI macros and UI pages that run on the server. The Jelly code, which is mostly XML code, converts to HTML before it is sent to the browser.

When creating UI pages and other artifacts, we can use Jelly and Glide tags, but also employ HTML and JavaScript codes. It is important to close all HTML tags within Jelly scripts, even if the tag in question is a `void` tag. For example, `<img>` is a void element as it doesn't require a closing `</img>` tag. There are many other void elements in HTML, such as `<br>`. The slash is syntactic sugar for these in which it is optional to close the element. However, when writing Jelly scripts, it is mandatory that we always close these tags.

# Namespaces and phases

Just like any language based on XML, Apache Jelly includes multiple namespaces. The `xmlns:j` is used for Jelly, whereas the `xmlns:g` is used to include the Glide namespace. When referring to tags within Jelly and `glide` namespaces, we only use the prefixes `j` and `g` respectively. There are two other namespaces available: `xmlns:j2` and `xmlns:g2`. These usually represent the phase of the script, where we either use `<j>` versus `<j2>`and `<g>` versus `<g2>`.

All Jelly script in ServiceNow will start with the following line of code:

```
<j:jelly trim= "false" xmlns:j= "jelly:core" xmlns:g= "glide" xmlns:j2=
"null" xmlns:g2= "null" >
```

In the preceding script, we include `jelly:core` and `glide` namespaces, and they will be referred to the script using the `j` and `g` prefixes respectively. The `j` prefix is used for tags that are native to Apache Jelly, whereas the `g` prefix is used for tags that ServiceNow platform extended and included in the platform. Similarly, the `j2` and `g2` prefixes are like `j` and `g`; however, they are processed only in the second phase:

```
<j:jelly trim="false" xmlns:j="jelly:core" xmlns:g="glide" xmlns:j2="null"
xmlns:g2="null">
<j:setvar="jvar_message" value="Hello" />
<j2:setvar="jvar_name" value="Sagar Gupta" />
${jvar_message} $[jvar_name]
</j:jelly>
```

In the preceding code, we have used the `j:set` and `j2:set` tags. The code will be parsed and executed twice in two different phases, namely phase I and phase II. Furthermore, variables in phase I are enclosed in curly brackets prefixed with a dollar sign, such as `${jvar_variable_1}`, and in phase II are enclosed in square brackets prefixed with a dollar sign, such as `$[jvar_variable_2]`.

The `j:set` tag, along with the `${jvar_message}`, will evaluate in phase I, and the code will be cached for all subsequent calls to this script. The cached code for phase II will appear to the system like the one shown here:

```
<j:jelly trim="false" xmlns:j="jelly:core" xmlns:g="glide"
xmlns:j2="jelly:core" xmlns:g2="glide">
<j2:setvar="name" value="Sagar Gupta" />
Hello $[jvar_name]
</j:jelly>
```

Note that in the preceding code, the `j:set` tag and `${jvar_message}` have already evaluated and are not part of the phase II code. Only `j2` and `g2` tags, along with the variables enclosed in `$[jvar_square_brackets]`, are available for subsequent execution.

Let us now go through some of the Jelly and Glide tags.

# Jelly tags

The following are a few of the core tags of Apache Jelly.

## j:if tag

The `j:if` tag is used to conditionally evaluate its body based on some expression. Unlike other programming languages, there aren't any else-if or else options. It accepts the following attribute:

- `test`: This is used to specify the Jelly expression (condition) to evaluate. If the expression evaluates to `true`, the body of the tag is evaluated.

For example:

```
<g:evaluatevar="jvar_gr" object="true">
var gr = new GlideRecord("x_8940_travel_book_booking_request");
gr.addQuery("active", true);
gr.query();
gr;
```

```
</g:evaluate>
<j:if test="${!jvar_gr.hasNext()}">
We did not find any active incidents.
</j:if>
<j:if test="${jvar_gr.next()}">
We found ${jvar_gr.getRowCount()} active incidents.
</j:if>
```

# j:choose, j:when, and j:otherwise

Similar to the `j:if` tag, the `j:choose` tag is used to conditionally evaluate its body based on an expression. Each of the `j:when` tags within the body of the `j:choosetag` is evaluated in the order it is written. If one of the `j:when` tags evaluates to true, the block of the j:when tag is executed and the rest are ignored. When no `j:when` conditions evaluate to true, the `j:otherwise` block is executed. The `j:choose` and `j:otherwise` tags don't require any attributes. The `j:when` tag accepts the following attribute:

- `test`: This is used to specify the Jelly expression (condition) to evaluate. If the expression evaluates to `true`, the body of the tag is evaluated.

For example:

```
<j:choose>
<j:when test="${jvar_gr.getRowCount() ${AMP}lt; 1}">
  We found multiple matching records!
</j:when>
<j:when test="${jvar_gr.next()}">
  We found ${jvar_gr.getValue('number') record}
</j:when>
<j:otherwise>
  Sorry no record found.
</j:otherwise>
</j:choose>
```

# j:set

The `j:set` tag is used to set a variable and its value. It accepts the following attributes:

- `var`: The name of the variable
- `value`: The value of the variable. This is a Jelly expression and can be used to include variables that contain `${jvar_curly_brackets}` and `$[jvar_square_brackets]`

- `defaultValue`: If the value evaluates to null or is empty, then the value specified in the `defaultValue` attribute is set to the variable

For example:

```
<j:setvar="jvar_booking_request_number"
value="${jvar_gr.getValue('number')}"/>
```

# The j:set_if tag

The `j:set_if` tag is used to set the value of a variable based on a condition. If the condition evaluates to `true`, the value specified in the `true` attribute is set. Otherwise, the value specified in the `false` attribute is set. It is similar to the ternary operator in many programming languages--`var x = test ?true : false`. It accepts the following attributes:

- `var`: The name of the variable to set. We usually use the `jvar_` prefix for consistency.
- `test`: The test expression to be used to determine whether to evaluate the `true` or `false` value. This should be a Jelly expression enclosed in `${}` or `$[]`, and must evaluate to boolean value.
- `true`: The value to set the variable to if the expression in the `test` attribute evaluates to `true`.
- `false`: The value to set the variable to if the expression in the `test` attribute evaluates to `false`.

For example:

```
<g2:set_if
var="jvar_style"
test="$[gs.getPreference('table.compact') != 'false']"
true="margin-top:0px; margin-bottom:0px;"
false="margin-top:2px;
margin-bottom:2px;" />
```

## The j:while tag

The `j:while` tag is used to perform the `while` loop. The `while` loop continues till the `test` expression condition evaluates to `true`. The `while` loop breaks once the condition evaluates to `false`. We can also manually break out of the `j:while` loop using the `j:break` tag. The `j:while` tag accepts the following attributes:

- `test`: This is used to specify the Jelly expression (condition) to evaluate. If the expression evaluates to `true`, the body of the tag is evaluated.

For example:

```
<g:evaluatevar="jvar_gr" object="true">
  var gr = new GlideRecord("incident");
  gr.addQuery("active", true);
  gr.query();
  gr;
</g:evaluate>
<ul>
  <j:while test="${jvar_gr.next()}">
    <li>${jvar_gr.getValue('number')}</li>
</j:while>
</ul>
```

# Glide tags

Let us now go through some of the Glide tags in the ServiceNow platform.

## g:evaluate

The `g:evaluate` tag is used to execute server-side JavaScript code. The body of the tag is used to write JavaScript code. The code written in the `g:evaluate` tag has the same scope as a script include, and can make use of server-side Glide APIs such as `GlideSystem` and `GlideRecord`. It is also useful to make calls to global business rules and script includes. Furthermore, it can also access variables defined in the Jelly code when the `jelly` attribute is set to `true`. It accepts the following attributes:

- `var`: The name of the variable that will be used to set the output.

- `object: Boolean`: If `true`, the output is considered to be an object (array, `GlideObject`, and so on); otherwise, it is treated as a primitive object, like an integer or string.
- `jelly`: When set as `true`, the variables in the Jelly context are made available to the script. The Jelly context variables are referenced using the `jelly.` prefix within the `g:evaluate` block.
- `copyToPhase2`: (Optional) If set to true, the
- `expression`: This can be optionally used to specify the JavaScript code instead of writing it in the body of the `g:evaluate` tag.

Example 1--standard `g:evaluate` script:

```
<g:evaluatevar="jvar_gr" object="true">
var gr = new GlideRecord("x_8940_travel_book_booking_request");
gr.addQuery("active", "true");
gr.query();
gr;
</g:evaluate>
```

Example 2--using the `expression` attribute instead of the code block:

```
<g:evaluatevar="user" expression="gs.getUser()"/>
```

Example 3--using the `copyToPhase2` attribute:

```
<g:evaluatevar="jvar_special_var" copyToPhase2="true">
varspecialVar = gs.tableExists("x_8940_travel_book_booking_request");
 specialVar; //last line is used to set the output to var
</g:evaluate>
<b>$[jvar_special_var]</b>
```

In the preceding code, the value of the `gr` object will be available in the Jelly code using the variable name `jvar_gr` specified in the `var` attribute. The last line is used to set the (return) value to the specified variable.

## g:breakpoint

The `g:breakpoint` tag can be used to dump the values of all variables or a specific variable into the system log. It is useful for debugging purposes while developing Jelly scripts. It accepts the following attributes:

- `var`: (Optional) The `var` attribute can be used to specify the name of the variable whose value needs to be dumped into the system log. If no `var` attribute is specified, then the system dumps all variables (including values) into the Jelly context available until the current execution.

Example 1--dumping all variables:

```
<g:breakpoint />
```

Example 2--dumping a specific variable:

```
<g:breakpointvar="sysparm_view"/>
```

## g:macro_invoke

The `g:macro_invoke` tag can be used to call a UI macro. The name of the macro needs to be specified in the `macro` attribute. Alternatively, a macro can be included by calling `g:name_of_a_macro`, as illustrated in the following examples. It can accept the following attributes:

- `macro`: The name of the macro to be executed. This attribute is required when using the `g:macro_invoke tag`; however, it can be ignored if you are using the `g:name_of_the_macrosystax`.

We can pass other attributes to this tag. All the attributes that we pass here will be available in the scope of the UI macro that is being invoked.

Example 1--using `g:macro_invoke` with the macro attribute:

```
<g:macro_invoke macro="sample_macro" message="This is a sample macro
variable." />
```

Example 2--using the `g:name_of_the_macro` syntax without the `macro` attribute:

```
<g:sample_macro message="This is a sample macro variable." />
```

# g:ui_form

The `g:ui_form` is used to define an HTML form. For example:

```
<g:ui_form>
<p>This is a form generated using &lt;g:uiform&gt;</p>
<g:dialog_buttons_ok_cancel ok="return true" />
<input type="hidden" name="hidden_field_name"
value="some value"/>
</g:ui_form>
```

# g:ui_input_field and g:checkbox

The `g:ui_input_field` and `g:checkbox` tags can be used to add HTML text input and checkbox fields respectively in any `g:ui_form`.

For example:

```
<g:ui_form>
<table>
<tr>
<tdnowrap="true"><label>WeatherProvider:</label></td>
<td><g:ui_input_field name="weather_provider"
value="Default"
size="50"/></td>
</tr>
<tr>
<tdnowrap="true"><label>Check Weather:</label></td>
<td><g:ui_checkbox name="check_weather_active"
value="checked"/></td>
</tr>
</table>
</g:ui_form>
```

# g:dialog_buttons_ok_cancel

The `g:dialog_buttons_ok_cancel` tag can be used to show the **Submit** or **Cancel** button in a UI page. When it is specified inside the block of a `g:ui_form` tag in a UI page, it can submit the form and execute the processing script defined in the UI page. Either the `ok` or `cancel` attribute must be set, and it must be an expression that evaluates to a Boolean value:

```
<g:ui_form>
<p>Click OK to run the processing script.</p>
<g:dialog_buttons_ok_cancel ok="return true"/>
<input type="hidden" name="application_sys_id"
value="499836460a0a0b1700003e7ad950b5da"/>
</g:ui_form>
```

# g:ui_reference

The `g:ui_reference` tag can be used to include a reference field within a UI page. The reference field accepts the following parameters:

- `name`: The name of the field that can be used to refer to it in the processing script and JavaScript
- `id`: The identifier to be used in the DOM element
- `table`: The name of the table that the reference field will be pointing to
- `query`: The string query value that can be used to filter data available to be selected in the field
- `columns`: The list of columns available while selecting values

For example:

```
<g:ui_reference name="booking_req_id" id="booking_req_id"
table="x_8940_travel_book_booking_request"
query="active=true"
columns="number;short_description"/>
```

## g:insert

The `g:insert` tag can be used to insert the Jelly code in a different file (UI page or macro) into your Jelly in a new context. When the Jelly code is inserted in a new context, the variables previously established in your Jelly are not available to the new code.

For example:

```
<j:setvar="jvar_message" value="Hello World!" />
<g:insert template="hello.xml" />
```

In the preceding example, the `jvar_message` variable will not be available to the included `hello.xml` template.

## g:inline

The `g:inline` tag can also be used to insert code into Jelly; however, unlike the `g:insert` tag, it makes the variables available to the included Jelly code.

For example:

```
<j:setvar="jvar_message" value="Hello World!" />
<g:inline template="hello.xml" />
```

In the preceding example, the `jvar_message` variable will be available in the `hello.xml` template.

## g:function and g:call

The `g:function` and `g:call` tags can be used to implement much better encapsulation than that offered by the `g:insert` and `g:inline` tags. The `g:function` tag can be added to your Jelly code to define the parameters it can accept by specifying them as one of the attributes of the tag. If we want to mark one of the attributes as required, we have to set its value to `REQUIRED`. Any other value will mean that the field is not required and will have a default value.

For example -`g:function`:

```
<g:function id="REQUIRED" city="REQUIRED" address="" zipcode="REQUIRED"/>
```

In the preceding example, the attributes `id`, `city`, and `zipcode` are required. The `address` attribute is marked as nonmandatory and doesn't have a default value.

The g:call, on the other hand, is used to include code and pass parameters to a Jelly code that has implemented the g:function tag.

For example - g:call:

```
<g:call function="demo_code.xml" id="${jvar_id}" city="New
York"zipcode="10006" />
```

In the preceding example, we include the demo_code.xml Jelly script and pass values from the current scope to the included file using attributes.

# Special characters in Jelly

When writing code in Jelly, we have to take special care when using some special characters, such as & (Ampersand), < (LESS THAN), and && (AND), among others. Let us take a look at how to write these special characters in Jelly scripts.

## Ampersand--&

The ampersand sign (&) causes Jelly scripts to get into a lot of errors as it is based on XML. To avoid causing Jelly scripts to break, we need to use ${AMP} or $[AMP], depending on the phase in which we insert the ampersand.

For example:

```
someArray = x.split('$[AMP]');
```

## AND--&&

The double ampersand is usually used as an AND condition within the if statement in JavaScript and other programming languages. However, using && in Jelly script may cause errors. We can use the ${AMP} or $[AMP] tag, depending on the phase.

For example:

```
if (x == y ${AND} a != b ) varc = d;
```

## LESS THAN--<

The LESS THAN sign (<) can cause a lot of <indexentry content="Jelly:LESS THAN--error in any XML-based language, including Jelly. To avoid errors when using the < sign, use `${AMP}lt;` instead.

For example:

```
if ( x ${AMP}lt; y ) a = x;
```

## Whitespace

The Jelly script usually trims the whitespaces, which is good for reducing the output size. However, there might be conditions where we want to preserve whitespaces. To do this, simply use the `j:whitespace` tag with the `trim` attribute set to `false`.

For example:

```
<j2:whitespace trim="false">${gs.getMessage('City Name')}: </j2:whitespace>
```

## Space

The space can be encoded just like the HTML entity ` ` by using the special Jelly variable `${SP}` or `$[SP]`, depending on the phase.

For example:

```
<span id="gsft_domain" style="display: inline">
${gs.getMessage('Weather')}:$[SP]
${gs.getMessage("Loading...")}
</span>
```

Now that we have learned the basics of Jelly and Glide tags, let us employ this newly acquired knowledge to create some UI pages, UI macros, and formatters.

# UI pages

Now let us create our first UI page that will show the statistics of the records stored in the `Booking Request` table. To create a new UI page, open **Studio** and in the **Create Application File** wizard, select **Forms & UI** | **UI Page** and click on the **Create** button, as shown here:

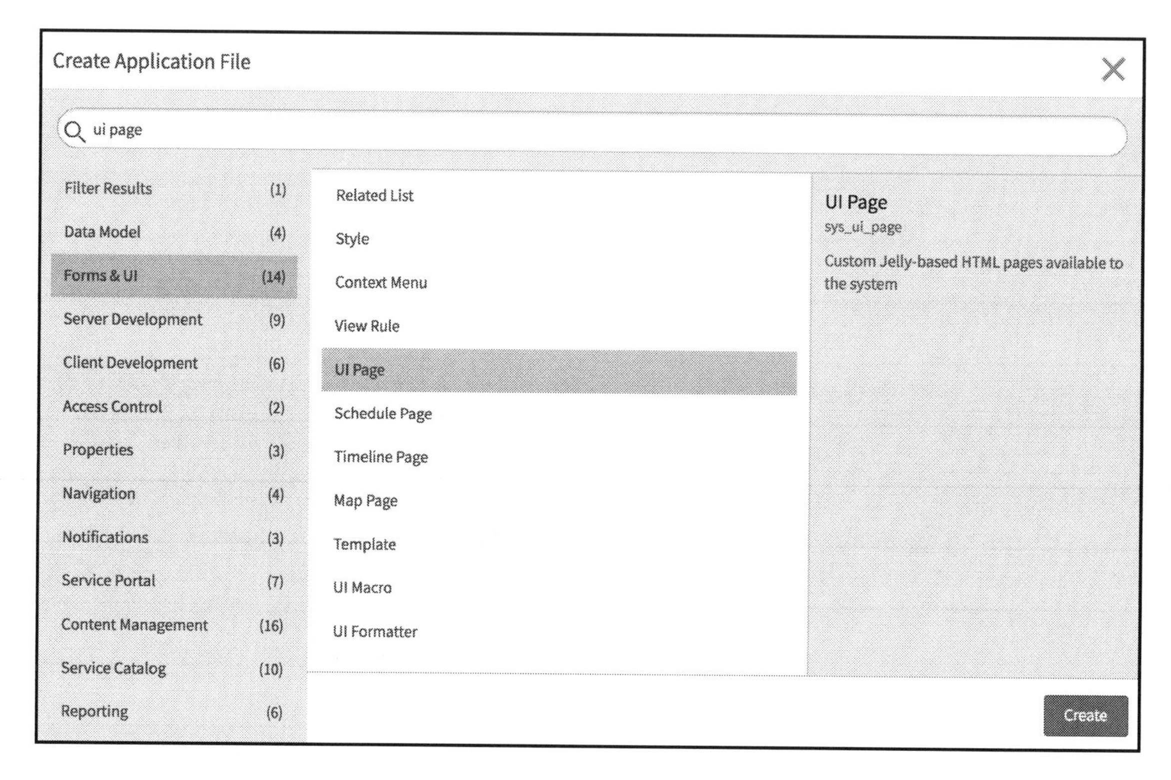


The UI page new record form will be shown. Now populate the field with the following values:

- **Name**: `app_properties` (the name field must not contain any spaces)
- **Category**: **General**
- **Endpoint**: (This will be automatically generated when we enter a name)
- **HTML**: (Use the code mentioned after the following screenshot)

- Leave the **Client script** and **Processing script** empty for now

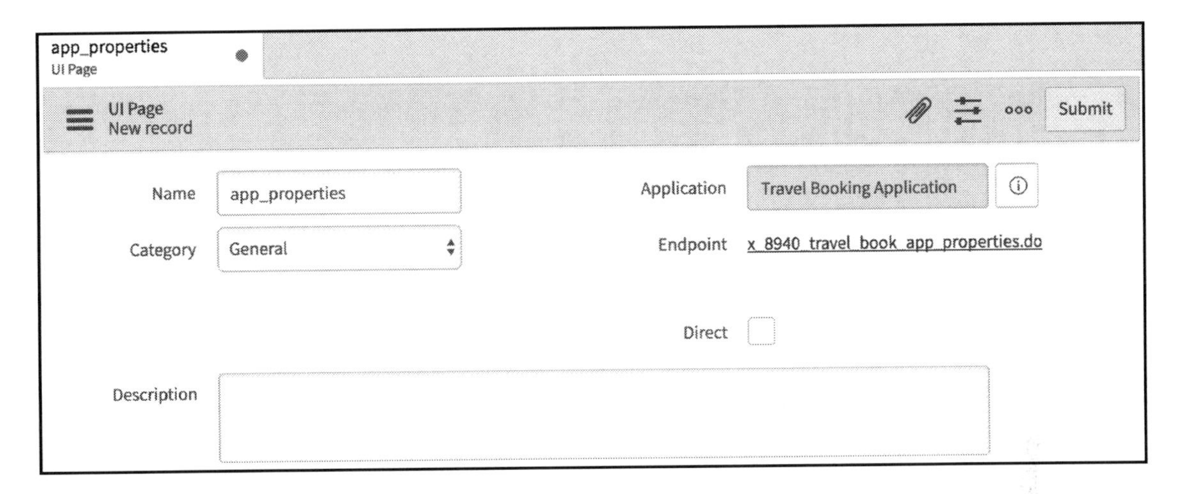


Use the following code in the **HTML** field:

```
<?xml version="1.0" encoding="utf-8" ?>
<j:jelly trim="false" xmlns:j="jelly:core" xmlns:g="glide" xmlns:j2="null"
xmlns:g2="null">
<g:ui_form>
   <table style="border-collapse: separate; border-spacing: 5px 5px;">
   <tr>
         <th></th>
         <th>Travel booking application settings description</th>
   </tr>
   <tr><td colspan="2" height="15px"></td></tr>
   <tr>
         <td><g:ui_checkbox name="check_weather_from" /></td>
         <td> Do you want to check latest weather condition at From
location? </td>
   </tr>
   <tr>
         <td><g:ui_checkbox name="check_weather_destination" /></td>
         <td> Do you want to check latest weather condition at Destination
location? </td>
   </tr>
   <tr><td colspan="2" height="15px"></td></tr>
   <tr><td colspan="2">
         <g:dialog_buttons_ok_cancel ok="return true"/>
   </td></tr>
   </table>
</g:ui_form>
</j:jelly>
```

The preceding Jelly script includes HTML and glide-specific UI elements. The output will contain a table and two checkboxes named `check_weather_destination` and `check_weather_from`.

Now click on the **Submit** button to create our new UI page. We can test the page by clicking on the endpoint URL and opening the link in a new tab. In order to open the newly created UI page in the content frame of the main interface of ServiceNow, we will have to create a new module and link it to the UI page.

In **Studio**, open the **Create Application File** wizard and select **Navigation** | **Module,** as shown in the following screenshot, and click on the **Create** button. This will open up the **New Module Record** page:

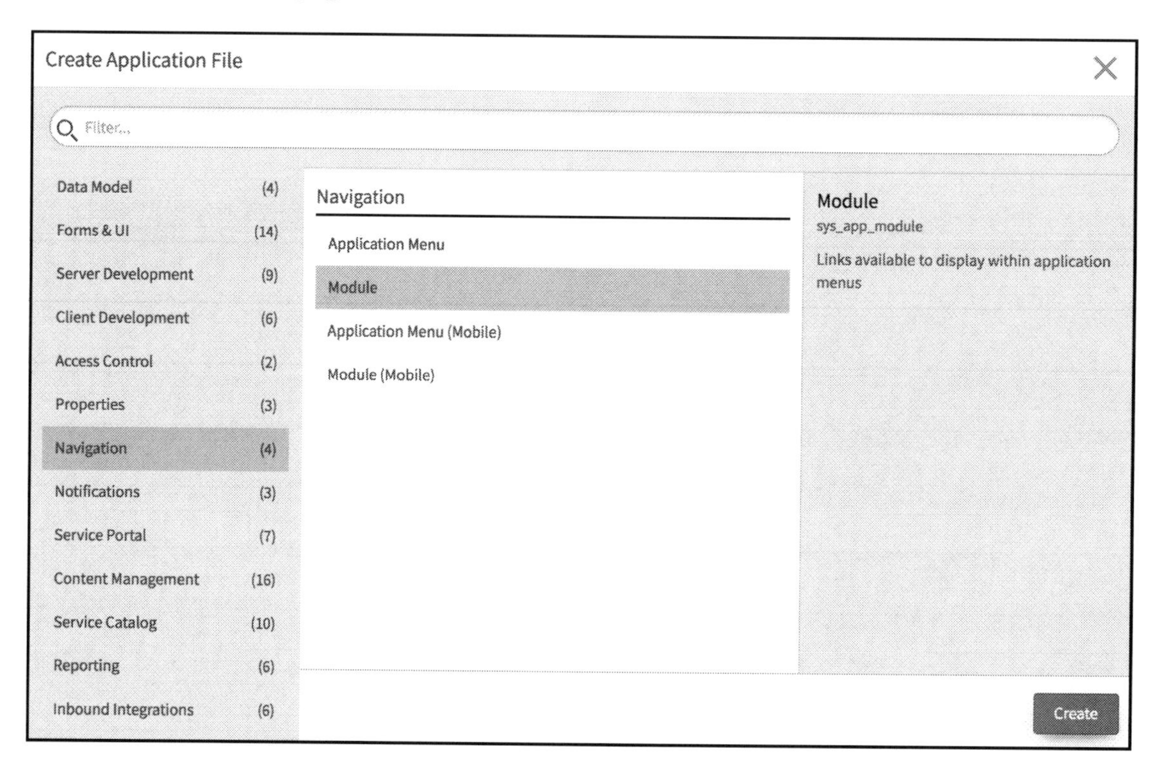


In the **New Module Record** form, enter the following values:

- **Name:** `Travel Booking Properties`
- **Application menu**: **Travel Booking Application**

- **Order**: `70`
- **Link type: URL (from Arguments:)**
- *** Arguments**: `/x_8940_travel_book_app_properties.do` (replace `8940` with your company code)

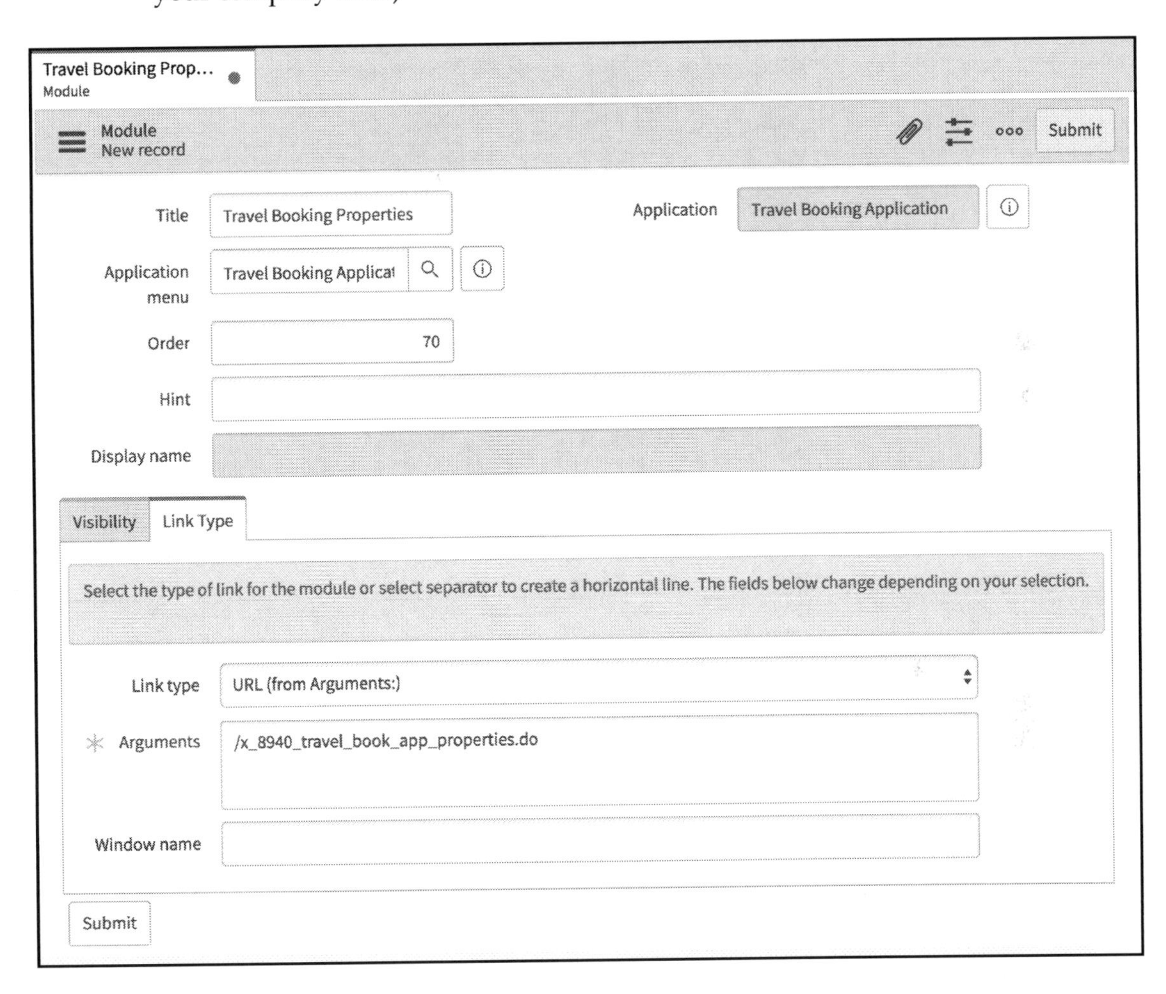

Once you populate the fields, click on the **Submit** button to create a new navigation link under the **Travel Booking Application**. The navigation link for the new module will appear in the navigation section of the main ServiceNow interface, as shown in the following screenshot:

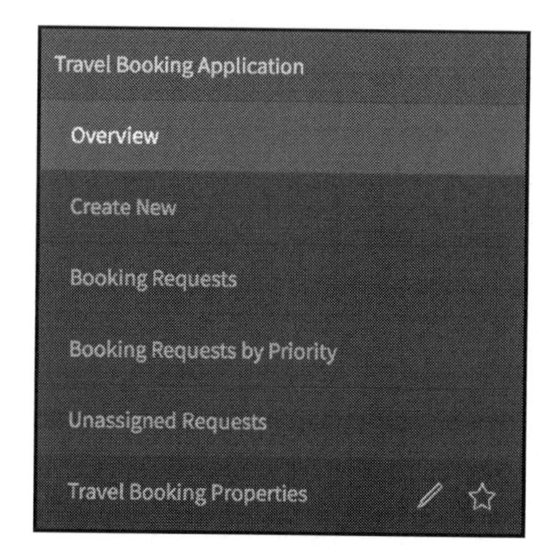


As shown in the following screenshot, when we click on the **Travel Booking Properties** navigation link under **Travel Booking Application**, the content frame of the interface will load the UI page we created in the previous step:

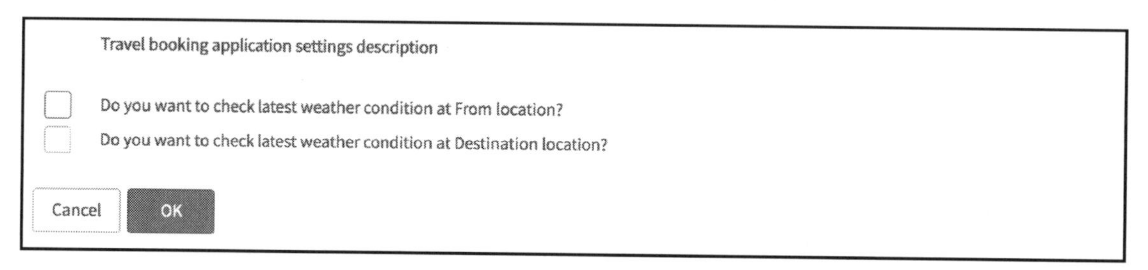


When we click on the **OK** button, the page will submit the form and try to execute the processing script part of the UI script, which is currently blank. So let us now create the functionality to save the values of the two checkboxes in **System Properties**. To do this, we will first define two system properties for both of the fields.

To create a new system property, open the **Create Application File** wizard in **Studio**, select **Properties** | **System Property**, as shown in the following screenshot, and click **Create**:

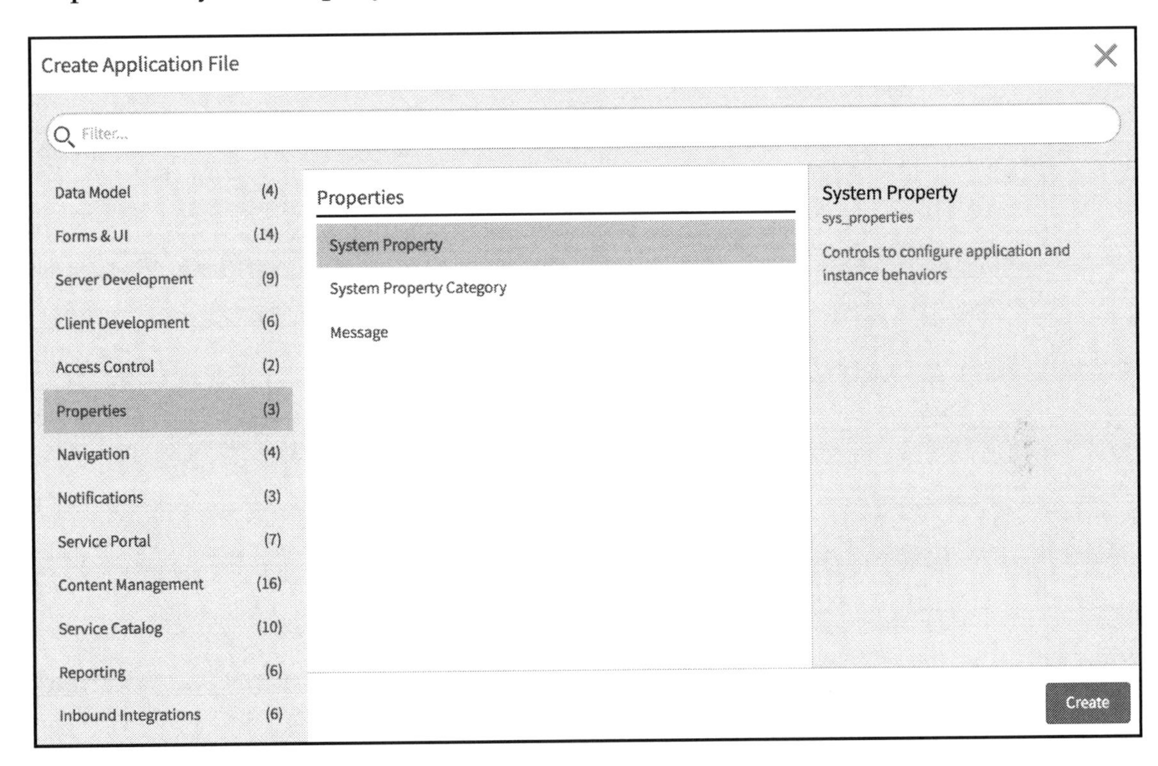


This will open up the **System Property New Record** form. Fill in the form with the following values:

- **Suffix**: `check_weather_from`
- **Name**: `x_8940_travel_book.check_weather_from`

- **Description:** `Check weather at From location`
- **Type: true | false**
- **Value:** `false`

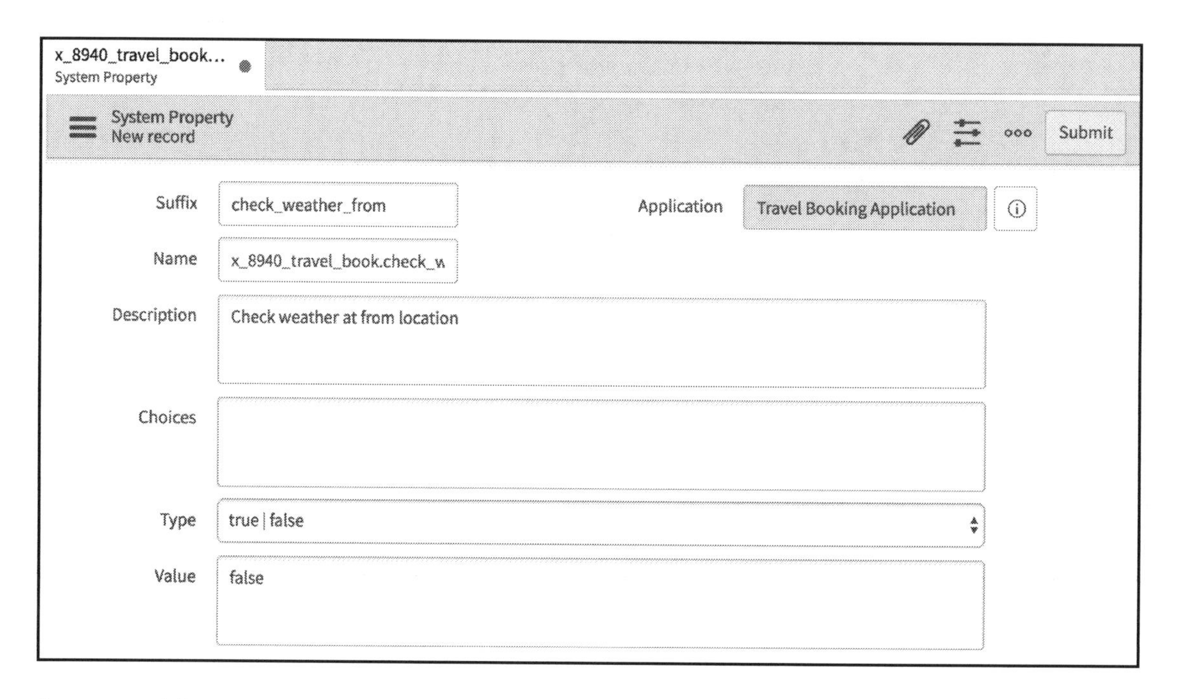


Once you fill in the form, click on the **Submit** button to create our first system property named `x_8940_travel_book.check_weather_from`. Similarly, create a new system property with the suffix `check_weather_destination` by repeating the steps we followed for the first property.

As shown here, the newly created system properties will appear under the **Properties** tree in the **Application Explorer** section of the **Studio**:

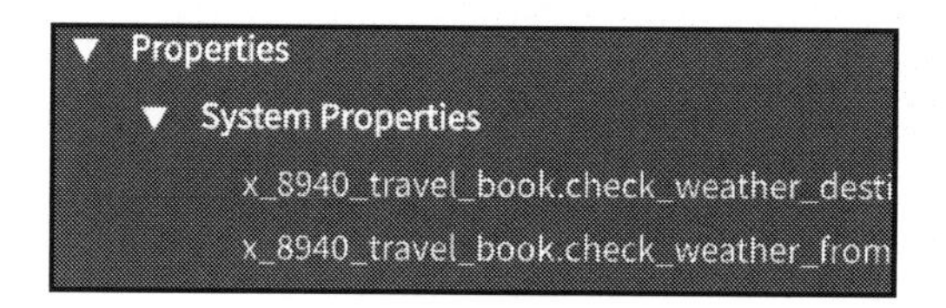

Once we have the properties created, we can now create the processing script of our UI page.

## Processing script

Let us now write our first processing script code that will enable the functionality to store the values of the checkboxes in the UI page in the system properties we just defined. The processing script is written while defining the UI page and is executed when we submit the form in the UI page.

Open the UI page named `app_properties` that we created earlier in the chapter. Scroll to the processing **Script** field and write the following code:

```
//set the value of the check_weather_from system property
gs.setProperty("x_8940_travel_book.check_weather_from",
check_weather_from);

//set the value of the check_weather_destination sys property
gs.setProperty("x_8940_travel_book.check_weather_destination",
check_weather_destination);
```

The preceding code makes use of the `GlideSystem` server-side glide API, and sets the values to the properties we created in the previous step. The `setProperty` method accepts the name of the property along with the value. The value is passed to the processing script through the form we created in the HTML section of the UI page.

We will also add the following lines of code prior to the `table` tag in the **HTML** field:

```
<g:evaluatevar="jvar_weather_from">
   varweather_from =
gs.getProperty('x_8940_travel_book.check_weather_from');
   weather_from;
</g:evaluate>
<g:evaluatevar="jvar_weather_destination">
   varweather_destination =
gs.getProperty('x_8940_travel_book.check_weather_destination');
   weather_destination;
</g:evaluate>
```

The preceding `g:evaluate` tag will make use of the `getProperty` method of the `GlideSystem` API and set the values to the `jvar_weather_from` and `jvar_weather_destination` variables. The variables will be used to set the values of the `g:ui_checkbox` tags, as seen in the following code:

```
<g:ui_checkbox name="check_weather_from"
        value="${jvar_weather_from}" />
...
<g:ui_checkbox name="check_weather_destination"
        value="${jvar_weather_destination}" />
```

The entire code of the **HTML** field is shown here:

```
<?xml version="1.0" encoding="utf-8" ?>
<j:jelly trim="false" xmlns:j="jelly:core" xmlns:g="glide" xmlns:j2="null"
xmlns:g2="null">
<g:evaluatevar="jvar_weather_from">
    varweather_from =
gs.getProperty('x_8940_travel_book.check_weather_from');
    weather_from;
</g:evaluate>
<g:evaluatevar="jvar_weather_destination">
    varweather_destination =
gs.getProperty('x_8940_travel_book.check_weather_destination');
    weather_destination;
</g:evaluate>
<g:ui_form>
    <table style="border-collapse: separate; border-spacing: 5px 5px;">
    <tr>
            <th></th>
            <th>Travel booking application settings description</th>
    </tr>
    <tr><td colspan="2" height="15px"></td></tr>
    <tr>
            <td><g:ui_checkbox name="check_weather_from"
            value="${jvar_weather_from}" /></td>
            <td>Do you want to check latest weather condition at From
location?</td>
    </tr>
    <tr>
            <td><g:ui_checkbox name="check_weather_destination"
            value="${jvar_weather_destination}" /></td>
            <td>Do you want to check latest weather condition at Destination
location?</td>
    </tr>
    <tr><td colspan="2" height="15px"></td></tr>
    <tr><td colspan="2">
```

```
            <g:dialog_buttons_ok_cancel ok="return true"
                cancel="return false"/>
        </td></tr>
        </table>
    </g:ui_form>
    </j:jelly>
```

To ensure our code is working properly, open the page in the main interface using the **Travel Booking Application | Travel Booking Properties** module. As shown in the following screenshot, try to check one or both of the checkboxes and click on the **OK** button. If everything goes well, the form will reload and we can see the values getting stored and retried properly:

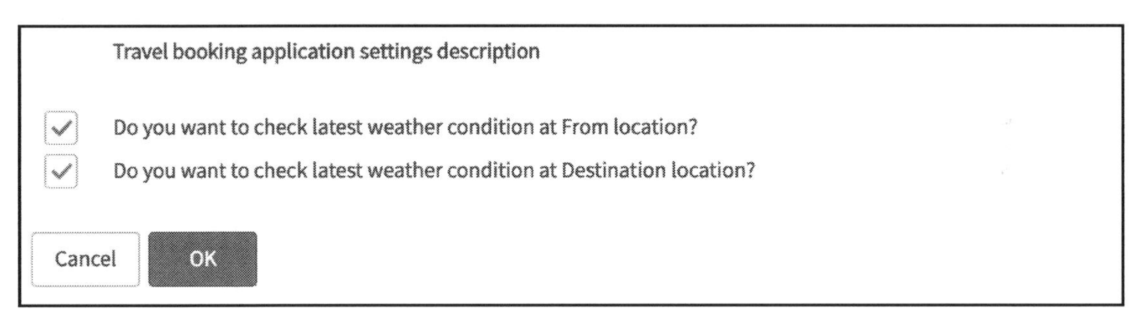


Let us now create a UI macro, which is also created by writing Jelly script similar to the HTML section of the UI page.

# UI macros

A UI macro is similar to the HTML section of the UI page and consists of Jelly code. The UI macro, however, is not tied to any page, and can be reused in multiple places in the system, including (using `g:insert`, `g:inline`, or `g:call`) other UI macros and UI pages. It can also be added to a form by creating a formatter and adding it to the form. Let us now create our first UI macro.

In **Studio**, open the **Create Application File** wizard and select **Forms & UI** | **Macro**, as shown in the following screenshot, and click on the **Create** button:

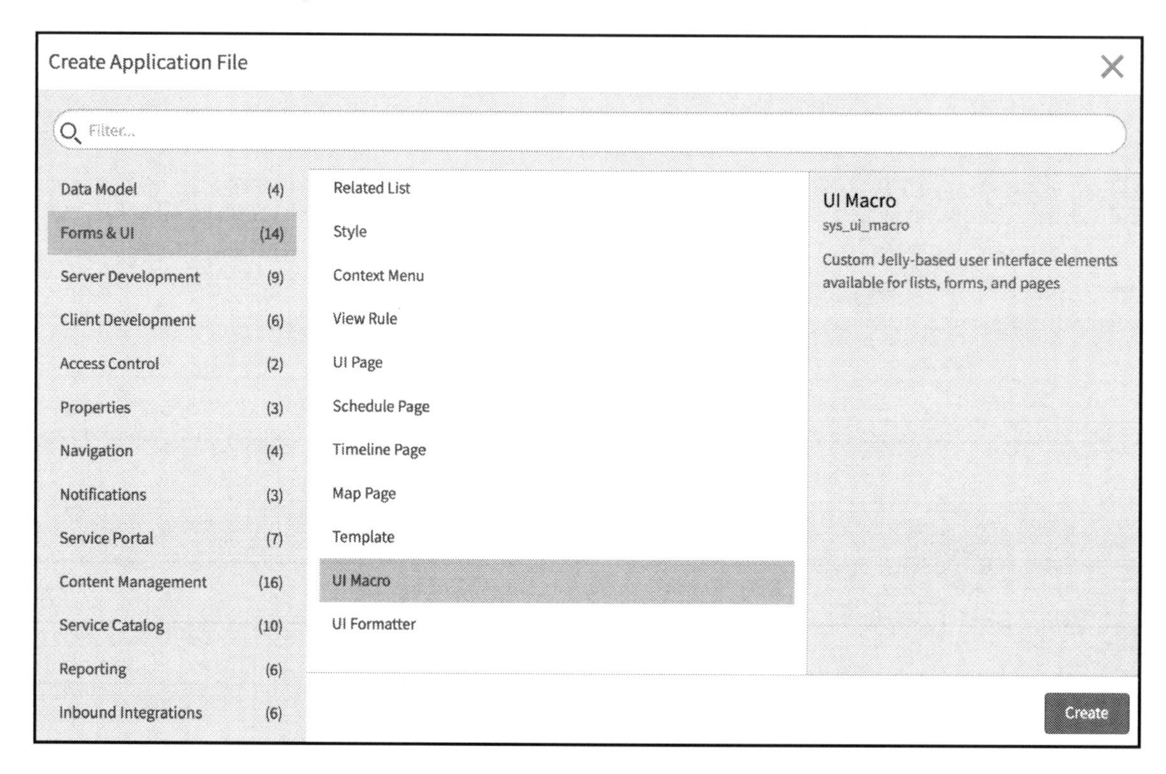


It will bring us to the new record form for a UI macro. Fill in the form fields with the following values:

- **Name**: `international_notice` (make sure the name doesn't contain any spaces)
- **API Name**: (This will be automatically populated)
- **Description**: `Shows a link to state.gov site where end-users can find more details about their international trips`

- **Active**: Checked
- **XML**: (Write the code mentioned after the following screenshot)
- **Protection policy**: **--None--**

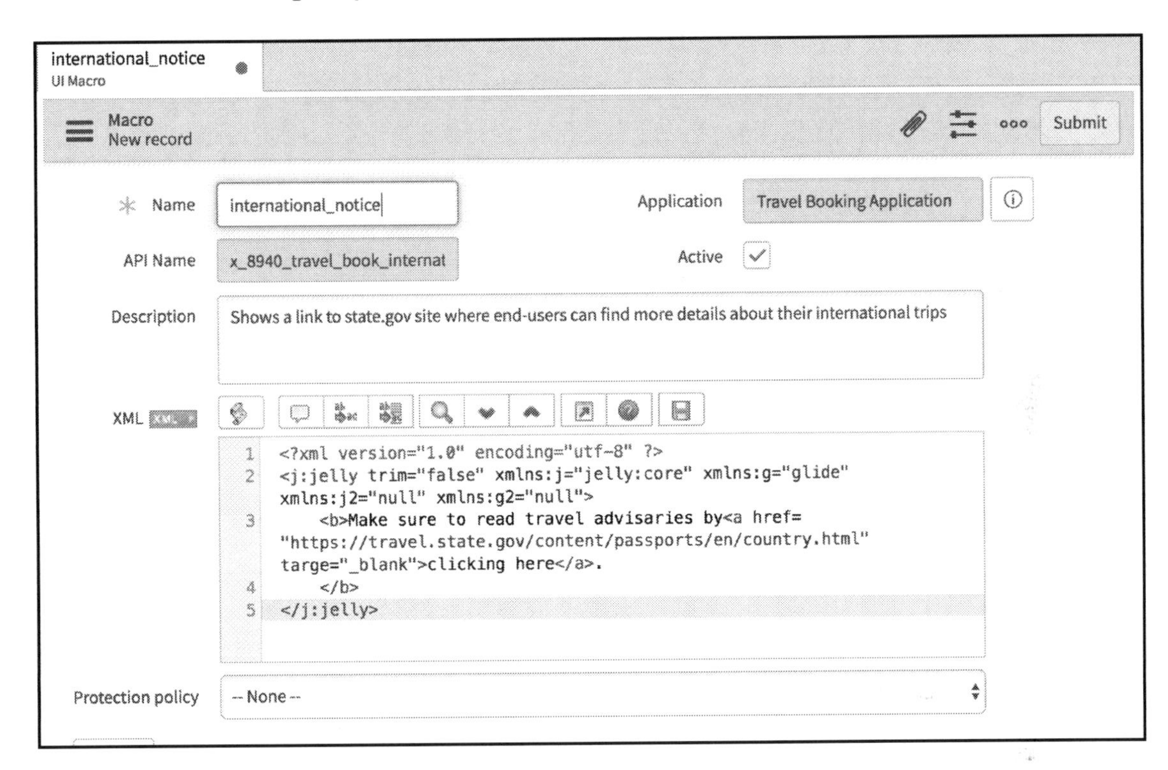


Write the following Jelly code in the **XML** field:

```
<?xml version="1.0" encoding="utf-8" ?>
<j:jelly trim="false" xmlns:j="jelly:core" xmlns:g="glide" xmlns:j2="null"
xmlns:g2="null">
        <b>Make sure to read travel advisaries by<a href=
"https://travel.state.gov/content/passports/en/country.html"
targe="_blank">clicking here</a>.
        </b>
</j:jelly>
```

Click on the **Submit** button to create the UI macro. The new UI macro needs to be added to either a UI page or form, or another UI macro that is part of a page or form. Let us add the UI macro we just created to the **Booking Request** form, for which we first need to create a UI formatter.

# UI formatters

Once we have created a UI macro, we can create a UI formatter. An existing UI macro is required in order to create a UI macro. This is because the UI macro provides the Jelly (XML) code to be used by the formatter.

To create a UI formatter, open **Studio**, select **Forms & UI** | **UI Formatter** in the **Create Application File** wizard, as shown in the following screenshot, and click on the **Create** button:

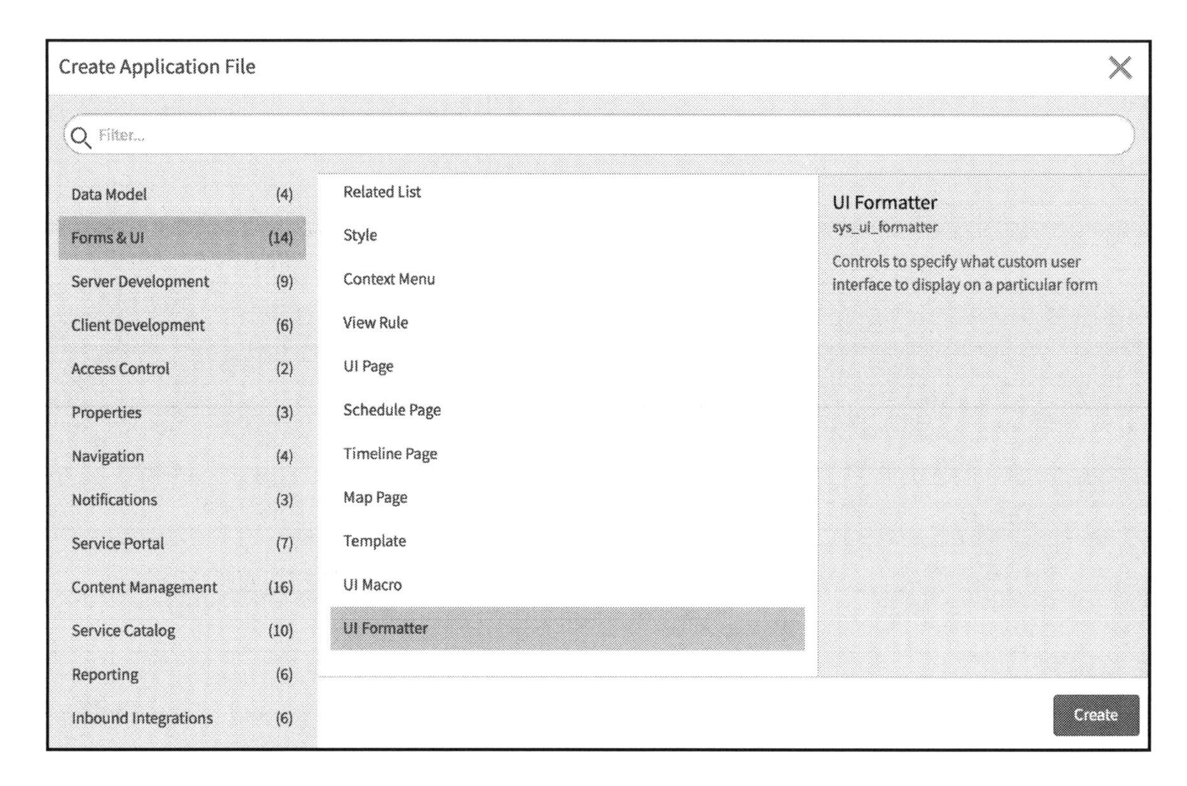


Fill in the new record form for the UI formatter with the values mentioned here:

- **Name**: `International Notice`
- **Formatter**: `international_notice.xml` (the name of the UI macro appended with `.xml`)

- **Table**: **Booking Request**
- **Type**: **Formatter**

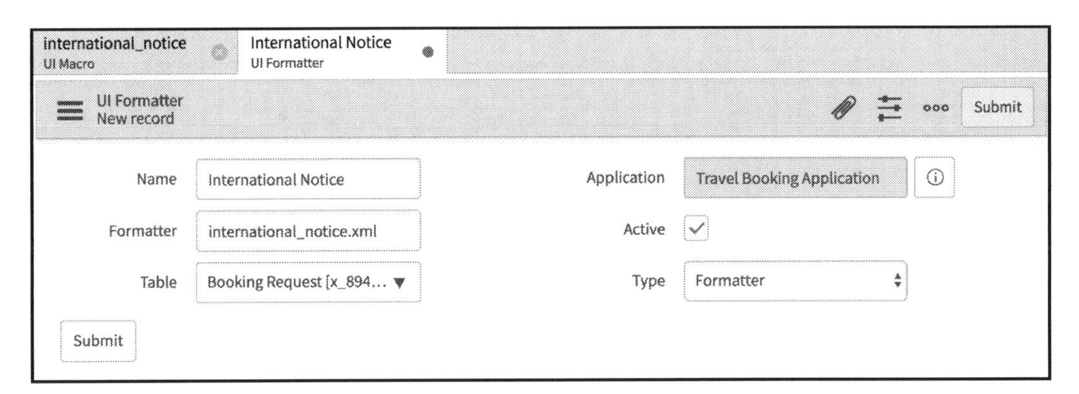


Click on the **Submit** button to finish creating the formatter. The newly created formatter will be added to the `Booking Request` table. We can open any form view of the table to bring the formatter into the view and arrange it just like any other form field.

To bring the **International Notice** formatter we just created to the **Employee** view of the `Booking Request` table, open the view in the **Form Designer** in **Studio**, as shown in the following screenshot, and bring in the **Formatters** from the **Fields** tab on the left to one of the sections on the right:

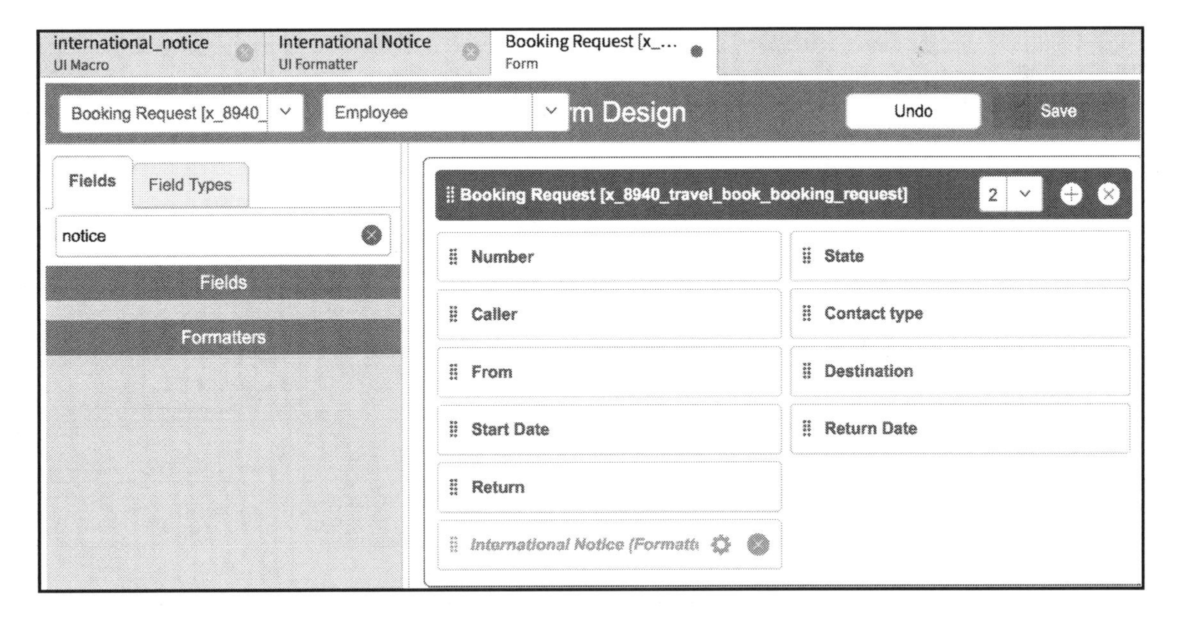

Click on the **Save** button on the top left of the **Form Designer** once you are satisfied with the layout of your form. We can confirm the changes and whether our UI macro and formatter are working properly by opening the Booking Request form in the Employee view, as shown in the following screenshot, by clicking on the **Travel Booking Application | Create new** module in the main ServiceNow interface:

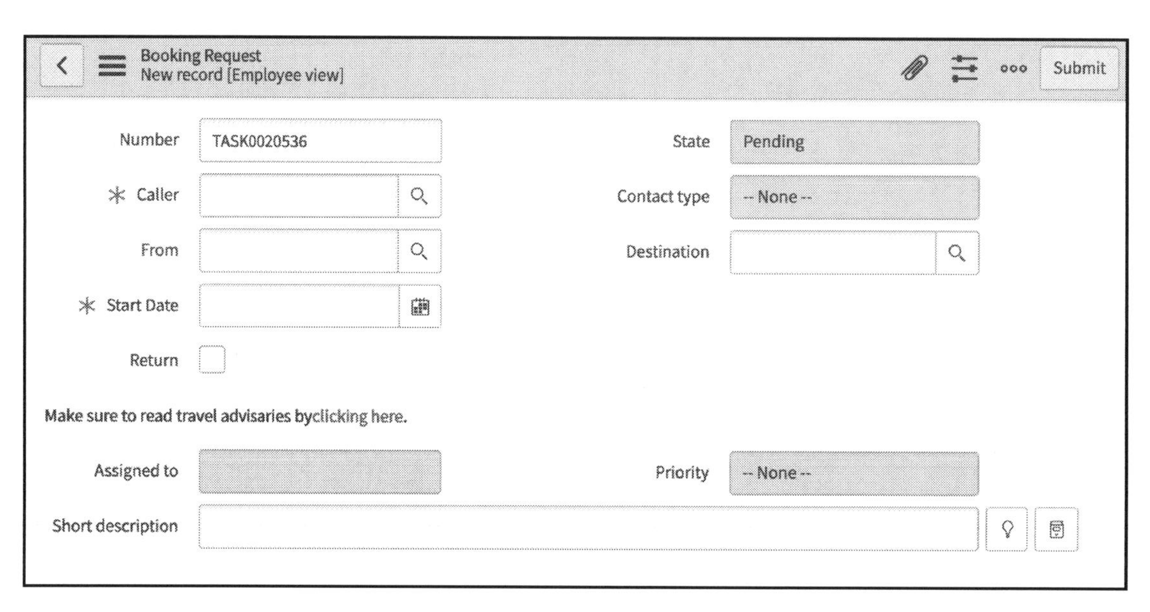


As you can see in the preceding screenshot, the UI formatter brings in the code written in the UI macro in order to enhance the form by bringing in external elements. The set of UI macros and forms can be used to create endless UI features and include codes to show highly dynamic content, such as maps or images.

# Summary

In this chapter, we learned how to use Jelly scripting to create UI pages and macros to create custom pages. We also learned how to incorporate the knowledge of HTML with Jelly code to create a properties page and how to make use of the processing script to perform server-side processing. We also learned how to use UI macros and formatters together to enhance the look of our forms.

In the next chapter, we will learn how to trigger events and handle them using script actions and notifications.

# 10
# Events and Notifications

Now that we have learned about and created client and server-side scripts, including UI pages and macros with Jelly scripts, let us learn about the concepts of events and notifications.

In the ServiceNow platform, events and notifications are among the features that are the easiest to implement. Events are used to monitor changes or *events* by event handlers, just like in any other programming language. Events in ServiceNow are stored in a table named `Event (sysevent)`, which is also referred to as **Event Log** or **Event Queue**. Events in the queue are consumed by script actions or notifications that in turn execute scripts or trigger notifications.

Notification, on the other hand, is the system in place within the ServiceNow platform to send our e-mail or SMS notifications to the end users. Any form or script sending out an e-mail replies to the notification feature of the platform. Notifications can be sent when an event occurs or is scheduled to go out at a particular time. All incoming and outgoing e-mails are monitored using the **System Mailboxes** application. Notifications are stored in the appropriately named `Notification (sysevent_email_action)` table.

In this chapter, we will learn how to trigger events when the values of a field in the **Booking Request** form are changed, as well as how to send out an e-mail based on events.

In this chapter, we will cover the following topics:

- Events
- Triggering events
- Notifications

# Events

While the events are triggered from scripts or workflow when a form field is updated, each event needs to be registered in the **Event Registry** within the platform. An event registry is a list of all the events that might be triggered from any of the sources and that are available for the handler to monitor.

# Registering events

The following steps show you how to register a new event:

1. Open the **Create Application File** wizard in **Studio** and, as shown here, select **Server Development** | **Event Registration** and click on the **Create** button:

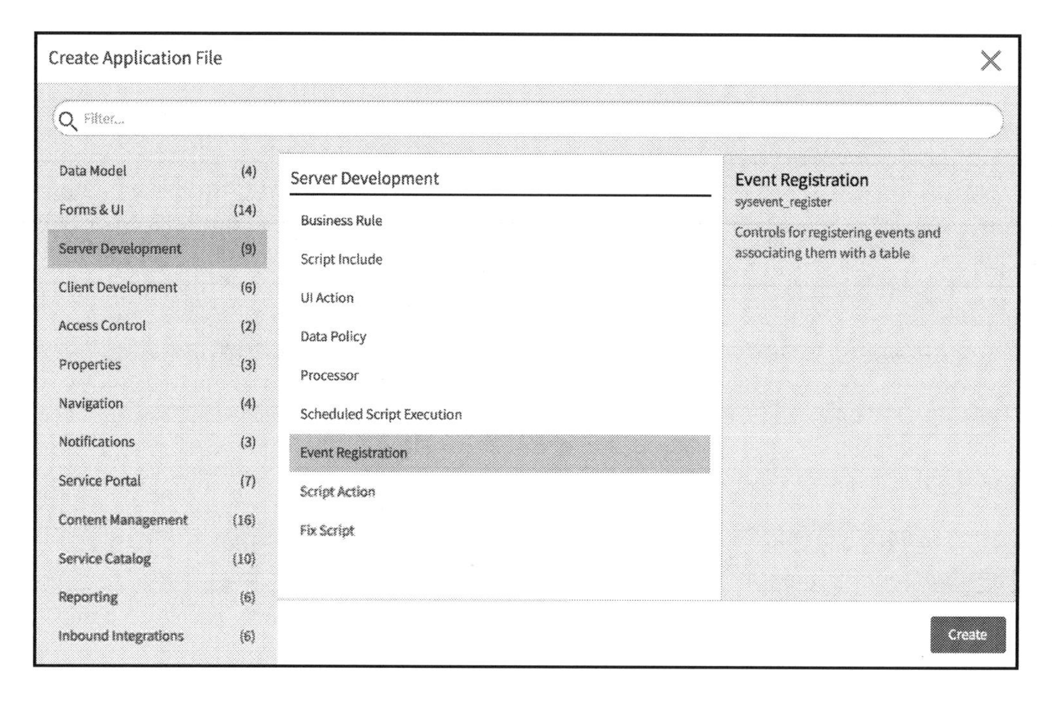


2. Now fill in the new record form for **Event Registration** with the following values:
    - **Suffix**: `assigned_to_changed`
    - (Suffix must not contain any spaces)
    - **Event name**: `x_8940_travel_book.assigned_to_changed`

(The value of the **Event name** field will be automatically generated once we populate the suffix, and just like the **Suffix** field, the **Event name** also cannot contain any space).

- **Table:** `Booking Request`
- **Description:** `Send email notification when assigned to field is changed`

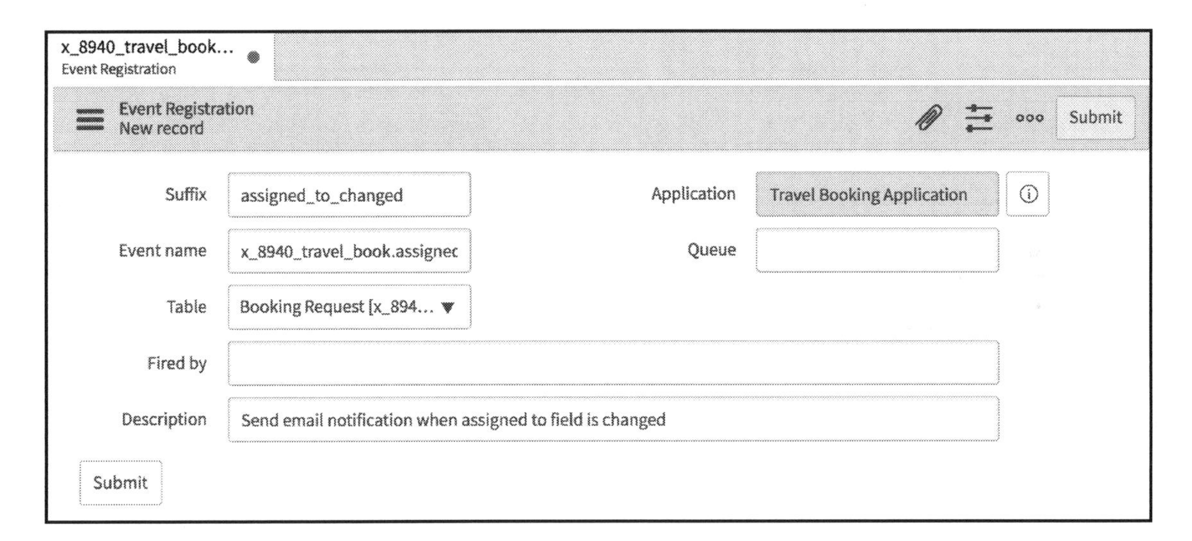

The **Fired by** field can be used to enter the name of the business rule or script that fires the script, and the **Description** field can be used to enter a description of what the event is supposed to do. The name of the queue is required only if the business rule or script that is going to trigger the event has a queue name specified. The queue can be used to segregate the types of events within a table.

3. Click on the **Submit** button to register the event in the event registry. This will create a record in the event registry (`sysevent_register`) table.

Now let us create a new business rule that will trigger the event we have added to the registry. Triggered events are stored in the `Event (sysevent)` table.

# Using a business rule to trigger events

The following steps show you how to create a business rule:

1. In **Studio**, open the **Create New Application File** wizard, select **Server Development** | **Business Rule**, and click on the **Create** button to open the new **Business Rule** record form.
2. Populate the form with the following values:
    - **Name**: `Monitor changes to assigned to field`
    - **Table**: `Booking Request`
    - **Active**: Checked
    - **Advanced**: Checked
    - **When**: **before**
    - **Order**: `200`
    - **Insert**: Unchecked
    - **Update**: Checked

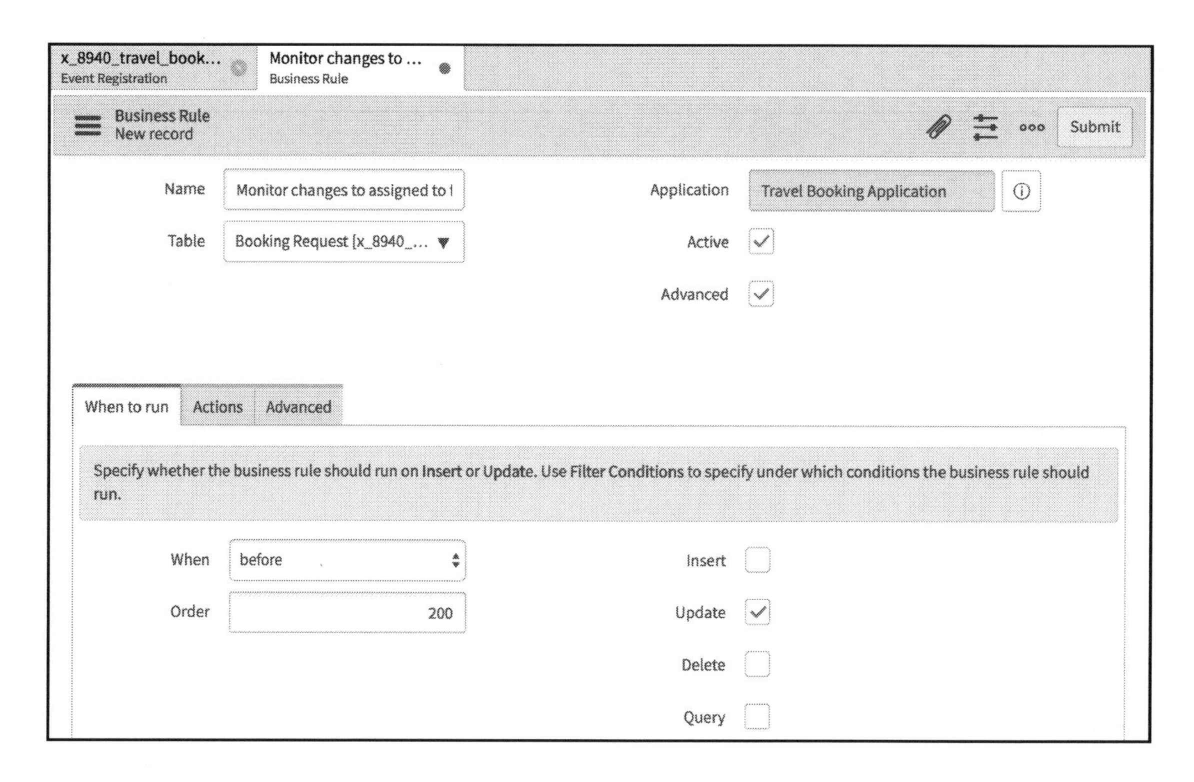

- Filter conditions:
    - **Assigned to** | **changes**
    - **Assigned to** | **is not empty**

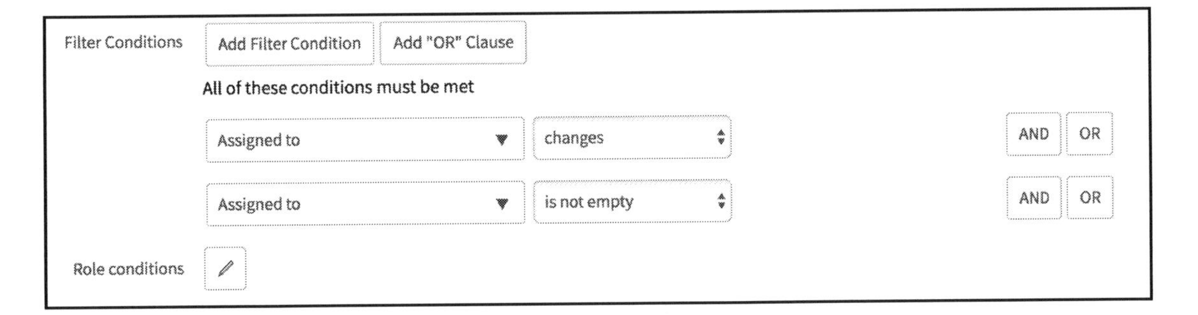


3. Navigate to **Advanced** tab | **Script**:
4. Write the following code in the **Script** field:

```
(function executeRule(current, previous /*null when async*/) {
  if (!previous.assigned_to.nil())
  gs.eventQueue("x_8940_travel_book.assigned_to_changed", current);
})(current, previous);
```

5. Click **Submit** to create the business rule:

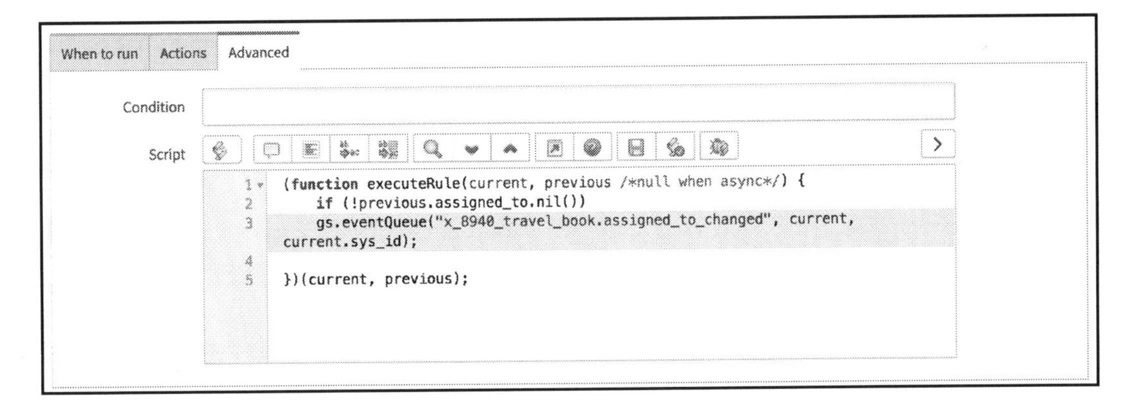


The code makes use of the `eventQueue` method in the `GlideSystem` API. The `eventQueue` method is used to trigger an event, which is added to the event queue (the `sysevent` table.) We pass the name of the event we created in the previous step. The current object is passed to the `GlideRecord` object that will be made available to any handlers of the event.

# Checking event logs

Once the business rule is created, we can confirm whether our code is working fine by creating an entry in the `Booking Request` table and updating the record while changing the **Assigned to** field. If everything goes well, we will be able to see the event in the events log module (**System Logs** | **Events**), as shown in the following screenshot:

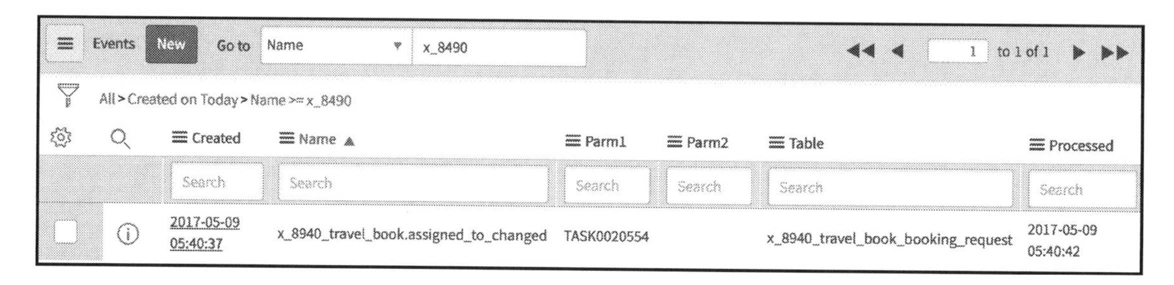


Once we are sure that events are being triggered properly, let us now create handlers for these events. The handlers could be either a script action that can execute server-side scripts or a notification.

For the purpose of this book, we are going to first create a script action that will increment the value of the reassignment count field, which is inherited from the task table. Next, we will create a notification that will be sent based on the similar condition we selected in our business rule.

# Script actions

Script actions are server-side JavaScript code that is executed when an event it is listening to is triggered on the specified table. Just like any other server-side script, script actions have access to all the server-side glide APIs, script includes, and other server-side resources.

The following steps show you how to create a script action:

1. Open the **Create New Application File** wizard in **Studio**, select **Server Development** | **Script Action**, and click on the **Create** button.
2. Fill in the new script action record form with the following values:
    - **Name**: `Update Reassignment Count`
    - **Event**: `x_8940_travel_book.assigned_to_changed`
    - **Active**: Checked
    - **Script**: (Use the following mentioned code)

3. Write the following code in the script field:

```
current.reassignment_count += 1;
current.update();
```

In the preceding code, we are incrementing the `reassignment_count` field by `1` and then updating the record. The system usually takes a few seconds to update the record because the control is returned back to the user when the record is updated and the event is added to the queue. It usually takes some time for the script action or any other event handler to pick up the event and process it. This event-queue-based development is good for updating hidden fields, invoking remote calls, or passing values to external tools as it frees up the normal form and database processes the user is interacting with.

In essence, whenever the **Assigned to** field of a record in the `Booking Request` table is modified, then the business rule will be triggered. The script in the business rule will trigger an event that we have registered in the system named `x_8940_travel_book.assigned_to_changed`. The script action handler we just created is monitoring this event. Finally, the script in the script action will increment the value of the reassignment count field within a few seconds.

Make sure to always replace company code with your own company code when trying to follow steps or copy scripts mentioned in this book. Thus, replace `8940` with you own company code. Read previous chapters of this book to understand the concept of the company code.

Now, before we move on to the next topic, let us register a second event named `x_8940_travel_book.assigned_to_notification` on the `Booking Request` table and also update our business rule script to trigger this new event, along with the existing one. So our second event will look like the one mentioned here:

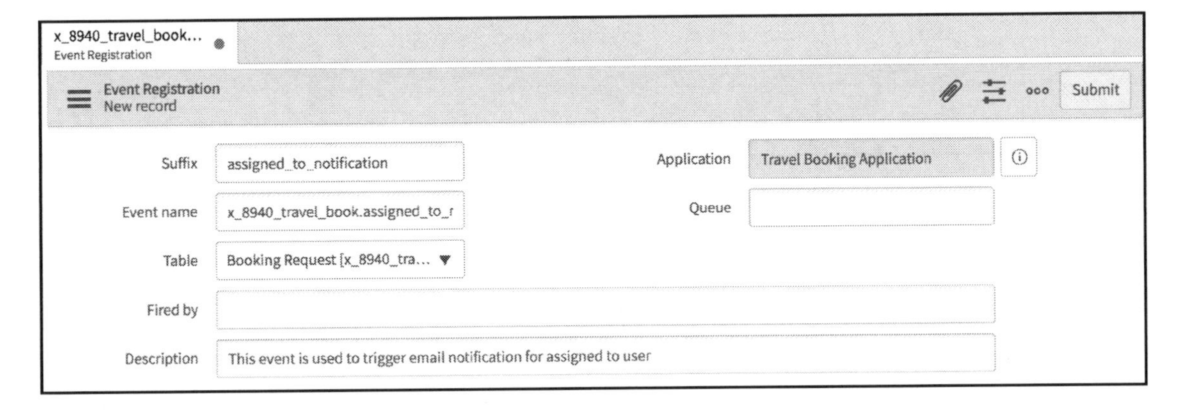

Now let us ensure that we are queuing the second event along from the business rule. The update script on the business rule we created earlier in the chapter is mentioned here:

```
(function executeRule(current, previous /*null when async*/) {
  if (!previous.assigned_to.nil())
  gs.eventQueue("x_8940_travel_book.assigned_to_changed", current);
  gs.eventQueue("x_8940_travel_book.assigned_to_notificat", current);
})(current, previous);
```

In the preceding code, we have added another call to the `eventQueue` method. We add another entry to the event queue, and the name of the event is `x_8940_travel_book.assigned_to_notificat`:

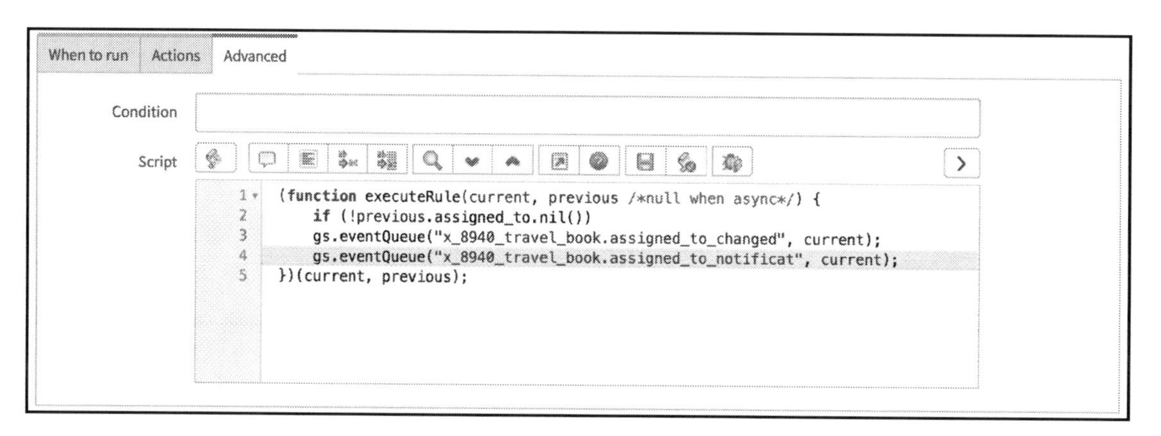

It is important that we use the correct name of the event as defined in the event registry. There is a limitation on the number of characters, and ServiceNow can trim the event name if the suffix is too long. If the event name in the code and registry doesn't match, invoking the `gs.eventQueue` method may throw the error `Access to event 'assigned_to_notification' from scope 'Travel Booking Application' has been refused. The event is not defined.`

Now whenever the **Assigned to** field is modified, the script mentioned in the business rule will execute and, based on the condition, will queue either one or both of the events. That is, the first event will be triggered only when the previous value of the **Assigned to** field is not set. Rest assured that everything will work the same and we will be able to see our reassignment count increasing every time we reassign the booking request task to another user. This can be confirmed by temporarily bringing in the **Reassignment Count** field to the **Booking Request** form using the **Form Designer**. Now let us see how to send notifications based on events.

# Notifications

Notifications can be scheduled to be autodelivered or sent when an event occurs. When an event is triggered, the `GlideRecord` object of the record that triggered the event is sent to the notification. This `GlideRecord` object is an important aspect of the event as it provides notification access to data fields available in the record, thus enabling developers to create dynamic e-mails with custom data fields. Before we create an e-mail action (notification), we will create an e-mail template.

The following steps show you how to create a new e-mail template:

1. Open **Studio** and in the **Create Application File** wizard select **Notifications** | **Email Template**, as shown here, and click on the **Create** button:

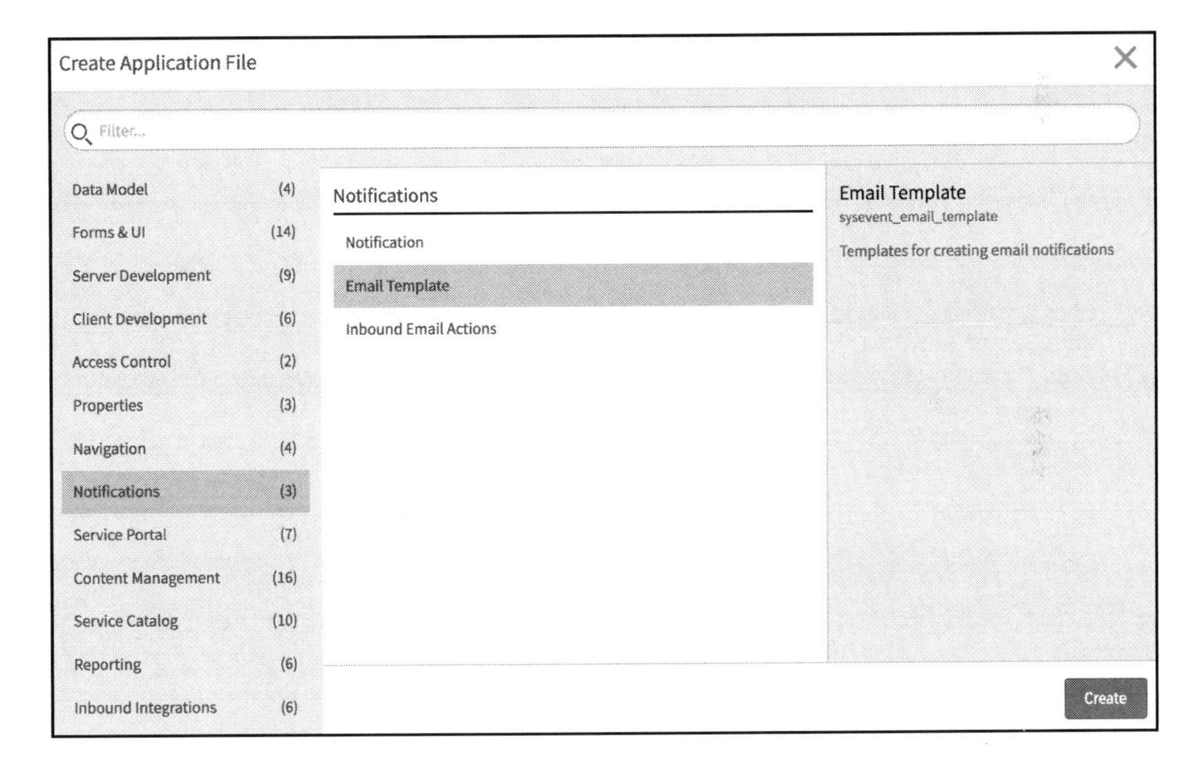

2. Fill in the new **Email Template** form with the following values:
    - **Name**: `Booking Request Template`
    - **Travel: Booking Request**
    - **Subject**: `Travel Booking Request - ${number}`
    - **Message HTML**: (As mentioned in the screenshot)

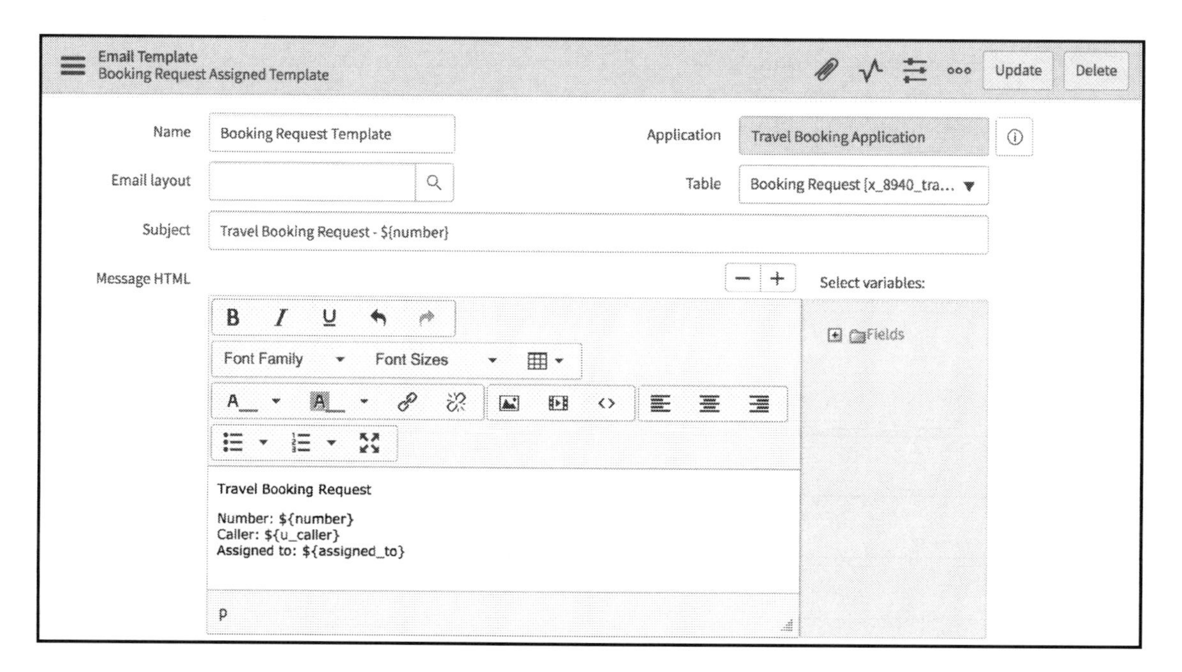


3. Enter the following text in the **Message HTML** field:

```
Travel Booking Request
Number: ${number}
Caller: ${u_caller}
Assigned to: ${assigned_to}
```

4. Leave the **Message text** and **SMS alternate** fields empty and click on the **Create** button.
5. Once the template is saved, scroll down to the **Notification**-related list as shown here and click on the **New** button.

6. Alternately, you can open the **Create Application File** wizard in **Studio**, select **Notifications** | **Notification** as shown here, and click on the **Create** button:

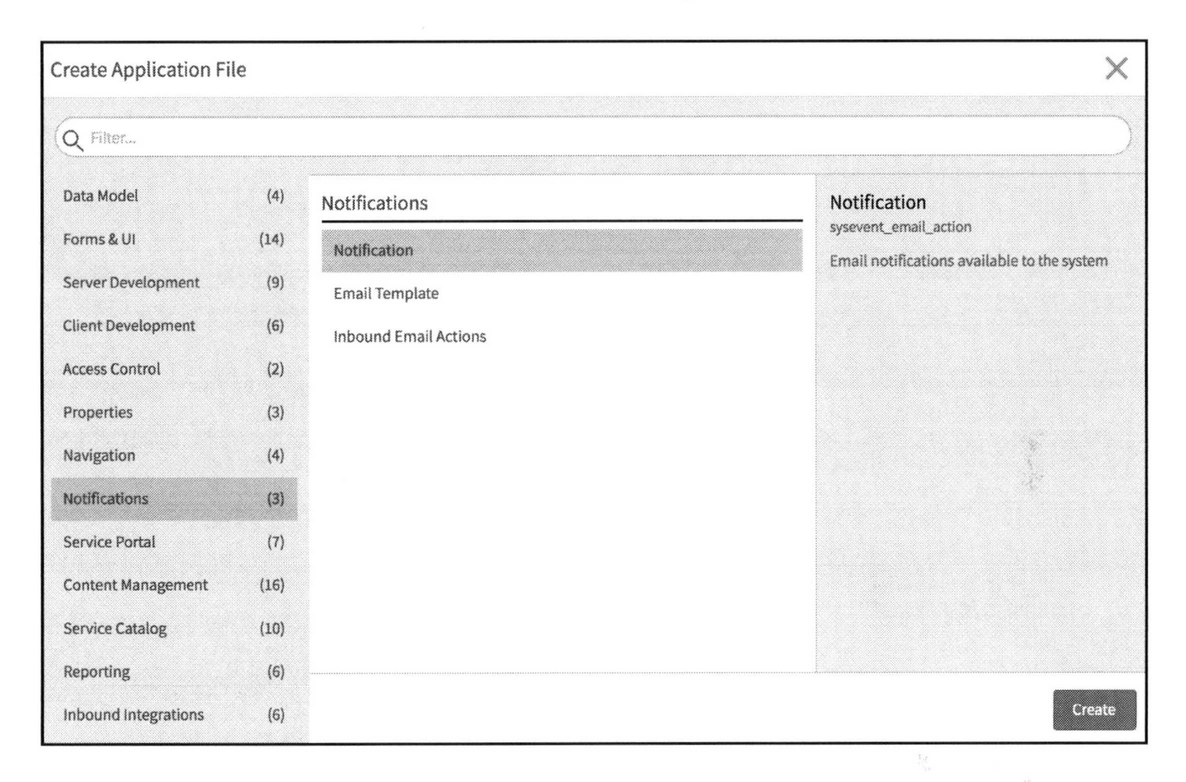

7. In the **Notification New record** form, click on the **Advanced View**-related list at the bottom of the form, as shown here:

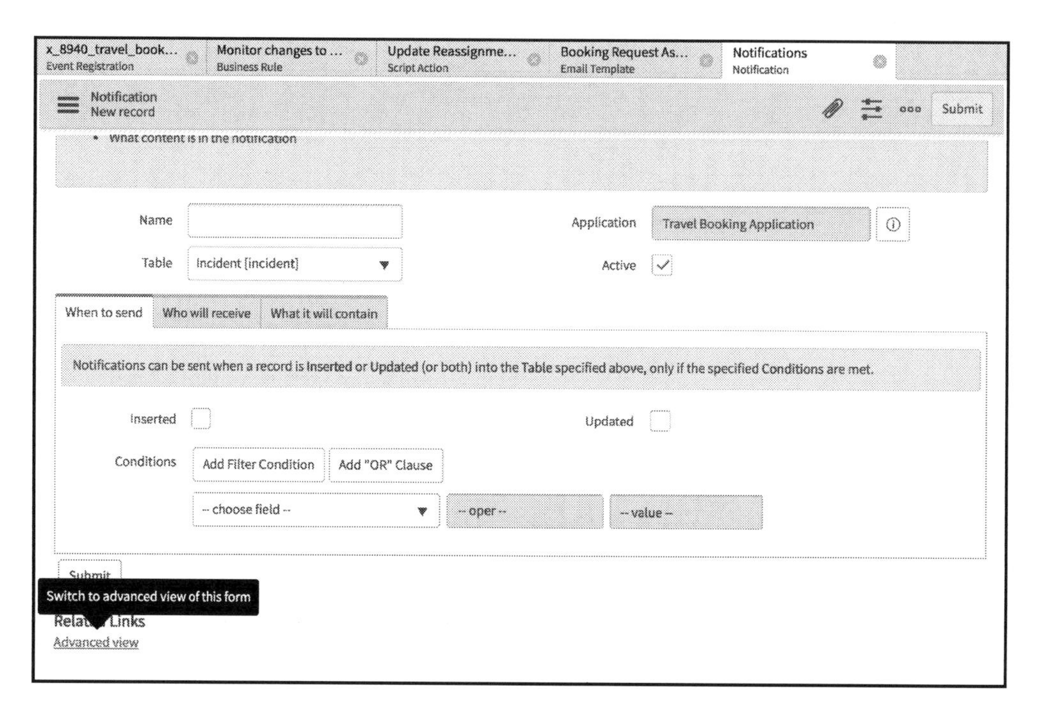


8. This will bring up the advanced form view of the **Notification** table. Now fill in the form with the following values:
   - **Name**: `Booking Request Assigned`
   - **Table**: **Booking Request**
   - **Type**: **EMAIL**
   - **Active**: Checked

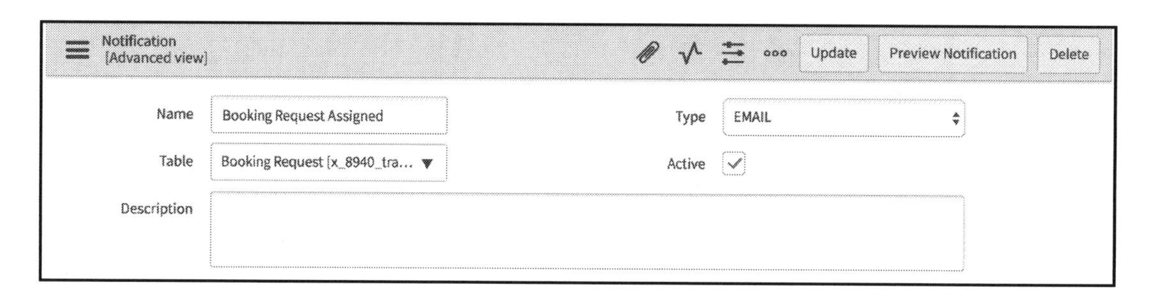

9. Next, in the **When to send** tab, fill in the form with the following values:

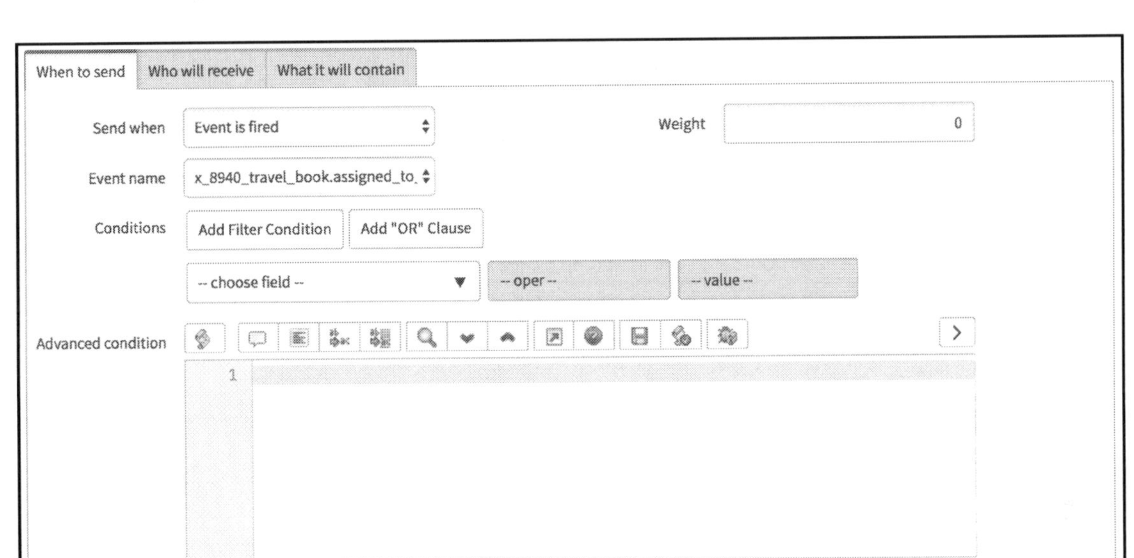


- **Send when**: **Event is fired**
- **Event name**: `x_8940_travel_book_assigned_to_notificat`

10. Now switch to the **Who will receive** tab and fill in the form with the following values:

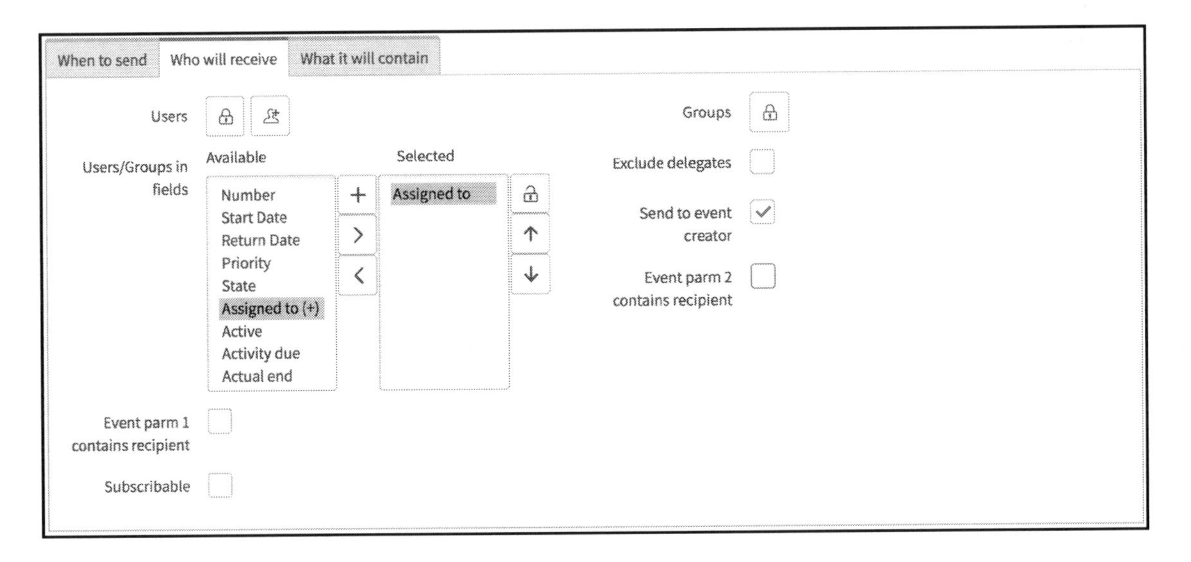

- **Users/Groups in fields**: Include **Assigned to (+)** in the **Selected** list

11. Now switch to the **What it will contain** table and fill in the form with the following values:

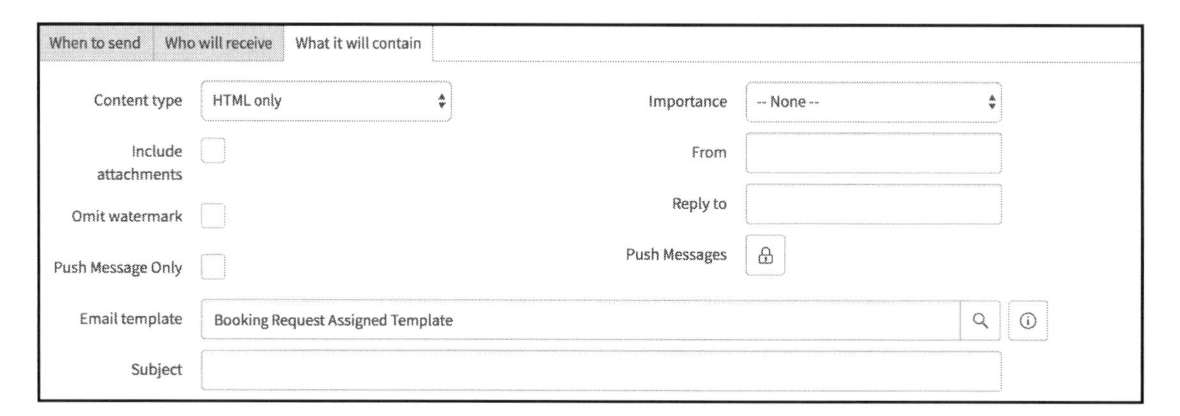


- **Content type: HTML only**
- **Email template: Booking Request Template**

(Select the template we created in the previous step)

12. Now click **Create/Update** to save the notification.

Going forward whenever the `x_8940_travel_book_assigned_to_changed` event is triggered by the business rule, the notification we just created will also be sent to the e-mail ID of the user that the booking request task is assigned to.

# Testing notifications

In ServiceNow, during development, we can forward all outgoing e-mails to one of the desired e-mail addresses. Also, we can use the **Preview Notification** feature in the **Notification** form to see a live preview based on the existing event or by generating a demo event. Let us now learn how to preview the notification and generate test e-mails.

# Previewing notifications

Click on the **Preview Notification** button on the form header, as shown previously, to open the **Notification Preview** modal window:

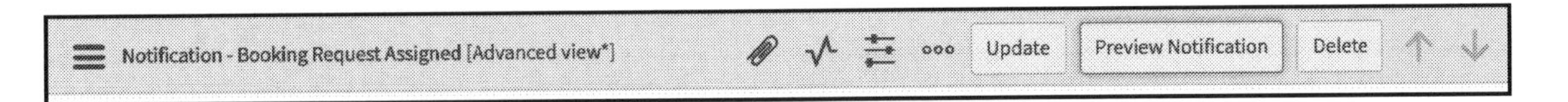


In the **Notification Preview** modal window, as shown in the following screenshot, select an existing task in the **Preview Record** reference field to see the preview of the **Subject** and **Body** of the e-mail:

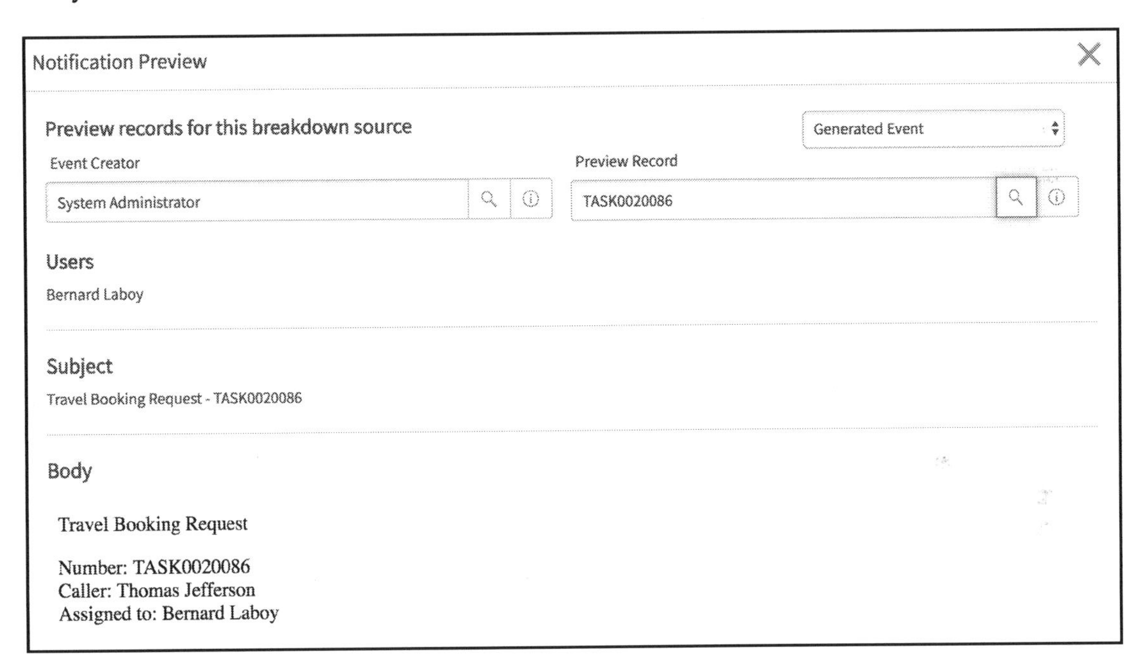


The notification is working properly if you can see information from the selected task in the **Subject** and **Body** section of the preview window.

# Forward outgoing e-mails

For testing purposes, it is recommended that we forward all outgoing e-mail to a private e-mail address. We can do this by updating the following two e-mail properties in the **System Mailboxes** | **Administration** | **Email properties** module:

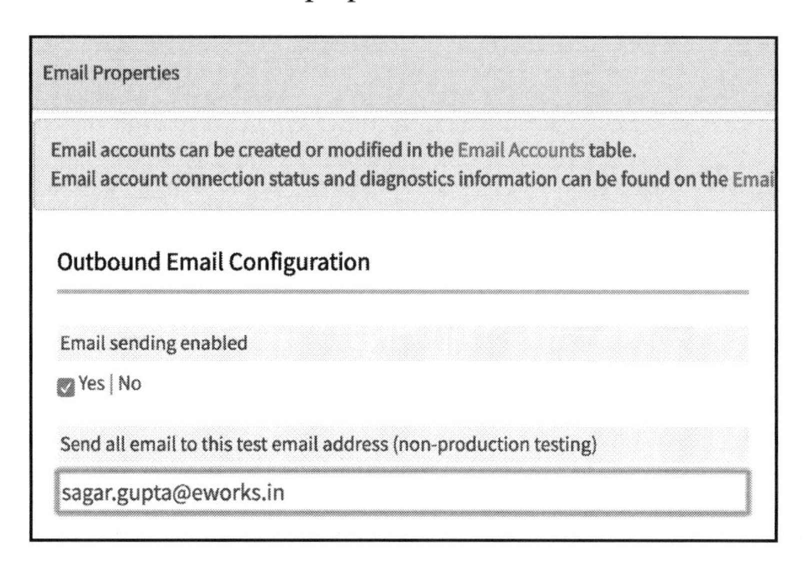


- **Email sending enabled**: Checked
- **Send all email to this test email address (non-production testing)**: (Specify your private e-mail ID here)

Now all outgoing e-mails will be forwarded to the e-mail ID we specified in the e-mail properties. This is very useful for testing the notification features and ensuring that test e-mails do not land up in end users' mailboxes. You may receive tons of pending e-mails from the system, so ensure that you only specify an e-mail address you are authorized to use.

You must switch to the **Global** application scope to make changes in the **Email Properties** page. You can switch to a global scope by using the application scope drop-down menu in the **Developers** tab of the **System Settings** dialog window, which is shown when you click on the cog (settings) icon on the top-right of the main ServiceNow interface. Once you modify the e-mail properties, click on the **Save** button on the page header to confirm your changes, and ensure that you revert back to the `Travel Booking Application` we have been working on in this book.

Now that the notification and the e-mail template we created are working as expected, let us test the notification by trying to send the e-mail by assigning a travel-booking request to a user.

## Updating a travel-booking request

In the main ServiceNow interface, go through the following steps:

1. Open one of the existing travel-booking requests, select a new user in the **Assigned to** field, and click **Update**:

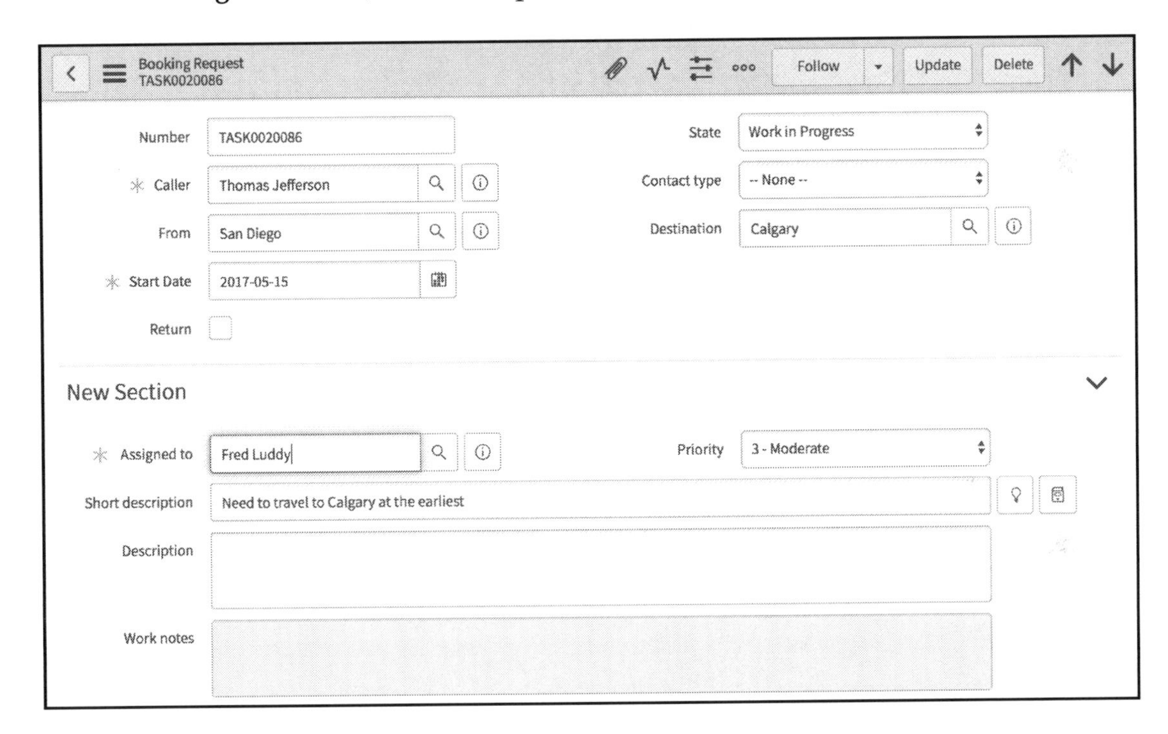


2. If everything works well, the e-mail should be sent to the **Assigned to** user, or else to **the Forward all** e-mail address you have set in the e-mail properties.

3. We can confirm the outgoing e-mail by using the modules available in the **System Mailboxes** application by switching over the main ServiceNow interface:

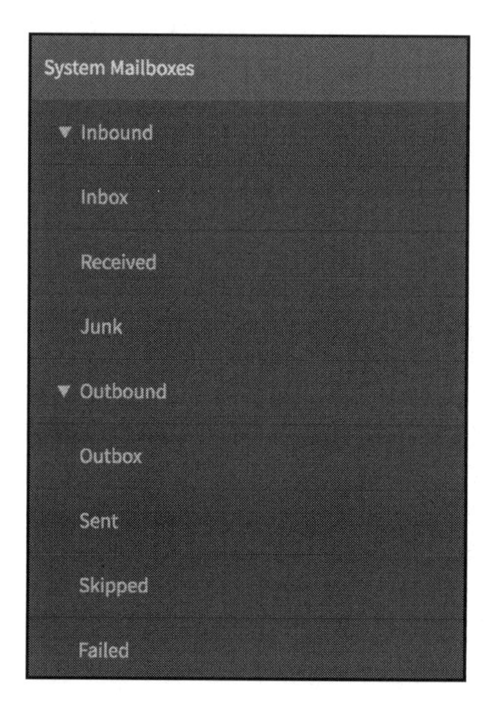


4. The module **System Mailboxes** | **Outbound** | **Sent** can be used to list all sent e-mails, as shown here:

You can click on the info icon against any sent e-mail record to view the content of the e-mail, along with the target record that triggered the e-mail. These modules are useful when trying to figure out if e-mails are being sent properly or failing for various reasons.

# Summary

In this chapter, we learned how to trigger events and handle e-mail notifications. We looked at the concept of event registry, along with the different ways events can be handled. We learned how to use business rules to queue events using the `eventQueue` method. Furthermore, we learned how to create e-mail templates and use them in notifications. In the next chapter, we will learn how to design workflows and use different kinds of activities to visually enhance the out-of-the-box features available in the ServiceNow platform without writing code.

# 11
# Workflow Development

We have learned many different features of the ServiceNow platform so far, including user administration, data dictionary, application scopes, modules, home page customization, reporting, events, and notifications, and have also written client-side and server-side code, including client scripts, business rules, script includes, script actions, and UI macros and UI pages using Jelly. The ServiceNow platform offers many such features and functionalities to administrators and developers to automate and extend the platform. Another such feature is workflows. Using workflows, developers can automate the platform visually without having to write much code.

The ServiceNow platform offers a web-based visual workflow designer known as workflow editor. A workflow is made up of activities and always consists of a **Begin** activity and an **End** activity that mark the start and end of the workflow. Workflow editor can be used to design, modify, and validate the workflows. Each activity in a workflow has its own variable scope and can output objects that can be used by subsequent activities. Activities defined within a workflow can also access workflow-level variables referred to as workflow scratchpad variables.

In this chapter, we will cover the following topics and learn how to use many of the different available standard workflow activities:

- Workflow basics
- Using workflow editor
- Workflow activities
- REST calls using workflows

# Workflow basics

Workflows are one of the most important features available in the ServiceNow platform. They can be used to perform server-side automation visually without having to write much code. They also offer a way to monitor running workflow context and activities. A workflow executes only when it is in published state. The workflow starts in draft (unpublished) state and once published cannot be edited unless we manually check out the workflow. Workflows have turned out to be the bread and butter of ServiceNow developers and are implemented in almost all custom applications due to their innovative graphical interface and ease of monitoring.

Many applications, including standard ones such as incident, change, problem, service-level management, and service catalog, rely heavily on workflows. Similarly, other applications such as orchestration, HR suite, and security operations also rely on workflows.

Each workflow comprises one or more activities, which are executed in sequence, beginning from the **Begin** activity and ending when it reaches the **End** activity. A workflow usually executes when a record in the table it is attached to is either inserted or updated and the start condition defined in the workflow properties evaluates to true. Workflows can also be executed based on an event or from scripts.

When the start condition matches, the workflow execution starts and a context of the workflow gets attached to the record. All the activities of the workflow are executed within this context. The workflow context is protected from any future changes to the workflow. If a workflow is modified or deleted after the context has been attached, it doesn't affect the context and the flow of the workflow.

If there are multiple workflows defined in a table, we can specify the order in which workflows are executed. Furthermore, we can also specify whether a workflow that has a lower order will execute or not if another workflow in higher order has already executed. This is achieved by specifying the execution order of the workflow in the workflow properties.

The following properties can be configured when defining a workflow:

- **Name**: A unique name for the workflow that can be used to distinguish it from other workflows.
- **Table**: Name of the table on which the workflow will be applied.

- **Description**: This field can be used to write details about the workflow, such as what the purpose of the workflow is and how it works, and can also mention some requirements and test cases.
- **If condition matches**: This property can be used to define when and how the workflow will execute. There are three possible options:
    - **Run the workflow**: If this option is selected, the workflow will execute when the workflow's condition field evaluates to `true`.
    - **Run if no other workflows matched yet**: If this option is selected, the workflow will execute when the workflow's condition field evaluates to `true` and no other workflows are running on the record.
    - **None**: This option can be used to ignore the condition filed and use a subflow or script to execute the workflow:

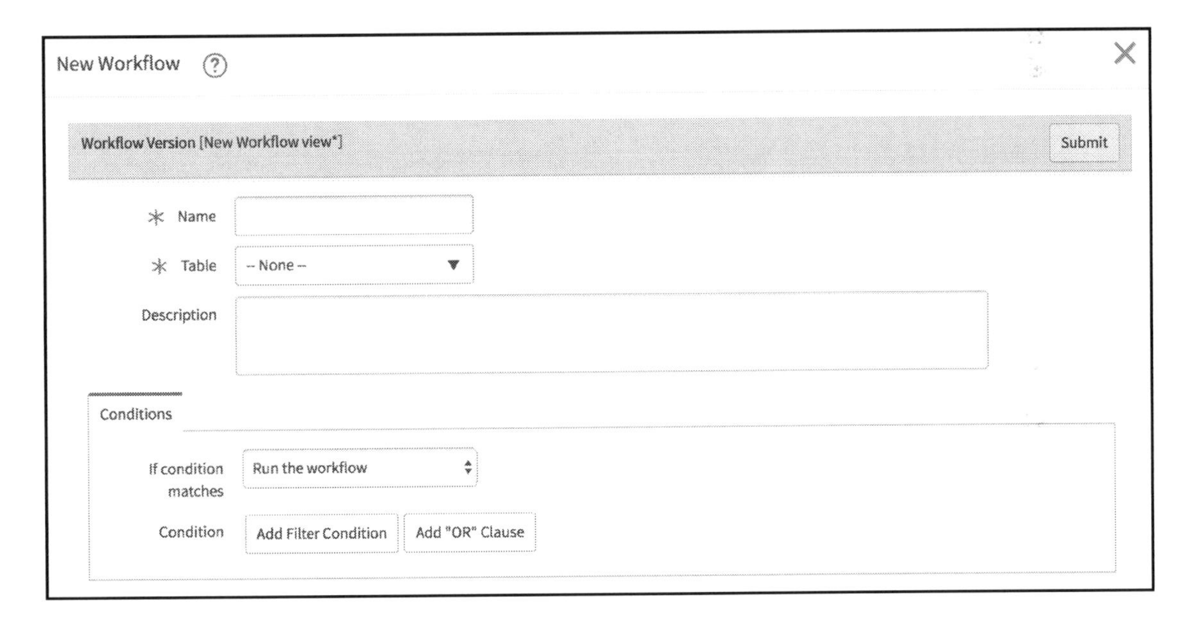

# Using workflow editor

Workflow editor is a graphical tool that is used to design workflows by arranging and connecting activities to automate a process. The workflow editor can be launched using Studio by selecting **Workflow** | **Workflow** in the **Create Application File** wizard as shown here:

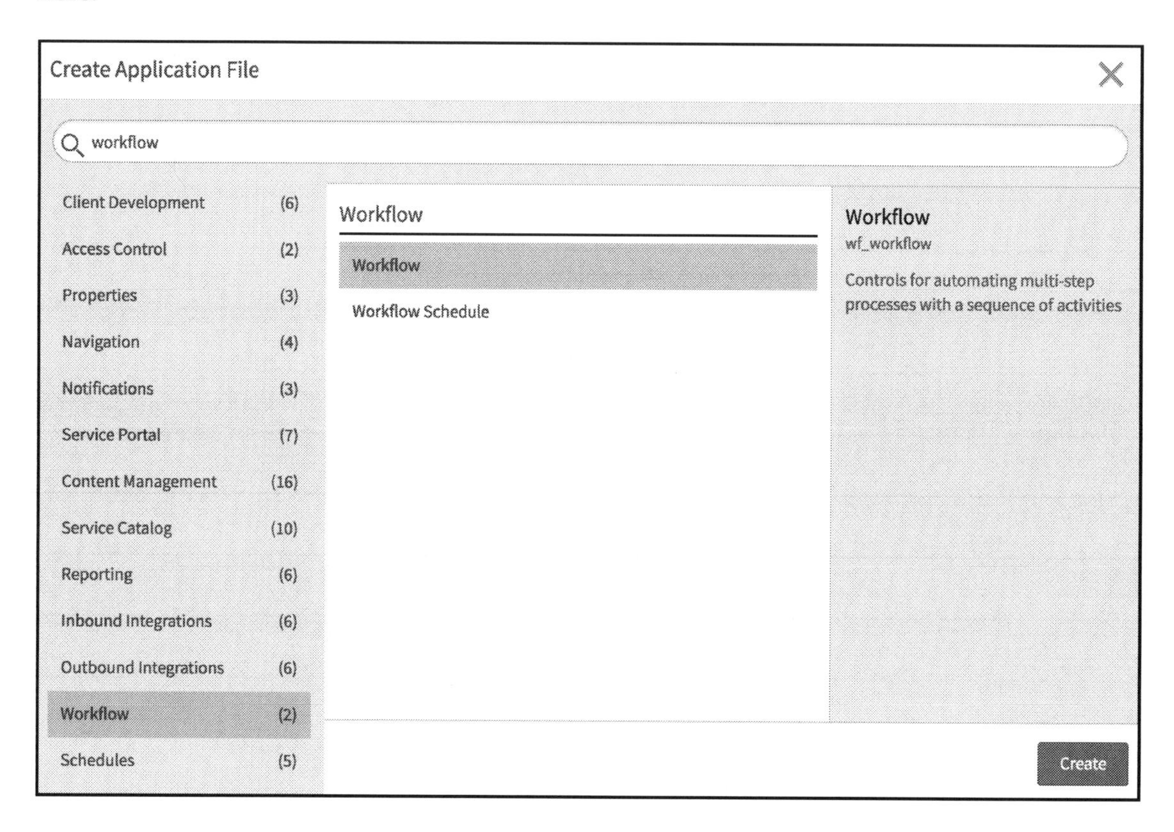

Workflow editor can also be launched by clicking on the **Workflow Editor** navigation link in the standard ServiceNow interface as shown here:

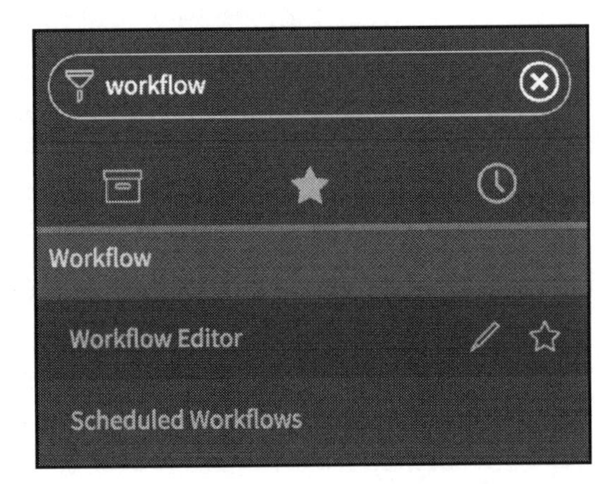

**Workflow Editor** opens up in a new browser window. Make sure to allow pop-up windows from your ServiceNow instance URL as it may cause problems when pop-up blockers are active.

Workflow editor features a tab-based interface as shown here:

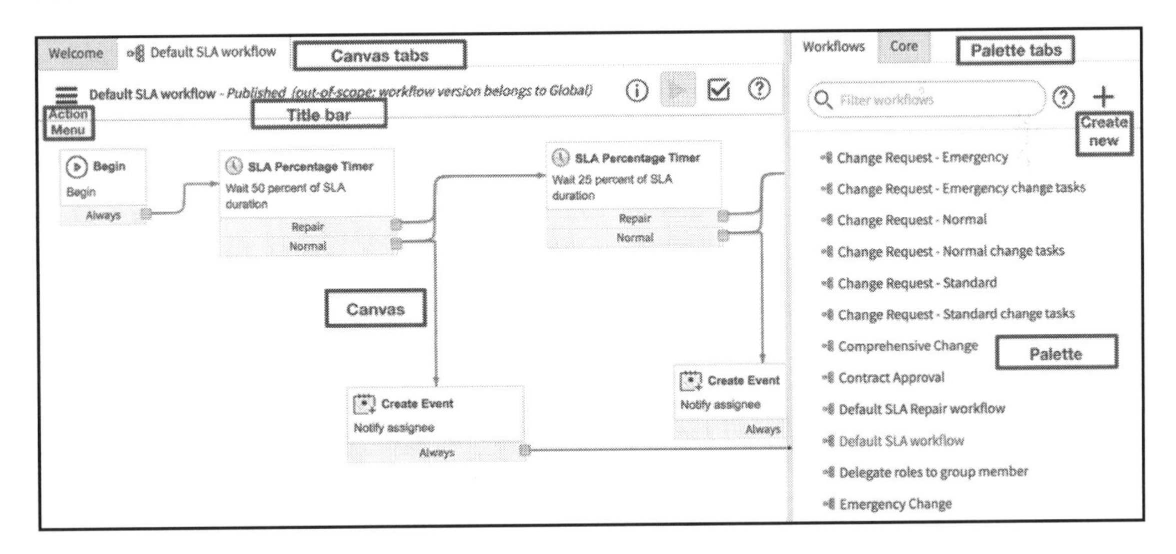

The section on the left includes the **Welcome** tab and other dynamic tabs for new and existing workflows, referred to as **Canvas tabs**. The **Welcome** tab has links to online documentation and other resources related to the workflow concept.

The canvas section in workflow editor consists of a **Title bar** and a workflow **Action Menu** at the top that can be used to perform operations such as editing workflow properties, publishing the workflow, checking out a published workflow, validating the workflow, and copying or deleting the workflow.

The section on the right is collapsible and is referred to as the **Palette tabs**. Initially, it includes the **Workflows** and **Core** tabs, and data- and orchestration-related tabs are visible when available.

The **Workflows** palette consists of a filter and a list of all existing workflows in the system. It can be used to open and modify existing workflows by double-clicking on a workflow name. A workflow can also be dropped on another workflow to include it as a subflow.

We can create a new workflow by clicking on the **+** icon next to the filter field, which opens a new workflow drawing canvas under a new tab in the left section as shown in the following screenshot:

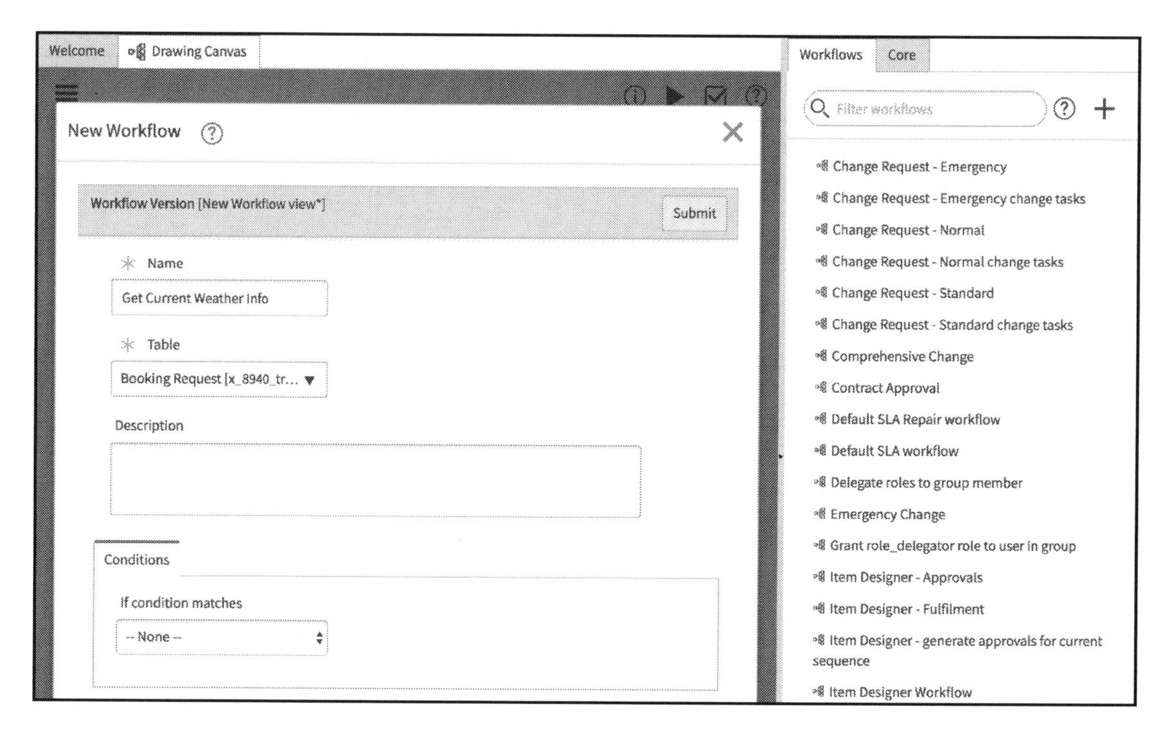

As detailed earlier in this chapter, we must specify a unique name for our workflow and select a table. For this section, we will specify **Demo Workflow** as the name and **Booking Request** as the table.

As shown in the following screenshot, the **Core** palette consists of activities that are available in the base system. One or more of these activities can be added to any workflow to graphically automate a process. Each activity has its own set of properties that must be defined in order for the activity to execute properly:

The content of the **Core** tab is available only when we are designing a new workflow or modifying an existing workflow. A workflow must be in checked-out state in order for us to modify it.

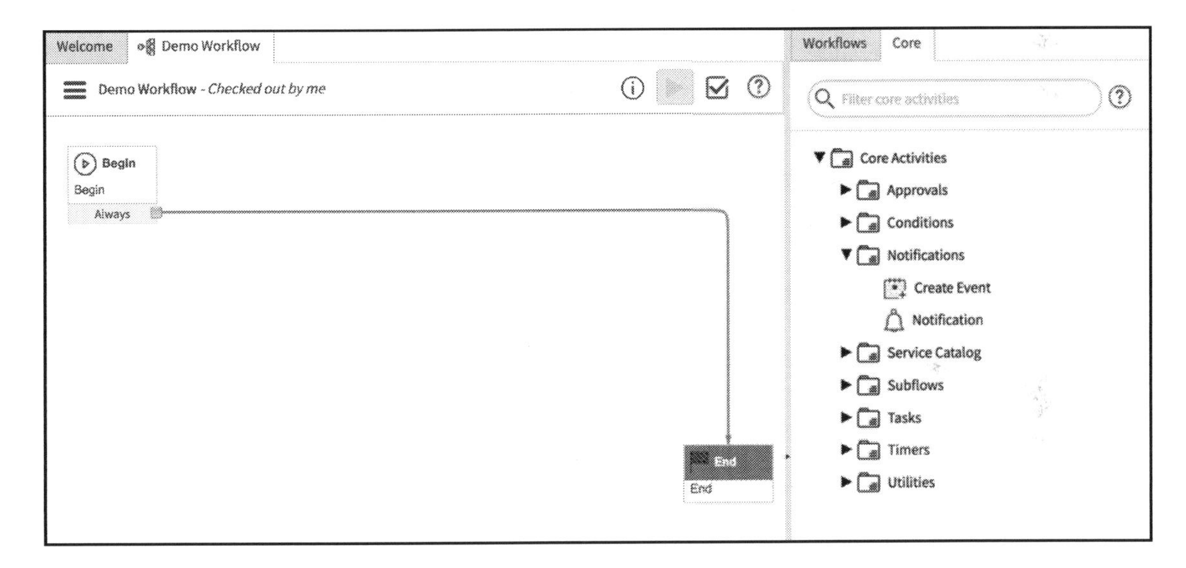

## Workflow actions menu

The workflow actions menu, as shown in the following screenshot, in the title bar of the canvas, can be used to perform many different actions related to the current workflow. It can be used to publish, copy, or delete the workflow. It can also be used to validate the workflow and access workflow contexts that are currently associated to any record. We will be using these action menu options during the course of this chapter:

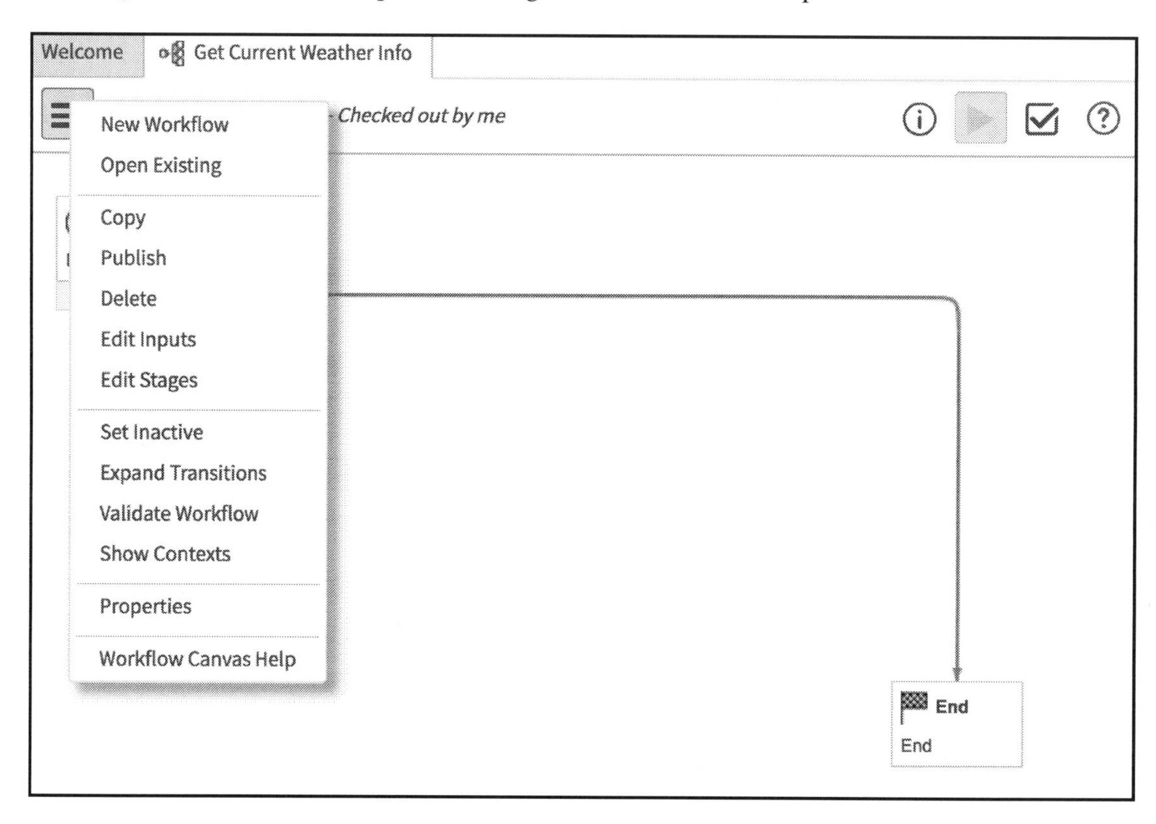

## Workflow development state

A workflow could either be in published, checked-out, or inactive state. A workflow executes only when it is in published state. We can publish a workflow using the **Publish** option in the actions menu. The status of the workflow is always visible in the title bar. If a workflow is in published state, we cannot modify its properties or make any changes to any of its activities.

In order to modify a workflow that is in published state, we must manually check out the workflow from the actions menu. A workflow must be in checked-out state in order for us to modify it. When we create a new workflow, it is by default in checked-out state and we can modify its content--add or modify activities or change workflow properties such as name, table, description, and condition.

All changes to a *checked-out* workflow are saved in a newer version of the workflow and are not available to the system till we publish the workflow back again.

When a developer checks out a workflow, two versions of the workflow are available in the system. The checked-out version of the workflow is available only to the developer. And the previously published version remains available to all other users. Once the checked-out version of the workflow is published, the system activates the new version of the workflow for all users.

## Workflow properties

We can modify properties of any checked-out workflow at any time. We can open the **Workflow Properties** dialog using the **Properties** option in the action menu in the title bar. The **Workflow Properties** dialog, as shown in the following screenshot, has many different workflow options segregated by tabs.

We can switch to the relevant tab to modify the appropriate property:

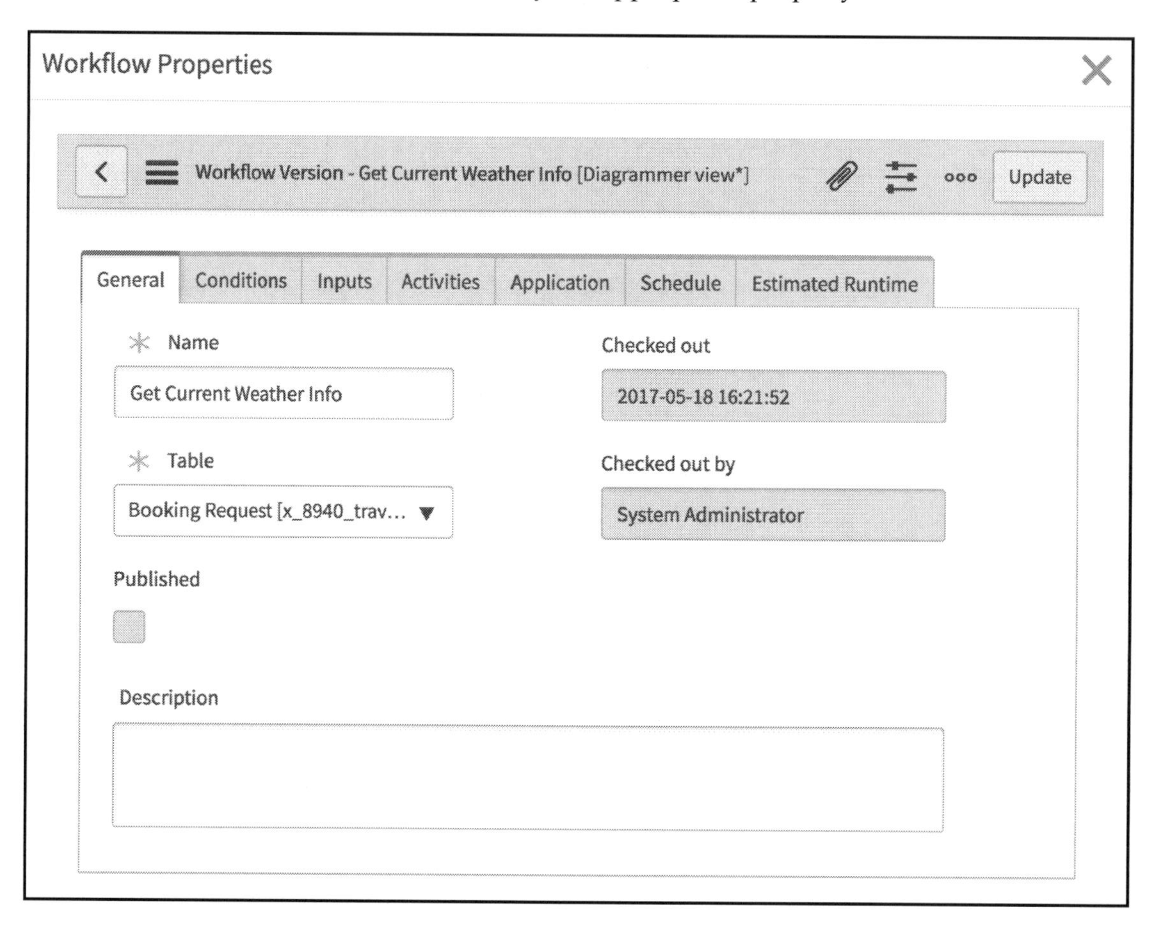


The following different tabs are available in the **Workflow Properties** dialog:

- **General**: This tab can be used to modify the basic information, such as name, table, and description of the workflow. Other fields such as the **Published** checkbox, **Checked out date**, and **Checked out by field** are read-only and cannot be modified by the developer.

- **Conditions**: As shown here, the **Conditions** tab can be used to set the **If condition matches** execution order and conditions of the workflow. In our case, we have set **If condition matches** to run the workflow and have set a simple condition that ensures the **Assigned to** field **is not empty**:

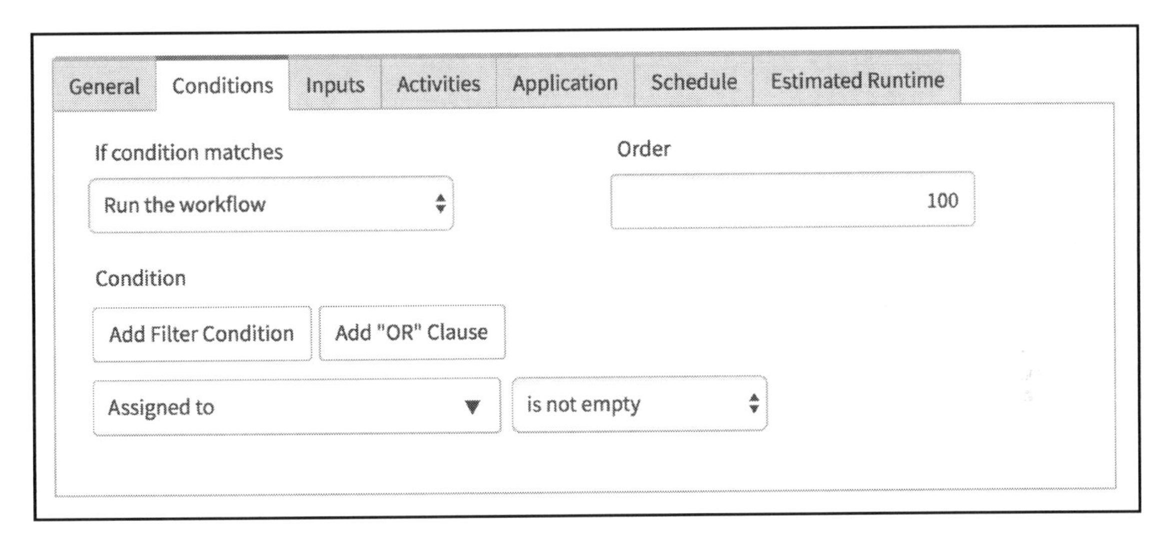


- **Inputs**: This tab is used to define optional workflow-level input parameters that can be passed when the workflow is called from script and used during the execution of the workflow.
- **Activities**: This tab is used to change the maximum number of activities to be supported by the workflow. We can also set the activity-pinning settings in this tab, which are used to prevent the system from updating custom activities downloaded from the ServiceNow store.
- **Application**: The application tab can be used to change the scope of the workflow. We can allow the current workflow to be invoked from artifacts in other application scopes:

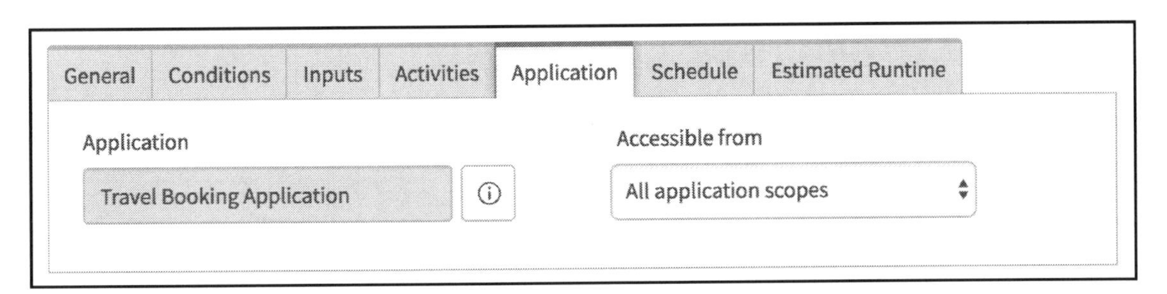

- **Schedule**: This tab can be used to run the workflow at a specific schedule. We can select an existing schedule defined in the system and also set the time zone. The schedule execution of the workflow will be active only when we populate the **Schedule** field:

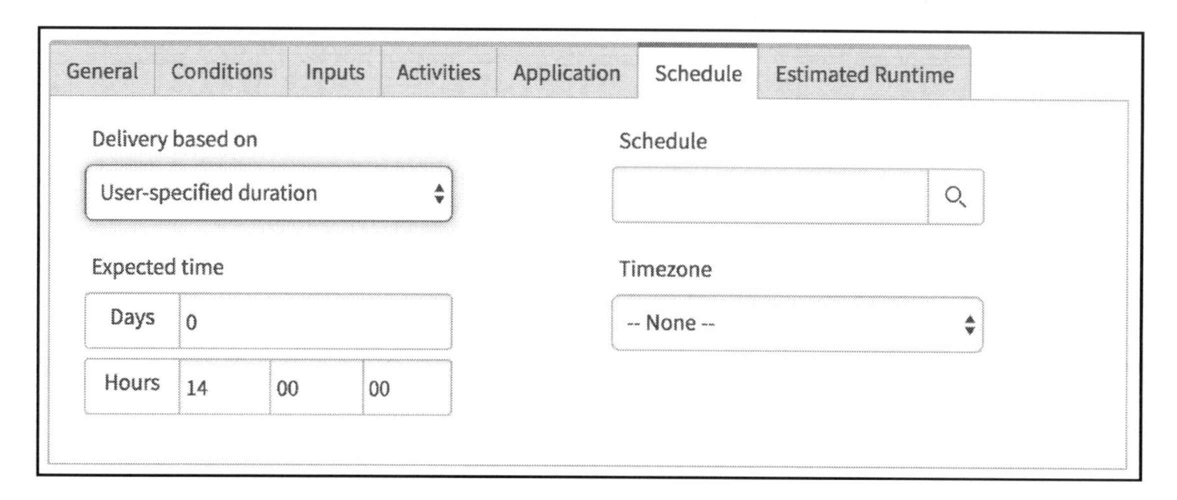


- **Estimated Runtime**: This tab can be used to calculate the estimated runtime based on the estimated runtime configurations. It can be used for larger workflows to improve the processes and flow of the workflow.

# Workflow transitions and activity exit conditions

Once the workflow's start condition evaluates to true, the workflow transition logic comes into play and determines which activity is performed next. Graphically, the workflow transition is represented using arrows.

The transitions can be created by taking the pointer over to one of the exit conditions and dragging and dropping the arrow on top of the activity we wish to execute next. We can select an existing transition and hit the *Delete* key to remove it from the workflow.

The branch activity can be used to transition into more than one activity and the join activity can be used to merge more than one workflow transition into a single activity.

The workflow transition logic continues to find the next activity based on the output and the exit conditions of the activity till it reaches the **End** activity.

Each activity can have more than one exit condition. Exit conditions are usually based on the condition evaluation or output of the activity. For example, as shown below, the `if` activity has two exit conditions, Yes or No, whereas the **Log Message** activity just has one exit condition, `Always`:

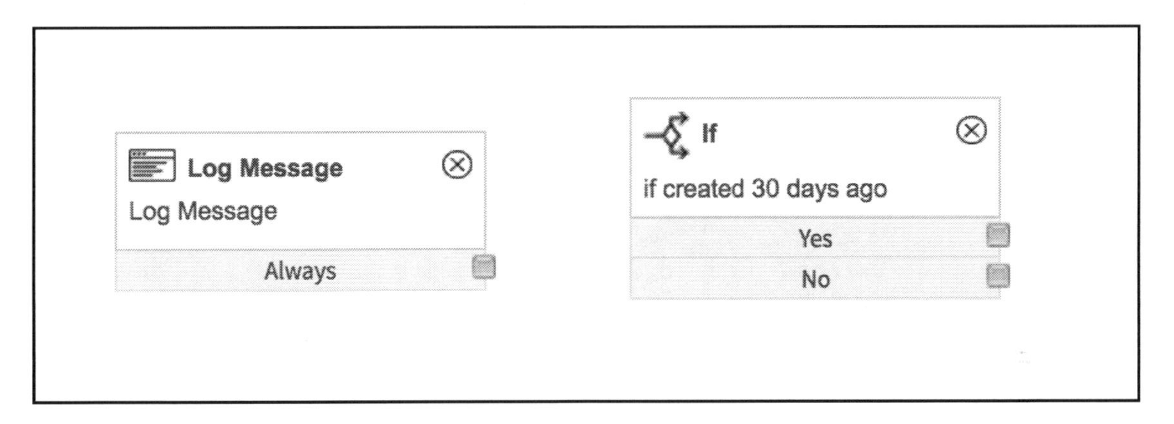


## Adding exit conditions

We can add exit conditions on most of the base activities by right-clicking on the activity title and selecting the **Add Condition** option. We can also add an error condition, as shown in the following screenshot, that will be used as transition in case the activity fails to execute properly. The menu can also be used to copy and pin/unpin an activity:

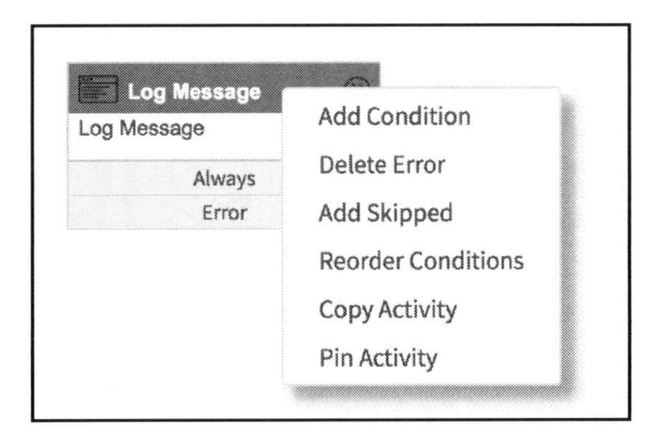

# Adding activities to a workflow

There are two ways to add activities to a workflow. Using the **Core** palette, we can either drag and drop an activity onto the workflow canvas or double-click on the activity type to add it to the workflow canvas. The **New Activity Property** dialog window is shown as soon as we add a new activity.

# Removing an activity from a workflow

We can easily remove any activity from a checked-out workflow simply by clicking on the cross icon in the top-right corner of the activity, as shown in the screenshot of *Validating a workflow* section. The **Begin** and **End** activities cannot be removed from the workflow.

# Validating a workflow

We can use the Validate icon in the title bar of the canvas to validate a workflow. A workflow must transition properly from the **Begin** activity and reach the **End** activity at the end of the process:

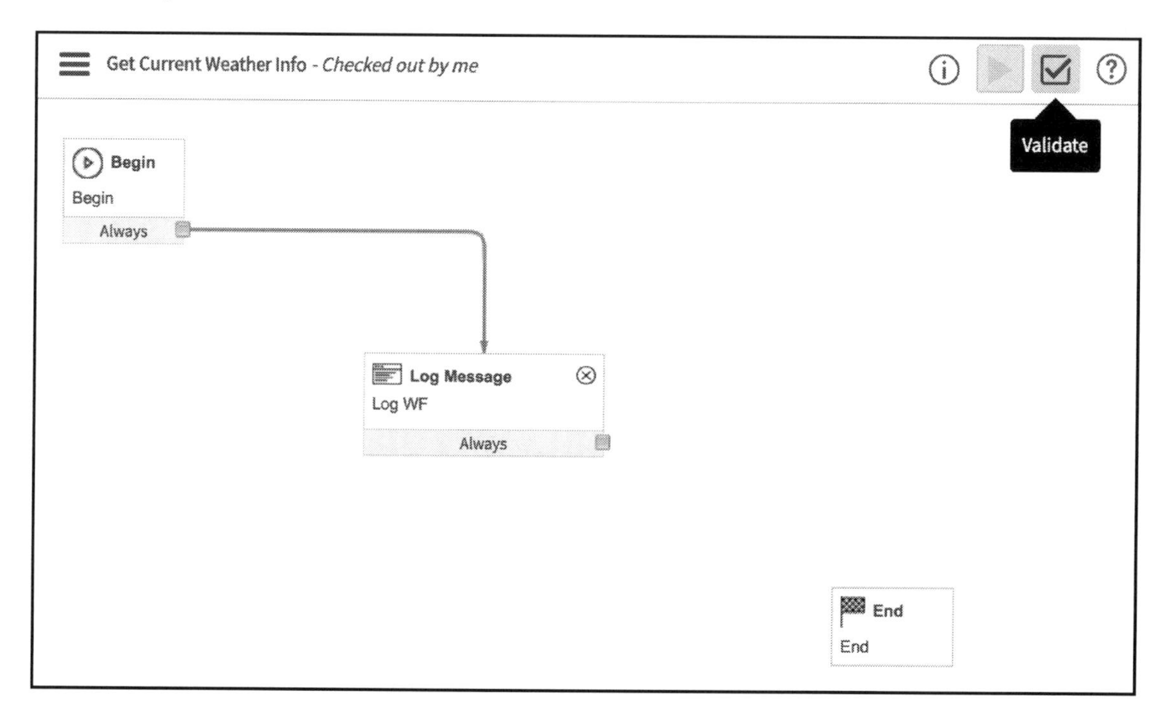

The ServiceNow platform doesn't allow broken workflows to be saved or published. A workflow must pass the validation in order to be published. We can click on the Validate icon to open the **Workflow Validation Report** window, as shown in the following screenshot:

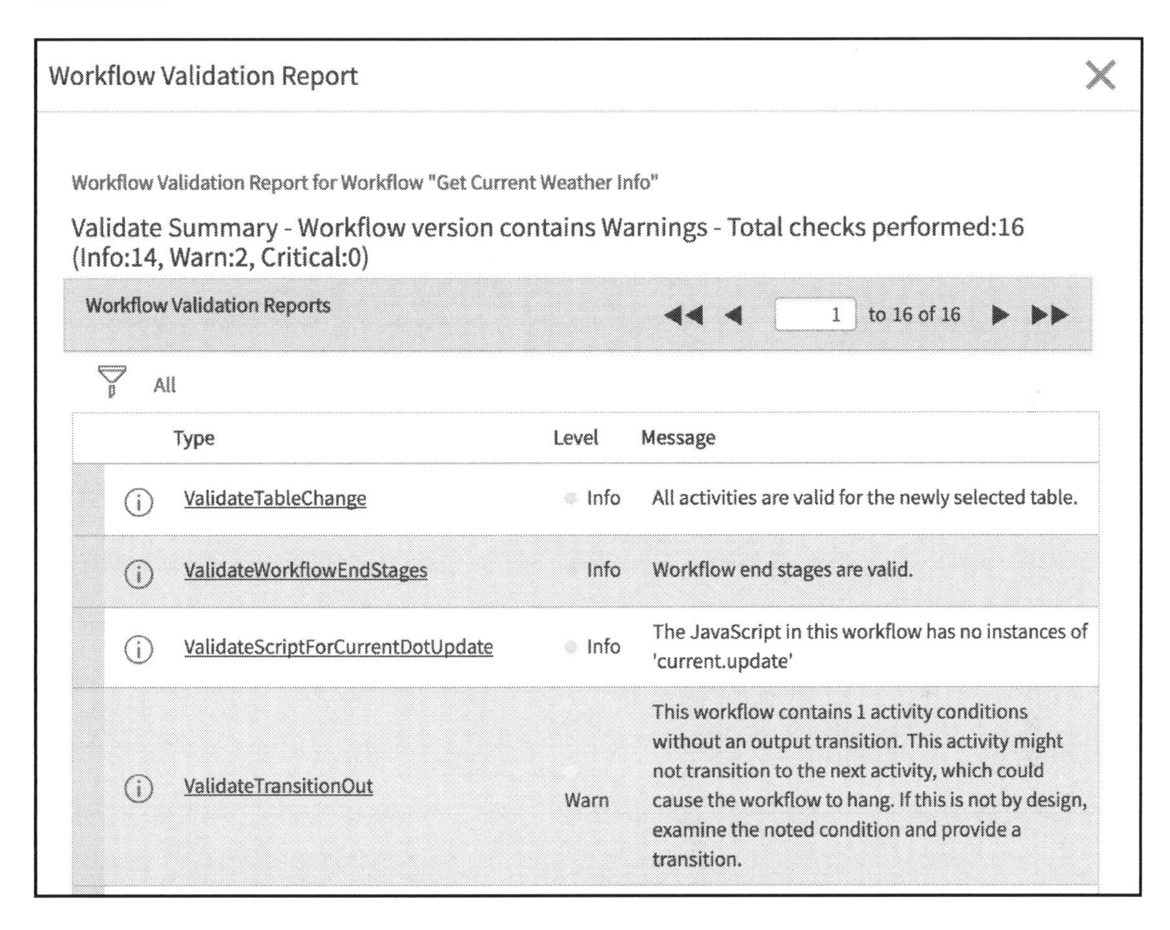


It is clear from the validation summary listed that our workflow contains one warning. At least one of the activities in our workflow version doesn't have an output transition. We can fix this by dragging the square icon next to the exit condition of the log message activity and dropping it on top of the **End** activity.

The final workflow should look similar to the one shown here, where all exit conditions of all the activities are transitioning to another activity and reaching the **End** activity at the end:

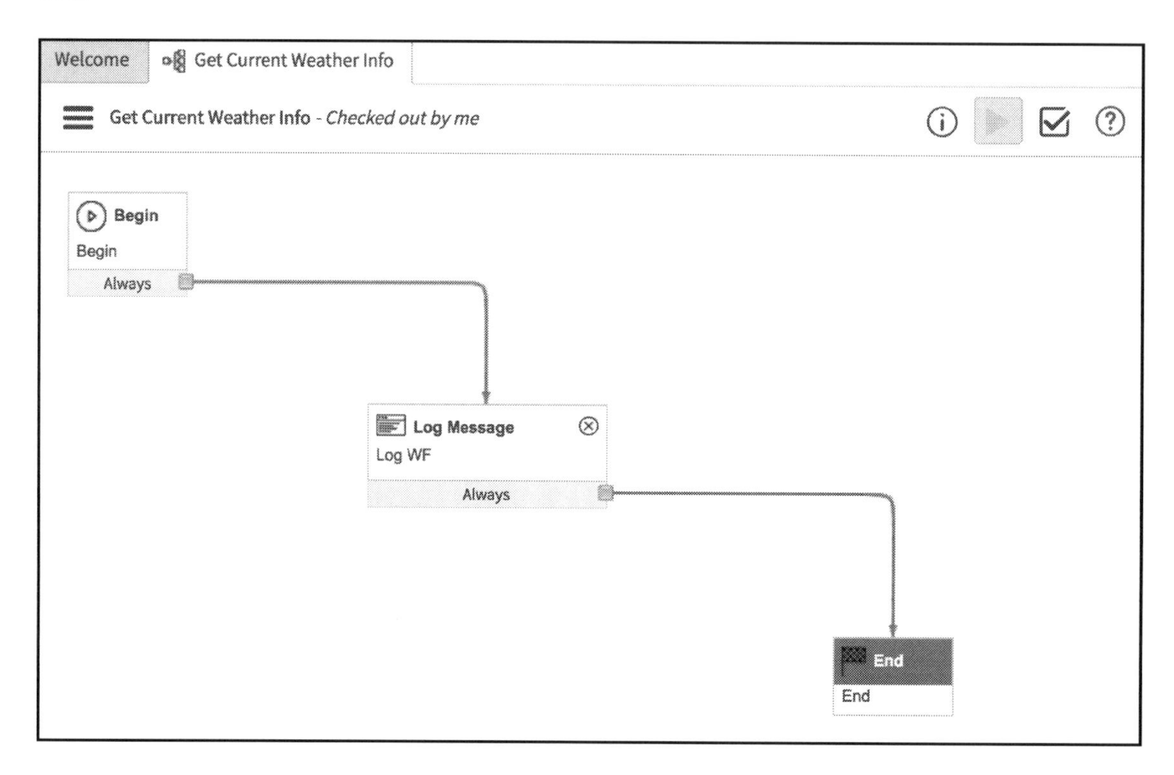


# Workflow activities

Let us now go through some of the most important core activities available in the ServiceNow platform. These core activities can be used in any workflow and one workflow can reuse the same core activity multiple times. An instance of the activity is created when we add it to the workflow.

The core activities provided by ServiceNow can be used to perform many different tasks, such as running a script, triggering an event, waiting (listening) for an event, logging a message, invoking rest calls, sending notifications, creating tasks, or requesting approvals.

# Approval and rollback activities

The approval and rollback activities, as shown here, are available only for tables that extend from the `Task` table. If the table doesn't extend from the task table, then all the activities except **Approval - User** and **Approval Action** are grayed out and not available:

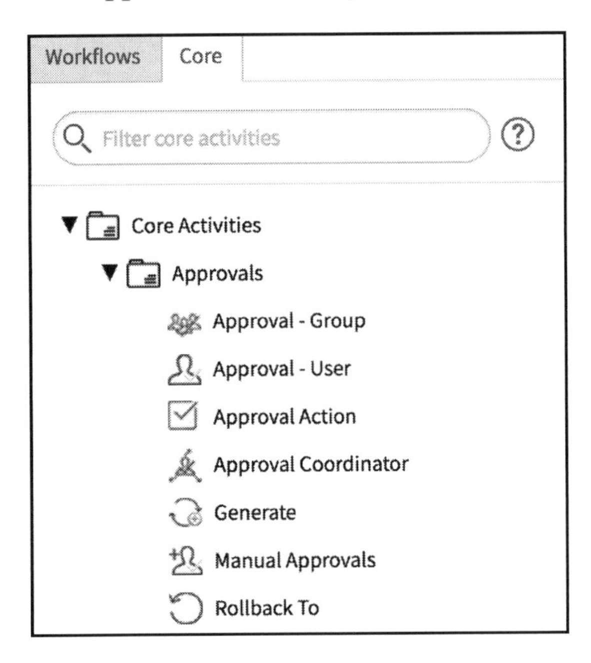


The following different activities are available under the approval and rollback activities:

- **Approval Action**: This activity is used to perform an approval action on the current task and mark the task as approved or rejected.
- **Approval Coordinator**: This activity is used to create an approval whose result depends on the output of one or more child activities, which usually includes one or more of the **Approval - User**, **Approval - Group**, and/or **Manual Approval** activities.
- **Approval - Group**: This activity can be used to create approval requests for each member of a specific group.

- **Approval - User**: This activity creates one or more individual user approval request. We can specify whether the request will be approved if one of the selected users approves, if everyone approves, or run a script to determine the outcome.
- **Generate**: This activity can be used to create task or approval records from any task or approval activities placed after it. If the **Generate** activity is not used, the workflow engine waits to create any records until reaching the associated activity during workflow execution.
- **Manual Approvals**: This activity watches any approvals that are added manually outside of the workflow process. It basically monitors the status of the approval field.
- **Rollback To**: When the **Rollback To** activity is triggered, the workflow moves processing backward to a specified activity in the workflow and resets overlapping activities that have already executed back to their original state.

# Condition workflow activities

The following four core activities are available under the condition workflow activities: **If**, **Switch**, **Wait for condition**, and **Wait for WF Event**:

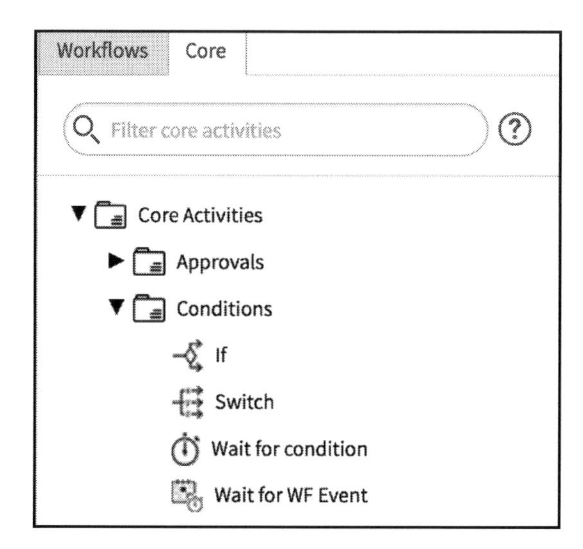

- **If**: The **If** activity is used to check for a condition or execute a script to evaluate whether `Yes` or `No` exit conditions are met.
- **Switch**: Unlike the **If** activity, the **Switch** activity can be used to determine whether the value of a field or workflow variable matches one of several case values. The case values are used as the exit conditions.
- **Wait for Condition**: The **Wait for Condition** activity can be used to cause the workflow to pause its execution path and wait at this activity until some specified condition evaluates to `true`.
- **Wait for WF Event**: Similar to **Wait for Condition**, the **Wait for WF Event** activity causes the workflow to pause its execution path and wait at this activity until the specified event is fired. The event could be fired from another activity in a parallel execution path. Events are fired in a script using the `workflow.fireEvent('eventName')` method.

# Workflow notification activities

Workflow notification activities can be used to notify create event or to send out notifications. The following two notification activities are available as part of the core workflow activities:

- **Create Event**: The **Create Event** activity can be used to add an event to the event queue.
- **Notification**: This activity can be used to send an email or SMS message to specific users or groups. An advanced script can also be used to determine the recipients.

# Subflow activity

The subflow activity, referred to as the **Parallel Flow Launcher** activity, can be used to launch another workflow as an activity. The parent workflow will wait for the completion of the child (sub) workflow before continuing execution. The child workflow must not be marked as inactive as it may cause the workflow to hang.

# Task activities

The task activities can be used to perform certain operations on records in tables that extend from the `Task` table:

- **Attachment Note**: The **Attachment Note** activity can be used to add an attachment to the current record
- **Create Task**: The **Create Task** activity can be used to generate a record on any of the tables that extend the `Task` table

The availability and functionality of some of the activities depends on the table on which the workflow is being applied. The **Create Catalog Task** feature is also available when we are defining a workflow that is applied on any service catalog related tables such as `Requested Item`.

# Timer activity

The **Timer** activity can be used to pause the workflow for a specified period of time. The duration can either be an absolute time value or a relative value based on a defined schedule.

The **SLA Timer** activity is available when we apply the workflow on the `task_sla` table.

# Utility workflow activities

The utility workflow activities, as shown in the following screenshot, offer various tools to enhance the flow and process of the workflow:

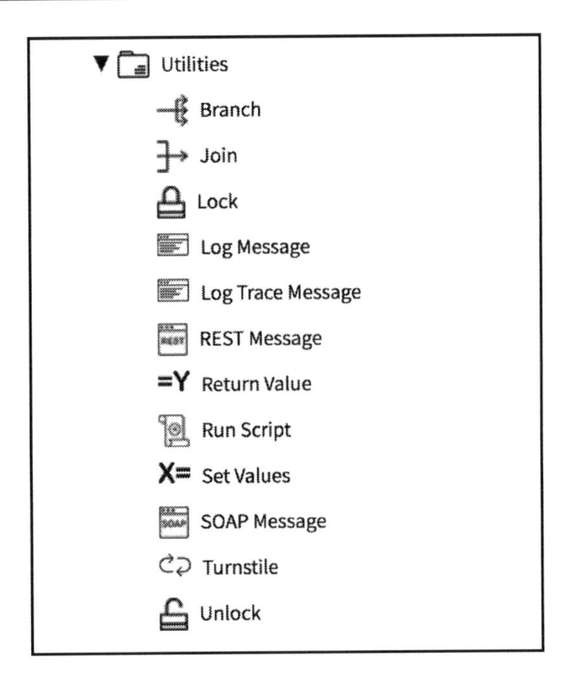


The following different activities are available under the utility category:

- **Branch**: The **Branch** activity is used to split the transition of the workflow into multiple paths.
- **Join**: The **Join** activity is used to merge two or more execution paths into one transition.
- **Lock**: This activity can be used to prevent contexts of the current workflow from transitioning past the lock activity. Other contexts pause when they reach the lock activity until the lock is released.
- **Log Message**: The **Log Message** activity can be used to log (write) an entry (message) to the workflow log. It is useful for logging outputs from scripts or other activities.

- **Log Trace Message**: The **Log Trace Message** activity can be used to log a trace message, which is useful for understanding the execution of activities and other system modules, to the workflow log.
- **REST Message**: The **REST Message** activity is used to make outgoing REST calls. The activity allows the REST endpoint URL configured in the **REST Message** module to be overridden and also supplies the dynamic values to the variables.
- **Return Value**: The **Return Value** activity is used in child workflows to return a value to a parent workflow.
- **Run Script**: The **Run Script** activity is used to execute scripts.
- **Set Values**: The **Set Values** activity is used to set the values of the fields in the current record.
- **Turnstile**: When working with large workflows, there might be a scenario where a workflow passes from the same activity multiple times. The **Turnstile** activity can be used in such scenarios to limit the number of times a workflow can pass through the same point.
- **Unlock**: The **Unlock** activity is used in conjunction with the lock activity. It is used to release a lock that was previously placed using the **Lock** activity.

# REST calls using a workflow

Now that we have learned the basics of workflows, let us now create a workflow that will use the REST Message activity to make a call to a remote REST endpoint to get the weather conditions at the From and Destination locations. However, before we create the workflow, we must define the REST endpoint in the **REST Message** module.

# Defining a REST endpoint

We must define every REST endpoint using the **REST Message** module. To define the REST endpoint, open **Studio** and in the **Create Application File** wizard, select **Outbound Integrations** | **REST Message**, as shown in the following screenshot, and click **Create**:

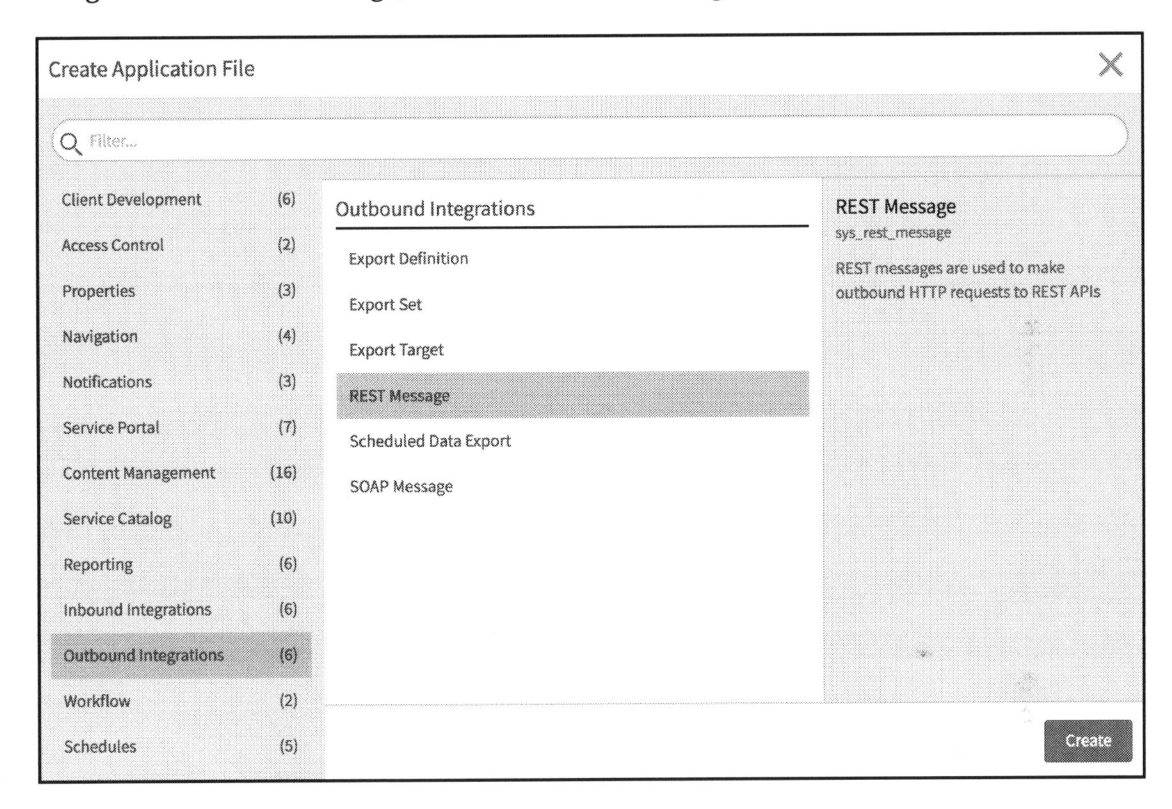

The **REST Message** new record form, as shown in the following screenshot, will open in **Studio**:

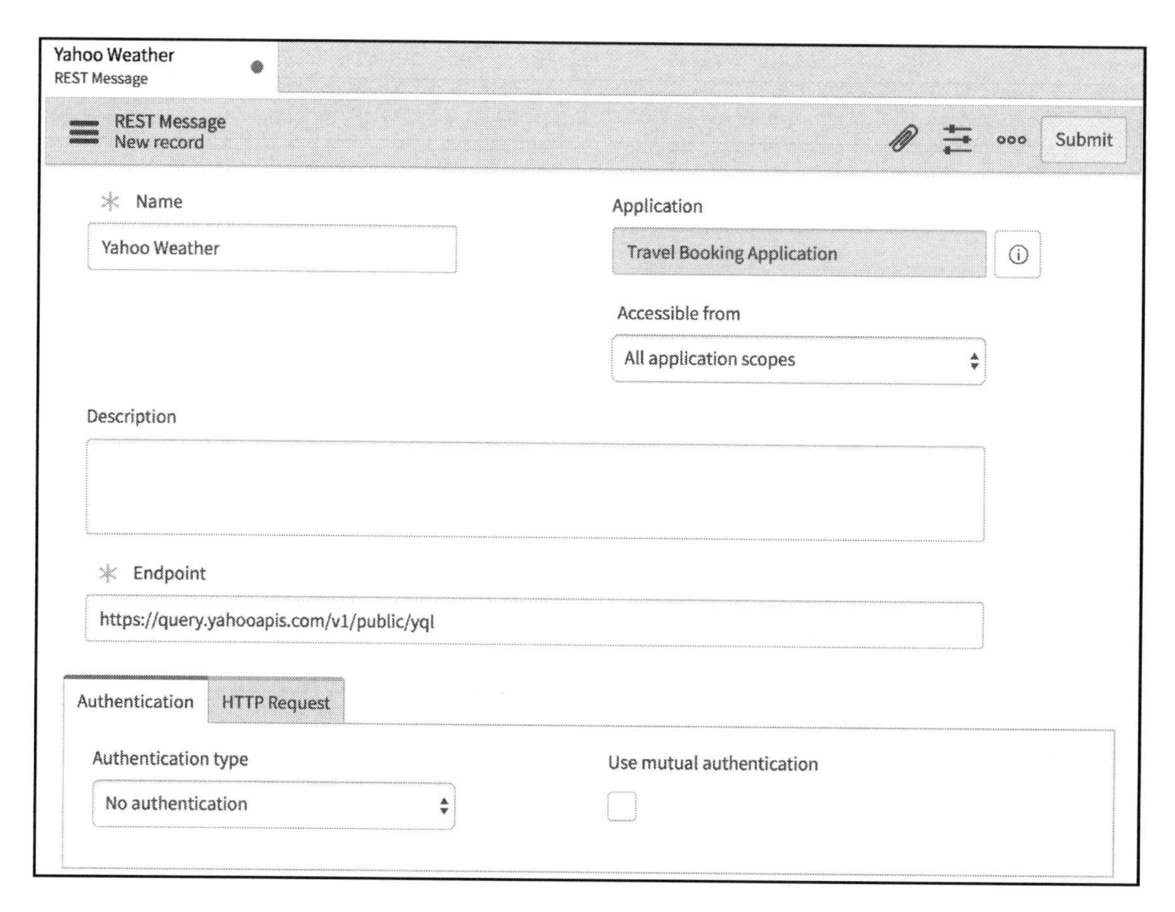


Fill in the form with the following values:

- **Name**: `Yahoo Weather`
- **Accessible from**: **All application scopes**
- **Endpoint**: `https://query.yahooapis.com/v1/public/yql`

Click on the **Submit** button to create the endpoint definition. Now scroll down to the **HTTP Methods** related list, as shown in the following screenshot:

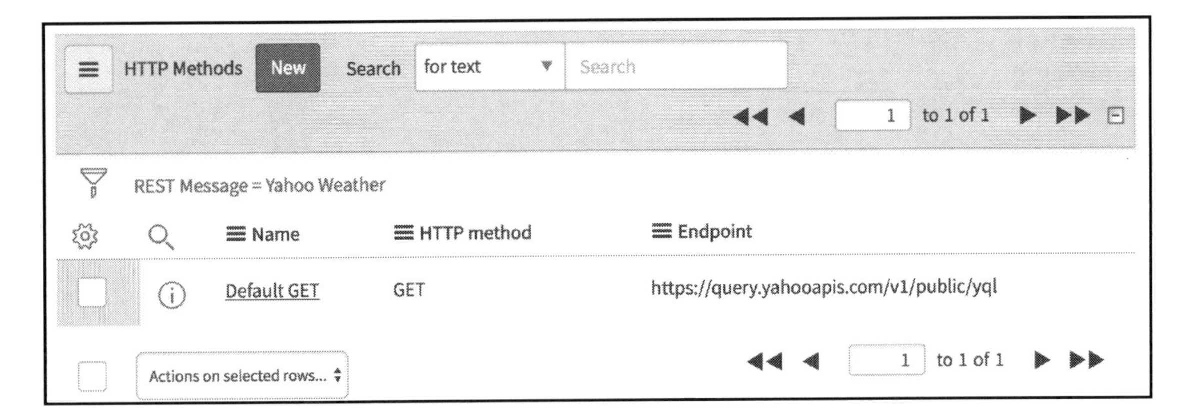


The system will automatically create the **Default GET** method entry for us. Click on the info icon next to the **Default GET** method and edit the form as shown in the following screenshot:

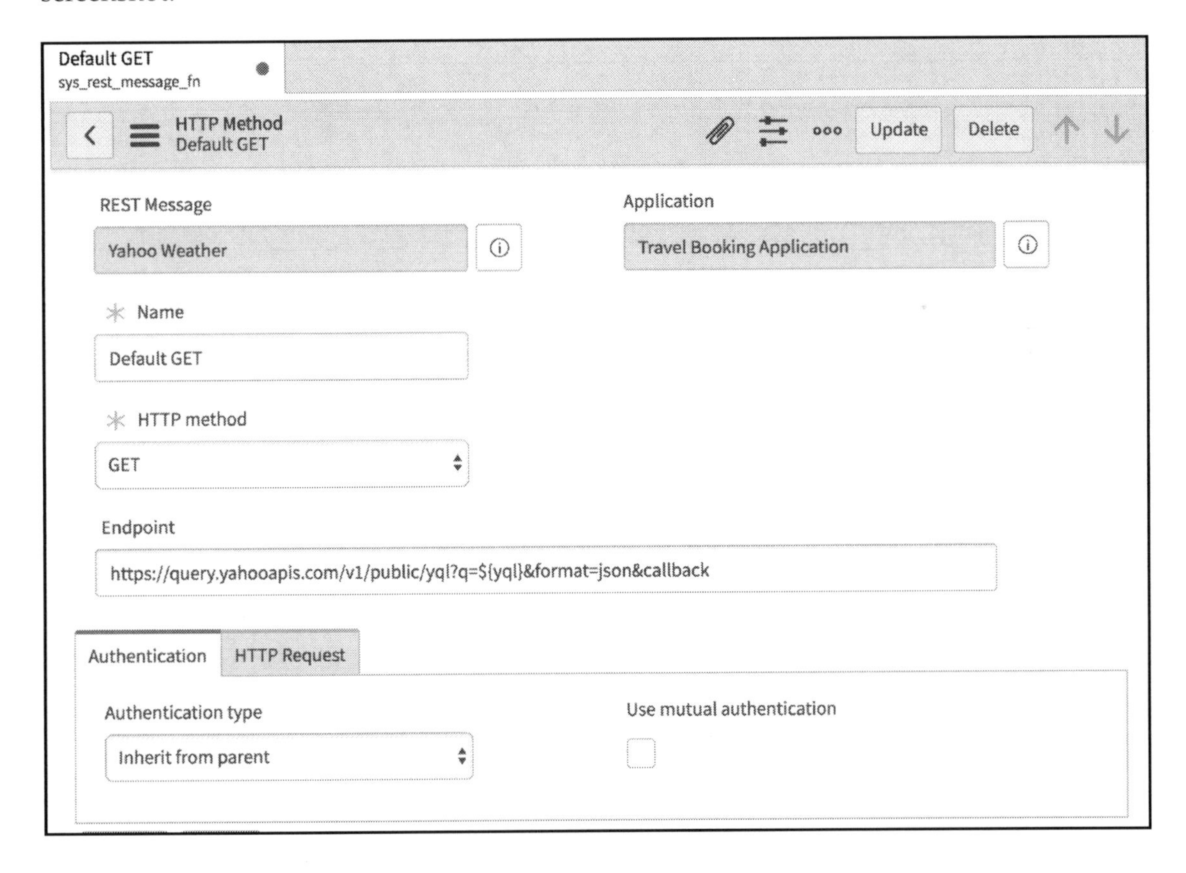

Make sure to change the endpoint URL to `https://query.yahooapis.com/v1/public/yql?q=${yql}&format=json&callback`.

`${city}` is a placeholder for the variable of the same name city. We will pass a value to the variable from the workflow to fetch the weather conditions of the city we are interested in.

**YQL** is short for **Yahoo Query Language**. You can learn more about Yahoo's YQL and Yahoo Weather API by visiting the API home page at `https://developer.yahoo.com/weather/`.

# Making a REST request using a workflow

To create a new workflow, open **Workflow Editor** and click on the **New** button under the **Workflows** palette tab and fill in the new workflow form as detailed here:

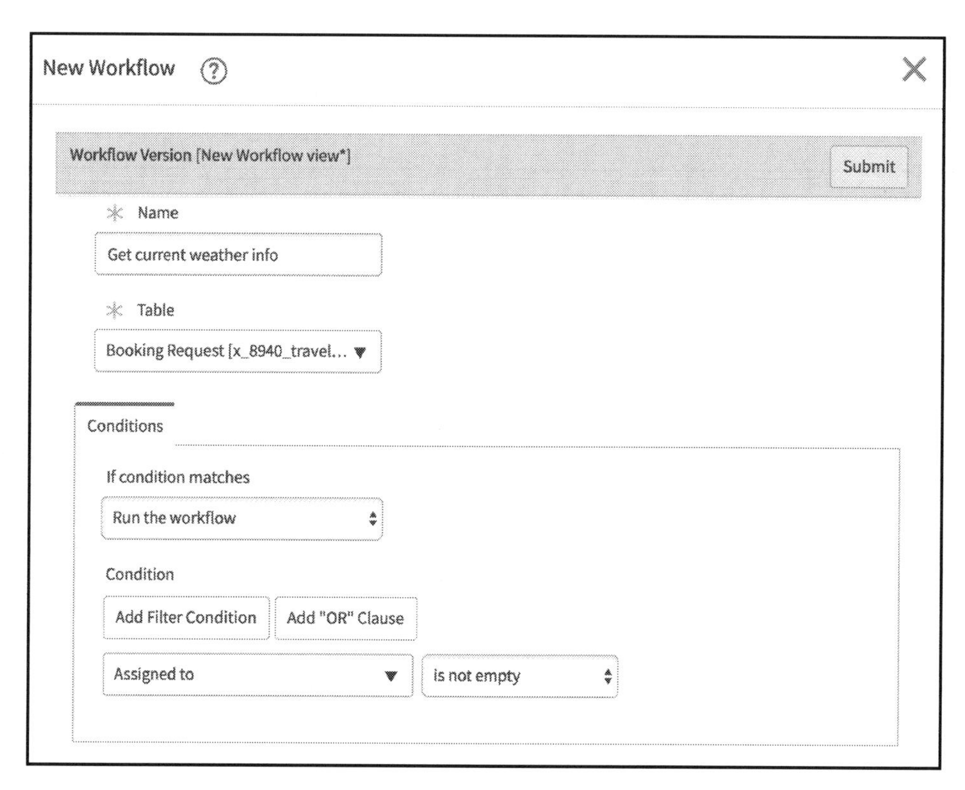

Fill in the form with following values:

- * **Name**: `Get current weather info`
- * **Table**: `Booking Request`
- **Condition**: **Assigned to | is not empty**

Click on the **Submit** button to create a workflow named **Get current weather info** on the `Booking Request` table. The workflow canvas will look similar to the one shown in the following screenshot:

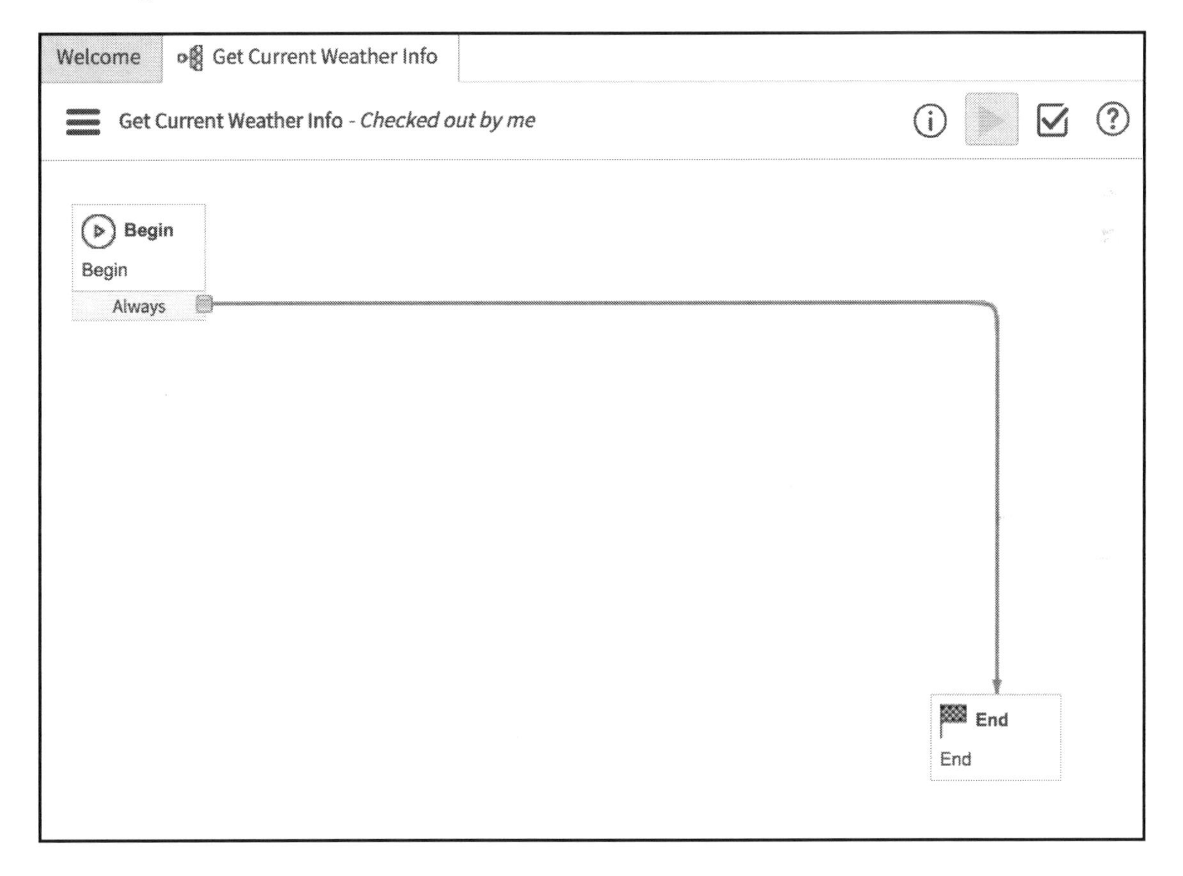

Now drag and drop the **Run Script** activity on the workflow canvas. The **New Activity** form dialog will open up in a modal window. Fill in the form with the following values:

- **Name**: `Call Yahoo Weather Service`
- **Script**: Populate the **Script** field with the following code:

```
var yql = 'select item from weather.forecast where woeid in (select woeid
from geo.places(1) where text="'
   + current.u_from_location.name
   + '")';
try {
 var r = new sn_ws.RESTMessageV2('x_8940_travel_book.Yahoo Weather',
'Default GET');
//replace 8940 with your company code
r.setStringParameterNoEscape('yql', encodeURI(yql));

 var response = r.execute();
 var responseBody = response.getBody();
 var httpStatus = response.getStatusCode();
    gs.addInfoMessage(httpStatus);
 if (httpStatus==200) {
  gs.addInfoMessage(responseBody);
  var weatherJSON = JSON.parse(responseBody);
  var currTemp = weatherJSON.query.results.channel.item.condition.temp;
  var currText = weatherJSON.query.results.channel.item.condition.text;
workflow.scratchpad.currentCondition = "Current condition at "+
current.u_from_location.name + ": " + currTemp + " - " + currText;
 gs.addInfoMessage("Current condition at "+ current.u_from_location.name +
": " + currTemp + " - " + currText);
 }
}
catch(ex) {
 var message = ex.getMessage();
}
```

The preceding code makes use of the `RESTMessageV2` API and creates an instance of the `Default GET` method defined in the `Yahoo Weather` method in the outbound **REST Messages** module.

The YQL we are using will help us fetch the current weather conditions from the Yahoo Weather service.

The name of the city is picked from the `From (u_from_location)` field in the `Booking Request` table. Furthermore, we are employing a workflow scratchpad to pass values set in one activity to subsequent activities.

The completed form will look similar to the one shown here:

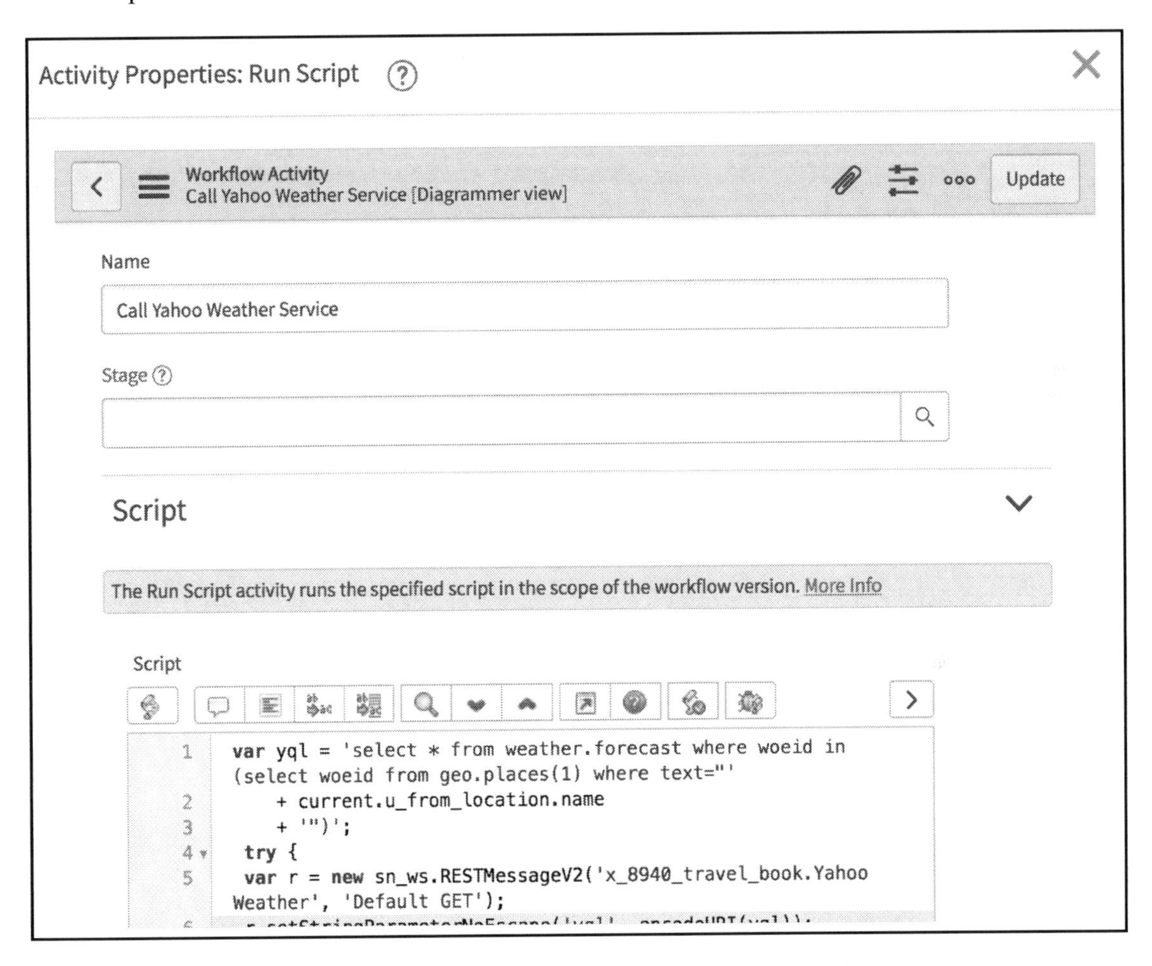

Let us now add another activity to our workflow--**Set Values**. As shown here, we will use the **Set Values** activity to update the **Work Notes Journal** field:

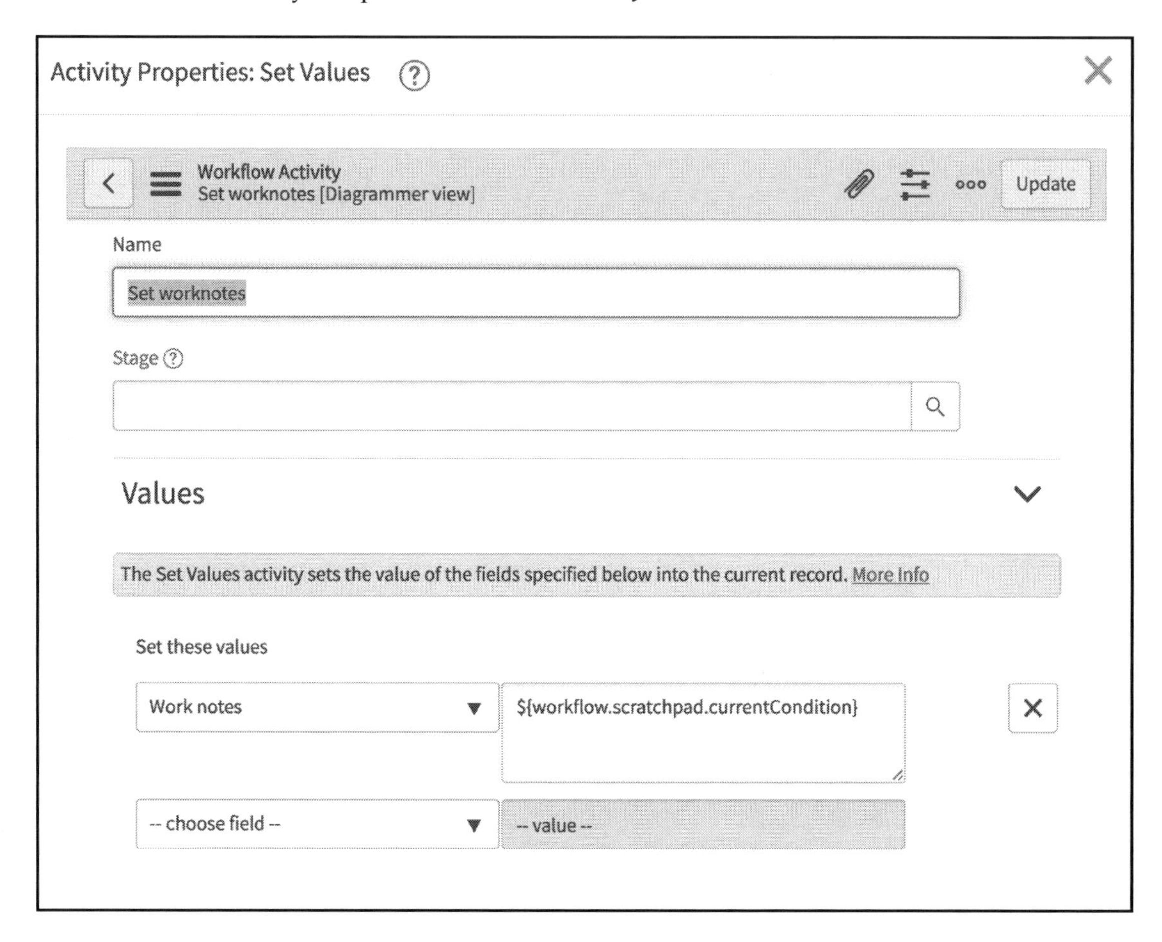


Fill in the **Set Values** new activity form with the following values:

- **Name**: `Set worknotes`
- **Set Values**: **Work notes** | `${workflow.scratchpad.currentCondition}`

The `workflow.scratchpad.currentCondition` variable is set in the workflow scope in the previous **Run Script** activity.

Change the existing transition on the **Begin** activity to point to the new **Run Script** activity and then to **Set Values** and then publish the workflow.

The completed workflow will look similar to the one shown here:

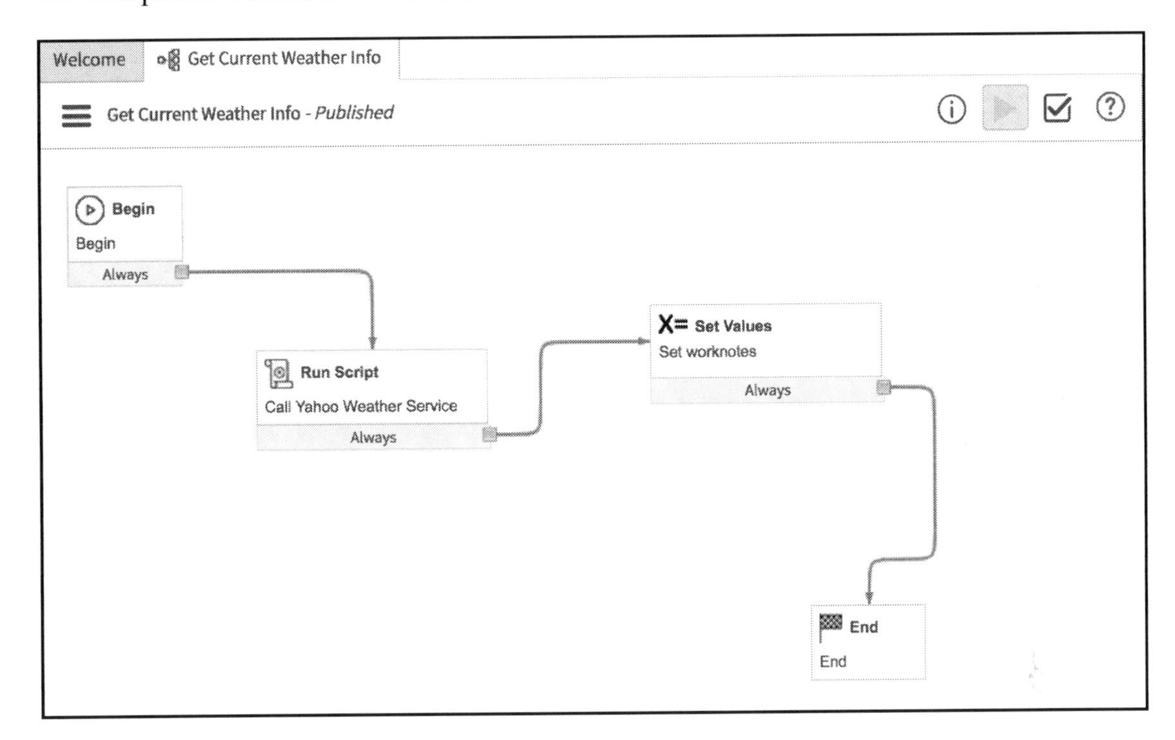

Let us now test our workflow by creating a new entry in the `Booking Request` table and then setting the **Assigned to** field. Subsequently, when we set the **Assigned to** field, an instance of the workflow, known as a workflow context, is triggered because the `start` condition of the workflow is met. If everything goes well, we can see the Work notes entry in the **Activities** (filtered) formatter, as shown in the following screenshot:

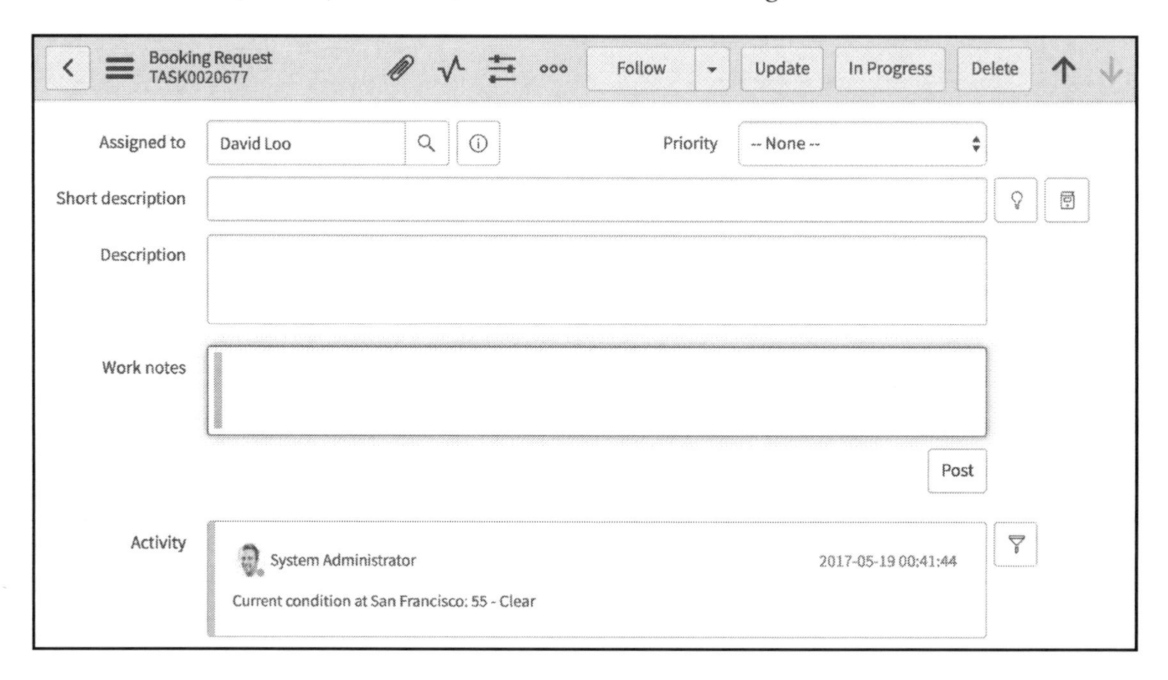


We can also monitor the execution of a workflow instance, known as a workflow context, graphically using the **Active contexts** or **All contexts** navigational module.

# Summary

In this chapter, we learned the concept of workflows and about different core activities. We learned in depth about the concepts of workflows and how they can be used to bring more visibility to the development process. We learned how to make use of the **Run Script** and **Set Values** activities. We also learned how to create an outbound REST message and invoke outbound REST calls using only scripts.

In the next chapter, we will learn how to debug the different server- and client-side scripting options available in the ServiceNow platform.

# 12
# Debugging in ServiceNow

We have learned how to write client-side and server-side code, including client scripts, business rules, script includes, script actions, UI macros, and UI pages using Jelly, and we have also learned how to design workflows. While there are many different kinds of scripting features available in the platform, developers usually also require a set of tools and features to debug their code. The ServiceNow platform offers developers many different ways to debug, troubleshoot, and optimize their code.

Within the ServiceNow platform, we write both server-side and client-side code. The ways to troubleshoot them more or less remain the same but the approach differs. In this chapter, we will cover the many different troubleshooting and debugging techniques available within the platform. We will also cover some coding best practices and understand the flow and execution of the different available scripting options, including server-side scripts, client-side scripts, and workflows.

In this chapter, we will cover the following topics and learn how to use the many features to debug and troubleshoot scripts in the ServiceNow platform:

- Syntax editor
- Script Debugger
- JavaScript log
- Field watcher

# Syntax editor

The syntax editor helps developers to write JavaScript code when working with scripts. It is enabled by default on all instances. The syntax editor is ubiquitous in the ServiceNow platform and is available on all forms where we have a field to write JavaScript code:

```
(function executeRule(current, previous /*null when async*/) {

    // Add your code here
    var gr = new GlideRecord(current.getTableName());
    gr.addActiveQuery();
    gr.addQuery("u_caller",current.u_caller);
    var state_qry = gr.addQuery("state","-5");
    state_qry.addOrCondition("state","IS","1");
    gr.query();
    if ( gr.hasNext() ) {
        gs.addErrorMessage("Unable to "+current.operation()+" the record as there is already an existing travel booking request by the user in pending or open state.");
        current.setAbortAction(true);
    }

})(current, previous);
```

The syntax editor, as shown in the preceding screenshot, may look like a simple text editor with syntax highlighting and formatting support; however, the syntax editor in the ServiceNow platform has lots of features developers must be aware of. The following are the different action buttons available in the syntax editor:

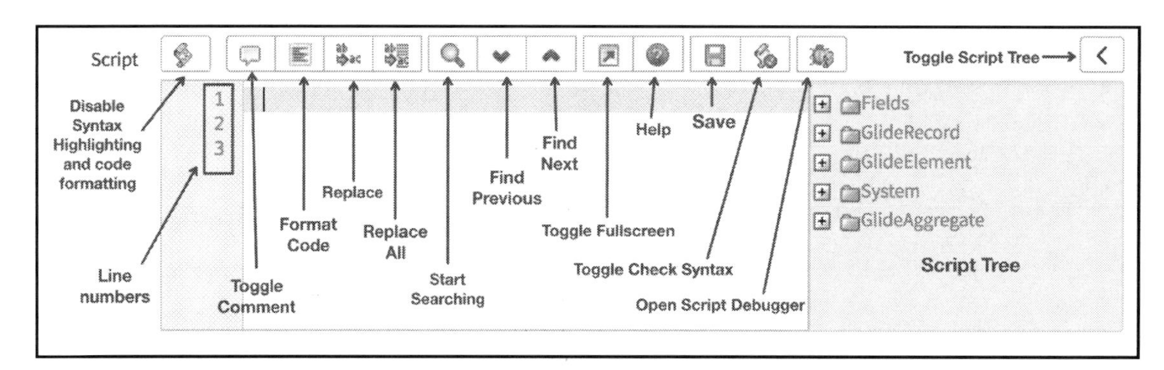

All of these features are simple to follow and understand but keeping them in mind when writing code can be very useful. The following are some of the features available in the syntax editor.

# Context-sensitive help

One of the most important features of the syntax editor is that it can help display context-sensitive API information when writing code, commonly known as autocomplete.

The context-sensitive help in the syntax editor is intelligent enough to offer suggestions based on the script type. For example, when writing a business rule, as shown here, it only offers suggestions from the server-side Glide API and objects such as current and previous. Similarly, when writing a client script, it displays suggestions from the client-side Glide API, such as `g_form`:

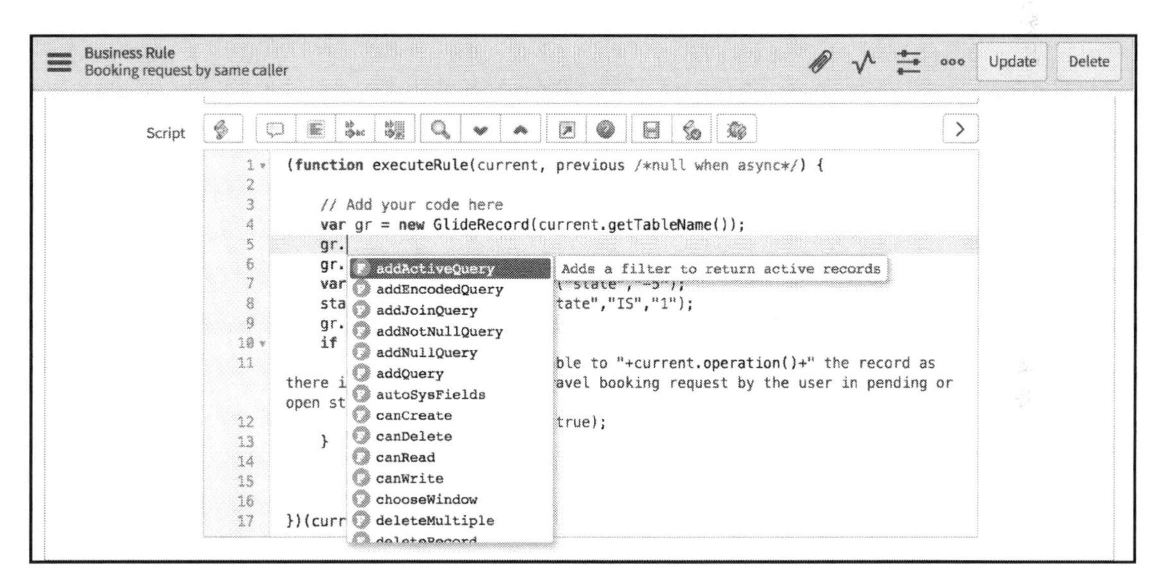


# Syntax editor keyboard shortcuts

The syntax editor has support to perform many actions using keyboard shortcuts.

# Scripting assistance

Pressing the *Ctrl* and spacebar keys together triggers the scripting assistance feature of the syntax editor. It displays a list of possible class names, function names, object names, and variable names that can be inserted at the cursor position.

# Period (.) key

The period (.) key can be pressed after any valid class name to see a list of methods for that class, as shown in the following screenshot:

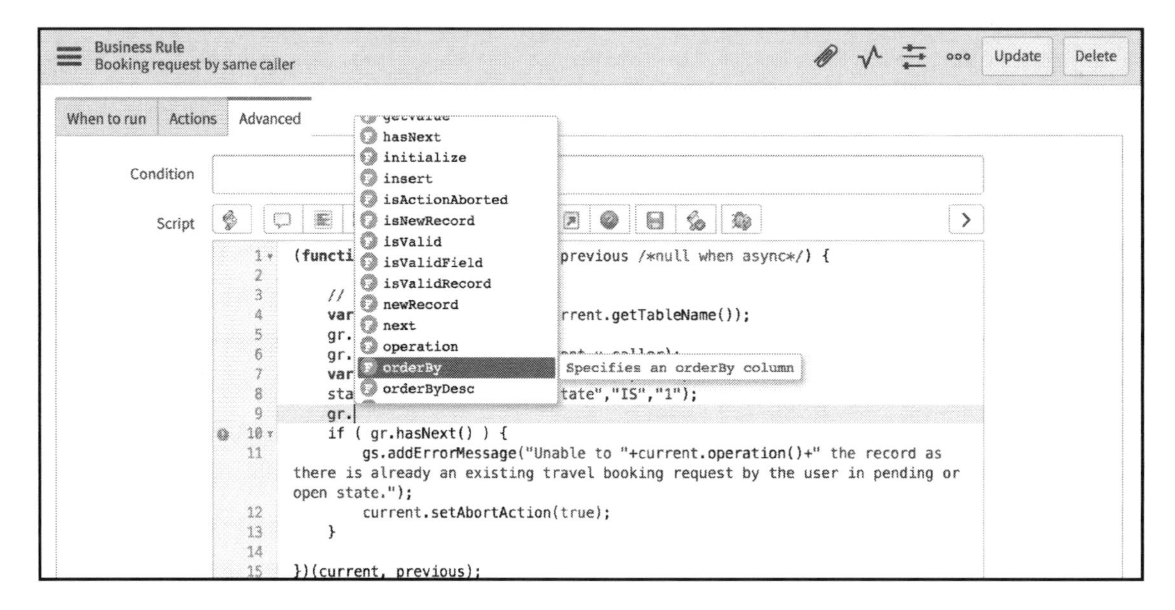


# Open parenthesis

The open parenthesis character can be pressed after any valid class or method name to see all possible parameters, as shown here:

```
4       var gr = new GlideRecord(current.getTableName());
5       gr.addActiveQuery();
6       gr.addQuery()
7       var state_qr addQuery(name: string, value: string) -> GlideQueryCondition
8       state_qry.addOrCondition("state","IS","1");
9       gr.query();
```

## Toggle full screen mode

The toggle full screen icon on the top button can be used to switch between displaying the syntax editor in full screen or normally. Alternately, the *Ctrl* + *M* keys can be pressed to toggle between full screen and normal mode.

## Start search

We can start a search for a string within the **Script** field by pressing the *Ctrl* + *F* keys on windows or command + *F* on macOS. Clicking on the start search button icon on top of the syntax editor can also be used to perform a search. The search query could be a normal string or a regular expression enclosed within backslashes (`/^[a-z][0-9]/`).

As shown in the following screenshot, the **Search** field appears on top to the syntax editor just below the action buttons. We can type in the search term we are searching for and then hit **Return** to jump to the first occurrence of the string within the **Script** field:

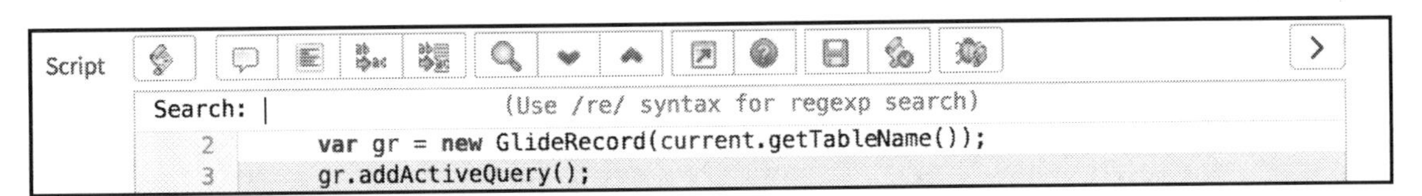


## Find next

The find next operation can be performed while there is an active search. Pressing *Ctrl* + *G* on windows or command + *G* jumps the cursor to the next occurrence of the search term.

## Find previous

The find previous operation, similar to find next, can be performed while there is an active search. Pressing the *Ctrl* + *Shift* + *G* on windows or command + *Shift* + *G* on macOS locates the previous occurrence of the search term.

## Replace

The `replace` command can be triggered by either clicking on the replace icon or by pressing the *Ctrl* + *E* keys on windows or command + *E* keys on macOS. It first asks for the search term, then a string to replace the search term with, and finally confirms before replacing the search term with the string.

## Replace all

The `replace all` command can be triggered by either clicking on the replace all icon or by pressing the *Ctrl*+ *;* keys on windows or command + *;* keys on macOS. Unlike the `replace` command, the replace all feature replaces all occurrences of a search term.

# Syntax editor macros

Script macros can be used as shortcuts for typing commonly used code. For example, we can type `vargr` anywhere in the code and press the *Tab* key to insert macro text defined for the macro named `vargr`.

That means we can type the name of any of the predefined macros, such as `vargr`, as shown in the following screenshot:

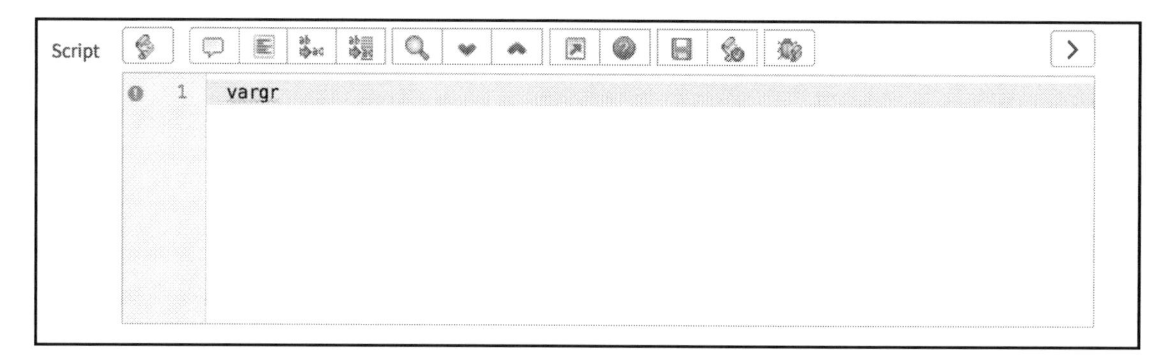

Then press the *Tab* key to write the following output:

```
Script
1  var gr = new GlideRecord("");
2  gr.addQuery("name", "value");
3  gr.query();
4  if (gr.next()) {
5
6  }
7
```

## Available macros

To see a list of available macros, we can type `help` and press the *Tab* key, which will show a list of all available macros with their description, as shown in the following screenshot:

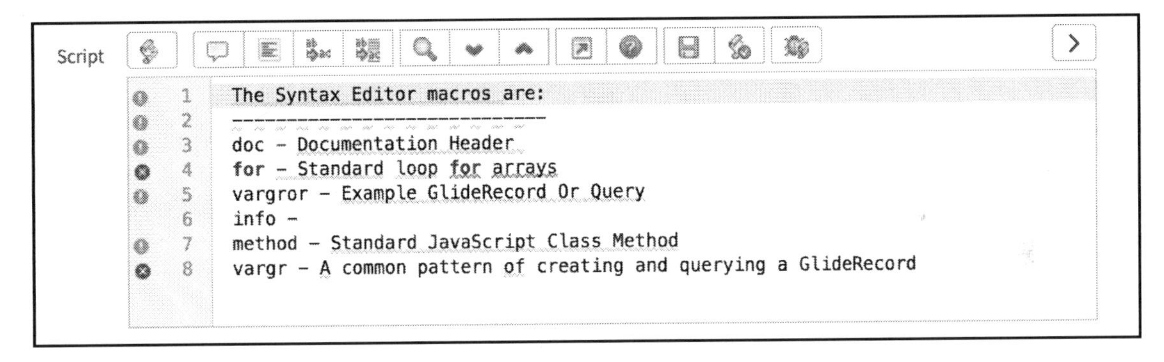

Script
The Syntax Editor macros are:
-----------------------------
doc - Documentation Header
for - Standard loop for arrays
vargror - Example GlideRecord Or Query
info -
method - Standard JavaScript Class Method
vargr - A common pattern of creating and querying a GlideRecord

Notice that the output of the `help` macro is not a valid JavaScript code and will cause your script to fail if you forget to remove or comment it.

# Creating a custom macro

We can create a custom script macro for use with the syntax editor. To create a new syntax editor macro, switch to the main ServiceNow interface and open the **System Definition** | **Syntax Editor Macros** module. Click on the new button to open the new syntax editor macro form, as shown in the following screenshot:

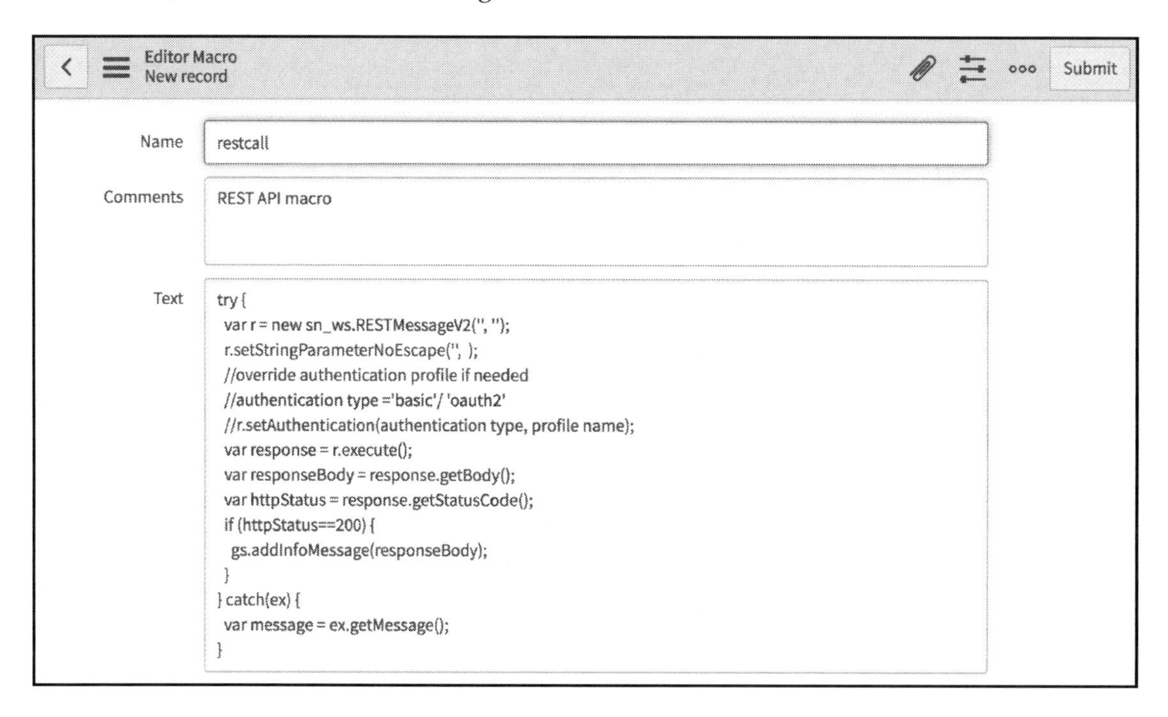


Fill in the form with the following values:

- **Name**: `restcall`
- **Comments**: `REST API macro`
- **Text**: Use the following code as the value of the **Text** field:

```
try {
var r = new sn_ws.RESTMessageV2('', '');
r.setStringParameterNoEscape('',  );
  //override authentication profile if needed
  //authentication type ='basic'/ 'oauth2'
  //r.setAuthentication(authentication type, profile name);
var response = r.execute();
var responseBody = response.getBody();
var httpStatus = response.getStatusCode();
```

```
if (httpStatus==200) {
gs.addInfoMessage(responseBody);
  }
} catch(ex) {
var message = ex.getMessage();
}
```

Click on the **Submit** button to create a new macro. Now open any of the server- or client-side script form, that have the syntax editor and type in the name of the macro we just created-- `restcall` --and press the *Tab* key:

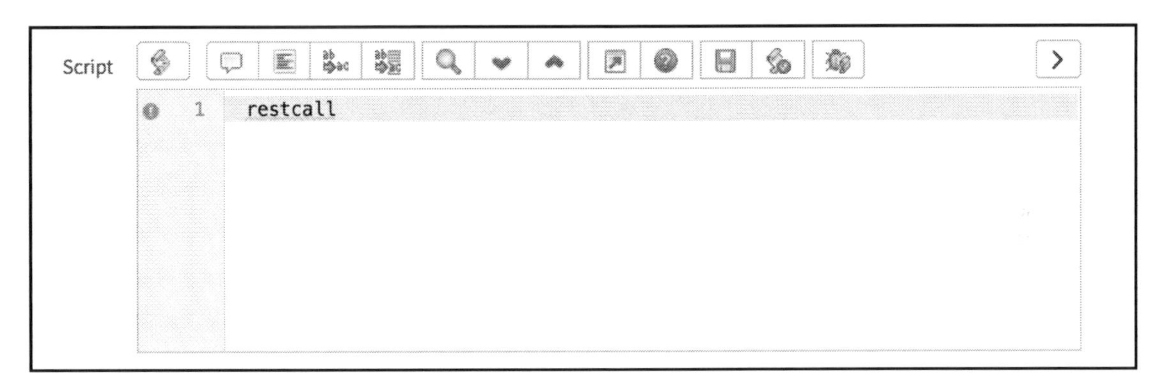


Pressing the *Tab* key will replace the `restcall` string with the value of the macro text field:

```
Script
1  try {
2    var r = new sn_ws.RESTMessageV2('', '');
3    r.setStringParameterNoEscape('',  );
4    //override authentication profile if needed
5    //authentication type ='basic'/ 'oauth2'
6    //r.setAuthentication(authentication type, profile name);
7    var response = r.execute();
8    var responseBody = response.getBody();
9    var httpStatus = response.getStatusCode();
10   if (httpStatus==200) {
11     gs.addInfoMessage(responseBody);
12   }
13 } catch(ex) {
14   var message = ex.getMessage();
15 }
```

We can create as many syntax macro texts as needed; however, we must keep in mind that it is loaded and included in all the pages where the syntax editor is available. So we must avoid creating syntax editor macros unless the code snippet will be used quite often.

## Script syntax error checking

The syntax error checking feature is another very useful feature of the syntax editor. It is useful for locating a script error easily when one occurs.

We can press the syntax check icon at the top of the syntax editor to check for script errors. The syntax editor will place the cursor at the line and position of a syntax error and, as shown in the following screenshot, highlight the line number with yellow or red icons for syntax warnings and errors respectively:

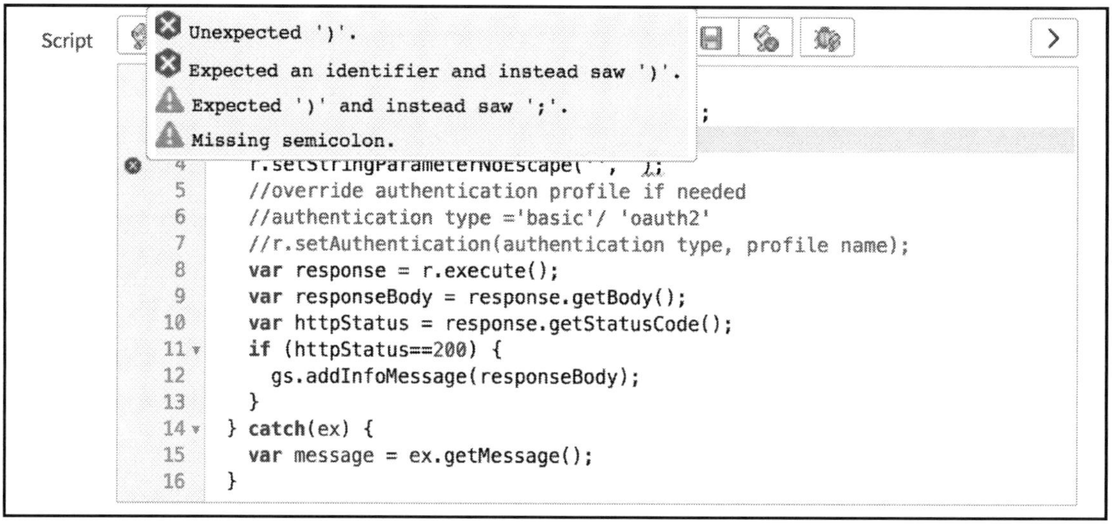

Script

Unexpected ')'.
Expected an identifier and instead saw ')'.
Expected ')' and instead saw ';'.
Missing semicolon.

```
4     r.setStringParameterNoEscape('', );
5     //override authentication profile if needed
6     //authentication type ='basic'/ 'oauth2'
7     //r.setAuthentication(authentication type, profile name);
8     var response = r.execute();
9     var responseBody = response.getBody();
10    var httpStatus = response.getStatusCode();
11    if (httpStatus==200) {
12      gs.addInfoMessage(responseBody);
13    }
14  } catch(ex) {
15    var message = ex.getMessage();
16  }
```

Furthermore, if we try to save a form that contains a **Script** field with some error, we will be presented with an appropriate error message, as shown in the following screenshot, with the line number of the syntax error:

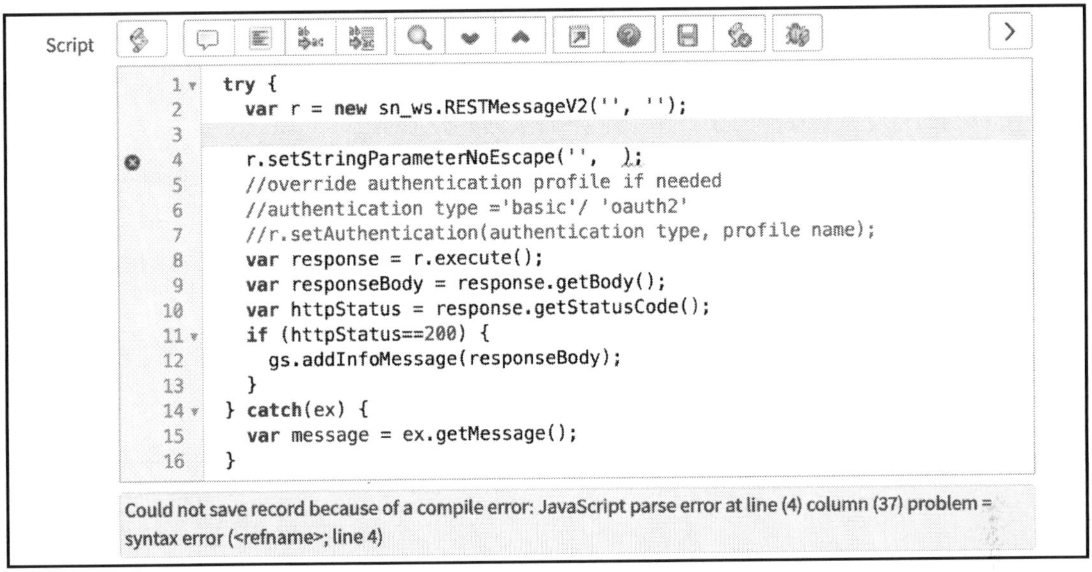

Script

```
1  try {
2    var r = new sn_ws.RESTMessageV2('', '');
3
4    r.setStringParameterNoEscape('',  );
5    //override authentication profile if needed
6    //authentication type ='basic'/ 'oauth2'
7    //r.setAuthentication(authentication type, profile name);
8    var response = r.execute();
9    var responseBody = response.getBody();
10   var httpStatus = response.getStatusCode();
11   if (httpStatus==200) {
12     gs.addInfoMessage(responseBody);
13   }
14 } catch(ex) {
15   var message = ex.getMessage();
16 }
```

Could not save record because of a compile error: JavaScript parse error at line (4) column (37) problem = syntax error (<refname>; line 4)

In the preceding example, the error occurred at line number **4** and column position **37**. We can save the code once we resolve all compile errors.

Now that we have learned how to use the syntax editor, let us learn how to debug server-side interactive scripts using Script Debugger.

# Script Debugger

Script Debugger can be used to perform line-by-line debugging of server-side scripts such as business rules, script includes, script actions, or UI actions that are running in interactive mode. An interactive script is one that is being executed as part of page processing that will display some output to the end user.

For example, consider a script include which we intend to debug and have set a breakpoint in the code. If we submit a form that triggers a business rule, which in turn runs the script include, then the said script is in interactive mode because it is executed as part of an action that requires an output. On the other hand, if the same script include is called from a processing script that runs at a particular schedule, the debugging will not pause at the breakpoint because the script is not in interactive mode.

# Launching Script Debugger

We can open Script Debugger for any server-side script by clicking on the Open Script Debugger icon on top of the script field as shown here:

Booking request by ...
Business Rule

Business Rule
Booking request by same caller

Update Delete

Script

Open Script Debugger

```
(function executeRule(current, previous /*n
    var gr = new GlideRecord(current.getTa
    gr.addActiveQuery();
    gr.addQuery();
    var state_qry = gr.addQuery("state","-5");
    state_qry.addOrCondition("state","IS","1");
    gr.query();
    if ( gr.hasNext() ) {
        gs.addErrorMessage("Unable to "+current.operation()+" the record as there is already an existing travel booking request by the user in pending or open state.");
        current.setAbortAction(true);
    }

})(current, previous);
```

The debugger can be used only when the script is executed in an interactive session. It becomes active only for the current (logged-in) session and doesn't affect other logged-in sessions or users executing the same code. Furthermore, breakpoints set in one session don't affect other developers trying to debug the same code with their own set of breakpoints.

The `GlideSystem` method `isInteractive()` can be used to determine whether the script is running in interactive mode or not. If the return value is `true` then the script is in interactive mode. A user must have the `script_debugger` role granted and at least read-only access to the script in order to use Script Debugger to debug the code. The major part of this chapter is relevant to the latest version of ServiceNow --**Istanbul**.

# Script Debugger interface

To properly use Script Debugger, it is important to understand its interface. Clicking on the Open Script Debugger icon in any **Script** field opens up the debugger in a new window. The debugger will open in active (running) state, as shown here:

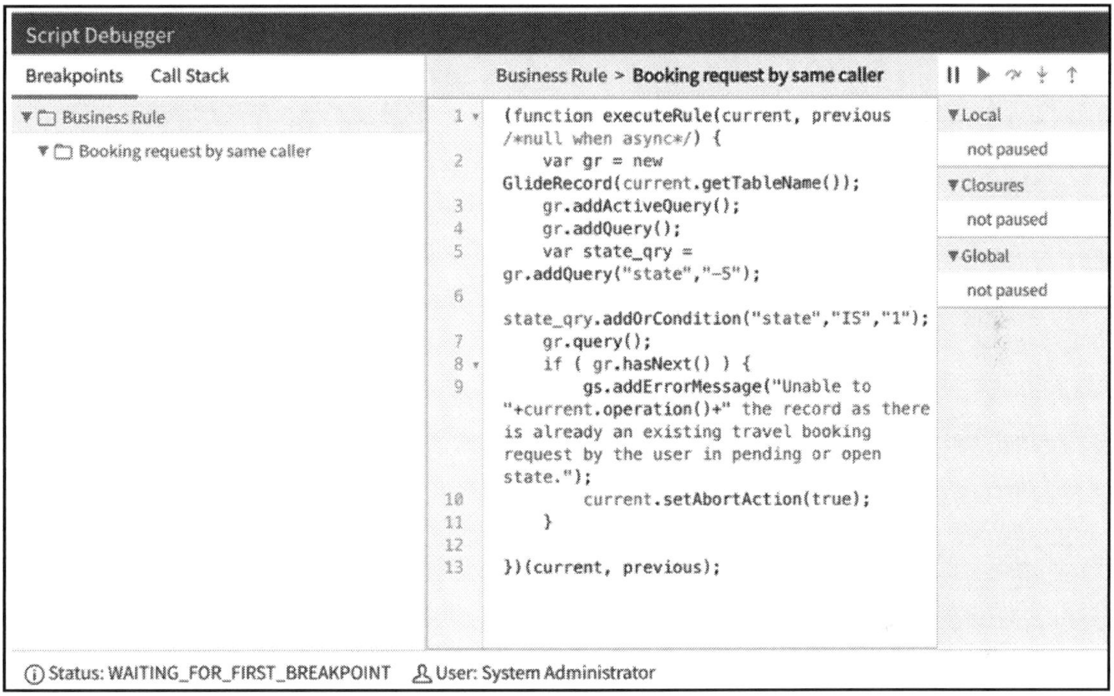

Script Debugger

Breakpoints Call Stack

Business Rule > **Booking request by same caller**

Business Rule
Booking request by same caller

```
1  (function executeRule(current, previous
   /*null when async*/) {
2      var gr = new
   GlideRecord(current.getTableName());
3      gr.addActiveQuery();
4      gr.addQuery();
5      var state_qry =
   gr.addQuery("state","-5");
6
   state_qry.addOrCondition("state","IS","1");
7      gr.query();
8      if ( gr.hasNext() ) {
9          gs.addErrorMessage("Unable to
   "+current.operation()+" the record as there
   is already an existing travel booking
   request by the user in pending or open
   state.");
10         current.setAbortAction(true);
11     }
12
13 })(current, previous);
```

Local
not paused
Closures
not paused
Global
not paused

Status: WAITING_FOR_FIRST_BREAKPOINT User: System Administrator

We can set breakpoints by simply clicking on the line numbers. The line number will be highlighted with bookmark-shaped break icons as shown in the following screenshot:

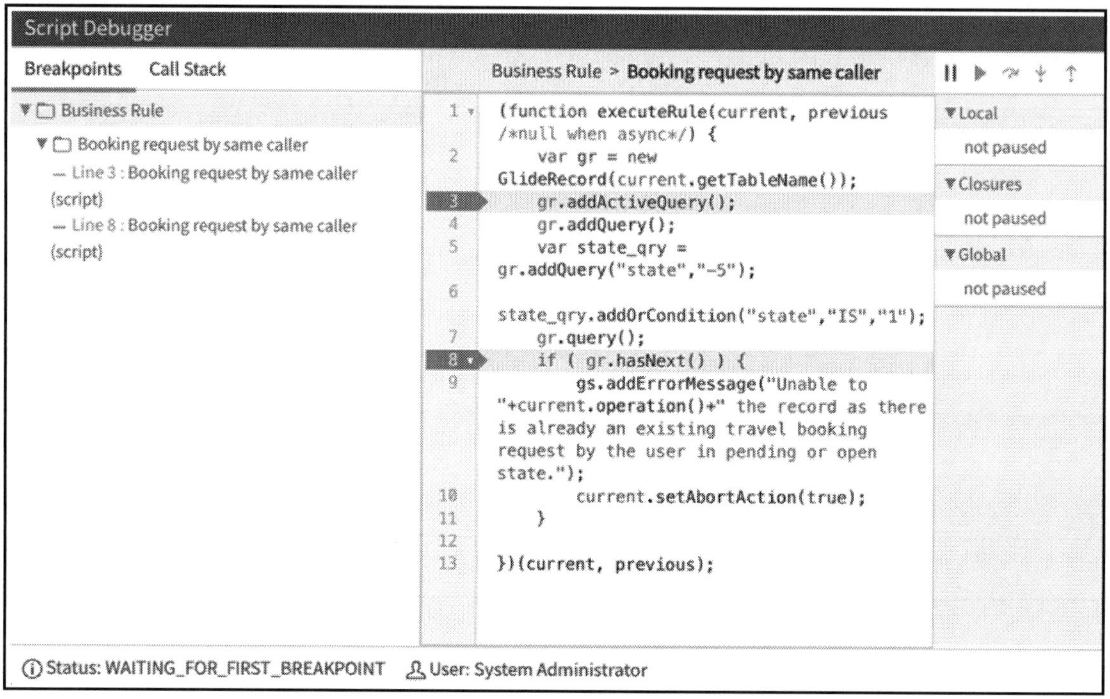

Script Debugger

Breakpoints Call Stack

Business Rule

Booking request by same caller

— Line 3 : Booking request by same caller (script)

— Line 8 : Booking request by same caller (script)

Business Rule > **Booking request by same caller**

```
1  (function executeRule(current, previous /*null when async*/) {
2      var gr = new GlideRecord(current.getTableName());
3      gr.addActiveQuery();
4      gr.addQuery();
5      var state_qry = gr.addQuery("state","-5");
6      state_qry.addOrCondition("state","IS","1");
7      gr.query();
8      if ( gr.hasNext() ) {
9          gs.addErrorMessage("Unable to "+current.operation()+" the record as there is already an existing travel booking request by the user in pending or open state.");
10         current.setAbortAction(true);
11     }
12
13 })(current, previous);
```

Local

not paused

Closures

not paused

Global

not paused

Status: WAITING_FOR_FIRST_BREAKPOINT User: System Administrator

The status bar of Script Debugger window can provide useful information, such as whether the debugger is running and waiting for the first breakpoint (see the preceding screenshot), paused on a breakpoint, has encountered any error, or is in off state as shown here:

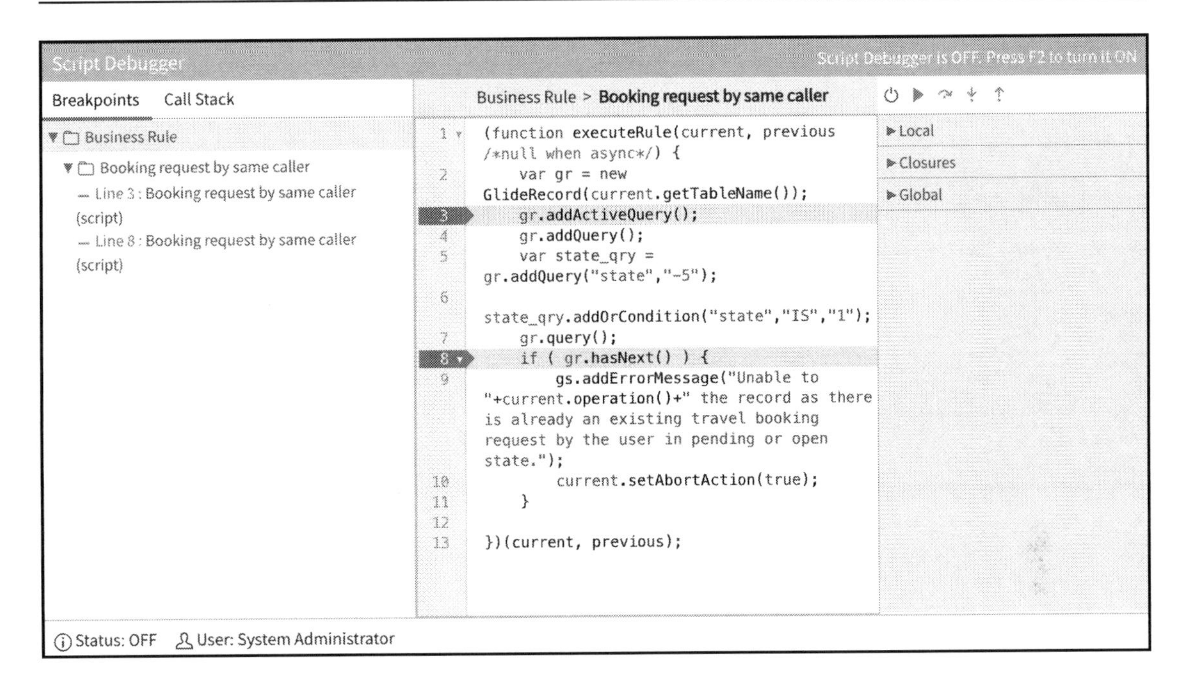


The off state means that Script Debugger is neither connected to the backend service nor waiting for the script to reach a breakpoint. We can toggle the active and off states by clicking on the Pause debugging and Start debugging icons available in the top-right section of the debugger along with other controls. Alternatively, we can press the *F2* key to toggle between active (waiting for breakpoint) and off states.

The name of the user is also displayed in the status bar at the bottom of Script Debugger. It is useful as Script Debugger remains active only for the current session and doesn't affect the sessions of other users or developers. Furthermore, if we impersonate a user, we must ensure that the user has the `script_debugger` role granted and at least has read-only access to the target script in order to debug the code.

Now that we have set a breakpoint, let us insert a new record to the `Booking Request` table that will trigger our business rule.

When the script reaches the first breakpoint, it will pause and we will be shown a modal window on the form as shown in the following screenshot:

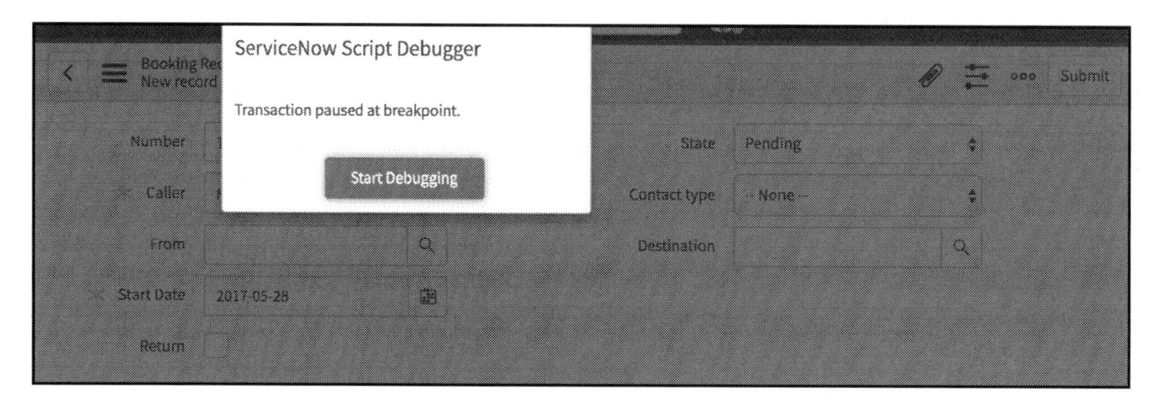


Click on the start debugging button to switch to **Script Debugger**, which will now provide us access to local and global variables along with the entire call trace as shown here:

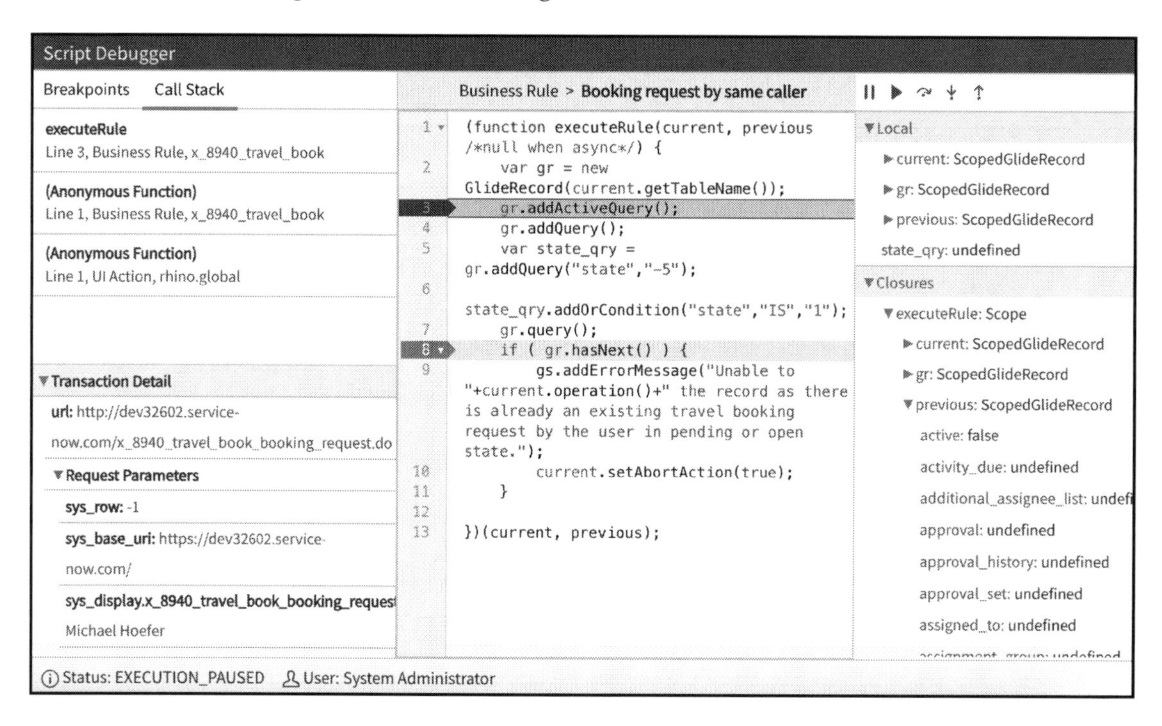

The status of Script Debugger with change to `EXECUTION_PAUSED`. The highlighted line of code in the editor section represents the current line where the debugger has paused. The **Call Stack**, **Transaction Detail**, and editor section, along with local, closure, and global variables will show all available information.

# Parts of Script Debugger

Let us go through what these different pieces of information mean and how they can be used:

- **Call Stack**: This is the list of script calls that preceded or invoked the current line (where the script is paused). It is useful to determine the flow of the execution and whether the flow is affecting any data or data validation, and so on:

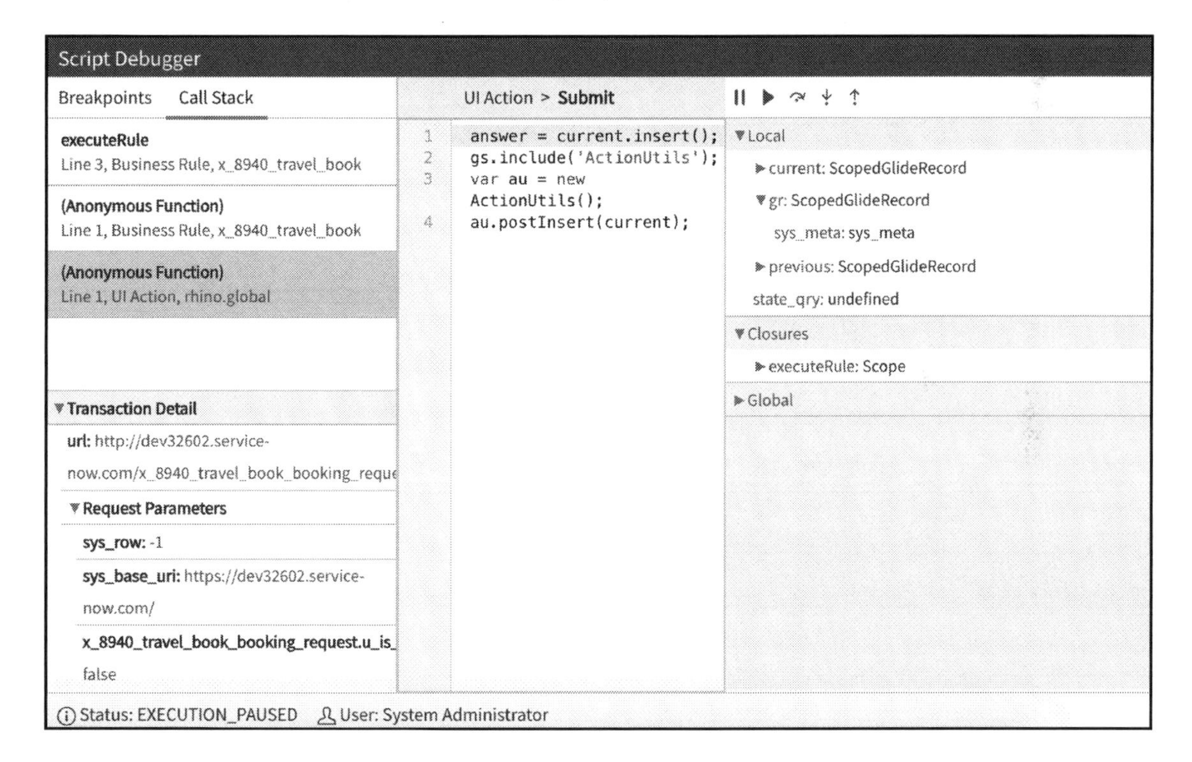

- **Transaction Detail**: This section contains a list of useful information such as the URL of the page, request parameters, (get and post) variables and their values, and instance and session details, and can be used to debug the values being passed from the form:

▼ **Transaction Detail**

**url:** http://dev32602.service-now.com/x_8940_travel_book_booking_request.do

▼ **Request Parameters**

**sys_row:** -1

**sys_base_uri:** https://dev32602.service-now.com/

**x_8940_travel_book_booking_request.u_is_return:** false

**sys_original.x_8940_travel_book_booking_request.number:** TASK0020730

**x_8940_travel_book_booking_request.number:** TASK0020730

**x_8940_travel_book_booking_request.u_start_date:** 2017-05-28

**isFormPage:** true

**sys_original.x_8940_travel_book_booking_request.state:** -5

**sys_display.original.x_8940_travel_book_booking_request.u_caller:** Michael Hoefer

**sysparm_ck:** 96934...f5a59 (length=72)

**sys_uniqueValue:** e3bfb2b24f3e72008522b5e18110c756

- **Variables**: The following three variable sections are available, segregated by scope, and are very useful when performing step over, step into, or step out as they can help monitor the list of available variables and changes to their values:
    - **Local**: This section lists all the local scope variables and their values
    - **Closures**: This section lists all the function scope variables and their values set and accessible within the function closures
    - **Global**: This section lists all the global scope variables and their values

# Debugging code

The following controls are available to perform line-by-line debugging:

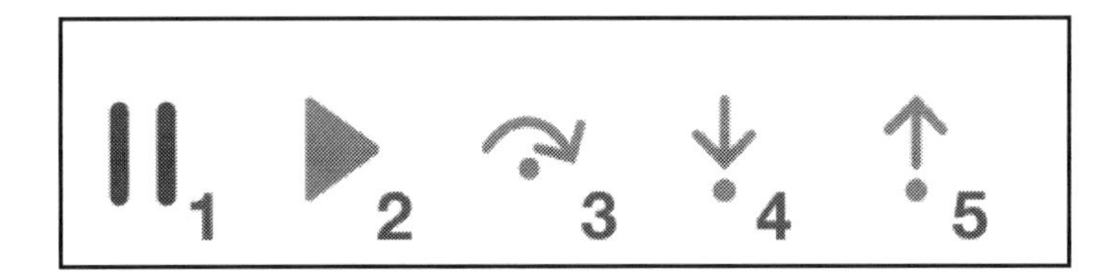


- **Pause/start debugging**: The first control is used to toggle the active and off states of the debugger. The same, as stated earlier in the chapter, can be achieved by pressing the *F2* key.
- **Resume script execution**: The second icon is active only when the debugger is paused on a breakpoint. We can click on the resume script execution icon to continue (advance) the execution of the code from the current breakpoint or line to the next breakpoint, which could be in the same script or another server-side code for this interactive session and call trace. Keyboard shortcut: *F9* key.

- **Step over next function call**: The third icon in the list of control is used to advance from the current line to the next evaluated line in the script that executes on the server. Keyboard shortcut: *F8* key. In the following code, we can notice that the line-by-line debugger is stepping inside the `if` condition block every time we submit the form. We can use the debugger to identify the error in our code and change the line `gr.addQuery()` to `gr.addQuery("u_caller",current.u_caller);`:

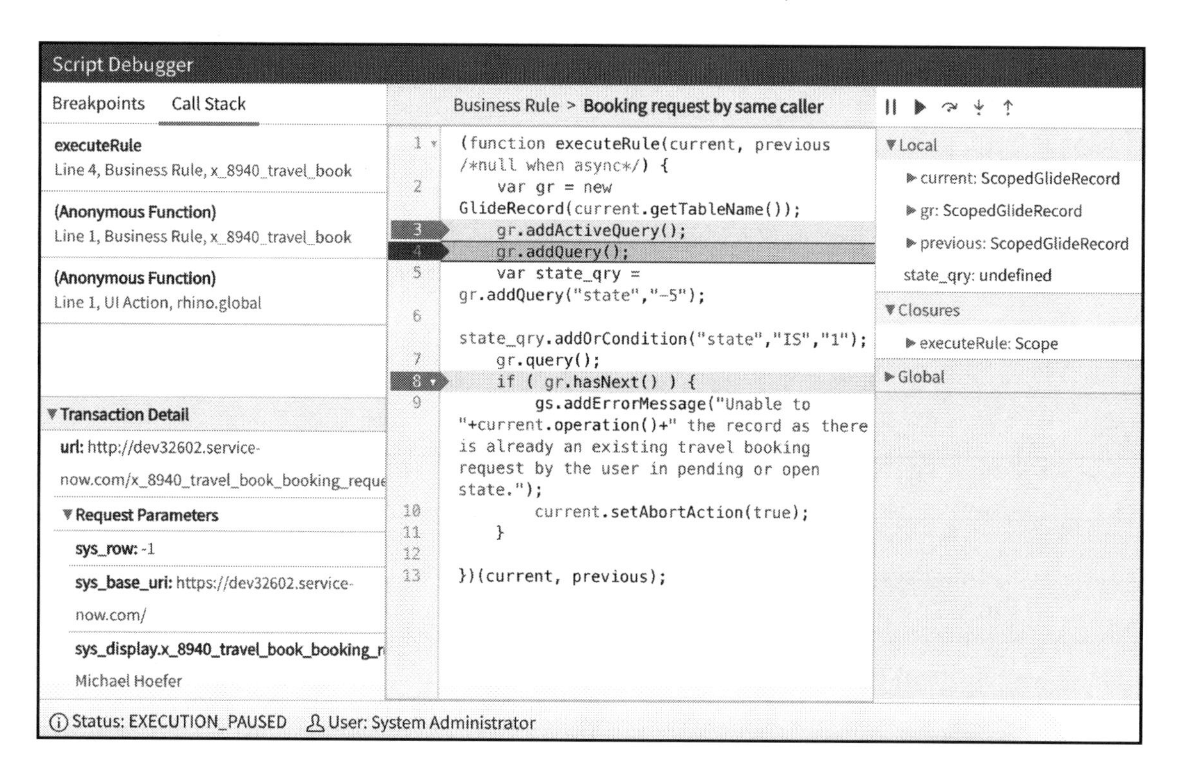


- **Step into next function call**: The fourth control icon is used to advance into the first executable line of code within the method call. The user must have read-only access to the target method if it is in a different script file, otherwise the control will act as step over. Keyboard shortcut: *F7* key.

- **Step out of current function**: The fifth and the last control icon is used to exit the current method call and return to the calling line of code in the calling script from the list of call stack. The control will act as step over if the user doesn't have process access to the code in the call stack or the debugger is not within a method call. Keyboard shortcut: *Shift* + *F8* key:

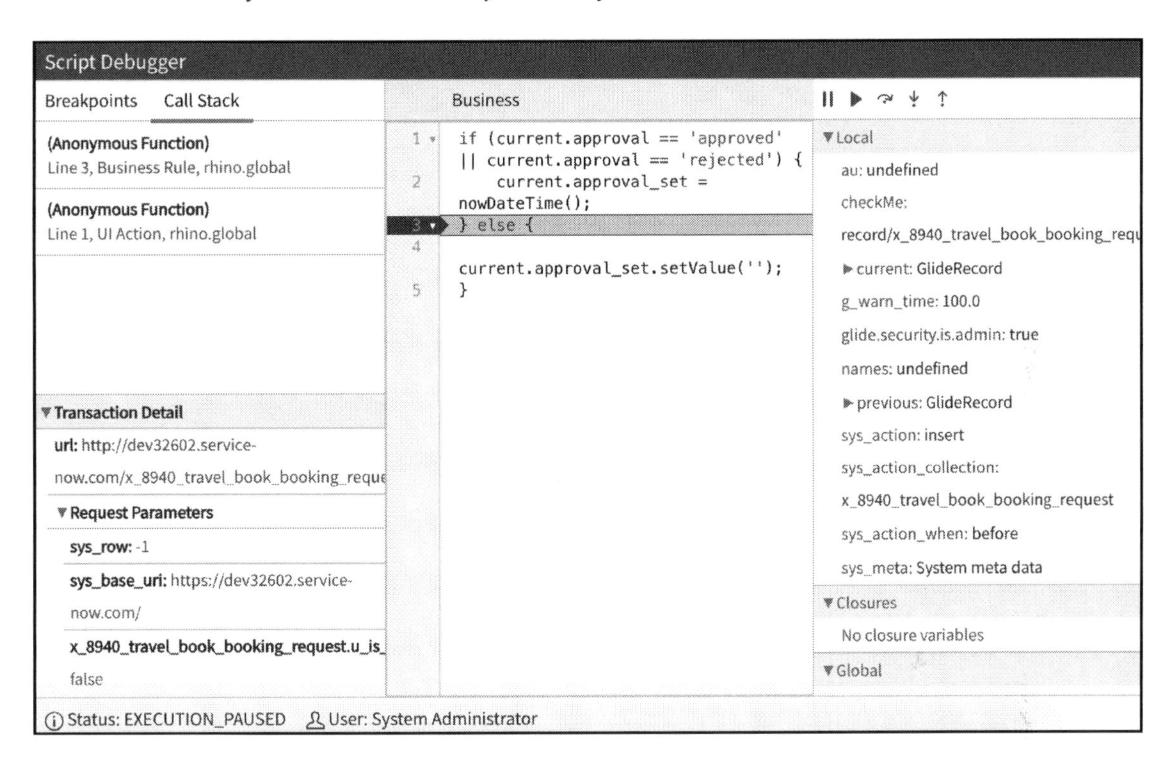

Make sure to remove breakpoints if you do not intend to further test your script using the logged-in user. This is to prevent any unplanned debugging alert and avoid confusion when debugging any other script.

# JavaScript Log

The **JavaScript Log** window along with **Field Watcher** appears at the bottom of the page when the **JavaScript Log and Field Watcher** setting, as shown in the following screenshot, is marked as active in the **Developer** pane of the **System Settings** page:

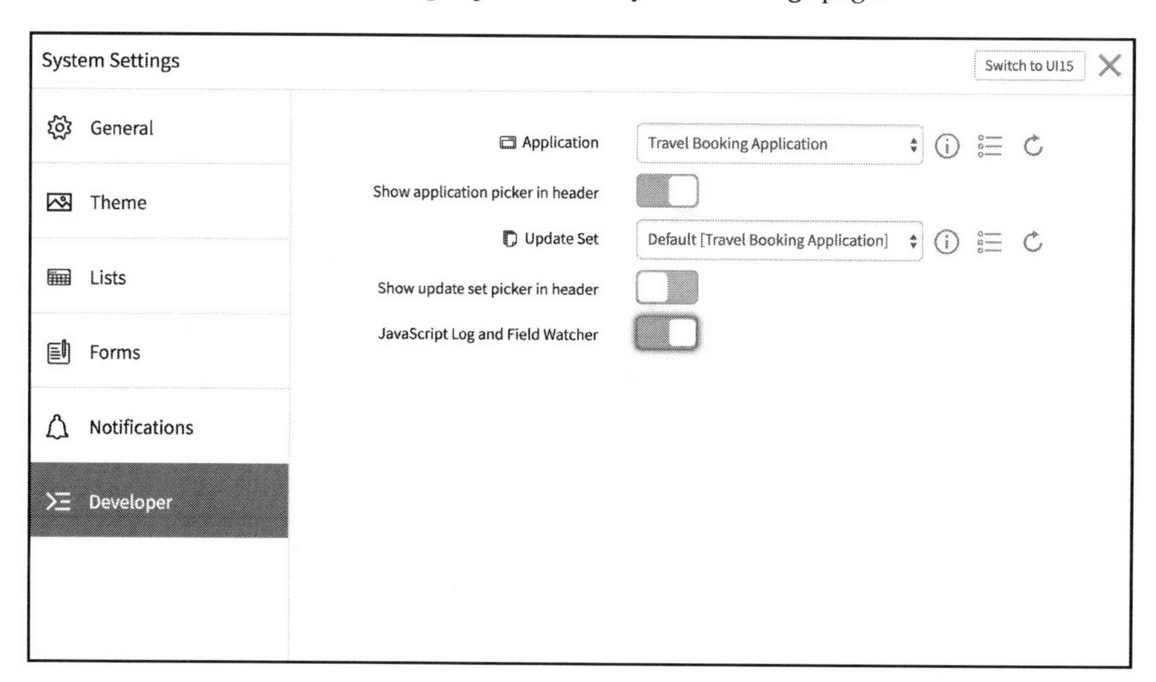


## JavaScript Log window interface

The **JavaScript Log** window will appear at the bottom of the page. It consists of the following controls:

- **Resize controls**: The size of the **JavaScript Log** window can be changed to one of the following three predefined settings:
    - **Small**
    - **Medium**
    - **Large**
- **Clear control**: When you click on the clear icon, all the log entries from the console will be cleared.

- **Minimize button**: The minimize control button can be used to close the **JavaScript Log** and **Field Watcher** windows. To reactivate the windows, we need to mark them as active in the **Developer** pane of the **System Settings** window:

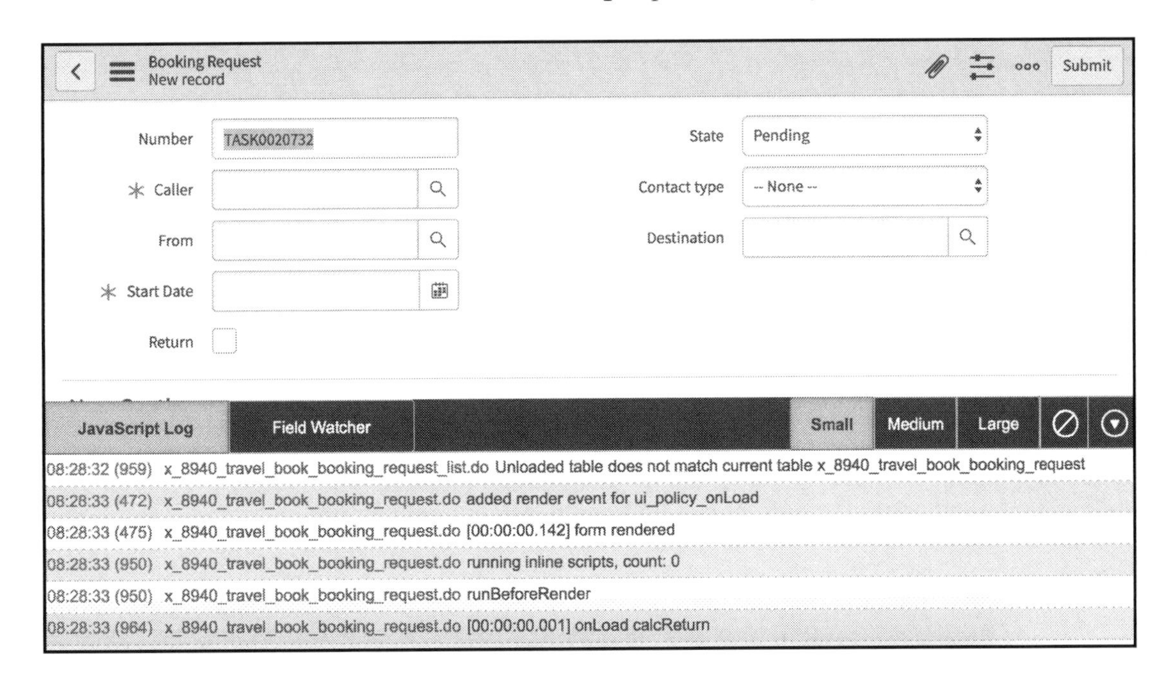


The **JavaScript Log** window output can be very useful when working with client scripts. When used along with the `jslog()` global function, it can help administrators and developers resolve lots of client-side script issues quickly without having to rely on the advanced interface of the browser-based JavaScript console, which might be difficult for some ServiceNow administrators to get used to.

While there is no built-in support for line-by-line debugging provided by the platform, any client-side script could be debugged using the browser-based developer tools or inspectors. This can usually be enabled by right-clicking on the page or the element you are interested in and selecting the **Inspect Element** option. You can switch over to the JavaScript console and also check the list of loaded resources. It is possible to set breakpoints in JavaScript code that runs on the client browser in the web developer tools offered by the browser.

# Using jslog()

The `jslog()` global function can be used in any client-side script. The output of the `jslog()` method is in the **JavaScript Log** window and visible only to users with the admin role.

As shown in the following screenshot, open the `Hide return date field on load` client script we created earlier in this book in **Studio**:

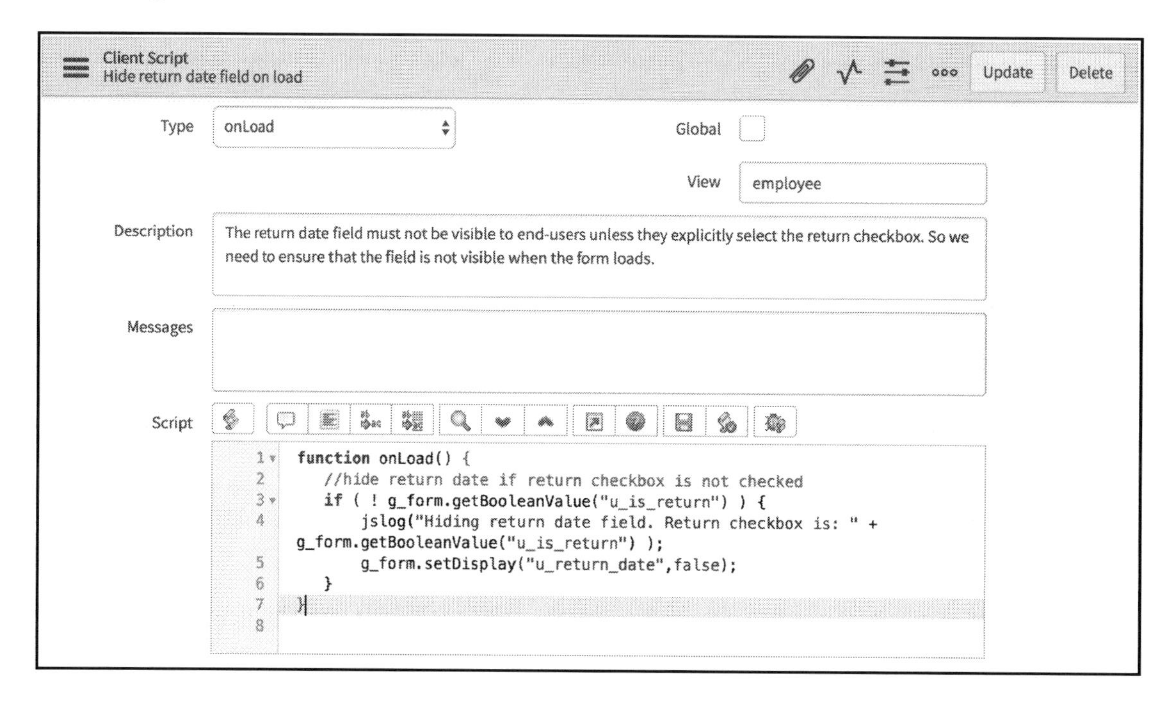


Now replace the code in the **Script** field with the following code:

```
function onLoad() {
   //hide return date if return checkbox is not checked
if ( ! g_form.getBooleanValue("u_is_return")) {
  jslog("Hiding return date field. Return checkbox is: " +
g_form.getBooleanValue("u_is_return") );
  g_form.setDisplay("u_return_date",false);
   }
}
```

Now with the **JavaScript Log** window active, switch to the **Booking Request** form in the employee view by opening the **Travel Booking Application** | **Create new** module. As shown in the following screenshot, you will notice a log entry created in the **JavaScript Log** window by the `jslog()` global function we just added in the client script:

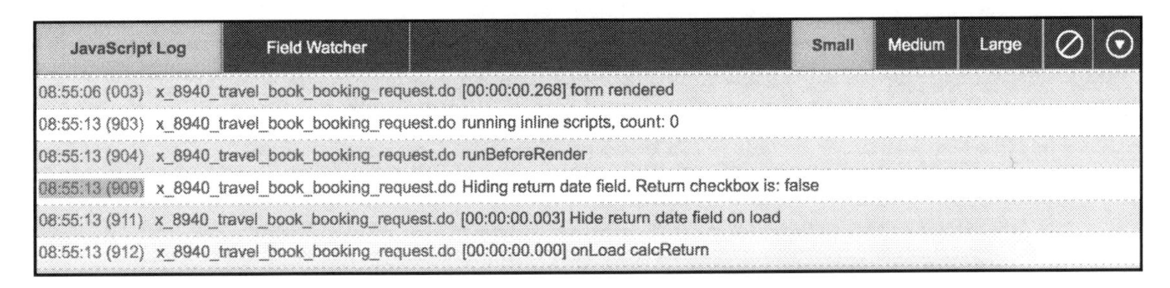


# Difference between console.log() and jslog()

The output of the `console.log()` method is visible in the JavaScript console available in the browser's developer tool. Whatever you output using `console.log()` will be available to all end users regardless of their group or roles. If they have access to the form or the page where the client-side script is included and that particular line of code executes, they can see the output in the browser's console log, as shown here:

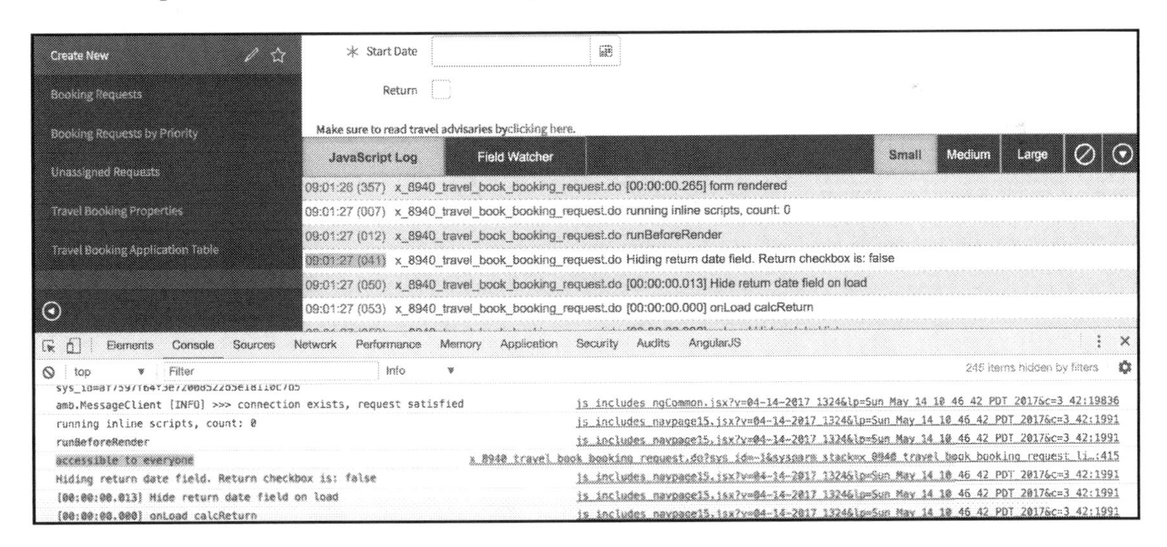

On the other hand, `jslog()` entries are only accessible by users with the admin role and the log entry can only be seen in the **JavaScript Log** window.

# Field Watcher

The **Field Watcher** window, which is available as a tab in the **JavaScript Log** and **Field Watcher** window, is useful to monitor changes to values of a particular field when server-side or client-side scripts perform any action. To watch a field, as shown in the following screenshot, we can right-click on the field label in the form and select **Watch Field**:

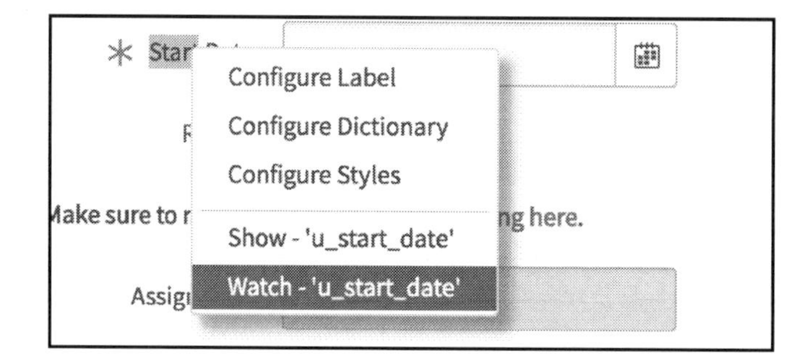


The **Field Watcher** window will automatically show up, if it is not already active, when we watch a field:

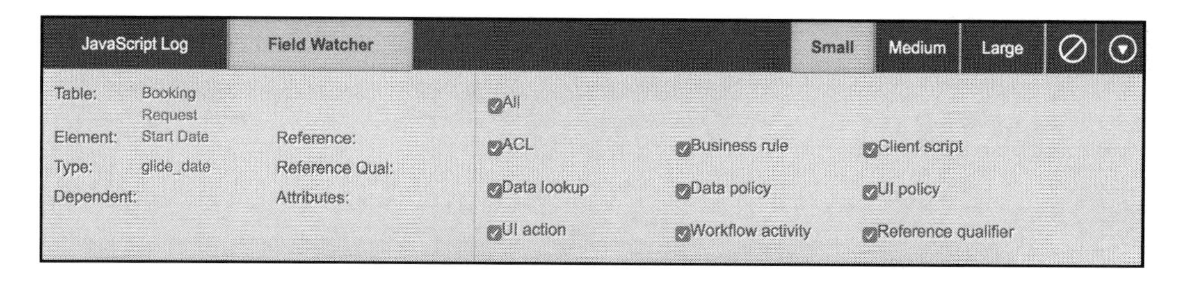

The **Field Watcher** window can help monitor changes to the field from the following artifacts:

- **ACL**
- **Business rule**
- **Client script**
- **Data lookup**
- **Data policy**
- **UI action**
- **UI policy**
- **Workflow activity**
- **Reference qualifier**

When we submit the form, if an ACL or business rule will act on the field or modify its value, we can see those details in the **Field Watcher** window as shown in the following screenshot:

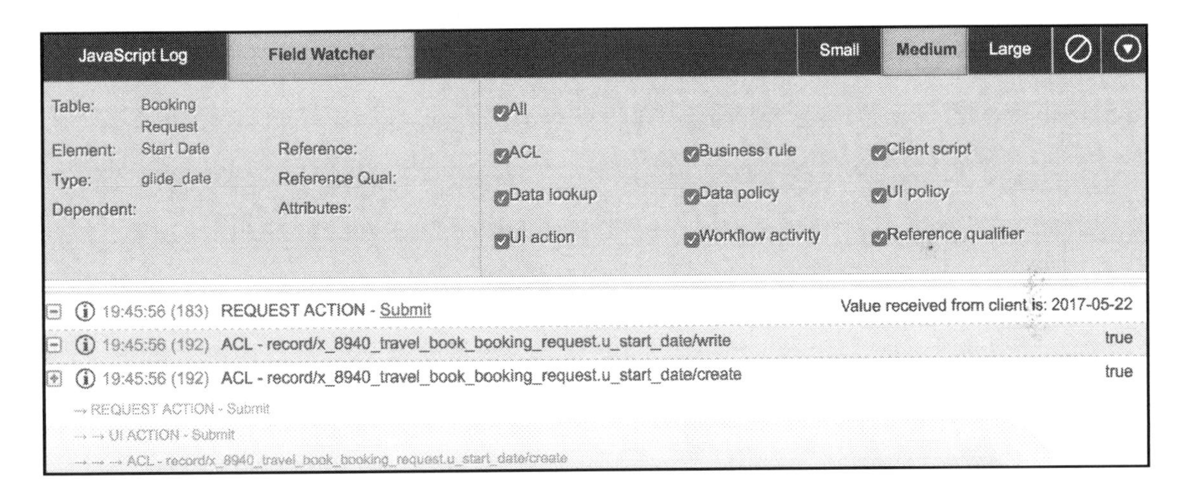

In the preceding screenshot, **Field Watcher** is informing us that the value received from the form was 2017-05-22 and the ACL entries are providing the information that the user has access to perform write and create. Similarly, the **Field Watcher** window can provide us details about changes to the field which may not be easily traceable. It is very useful when performing ACL checks. At any given time, we can only monitor one field. If we want to watch another field, we must first unwatch the existing watched field:

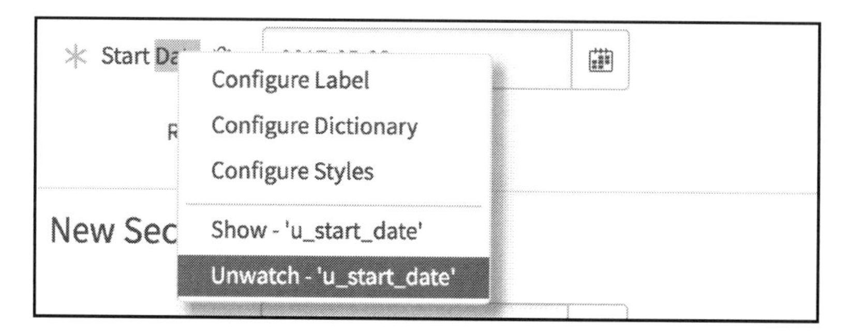


# Summary

In this chapter, we learned the concept of debugging server- and client-side code in the ServiceNow platform. We learned how to make use of the script editor macros and Script Debugger. We also learned how to set breakpoints in server-side code and access runtime variables by pausing the scripts in Script Debugger. Furthermore, we learned the concept of the **Field Watcher** window and the difference between `console.log()` and `jslog()`.

In the next chapter, we will learn different advanced ServiceNow data management and database features such as field overriding and defining relationships.

# 13

# Advanced Database Features

You have learned how to create workflows, write client-side and server-side scripts, design workflows, and how to debug different server-side and client-side scripting features. In this chapter, you will learn the different administration options and advanced features available in the platform.

The ServiceNow platform offers many features to improve the performance and overall functionalities of the ServiceNow applications. In this chapter, we will cover features such as table rotation, relationships, indexing and full-text search, and overriding field properties. We will also cover topics such as how to undelete records and override field properties in child tables.

In this chapter, we will cover the following topics:

- Relationships
- Overriding field properties
- Indexing
- Table auditing
- Restoring deleted records
- Database rotation and data archiving

# Relationships

When we open a record in the detailed view, we have an option to show related lists. Any two tables can have a logical relationship defined within the platform and appear as a parent/child pair via a related list. The relationship between two arbitrary tables can be used to create a related list that appears in the detail view of the form and displays a list of related records.

Examples of relationships that come defined in the platform include the following:

- **Incidents by same callers**: This relationship is defined in the incidents table, and it displays a related list to show other incidents opened by the same caller
- **Member of groups**: This relationship is applied to the users (`sys_user`) table and queries records from the groups (`sys_groups`) table to display them as a related list in the user's detail form

A list of all the existing relationships can be accessed using the **System Definitions** | **Relationships** module. When a new relationship is defined, it is available as a related list in the form of a specified table. To show or hide a related list in a form in a specified table, we need to configure a form-related list. A user must have the admin role granted in order to use define a relationship.

To show a related list that shows booking requests by the same user in the **Booking Request** form, we first need to define a relationship.

# Creating a new relationship

To create a new relationship, use the following steps:

1. Open **Studio** and in the **Create Application File** wizard, select **Data Model** | **Relationship**:

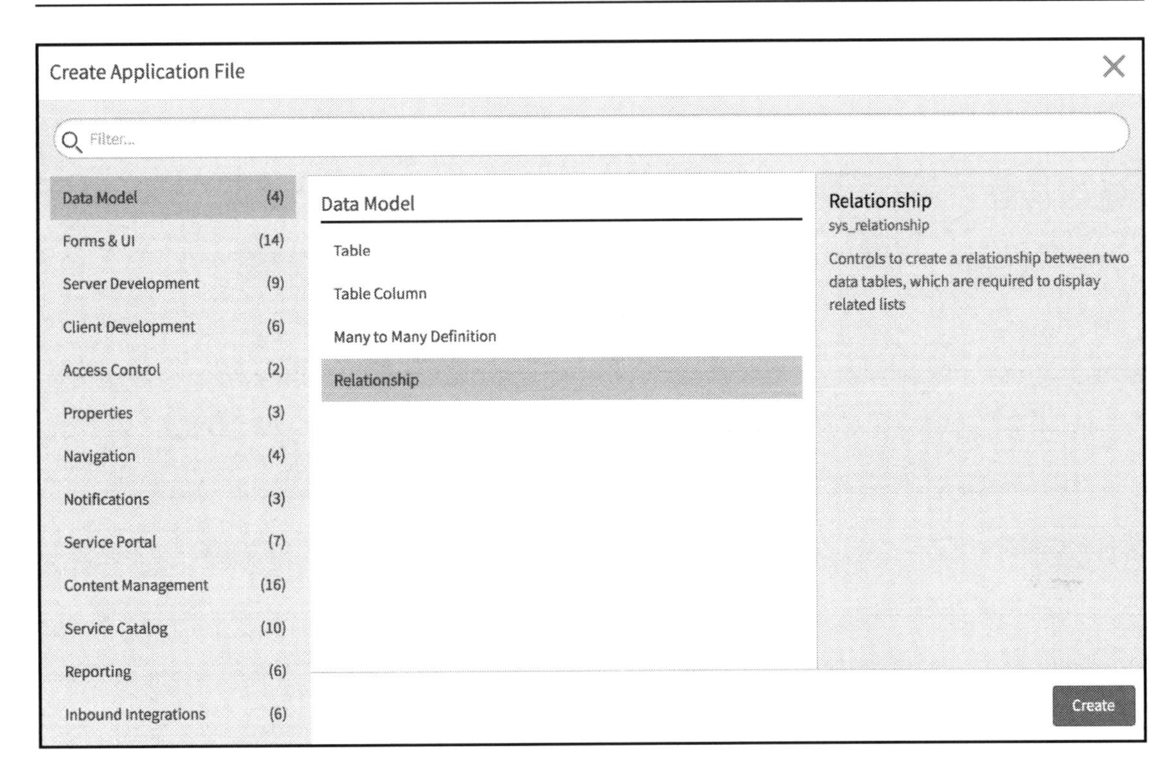


2. Now, fill in a new record form in the relationship table, as shown in the following screenshot, with the following values:
   - **Name**: `Booking requests by same caller`
   - **Applies to table**: **Booking Request**
   - **Queries from table**: **Booking Request**

- **Query with**: (Use the following mentioned script)

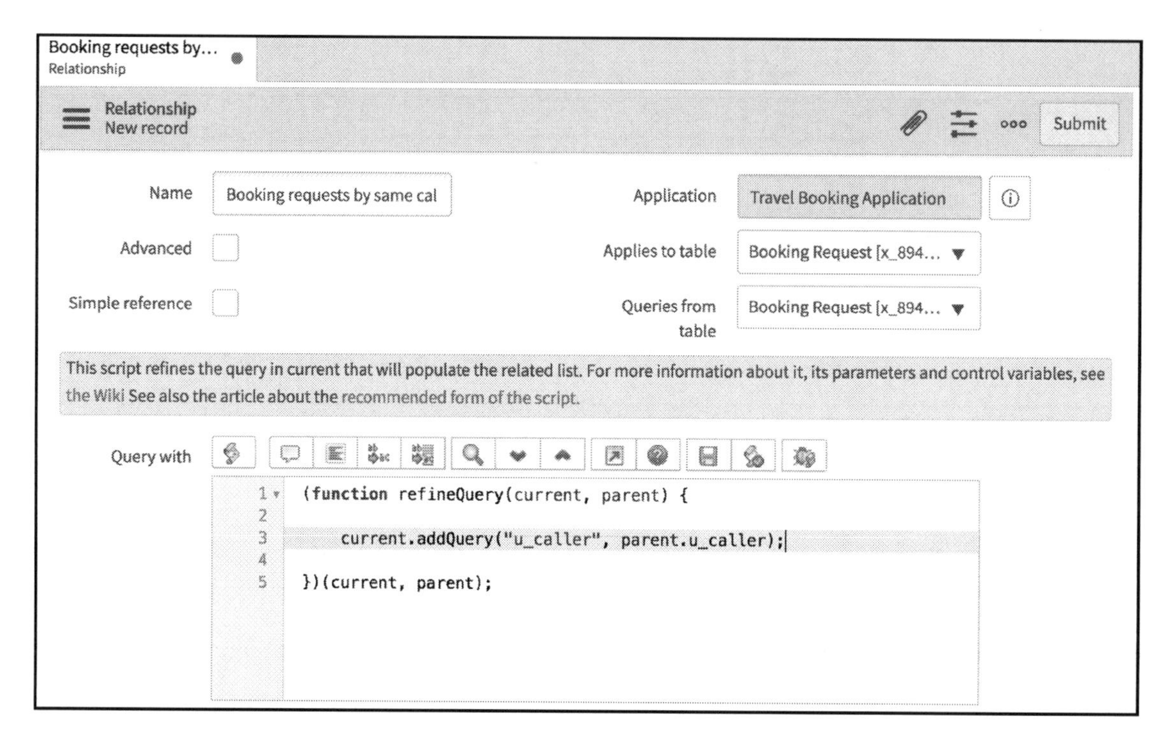


3. Populate the **Query with** field with the following script:

```
(function refineQuery(current, parent) {

  current.addQuery("u_caller", parent.u_caller);

})(current, parent);
```

The **Query with** field executes on the server side and has access to all server-side Glide APIs. It also has two special objects named `current` and `parent`. The `current` object is a `GlideRecordreference` to the table specified in the queries from the **Table** field and is used to retrieve the list of records displayed in the related list. The `parent` object, on the other hand, is a reference to the record being displayed on the form. The preceding script is going to add a filter to the current `GlideRecord` object to retrieve and show records that belong to the same user. Now, click on the **Submit** button to define a new relationship.

The relationship will add a related list to the table it is applied to, which in our case is the `Booking Request` table. However, to show a related list in the form, we need to configure the related list to the form view.

# Configuring forms to show related lists

To display a related list in the form, use the following steps:

1. Open any record in the **Booking Request** form. Clicking on the info icon against the record in the **Travel Booking Application** | **Booking Requests** module, select **Configure** | **Related Lists** from the form header menu, as shown in the following screenshot:

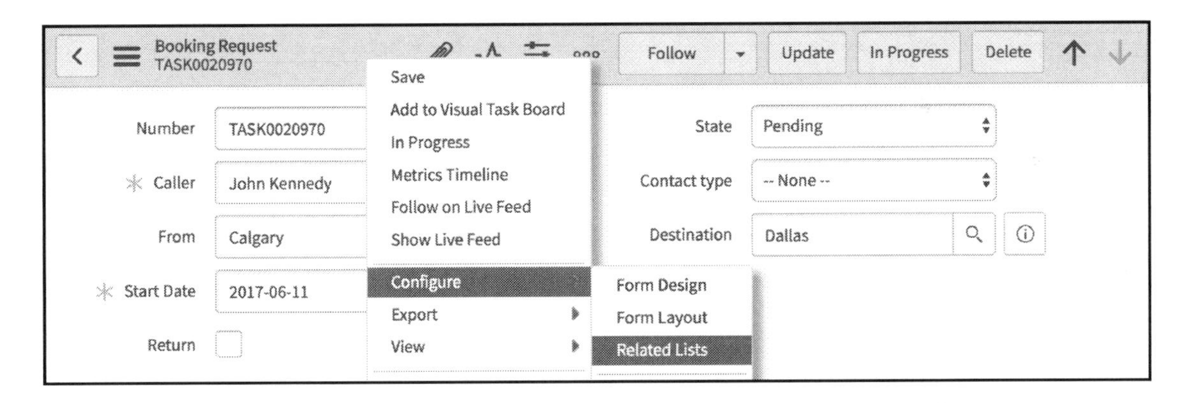

2. This will bring us to the **Related Lists** slush bucket list page for the `Booking Request` table in the default view. Now, as shown in the following screenshot, bring in the `Booking requests by same caller` related list from the available list to the selected list by selecting and clicking on the Add arrow icon or double-clicking on the entry:

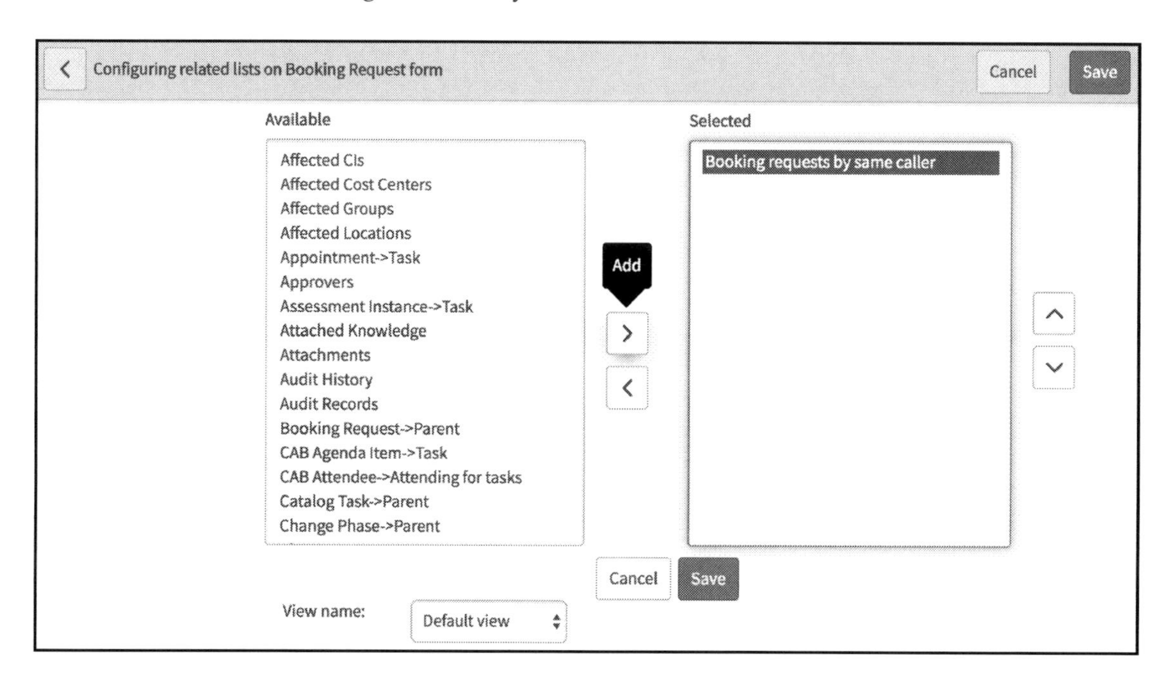

3. Click on the **Save** button to be taken back to the record you previously had open and scroll down to the bottom of the page to see the newly added related list titled `Booking requests by same caller`, as shown in the following screenshot:

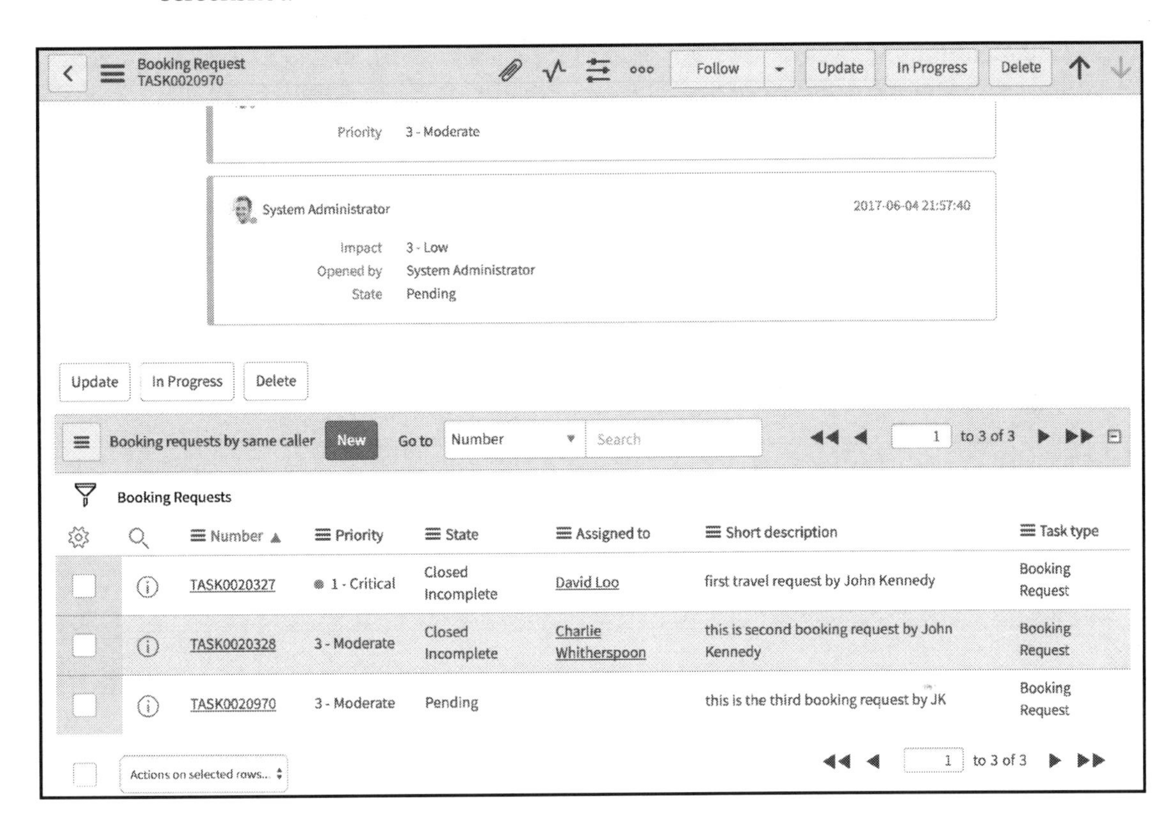

As you may notice in the preceding screenshot, the Booking Request number `TASK0020970` appears as a related record under the same **Booking Request**. This can be avoided by improving the relationship we just defined and adding another filter to the query:

```
current.addQuery("sys_id", "!=" , parent.sys_id);
```

The related list appears similar to the list of records module. It has controls to perform a quick search, apply advanced search filters, change ordering, configure available columns, and so on, and resembles a list of records page. The related list is very useful when working on records that are interrelated and need to be shown to users for enabling them to take better decisions. The preceding related list has listed all other booking requests opened by the same caller. It also displays a **New** button that can be clicked on to add a relevant record to the `Booking Request` table. We can show or hide the controls available on the list that can be configured using the **List Control** option.

## Modifying the list control options

To modify the list control options, use the following steps:

1. Right-click on the related list column header as shown in the following screenshot, and select **Configure** | **List Control**:

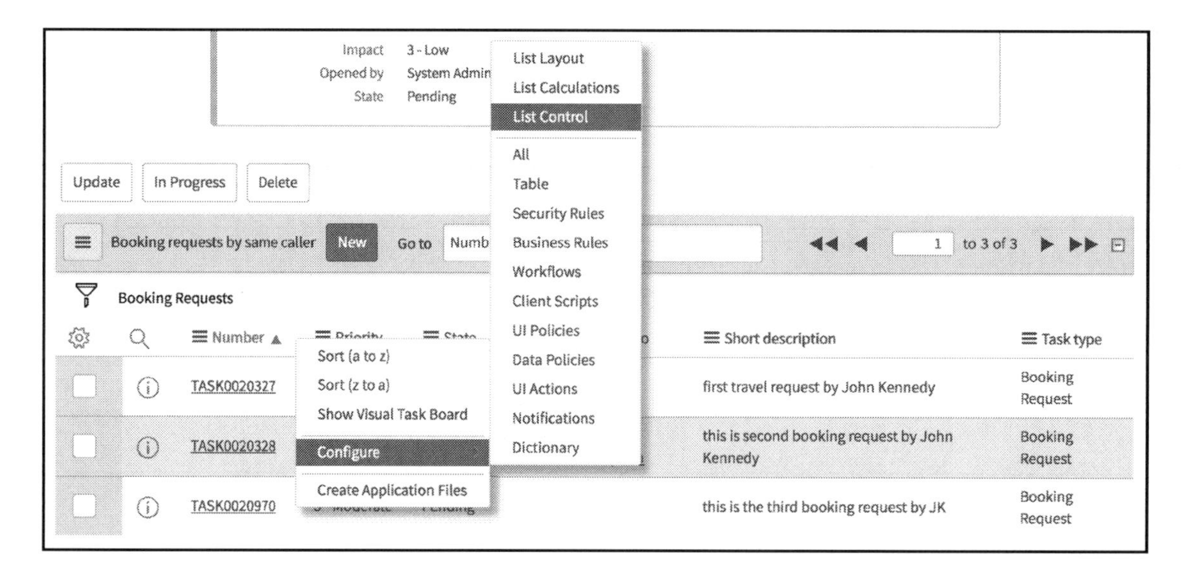

2. This will bring us to the **List Control New record** form, where we can configure display properties, labels, and roles requirements for different controls available in the list. As shown in the following screenshot, the **Related list** field will be auto-populated with the `sys_id` of the related list added to the **Booking Request** form:

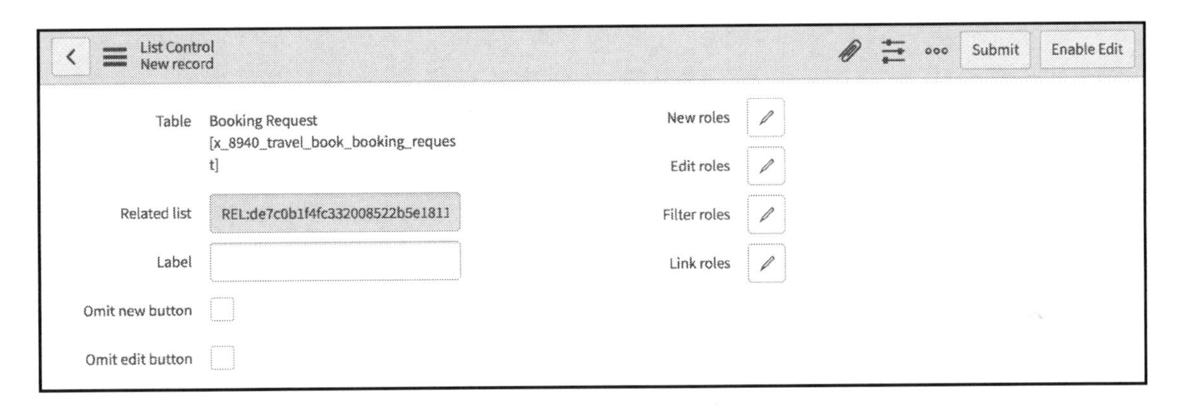


3. Fill in the form with the following information and leave other fields unchanged:
   - **Label**: `All booking request by same caller`
   - **Omit new button**: Checked
   - Click on the button next to the **Filter roles** field, as shown in the following screenshot:

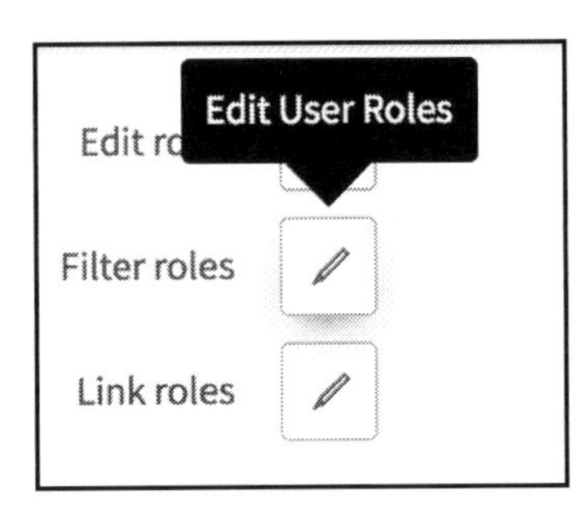

4. This will open a modal window with a slush bucket list to select roles required in order to use the filter control. Bring in the **admin** role to the selected list, as shown in the following screenshot, and click on **Done**:

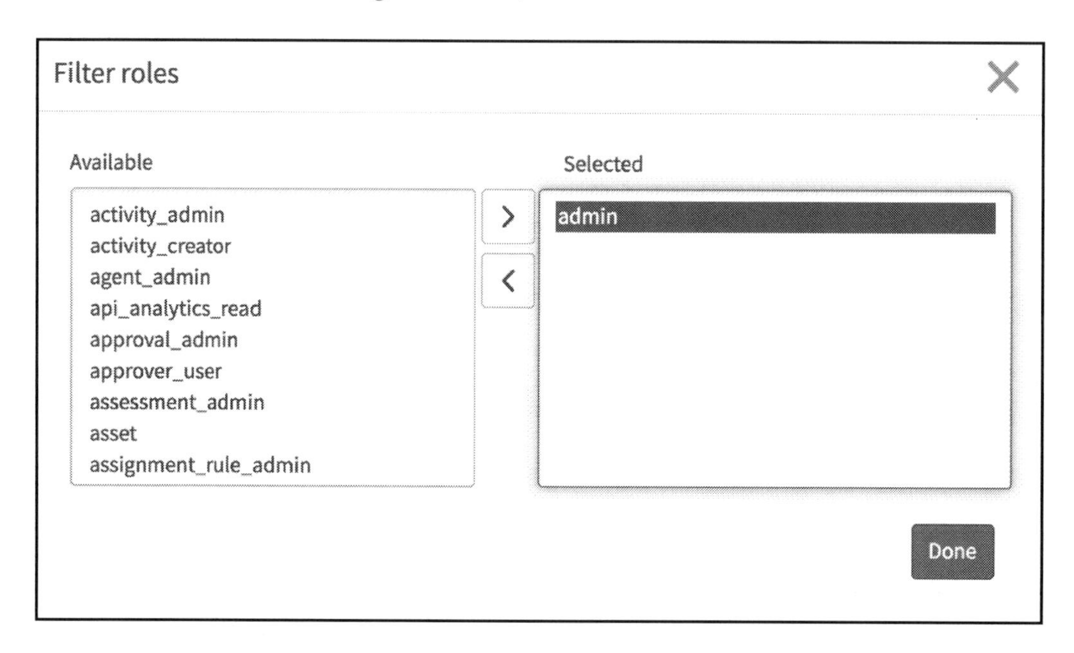


5. Now, ensure that the form has been populated properly, as shown in the following screenshot, and click on the **Submit** button to create the list control:

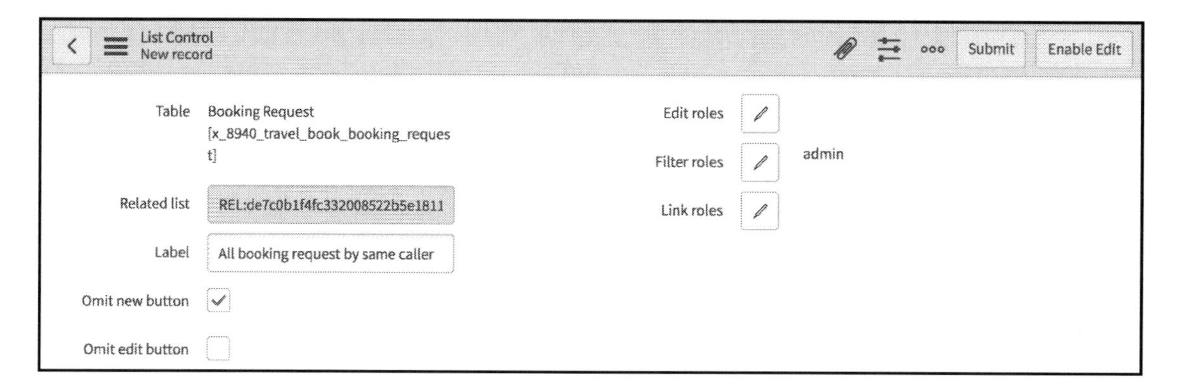

6. You will be brought back to the **Booking Request** record form. Scroll down to the bottom of the page to confirm that the **New** button is now hidden and the list has a new label, as was set in the **List Control** form. Furthermore, the advanced search filter will only be visible if you have the admin role:

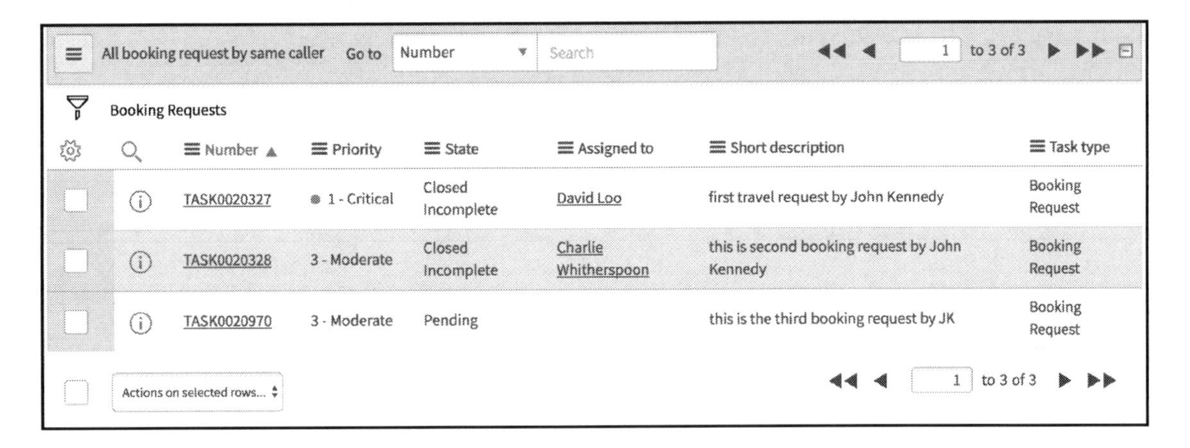


Using the list control, we can modify different display settings of the related list that can prove useful when working on complex applications with tables having varying requirements. In our **Travel Booking Application**, we are already aware that we do not allow a new request to be opened by a user if there is already one in a pending or work in progress state.

# Dictionary override

The dictionary override feature allows us to change the configuration of inherited fields in an extended table. We can define dictionary override on any table from which we have extended another table. The dictionary override must be defined in the same scope in which the extended table exists. In our **Travel Booking Application**, the `Booking Request` table extends from the `Task` table that is in the **Global** scope. However, we will define the dictionary override in the **Travel Booking Application** scope.

1. Open the **System Definition** | **Dictionary** module and open the entry for the `state` field in the `task` table by clicking on the info icon against the record, as shown in the following screenshot:

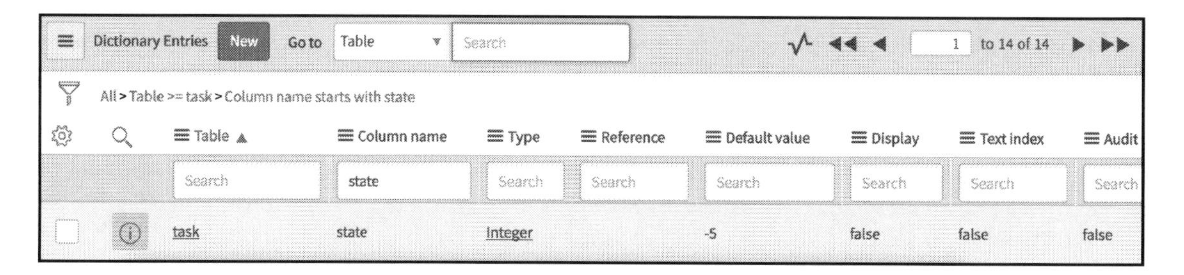


2. As the record is in the **Global** application, you may see information text below the form header, as shown in the following screenshot, which is what we expected, as we want to create the dictionary override entry for the `Booking Request` table that is in **Travel Booking Application**:

3. If you are not in the correct scope, make sure that the **Travel Booking Application** scope is selected in the application picker drop-down menu in the banner section, as shown in the following screenshot:

4. Now, scroll to the bottom of the dictionary entry form for the `state` field in the `task` table and click on the **New** button in the **Dictionary Overrides** related list:

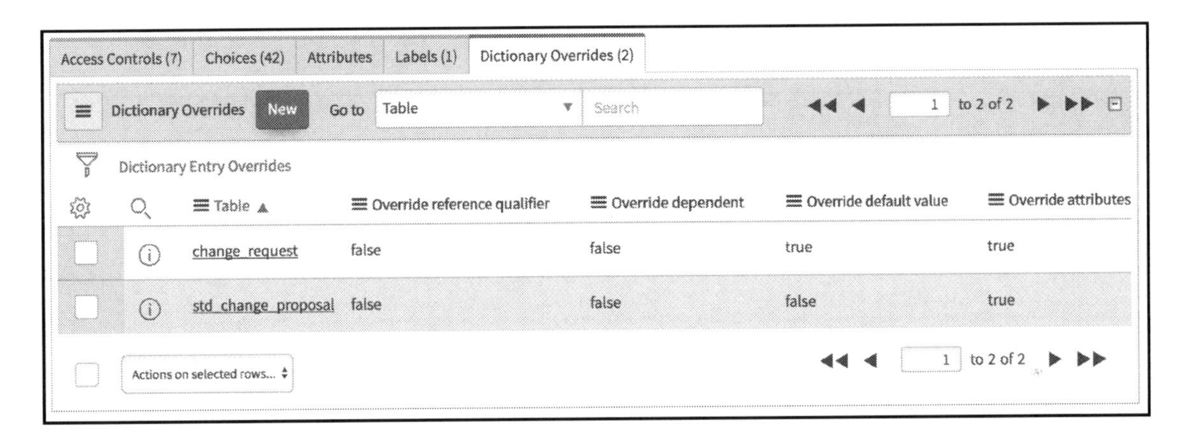


5. It will bring you to the new record form for **Dictionary Entry Override**, as shown in the following screenshot:

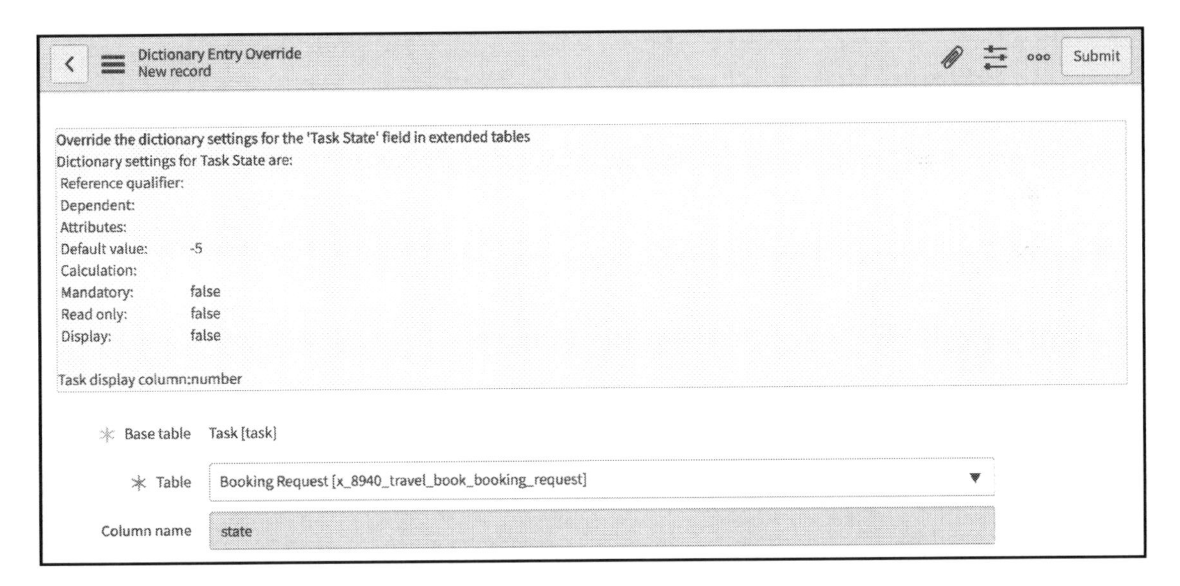

6. Navigate further down on the form and check the **Override mandatory** and **Mandatory** checkboxes, as shown in the following screenshot, to set the `state` field as mandatory in the extended `Booking Request` table:

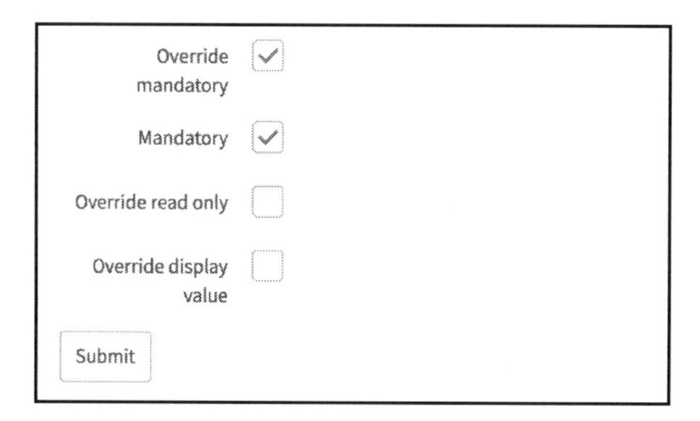


The `state` field in the `task` table remains non-mandatory; however, the field in the **Booking Request** child will become mandatory due to the dictionary override we just defined.

The dictionary override can be defined to change the following aspects of a field in the extended tables:

- Reference qualifiers
- Dictionary attributes
- Default values
- Field calculations
- Field dependencies property
- Mandatory property
- Read-only property

# Database indexing

Indexing is one of the most important database features and must be implemented properly where needed to improve response time. Just like in other database-based applications, creating an index must be dealt with carefully, and only the fields that will be looked up often must be indexed. Indexing will not just improve the response time; it also greatly improves the database performance and can help optimize slow queries:

1. In the ServiceNow platform, to create a database index, we can use the **System Definition** | **Tables** module. Let's create an index for the `Caller` field in the `Booking Request` table.
2. In the **System Definition** | **Tables** module, open the `Booking Request` table by clicking on the info icon next to the record:

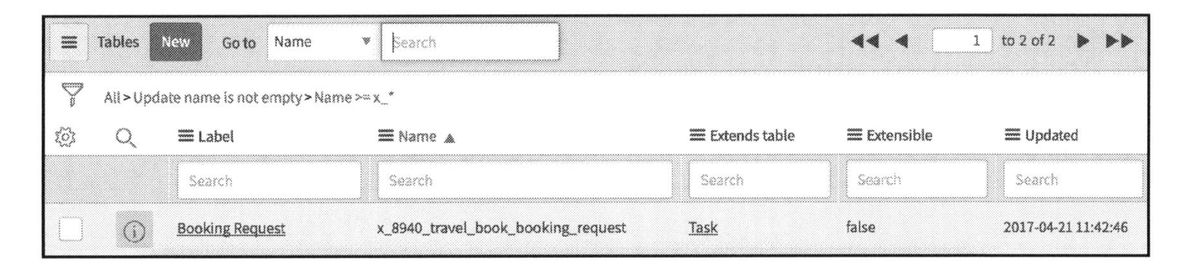


3. It will bring you up to the details page of the `Booking Request` table's configuration. Navigate to the bottom of the page and click on the **New** button in the **Database Indexes** related list, as shown in the following screenshot:

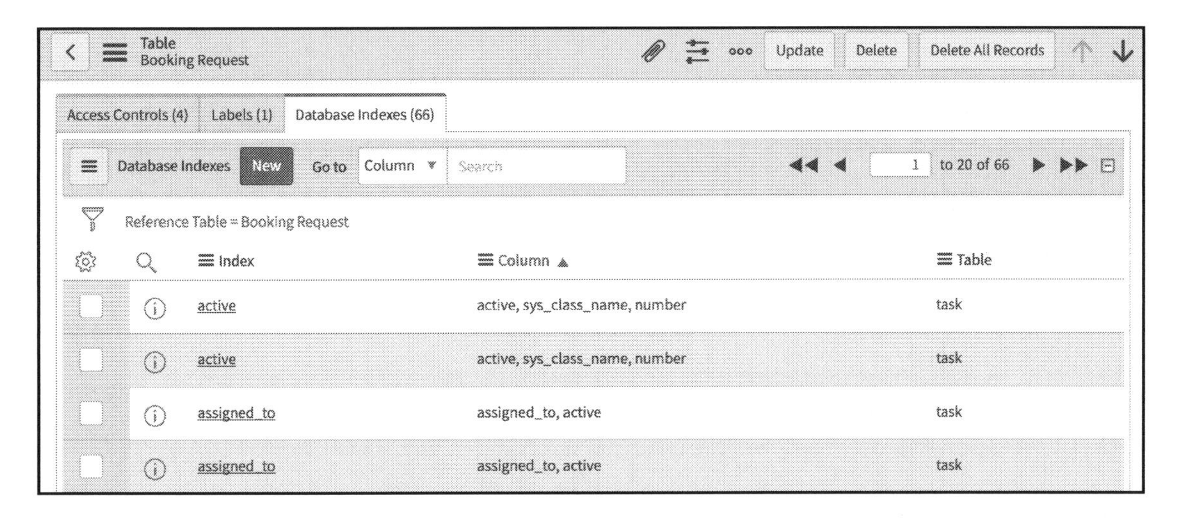


4. Clicking on the **New** button in the **Database Indexes** related list will open a modal window, as shown in the following screenshot.

5. Bring in the `Caller` fields from the available list to the selected list, and click on the **Create Index** button:

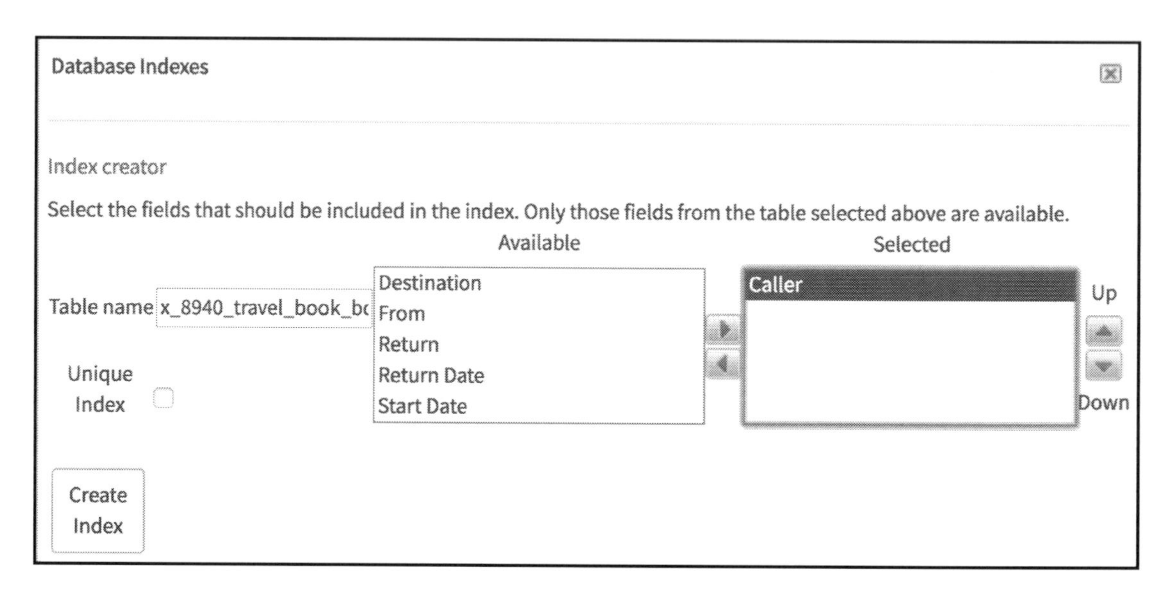


We can select multiple fields to index; however, we must be careful when selecting multiple fields as the order in which we select the fields can hamper the index performance.

The platform will usually generate the index in the background within a minute or two and prompt you to specify an email address to receive status notifications upon completion of the indexing process. An index can take anywhere between a minute to about an hour to generate depending upon the number of records that need to be indexed. Now that we have learned how to index a column in the ServiceNow platform, let us look at how to enable full-text indexing on a table.

# Full-text search

To enable full-text indexing on **Booking Request**, use the following steps:

1. Navigate to the **System Definition** | **Dictionary** module and open the table record by clicking on the info icon against the collection record, as shown in the following screenshot:

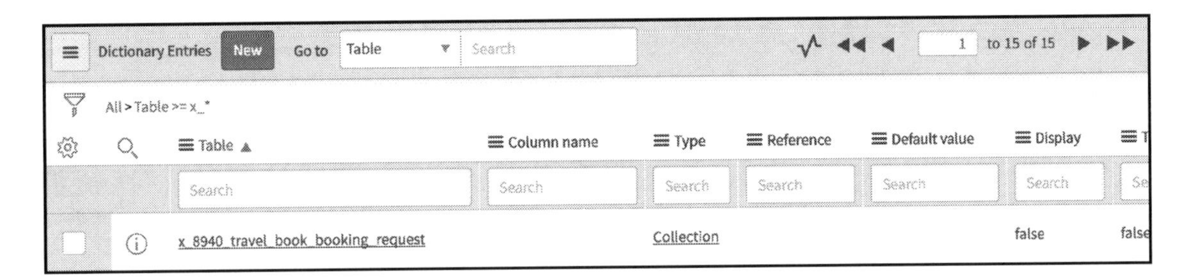


2. This will take you to the dictionary entry form for the `Booking Request` table, as shown in the following screenshot:

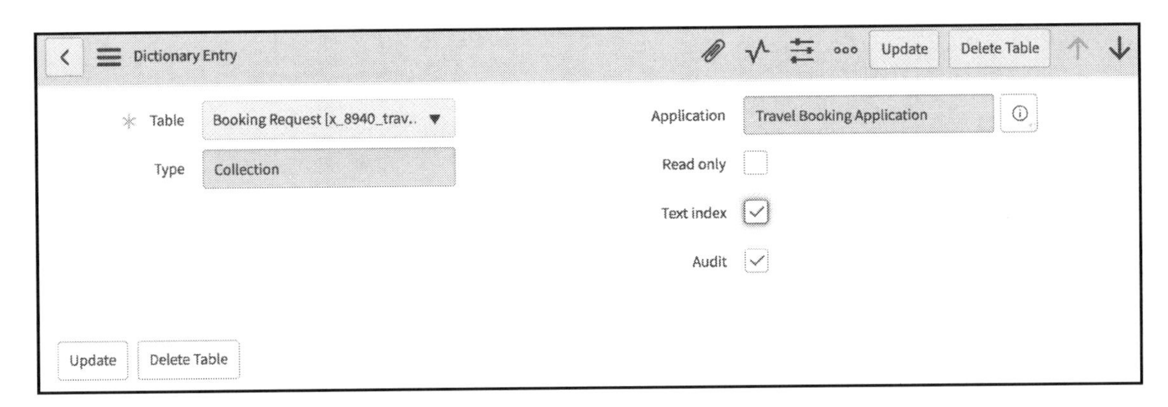


3. Check the **Text index** checkbox, and click on the **Update** button. Now, open the **Booking Request** collection record form again, and click on the **Generate Text Index** option under **Related Links**, as shown in the following screenshot, in order to generate the index:

Related Links
Generate Text Index
Show Table
Advanced view

4. This will open a modal window, as shown in the following screenshot, where you can specify an email address to receive a notification upon successful completion of the full-text index:

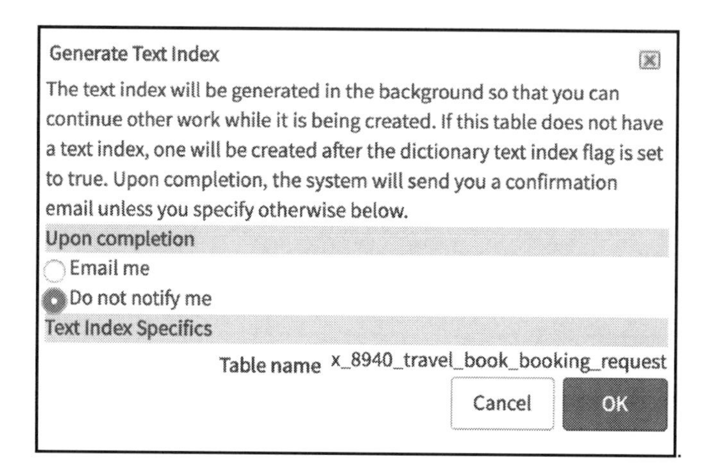


5. Select the **Do not notify me** option, and click on the **OK** button to schedule a full-text index of the entire table, which will complete within a minute or a few hours, depending upon the number of records in the table.
6. To monitor the status of the index or to evaluate the amount of time, an index may take navigating to the **System Definition** | **Text indexes** module and check the historical status of the previously completed index of the same table, if it exists.
7. Once a table has been fully indexed, we can perform fast text search in the list view, by selecting **for text** in the quick search option, as shown in the following screenshot:

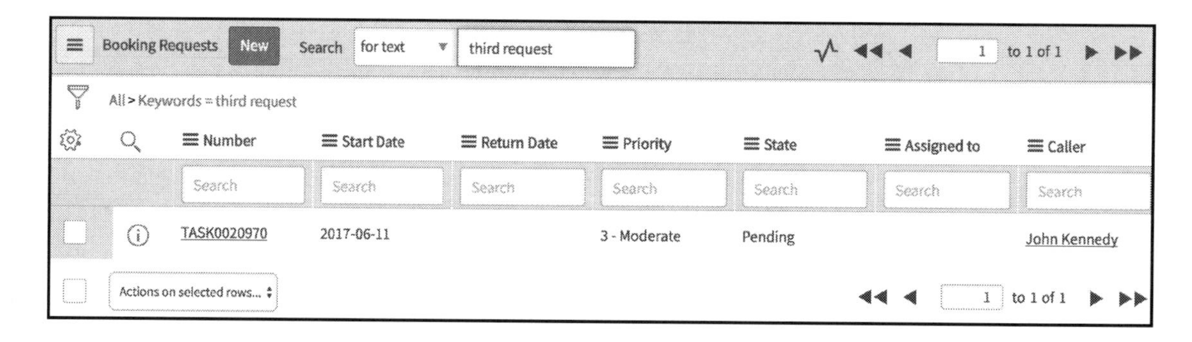

# Table auditing

The audit property of the collection dictionary entry can be used to monitor and track all changes to a record. If auditing is enabled for a table, then the system tracks insertion, update, and deletion of all records in the table. Let's enable auditing in the `Booking Request` table.

To enable auditing for the `Booking Request` table, open the dictionary entry for the table (collection) as described previously in the chapter. Now, check the **Audit** checkbox, as shown in the following screenshot, and click on the **Update** button:

Once the auditing is enabled on a table, the platform tracks all changes to a record and stores all changes to the `sys_audit` table. The `sys_id` of the record that changed is tracked, along with the following other information:

- Name of the table that contains the record that changed (table name)
- Name of the field that changed (field name)
- The new field value (new value)
- The old field value (old value)
- Number of times this record and field have been updated
- The date and time when the change occurred
- The details (`sys_id`) of the user who made the change (document key)
- The reason, if any, for the change
- The record's internal checkpoint ID when the record has multiple versions

While auditing track changes to all available columns (when auditing is enabled) any field that is with `sys_` is ignored, except the `sys_class_name` and `sys_domain_id` columns. It also ignores updates made through an import set (data import) or when the column has the `no_audit` field attribute specified.

# Excluding a field from being audited

We can disable auditing to track changes to a field by updating the dictionary entry for that column and specifying the `no_audit` attribute.

To exclude a field from being audited, open the dictionary entry for the field using the **System Definition** | **Dictionary** module and add a new entry to the attributes related list by clicking on the **New** button:

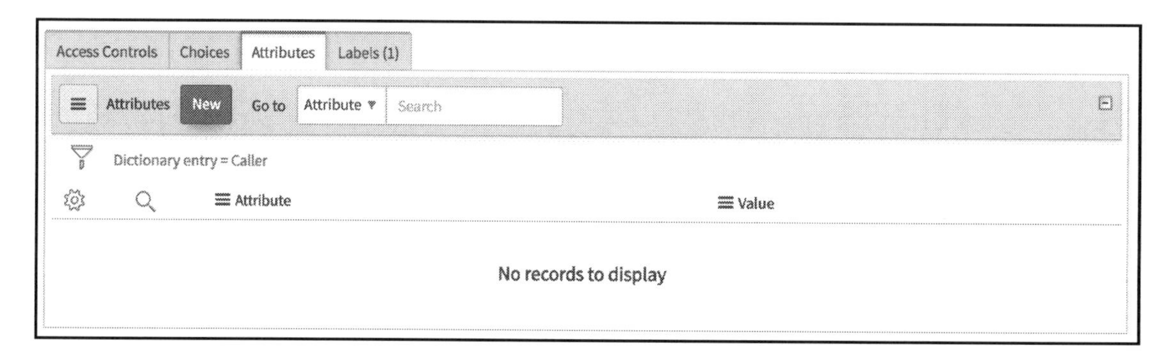


Fill in the form with the following values and click on the **Submit** button:

- **Attribute**: `No audit`
- **Value**: `true`

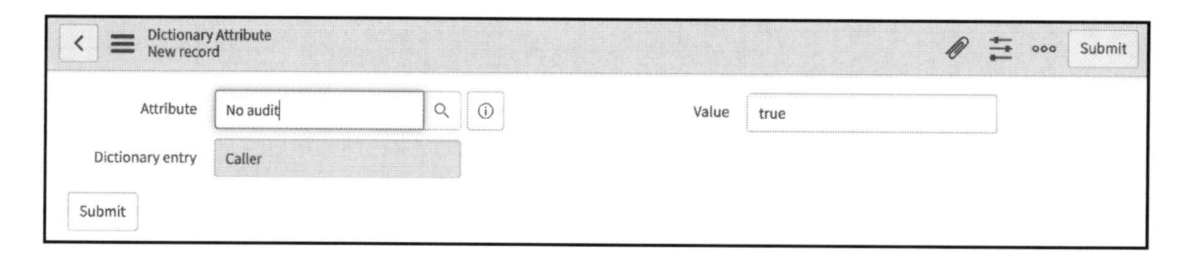

# Restoring deleted records

We can restore a deleted record by navigating the following steps:

1. Use the **System Definition** | **Deleted records** module:

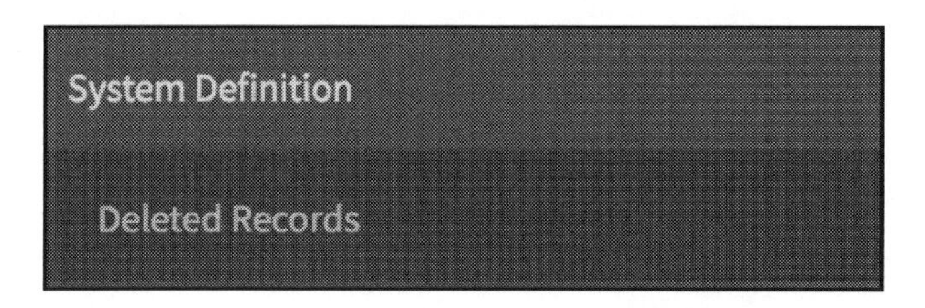


2. As shown next, in the list of records page, sort the table by the **Record deleted** field to see the recently deleted records on the top. Then, click on the info icon next to the record you want to restore:

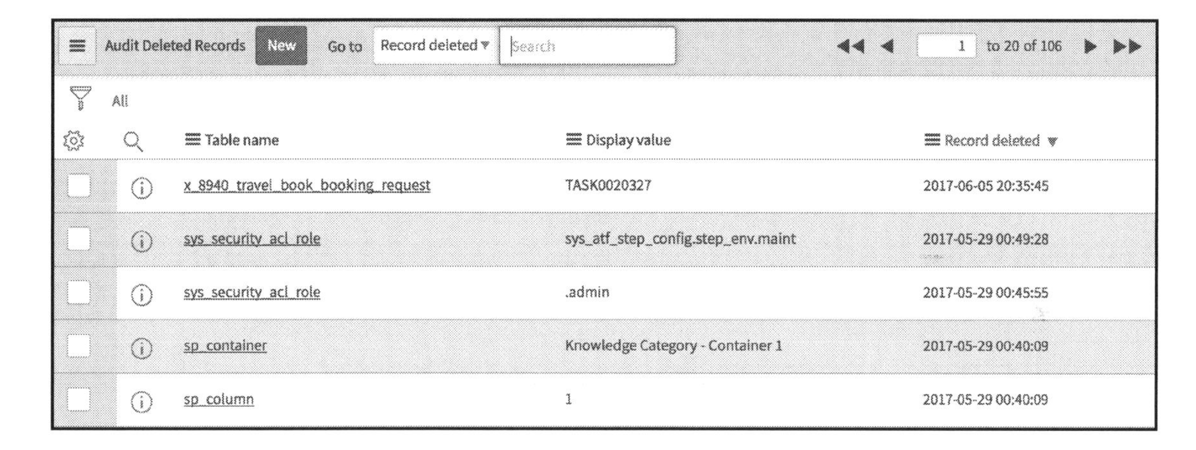

3. In the form, as shown in the following screenshot, confirm if this is the record you want to undelete, and then click on the **Undelete Record** button on the form header:

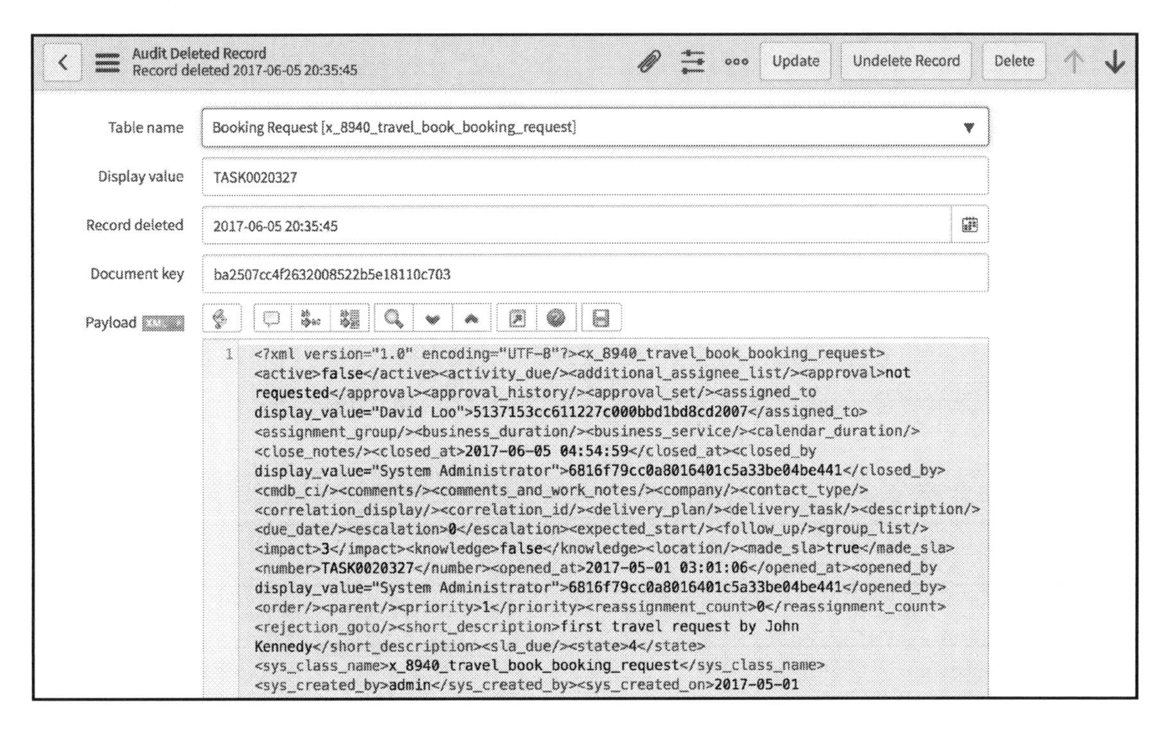


4. The record will be restored and be available in the original table as if it was never deleted. If you want to restore the record along with deleted reference records, use the **Restore Record** and **References** related links instead of the **Undelete Record** button.

The insert business rules, if any, will still execute on the record being moved from the `Audit Delete` table to the original table.

# Limitations of the undelete feature

There are some limitations of the undelete feature. It only works for tables that audit deletions, that is, tracks deletion. The following are the limitations of the restore deleted record feature:

- Record deletions are not tracked for tables with `the no_audit_delete=true` dictionary attribute
- Record deletions from tables with a `sys` prefix are also not tracked by default
- Any attachments associated with the record are not restored when the record is restored
- References are restored only if the reference field is on an audited table

We can overcome some of these limitations, such as restoring configuration record such as, **Business Rule**, and **Script Includes**, using the app creator.

We can configure specific system tables to audit deletions by adding the specified table to the `glide.ui.audit_deleted_tables` property using the **System Properties** | **UI Properties** module.

# Database rotation

The longer an instance runs and usage increases, the amount of data stored in tables increases over a period of time. More and more system logs and tasks are created each day causing the datasets to increase in size and negatively impact the database performance. Systems tasks, such as indexing can further impact the performance when the dataset in question is huge.

The database rotation feature available in the ServiceNow platform can be used to improve the database performance and avert any unknown risks associated with large datasets. The database rotation can be used to separate a large dataset into smaller ones thus improving the system performance.

The database rotation feature offers two possible techniques to administrator and to improve the performance by reducing the amount of data in a table:

- **Table rotation**: A table rotation works by creating a subset of data at a regular specified interval and maintains the records in subset tables till the number of rotations reaches the specified limit. The datasets stored or captured before the specified rotation limit is discarded from the system.
- **Table extension**: A table extension, on the other hand, works similar to the table rotation; however, it doesn't have any limit on the number of rotations and maintains the subsets of data till they are manually removed from the system.

To view or create a new table rotation group, navigate to the **System Definition** | **Table Rotations** module:

1. As shown in the following screenshot, it will list all the existing **Table Rotation Groups** defined in the system. Let's explore the **Table Rotation Groups** defined for the `syslog` table:

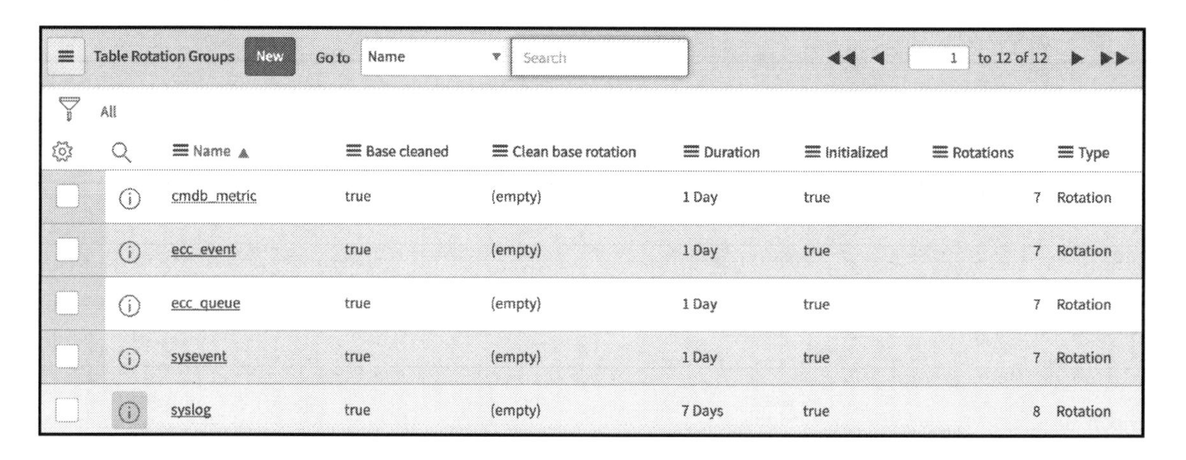

Table Rotation Groups New Go to Name Search 1 to 12 of 12

All

| Name ▲ | Base cleaned | Clean base rotation | Duration | Initialized | Rotations | Type |
|---|---|---|---|---|---|---|
| cmdb_metric | true | (empty) | 1 Day | true | 7 | Rotation |
| ecc_event | true | (empty) | 1 Day | true | 7 | Rotation |
| ecc_queue | true | (empty) | 1 Day | true | 7 | Rotation |
| sysevent | true | (empty) | 1 Day | true | 7 | Rotation |
| syslog | true | (empty) | 7 Days | true | 8 | Rotation |

2. As can be seen in the following screenshot, the `syslog` table rotation group definition is set to create a rotation every 7 days and maintain the data from the last `8` rotations:

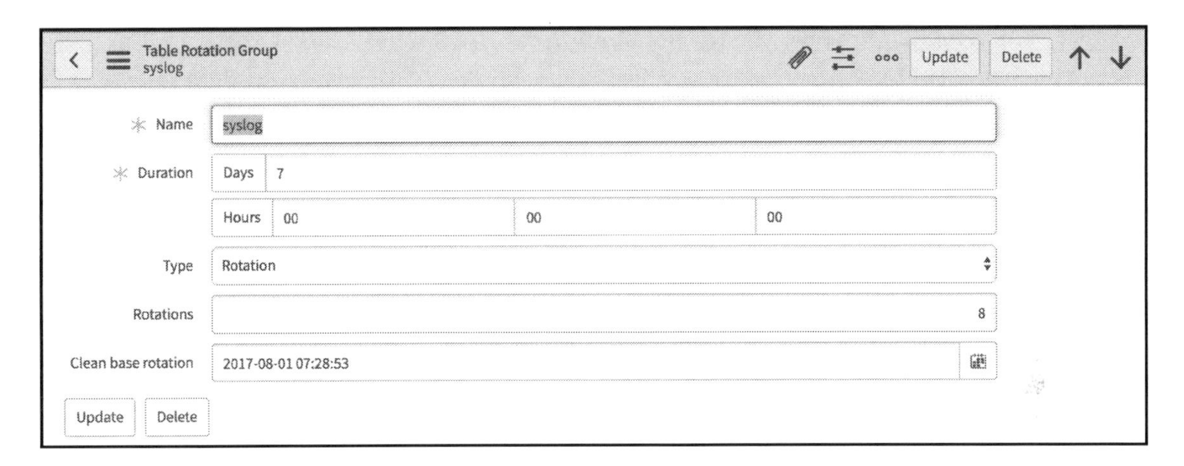


3. This eventually means that the system will create subsets of data in the `syslog` table every `7` days and maintain a subset of records for the last `8` rotations while discarding and taking offline the data stored in older subsets. The following related list **Table Rotation Schedule** lists all the subset data stored and maintained.

# Data archiving

Similar to table rotation, the data archiving feature in the ServiceNow platform can also be used to improve query and reporting performance by moving old data from the primary table to a set of archive tables. Furthermore, a destroy rule can be set to permanently delete data after a specified period of time, which should only be used when you do not require historical data for auditing or reporting purposes. For example, we can define data archiving on the `Booking Request` table to archive records that are a year old and further, to destroy them after a period of two years.

When we set data archiving on a table, a new table with the same name and prefix `ar_` is created. The data from the original data is flattened and stored in the archive table. For example, if we apply data archiving `Booking Request` table, then a new table comprising of fields from the base to the `Booking Request` table along with the parent task table will be created to store the archived data. All the reference fields will be converted to string and the `sys_id` of the referenced data will be stored. Furthermore, the archived data will be removed from the original table.

To enable archiving on a table, we need to create an archive rule. Archive rules are stored in the `sys_archive` table and can be created by users with an admin role.

# Creating an archive rule

To create a new archive rule, use the following steps:

1. Navigate to the **System Archiving** | **Archive Rule** module and click on the **New** button. Now fill in the form fields with the following values:
    - * **Name**: `Archive Old Booking Requests`
    - * **Table**: **Booking Request**
    - **Conditions**: **Updated** | **on** | **One year ago**

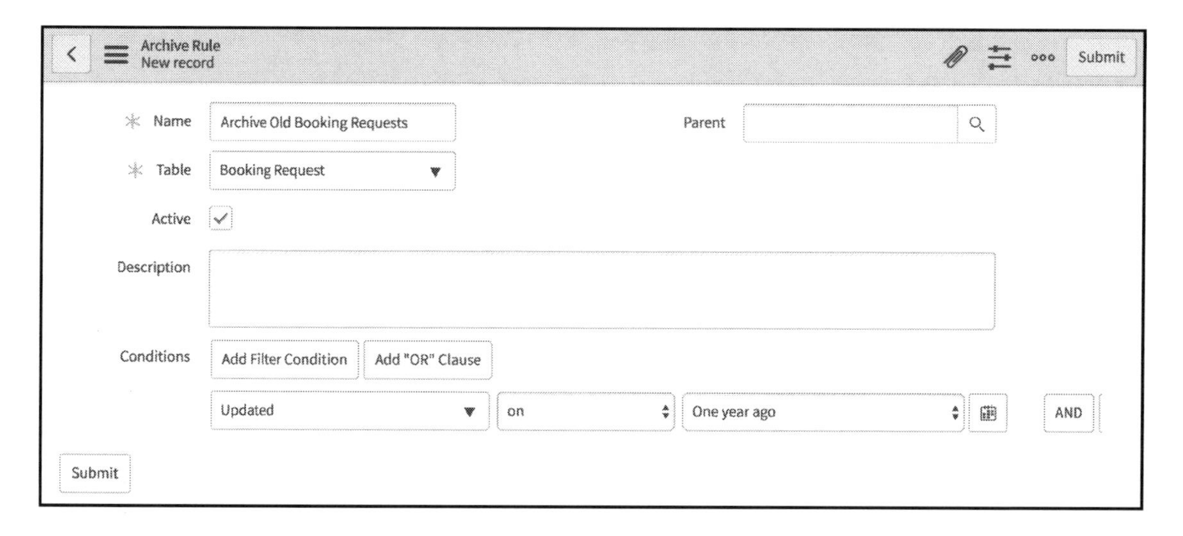

2. Now, click on the **Submit** button to create the archive rule. An estimate run date and record count will be shown in the form:

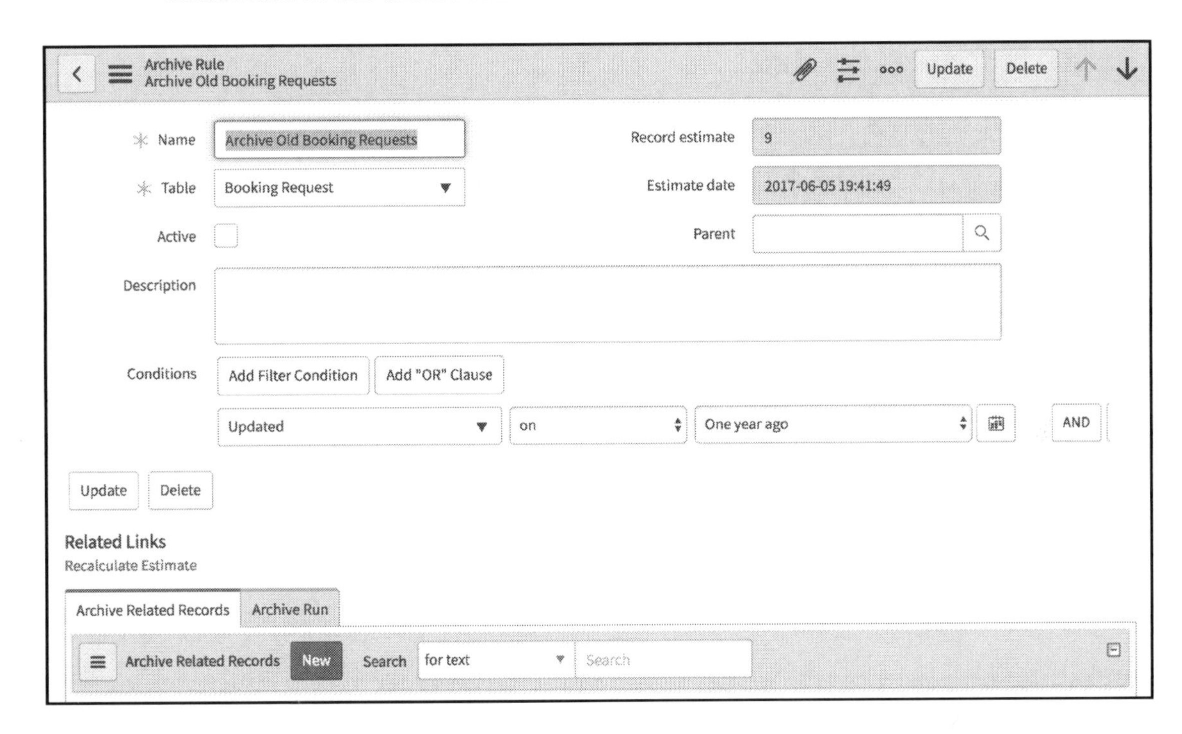


The **Recalculate Estimate** UI action under related links can be used to manually trigger the calculation of estimates. When the archive runs, it will archive all the data that matches the conditions we set in the archive rule.

If you want to archive the data stored in any reference field, you can create a new record using the **Archive Related Records** related list in the archive rule form. Furthermore, a destroy rule can also be created to permanently delete the data from the instance.

# Creating a destroy rule

A destroy rule works only on data stored in the archive tables. It cannot be implemented directly on target tables, such as booking request or incident:

1. To create a destroy rule, navigate to **System Archiving** | **Archive Destroy Rules**, and click on the **New** button.

2. Fill in the form with the following values:
    - * **Name**: `Destroy Older Booking Requests`
    - * **Table**: **Archive Booking Request**
    - **Archive Duration**:

    **Days**: `365`

3. Click on the **Submit** button to create the destroy rule. The data is kept in the `archive` table for the amount of time specified in the **Archive Duration** field in the destroy rule after which the records are permanently deleted from the `archive` table:

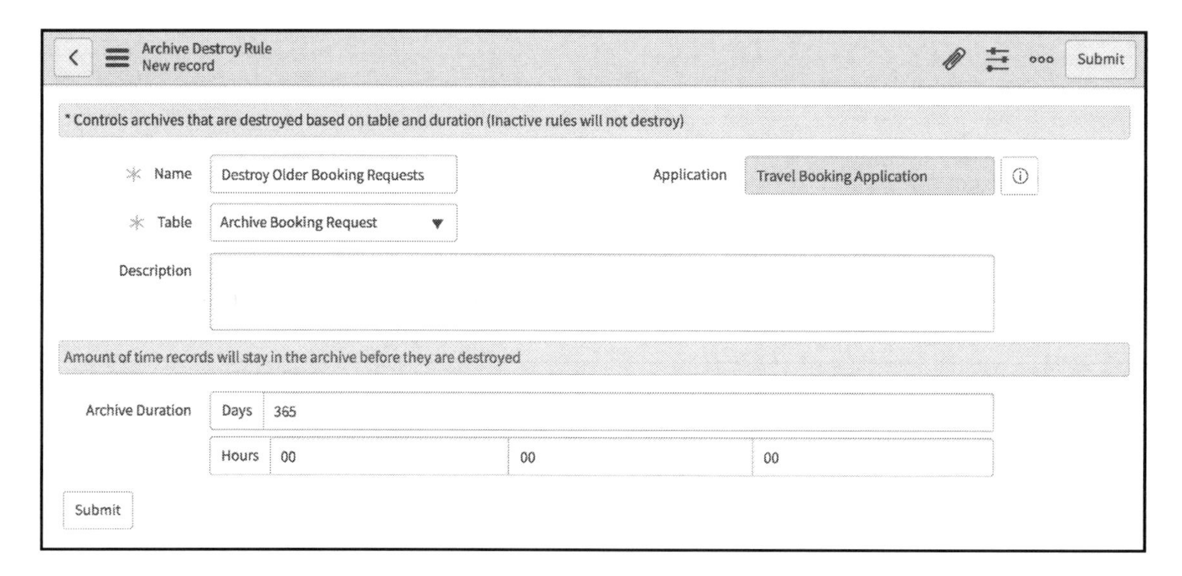


4. The **Archive Destroy Run** related list available in the destroy rule record form, as shown in the following screenshot, can be used to inspect details about the past destroy runs on the `archive` table:

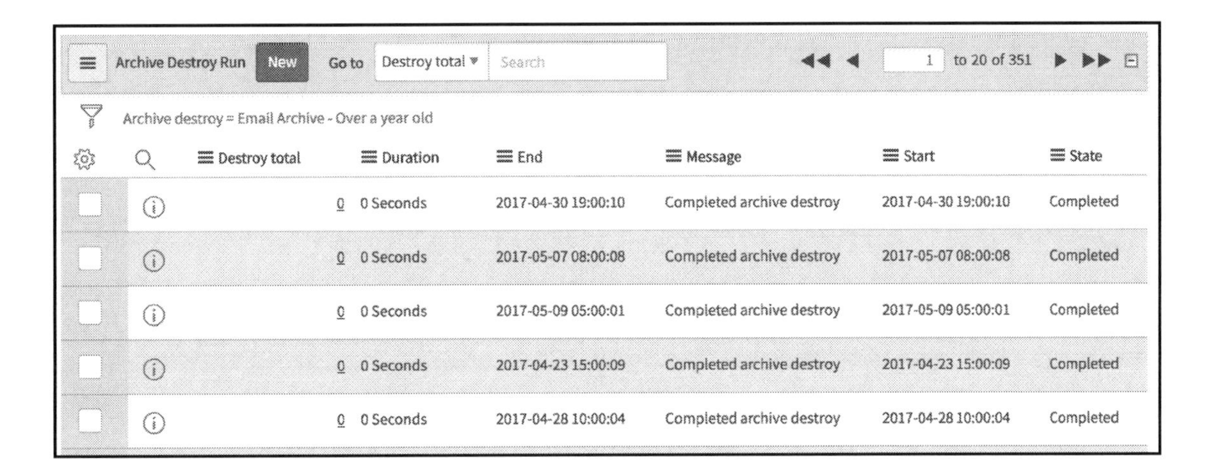


# Summary

In this chapter, you learned different database-related features, such as relationships, configuring related lists, and enabling auditing in a table. You also learned how to enable indexing on a field and perform a full-text search in a table. Furthermore, you learned how to configure table rotation and archive and destroy rules.

In the next chapter, we will cover some other advanced topics, such as the service catalog, record producers, running schedule scripts, and performing other administrative tasks, such as using import sets and exporting table data.

# 14
# Job Scheduling and Data Export-Import

You have learned how to create workflows, how to write client-side and server-side scripts, and many different features of the ServiceNow platform, including user and table management. As we approach the final part of our book, you will now begin to learn some of the advanced scripting, integration, and administrative features available in the platform. In this chapter, you will learn about some administrative tasks that a developer must be aware of, such as scheduled script execution and data export and import.

In this chapter, you will learn how to run scripts in the background and how to export and import data. More specifically, you will learn the following topics in this chapter:

- Scheduled script execution
- Exporting data
- Importing data using Import Sets
- Configuring transform maps
- Using scripts to process import data

## Scheduled script execution

Using the scheduled script execution feature, we can execute a server-side code on a recurring schedule. This is useful for many scenarios, such as updating multiple records, purging old records based on criteria, or parsing or validating large datasets.

As a part of our **Travel Booking Application**, we will create a scheduled script to automatically close booking requests, where the state is *pending* (-5) and the travel start date is past the current date. In essence, we will mark the state field as **Closed Incomplete**, which corresponds to the value of 4.

You can view, add, or remove choices for any drop-down field using **Dictionary entry**, **Form Designer**, or **Update Choice List**.

To define a new script that executes on a recurring schedule, use the following steps:

1. Open **Studio**, select **Server Development** | **Scheduled Script Execution** as shown in the following screenshot, in the **Create Application File** wizard, and click on **Create**:

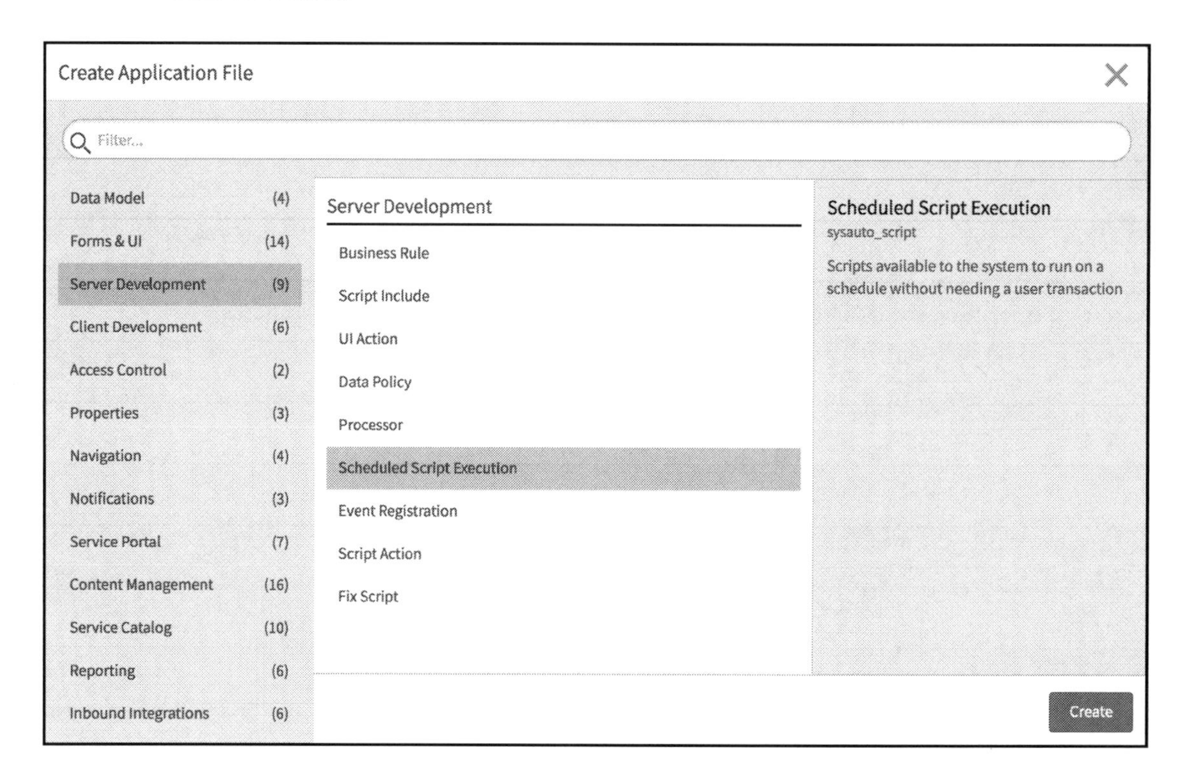

2. In the subsequent form that opens up (shown here), fill the fields with the following values:
    - **Name**: `Auto close expired booking requests`
    - **Active**: Checked
    - **Run**: **Daily**
    - **Time**: `08:00:00`
    - **Run this script**: (Use the following code)
3. Use this code:

```
var gr = new GlideRecord("x_8940_travel_book_booking_request");
//always use your company code
gr.addActiveQuery();
gr.addQuery("state", "!=",  -5 );
var dt = new GlideDateTime();
gr.addQuery("u_start_date", "<",  dt.getDate() );
gr.query();
while(gr.next()) {
     gr.state=4;
     gr.update();
}
```

4. The preceding code will create a `GlideRecord` object of the `Booking Request` table and query all records that are in a pending state and for which the travel start date is past the current date. The scheduled script execution is set to run every day at 08:00 hours:

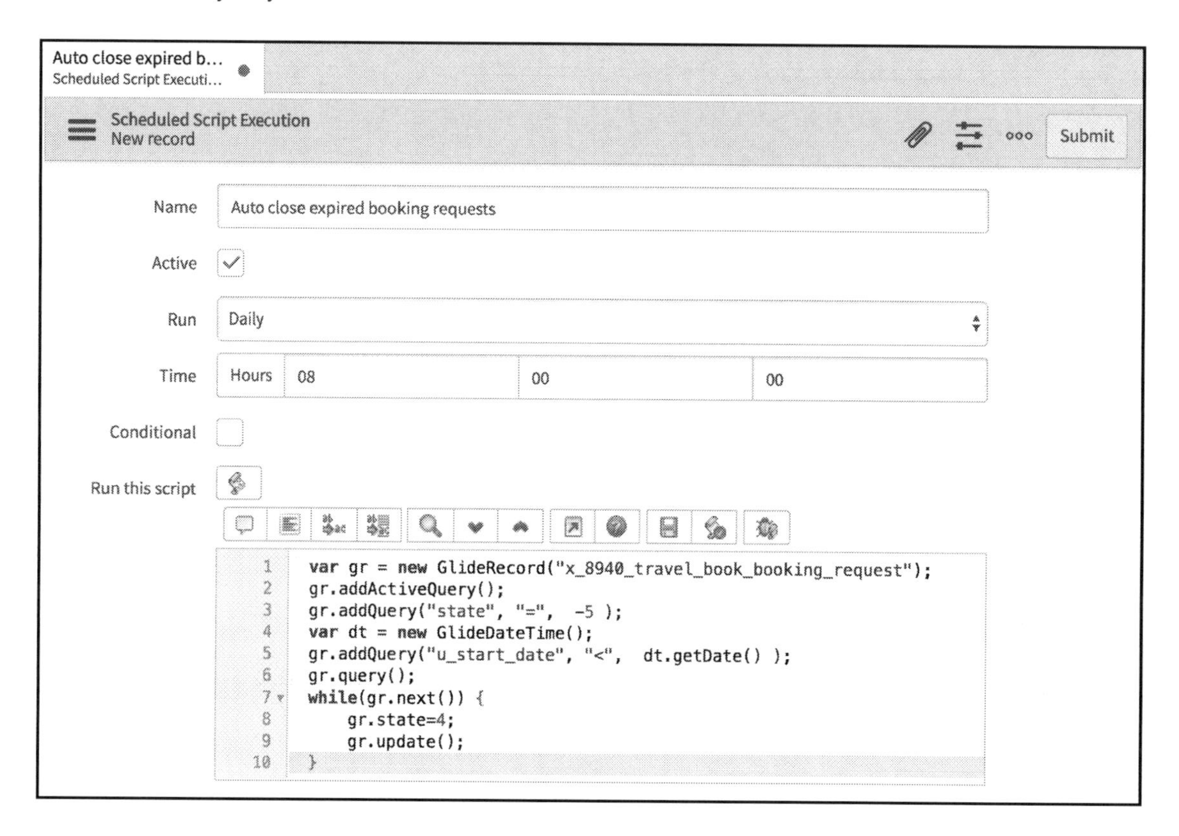


5. Click on the **Submit** button to create the scheduled script execution entry in the database. The SSE will execute at the specified time interval; however, we can manually execute the script by clicking on the **Execute Now** button on the form header.
6. When the SSE code executes, it will mark all records in the `Booking Requests` table that are in a pending state and have a start date past the current date as **Closed Incomplete**.

We can use the **Conditional** checkbox to execute the scheduled script execution based on some condition. The execution engine will look for the value of a variable named `answer`. The code in the **Run this script** field will execute only if the value of the `answer` variable in the condition script evaluates to `true`.

# Exporting data

In the ServiceNow platform, there are multiple options available for administrators and users to export data in various formats. The following options are available to export data:

- Form export
- List export
- Direct URL access

# Form export

The form export feature works only on any form that the user has access to. We can export data of a form using the **Export** option available in the form header, as shown in the following screenshot:

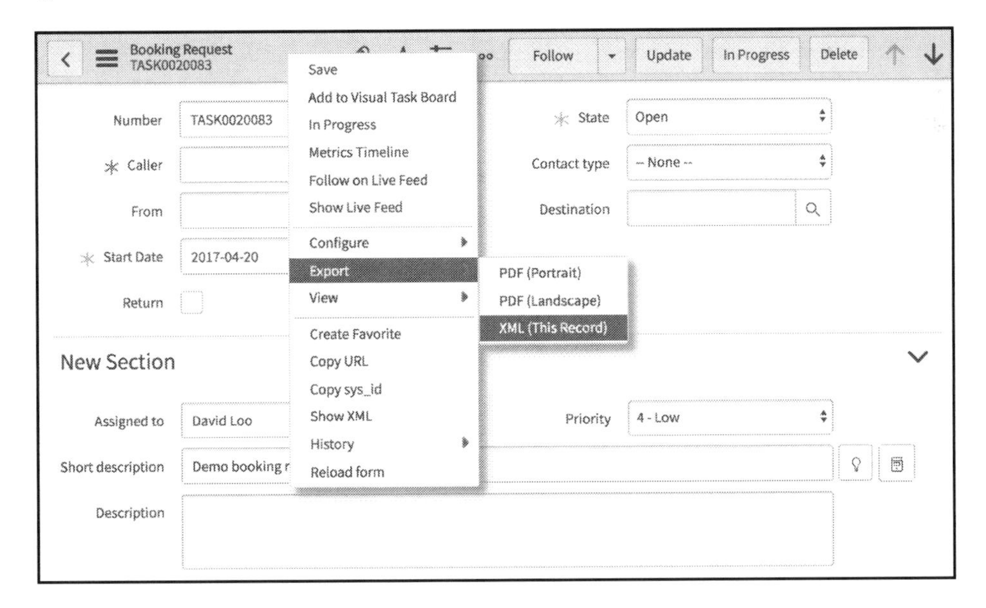

The export option can be used to export the data of the form comprising of the fields in the table in the following formats:

- **PDF (Portrait/Landscape)**: When exporting the data of a form in a PDF format, only the fields that are displayed in the view are visible in the form; however, it includes fields that might be hidden using the UI policy. A PDF can be exported in either a portrait or landscape format.
- **XML (This Record)**: When exporting form data in an XML format, all fields, irrespective of the view, are available.

# List export

The data in any list of a record page can be exported using the options available in the list column header, as shown in the following screenshot:

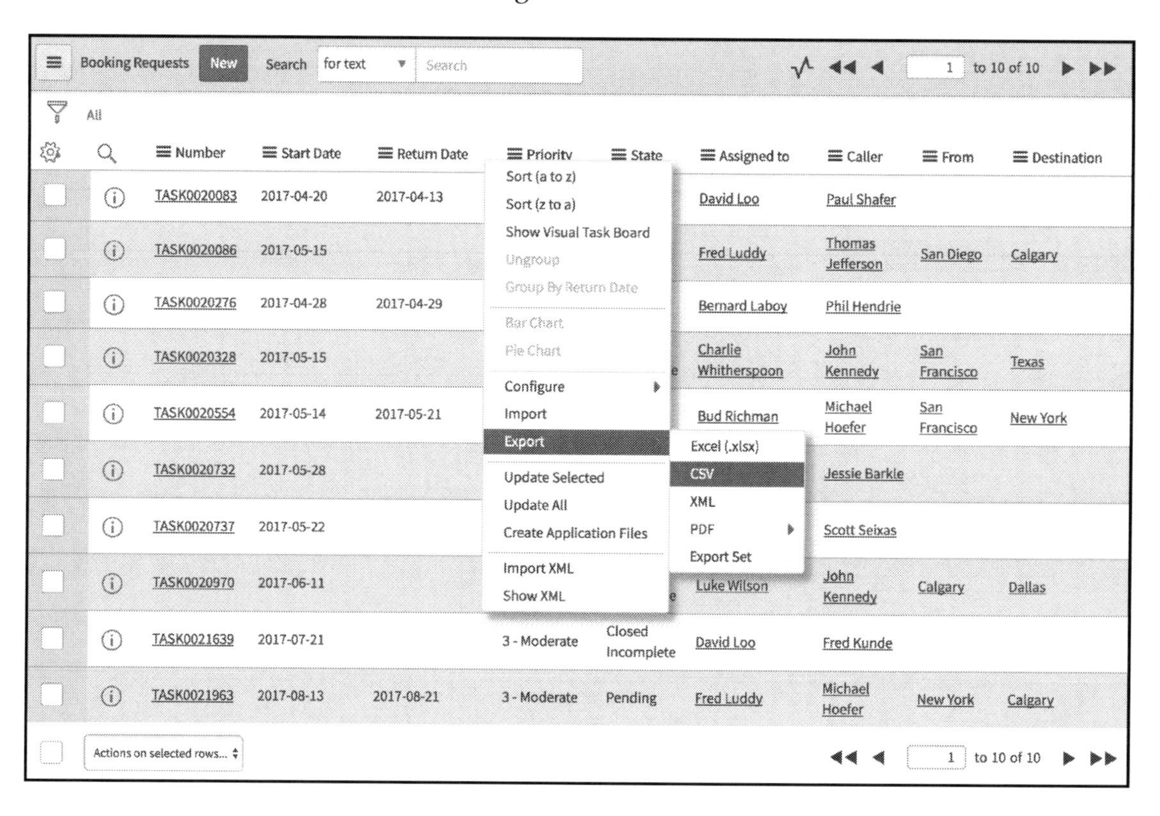

The records in the list can be exported in various formats, including **Excel (.xlsx)**, **CSV**, **XML**, and **PDF**. Furthermore, we can define an **Export Set** that can upload the data in one of the available formats to a MID server.

The `.xlsx` and CSV export formats will only include columns that are visible in the list of the record page. You can personalize the list layout to show or hide any columns to the list prior to exporting the record. Furthermore, you can also apply any filters to drill-down to the records you are interested in exporting.

# Direct URL access

The records stored in tables are accessible through a URL and passing a desired format as one of the query parameters. We can directly access records stored in the `Booking Request` table in CSV by hitting the following URL:

```
https://<instance>.service-now.com/x_8940_travel_book_booking_request_list.
do?CSV
```

We can also access the same data in an XML format using the following URL:

```
https://<instance>.service-now.com/x_8940_travel_book_booking_request_list.
do?XML
```

Make sure to replace `x_8940` with your company code in all the URL and code mentioned in this book.

## sysparam_view

We can also access columns in a specific view by specifying the view name in the `sysparam_view` query parameter; for example:

```
https://<instance>.service-now.com/x_8940_travel_book_booking_request_list.
do?XML&sysparm_view=employee
```

## sysparm_query

It is also possible to drill-down records in the direct URL output based on a sysparm_query search filter query parameter. In order to access just one record using its sys_id, we can use the following direct URL:

```
https://<instance>.service-now.com/x_8940_travel_book_booking_request_list.
do?XML&sysparm_query=sys_id%3D<sys_id of a booking request>
```

```
https://<instance>.service-now.com/x_8940_travel_book_booking_request_list.
do?XML&sysparm_query=sys_id%3D6e1df2c54f9232008522b5e18110c740
```

The %3D is the URL encoded form of = (equal) sign. The alphanumeric value, 6e1df2c54f9232008522b5e18110c740, that follows %3D is the sys_id of one of the records in the Booking Request table. When trying the previous mentioned URI, make sure to replace x_8940 with your company code and also use sys_id of one of the records stored in the Booking Request table in your instance.

We can use the following URL to fetch a list of booking requests that are in an *open* state in the XML format:

```
https://<instance>.service-now.com/x_8940_travel_book_booking_request_list.
do?XML&sysparm_query=state%3D1
```

## sysparm_record_count

The sysparm_record_count query parameter can be used to limit the number of records returned by the export processor; for example:

```
https://<instance>.service-now.com/x_8940_travel_book_booking_request_list.
do?XML&sysparm_query=state%3D1&sysparm_record_count=10
```

## sysparm_order_by

The sysparm_order_by query parameter can be used to sort the output from the export processor by a specific field; for example:

```
https://<instance>.service-now.com/x_8940_travel_book_booking_request_list.
do?XML&sysparm_query=state%3D1&sysparm_order_by=short_description
```

## Building queries using a list of records filters

You can copy complex queries to be used in direct access URLs by right-clicking and copying the query, as shown in the following screenshot, on the filter available in any list of the record module:

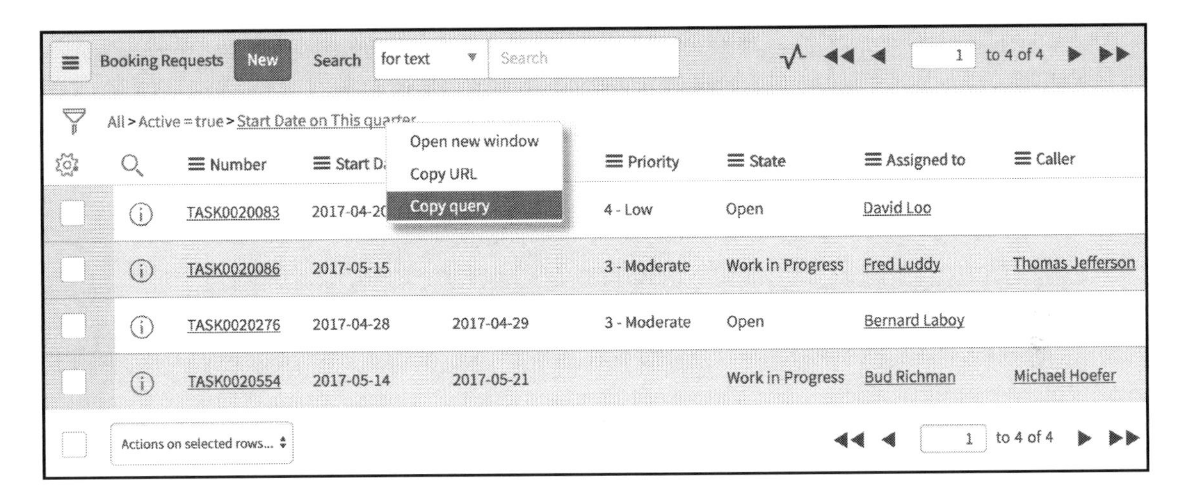


## Export limits

By default, the system limits the maximum number of records returned by the export processor based on the output format. The following system properties can be set to limit the number of records:

- **General output limit**: The general output limit can be configured using the `glide.ui.export.limit` system property and defaults to 10,000. The general output limit applies to the XML, CSV, and Excel format outputs.
- **XML**: The format specific output limit for an XML output format can be configured using the `glide.xml.export.limit` system property.
- **CSV**: The format specific output limit for a CSV output format can be configured using the `glide.csv.export.limit` system property.
- **Excel**: The format specific output limit for an Excel output format can be configured using the `glide.excel.export.limit` system property.

- **PDF**: The format specific output limit for a PDF output format can be used to control the maximum number of rows and columns using the `glide.pdf.max_rows` and `glide.pdf.max_columns` system properties respectively.

# Importing data using Import Sets

**Import Sets** allow administrators and developers to pull in data from different sources and import them into the ServiceNow platform. The import set application has all the modules one may require to define external sources and import data to the target (destination) table. During a normal import from an external source, the data is first stored in an import set table and then copied to the target table based on a transform map.

The import set tool can be used to perform imports from various kinds of sources and can be configured to be run in different ways. Most commonly, the import set tool can be used to perform the following tasks:

- Manual import of data from a file source, such as CSV, XLS, or XML, and optional parse and process of data through a script
- Manual import of data from an online data source, such as HTTP, FTP, LDAP, or JDBC
- Import data periodically from a data source by defining scheduled imports
- Import data from a web service

There are four key aspects when working with the import set tool:

- **External data source**: The source from where the data needs to be imported. The ServiceNow import tool supports multiple sources, such as JDBC, LDAP, HTTP, FTP, Excel, CSV, and XML.
- **Import set table**: An import set table is a temporary staging table used to store raw data imported from an external source. It consists of sets of columns and rows imported from external sources. The system also adds a few columns that are used to identify the status of the import process.
- **Transform map**: A transform map is used to establish a relationship between fields in the import set table and the target table. A transform map is designed graphically using the transform map designer interface and optionally can be automatically generated by the system.

- **Target table**: A target table is the one into which the data being imported is either inserted or updated. The system will skip rows when the data being imported matches the data in the table or if it encounters an error.

Before we begin importing data using the import set tool, let's first go through different modules available under the **System Import Sets** application:

The **System Import Sets** application, as shown in the preceding screenshot, is accessible from the left navigator in the main interface of the ServiceNow instance. The following are the key modules available under the **System Import Sets** application:

- **Load Data**: The **Load Data** module allows administrators and developers to create import set tables from an import source by either uploading a file source or specifying an online data source defined using the **Data Sources** module. It is also possible to pull new data from sources into one of the existing import set tables.
- **Create Transform Map**: The **Create Transform Map** module is used to define detailed customization of the import operation by mapping fields of the import set table (created using the **Load Data** module) to the target (destination) table. A transform script can be created in order to perform advanced import operations and pre- and post-data processing.
- **Run Transform**: The **Run Transform** module is used to push records from an import set table; through its respective transform map to the target table. Multiple Import Sets for which transform maps are already defined can be selected in one run. Furthermore, transform run can be scheduled to run at a particular time.
- **Administration | Data Sources**: The **Data Sources** module is used to define online data sources, such as LDAP, JDBC, HTTP, or FTP.
- **Administration | Transform Maps**: This module is useful for reviewing existing transform maps and creating new transform maps.
- **Administration | Scheduled Imports**: The **Scheduled Imports** module can be used to configure an import to run at a regular time interval. The external data source, if an online one, is refreshed before the transform operation.
- **Advanced | Import Sets**: A list of all Import Sets.
- **Advanced | Progress**: This displays the progress of on-going scheduled imports running in the background.
- **Transform History**: A list of log entries of import operations that are completed. An import operation is considered to be complete, with or without errors, when the records were transformed into a target table.
- **Transform Errors**: A list of all entries of all errors that were encountered during the import operation.
- **Import Log**: A list of log entries generated by the System Import Set tool about each import operation.

- **Import Set Tables**: The expandable tree menu can be used to see all individual import set tables created using the **Load Data** or **Scheduled Import** module. It also has the following two sub-modules:
    - **Clean Up**: The **Clean Up** module can be used to remove unwanted import set tables when they are no longer required and have already been transformed into a target table.
    - **Scheduled Cleanup**: The **Scheduled Cleanup** module can be used to schedule cleanup of the records stored in the import set tables on a regular interval.

# Importing data using CSV

Now, let's try to import booking requests from a CSV source file into the `Booking Request` table. To import data from a CSV file, we will first create an import set table that will act as staging table, by uploading the file, then configure the transform map, and finally, run the transformation to push the data from staging table to the target table.

## Import set table

As a first step, we will create an import set table using the **Load Data** module. Open the **System Import Sets** | **Load Data** module, as shown in the following screenshot, and fill in the form using the following values:

- **Import set table**: Select **Create table**
- **Label**: `Booking Req Import`
- **Name**: (This field will be automatically populated)
- **Source of import**: Select **File**
- **File**: (Choose the file we exported earlier in the chapter)
- **Sheet number**: `1`
- **Header row**: `1`

The **Label** and **Name** fields tell us the label and name of the new table that will become our import set staging table. The source of the input that we are selecting here is a file, as we will upload a CSV file that contains rows that will be inserted into the new staging table being created. The sheet number is useful when we are trying to upload an Excel file that may contain more than one worksheet. Similarly, the header row number field is used to specify the row number that contains the column headers. Selecting an existing table option is useful when we are uploading a file the with same columns (but updated or newer rows entries) for which we have already created an import set table:

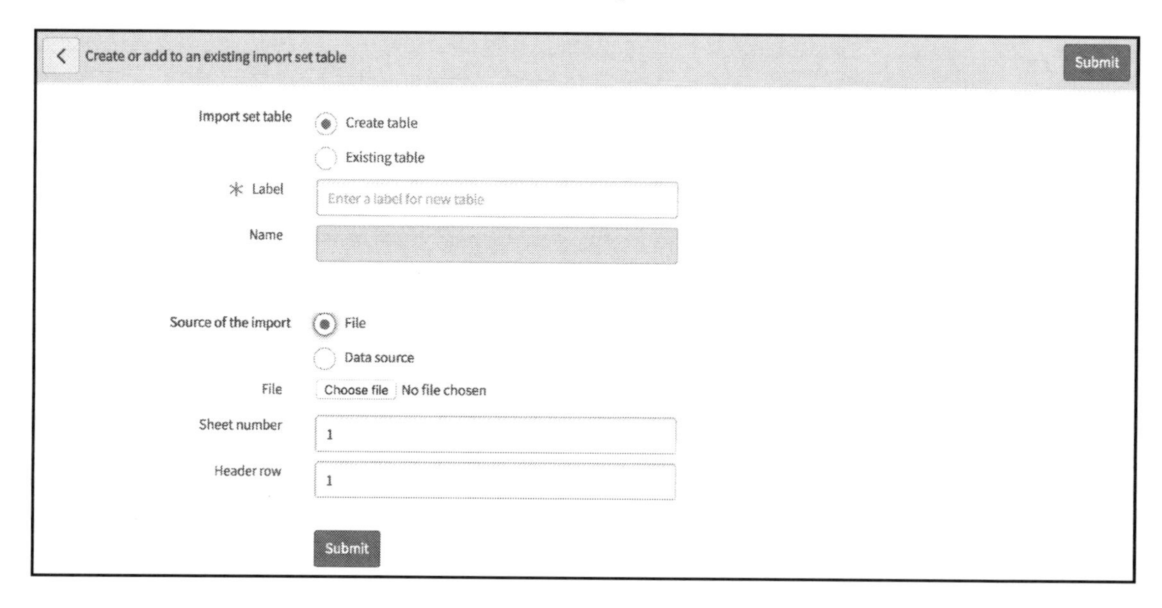


Now, click on the **Submit** button to upload the CSV file and be taken to the next page. Depending on the size of the file that you select, it may take some time for the upload to complete.

When the file is uploaded, the first task that the system performs is to create a new import set table. The system parses the columns in the header row of the uploaded file and creates columns with the same name in the import set table. Furthermore, the system samples only the first 20 rows of the uploaded file in order to determine the data type and size of each column.

Once the import set table is created, the system picks each row from the uploaded CSV file and inserts records into the import set table. If the system fails to insert a row, it jumps to the next row and continues trying to insert the remaining records. The system may update a record if all the values of a row match a record in the import set table. We can control these behaviors by changing the system properties, which you will learn about later in the chapter. Once the process is complete, we will be presented with a confirmation message, as shown in the following screenshot, along with the total number of rows processed and the number of records inserted, updated, or skipped:

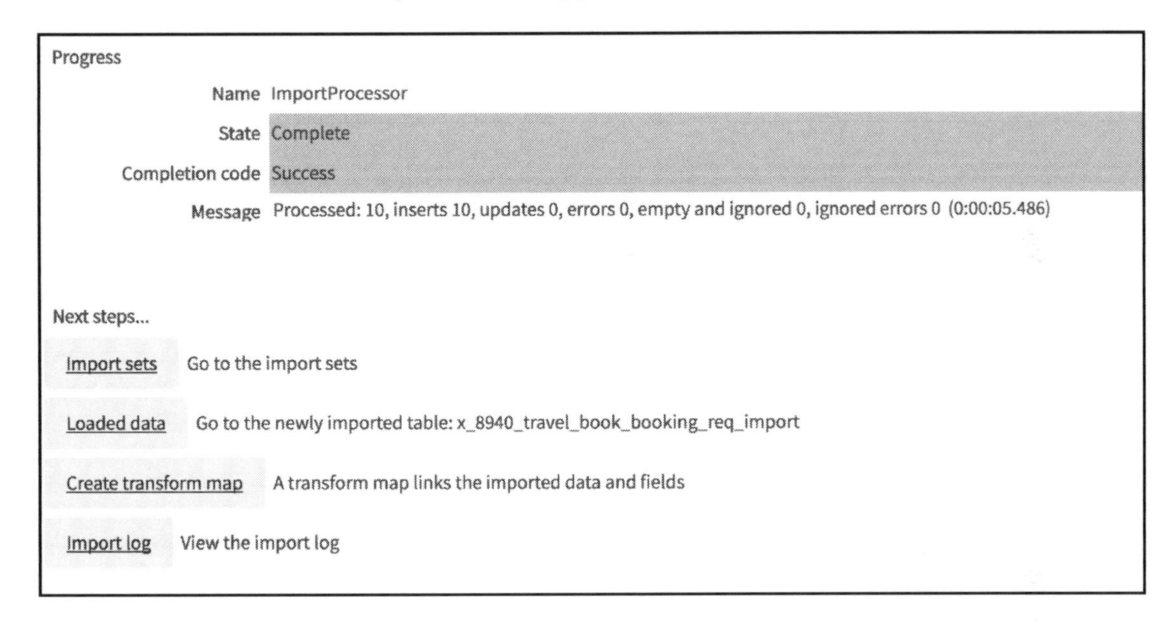


The next step is to ensure that the data we uploaded has inserted properly into the import set table. We can open the **Import Sets** module by clicking on the **Import Sets** links under the **Next steps...** section. As shown in the following screenshot, the list of records page will show us the newly created import set:

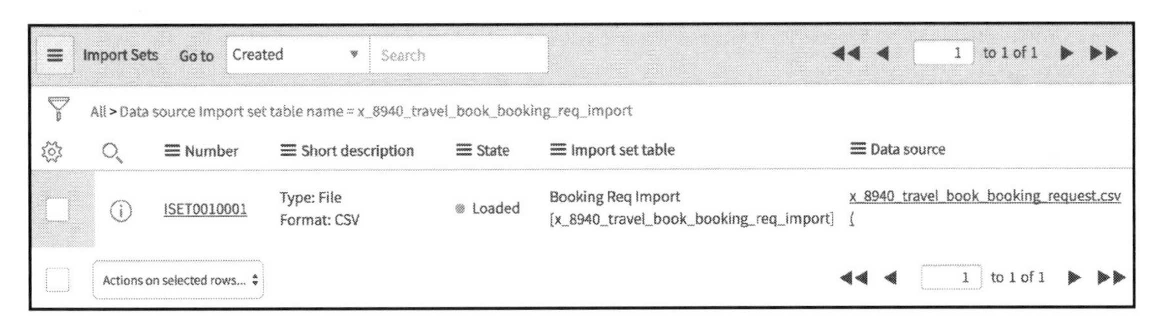

Every attempt to upload new data will create a new Import Sets entry and will be linked to at least one import set table and a source. Each Import Sets is given a unique number that begins with ISET and is followed by 7 digits. The state of the import set is used to determine the status of the import set and tell whether the data is currently loading, loaded, processed, or canceled.

Now, click on the import set number to be taken to the detail page of the import set, as shown in the following screenshot. It is recommended not to change any values in any fields, except the **Short description** field. The transform related link under the form can be used to configure the transform map for the import set if it is already not defined or to run an existing transform map if it is already defined:

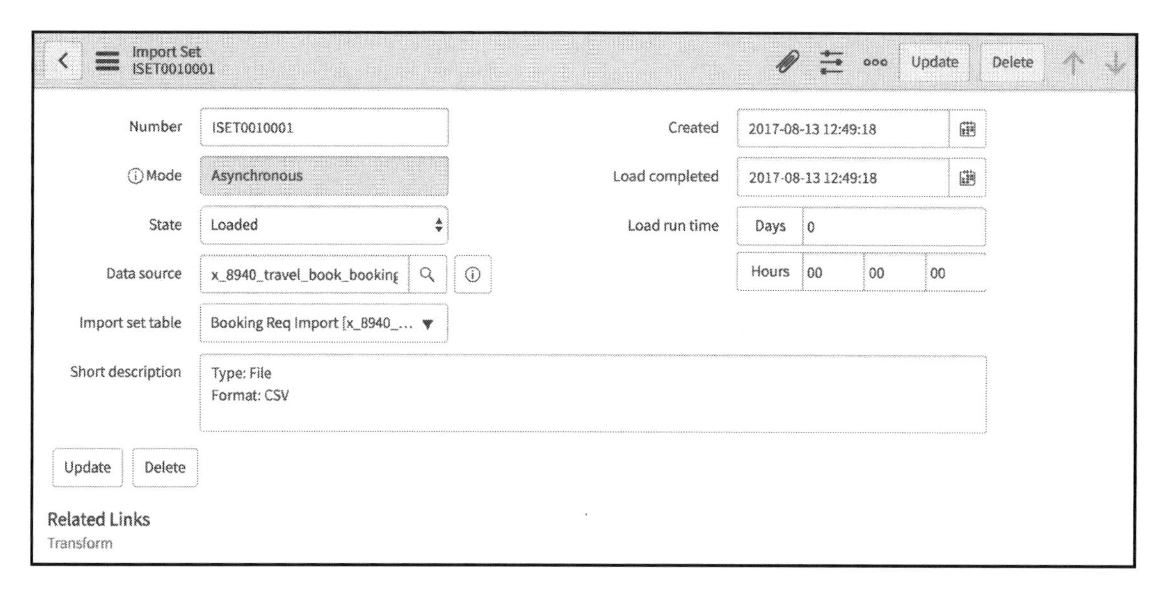


The **Import Sets Rows** related list below the main form, as shown in the following screenshot, can be used to view all the records that are uploaded to the instance using the load data module. The list is useful for determining if there were any errors while loading the data. It can also be used to find the target record that will be inserted or updated when we transform the import set.

Furthermore, the **State** field can be used to learn about the status of the transform process. If the row gets properly inserted or updated into the target table, the **State** field will be marked as inserted or updated, respectively. In case there is an error while trying to insert the row into the target table, the **State** field will be marked as an error. The state of pending means that the records have been inserted into the staging table and are awaiting the transform process to be completed, which you will learn next:

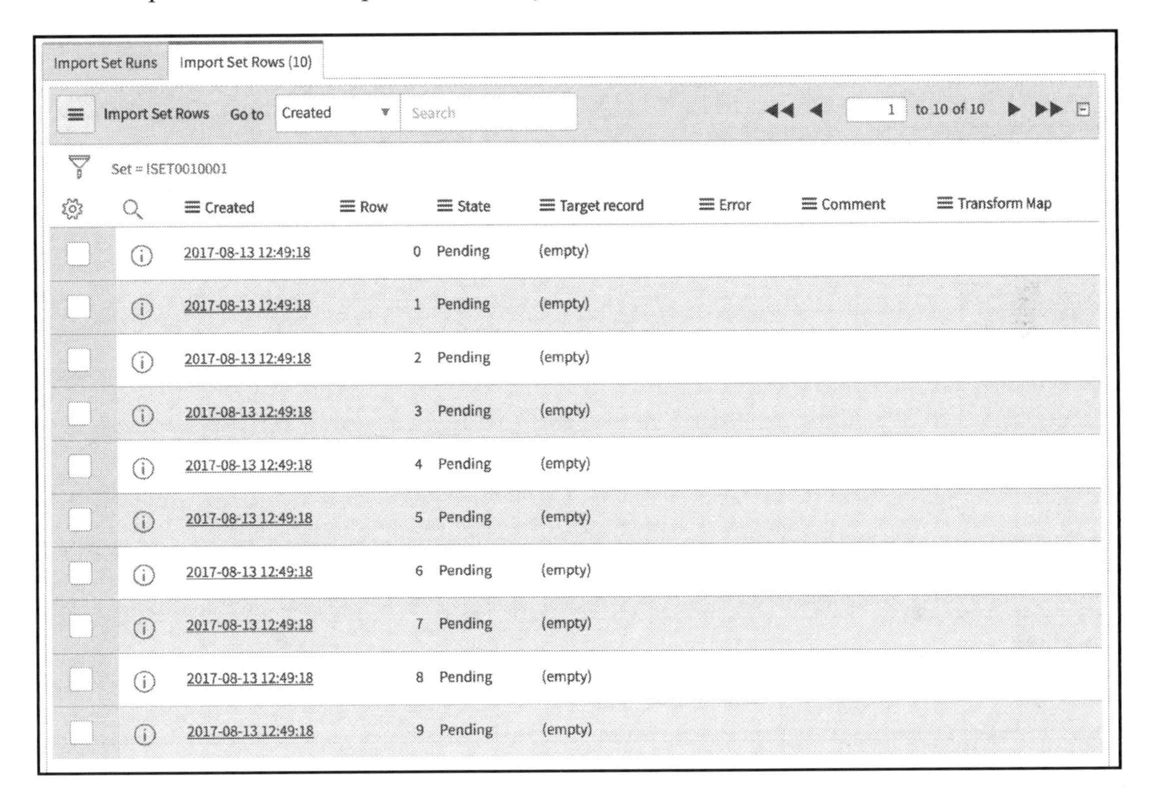

As shown in the following screenshot, we can take our mouse over to each info icon to quickly look through some records to determine if the column headers and row values in the source CSV file mapped and uploaded into the import set table properly. This is a recommended process for when we are trying to use an existing table while loading the data, as, chances of selecting a different source that might have a different column structure is high in such a case:

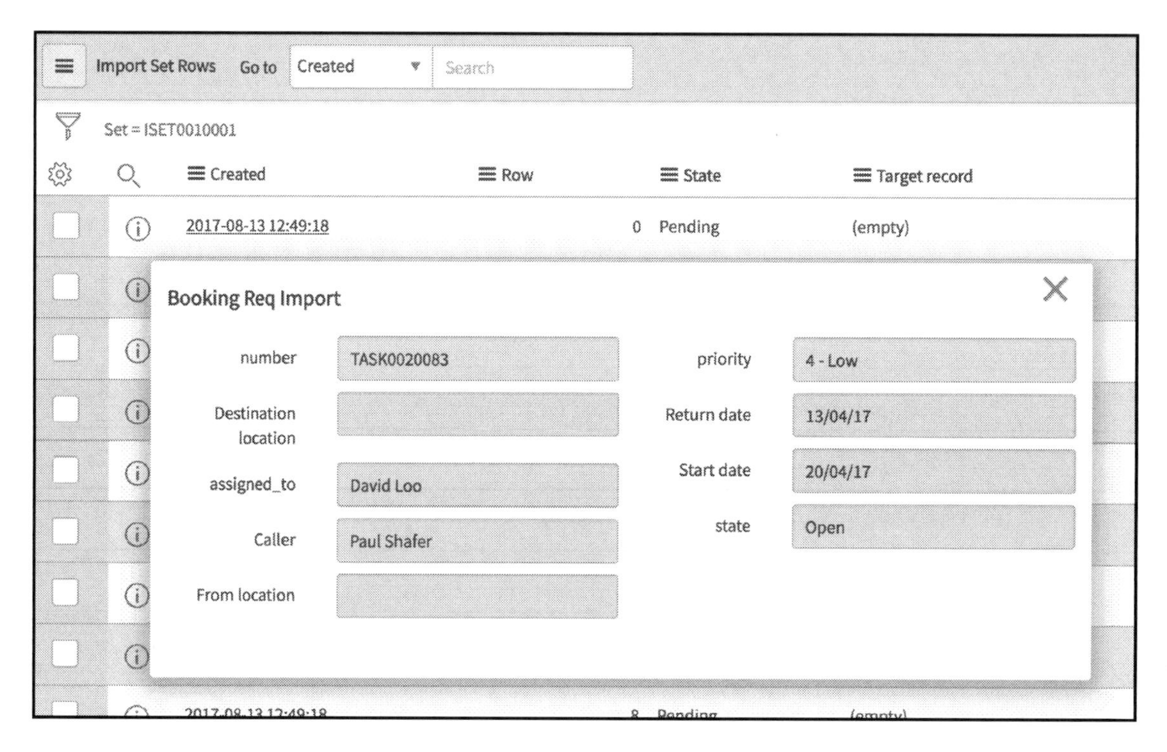


## Checking the import log

At any step of the import process, you can look into the import log by clicking on the **System Import Sets | Advanced | Import Logs** module. The module, as shown in the following screenshot, will list all the entries for different import actions performed in the instance:

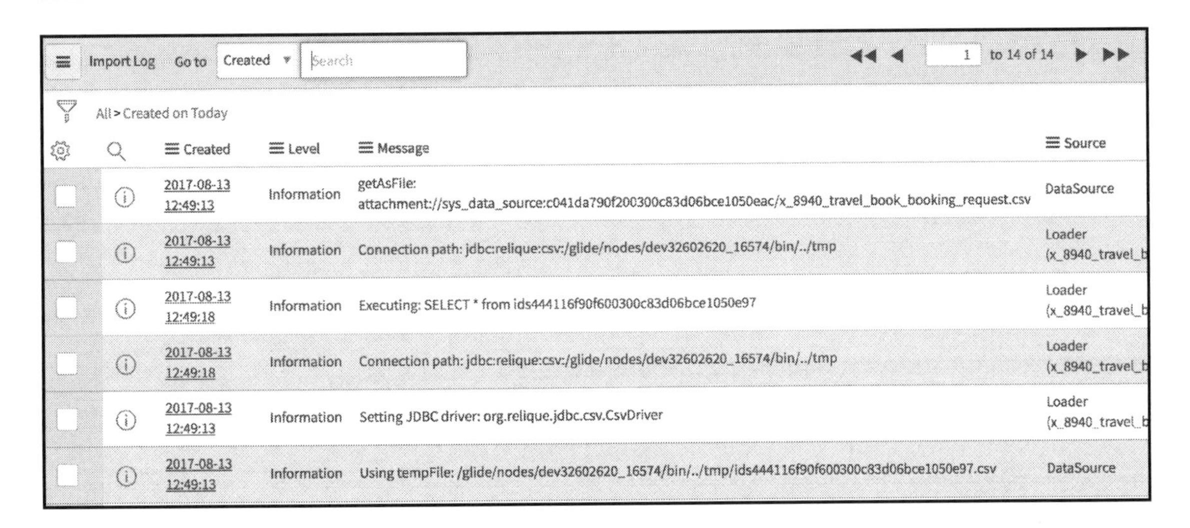


The next step is to create a transform map. To create a transform map, click on **Transform related link** under the **Import Sets** detail form. If the map doesn't already exist for the import set, you will be asked to first configure the transform map.

# Creating the transform map

The transform map acts as a link between the columns in the import set table and the target (destination) table. The target table may have more or fewer columns compared to the columns in the import set table. Depending on the source CSV file we used, the columns of the import set table may not always have corresponding columns with matching names in the target table.

The transform map can either be created manually using the map assist tool or else using the automap matching fields feature that relies on matching column names. As a part of this book, we will use the manual process to create the transform map to better understand the features available for mapping fields using the transform map assist tool.

Once you are in create new transform map form page, fill in the form with the following values:

- * **Name**: `Booking Request CSV Source`
- * **Source table**: (Select the import set table we created in the previous step)
- **Active**: Checked
- **Run business rules**: Unchecked (If unchecked, business rules will not get executed)
- **Enforce mandatory fields**: **Only Mapped Fields** (The option selected here can change the way values of mandatory fields are handled)
- **Copy empty fields**: Checked (When checked, the empty values from the staging table copied to the target table instead of leaving it as `NULL`)
- * **Target table**: **Booking Request**
- **Order**: `100`
- **Run script**: Unchecked (When checked, the transform map script executes during the transform process. Leave it unchecked for now. We have covered the topic in detail later in the chapter.)

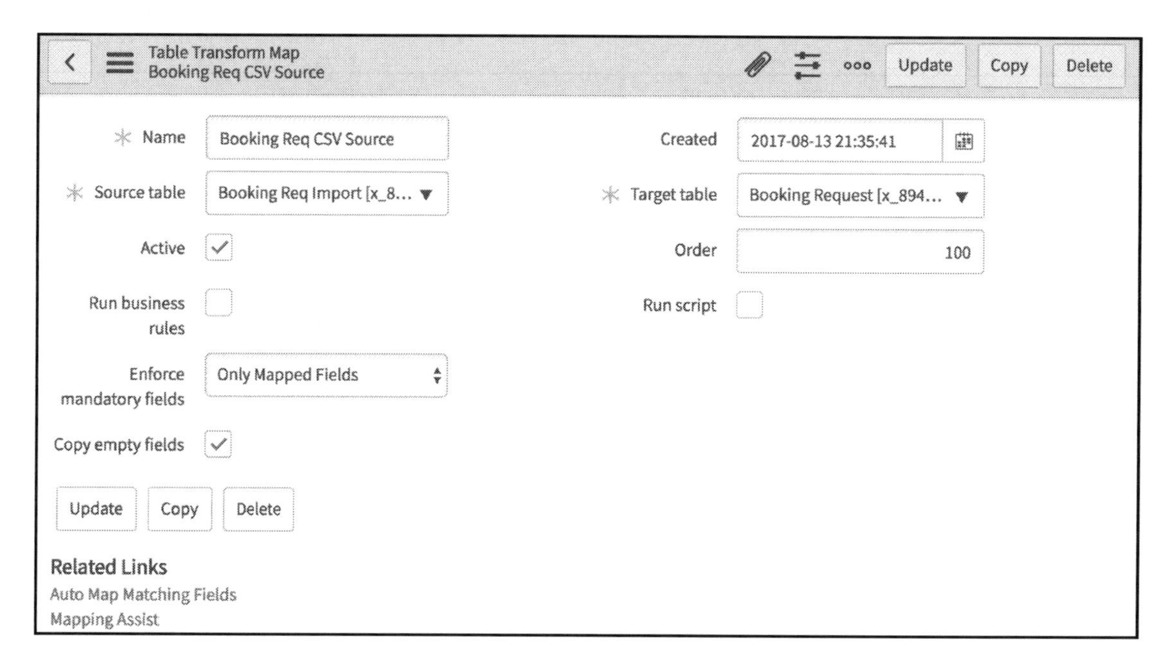

Now, instead of clicking on the **Submit** button, click on the **Mapping Assist** related link to be taken to the transform map assist tool page, as shown in the following screenshot:

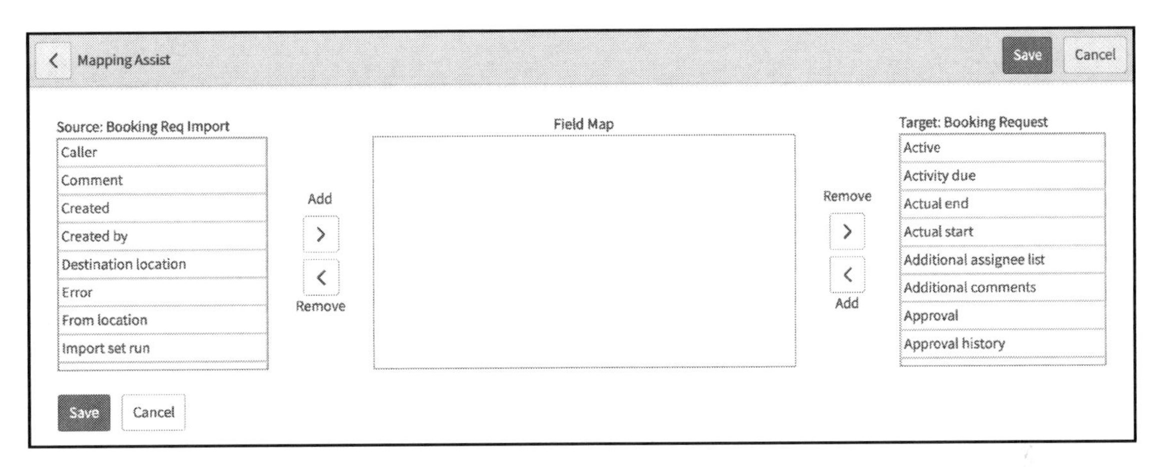


The columns (fields) of the import set staging table are shown on the left, whereas columns of the `Target: Booking Request` table will be shown on the right side list. The center **Field Map** grid is used to configure mapping and map fields on the left to the fields on the right. To map a field on the left to a field on the field list, both the fields must be in the same position in the field map grid.

Now, follow the following steps to manually map the fields of the import set table with the fields of the target booking request table:

1. Double-click on the **Caller** column entry in the import table on the left to bring it into the **Field Map** grid:

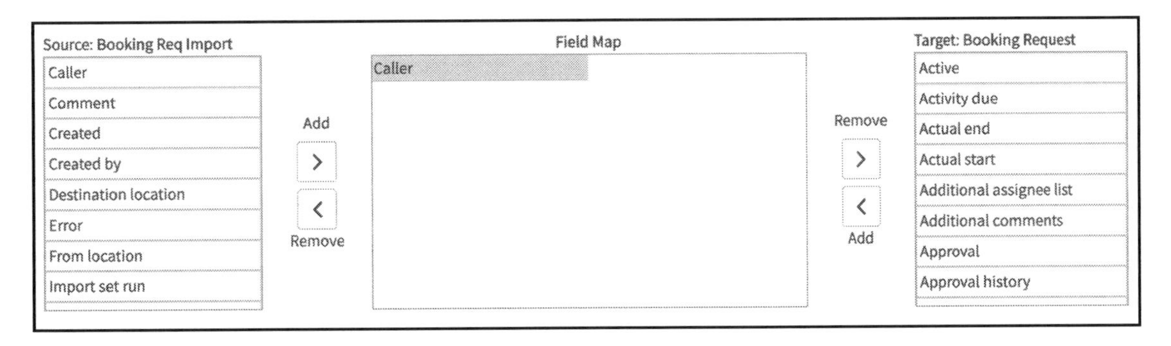

2. Bring in the corresponding **Caller** field from the target table to the field mapping grid either by double-clicking or else by selecting the entry and clicking on the Add icon:

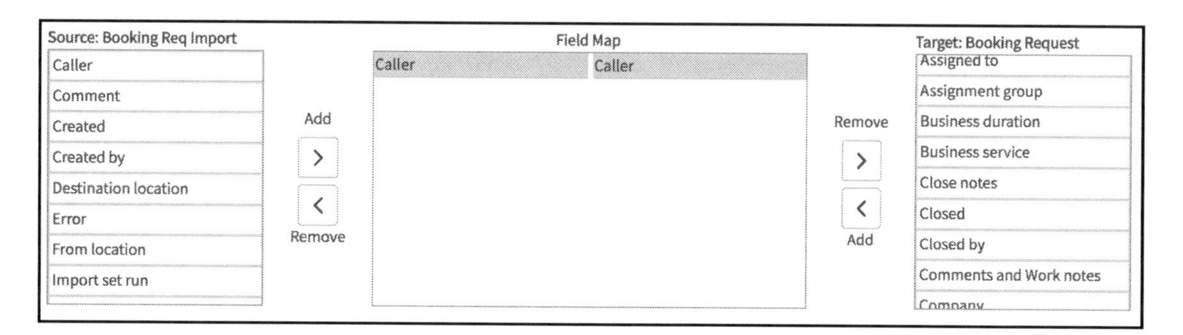


3. Now, double click on all required fields in the `Source: Booking Req Import` table list to add them all to the **Field Map** grid. Unless explicitly required for your project, we need to take care about not mapping fields, such as **Error**, **Created**, and **Created by**, which were created by the system in the staging import set table and were not a part of the CSV source:

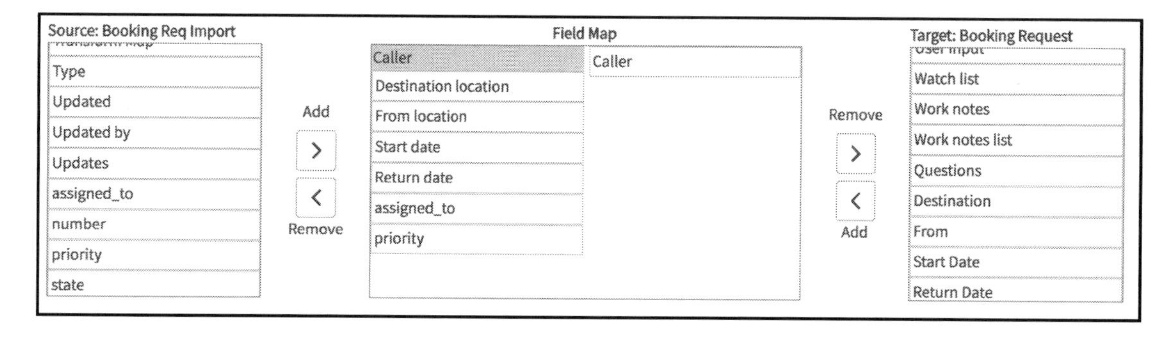

4. Next, bring in all the corresponding fields from the `Target: Booking Request` table list to the **Field Map** such that all the corresponding fields are positioned next to the source field names:

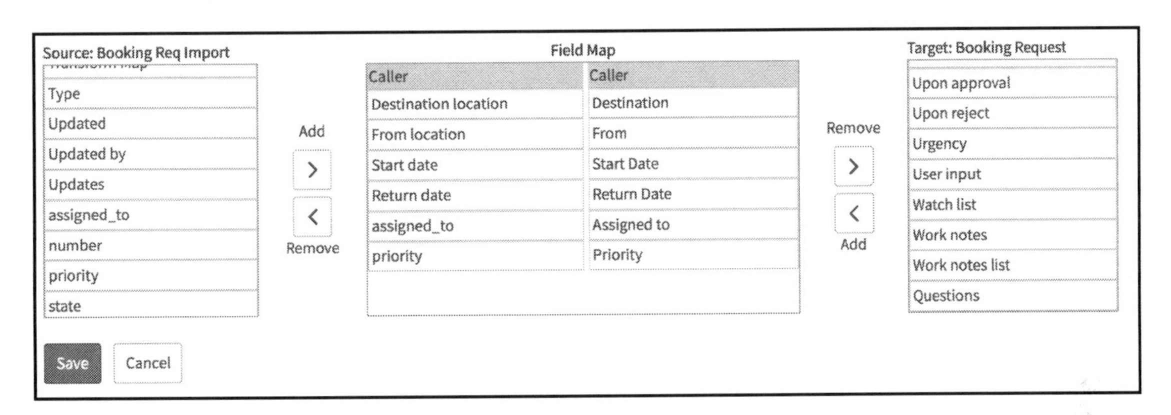


5. As shown in the following screenshot, confirm the mapping by clicking on the **Show Mapped Fields** radio button under the **Data Viewer** section of the page to view values of the mapped fields in the respective tables. By default, the first row of both the tables is shown. You can jump between rows by clicking on the arrow sign next to the **Viewing** label. The number adjacent to the **Viewing** label denotes the row number you are looking at:

6. If required, you can rearrange or reposition the mapped fields in the **Field Map** grid.
7. Click on the **Save** button to be taken back to the transform map form.

When in transform map detail page, you can confirm that fields are mapped correctly by looking at the **Field Maps** related list, as shown in the following screenshot:

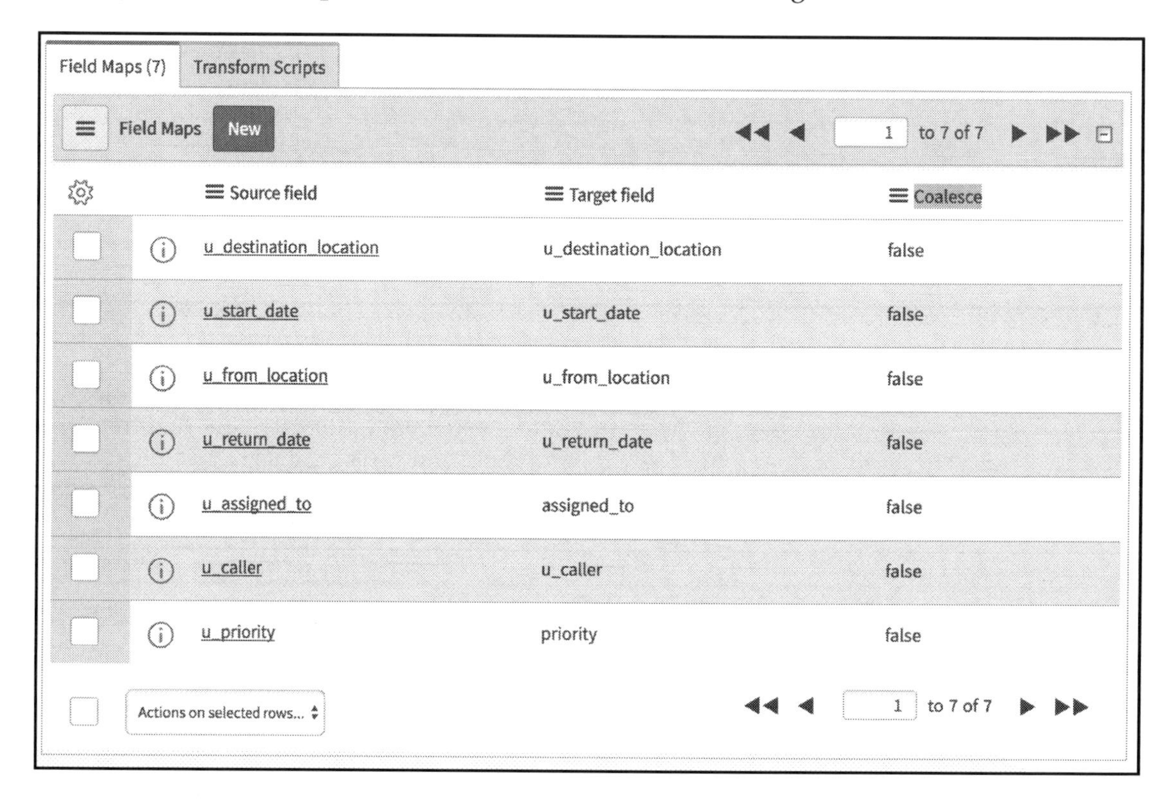


The import tool offers us the ability to fine grain how these mapping work based on data types and parse source field values using scripts. We can also define coalesce on one or more fields. When a field mapping is marked as coalesce, the field is used as a unique key, such that when a match is found in the target table, the existing row is updated and if a match is not found in the target table, the row is inserted.

The detail form of the field maps entries can allow us to configure and parse values by specifying the format of a date-time field; configure how choice list values will act when a new value that is not in the choice list is being added. We can also specify a script to parse and create a new value for the destination column. Let's change how the priority field mapping will work by editing the **Field Map** properties.

## Changing Field Map properties

To modify a property of a field mapping, click on the info icon next to the map entry in the **Field Maps** list in the transform map detail form.

We will open the entry for the priority field to change its property:

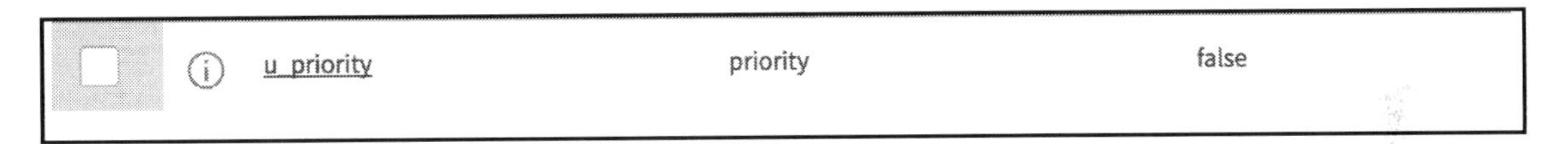


In the field map entry's detail form, as shown in the following screenshot, change the value of the **Choice action** field to **ignore**:

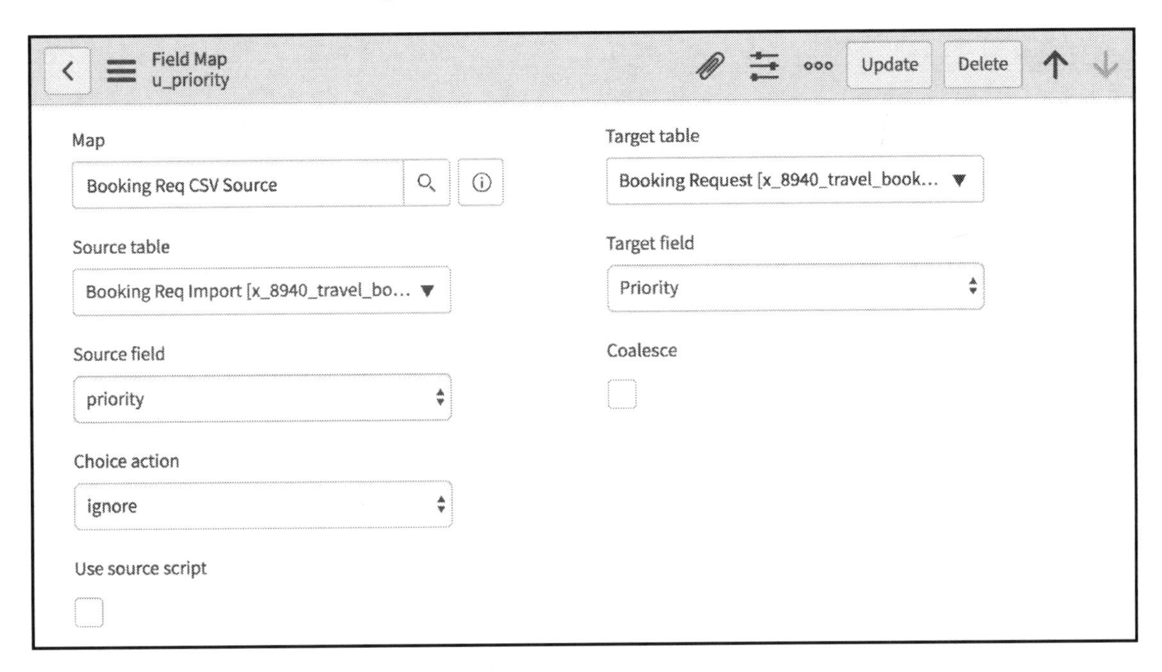

Click on the **Update** button to return to the transform map detail page. We can modify the property of any field that we would like to have more control over. We can also optionally set referenced value field names in order to properly map any referenced field to the correct entry.

Let's set format for date time fields, such as **Start Date** and **Return Date** to ensure that system understands that date format used in the CSV source file. Open each **Start Date** and **Return Date** field map entry and change the value of the **Date format** field to `mm/dd/yy`, as shown in the following screenshot:

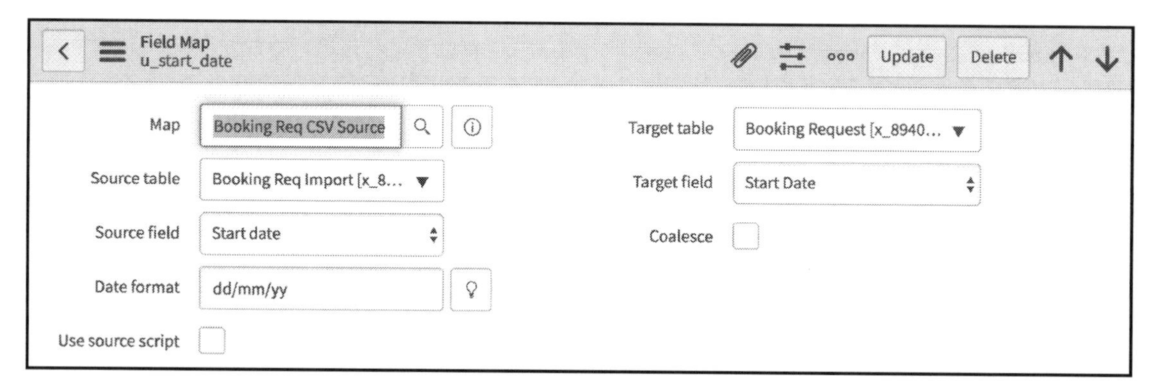


The **Date format** field is used to specify the format to be used when inserting or updating any record to a date field. Now, let's see how we can employ scripts to parse and override field values.

## Scripting to override field values

Open the entry for the priority field map property again and check the **Use source script** field. As shown in the following screenshot, the **Source script** field will now be visible:

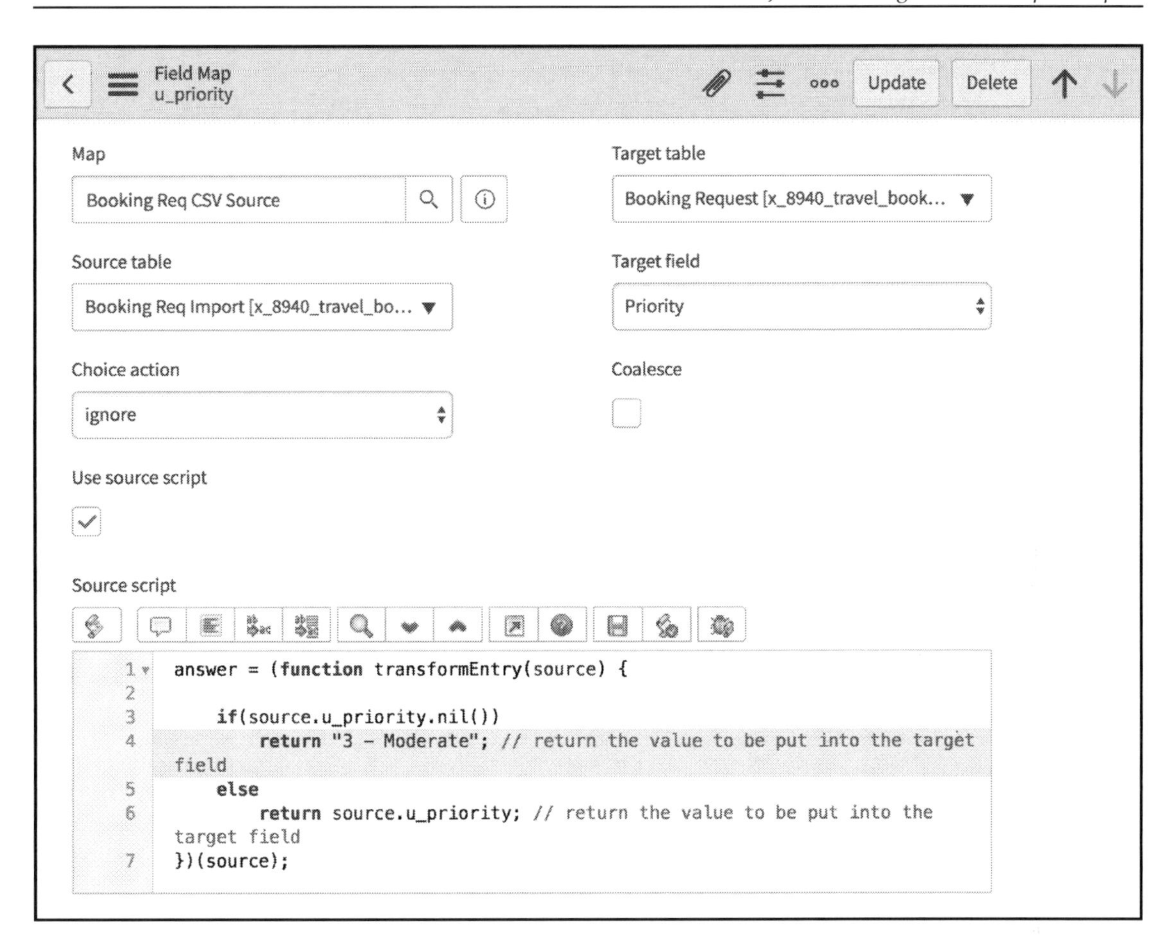


Use the following code in the **Source script** field:

```
answer = (function transformEntry(source) {
  if(source.u_priority.nil())
    return "3 - Moderate"; // return the value to be put into the target
field
  else
    return source.u_priority; // return the value to be put into the target
field
})(source);
```

In the preceding code, we have used the source `GlideObject` object available to us to check the value of the `u_priority` (priority) field in staging the import set table. We have set `3 - Moderate` as the default value if the value of the priority field in the staging table is nil. Thus, whenever a row that has a nil or blank value, the value `3 - Moderate` will be inserted into the priority field of the target `Booking request` table. Click on the **Update** button to save the **Field Map** property. In the field maps related list in the transform map detail form, you may notice that the value of the Source field column for the field map entry we just edited, as shown in the following screenshot, has been changed to `[Script]`:

| | | | |
|---|---|---|---|
| ⓘ | [Script] | priority | false |

This is an absolutely normal system behavior because we are now using a script as a source to calculate the value for the target priority field.

We can employ field map level scripting to concatenate values, perform system properties checks, database lookup by creating `GlideRecord` objects, and so on, to accomplish different project solutions. While field level scripting is good for cases where we want to parse, override, check, or validate field values, we can also specify scripts at the transform map level to control row-level actions, such as insert, update, and skip. Let's write a transform map script that will control how the rows will be inserted programmatically.

## Transform map scripts

The transform map scripts can be used to control the behavior of the transformation process. When we check the **Run script** checkbox in the transform map form, we can see the essential script already mentioned in the **Script** field, as shown in the following screenshot:

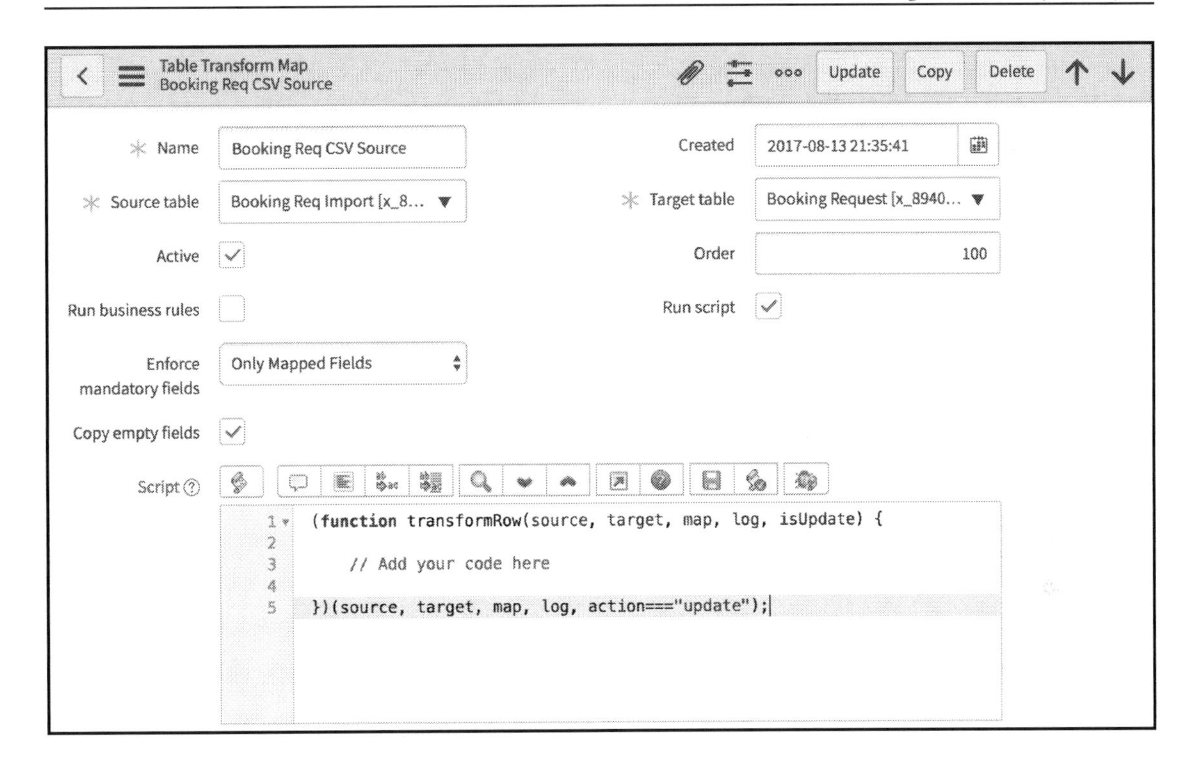


The following are the objects available to us when writing transform map scripts:

- `source`: A `GlideRecordobject` that refers to the row in the staging import set table
- `target`: A `GlideRecord` object that refers to the record being inserted into the target table
- `map`: A `GlideRecord` object that refers to the transform map entry stored in the `sys_transform_map` table
- `log`: This object has quick access to write log entries to the system log table. Supported methods includes `log.info()`, `log.warn()`, and `log.error()`
- `action`: A string identifier that returns a value or either inserts or updates based on whether the target object is being inserted or updated
- `ignore`: A `boolean` value that can be used to skip one or more records
- `error`: A `boolean` value that can be used to cause the current row to stop processing and log an entry into the import set log

Let's now write a simple transform map script that will create a log entry and skip the row whenever the destination field is empty. The transform map script will execute after the values from the source import set table have been copied to the target object, however, before the insert or update operation has been performed.

The following code will skip and create a log entry whenever the destination field on the import set staging table is empty:

```
(function transformRow(source, target, map, log, isUpdate) {

  if( source.u_destination_location.nil() ) {
    ignore = true; //skip the record
    log.info("Ignoring empty record: "+source.u_number); //create log entry
  }

})(source, target, map, log, action==="update");
```

Make sure that the **Run script** box is checked. The transform map form will look as shown in the following screenshot:

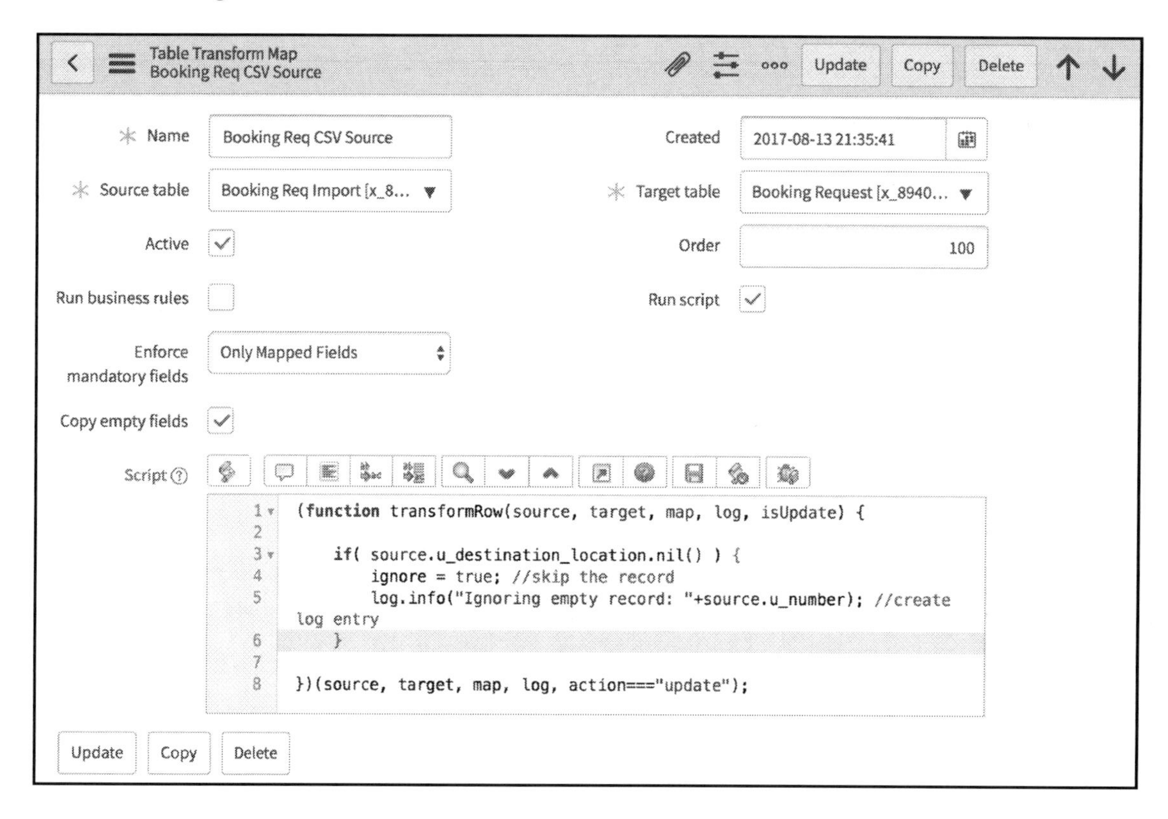

## Running the transform

The last step, apart from performing import validation, is to execute the transformation map. Once we have loaded the data and configured the transformation map, we can click on the **Transform** action under the related links in the transform map form or else click on the **System Import Sets** | **Run Transform** module link.

As shown in the following screenshot, we will be presented with a screen to select one or more transform maps for which there are records in a pending state in the import set table:

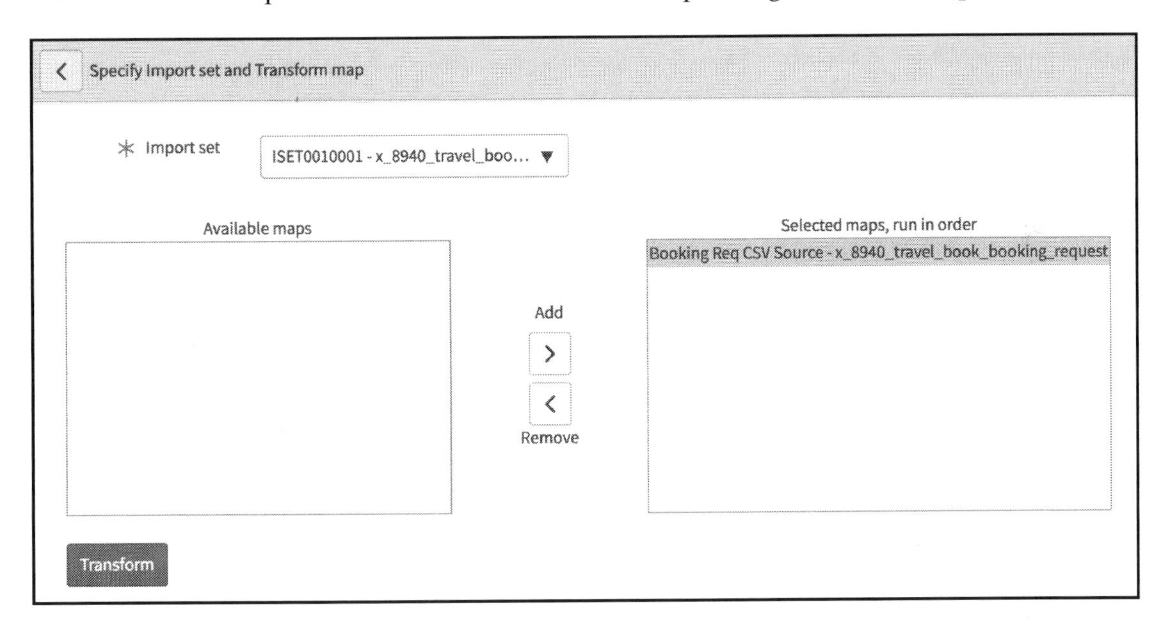


We can select one or more transform maps at any given time and click on the transform button. The transformation process will start processing each row in the import set table and copy them to the target table based on the field mapping and scripts we have configured while creating the transform map.

The business rules for each insert operation (whether before, after, or async) will execute only if the **Run business rules** checkbox was checked while configuring the transform map.

When uploading a large number of records, it is advised to keep the **Run business rules** checkbox unchecked, unless explicitly needed, to ensure a quick data transformation.

The process can take some time depending on the number of records being copied and progress will be visible, as shown in the following screenshot:

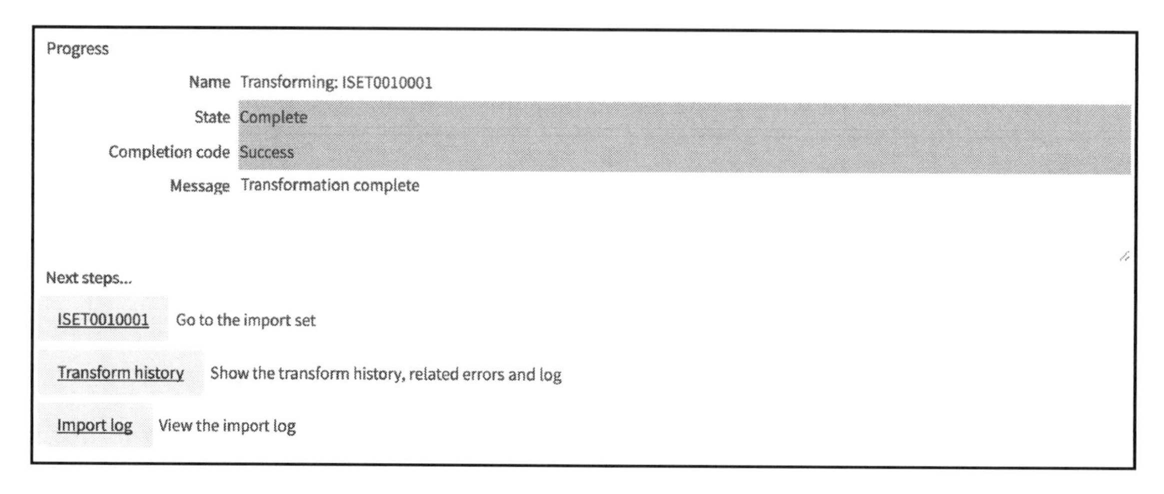


## Monitoring transform progress

Click on the **Transform history** link under the **Next steps...** section to be taken to the **Transform Histories** module, where we can see a list of entries, as shown in the following screenshot, each of which points to a transform action:

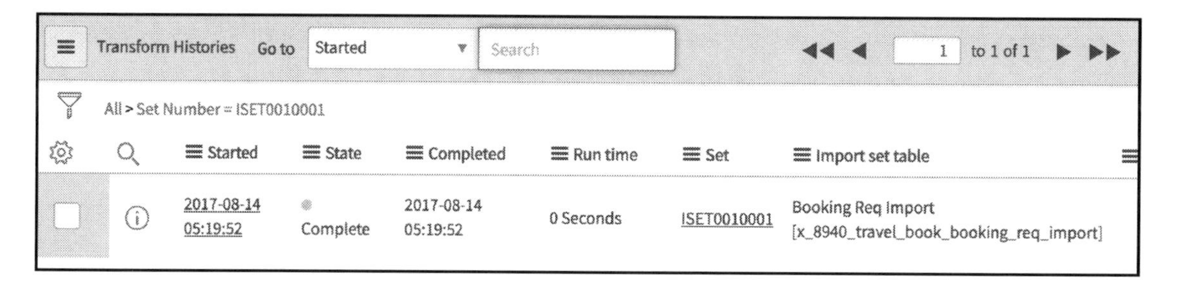


Find the entry for the import set we just transformed and click on the info icon to be taken to the detail form.

The **Transform History** detail form can be used to figure out the total number of records processed, along with the number of rows inserted, updated, ignored, skipped, or which had errors:

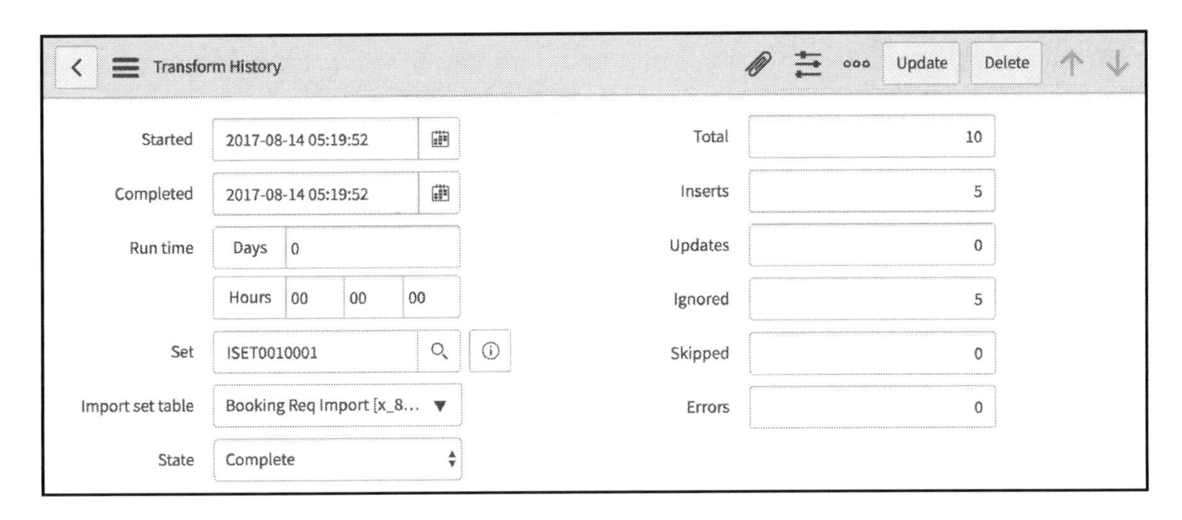


The import set row errors and import log sections below the main form can be used to find the relevant error and log entries created during the transformation process. As shown in the following screenshot, the import log list contains some log entries created by the `log.info` method used in the script we created in the previous step:

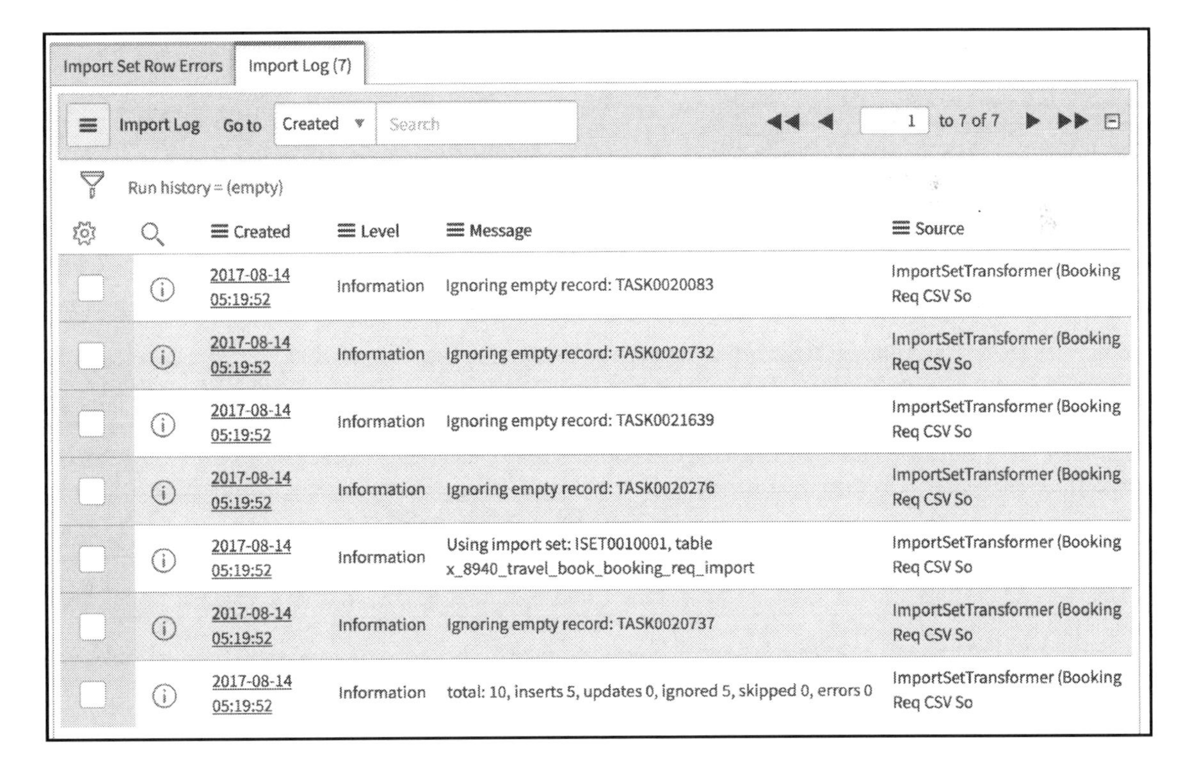

This means that there were no import errors and all records were processed properly. Furthermore, as mentioned in the transform map script, the rows where the destination field was empty was ignored and the remaining rows were inserted properly.

We can also open the **Booking Request** list of the record module, as shown in the following screenshot, to ensure that we can access the five records mentioned in our import logs:

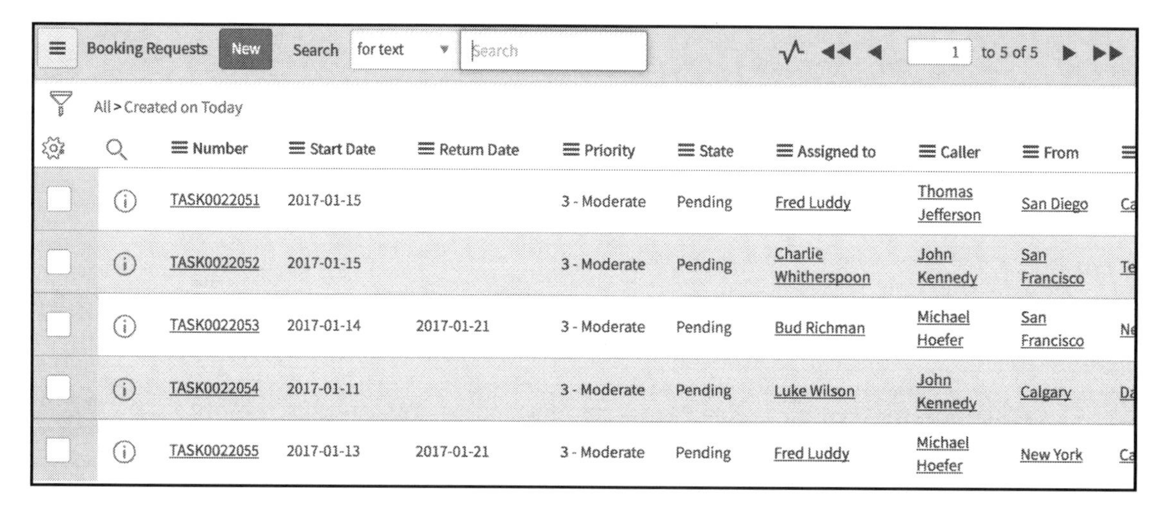
Booking Requests New Search for text Search 1 to 5 of 5

All > Created on Today

| Number | Start Date | Return Date | Priority | State | Assigned to | Caller | From |
|---|---|---|---|---|---|---|---|
| TASK0022051 | 2017-01-15 | | 3 - Moderate | Pending | Fred Luddy | Thomas Jefferson | San Diego |
| TASK0022052 | 2017-01-15 | | 3 - Moderate | Pending | Charlie Whitherspoon | John Kennedy | San Francisco |
| TASK0022053 | 2017-01-14 | 2017-01-21 | 3 - Moderate | Pending | Bud Richman | Michael Hoefer | San Francisco |
| TASK0022054 | 2017-01-11 | | 3 - Moderate | Pending | Luke Wilson | John Kennedy | Calgary |
| TASK0022055 | 2017-01-13 | 2017-01-21 | 3 - Moderate | Pending | Fred Luddy | Michael Hoefer | New York |

We can see that the records were imported properly to the target (destination) table - `Booking Request`. Furthermore, the date field and the priority field map properties that we defined in the previous steps worked properly.

# Summary

In this chapter, you learned different features such as scheduled script execution and understood how to export data in various formats. You also learned how to import data from an external source, along with different ways to parse and override fields and properties using field map and transform map scripts.

# Index

## A



## B



## C

# D



# E



# F



# G

# H



# I



# J

## R



## S

## Y

Made in the USA
Columbia, SC
15 February 2019